Guarini's "Il pastor fido" and the Madrigal

Battista Guarini's pastoral tragicomedy *Il pastor fido* (1589) began its life as a play, but soon was transformed through numerous musical settings by prominent composers of the late sixteenth and early seventeenth centuries. Through the many lives of this work, this book explores what happens when a lover's lament is transplanted from the theatrical stage to the courtly chamber, from speech to song, and from a single speaking character to an ensemble of singers, shedding new light on early modern literary and musical culture.

From the play's beginnings in manuscripts, private readings, and aborted stage productions in the 1580s and 1590s, through the gradual decline of *Pastor fido* madrigals in the 1640s, this book examines how this widely read yet controversial text became the center of a lasting and prolific music tradition. Using a new integrative system of musical–textual analysis based on sixteenth-century theory, Seth Coluzzi demonstrates how composers responded not only to the sentiments, imagery, and form of the play's speeches, but also to subtler details of Guarini's verse. Viewing the musical history of Guarini's work as an integral part of the play's roles in the domains of theater, literature, and criticism, this book brings a new perspective to the late Italian madrigal, the play, and early modern patronage and readership across a diverse geographical and temporal frame.

Seth J. Coluzzi is an Assistant Professor of Music at Colgate University and a scholar of the music, poetry, and culture of late-Renaissance Italy. His work focuses on issues of analysis, mode, interpretation, and text–music relations in the Italian madrigal and has appeared in *Journal of Musicology*, *Music and Letters*, *Music Theory Spectrum*, *Early Music*, *Studi musicali*, and other journals and collections.

Guarini's "Il pastor fido" and the Madrigal

Voicing the Pastoral in Late Renaissance Italy

Seth J. Coluzzi

Routledge
Taylor & Francis Group

LONDON AND NEW YORK

First published 2023
by Routledge
4 Park Square, Milton Park, Abingdon, Oxon OX14 4RN

and by Routledge
605 Third Avenue, New York, NY 10158

Routledge is an imprint of the Taylor & Francis Group, an informa business

British Library Cataloguing-in-Publication Data
A catalogue record for this book is available from the British Library

ISBN: 978-1-138-20709-7 (hbk)
ISBN: 978-1-032-42385-2 (pbk)
ISBN: 978-1-315-46305-6 (ebk)

DOI: 10.4324/9781315463056

Typeset in Times New Roman
by codeMantra

Access the Support Material: www.routledge.com/9781032423852

Printed in the United Kingdom
by Henry Ling Limited

Contents

Acknowledgments

Guarini's *Il pastor fido* and the late-Renaissance madrigal have been a central part of my life for some time now. Through such a period, it is almost without question that life will yield many experiences, both enjoyable and challenging, yet often unexpected, and always enlightening. I have been very fortunate through this book's development to find myself surrounded by many remarkable people, whose encouragement, direction, and generosity have been invaluable, and to whom I owe the sincerest thanks.

It was during my time as a fellow at Harvard University's Center for Italian Renaissance Studies at Villa I Tatti in Florence in 2010–11 that I was able to lay the foundation for this work in the idyllic space and with the abundant resources of I Tatti itself, along with the access it offered to libraries and archives across Italy and beyond. I am especially thankful to Kathryn Bosi, scholar and librarian of I Tatti's Biblioteca Berenson, for her assistance in acquiring microfilms of countless madrigal partbooks, and for her wealth of knowledge on late-Cinquecento court culture and the madrigal. I am also grateful to the staff of numerous libraries and archives, in particular the Biblioteca Comunale Ariostea in Ferrara, the Biblioteca Nazionale Marciana in Venice, and the Archivio di Stato di Mantova.

I am tremendously indebted to the colleagues and scholars whose work and shared ideas have continued to teach and inspire me. These include fellow members of the Madrigal Study Group for their passion for early modern culture and music, and for providing a welcoming and supportive setting in which to share new work. In particular, I thank Massimo Ossi, who first introduced me to *Il pastor fido* and the madrigal as an undergraduate at the University of Rochester, and who has remained a source of inspiration and guidance ever since.

My burgeoning interest in the music and culture of Renaissance Italy could not have been nurtured more than in the company of John Nadàs and the late James Haar as a graduate student at UNC Chapel Hill and thereafter over coffees, dinners, and strolls through the streets of Florence. Their encouragement was formative in my early stages as a developing scholar, and their approach to investigative research exemplified for me the healthy mix of enjoyment, seriousness, and fellowship that could be found in academic life.

There are so many others that I must thank for their support in varying ways, especially John Brackett, Mauro Calcagno, Giuseppe Gerbino, Severine Neff, and Emiliano Ricciardi. I also owe tremendous gratitude to the anonymous reviewers for their invaluable comments on earlier versions of this book, and to the editors with whom I have worked, beginning with fellow madrigal scholar and UNC alum Laura Macy, who took on this project with Ashgate Publishing, followed by Emma Gallon and Genevieve Aoki after Ashgate merged with Routledge. I am especially grateful to Genevieve for her support and guidance through the book's long gestation and the disruptions that emerged along the way. I would also like to acknowledge Maria Sullivan for her invaluable help with the index on short notice under an unexpectedly tight circumstances.

It is difficult to find the words with which to thank someone who has been seemingly boundless in their generosity, dependability, and insight, as Tim Carter has been for me through the years of this project's development. Tim's model of care, vivacity, and creativity as a scholar and mentor is something toward which I can only strive, and this book has benefitted immensely from his comments and inspiration.

Finally, I thank my family for having tolerated Mirtillo, Amarilli, Corisca, and the many other inhabitants of this book, real and fictitious, who have occupied my mind for a considerable part of our lives. To my mother Linda, my late father Richard, Chrissy, Jens, Tory, Melissa, and, most of all, Michelle: thank you for your support, understanding, and patience. And Michelle, thank you for waiting late into so many nights for me. I look forward to spending more time with you all among the real *selve* and *augelli*, rather than so much among the imagined ones of Arcadia. Perhaps I shouldn't jinx myself by saying that the next book will be much easier.

Editorial Principles

Translations throughout are my own unless otherwise noted. The original Italian for lengthier citations is available in the Support Material (www. routledge.com/9781032423852) for rare sources and where subtleties of the original language are important to the discussion. In most cases, for the sake of clarity and consistency, I have not modernized the Italian in prose citations, even if it has meant retaining odd usages. Likewise, poetic texts transcribed from primary print and manuscript sources, particularly for purposes of comparison and lineage, are left unedited, and hence follow the spelling, punctuation, accents, and abbreviations of the originals. In other instances, poetic texts are minimally edited, generally by way of added punctuation, when it is important to the sense of the passage. I have made the poetic translations as literal as possible, including in terms of lineation and syntax, in order to facilitate line-by-line references and comparisons for musical and textual analysis, even if this has come with slight sacrifices in elegance. I also adopt the convention here of capitalizing the beginnings of poetic lines, including for partial verses and in musical settings, in order to convey the formal layout and treatment of the text.

All music examples have been newly edited based on image files or microfilms of the princeps, when extant. Music examples are provided for the most relevant passages when dealing with works for which modern editions are readily available. For works that are difficult to access in modern edition—namely, the three madrigals of Gian Giacomo Gastoldi and three of Salamone Rossi discussed in Chapter 8—I have provided complete scores in the Support Material.

Throughout the study, for madrigals consisting of multiple "*parti*" (parts) or sections—similar to movements in later music or acts in a play—these component sections are referred to as *parti* to avoid confusion with the connotation "voice parts." Such multi-*parte* madrigals, in turn, are considered and counted as single madrigals; thus, Monteverdi's five-*parte* setting *Ecco, Silvio, colei che 'n odio hai tanto* in his Fifth Book constitutes a single work (rather than five individual madrigals). All references to madrigal books not specifying the number of voices refer to collections for five voices: for example, Marenzio's Seventh Book implies the Seventh Book for five voices.

Collections of madrigals calling for any other number of voices will be specified, as in "First Book for four voices." The shorthand *a4*, *a5*, and so forth likewise refer to the number of voices in a work or collection.

References to general pitch classes take the form of roman upper-case letter names: for instance, "a cadence on A," or "the continuous presence of A." Sonorities ("triads") similarly appear in roman with upper case denoting major (D) and lower case, minor (d), except where the quality is written out ("a D-minor sonority"). Specific pitches are indicated by italics and use primes and case to indicate register in the manner:

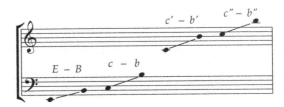

Pitch classes are also indicated at times based on their position in the mode (i.e., relative to the modal final): for example, G represents the "modal fourth" or "$\hat{4}$" of the D-dorian mode. The terms *diapason*, *diapente*, and *diatessaron* of sixteenth-century modal theory refer to the octave, fifth, and fourth, respectively, and often carry with them the connotation of the role of these intervals—with their internal intervallic makeup—in defining the mode. Importantly, true cadences are distinguished from non-cadential arrivals (especially in examples and tables) using parentheses for the latter: hence, "D" represents a cadence on that pitch, while "(D)" denotes a non-cadential ending. The basic principles of cadences and mode are discussed in Chapter 1. Finally, I refer to the specific voice parts of the madrigal with the Italian names used in contemporary sources: Canto (soprano), Alto, Tenore, Basso, Quinto ("fifth," a variable part), Sesto ("sixth"), and so forth.

Introduction

Voice, Genre, and Interpretation in the Italian Madrigal

With its close musical readings of high Italian poetry, the madrigal represents a culmination of musical–literary innovation and technique in the early modern period not only in Italy, but throughout Europe. The flourishing of the genre through the sixteenth and early seventeenth centuries followed the literary fashions of the age, conveying the poems, epics, romances, and plays of poets such as Petrarch, Ariosto, Sannazaro, Tasso, Guarini, Marino, and countless others in settings for an unaccompanied vocal ensemble (typically from four to six voices), and later, after c.1600, increasingly for vocal ensemble, solo voice, or duet with instrumental accompaniment. This introspective and rhetorically sophisticated verse inspired bold, new means of musical expression that pushed the bounds of accepted practice.

Yet, the transition from lyric poem to music—from the act of silent or spoken reading to the experiences of singing, listening, and observing—brings significant consequences to the text in terms of perception and perspective. Take, for example, the first lines of a poem by Giovanni Guidiccioni of which composer Jacques Arcadelt produced a notable setting:

Il bianco e dolce cigno	The white, sweet swan
Cantando more, et io	dies singing. And I,
Piangendo giungo al fin del viver mio.	weeping, reach the end of my life.

Thus begins the poem, and thus sing the three, then four, voices in Arcadelt's celebrated madrigal first published in 1539 (see Example I.1). But just what happens when the text is transferred from lyric poem to polyphonic madrigal, from the perspective of a single poet-speaker to an ensemble of four voices? Such questions of voice and interpretation have stood at the center of madrigal studies in recent years, with the two principal views arguing that the genre renders the poetic voice as a shared, universal "I" voiced collectively by the ensemble, at times with individual voices coming to the fore for expressive effect, verisimilitude, or variety; or as a singular subjectivity located primarily in a specific voice part. The latter view sometimes comes with a teleological framing of the madrigal as in some sense "dramatic" or

DOI: 10.4324/9781315463056-1

Example I.1 Arcadelt, *Il bianco e dolce cigno*, mm. 1–15

mimetic, a precursor to opera, whereby the polyphonic setting represents a type of conventionalizing garb for an underlying representational or soloistic treatment.

Analyses of any madrigal's manner of reading, furthermore, tend to focus overwhelmingly on texture, whereby homophonic declamation represents a collective unity to some, a centered Self to others, and a plainly accompanied principal voice to others still. A rhythmically offset voice, in turn, marks that part as the speaking subject, while polyphony represents a fractured or conflicted Self, despite the lack of a systematic framework (not to mention historical backing) for such straightforward associations and how they are applied. The lack of contemporary sources on the subject and the variety of modern hermeneutical–analytical approaches have led to a plurality of assertions about the madrigal's narrative mode or "voice." This outcome may, on the one hand, be part of the point: that the genre facilitates a variety of interpretative readings. But on the other hand, it gets us no closer to a reliable and historically informed understanding of how madrigals read and were read.

Two relatively recent analyses of Arcadelt's *Il bianco e dolce cigno* illustrate the point. The text opens by evoking the white swan's singing at its death in the first clause—"Il bianco e dolce cigno cantando more"—and contrasting it with the first person's weeping at the end of his life in the second—"et io piangendo giungo al fin del viver mio." The poem stresses this change of focus from swan to Self with the inward gesture of the first-person pronoun at "et io" (and I) at the end of verse 2, the first-person verb "giungo" (reach) and possessive "mio" (my) in verse 3, and the end-rhyme *io–mio* between the two verses.

In *Modal Subjectivities* (2004), Susan McClary interprets Arcadelt's madrigal as a rendering of an individual Self divided between a rational, unified persona (portrayed with homophony) and a decentered, irrational interiority (rendered through polyphony). Thus, through most of the madrigal's prevailing homophony, McClary explains that "all four voices declaim the text at the same time to produce the image of a single [centered] speaking subject," while at the later shift to imitation, "the speaker becomes riddled with inner conflict." Here, McClary reads the Tenore as the predominant voice, while the delayed entrance of the Basso at "et io" in mm. 5–6 strengthens "the contrast between the swan…and the masculine Self."[1]

In analyzing the same passage in *From Madrigal to Opera: Monteverdi's Staging of the Self* (2012), Mauro Calcagno focuses on a reading of the Basso as a representation of the poem's speaker, "who is silent for the first clause (dominated by the swan's singing), but 'steps forward' for the second clause, singing the word *io* (and then *mio*)."[2] Calcagno continues by noting that this textual device results in:

> a conflation, a merging of the *persona* of the composer—the musical narrator—with the *persona* of the poet, the literary narrator, via the protagonist/character of the poem, coalescing into the actual singer [the Basso] at the moment in which he sings the word *io*.[3]

A different perspective, focusing on the second clause (mm. 5–10), however, reveals another potential reading, one in which, while the Basso "steps forward" and *joins* the ensemble, the Canto steps *away from* it, and in its rhythmic displacement, enunciates the first-person pronoun, "et *io*," and verb, "giungo" (I reach), independently. The varied restatement of this passage in mm. 10–15 further emphasizes the Canto's singularity by combining its rhythmic separation with the pre-cadential syncopation from the Tenore's earlier statement of "viver mio" in mm. 7–10. To all of these readings, furthermore, could also be added the general views of the madrigal's rendering of the lyric *io* as a shared, plural identity throughout; as narrated (or reported) speech; and as a quasi-dramatic persona, whose location in the Canto is supported by that part's consistent presence and frequent textural, rhythmic, and registral prominence across the piece amidst a largely homophonic setting. All of these readings prove plausible and demonstrate the inevitable inconsistencies—or, to put it more positively, variety—inherent in interpretative analyses of voice and subjectivity based chiefly on superficial features, such as texture, register, and offset phrasing.

My study further explores such questions of poetic genre, voice, and perspective as part of a broader investigation into compositional and interpretative strategies in the madrigal by looking at a distinctive and prominent trend in the genre in the decades around 1600: the setting of texts not from a lyric source, as was typical, but from a play, Battista Guarini's pastoral tragicomedy, *Il pastor fido*, published in December 1589. The play's single speeches for the most part transitioned seamlessly from their theatrical contexts to the self-contained madrigal, where they prove largely indistinguishable from lyric poems (which is what some of them likely originally were). Yet, these extracted passages cannot be considered solely *in vacuo*, as autonomous poems, from the standpoint of readership, owing to their inherent interpretative ties to their dramatic source. As the studies of the musical works in later chapters will show, composers, indeed, heeded this distinction. For despite the texts' removal from the play and any modifications they underwent, composers often responded to them in ways that entertain both independent and intertextual readings by evoking aspects of the external plot, attributes of their speakers and other relevant personas, and veiled intentions that lie behind the speech in the play. The *Pastor fido* madrigal, as a documented close interpretative reading by its composer–author, then, is by nature discursive—with its textual source, with other madrigals within and between collections, and with its readers, taken at large to include performers, listeners, and readers of the page—and, hence, is invested with multiple layers of meaning and an extended capacity of referentiality and interpretative play. *Il pastor fido* and the madrigal, therefore, held a reciprocal, or mutualistic, relationship: while the play enriched the madrigal with the expanded backgrounds and scenarios of its speaking characters and verse, the madrigal, in turn, potentialized the speeches through its own non-verbal means of expressive reading.

The rendering of speeches from the play polyphonically in the madrigal foregrounds further these issues of voice, perspective, and poetic genre as the words of a single embodied character enacted onstage or imagined in a silent reading are sounded through multiple voices collectively in the intimate setting of a courtly chamber, intellectual *ridotto*, or private household. The difference, for example, is comparable to reading the well-known passage *Cruda Amarilli, che col nome ancora* as a generic complaint of unrequited love, and reading it through the lens of the protagonist Mirtillo (the "faithful shepherd") in *Il pastor fido*, with knowledge of the dramatic irony that lies behind his beloved's spitefulness and the responsibility she bears in the context of the play.

The multi-voice madrigal, thus, presents the inherent incongruities that it is neither dramatic nor, as a component of this, verisimilar, by virtue of the fact that performing polyphony is a collaborative endeavor, as well as a cross-gendered one, and, hence, no individual "voice" (part) has exclusive claim to the singular first-person identity (*io*). This is not the concern of the madrigal. For, as contemporaneous accounts and modern-day performances attest, singers of madrigals do not only deliver the speaker's words; they also interact with one another vocally and aurally by coordinating tempo, rhythm, and intonation; semantically and grammatically by sharing, trading, and completing a common text; and visually and physically by exchanging glances, facial expressions, and movements. In other words, they are acting, and interacting, as an ensemble of reader–reporters of the speaker's words, rather than truly acting out individually and dramatically as the speaker. This mode of delivery is exemplified well in the opening of Arcadelt's *Il bianco e dolce cigno*, where separate voices play distinct yet interdependent roles in voicing the text. This view contrasts with Mauro Calcagno's assertion that madrigal "composers were able to empower performers to become in effect flesh-and-blood characters, not merely conveyors of 'readings' or 'exegeses'."[4] It also vindicates the madrigal as a free-standing genre rather than as a harbinger of any musical drama to come, and it obviates the need (to return to McClary) to identify rational personas and irrational interiorities with musical settings that, instead, celebrate the act of reading.

The extension of this narrative (or diegetic) conception to a madrigal such as *Il bianco e dolce cigno*, for instance, would effectively hem the work in implied quotation marks, as if to include the caption, "He [the unnamed poet-lover] said: 'Il bianco e dolce cigno...'"[5] This view rationalizes the fact that, for example, the Basso and Canto both play prominent, but complementary roles in the opening passage: while the Basso's entrance adds an effect of verisimilitude by evoking what McClary calls a "masculine Self," the Canto's rhythmic displacement conjures the speaker's desolation at the hyperbolic end of his life while dismissing any designations of gender. The basic expression, therefore, becomes universal. Likewise, the transferal of Mirtillo's widely set entrance monologue from Guarini's play to five-voice madrigal would involve the implicit introduction: "Thus cried the faithful shepherd, 'Cruda Amarilli, che col nome ancora...'" The madrigals present the words and passions of the characters, but they do not act their parts, as in the play.

As Arcadelt's madrigal and the settings from *Il pastor fido* show, even at times when a single voice is highlighted or briefly alone, that voice, indeed, speaks *for* (not *as*) the speaker—i.e., relates his or her words—but also for the ensemble, as collective, underlying narrator. Thus, in *Il bianco e dolce cigno*, the swan sings (*cantando*); the lover weeps (*piangendo*); the performers narrating the lover sing about weeping, even as individual voices "step forward" in various ways (e.g., the Basso by entering and the Canto through rhythmic displacement). The same is true of settings of dialogues from *Il pastor fido* that preserve superficially the distinction between two characters (for example, by way of voice-groupings or of other textural means) but which remain grounded within a polyphonic ensemble. There is always a conceptual separation between singer(s) and speaker(s), even as the singers imitate the speaker's words and affects. This means of realization is distinct from that of true drama, or *mimesis*, where the audience lets itself believe that the actor truly *is* the speaking persona. Even if one voice is singled out metrically, registrally, through dissonance, or by another means, it becomes more prominent in the madrigal's expressive/rhetorical delivery, but it does not become *more* the speaker than any of the other voices. In this respect, all of the active voices are always participants, with some more conspicuous than others, yet without a separation between true (or truer) speaker and mere background support.

All of these strategies of distinguishing individual voices suggest that while verisimilitude can be invoked for semantic and expressive effect, true enactment or personification is not part of the madrigal's means. It could hardly be considered plausible, after all, that Mirtillo would apostrophize polyphonically, with the expressive and oratorical focus shifting from one voice to another. Instead, the madrigal presents its texts in ways that not only recount linear narratives, but prompt non-linear reflection on their emotional and other consequences; the aim is not so much to experience these consequences as to consider them in whatever ways the listener (and the performer) might prefer.

Whereas many recent studies have seemed intent on uncovering signs of soloistic, representational, or even operatic tendencies in the madrigal based on their texts, textual sources, musical texture, and the imminent rise of opera, the texts and paratexts of these *Pastor fido* settings contend otherwise: madrigal composers and performers do not create flesh-and-blood personas, but rather rendered these characters' words framed in narrative terms. Despite conflicting views even on the poetic mode of lyric poetry—pure narration according to Plato, pure *mimesis* to Aristotle, or a mix of both to Renaissance literary theorist Antonio Minturno, to list a few—it was, by function, poetry to be read or sung, as opposed to acted onstage. The examples here suggest that these madrigals—if not *the* madrigal—too, act as readings, not enactments, both in performance and in interpretation, whatever the genre and source of their texts.

The musical–textual and cross-generic tradition of the *Pastor fido* madrigal, therefore, in turn, was rooted not in enactment or in the polyphonic simulation of drama, but in adapting the pastoral's speeches to the intimate domains of aristocratic households and solitary readings as heightened retellings of the Arcadians' thoughts and orations, as depictions of their interior and external states, and as incisive interpretations of the poet's witty, sophisticated, and affecting verse. For performers and listeners alike, the madrigal allowed the vicarious and empathic experience of the subjectivities of the text, rather than immediate embodiments or representations as carried out on stage. This manner of presentation, in fact, suited Guarini's play distinctly well. For despite its label as a *tragicommedia pastorale*, from its earliest exposure in Guarini's spoken readings, *Il pastor fido* proved a work to be read more than staged. The madrigal continued this practice in music, as composers' readings of characters' speeches were conveyed through sung performance.

Pastoral Personas in a Tragicomic Plot

In the fourth scene of act 3 in *Il pastor fido*, the nymph Amarilli finds herself torn between her love for the shepherd Mirtillo and an obligation to marry the callous huntsman Silvio. Up to this point in the play, Amarilli had stood firm in her obedience to patriarchal order, feigning an air of indifference and even cruelty toward Mirtillo. But after Mirtillo sneaks his way into a game of blind man's buff (*Il gioco della cieca*) between Amarilli and a band of nymphs and steals a kiss from his blindfolded beloved, Amarilli's front begins to crumble. She scornfully rejects Mirtillo, but once alone reveals the conflict she faces between love and law, between personal desire and civic duty. Her speech begins with the cry "O Mirtillo, Mirtillo anima mia" and the verses set by more than twenty composers, then continues with lines cited by critics of the play for their illustration of Amarilli's defiant inclinations and impractical capacity to reason:

Se 'l peccar è sì dolce,	If to sin is so sweet,
E'l non peccar sì necessario, o troppo	and not to sin so necessary: Oh, too
Imperfetta natura,	imperfect nature
Che repugni a la legge;	that opposes law;
O troppo dura legge,	Oh, too harsh law
Che la natura offendi.[6]	that offends nature.

The responsibility that lies in Amarilli's hands, however, involves much more than her own well-being and the political and financial interests of an arranged marriage. Though set in the mythical pastoral land of Arcadia, typically seen as an idyllic home of shepherds and nymphs far removed from the clamor and depravity of the city, Guarini's Arcadia is threatened by a curse of the goddess Diana that requires either the marriage of two progeny of divine blood or the sacrifice of a chaste nymph in order to spare its citizens from severe misfortune. Thus, it has been arranged that Silvio, son of Montano and a descendant of Achilles who wants nothing to do with love, will marry Amarilli, daughter of Titiro and a descendant of Pan. All would be well and good for Silvio and Amarilli to wed, except that Mirtillo (an outsider to Arcadia) is determined to win Amarilli's heart and, unknowingly, has succeeded in doing so.[7]

But in spite of her intense love for Mirtillo, Amarilli remains steadfast in her role of dutiful daughter and citizen, acting bitterly toward Mirtillo so as not to compromise her betrothal to Silvio and, in turn, jeopardize the fate of Arcadia. Thus, with its impending curse, imposed marriage, and thwarted love, Guarini's Arcadia is hardly a refuge from the troubles of Renaissance life. Even more unsettling for some readers of the play was the notion that the fate of this imperiled Arcadia lay in the hands of a love-torn nymph, who weighs her own natural inclinations against social obligation and divine and patriarchal authority.[8]

Indeed, the image of Arcadia as sensual bliss and utopian freedom represents only half of the picture of the late-sixteenth-century pastoral. Instead, Arcadia is often portrayed as a land fallen from grace, whose inhabitants suffer of love-sorrow, unattainable desires, and the confines of social codes, and look back longingly to a past Golden Age. This is a far cry from simple rustic life, and as we shall see, the music inspired by the speeches of Arcadian inhabitants could be far from simplistic as well.[9]

The play, like the madrigals derived from it, centers principally on the forbidden love between Mirtillo and Amarilli and the dichotomy of their predicaments—Mirtillo's constancy in the face of despair and humiliation, and Amarilli's struggle to conceal her passion with outward coldness—and secondarily on the innocent Dorinda's love for the heartless Silvio, and her desperate (indeed, nearly fatal) efforts to open his eyes to love (Figure I.1). These alternating storylines remain largely separate in the play, but are connected crucially through the imposed vow between Amarilli and Silvio. While the devoted and desperate Mirtillo and Dorinda pursue their cruel beloveds, the tragic dimension (and ultimately resolution) of the plot arises from the devious Corisca's hidden passion for Mirtillo, and her willingness to remove any obstacle that stands in her way—namely Amarilli. The duplicitous nymph is, in turn, supposedly sworn to the shepherd Coridone, while also sought by the lustful Satiro.

Over the course of act 3, Corisca takes advantage of Amarilli and Mirtillo when they are at their most vulnerable—after their distressing exchange following the *Gioco della cieca*—to set her machinations into motion. Whereas several fashionable madrigal texts came from the early expository acts of the play—including the elder Linco's *Quell'augellin, che canta* (I,1), Mirtillo's *Cruda Amarilli* (I,2), and Dorinda's *O misera Dorinda* (II,2)—act 3 generated more musical settings than any other act in the play. The musical texts focus on six main episodes of scenes 1–4 and 6:

1   Mirtillo's anxious monologue ahead of Amarilli's arrival that makes up the whole of scene 1 (*O primavera, gioventù dell'anno*);
2   the *Gioco della cieca* in scene 2 with sung and danced choruses intermixed with dialogue from Mirtillo, Amarilli, and Corisca (*Ecco, la cieca...*);
3   Mirtillo's tearful farewell following Amarilli's humiliating rebuke in scene 3 (*Ah, dolente partita*);

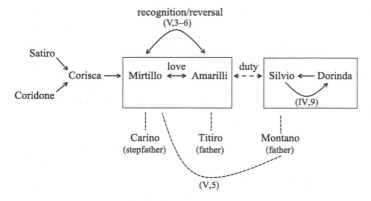

Figure I.1 Pastor fido Characters

4 Amarilli's private confession of her true love for Mirtillo in scene 4 (*O Mirtillo, Mirtillo anima mia*) that the eavesdropping Corisca overhears, before convincing Amarilli in scene 5 to follow the more ancient law of Venus, rather than restrictive one of Diana;

5 Mirtillo's apostrophe at the start of scene 6—also overheard by Corisca—bemoaning the perpetual torment of loving a cruel lady (*Udite, lagrimosi*); and

6 Corisca's futile effort through the remainder of the scene to tempt Mirtillo with the prospect of enjoying other affectionate lovers with the intent of winning him for herself, which only prompts the faithful shepherd to double down on his commitment to constancy (*M'è più dolce il penar per Amarilli* and other passages) and leads to Corisca's intricate scheme to dispose of her rival by framing Amarilli as unfaithful in her engagement to Silvio.

The last two acts proved the least fruitful in terms of madrigal texts, perhaps because they focus much more on dramatic action and development, rather than introspection and background. In act 4, Corisca's ploy goes seriously awry when the elders of Arcadia find Amarilli in a cave alone with Mirtillo instead of Coridone, as Corisca had designed. The oracle dictates that any adulterous woman must be sentenced to death, unless a faithful shepherd offers to die in her place. Thus, Amarilli faces the sacrificial altar, before Mirtillo insists on giving his own miserable life to spare hers.

This sudden shift toward a tragic scenario, however, is but the first of two dramatic reversals. For, in keeping with the tragicomic design, the second reversal leads to a narrow escape and a providential end. Carino, while passing by the temple, realizes that the unfortunate victim at the altar is not the usual virgin or perfidious nymph, but his son, Mirtillo. A moment before the priest (Montano) delivers the fatal blow, Carino begs to embrace Mirtillo one last time, which prompts the shepherd to speak, thus defiling the sacrifice and requiring that the preparations begin again. The delay allows for a conversation between Montano and Carino, in which the latter explains Mirtillo's backstory: how some twenty years ago after the great flood, Carino found him floating, like Moses, in a cradle in the river Alfeo, and named him Mirtillo. The tale ends in Montano's recognition of Mirtillo as his lost firstborn son, Silvio, whose name he then gave to his second son (the hunter betrothed to Amarilli). The priest now faces the grave task of executing his own child. All is finally resolved, however, when the prophet Tirenio points out that Mirtillo fulfills the same requirements as Silvio, being of divine lineage and having the birth name Silvio. Thus, the sequence of recognitions and reversals in act 5 incrementally divulges the true destiny of Amarilli and Mirtillo's love.

Meanwhile, as Amarilli, then Mirtillo, escape death at the altar, Dorinda likewise finds herself fighting for her life, as the inadvertent victim of Silvio's arrow. The distressing episode in act 4, scene 9 that shows Dorinda begging for Silvio's blessing, and Silvio's reversal as his heart warms with pity, forms the basis of Monteverdi's lengthy dialogic madrigal, *Ecco, Silvio, colei che 'n odio hai tanto* (1605), discussed in Chapter 7. Like Amarilli and Mirtillo, Dorinda, too, evades death—in this case, by a medicinal herb for healing wounds known to Silvio. In the end, with Silvio transformed and replaced by Mirtillo as Amarilli's betrothed, all of the protagonists fulfill their longings, and the potential tragedies of the dual plot dissolve into a *lieto fine*—a distinguishing mark of Guarini's new hybrid genre. Corisca, too, repents and is fully forgiven by Amarilli and Mirtillo in the work's closing lines.

Guarini's ties to the Este court in Ferrara—a center famed for its activities in music, poetry, and theatrical entertainment—and his reputation as a poet of lyric verse suited to the polyphonic madrigal likely also contributed to the early acceptance of his pastoral tragicomedy as a source of musical texts. The attention that it garnered both in the theater and out of it—from literary critics and readers of the printed text—seems only further to have stoked this demand for musical treatments of its extracted passages. But whereas the pastoral play *Aminta* (1573) by fellow Ferrarese poet Torquato Tasso proved less difficult as a theatrical work and enjoyed comparable success as a printed text, its musical legacy was isolated and short-lived. Something, in short, set Guarini's work apart not only from Tasso's play, but also from all other plays of Renaissance Italy as a promising, plentiful, and inspiring source of madrigal texts. Indeed, in contrast to the simple, rustic characters and taut plots of conventional pastoral comedies, the individuals of Guarini's Arcadia are cultured and complex, and bring forth a range of dispositions and tragicomic scenarios with an exceptional number of divulging and impassioned soliloquies. The following chapters explore the play through these various dimensions of its history: as a developing text, in the theater, as a catalyst of controversy, and in musical setting, where the polyphonic madrigal served not only as annotated reading, but also, as we will see, as a means of discourse between text, composer, performers, and listeners, as well as between madrigals and the books in which they reside.

Notes

1 Susan McClary, *Modal Subjectivities: Self-Fashioning in the Italian Madrigal* (Berkeley: University of California Press, 2004), 63–64.
2 Mauro Calcagno, *From Madrigal to Opera: Monteverdi's Staging of the Self* (Berkeley: University of California Press, 2012), 110.
3 Calcagno, *From Madrigal to Opera*, 112.
4 Calcagno, *From Madrigal to Opera*, 101.
5 While this framework conflicts with Calcagno's reading of the Basso as representing the first-person *io* of the poem, it does complement his later expansion of that voice's role to comprise "a conflation…of the *persona* of the composer…with the *persona* of the poet, coalescing into the actual singer at the moment in which he sings the word *io*."
6 Battista Guarini, *Il pastor fido* (Venice: Bonfadino, 1589 [dated 1590]).

7 This scenario reverses the customary male and female roles of earlier neo-Latin plays in the Renaissance, such as Tommaso Mezzo's *Epirota* (Venice, 1483), Giovanni Antonio Marso's *Stephanium* (Venice, n.d., written in 1502), and Bartolomeo Zamberti's *Dolotechne* (Venice, 1504), wherein a daughter of noble standing, who has long been separated from her family, falls in love with a young aristocrat but is forbidden to marry him due to her lack of a dowry and her low social status. The opposition between patriarchal interests (for the groom's father to acquire a dowry and lucrative relations through the son's marriage) and love is resolved through the discovery of the young woman's father, who turns out to be a former, wealthy acquaintance of the groom's father.

8 As Joseph Addison wrote over a century after the play's publication:

> In the *Pastor Fido*, a shepherdess reasons after an abstruse philosophical manner about the violence of love, and expostulates with the gods for making laws so rigorous to restrain us, and at the same time giving us invincible desires. Whoever can bear these, may be assured he hath no taste for pastoral.

The Guardian (no. 28, 13 April 1713), as cited in Nicolas Perella, "Amarilli's Dilemma: The *Pastor fido* and Some English Authors," *Comparative Literature* 12 (1960): 348–59, at 353.

9 On the double-sided nature of Arcadia and its function for Renaissance courtly society, see Giuseppe Gerbino, *Music and the Myth of Arcadia in Renaissance Italy* (Cambridge: Cambridge University Press, 2009), especially 256–91.

References

Calcagno, Mauro. *From Madrigal to Opera: Monteverdi's Staging of the Self.* Berkeley: University of California Press, 2012.

Gerbino, Giuseppe. *Music and the Myth of Arcadia in Renaissance Italy.* Cambridge: Cambridge University Press, 2009.

Guarini, Battista. *Il pastor fido.* Venice: Bonfadino, 1589 [dated 1590].

McClary, Susan. *Modal Subjectivities: Self-Fashioning in the Italian Madrigal.* Berkeley: University of California Press, 2004.

Perella, Nicolas. "Amarilli's Dilemma: The *Pastor fido* and Some English Authors." *Comparative Literature* 12 (1960): 348–59.

1 Reading the Madrigal

Mode, Structure, and the Analysis of Late-Renaissance Music

On Mode

The multivalent view of the madrigal as affective reading likewise requires an innovative approach to analysis that is at once informed by musical thinking of the time and forceful in handling both text and music. Analyses of late-Renaissance vocal polyphony in recent years have focused predominantly on surface- and phrase-level features of the music, such as texture, melodic contour, rhythmic character, motions between sonorities, dissonance, cadences, and so forth. Such foreground activity is, indeed, vital to the delivery and expression of the text, and to the delineation of its formal layout. Equally essential, however, is the consideration of how the individual passages and isolated details relate to one another and to the whole in a coherent and integrated way to create a work that has a discernible beginning, middle, and end. This conception of the "whole" in a composition is defined most fundamentally by the frameworks of mode and the poetic text.

According to Renaissance theorists, mode was not only indispensable, it was to be heeded and made apparent at all times in a composition. Pietro Pontio, a practicing composer and a student of Cipriano de Rore in Parma, writes in his *Dialogo, ove si tratta della theorica e prattica di musica* (1595) that "the mode must be observed above anything else in a composition; otherwise, the whole would be constructed haphazardly."[1] Seven years earlier, in his *Ragionamento di musica*, Pontio stressed that in addition to knowing counterpoint, it is imperative that a composer also have a thorough comprehension of mode:

> because, even if you understood consonances and dissonances…and you did not understand the modes, and consequently, their cadences, you would be like a blind man, who just goes around and has no guide and at last finds that he has lost the way; this, I say, would happen to you if you did not understand the modes.[2]

According to Gioseffo Zarlino, a student of Adrian Willaert and teacher of theorist Giovanni Maria Artusi (who will return later in the chapters on

DOI: 10.4324/9781315463056-2

Monteverdi's madrigals), not only did mode exist, but it played a discernible part in the overall process—"the whole form"—of a work. In his influential *Le istitutioni harmoniche* (1558), Zarlino writes:

> It should be noted that the mode of a composition can be judged by two things: first by the form of the entire composition, and second, by the ending of the composition, namely, by its final note. Since it is form which gives being to a thing, I would consider it reasonable to determine the mode of a composition not merely by the final note, as some have wanted, but by the whole form contained in the composition.[3]

Zarlino continues by condoning the ending of a work on a pitch other than the final (namely the fifth), as long as the mode is clearly upheld in the overall form.[4]

While Renaissance theorists stand notoriously at odds about the affects of the modes, their proper cadence pitches, and (following the proposal of a twelve-mode theory in Heinrich Glarean's *Dodecachordon* of 1547) their number, most do agree on the basic means by which to establish and identify mode. Beyond merely observing the starting and ending sonorities (which, theorists tell us, are not sufficient for judging the mode), there are four principal ways by which to determine a work's mode: the ambitus, or ranges, of the voices; the melodic outlining of the intervallic species of the mode; reciting pitch; and cadence plan.[5]

The ambitus of each voice generally centers on a principal octave, including its neighboring pitches above and below. Through melodic behavior, this octave should bear a distinct division into perfect fifth (*diapente*) and perfect fourth (*diatessaron*), the placement of which determines whether the mode is authentic or plagal (see Example 1.1). It is the intervallic makeup of the octave species and its component *diapente* and *diatessaron* that gives each mode its distinctive features. As Renaissance theorists explain, these basic species of perfect consonances—octave, fifth, and fourth—should be emphasized regularly across a piece as melodic boundaries and at the beginnings and endings of phrases, particularly in the voices regarded as the principal bearers of mode, the Tenore and (increasingly after the mid-sixteenth century) the Canto. Moreover, contemporary theorists identify the final of a mode as the lowest pitch of the modal *diapente*—not the base of an octave scale or the root of a sonority—and in turn consider the *diapente* "more noble" than the *diatessaron*.[6]

After ambitus and melodic character, a third means of delineating the mode is through the "reciting tone": the interval above the final that characteristically figures prominently as a melodic boundary and cadence goal of a given mode (marked "R" in Example 1.1).[7] Finally, mode may be distinguished by the cadences deployed across a piece, and in particular, by the differentiation between the various cadential goals in terms of frequency and structural weight—the relative weight being influenced by factors such

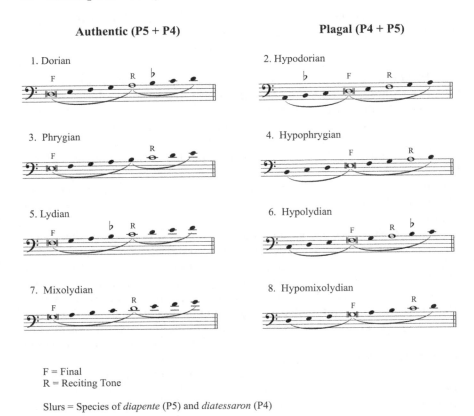

F = Final
R = Reciting Tone

Slurs = Species of *diapente* (P5) and *diatessaron* (P4)

Example 1.1 The Modes and Their Interval Species

as voicing, the fruition of each individual cadential part, the duration of the preparation and conclusion, position in the tactus, and placement in the text (discussed below). Despite theorists' notorious disagreements over the principal cadence degrees and the hierarchy among them, in practice most modes favor cadences on the principal boundaries of the modal octave and its division—i.e., on the final, $\hat{1}$, and cofinal, $\hat{5}$—as well on the reciting tone (when it differs from the cofinal).

Likewise, though not widely acknowledged in contemporary treatises, the music itself reveals that the modes may borrow features such as the reciting tone and principal cadences from their collateral forms. Thus, for example, it is not uncommon for G-mixolydian works to have a strong tendency toward C (the reciting pitch of the mode's plagal partner, G-hypomixolydian), and E-phrygian works, toward A (the reciting pitch of E-hypophrygian) as a cadence goal and melodic boundary.

Moreover, all of the eight modes may also appear in transposed form downward by fifth (using the flat system) or up a fifth. As early as 1476, theorist Johannes Tinctoris, in fact, supports that the four modal finals may appear at any pitch-level through transposition:

> Four places...are regularly attributed to our four tones [modes], hence when they finish on these they are called regular. However, these tones can finish in all places by other rules, coming about through true or *ficta* music, either within or without the [Guidonian] hand, and then they have been called irregular.[8]

Tinctoris then gives the example of transposing the F-lydian mode not only up a fifth to C, but also down a fifth to B♭, although this is seldom seen in extant works.[9] Hence, the seven octave species and their viable divisions (Example 1.2) include four modes with irregular finals (A and C), labeled in parentheses in Example 1.2, that result from transpositions of modes from their natural octaves. For instance, the C-lydian mode is a transposition of F-lydian down a fourth to the C octave. In the twelve-mode system, these transposed forms came to signify two new modal families: aeolian and ionian.

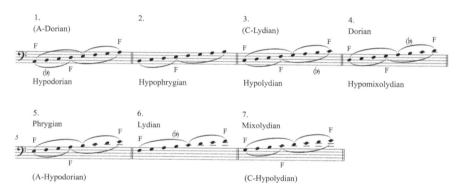

Example 1.2 The Seven Octave Species (Eight-Mode System)

It is important to note also that while the species of octave, fifth, and fourth are elemental to modal identity, the D-dorian/hypodorian and F-lydian/hypolydian pairs often make widespread use of B♭, notated either locally as an accidental or with a flat system (*cantus mollis*), as indicated in Examples 1.1 and 1.2 (and as seen in Arcadelt's *Il bianco e dolce cigno* in the Introduction). The transposed forms of these modes likewise maintain the use of ♭$\hat{6}$ (dorian/hypodorian) and ♭$\hat{4}$—for instance, through notated E♭ in the *cantus-mollis* system for G-(hypo)dorian, or the inclusion of ♭$\hat{4}$(F) through the *cantus-durus* system of C-(hypo)lydian. Defenders of the eight-mode theory found various ways to justify these inflections, in contrast to Glarean and later twelve-mode proponents, who dealt with them by championing new aeolian and ionian modal pairs in the sixteenth century. In practice, however, the deployment and even predominance of B♭ in the D-dorian- and F-lydian-type modes (and of E♭ in the G-dorian modal pair) was widespread and, it seems, an inherent and long-standing convention of these modes. Theoretical justification for the use of the lowered $\hat{6}$ in Modes 1 and 2 and the lowered $\hat{4}$ in Modes 5 and 6, in turn, comes from as early a source as Marchetto da Padova's *Lucidarium* (c.1317).[10]

The devising of a new modal pair to accommodate D- and F-final works with B♭ under the twelve-mode system—namely the D-aeolian/hypoaeolian and F-ionian/hypoionian modes—in effect rendered the designations "dorian" and "lydian" largely obsolete, for by the sixteenth century D- and F-final works in "pure" *cantus durus* (i.e., without "accidental" B♭) prove scarce. Hence, the two new modal pairs—aeolian and ionian—did little more than replace the traditional dorian and lydian modes used overwhelmingly in practice, which likely explains why both eight- and twelve-mode theories continued to coexist long after Glarean's *Dodecachordon* (1547): both systems were, in effect, eight-mode theories, only that the "twelve-mode" version effectively renamed the dorian and lydian types used in practice and relegated their traditional names to disuse. As Glarean himself remarks as early as 1547:

> Certainly our time does not use the old fifth mode and also the old sixth mode as frequently as the present new fifth and sixth modes, namely, the eleventh and twelfth or Iastian [Ionian] and Hypoiastian [Hypoionian].[11]

In this study, I will adhere to the traditional eight-mode nomenclature, whereby dorian comprises what some would consider aeolian, and lydian encompasses what some would call ionian, as shown in Example 1.2.

The Contrapuntal Cadence as Syntactic Musical–Textual Marker

Despite the notorious disagreements among Renaissance theorists on the number and proper cadences of the modes, and the *ad hoc* and often anachronistic valuation of cadences in many modern analyses, contemporaneous sources prove remarkably consistent when it comes to the basic structure and formal–rhetorical roles of cadences. The cadence in pre-tonal polyphony is fundamentally a contrapuntal event formed by two voices moving stepwise in contrary motion toward a common pitch—either as a major sixth expanding to an octave (Example 1.3a), or its inverse, a minor third (or tenth) converging on a unison (or octave; Example 1.3b).[12] Bernhard Meier usefully termed these two integral components the *clausulae tenorizans* ($\hat{2}$–$\hat{1}$) and *cantizans* ($\hat{7}$–$\hat{8}$) after the voices in which they characteristically appear in medieval and early-Renaissance polyphony, although they may occur in any voice part. This basic two-part design may be enhanced in a number of ways rhythmically and contrapuntally, such as by incorporating a 7–6 (or 2–3) suspension in the *clausula cantizans* (Example 1.3c), or by adding other parts to the two-part structure (Examples 1.3d–f). By the sixteenth century, the support of a leap from $\hat{5}$ to $\hat{1}$ in the lowest sounding voice (the *clausula basizans*) became standard for assertive cadences, particularly at the end of a work or at major sectional divisions. Though the formations for three or more voices resemble the common harmonic cadential patterns of tonal music—namely vii°⁶–I and V–I—the cadence in late-Renaissance and early-Baroque polyphony remains essentially linear in conception. Voices added to the underlying motion from a major sixth to an octave (or its inversion)—including the $\hat{5}$–$\hat{1}$ bass—therefore act as subsidiary contrapuntal support to the cadence and hence affect its relative weight. Likewise, the common raising of the third above the cadential goal represents a transient, superficial inflection, similar to a "Picardy third," and therefore does not signal a change of mode, as many studies have construed it.[13] Composers could also weaken the conclusiveness of a cadence through various means of *fuggire la cadenza* (evading the cadence)—for instance, by diverting one of the component voices from the final (such as $\hat{2}$–$\hat{3}$, $\hat{2}$–$\hat{5}$, $\hat{5}$–$\hat{6}$, and so forth) or having a voice rest at the moment of resolution—by shortening the duration of the preparation or arrival, or by aligning the cadence with an inconclusive moment in the text.

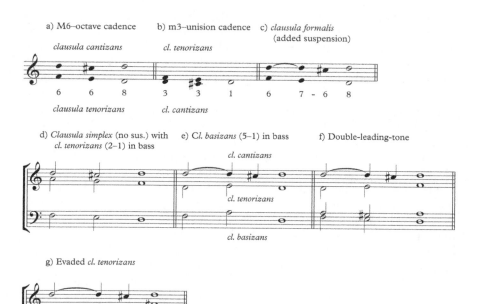

Example 1.3 The Contrapuntal Cadence

Through the sixteenth century, both theory and practice showed a growing focus on a two-voice framework between soprano and bass in place of the traditional soprano–tenor skeleton, particularly in homophonic settings. In his *Antica musica ridotta alla moderna prattica* (1555), Nicola Vicentino testifies to the privileging of the outer voices when it comes to recognizing the mode, revealing his own preference for the lowest voice when he writes:

> When getting acquainted with a composition, many composers look at the soprano, from which part they cannot securely judge the mode of the work. Let students first rely on the bass, for in that part, there appear the fourths and fifths that form all the modes.[14]

The increasing emphasis on the bass over the tenor led not only to a more structural relationship between the outer voices, but also at times to the prioritizing at cadences of the integrity of the *clausulae cantizans* ($\hat{7}$–$\hat{8}$) and *basizans* ($\hat{5}$–$\hat{1}$) over that of the essential *clausula tenorizans* ($\hat{2}$–$\hat{1}$), the latter often being implied but evaded in a closing $\hat{2}$–$\hat{3}$ motion (Example 1.3g).[15] The outer-voice framework gained supremacy through the seventeenth century and took shape elementally in accompanied solo song and in the advent of basso continuo around 1600.

The opening of Arcadelt's *Il bianco e dolce cigno*, shown in Example I.1 in the Introduction, demonstrates well the use of a range of cadence types as syntactical markers in coordination with the grammar and sense of the text, rather than with its line breaks. Following a three-part, "vii^{o6}–I"-type arrival to F with sixth-to-octave motion in the Tenore and Alto in mm. 4–5 come two statements of "Et io / Piangendo giungo al fin del viver mio," both based on the same Basso line and ending in F cadences with the same *clausula cantizans* (mm. 6–10 and 10–15). Arcadelt revoices and reworks these two cadences, however, so that the second carries more weight. The first shows the M6–octave formula again in the Tenore and Alto, now with 5–1 Basso, but the Alto evades the *tenorizans* by leading 2–3 (*g–a*), as in Example 1.3g. The restatement then transfers the 7–8 (*cantizans*) motion to the Canto, completes the *clausula tenorizans* (*g–f*) in the Tenore, and maintains the 5–1 *basizans* (Example 1.3e). While all three arrivals lead to the F final, the increasing finality of the cadences reserves the strongest for last, thereby marking both the end of the syntactical unit and the "fin del viver mio" (end of the speaker's life). This increase in cadential strength also helps explain why the Canto adopts the Tenore's line (from mm. 7–10) in mm. 12–15. All of these features of the cadence in terms of formation, voicing, and varying degrees of rhetorical and structural weight play an integral role as well in composer's renderings of Guarini's verse, and serve as the basis for individualized and sometimes strikingly idiosyncratic modifications of the basic cadential motion for text-expressive purposes.

Theorists maintain that cadences should be made predominantly on the pitches appropriate to each mode. The problem, however, is that they often disagree about what these proper cadences are, thus demonstrating the difficulty of identifying a reliable hierarchy of cadence pitches for the modes, as well as deviations from standard practice. Zarlino, for example, is unusual in his strict, systematic derivation of a hierarchy of three regular cadence pitches for each mode: $\hat{1}$, $\hat{5}$, and $\hat{3}$. All other cadence degrees, Zarlino asserts, are irregular. The reasoning behind Zarlino's scheme is that regular cadences are formed only on "the true and natural initial tones" of a mode, which are "on the extreme notes of the *diapente* and *diatessaron*, and on the median note which divides the *diapente*."[16] These pitches also happen to coincide with those pitches contained in a sonority built on the modal final. Many later theorists, including Seth Calvisius, Orazio Tigrini, Joachim Burmeister, and others, follow Zarlino's system, but tend to be more willing to admit exceptional cases.[17] The hierarchies of cadence pitches proposed by Pietro Aron, by contrast, prove highly unsystematic and loosely defined, owing largely to his agenda of aligning them with the psalm tones and the variable endings (*differentiae*) thereof, and to his tortuous efforts to assign works in transposed modes to a mode on one of the four "regular" (untransposed) finals: D, E, F, and G. For the mixolydian mode, for example, Aron cites all five pitches in the modal *diapente*—G, A, B, C, and D—as appropriate cadences, yet he offers no further insight as to how they rank among themselves.[18]

In practice, the proper cadences of the modes often do fall on the modal $\hat{1}$, $\hat{5}$, and $\hat{3}$, but with two important exceptions that affect four of the eight modes. First, if the third or the fifth degree of a mode is B-*mi*, preference is given to the pitch a semitone above it, C, owing to the lack of a perfect fifth above B-*mi*.[19] This situation applies to the phrygian and mixolydian modal pairs. Second, the anomalous phrygian-type modes have a distinctive inclination toward the fourth degree, A, over the third degree, G, as a cadence pitch, sonority, and melodic boundary, to the extent that A rivals the final in terms of salience, particularly toward the openings of works. In all, then, the mixolydian-type modes favor cadences on $\hat{1}$ (G), $\hat{4}$ (C), and $\hat{5}$ (D), and the phrygian-type, on $\hat{1}$ (E), $\hat{4}$ (A), and $\hat{6}$ (C), although arrivals on $\hat{3}$ (G) and $\hat{5}$ (B-*mi*) are neither uncommon nor disruptive in the latter.[20]

These principal cadences of the modes observed in practice, however, can be accounted for straightforwardly by the fact that they correspond to a given mode's final plus the reciting tones of *both* the mode itself and its collateral (i.e., authentic/plagal partner). This general principle, thus, rationalizes the seeming inconsistencies in the primary cadences seen in practice for the phrygian pair ($\hat{1}$, $\hat{4}$, and $\hat{6}$) and the mixolydian pair ($\hat{1}$, $\hat{4}$, and $\hat{5}$), while the dorian and lydian pairs favor $\hat{1}$, $\hat{3}$, and $\hat{5}$. At the same time, theorists regard cadences on pitches other than these customary sites as foreign—*cadenze irregolari* (Zarlino), *peregrine* (Tigrini and Dressler), *per transito* (Pontio), and *affinales* (Burmeister)—thus underscoring the instability, or structural "dissonance," that such gestures introduce to a piece. Such effects of cadential disruption and conflict with the underlying mode, of course, also carry expressive potential. Moreover, while foreign cadences may be localized in their effect and, thus, carry little structural weight, in other instances they may form part of a broader shift into an entirely new modal context and bring more integral and lasting consequences.

Modal Unity within Diversity: *Commixtio Tonorum*

While establishing and maintaining accountability to the underlying mode is of utmost importance in a composition, the introduction of other modal contexts in the course of a work likewise proves a key rhetorical–structural strategy. Changes of mode on a local level were by no means rare in Renaissance music, and theorists widely recognized and accepted the practice. Just as Zarlino describes that "dissonances are used incidentally and secondarily... [to] pass from one consonance to another,"[21] so the underlying mode may give way in the course of a composition to a mode that is considered unstable and subsidiary. That is to say, the mode that governs the larger framework of the piece may at times be temporarily displaced by modes that are structurally foreign or dissonant. This process, referred to in sixteenth-century theory as *commixtio tonorum*, ranges from localized emphases of the *diapente* or *diatessaron* of a foreign mode to an extended portion of a work in which a new mode becomes fully operative. Such a departure from the fundamental mode generally occurs in the middle of a piece and often comes as a reflection of the text, [22] yet certain theorists also admit that a long piece may use *commixtio* purely for the sake of variety.[23] In Renaissance polyphony, *commixtio tonorum* is manifest in the concerted emphasis in the full texture of a foreign mode through the delineation of its principal boundary pitches and species of perfect consonances (i.e., the modal octave plus its divisions into fifth/fourth) in melodic motion, cadential centricity, and the sonorities that figure prominently at phrase beginnings and endings and in duration.

In the works of composers such as Orlando di Lasso, Cipriano de Rore, Giaches de Wert, Luca Marenzio, and others in the second half of the sixteenth century, *commixtio tonorum* becomes increasingly prominent and distinct. Entire verses of the text are set apart modally by way of melodic behavior, cadential centricity, and ambitus. At times, a madrigal or motet might comprise an entire series of juxtaposed modal contexts, some so clearly articulated as to effect the full abandonment of one mode for another. Yet, while Renaissance theorists stress the need to distinguish hierarchically between these subsidiary, foreign modes and the true fundamental one, precisely how these differing modal contexts interrelate as components of an integrated, coordinated structure has remained open to question. This comes as little surprise, given the resistance that even the notion of large-scale unity in pre-tonal music has faced from some modern analysts.

Heinrich Schenker, for instance, throughout his writings makes clear his view of early music as "irrational."[24] According to Schenker, the shortcomings of early music stemmed above all from the inadequacies of the modal system, which Schenker describes as "often beset with unnatural, vexed, and tortuous features."[25] In his *Counterpoint* of 1910, Schenker proposed that, "provided with only a small stock of technical devices... composers still meandered along the text from passage to passage and from cadence to cadence."[26] The basic idea that early music lacks unity and integration is echoed in Don Harrán's assertion that the madrigal specifically "is a form...without focus or orientation," the phrases of which "follow cumulatively upon one another, too individualized to sustain a general mood or to impart a sense of direction."[27]

Nevertheless, numerous studies in more recent years have sought to demonstrate deeper-level structural processes in pre-tonal music, many making use of Schenkerian reductive techniques (some in more orthodox ways than others). Most of these analyses, however, have stopped short of explaining how more localized structures form part of any far-reaching, coherent process in a way that is at once sensitive to contemporary thinking and paradigmatic to music of the period.

Analytical Approaches to Late-Renaissance Polyphony

Many systems of analysis for pre-tonal music have appeared in recent scholarly literature, but few of these methods meet the challenge of providing a rigorous, systematic means of analysis while still remaining accountable to contemporaneous musical thinking. Numerous studies, for example, have applied tonal theory to medieval and Renaissance music, even reducing the music to a large-scale harmonic unfolding in traditional Schenkerian fashion devoid of any modal implications. Others have applied more historically informed ideas to the music with varying degrees of success in terms of achieving a normative and informative analytical model. Cristle Collins Judd, for example, has examined middleground melodic behavior in Josquin's motets using what she terms "modal types": melodic–contrapuntal paradigms based on three "tonalities"—*ut*, *re*, and *mi*—and characteristic intervallic patterns denoted by solmization syllables (e.g., *re–la* for D-final works with prominent D–A motion in the contrapuntal upper voice).[28] Although compelling in its application to Josquin's sacred works and its grounding in practice as well as theory, the method has limited applicability outside the domain of sacred polyphony around 1500 and, thus, falls short of providing a paradigmatic analytical model for Renaissance music at the fundamental level. Moreover, Judd's focus almost exclusively on melodic boundaries above the final neglects fundamental distinctions between the *diatessaron* of the modes. This oversight proves particularly consequential in the cases of the lydian and mixolydian modal pairs, all of which are reduced to a single tonality (*ut*), which, in turn, likewise overlooks the characteristic variability of the lydian modal $\hat{4}$ (B-*mi/fa*) and the mixolydian $\hat{7}$ (F$\sharp$/$\natural$).

The hexachords have also become the basis of an analytical system aimed at exploring harmonic and tonal behavior in Renaissance and early-Baroque music. The technique views the hexachordal degrees not only as pitches, but also, problematically, as chordal roots that together form a partial circle-of-fifths series reaching from *fa* on the flat (*mollis*) side to *mi* on the sharp (*durus*) side. Any harmonic movement beyond these boundaries brings a shift of hexachord and possibly a shift of system in the *mollis* or *durus* direction, similar to the way a foreign harmony in tonal music might effect a change of key. This kinship with tonal harmony is a central feature of the analytical model, as its earliest exponents (Carl Dahlhaus and Eric Chafe) applied it to illuminating tonal behavior in early music, centering on the works of Claudio Monteverdi.[29]

Despite its integral use of hexachords, the method raises many discordances with pre-Baroque thought and practice. To begin, there is no evidence that musicians of the time perceived the hexachordal degrees as parts of a perfect-fifth series or as chordal roots. In fact, the very notion of "chords" did not exist until the seventeenth century. Rather, Renaissance musicians viewed vertical sonorities as products of the contrapuntal interactions of the voices. Further, the theory overlooks the fact that the hexachords represented a means of conceptualizing individual lines of a composition, so any "chord" would more appropriately comprise three separate syllables, each depending on the solmizations surrounding it, not a single syllable tied to the root pitch alone. Hexachordal analyses also tend to prioritize harmonic explanations of the music over contrapuntal considerations (such as *mi contra fa*). Lastly, the theory's failure to distinguish systematically between hexachord, system, and mode seems to facilitate a noncommittal approach to mode, calling instead for designations by pitch-center and system (e.g., G-*mollis* instead of G-dorian/hypodorian) and for descriptions of shifts in a *mollis* or *durus* direction where, in fact, modal mixture might be at play. *Mollis/durus* shifts, in other words, are often products of modal mixture, not equivalent to it, as Dahlhaus and Chafe contend. These hexachord-driven readings by Dahlhaus and Chafe of certain *Pastor fido* madrigals will be addressed in the later discussion of Monteverdi.

Many studies have incorporated aspects of Renaissance theory and practice with Schenkerian-style reductive techniques, some with more accountability to the tenets of Renaissance thinking than others.[30] Along the more tonal end of this spectrum falls the work of Felix Salzer, William Mitchell, Peter Bergquist, and David Stern.[31] Their analyses rely heavily on triadic readings of the music, and lead either to a quasi-tonal background or to piece-specific structures that seem to dispense with any aim at a normative background.

Other reductive-style approaches have remained more mindful of Renaissance precepts on the musical surface in their analyses, yet fall short of attaining what a true background model should define: a unified, stylistic paradigm that prevails in a given historical–cultural period and that provides a touchstone by which to measure how pieces of the period uphold or deviate from convention.[32] Some scholars, however, have indeed made considerable advances in the application of Schenkerian methods toward such an end, often adopting a structural model based on $\hat{5}-\hat{1}$ (*diapente*) descents or on stock bass or melodic patterns, such as the *romanesca*.

In her revealing study "The Transition from Modal to Tonal Organization in the Works of Monteverdi" (1976), for example, Susan McClary demonstrates the projection of mode through chains of upper-voice descents of a fifth, a pattern derived (along with their typically attendant bass progressions) from secular melodic prototypes, such as the *romanesca*, *passamezzo*, and *folia*.[33] With its focus on surface and middleground fifth descents, McClary's analyses at times overlook other means of local expansion (some of which we will encounter below) and how these processes derive from a deeper-level structure (although her very useful notion of parenthetical expansion offers a glimpse of such a synthesis). Instead, structure is portrayed in McClary's work as a series of descents, the hierarchical rankings of which are determined principally by placement—those at the beginning and, especially, the end typically carry the most weight—and frequency. In this respect, McClary's theory refashions the troublesome attempts in Renaissance theory to explicate modal structure using cadential hierarchies, also allowing a means to identify and explain modal mixture (as subsidiary descents from individual notes within the background descent). Also with notable effectiveness, Geoffrey Chew similarly explicates the "prototonal" behavior (or "directedness") of Monteverdi's music as a system of interlocking descents of an octave, fifth, or fourth. Chew's method, however, stops short of revealing a systematic means by which to differentiate structural weight among these various descents (other than by virtue of placement) and, hence, to distinguish middleground processes from a more fundamental, determining course.[34]

The analytical method used here for the study of early settings of *Il pastor fido* aims to illustrate long-ranging structural processes in the music by incorporating aspects of a Schenkerian-style system of hierarchical levels (and the means of notating them) into a framework rooted in Renaissance contrapuntal and modal theory.[35] While utilizing the principles of voice-leading and contrapuntal diminution common to both Renaissance and Schenkerian theory, the technique could hardly be considered truly Schenkerian with its foregoing of the notion of a controlling background triad and tonal harmonic syntax in favor of a modal framework more relevant to this repertory.[36] This modal structure, at its most basic level, takes the form of a linear descent across a work through the steps of one of the mode-defining interval species, typically the species of fifth ($\hat{5}-\hat{1}$). This is, in essence, a monophonic structure, since it is the arrangement of tones and semitones within the fifth that defines the identity of the mode, and not the interval of the fifth itself or a triad built on its final. Nicola Vicentino describes the fundamental importance of the basic, mode-defining interval species—octave, fifth, and fourth—with language that resonates strongly with Schenker's later conception of a background structure realized through linear unfolding. Vicentino writes:

> The most important foundation a composer must have in mind is this: he should consider what he plans to build his composition on, in keeping with the words, be they sacred or on another subject. The foundation of this building is the selection of a tone or mode suitable to the words or to another idea. On that foundation, then, he will use his judgment to measure well and to draw over this good foundation the lines of the fourths and fifths of the chosen mode, which lines are the columns that support the building of the composition and its boundaries, even though the fourths and fifths of other modes may be placed between them. These [other fourths and fifths] do no harm to this edifice when they are disposed and matched gracefully in a few locations in the middle of the work. It is with such architectural variety that composers adorn the building of their composition, as do good architects...[37]

The crucial role of linear descents, particularly those of a perfect fifth, at various levels of structure in late-Renaissance polyphony has long been recognized in modern scholarship. An especially lucid example of the process can be seen in middleground structures based on strophic aria formulas, such as the *romanesca*, in which an upper-voice descent supported by a standard bass pattern serves as a basis for elaboration. Whereas scholars such as David Gagné and Susan McClary have explored the role of these formulas as outer-voice frameworks, Claude Palisca provides evidence that such arias were defined fundamentally by the progression of the upper voice alone, and, hence, not by the outer voices together, or by the bass or chord patterns, which became somewhat standardized only later and remained flexible.[38] Palisca's finding is consistent with the model employed here of a basic upper-voice framework supported by a variable, structurally subordinate, and often disjunct lower voice (or voices). Moreover, as described above, while the Tenore and Canto maintained their status as the principal bearers of mode according to many contemporary theorists, the conception of the outer voices individually as modal determinants finds growing support through the sixteenth century.[39]

Example 1.4 illustrates the possible means by which the G-dorian mode may be projected as a background across an entire work. The upper staff contains the fundamental stepwise descent through the G-dorian *diapente* from *d″* to *g′* in *cantus mollis*. The middle staff, labeled "Viable contrapuntal support," shows all options for lower-voice consonant support of the large-scale structure. Accordingly, the lower voice buttresses the pitches of the upper voice at the intervals of octave, fifth, or third below. The definitive contrapuntal support may assert itself in a multitude of ways on the surface of a composition: as cadential center, through relative salience (duration, rhythmic character, texture, register, etc.), by its association with the text or with a musical motive, and so forth. In practice, only a selection of these fundamental lower-voice pitches will be employed in a single composition, so long as each of the background pitches receives contrapuntal support. The final itself may appear as structural underpinning for three of the *diapente* pitches: $\hat{5}$, $\hat{3}$, and $\hat{1}$, respectively. The lower-voice support, in turn, might change while a given background pitch remains active in the upper voice. As the analyses here will show, the degrees of this background structure in any mode are typically articulated with an event of distinctive musical–textual salience and contextual support on the musical surface and maintained (prolonged) through modal and contrapuntal means, such as local modal context (including *commixtio tonorum*), cadential focus, intervallic boundaries in melodic motion, voice-leading, and contrapuntal diminution.

Example 1.4 Options for Supporting a G-Dorian Background

The lowest staff, "Potential modal contexts," in Example 1.4 shows the possible means by which the upper-voice descent may be supported and delineated specifically by *commixtio tonorum*, by way of shifting the octave species and its division. The changing modal contexts allow for the correlation between operative modal/intervallic species and background structure, thereby allowing each fundamental pitch to appear within a region in which it is locally (modally) "consonant," but that may conflict with the underlying mode and, hence, be "dissonant," unstable, and yet subsidiary on the broader scale. Such internal modal contrasts play an important role not only in supporting and expanding the structural line and reflecting notions of conflict and instability in the text, but also in generating a sense of forward thrust and end-driven motion toward modal–structural resolution.

Like the "Viable contrapuntal support," the "Potential modal contexts" of Example 1.4 are merely an illustration of the potential *options* available to a composer. In practice, only a limited number of modal contexts are typically used in any given composition, and in some instances, *commixtio* plays no part at all, either in the long-range structure or at a local level. *Commixtio tonorum*, therefore, is not a requisite means of projecting the modal framework, but, rather, one of various potential means.

There are two notable features of the background of Example 1.4 that distinguish it from other models for tonal and early music. First is the manner by which the fundamental descent may be distributed across the piece through the use of *commixtio tonorum*. These changing modal contexts expand the basic framework by providing localized modal support for several individual pitches of the underlying diapente descent, each of which, in turn, is prolonged contrapuntally at more foreground levels.[40] This modal–structural partitioning, furthermore, tightly adheres to the formal, rhetorical, and expressive features of the text, thereby linking text and musical structure at the most basic level. Moreover, the distinct structural divisions created by the background motion are generally a direct consequence of the form of the text: the positions of prominent rhetorical pauses, verse structure, rhyme scheme, change of voice (speaker to imparted speech, for example), the interjection of an exclamation, and so forth. The influence of the text on the placement of the fundamental pitches reflects a concern for rhetorical presentation that characterizes this repertory as a whole, meaning that the spacing of the background may vary from work to work depending on both the disposition of the text and the composer's interpretation of it.

The second notable feature of Example 1.4 is the notion that linear structures derive not from harmonic unfoldings and progressions as in tonal music, but exclusively through contrapuntal and modal means. As a result, the second degree of the background structure may be supported by a context other than the modal $\hat{5}$—what we might consider the "dominant" in a tonal context. While such support is possible—and, indeed, common, given that it had by the late sixteenth century become a conventional part of the terminal cadential approach in non-phrygian works—it is not an essential structural feature of pre-tonal music. While often pointed out by analysts as evidence of emerging tonal functions, the dominant-to-tonic-type bass motion, as we have seen, played a subsidiary role in the Renaissance conception of cadence, which theorists defined invariably as a contrapuntal, and not a harmonic, procedure, even as the $\hat{5}$–$\hat{1}$ motion gained importance as a marker of cadential finality.

The subsidiary status of the lower voice and its terminal $\hat{5}$–$\hat{1}$ cadential motion extends as well to the status of the lower voice overall in the fundamental structure. As the basic framework derives essentially from the stepwise unfolding of a mode-defining interval in the structural upper voice, and not from the projection of a vertical, controlling triad as in tonal music, the lower voice in sixteenth-century music serves primarily as contrapuntal support to the directed course of the fundamental line and may therefore take a number of forms. This is certainly not to say that the lower voice is irrelevant or even unimportant, for it plays an integral role in defining modal boundaries, differentiating cadential weight, and providing a harmonic foundation to the contrapuntal fabric at more local levels.

As a systematic structural model for late-Renaissance polyphony, this approach provides a stylistic archetype for the basis of comparative studies of composer's individual strategies tailored to each text. Moreover, knowledge of such a model is crucial for identifying departures from contemporary norms and expectations, and, hence, how much subversions act as responses to the text. Factors such as the pacing of the background motion, the turbulence or stability of its unfolding, the positioning of structural events within the text, and the interplay between features on the musical surface and deeper-level processes that are generally overlooked by superficial analyses play a central part in composers' interpretative readings, particularly in conveying aspects of the speaker's affective state and intrinsic character and the rhetorical–expressive trajectory of the text.

Notes

1 Pietro Pontio, *Dialogo, ove si tratta della Theorica e Prattica di Musica* (Parma: Viotto, 1595), 25. This passage is translated in Bernhard Meier, *The Modes of Classical Vocal Polyphony, Described According to the Sources*, trans. Ellen Beebe (New York: Broude Brothers, 1988), 25.

2 Pontio, *Ragionamento di musica* (Parma: Viotto, 1588), 26; trans. in Meier, *The Modes of Classical Vocal Polyphony*, 94.

3 Gioseffo Zarlino, *Le istitutioni harmoniche* (Venice: Pietro da Fino, 1558), Book 4, Chapter 30; trans by Vared Cohen as *On the Modes* (New Haven, CT: Yale University Press, 1983), 90.

4 "Hence I say that if I had to judge a composition by its form, that is, by its manner of proceeding, as should be done, I would not consider it amiss for a principal mode to end on the median note of its diapason, divided harmonically, and, in a similar way, for a collateral mode to end on the extreme notes of its diapason, divided arithmetically, the final note having been laid aside" (Zarlino, *Le istitutioni harmoniche*, Book 4, Chapter 30; trans. in *On the Modes*, 90).

5 Heinrich Glarean writes:

> For although some contend that they [the modes] are distinguished by the final key and others by different fifth-species, these are not satisfactory to the discerning reader. Indeed the final key was discovered later and has not always been preserved in the same way, as usage demonstrates... And the same final key of two modes as well as their common fifth refutes this.

Dodecachordon (Basel: Heinrich Petri, 1547); trans. Clement Miller (Münster, Germany: American Institute of Musicology, 1965), Book II, Chapter 1, 103–104. Glarean's statement infers that the fifth-species (*diapente*) is insufficient only in determining the form, authentic or plagal, of a given mode. He argues instead that the entire octave-species and its constituent *diapente* and *diatessaron* are necessary to determine the mode.

6 In Book IV, Chapter 12 of *Le istitutioni harmoniche*, Zarlino writes: "The modes of the first group [the authentic] were called principal, for honor and preeminence are always given to those things which are more noble" (*On the Modes*, 41). In Chapter 13, he writes: "Modern musicians take as the final note of each mode the lowest note of the diapente, and it makes no difference whether the diatessaron is placed above or below it" (43).

7 This tendency of the modes toward a secondary pitch, or "reciting tone," may derive from their historical comingling with the psalm tones, whereby the prominent pitch used for reciting verses in a given psalm tone likewise took on a distinguishing and salient role in the most closely related mode. The locations of the reciting tones in these mode/psalm tone pairs, however, may themselves derive from the particular intervallic makeup of each pair, as seen, for example, in instances where the reciting tone lies a semitone above B-*mi* (i.e., phrygian and hypomixolydian). In a polyphonic context, particularly by the sixteenth century, the reciting tones of both members of a authentic/plagal modal pair generally play important structural roles in both modes—for example, A and F in both dorian and hypodorian, and A and C in phrygian and hypophrygian—as discussed below.

8 Johannes Tinctoris, *Liber de natura et proprietate tonarum* (1476), Chapter 45; translated by Albert Seay as *Concerning the Nature and Propriety of Modes* (Colorado Springs: Colorado College Music Press, 1967), 41.

9 "The fifth tone and the sixth could finish irregularly within the hand on C *fa ut* through the natural and through the hard *quadro* and on B *fa quadro mi* acute through soft *fa* and through the natural and through the *coniuncta* E la mi acute, if it be necessary" (Tinctoris, *De natura et proprietate tonarum*, Chapter 48; trans. in *Concerning the Nature and Propriety of Modes*, 44). Similar descriptions of modal transposition appear throughout mid- to late-Renaissance theory. For example, Johannes (Turmair) Aventinus writes in 1516:

> The first and second modes are commonly transposed to a la mi re and g sol re ut. The third and fourth modes are transposed to b mi and a la mi re. The fifth and sixth modes are transposed to c sol fa ut, and the seventh and eighth modes are transposed to d la sol re (however we rarely transpose the eighth).
> (*Musicae Rudimenta*, trans. T. Herman Keahey
> [New York: Institute of Medieval Music, 1971], 27)

Also, Adrian Coclico shows all eight modes transposed up and down by fifth in his *Compendium musices* [1552], trans. Albert Seay (Colorado Springs: Colorado College Music Press, 1973), 12 (Coclico's Examples 7 and 8).

10 See Marchetto Da Padova, *The Lucidarium of Marchetto da Padova: A Critical Edition, Translation, and Commentary*, ed. and trans. Jan Herlinger (Chicago, IL: University of Chicago Press, 1985), 399–401.

11 Glarean, *Dodecachordon*, Bk. 2, Ch. 5; trans. in Miller, 111.

12 Many Renaissance treatises deal with the construction of cadences, some of which are summarized in Meier, *The Modes of Classical Vocal Polyphony*, 89–101. Stefano La Via also provides a detailed discussion of cadential structures in sixteenth-century theory and practice in "'Natura delle cadenze' e 'Natura contraria delli modi': Punti di convergenza fra teoria e prassi nel madrigale cinquecentesco," *Saggiatore musicale* 4 (1997), 5–51. See also, for example, Gioseffo Zarlino, *Le istitutioni harmoniche*, Book 3, Ch. 53; trans. Guy Marco and Claude Palisca as *The Art of Counterpoint* (New Haven, CT: Yale University Press, 1968), 141–51 and Joachim Burmeister, *Musica poetica* (Rostock: Mylian-der, 1606), Chapter 5; trans. by Benito Rivera as *Musical Poetics* (New Haven, CT: Yale University Press, 1993), 107–21.

13 Such theoretically incongruous views of raised thirds in cadential sonorities (and elsewhere) occur throughout Susan McClary's *Modal Subjectivities*, for example, where they are frequently construed in tonal terms as denoting "dominant" sonorities, even at points of resolution. In the first analysis of the book, of Monteverdi's *Ah, dolente partita*, McClary goes so far as to assert that the terminal cadence on A "contains a C♯, which can be—indeed, given the context

of this piece, *must* be—heard doubly: as the conventionally raised mediant in a final chord (the *tierce de Picardie*) or as the dominant of D," which, in turn, "produces the musical equivalent of Mirtillo's immortal undeath" (*Modal Subjectivities*, 35). For Gesualdo's madrigals, McClary's reading of a raised pitch as leading-tone is extended to any degree; hence, in the C♯-major sonority that opens *Moro, lasso, al mio duolo*, "C♯ could only be a leading tone to D, G♯ only a leading tone to A, and E♯...a leading tone to F♯?" (165). Such readings overlook the clear and consistent principles of cadences in contemporary theory.

14 Nicola Vicentino, *L'antica musica ridotta alla moderna prattica* (Rome: Antonio Barre, 1555), fol. 48r; trans. By Maria Rika Maniates in *Ancient Music Adapted to Modern Practice* (New Haven, CT: Yale University Press, 1996), 151.

15 In his analysis of Arcadelt's madrigals of the 1530s, for example, Benito Rivera notes that "all the homophonic non-imitative sections of Arcadelt's First Book of Madrigals are built on a soprano–bass rather than soprano–tenor framework" ("The Two-Voice Framework and Its Harmonization in Arcadelt's First Book of Madrigals," *Music Analysis* 6 [1987]: 59–88, at 64). Rivera also cites numerous examples from contemporary theory supporting that, through the course of the sixteenth century, "the bass is gradually emancipated—in practice and in theory—from the crutch of the discant–tenor structure" ("Harmonic Theory in Musical Treatises of the Late Fifteenth and Early Sixteenth Centuries," *Music Theory Spectrum* 1 [1979]: 80–95, at 81). Most theorists, however, maintain the primacy of the traditional mode-bearing voices, the discant and tenor, which lie within the principal range of the mode. See Meier, *The Modes of Classical Vocal Polyphony*, esp. 56–60.

16 Zarlino, *Le istitutioni harmoniche*, Book 3, Ch. 18; trans. *On the Modes*, 55. Zarlino continues:

> The regular cadences are those which are always made on the extreme sounds or notes of the modes, and on the median note by which the diapason is mediated or divided harmonically or arithmetically. These are the extreme notes of the diapente and the diatessaron. The regular cadences are also made on the median note by which the diapente is divided into a ditone and a semiditone.

17 For a summary of the cadence-pitch hierarchies of Zarlino, Calvisius, Tigrini, and others, see Meier, *The Modes of Classical Vocal Polyphony*, 105–11.

18 Pietro Aron's ranking of cadence pitches occurs in Chapters 9–12 of the *Trattato della natura et cognitione di tutti gli tuoni* (Venice: Bernardino de Vitali, 1525).

19 As Pontio writes: "talche il fine non sarebbe perfetto"—that is, it lacks a "perfect" cadence with 5–1 motion in the lowest voice (*Ragionamento di musica*, 107).

20 Zarlino, in fact, concedes that the phrygian-type and hypomixolydian modes are exceptions to his rigid cadential scheme. Rather than accepting their "aberrant" behaviors as innate characteristics of the modes themselves, he rationalizes them by invoking modal mixture: the phrygian-type modes, he explains, are typically mixed with A-aeolian and, therefore, cadence commonly on A, and G-hypomixolydian is generally mingled with C-ionian and gravitates toward C. This innate "mingling" of the G-mixolydian-type modes with C, in fact, becomes a crucial point of contention in the debate between Zarlino's student, Artusi, and composer Claudio Monteverdi over one of the latter's celebrated *Pastor fido* madrigals, *Cruda Amarilli* (see Chapter 7).

21 *Le istitutioni harmoniche*, Book III, Ch. 27; trans. in *Art of Counterpoint*, 53. The title of the chapter is "Compositions Must Be Composed Primarily of Consonances and Only Incidentally of Dissonances." This hierarchical conception parallels contemporary theorists' assertions of the secondary status of foreign modes in relation to the underlying mode.

22 See, for example, Meier, *The Modes of Classical Vocal Polyphony*, 286–354. In 1476, Tinctoris advises taking caution when determining the mode of a work, for "there may be repeated in the course of this tone [i.e., mode] a type of diapente or diatessaron of one or more other tones frequently and more often than its own" (*Concerning the Nature and Propriety of Modes*, 18). Likewise, Zarlino states:

> When in any of the modes set forth, whether authentic or plagal...a diapente or diatessaron used in another mode is repeated many times...the mode can be called mixed, because the diapente or the diatessaron of one mode becomes mixed with the melodic line of another.
>
> (*On the Modes*, 46)

Similarly, Vicentino asserts that in secular music, "a composer may forsake the modal order in favor of another mode," for in such works,

> the composer's sole obligation is to animate the words and, with harmony, to represent their passions—now harsh, now sweet, now cheerful, now sad—in accordance with their subject matter. This is why every bad leap and every poor consonance, depending on their effects, may be used to set the words. As a consequence, on such words you may write any sort of step or harmony, abandon the mode, and govern yourself by the subject matter of the vernacular words, as was said above.
>
> (*Ancient Music Adapted to Modern Practice*, 149)

23 See, for example, the theory of Illuminato Aiguino (1581), discussed in Peter Schubert, "The Fourteen-Mode System of Illuminato Aiguino," *Journal of Music Theory* 35 (1991): 174–210, especially 191–93.

24 See, for example, Heinrich Schenker, *Kontrapunkt. Neue musikalische Theorien und Phantasien II* (Vienna: Universal, 1910); trans. J. Rothgeb and J. Thym. as *Counterpoint* (New York: Schirmer, 1987), 21–22.

25 Schenker, *Harmonielehre: Neue Musikalische Theorien und Phantasien I* (Vienna: Universal, 1906); trans. E. Borgese as *Harmony*, ed. O. Jonas (Chicago, IL: Chicago University Press, 1954), 59.

26 Schenker, *Harmony*, 2. Pietro Pontio seems to have preemptively refuted Schenker's denial of synthesis and direction in pre-tonal music in his *Ragionamento di musica* (1588):

> Even if you understood consonances and dissonances...and you did not understand the modes, and consequently, their cadences, you would be like a blind man, who just goes around and has no guide and at last finds that he has lost the way; this, I say, would happen to you if you did not understand the modes.
>
> (94)

Translated in Meier, *The Modes of Classical Vocal Polyphony*, 26.

27 Don Harrán, "'Mannerism' in the Cinquecento Madrigal?" *Musical Quarterly* 4 (1969): 521–44, at 539.

28 Cristle Collins Judd, "Modal Types and 'Ut, Re, Mi' Tonalities: Tonal Coherence in Sacred Vocal Polyphony from about 1500," *Journal of the American Musicological Society* 45 (1992): 428–67 and "Aspects of Tonal Coherence in the Motets of Josquin," Ph.D. diss., King's College London, 1994. Judd derives the three basic "tonalities" from Glarean's statement that "the same men teach in this way concerning the ending of songs in all modes: Every song ends either on *re* or on *mi* or on *ut*" (*Dodecachordon*, Book 1, Ch. 12; trans. Miller, I, 70).

29 Carl Dahlhaus introduced hexachordal analysis in his *Studies on the Origin of Harmonic Tonality*, trans. Robert Gjerdingen (Princeton, NJ: Princeton University Press, 1991), which Eric Chafe developed further in *Monteverdi's Tonal Language* (New York: Schirmer, 1992).

30 David Stern examines many of the central issues concerning Schenkerian analysis of early music in his "Schenkerian Theory and the Analysis of Renaissance Music," in Siegel Hedi, ed., *Schenker Studies* (Cambridge: Cambridge University Press, 1990), 45–59.

31 See Felix Salzer, *Structural Hearing: Tonal Coherence in Music* (New York: Boni, 1952); William Mitchell, "The Prologue to Orlando di Lasso's Prophetiae Sibyllarum," *The Music Forum* 2 (1970): 264–73; Peter Bergquist, "Mode and Polyphony around 1500: Theory and Practice," *Music Forum* 1 (1967): 99–161; and David Stern, "Tonal Organization in Modal Polyphony," *Theory and Practice* 6 (1981): 5–39.

32 See, for example, the piece-specific structures that result from Frederich Bashour's analyses of Dufay in "Towards a More Rigorous Methodology for the Analysis of the Pre-Tonal Repertory," *College Music Symposium* 19 (1979): 140–53.

33 Susan McClary, "The Transition from Modal to Tonal Organization in the Works of Monteverdi," Ph.D. diss., Harvard University, 1976.

34 Geoffrey Chew, "The Perfections of Modern Music: Consecutive Fifths and Tonal Coherence in Monteverdi," *Music Analysis* 8/3 (1989): 247–73.

35 Literature on the applicability of Schenkerian analytical techniques to early music is vast. Many of the most imperative issues are summarized in David Stern, "Schenkerian Theory and the Analysis of Renaissance Music." Examining primarily the music of Josquin of the late-fifteenth and early-sixteenth centuries, Stern cites "the absence of the second scale degree as a structural tone" in the upper voice, along with the lack of a possibility for substitution (owing to the $\hat{2}$–$\hat{1}$ residing characteristically in the tenor), as an obstacle to fundamental $\hat{5}$–$\hat{1}$ descents. Not only does this deficiency diminish through the first half of the sixteenth century through the growing prevalence of the three-part cadence and a soprano–bass contrapuntal framework, and through the dissociation of upper voice parts from their respective cadential roles, but substitution in cadential formulations does indeed seem to be operative, as the $\hat{7}$–$\hat{8}$ motion implies a complementary $\hat{2}$–$\hat{1}$ descent in the presence of the $\hat{5}$–$\hat{1}$ bass—witnessed most transparently in three-voice context—often allowing a terminal $\hat{2}$–$\hat{3}$ in the topmost voice, a construction common to late-Renaissance polyphony. On the changing conception of the voices in the sixteenth century and its implications on cadential structure, see Rivera, "Harmonic Theory."

36 For a detailed description of this analytical model, its relationship to sixteenth-century theory, and a more thorough review of earlier studies applying Schenkerian analysis to early music, see also Coluzzi, "Structure and Interpretation in Luca Marenzio's Settings of *Il pastor fido*," Ph.D. diss., University of North Carolina at Chapel Hill (2007), especially Chapter 3, "The Analysis and Interpretation of Late-Renaissance Polyphony," 119–202.

37 Vicentino, *L'antica musica*, Book 3, Ch. 15, fol. 47v; trans. in *Ancient Music Adapted to Modern Practice*, 149. Vicentino continues by comparing the use of fourths and fifths from other (foreign) modes to architects who mix to good effect the Doric and Attic modes (for columns), or the Corinthian and the Ionian. Referring to the passage cited above, David Stern writes:

> Vicentino expresses with exemplary clarity the concept that the modal species form a structural framework which serves as the basis for melodic diminutions and elaborations. While Vicentino's modal framework is not the same as Schenker's *Ursatz* or fundamental structure, the idea that music consists of the elaboration of an underlying structure is common to both theorists.

> ("Schenkerian Theory," 52)

38 David Gagné, "Monteverdi's *Ohimè dov'è il mio ben* and the Romanesca," *The Music Forum* 6 (1987): 61–91; McClary, "The Transition from Modal to Tonal Organization"; and Palisca, "Vincenzo Galilei and Some Links between 'Pseudo-Monody' and Monody," *Musical Quarterly* 46 (1960): 344–60. Palisca cites a variety of sixteenth and early seventeenth century sources to support the notion of *arie* as melodic formulas, including Petrucci's Fourth Book of frottole (Venice, 1505), Baldassarre Castiglione's *Il libro del cortegiano* (Venice, 1528), Vincenzo Galilei's *Dialogo della musica antica et della moderna* (Florence: Marescotti, 1581), and Giulio Caccini's *Nuove musiche* (Florence: Marescotti, 1601). Gagne's study of the role of the *romanesca* as a contrapuntal framework in Monteverdi's *Ohimè, dov'è il mio ben* (1619) many times asserts the support of $\hat{5}$ (D) with III (B♭), even when support with G is quite evident. This is presumably not only to uphold the expected *romanesca* pattern, but also to avoid parallel fifths resulting from the support of $\hat{5}$–$\hat{4}$ (D–C) with $\hat{1}$–$\hat{7}$ (G–F). As Geoffrey Chew ("Perfections of Modern Music") has shown, however, such motion by parallel perfect consonances between outer voices proves characteristic of deeper-level linear descents in Monteverdi's music, which, even with the presence of a standard bass pattern, only underscores the essentially monophonic nature of such structures.
39 See above, note 15.
40 McClary ("The Transition from Modal to Tonal Organization") observes the presence of subsidiary descents from the individual pitches of the primary descent, which may or may not entail an articulated shift in modal context. McClary identifies these subsidiary *diapente* descents with contemporary contrapuntal paradigms such as the *passamezzo* and *romanesca*, and recognizes the role of these paradigms in expanding the principal scale degrees above the modal final—namely $\hat{4}$ and $\hat{5}$—but does not incorporate *commixtio tonorum* as an agent of middleground expansion in her model.

References

Aron, Pietro. *Trattato della natura et cognitione di tutti gli tuoni*. Venice: Bernardino de Vitali, 1525.

Aventinus, Johannes [Turmair]. *Musicae Rudimenta [1516]*. Trans. by T. Herman Keahey. New York: Institute of Medieval Music, 1971.

Bashour, Frederich. "Towards a More Rigorous Methodology for the Analysis of the Pre-Tonal Repertory." *College Music Symposium* 19 (1979): 140–53.

Bergquist, Peter. "Mode and Polyphony around 1500: Theory and Practice." *Music Forum* 1 (1967): 99–161.

Burmeister, Joachim. *Musica poetica*. Rostock: Stephan Myliander, 1606. Trans. by Benito Rivera as *Musical Poetics*. New Haven, CT: Yale University Press, 1993.

Chafe, Eric. *Monteverdi's Tonal Language*. New York: Schirmer, 1992.

Chew, Geoffrey. "The Perfections of Modern Music: Consecutive Fifths and Tonal Coherence in Monteverdi." *Music Analysis* 8/3 (1989): 247–73.

Coclico, Adrian. *Compendium musices [1552]*. Trans. by Albert Seay. Colorado Springs: Colorado College Music Press, 1973.

Coluzzi, Seth. "Structure and Interpretation in Luca Marenzio's Settings of *Il pastor fido*." Ph.D. diss. University of North Carolina at Chapel Hill, 2007.

Dahlhaus, Carl. *Studies on the Origin of Harmonic Tonality*. Trans. by Robert Gjerdingen. Princeton, NJ: Princeton University Press, 1991.

Da Padova, Marchetto. *Lucidarium [c.1317].* Ed. and trans. by Jan Herlinger as *The Lucidarium of Marchetto da Padova: A Critical Edition, Translation, and Commentary.* Chicago, IL: University of Chicago Press, 1985.

Gagné, David. "Monteverdi's *Ohimè dov'è il mio ben* and the Romanesca." *The Music Forum* 6 (1987): 61–91.

Glareanus, Heinrich. *Dodecachordon.* Basel: Heinrich Petri, 1547; facsimile repr. New York: Broude Brothers, 1967. Trans. by Clement Miller, in series Musicology Studies and Documents No. 6, 2 vols. Münster: American Institute of Musicology, 1965.

Harrán, Don. "'Mannerism' in the Cinquecento Madrigal?" *Musical Quarterly* 4 (1969): 521–44.

Judd, Cristle Collins. "Aspects of Tonal Coherence in the Motets of Josquin." Ph.D. diss., King's College London, 1994.

―――. "Modal Types and 'Ut, Re, Mi' Tonalities: Tonal Coherence in Sacred Vocal Polyphony from about 1500." *Journal of the American Musicological Society* 45 (1992): 428–67.

La Via, Stefano. "'Natura delle cadenze' e 'Natura contraria delli modi': Punti di convergenza fra teoria e prassi nel madrigale cinquecentesco." *Saggiatore Musicale* 4 (1997), 5–51.

McClary, Susan. *Modal Subjectivities: Self-Fashioning in the Italian Madrigal.* Berkeley: University of California Press, 2004.

―――. "The Transition from Modal to Tonal Organization in the Works of Monteverdi." Ph.D. diss., Harvard University, 1976.

Meier, Bernhard. *The Modes of Classical Vocal Polyphony, Described According to the Sources.* Trans. by Ellen Beebe. New York: Broude Brothers, 1988.

Mitchell, William. "The Prologue to Orlando di Lasso's Prophetiae Sibyllarum." *The Music Forum* 2 (1970): 264–73.

Palisca, Claude. "Vincenzo Galilei and Some Links between 'Pseudo-Monody' and Monody." *Musical Quarterly* 46 (1960): 344–60.

Pontio, Pietro. *Dialogo, ove si tratta della Theorica e Prattica di Musica.* Parma: Viotto, 1595.

―――. *Ragionamento di musica.* Parma: Viotto, 1588.

Rivera, Benito. "The Two-Voice Framework and Its Harmonization in Arcadelt's First Book of Madrigals." *Music Analysis* 6 (1987): 59–88.

―――. "Harmonic Theory in Musical Treatises of the Late Fifteenth and Early Sixteenth Centuries." *Music Theory Spectrum* 1 (1979): 80–95.

Salzer, Felix. *Structural Hearing: Tonal Coherence in Music.* New York: Boni, 1952.

Schenker, Heinrich. *Kontrapunkt. Neue musikalische Theorien und Phantasien II.* Vienna: Universal, 1910. Trans. by J. Rothgeb and J. Thym. as *Counterpoint.* New York: Schirmer, 1987.

―――. *Harmonielehre: Neue musikalische Theorien und Phantasien I.* Vienna: Universal, 1906. Trans. by E. Borgese as *Harmony,* ed. O. Jonas. Chicago, IL: Chicago University Press, 1954.

Schubert, Peter. "The Fourteen-Mode System of Illuminato Aiguino." *Journal of Music Theory* 35 (1991): 174–210.

Stern, David. "Schenkerian Theory and the Analysis of Renaissance Music." In *Schenker Studies,* ed. Siegel Hedi, 45–59. Cambridge: Cambridge University Press, 1990.

Tinctoris, Johannes. *Liber de natura et proprietate tonarum [1476].* Trans. by Albert Seay as *Concerning the Nature and Propriety of Modes.* Colorado Springs: Colorado College Music Press, 1967.

Vicentino, Nicola. *L'antica musica ridotta alla moderna prattica.* Rome: Antonio Barre (1555). Trans. by Maria Rika Maniates as *Ancient Music Adapted to Modern Practice.* New Haven, CT: Yale University Press, 1996.

Zarlino, Gioseffo. *On the Modes. Part Four of Le istitutioni harmoniche* [Venice, 1558]. Trans. by V. Cohen, ed. C. Palisca. New Haven, CT: Yale University Press, 1983.

———. *The Art of Counterpoint. Part Three of Le istitutioni harmoniche* [Venice, 1558]. Trans. by G. Marco and C. Palisca. New Haven, CT: Yale University Press, 1968.

2　The Play and Its Early Audiences

On the title page of a 1585 draft of *Il pastor fido*, the Ferrarese poet Battista Guarini scribbled out the conventional label "favola pastorale," renaming it "tragicomedia pastorale."[1] The poet would undoubtedly have been aware of the consequences of this change. For the following year, when the play was thrust into the center of intense critical debate, on the heels of the quarrels surrounding Dante's *Divina commedia* and Ariosto's *Orlando furioso*, Guarini was well prepared to defend himself. Conservative critics condemned the play primarily for its mixing of the two classical genres of tragedy and comedy into a single genre not explicitly sanctioned by Aristotle, and even further for mixing this hybrid genre with the pastoral. They also faulted the play on numerous other fronts, including its excessive sensuality and length, its lyrical style, and the lack of verisimilitude in the sophisticated, philosophical discourse of Guarini's shepherds and nymphs. Guarini's defense was significant for its justification of the new genre based on the demands of the present: tragedy and comedy were no longer useful and desirable to modern audiences, and tragicomedy sought to please through delight. Much of this dispute had taken place by the year 1588, still over a year before the play would even go to print.

Alongside the literary debates that trailed the play well into the seventeenth century, *Il pastor fido* functioned prominently in three other realms in early modern Europe: theatre, literature, and music. While in the domains of music and literature the play's fortunes proved generally much more favorable than its reception in critical spheres, its introduction to the stage from 1585 to 1598 has been widely recognized as another tumultuous story. This, however, is only part of the picture, a part focused chiefly on a handful of major cultural centers with which Guarini was directly involved—especially Mantua and Ferrara—that has been passed down through the past two centuries in the important work of Alessandro d'Ancona, Vittorio Rossi, Iain Fenlon, and others. But, as we will see, there are more sides to the play's early history in the theater that reach further corners of the Italian peninsula, the traces of which survive through only the scantiest of known sources. Indeed, the poet himself, who was particularly sensitive when it came to the success of the work that had troubled him for nearly a decade, seemed content when he wrote to the Venetian ambassador of France,

DOI: 10.4324/9781315463056-3

Pietro Duodo, in 1595, acclaiming the play's reception throughout Italy and abroad, and now by the readers of France (particularly female ones) in their own language:

> I never believed that my *Pastor fido* should rise so high, either in fortune or in honor, that it would make me envious of its wellbeing, that being read and discussed through all of Italy (having been already many times staged in theatres) and of major cities; having crossed both mountains and seas so quickly; having become so beloved and familiar to the most noble foreign nations that it may already speak in their tongues; and entering those famous kingdoms of the ocean (into which, they say, our world is divided), having had from them the esteem of print, the honor of the stage, and the applause of the people—all these great and excessive favors never had the force to give me the jealousy that your letter has done, which was so kind as to give me notice that *Il pastor fido* has become the delights of those beautiful and never adequately exalted and revered Ladies of France.[2]

Even before its completion, let alone publication, the courts of northern Italy—in particular those of Ferrara, Mantua, Turin, and Florence—sought vigorously to stage the play. In the cases of the Gonzaga, Este, and Savoy courts, the race to stage *Il pastor fido* in the 1580s and 1590s resulted, for various reasons, in a run of failures—sometimes quite costly. All the while, Guarini—always the deft diplomat—was wooing a number of prominent figures with the prospect of a prestigious stage spectacle, even managing with no apparent difficulty to cultivate at once the interests of two of Italy's bitterest rivals, Duke Vincenzo Gonzaga of Mantua and Duke Carlo Emanuele I of Savoy.

Guarini's Readings of the Early 1580s

Although *Il pastor fido* was not finished and polished for publication until the end of 1589—and even then, as we will see, rather rashly—Guarini's efforts to publicize it had already begun at least six years earlier in a series of readings before prominent *letterati* and patricians as the poet moved between the Este court in Ferrara; his family estate, the Villa Guarina, at San Bellino in Polesine (Veneto); and the vibrant, yet fierce, academic setting of Padua. The first record (to my knowledge) of such a reading comes from a letter of 22 July 1583 to Francesco Maria Vialardi in Turin. Guarini, who had retreated to his villa "to be a good father of the family, rather than a useless courtier"[3] (and also, no doubt, to work on his play, which "suffers as much from delay as I suffer torment of the heart"), describes his stay at the court of Ferrante Gonzaga in Guastalla:

> In my return from Milan, I was welcomed by Signor Don Ferrando [Ferrante] Gonzaga of Guastalla, who certainly can be called the

delight of the Muses, where I found Curzio Gonzaga, Muzio Manfredi, and still others, but yet more important, the most beautiful Countess of Sala with a squadron of the best-bred ladies. And there Signor Don Ferrando, who had heard a part of the *favola* other times in Ferrara, wanted to hear the same again in the presence of that most noble company. And they made and said so many wonderful things of it (particularly signor Curzio) that it [the play] had never heard the like, such that if one were to believe them, not for a good long while had anything so beautiful been seen...[4]

Given the company, this was surely an expedient, early opportunity for the poet to showcase his tragicomedy. It was also assuredly a lively affair with the presence of the Countess of Sala, Barbara Sanseverino, and her "drapello di gentilissime dame." Widely renowned for her extraordinary beauty, Barbara Sanseverino was a notorious instigator of the revels at Carnival at the court of Guarini's patron in Ferrara, Duke Alfonso II d'Este, in 1577, as well as an alleged mistress of both Alfonso II and Vincenzo Gonzaga of Mantua.[5] She was also an enthusiastic supporter of the arts, employing musicians and receiving lessons from the Neapolitan lutenist Fabrizio Dentice in her household in Rome in the early 1570s, and an inspiration to numerous poets, including in particular Torquato Tasso.[6] It is possible that among Sanseverino's *drapello* at Guarini's reading was Agnese Argotta, who was, like Sanseverino, keenly interested in the arts, a capable musician, and the dedicatee of works by notable artists, including poet and playright Muzio Manfredi (who was also present at the Guastalla reading) and composer Giaches de Wert (1535–96). She, too, was to be a mistress of Duke Vincenzo Gonzaga from about 1587 and would lead a diligent effort to stage *Il pastor fido* in 1591–92 in Mantua.[7]

In turn, the host of Guarini's 1583 reading, Don Ferrante II Gonzaga (1563–1630), the head of a cadet branch of the Gonzaga family in Guastalla, was himself a recognized poet and the author of his own *favola pastorale*, *Enone*, which was widely praised as a model of modern pastoral but evidently never published.[8] Ferrante's associations with Guarini and *Il pastor fido* do not end with this event: his name turns up frequently in Guarini's letters (including an update from the poet on the state of the 1584 staging attempt in Ferrara) and in the rolls of the Accademia degli Innominati of Parma alongside those of poets Guarini, Tasso, Manfredi, and Livio Celiano (Angelo Grillo), and he is listed with both Guarini and the Roman composer Luca Marenzio as a member of the Accademia Olimpica of Vicenza.[9] It comes as little surprise, therefore, that Luca Marenzio's Eighth Book and Lucrezio Ruffolo's First Book of five-voice madrigals, both early sources of musical settings from Guarini's play published some fifteen years after the Guastalla reading (1598), bear dedications to Ferrante Gonzaga.[10]

Despite the overwhelming praise of the Guastalla audience at the time, Guarini's hint of having reservations about his admirers' reactions to the play ("se si prestasse lor fede") seems to have been justified. For, by August 1590, only months after the play's printing, a notable attendee of the reading, Muzio Manfredi, showed a very different opinion of Guarini's work in a letter to Ferrante Gonzaga. After updating the Guastalla prince on the progress of his own pastoral, *Semiramide*, Manfredi launches into an extensive criticism of *Il pastor fido* framed by praise for Ferrante's own pastoral:

> And I still want to see your *Enone* finished, if not to see it [performed], so that at least I will see something other than the *parturient montes* ["mountains will labor"][11] of *Il pastor fido, tragicomedia pastorale*, which I have just been able to finish reading in five days in the month of July. It is so long, has so many vain discourses, so many characters, many types of vicissitudes; it is so intricate in its organization, so elevated in its elocution, and so flooded with conceits [designed] to make one cry that they make one laugh, and with civic axioms that would be a thousand times too many in a tragedy of monarchs, heroes, gods, and the like. Besides, when I read it, cursed be what I remembered of the plot; but what should I want to remember given that I do understand the prose *argomento* that it has in front? It has one thing of perfect beauty in someone's judgment: that it is most shameless. Oh! Resolve, Your Excellency, to provide yours [*Enone*], which will put all in checkmate.[12]

The next year, after having "read it a good four or five times," Manfredi manages to suppress his rancor for the work in his response to Guarini himself on 14 November 1591. Rather than full of excesses and artificiality, the play now struck Manfredi as being ripe with the "most beautiful and marvelous things," as well as departures from the models and teachings of the ancients that even Manfredi had not attempted.[13]

Guarini's account of the Guastalla reading gives us two further glimpses at the history of the play at this early stage, one pointing forward and the other glancing back. The remark that Ferrante Gonzaga "had heard a part of the *favola* other times in Ferrara" confirms that at earlier stages in the gestation of the play—that is, before July 1583—portions were read in the lively artistic circles of Alfonso II d'Este.[14] Given the intensely protective, even secretive, manner of the Ferrarese duke (and the unhappy outcome of the Este estate following his death), particularly with respect to the artistic work of his court, there is little wonder that no further details of these readings have survived. The duke, however, had every reason to be secretive about the fruits of his court poet, for the years immediately following these readings of *Il pastor fido* hosted by the Este and by the Guastalla branch of the Gonzaga witnessed the start of a race between both families to stage the work—a race that neither family, it seems, would end up winning.

In addition to its record of early Ferrarese readings, Guarini's letter foreshadows the future trend in the reception of his play of its having a marked appeal to women readers. We have already seen, for example, the specific mention of *Il pastor fido* becoming "the delights of those beautiful, and never adequately exalted and revered Ladies of France" in 1595, and both Barbara Sanseverino and Agnese Argotta hold distinctive places in the history of the play's reception and production. There are also numerous examples among Guarini's letters that show the poet responding to the favorable reactions by women of considerable social rank, including the Duchess of Urbino, Lucrezia d'Este (4 November 1592); the Countess of Scandiano, Laura Boiarda Tiene (1590); and Bradamante d'Este Bevilacqua.[15] This appeal among women readers, furthermore, may have inspired not only the 1591–92 staging attempt in Mantua, but also the lavish Mantuan performance of November 1598 for the newly married Queen of Spain, Margherita d'Austria.

Critics took note of this aspect of the play's readership. Paduan critic Faustino Summo, for example, at the end of his *Due discorsi: l'uno contro le tragicommedie e le pastorali, l'altro contro il pastor fido* (Padua, 1600), accuses Guarini expressly of trying "to show himself as fair and lascivious—a vice that he considers a virtue—to earn perhaps the hearts and favor of beautiful and courteous ladies and youths."[16] Summo and most other of the play's detractors likewise found fault with the sophisticated rhetoric and models of disobedience and cunning of the work's central female characters, Amarilli and Corisca. Of Amarilli's words (retold by the doting Mirtillo) in the nymphs' kissing game of act 2, scene 1, Summo exclaims:

> Is it possible, dear God, that such concepts are formed in the bosom of a well-mannered nymph? Is it conceivable that such filthy, crude, indecorous words should come out of the mouth of a true virgin and lady? I would certainly think that the public whores themselves should blush from them.[17]

Substantial portions of the play were also allegedly cut for the 1598 production for the fourteen-year-old Queen of Spain. As we shall see, among the excluded passages were two situations where Amarilli reasons about her struggle between true love and social duty—personal happiness and the general good—while the fate of Arcadia hangs in the balance (II,5 and IV,5), as well as the attempts by the duplicitous Corisca to persuade Amarilli of the merits of infidelity (III,5) and to entice the "faithful shepherd" himself, Mirtillo, with the prospect of enjoying multiple lovers (III,6).[18] Perhaps, the most fundamental theme of the play, after all, is the desire for personal freedom, which pertains equally to the male and female characters—thus, the nearly tragic conflicts between individual and society. In act 2, scene 5—one of the speeches sheared for the 1598 performance—Amarilli gives voice explicitly to her longing "to live for myself and have life conform to my wishes" (Di viver a me stessa e di far vita / Conforme a le mie voglie), and later—after Mirtillo has tricked her into unknowingly kissing him in the *Gioco della cieca*—she bemoans the conflict between desire (nature) and duty (unnatural law): "If to sin is so sweet and not sinning so necessary...

Oh, too imperfect nature that opposes law. Oh, too severe law that offends nature!" (act 3, scene 4).[19]

In the years 1583–85, when not at his family estate, Guarini divided much of his time between Vicenza, where he worked alongside the Venetian dramatist and theorist Angelo Ingegneri in preparing the inaugural performance of Sophocles' *Oedipus Rex* at the Teatro Olimpico (March 1585), and Padua, giving readings in both cities of his *Pastor fido*. Little is known of Guarini's readings in Vicenza.[20] His time in the city is significant, however, for the practical experience it gave him in stage production, which he would put to use in the fruitless attempts to stage *Il pastor fido* in Mantua and Ferrara.[21] Guarini's work in Vicenza also brought him into contact not only with the celebrated actor, Giovan Battista Verato—the namesake of the first two published defenses of Guarini's play of 1588 and 1591, the "Verrati," commonly attributed to Guarini himself—whom Guarini brought from Ferrara to play the blind prophet Tiresias, but also the highly regarded musicians of the Pellizzari family, who at the time were entrusted with a considerable share of the musical responsibilities for the Accademia Olimpica, including those for the 1585 performance of *Oedipus Rex*.[22] This latter connection might also have proved useful for the staging efforts in Mantua soon after, for by 1588, Antonio Pellizzari, his two daughters (Lucia and Elisabetta), and his sons (Annibale and Bartolomeo) were recruited for Vincenzo Gonzaga's chamber ensemble.[23]

That Padua held a particularly dear place in the poet's mind throughout his life is witnessed in the longing references to the city in his letters. After attending university there in the mid-1550s, it was his return in 1564–67, at the invitation of Scipione Gonzaga, that made a significant impression on the young poet, and that made Padua a refuge from the torments of his life at court and at home in later years. The importance of Scipione Gonzaga (1542–93) in Guarini's life and in the musical history of *Il pastor fido* is far-reaching.[24] Destined from early age to lead an ecclesiastical career, Scipione was given into the protection of his uncle, Cardinal Ercole Gonzaga, in Mantua in 1550. Here, Scipione was exposed to the thriving cultural scene of the city, which was essentially under Ercole's control as regent, until Duke Guglielmo Gonzaga (1538–87) had reached a suitable age to govern in 1558.

Scipione's own avid interests in the arts, particularly poetry and music, showed themselves soon after his move to Padua in 1558, where he took up studies first in philosophy, then in theology at the university, all the while continuing his studies and involvement in the arts. He formed close and lasting ties with Ferrarese poet Torquato Tasso in his early years in the city, and by 1564 he had published his own works of poetry and music.[25] Scipione's learning in the arts was no doubt cultivated through his involvement in several academies, including in particular the short-lived Accademia degli Elevati of Padua (1557–60), which was known for its active promotion of music by its members. In 1562, Scipione also became a founding member of the Accademia degli Invaghiti, which was established by Cesare Gonzaga of Guastalla (father of Ferrante Gonzaga) and met in his household in

Mantua.[26] The Invaghiti concerned themselves largely with oratory, letters, and festive ceremonies, but it was also through this academy that Scipione's first known poetry was printed, in a collection dedicated to the late Ercole Gonzaga, in 1564.

It was Scipione's own academy, however, that seems to have made the strongest impressions on both him and Guarini. Founded in 1564, the Accademia degli Eterei met twice weekly in the home of Scipione and his fellow academician, Stefano Santini, to devote themselves to oratory and discussions of literature, philosophy, ethics, and mathematics. Poetry, on the other hand, was reserved for the ends of meetings, where it functioned as a special enjoyment after weighty, intellectual subjects. Twenty Eterei were present at the inauguration of the academy in January of 1564, but it was not until March of that year that Torquato Tasso returned to Padua and was admitted. Guarini, who from the end of the previous year found himself in Ferrara contributing to the festivities for Carnival, returned in the following months to join the group, leaving behind the vibrant and progressive cultural life of the Este court for the ardent scholastic environment of Padua, possibly at Scipione's personal solicitation.[27]

The life of the Eterei was relatively short, dissipating after the departure of Scipione Gonzaga in the early months of 1567. The *Rime degli Accademici Eterei* (Venice: Comin da Trino, 1567)—signed "Di Padova il primo di Genaro, nel 1567" in Guarini's dedication to Margherita di Valois, Duchess of Savoy—is the single, lasting testament to the academy's activities, presenting a substantial number of early works by Tasso (Il Pentito), Guarini (Il Costante), Ridolfo Arlotti (Il Sicuro), and, among others, Scipione (L'Ardito) himself. The publication also demonstrates the early and enthusiastic appeal of Guarini's verse to composers. In 1569, three of Guarini's contributions appeared in the *Musica nuova* of Ferrarese composer Giulio Fiesco, which represent the first known musical settings of Guarini's poetry. Another setting followed two years later north of the Alps from the Kapellmeister at the court of Emperor Maximilian II in Vienna, Philippe de Monte (Fourth Book *a 5*, 1571). From there, Guarini's poems in the *Rime degli Accademici Eterei* continued to generate musical settings into the 1620s, including works by Marc' Antonio Ingegneri (1584), Francesco Guami (1598), Archangelo Crivelli (1606), and Giovanni Priuli (1622)—all composers who would also look to Guarini's *Pastor fido* for madrigal texts. Monte's attention to the poetry of Guarini at this early stage in the poet's career—and at such a distance as the emperor's court in Vienna—is particularly important, giving some indication of what would follow. For in the succeeding decades, Monte was to prove one of the most prolific composers not only of Guarini settings, but also specifically of settings from *Il pastor fido*, producing some twenty-three madrigals based on the play's texts in 1590–1600, including a volume entitled *Musica sopra Il pastor fido ... libro secondo a7* (Venice: Gardano, 1600).

Scipione Gonzaga would never return to Padua after 1567. After visiting Rome as a guest of Cardinal Ippolito d'Este, he spent several years traveling in the Alps before settling permanently in Rome in 1572, later to be appointed Patriarch of Jerusalem by Pope Sixtus V (1585) and then cardinal (1587). No longer concerned with his own writing of music and poetry, he nevertheless found himself again in the circles of literati and philosophers through his frequent visits to the renowned Villa d'Este at Tivoli, which was left by Ippolito d'Este to his nephew, Cardinal Luigi d'Este, soon after Scipione's arrival in Rome. Indeed, Scipione's involvement in the literary and musical world, and his contact with Guarini and Tasso, remained strong throughout his life. It will be here in Rome, by way of his associations with Guarini, the Duke of Mantua, and Luigi d'Este (patron of composer Luca Marenzio in the 1580s), that Scipione will weigh again with great importance in the history of *Il pastor fido* (discussed in Chapter 4).

For Guarini, on the other hand, Padua remained a primary refuge—as Guarini described it to Scipione in 1590, the "secure and usual port of my shipwrecks...*patria* without worries"[28]—where he could flee the troubles of courtly life and seek the company and counsel of old and close acquaintances, most of them directly tied to the university there. When the poet returned in 1584–85 bearing his nearly finished pastoral, the city's environment must have been markedly changed from that of the 1560s, with most of his fellow literati and versifiers of the Eterei now absent, and with the university's Studio of intellectuals deeply entrenched in debate over Aristotelian and Horatian poetics (discussed in the following chapter). Apparently, this new Paduan environment was no longer supportive of Guarini's work, for by the very next year (1586), the city was to become the central source of critical attacks waged on *Il pastor fido* for years to come.

Nevertheless, the critical tendencies of his Paduan connections must have served Guarini well during his visits in 1584–85, when the poet's attention turned increasingly from writing his tragicomedy toward revising and polishing it. During this time, Guarini discussed his *Pastor fido* closely with the notable academic and critic Antonio Riccoboni, and also likely with Jacopo Zabarella, a professor of logic and natural philosophy, and various other *letterati*.[29] Riccoboni (1541–99), also a former member of the Eterei, was a professor of humanities and rhetoric at the university, and specifically a scholar of Aristotle's theories of rhetoric and poetics—subjects that would prove especially useful to Guarini in defending his pastoral tragicomedy in writing. As the poet (so it is believed) relates under the pseudonym "L'Attizzato" in the second defense of the play, *Il Verato secondo* (1593), his and Riccoboni's conversations about "l'argomento" of the play took place in the bookshop of Paolo Meietti, "in the presence of many others [who] heard more than one time the author of *Il pastor fido* himself, from his own mouth, give long disquisitions [*propositi*]" on the play, and "discussing at length with many *letterati*."[30] Similar readings for "i letterati di Padova" took place on at least two other occasions "in the house of Signore Jacopo Zabarella, most honored Cavaliere, and the companion and most singular friend of the author," where the play was "instantly praised."[31]

If Guarini had any reason to be somewhat unsure of the genuineness of his audience in Guastalla, however, he should well have been doubly on his guard in Padua. For Meietti—"honored bookseller and most dear friend"[32] to the poet—was also the printer of the critical writings of moral philosopher Giasone Denores, including in the coming years his two bitter assaults against Guarini's work that would spark the *Pastor fido* debate. Thus, it is in this setting of Meietti's bookshop, as well as at Zabarella's house, that one gets a sense of the potentially treacherous environment of the academic circles of Padua. Guarini's two trusted acquaintances, Zabarella and Riccoboni, for example, agreed on many issues, but they did stand at odds over one of Zabarella's most prized theories: that poetry belonged to the rational sciences, namely logic as well as civics. Zabarella entered the literary debates on the relationship between poetry, rhetoric, and logic with his *De natura logicae libri duo* of 1578, while Riccoboni countered this position the following year in the preface to his translation of Aristotle's *Rhetoric* (*Aristotelis Ars rhetorica libri tres, graece et latine*). Importantly for Guarini, both Zabarella and Riccoboni agreed that pleasure was a principal end of poetry, which would become one of the poet's chief rationales for the legitimacy of the new hybrid genre of pastoral tragicomedy.[33] Thus, in 1586 when Denores criticized an unnamed work boasting the label *tragicommedia pastorale*, it is understandable that Guarini would assume that this was an attack on his yet-unpublished *Pastor fido*, being the only example of its kind. As Guarini ("L'Attizzato") writes in 1593:

> If *messer* Giasone has proved that there are other *tragicommedie pastorali*, absolve him, and if not, condemn him as a scandalous slanderer, who with invidious and dishonest manners has consciously sought to offend the work of a friend, in the capacity of which it was introduced to him.[34]

That Guarini's rebuttal is so personal and vindictive in tone is hardly surprising, for as the author points out, Denores was allegedly a friend of his, and was there "every day in the same bookshop" as the poet and his peers discussed and read *Il pastor fido*. Yet, the critic never voiced any misgivings to the poet before his public attack, and in his writings, he continued to insist that he was unaware of Guarini's work.[35] Although Guarini surely felt betrayed by his audience at Padua, it is thanks to his impulse to expose Denores as a coward, in addition to simply defending his work, that we have—among other things—any record at all of the role of the informal Paduan academic circles in the development of *Il pastor fido*. In all, one thing can be certain about Padua in the 1580s: it was a hostile critical environment, and the city's intellectual circles seemed to relish their controversies. (Indeed, many participants—as well as subjects—benefited from the robust stream of pamphlets, treatises, and exposure generated by this milieu, including, it seems, Guarini.) In his *De Gymnasio Patavino* of 1598,

Riccoboni records the "controversia Iasonis Denores habita cum Baptista Guarino equite" (along with those involving Zabarella, Piccolomini, and Bernardino Petrella) among the memorable happenings of those years at the university.[36]

As Guarini's biographer Vittorio Rossi writes,

> as in Padua in the house of Jacopo Zabarella, so in Venice in that of Jacopo [or Giacomo] Contarini and of Francesco Vendramin an audience of gentlemen and *letterati* had the occasion to hear many times from the mouth of the author, and to applaud, the new dramatic work.[37]

And likewise as with Padua, the records of these readings in Venice, which also took place in 1585, survive in the two published defenses against Denores. The first of these defenses, *Il Verrato* (1588), in fact, is dedicated to these "illustrissimi signori ... Jacopo Contarini e Francesco Vendramini" of Venice—the former a mathematician, and the latter a soon-to-be ambassador to Spain before achieving high ranks in the Church in Venice.[38] Little more is heard from these Venetians in relation to *Il pastor fido*, although both continue to appear among Guarini's letters of subsequent years, and Contarini appears as the chief authoritative figure in Guarini's dialogue, *Il segretario* (1594).[39]

While the hosts of Guarini's readings in Venice have rather different backgrounds than those of Padua, his audiences there were presumably still composed largely of *letterati*. As Guarini recounts, by this point in 1585, the play had "already been read and reread in Padua and Venice, and passed through the mouths of all—*letterati*, printers, and booksellers—as though it were already in public [i.e., printed] form."[40] The play's readership at this preliminary stage, still four years before its printing, however, reached beyond "the *letterati* of the courts of Italy ... since all their princes had had news of *Il pastor fido*, and had greatly honored and praised it."[41] Guarini may be somewhat exaggerating about the scope of his work's popularity, but his statement does underscore his consciousness about the public readership of the play, something that he very clearly and methodically worked to cultivate. Although it was still unfinished by the fall of 1585, three distinct courts had already put forth earnest attempts to mount productions of the tragicomedy, all of them, in the end, unsuccessful.

Signs of Stagings in the Mid-1580s

The rocky beginnings of the play's history on the stage began not at the court of Guarini's patron in Ferrara, as might be expected, but in Mantua at the court of Guglielmo Gonzaga. Yet, it was not the generally ascetic Duke Guglielmo himself who led the effort, but his son, Vincenzo, who was to be one of the play's most ardent and devoted supporters. Following the marriage of his sister, Margherita Gonzaga, to Duke Alfonso II d'Este in 1579,

Vincenzo developed extremely close ties with the Ferrarese court. The lavish and enthusiastic secular environment of Ferrara under Duke Alfonso II proved much more to Vincenzo's taste than the pious and austere character of his father's court under the firm influences of the Counter Reformation. Indeed, after 1579, Vincenzo became essentially, in Iain Fenlon's words, "a child of the Ferrarese court,"[42] absorbing its traditions in music and theater that made it the envy of courts throughout Italy and north of the Alps, and exploiting this learning in his own cultural enterprises as the Duke of Mantua after his father's death on 22 December 1587.

Two of the most important of these Ferrarese influences were its celebrated groups of women singers and dancers—the *concerto delle donne* and the *balletto della duchessa*—which formed a principal part of Alfonso d'Este's dearly cherished and highly exclusive court entertainments.[43] These two ensembles, however, seem to have originated more from Duchess Margherita's, rather than Alfonso's, devising. A *concerto delle donne* had existed at the Ferresese court for some years before Margherita's arrival, but this took the form more of a dilettante ensemble composed of a handful of noblewomen.

After 1579, the nature and function of the *concerto* changed drastically. A vigorous effort was launched to procure talented singers from the surrounding area, and through the early 1580s, four virtuoso sopranos— Laura Peperara, Tarquinia Molza, Anna Guarini, and Livia d'Arco—were employed as professional performers at the Ferrarese court, forming the basis of the duke's famed *musica segreta*. As the scattered accounts by ambassadors and visitors reveal, the four ladies—along with the Neapolitan bass Giulio Cesare Brancaccio—performed in various configurations, ranging from solo song to multi-part madrigals, sometimes also providing their own instrumental accompaniment. The *balletto della duchessa* also emerged during this time, and it, too, quickly became a key element of court spectacle and entertainment, demonstrating the versatile talents at Duke Alfonso's disposal with its incorporation of choreography, music, and verse.[44] Guarini was directly involved with both of these ensembles, supplying verses for musical works that were sung by the *concerto* or fitted to the choreography of the *balletto*, as Ferrarese practice at the time often required that the text be added only after the choreography and music were complete. In fact, as Kathryn Bosi has shown, the activity of the *balletto della duchessa* seems to have been tied specifically to Guarini's presence at the Este court, for the ensemble's activity diminished markedly during the poet's absence in 1583 (when he was in Guastalla and the Veneto) and again in 1588 (when he left Alfonso II's service). This experience in composing texts to suit choreography and music that had already been established would prove exceptionally useful to Guarini when it came time to create his own *ballo* for *Il pastor fido*.

The surviving documents and musical works for the two ensembles show that the level of training and expertise of the singers and dancers was exceptional. It is also evident that a substantial share of the court's artistic energy revolved around the groups, which required not only music, choreography, and poetic texts, but at times also elaborate set designs and stage machinery. Both Guarini—whose daughter Anna was a singer in the *concerto*—and Tasso were entrusted with providing verse to be set (or fitted) to music and dance for the two ensembles, and although it may be difficult to identify all of the works that were specifically designed for this purpose, the number is probably considerable.

Music for the two ensembles was furnished chiefly by composers at Alfonso II d'Este's court—the most notable of them being Luzzasco Luzzaschi and Ippolito Fiorino—but numerous composers from elsewhere also devoted works to the *concerto*, or sometimes to its individual members.[45] Included among these composers was a figure with particularly close Ferrarese connections dating back at least to the mid-1560s: the *maestro di cappella* of the Mantuan ducal chapel, Giaches de Wert. Wert became something of a fixture at the Ferrarese court in the 1580s, even to such an extent that his patron, Guglielmo Gonzaga, was compelled to write to Alfonso II demanding that the composer be returned to Mantua. Wert seems at first to have simply been enticed by the flourishing artistic climate of the Este court—as was his patron's son, Vincenzo—but in the mid-1580s, this fascination intensified with the composer's love affair with one of the *donne* of the duke's *concerto*, Tarquinia Molza, in 1584–89. This exposure to the *virtuose* of Ferrara had a marked effect on Wert's music of the 1580s, which witnesses a straightforward demand for vocal skill and virtuosity, frequent distinction of the upper voices, and a predilection for declamatory textures—not to mention a noticeable taste for Ferrarese texts. Thus, when Vincenzo succeeded his father as Duke of Mantua in 1587, Wert was well equipped for the task of providing music for Mantua's own *concerto delle donne*, and for a lavish series of court spectacles and entertainments strongly inspired by those of Ferrara.

Ferrara, however, was not the only court to have a profound influence on the young Vincenzo Gonzaga. For in 1584, after the failure of his marriage to Margherita Farnese three years before, Vincenzo married again, this time into the Medici family of Florence. While the Medici shared Duke Alfonso's taste for theater, dance, and music in the intimate settings of the ducal chambers and gardens—even emulating his *concerto delle donne*—the late 1580s in Florence also brought forth some notable displays of public pageantry and grandeur. This projection of court power and prestige took its most quintessential form in the production of *intermedi*: lavish stage spectacles between the acts of plays that combined music, dance, poetry, and often an extravagant arsenal of machinery, scenic designs, and special effects. The first of these that took place after Vincenzo's marriage to Eleonora de' Medici came at the 1586 performance of Giovanni de' Bardi's *L'amico fido*, with *intermedi* written by Bardi himself and stage sets devised by the talented Buontalenti. These were outdone three years later by the astonishing set of six *intermedi* that accompanied the performance of Girolamo Bargagli's comedy, *La pellegrina*, in celebration of the marriage of Grand Duke

Ferdinando de' Medici to Christine of Lorraine. The event brought together a number of prominent Florentine artists, including Bardi and Buontalenti, along with Emilio de' Cavalieri, Cristofano Malvezzi, and Jacopo Peri, but it also relied heavily on talents from elsewhere, including composer Luca Marenzio from Rome.[46] The most substantial source of these outside forces was the court of Vincenzo Gonzaga, which had developed considerably in the two years since Vincenzo had become duke and would soon rival the most distinguished courts in Europe in its artistic patronage.

Early signs of Vincenzo's cultural indulgence begin to appear in his planning for the celebrations of his marriage to Eleonora de' Medici. The union had considerable political importance to the Gonzaga, solidifying ties with the Medici and fortifying those already in place with Archduke Ferdinand of Austria and the future Queen of France, Maria de' Medici (to both of whom Vincenzo was brother-in-law). But by this time, Vincenzo had already developed strong ties to the Este court; hence, it was to this court that Vincenzo turned in early 1584 with hopes for a suitable way to honor his wedding. These hopes lay specifically on the play currently being composed by the Ferrarese court poet, Battista Guarini, who had given readings of the work not only in Guastalla, but also, "altre volte," in Ferrara.

If Vincenzo had not heard these readings of *Il pastor fido* in the early 1580s, he had at least heard of Guarini's work, for on 12 January 1584, he wrote directly to the poet in Padua requesting a manuscript of the play. Guarini's responses in subsequent months, in which he repeatedly denies Vincenzo a copy, establish several motifs that recur throughout Guarini's dealings with early solicitations of the play in the years that follow. In his initial response to the Gonzaga prince on 8 February, Guarini's reason for refusing the manuscript is straightforward: "In the fifth act, which is all that remains for me, I have hardly begun the first scene."[47] Beyond this, progress on the work had apparently been proceeding disappointingly slowly due to circumstances that were unfavorable to writing. As Guarini explains:

> My patron, the Muses—and particularly mine—do not willingly stay where the heart has little calm. Thus, they are so delicate and graceful by their nature that they will not be well at ease if they do not have at their disposal the entire room of our hearts.[48]

When Vincenzo writes again in April to inquire about performing "l'Egloga pastorale"—even suggesting that Guarini send him the unfinished draft, if the rest can be delivered "within twelve or fifteen days"—Guarini's refusal becomes more detailed and discouraging.[49] The play, Guarini claims, would not be ready "at least for all of this year": it lacked all of the fifth act and all the choruses, and there was little hope that the poet would be in the right state of mind anytime soon to produce verse that was up to his own standards.

On top of this, Guarini contends, a performance of the play simply "could not be put together in three months," as Vincenzo had in mind. The reasons for this have been noted frequently in the scholarship, and they are important for our purposes here, for Guarini's list of the difficult aspects of his play seems to foretell some of the downfalls that several future staging operations would encounter:

> Besides being comprised of many long parts from the first act forward, and full of novelty and of the grandest actions [*movimenti*] that need to be set to music [*concertati*] and rehearsed and re-rehearsed onstage, and even more a *giuoco* that comes in the third act, set in the form of a *ballo* done by a chorus of nymphs—this is still in the hands of Leone; neither the music is done, and even less, the words—now consider [*vegga*], Your Highness, how it is possible to perform [it], especially in such short time. I will not mention the many other difficulties: the scenery that is made with unusual artifice, the characters that are both diverse and of a presence and manner appropriate to the subject, which (as you know), although it pertains to shepherds, are, however, very noble, as those that come from a divine stock...[50]

Guarini's response to Vincenzo is especially revealing of several things, including his intention that various—indeed, *grandissimi*—parts of the play be set to music, and his aim at this early stage to compose verse for the *Gioco della cieca* of act 3 only after the choreography and music had been finished—a talent that he had developed undoubtedly through his work for the *balletto della duchessa* in the early 1580s.[51] In his *Annotazioni sopra Il Pastor fido*, published in the sumptuous authoritative 1602 Ciotti edition of the tragicomedy, Guarini reveals that this collaborative process involved not only "Leone"—likely the Ferrarese dancer–choreographer Leone Tolosa—but also Luzzasco Luzzaschi as composer.[52] Also evident in the letter to Vincenzo is Guarini's underlying concern for—even obsession over—the fate of his play both onstage and as a written work, which led to an extreme reluctance to let the play out of his hands before its well-being could be guaranteed.

The poet was also undoubtedly concerned about giving his play away too soon, before he had made the most of it for his bargaining between two other distinguished courts: that of his employer, Duke Alfonso d'Este, and that of the play's dedicatee, Carlo Emanuele, Duke of Savoy. To relieve himself of Vincenzo's prodding, Guarini assures him that there are many other plays from which to choose, probably even some new ones in his very own Mantua, where there can be found "ingegni nobilissimi,"[53] but just in case, he sends his own "nuova comedia," *L'idropica*—which was eventually performed in Mantua for the 1608 wedding of Prince Francesco Gonzaga and Margherita of Savoy.

Guarini is also already making a willful effort to establish his work as a novel type of dramatic poetry: whereas Vincenzo offhandedly requests "l'Egloga pastorale," Guarini corrects the prince at the start of his own letter by using its full label, "la mia Tragicomedia Pastorale." By the time he makes his next move to stage the play seven years later, Vincenzo—now the Duke of Mantua—had apparently forgotten Guarini's correction. For in a letter to the Mantuan ducal secretary, Annibale Chieppio, of 23 November 1591, Guarini (again in Padua) is quick to pounce on the problem:

> Yesterday Signor Strigio [*sic*] gave me the letter from Your Highness of 19 [November], by which I understood your order concerning the performance of my *Pastor fido*—which, so I believe, you meant by that *Egloga Pastorale*.[54]

That being said, Guarini announces plans to set out "immediately" for Mantua to help with the preparations.

The poet's reminder must have been effective, for Chieppio was sure to refer to the play correctly in his reply to Duke Vincenzo of 26 November, informing him of Guarini's intentions to go to Mantua "to take care that his *pastoral tragicomedy* is performed with good success, according to Your Highness's desire, in the entertainments of the coming Carnival."[55] It would seem, however, that Guarini had little reason to be so concerned about the Duke of Mantua's fumbling of the play's title, given that at this point, it had already been issued in at least six editions in Venice, Ferrara, Mantua, Pavia, and London, not to mention publicly debated in the pamphlets of Denores and the author (under the name "Verrato").[56] There had also been at least three other bids to stage the work by 1591, and in these dealings, Guarini seemed perfectly content with the terms *pastorale* and *favola*; but *Egloga*—a different poetic type altogether than drama, and a label implying considerably less scope and merit than comedy and tragedy, as the ensuing debate spells out—clearly did not suit his play (as we shall see in the following chapter). Nor was the Duke of Mantua the only figure to use the term when speaking of the new pastoral drama.

As the scribbled-out title "favola pastorale" on the 1585 draft witnesses, Guarini had his mind firmly set on his *Pastor fido* becoming the exemplar of a new breed of play. With this in mind, his preoccupation with—perhaps even offense at—Vincenzo's misidentification would not have been out of place. The poet's concern is especially understandable seeing that Vincenzo was not the only person to have made this mistake. The very same misconception of the play can, in fact, be traced to Guarini's own place of employment, Ferrara, where the play had been written and read aloud (possibly in Vincenzo's company), and where the first serious staging attempt was launched.

Guarini had been right about the slow progress of his writing in his letters to Vincenzo early in 1584. When Alfonso II d'Este contacted the poet in November of that year about his own plans to stage the play for the forthcoming Carnival festivities, still only the first four acts were ready. Guarini, of course, was already concerned about the shortness of time remaining to prepare the production: as he said before to Vincenzo Gonzaga, the play "could not be put together in three months," and this deadline was already upon them. On 25 November, Guarini responded to the Duke of Ferrara directly, urging that rehearsals of the unfinished play begin forthwith:

> I am sending the four acts of my *favola* to Your Highness, and these [are] hardly correct by fault of the copyists' lack of understanding. [...] All the parts are already transcribed, which need to be given out as demands the brevity of time and the length of many [of the parts], and also the need to rehearse them. They carry a great risk that they not be copied by those who will have to perform them.[57]

The poet, then, reveals another anxiety that would continue to harass him as long as the play remained unpublished: that unauthorized copies of the work would be leaked into the public by the actors. Consequently, Guarini implores the duke to command the actors "neither to show them, nor recite them to any person, much less make copies of them," adding that he will "truly make sure not to give them out without this protection."[58]

Two days later, Duke Alfonso—now referring to the play as "la trage-dia"—sent out an order for officials to search for boys suitable for the performance.[59] By 11 December, the preparations seemed to be taking shape. In a letter to Ferrante Gonzaga in Guastalla, Guarini reports that the parts had been distributed to the actors, and work on the sets was to be started presently. Still lacking, however, was a boy to play "a nymph sixteen or seventeen years old"—possibly Dorinda, a fairly major role—and it is hoped that Ferrante may know of a suitable one.[60] The produc-tion was still on track in early January, when Guarini informs Alfonso II that some days prior he had finished transcribing the play—presumably now completed, but by no means in its final form—but that he delayed sending it due to the duke's absence, presumably out of fear that the draft would fall into the wrong hands. At some point after this, however, the preparations evidently fell apart. In a letter of November of the following year (1585), the Ferrarese Filippo Montecatini—writing to Duke Alfon-so's brother, Cardinal Luigi d'Este, in Rome—references "the *Egloga* that was supposed to be performed here [in Ferrara] last year" (l'Egloga...che si doveva recitare qui l'anno passato).[61] As one who was quite aware of business pertaining to Guarini and his play, Montecatini was evidently oblivious to Guarini's sensitivity when it came to the play's label. Guarini, it seems, must have been fighting an uphill battle in Ferrara—as in Mantua—to attach the title "tragicomedia pastorale" both to his play, and to himself as the progenitor of the new genre, based on Alfonso d'Este's and Montecatini's letters.

The primary concern of Montecatini's reference to *l'Egloga* in 1585, how-ever, was not to inform Luigi d'Este of the staging attempt in Ferrara—the cardinal would surely already have heard news of this—but rather to relay matters surrounding another staging effort in the autumn of that year in

Turin. Guarini's dedication of *Il pastor fido* to the Duke of Savoy, Carlo Emanuele I, and Catalina Micaela of Spain on the occasion of their marriage would not appear in print until the first edition of 1589, but it became widely known well before this, when Guarini visited the court of Savoy in September 1585 to present a copy of the work in person. On the face of it, Carlo Emanuele was a fitting candidate for the dedication, being a capable poet himself and a generous supporter of the arts. But in the political climate of the time, this move put Guarini in a potentially perilous juggling act involving his possessive and secretive patron, Alfonso d'Este, and two increasingly bitter rivals, the Duke of Savoy and the Gonzaga, whose animosity intensified markedly following Guglielmo Gonzaga's decision in 1585 to build a major fortress in the disputed territory of Monferrato, to which both the Savoy and Gonzaga laid claim.[62] It was in this precise year that Guarini made his high-profile visit to the Savoy court, one year after denying Vincenzo Gonzaga a draft of the play.

Guarini, however, seems to have played his cards remarkably well. The poet arrived at the Savoy court toward the end of September 1585, presenting his work—still lacking the choruses (presumably so they could be tailored to the given circumstances) and requiring much further polishing—to the duke and duchess, whose wedding, as it was rumored, "had given beginning and birth to the poem."[63] (The play, in reality, had been conceived years before any plans for the Savoy wedding could have been known.) There were apparently hopes that Guarini would secure a position at the Savoy court with the gesture, but by 23 October, he had returned to Ferrara with an opposing offer by his own jealous patron: to become "court secretary" with a very high monthly salary of 51 *scudi*.[64]

There is no question that preparations were underway to stage the work during Guarini's visit in Turin, which progressed at least to the point of copies being dispersed to the "Compagnia dell'Isabellina"—the *Gelosi* acting troupe of Isabella and Francesco Andreini.[65] In a letter from Padua to Filippo d'Este in Turin, probably of the following year (1586), Guarini recounts of his *tragicommedia*:

> Since, divided in its parts, it was given into the hands of the actors by the order of that most serene prince in the hope of being performed, it goes out through the tattered copies of many, to the littlest reputation both of me who composed it, and of His Highness, to whom it was dedicated, and who has already shown to have much esteem for it.[66]

Iain Fenlon has claimed that "most authorities agree that the play was staged in some form in 1585," and numerous scholars have accepted this assertion.[67] However, aside from Guarini's reference to the distribution of the parts and a note in the 1602 edition of the play stating rather equivocally that "si rappresentava la favola" in Turin, the bulk of the evidence seems to point in the other direction.

The initial indications that the staging at the Savoy court failed come from November 1585, the month after Guarini's return from Turin. In a letter to Luigi d'Este—referring to the play as an *Egloga*—Filippo Montecatin writes from Ferrara:

> Signor cavalier Guarini, on the occasion of his trip to Turin with the ambassador of Venice, presented [*rappresentò*] to the duke his *Egloga* that should have been performed [*doveva recitare*] here last year, for which that Highness sent a courier here to present to him a chain of 500 *scudi*, and he [Guarini] hopes for a much bigger reward when it will be performed [*recitarà*] this Carnival.[68]

Here, Montecatini seems to make a distinction between "rappresentare" and "recitare," using the latter specifically to denote performance, and the former to denote a conferral. Thus, the play was presented [*rappresentò*] to the Duke of Savoy in Turin, "should have been performed" [*recitare*] in Ferrara, and "will be performed" [*recitarà*] in Turin during Carnival 1586 (or so it was thought). This reading is bolstered by a letter from Guarini to the Duke of Savoy of 15 November 1585 thanking him for the gold chain, and stating that the play had been "destined for the stage with the richest decoration" (alla scena con apparato ricchissimo destinata), but not that this staging had actually happened, and by a letter of 7 January 1586 to Eugenio Visdomini, secretary to the Duke of Parma, stating that he continued to lack the time and spirit to finish the play.[69]

There are additional letters from later years suggesting that the Turin performance never took place. On 2 November 1589, for example, Guarini remarked to the Duke of Urbino that he simply *presented* his play to Duke Carlo Emanuele ("la presentai al Serenissimo Duca di Savoia"), and the accounts of Florentine Roberto Titi and Ludovico Canobio of Crema state specifically that *Il pastor fido* "was not performed [*recitato*] in Turin for the nuptials of that Most Serene Duke, for which, it was composed."[70] Likewise, as Rossi notes, in none of the contemporary descriptions of the festivities for the Savoy wedding is there mention of such a performance, including in the expense records in the Archivio Camerale di Torino, and Guarini's stay in Turin, which lasted some twenty days, was too short to organize so demanding a production.[71] At the same time, the sources cited above, all of which have been taken as evidence that the Savoy effort was a failure, leave plenty of room for doubt owing to the use of ambiguous terminology or, as we will see, their origins in later, opposing efforts to stage the play, which fostered the disparagement of earlier efforts usually by larger courts.

There are, however, two other sources that have been overlooked which may add substantial weight to the matter because they come from the poet himself. The first is a letter from Ferrara written on 19 March 1587 to Barone Sfondrato, the ambassador for King Philip II of Spain at the Savoy court. The main purpose of the letter is to seek Sfondrato's support in obtaining a privilege in Turin to print the work, which was now becoming a major concern since the parts had been distributed for two separate staging attempts.[72] Sfondrato had apparently read a copy of the play, and Guarini's request for the privilege adroitly flatters Sfondrato for his praise of the work. In fact, the poet claims, Sfrondrato's fondness for *Il pastor fido* is of such value that in comparison, "any other honor either of the stage or of the printing *will be* of little worth" (ogn'altro honore ò della scena, o della stampa le dovrà esser di minor pregio).[73] The remainder of the letter then deals with how the play *will be* printed: "I nonetheless *will* hasten as much as *will* be possible so that it is printed..." (Io nondimeno m'affretterò quanto sarà possibile che si stampi). By coupling the staging of the play with its printing, both as honors that may come in the play's future (*dovrà esser*), Guarini seems to verify the absence of both before March 1587. As a diplomat at the Savoy court who had a copy of the play and was acquainted with Guarini, there is little question that Sfondrato would have been aware of the play's fate in Turin. He would also have been aware of how much Guarini would value a performance of the play, which is an essential part of the letter's rhetoric.

The second corroboration comes in the second published defense of the play against the criticism of Denores, *Il Verato secondo*, published in 1593. In picking apart Denores' argument, the author—widely believed to be Guarini himself under the pseudonym L'Attizzato—maintains that the critic had no grounds by which to judge the play's unity and singularity. His reasoning for this is simple, because at the time of Denores's initial attack (1586) he would not have had access to the entire play in any sanctioned format:

> Is it not enough to say, "I have not seen it, nor read it, nor heard it performed [*sentita rappresentare*]?" And who knows of it, being still neither printed, nor performed [*recitata*]; it being still in the hand of the author?[74]

The only way for Denores to access the entire work, the author alleges, would have been not through a performance, but through pirated copies from *commedianti*, or through recitations by such performers from memory, in which case the text would have been "fiercely contaminated by them" (fieramente da loro contaminato).[75] Hence, from what we learn from "L'Attizzato," no performances had occurred by 1586—when Denores initially attacked the play—which includes both the attempts of Ferrara and Turin.

Although progress on the tragicomedy was slow and laborious following the presentation of the text to the Duke of Savoy in 1585, the following years proved as busy as ever for Guarini. To begin, the position of court secretary that had prompted Guarini's hasty return from Turin was not turning out nearly as well as he had likely expected. In another letter to Barone Sfondrato of 15 February 1586, the poet laments profusely about the demands of the job and of how he is treated—of, as Guarini puts it, "being the old servant and new secretary, for which things go very badly when labor happens in the place of honor."[76] "Needing to write as others want," Guarini is no longer free to think and write as he wishes. At about this time in February, Guarini initiated contacts with the well-known Florentine linguist and philologist Lionardo Salviati of the Accademia della Crusca, and by July of that year had prepared a draft of the play suitable enough to send to Salviati and the Crusca for suggestions—a process that was repeated the following year with his old friend Scipione Gonzaga in Rome (discussed in Chapter 4).

By mid-1587, there had been no attempts to stage *Il pastor fido* since the wedding celebrations in Turin, but Guarini soon found the opportunity to be involved in the lavish production of a different play, Agostino Beccari's *Il sacrificio* (1554), in the small Ferrarese feudal state of Sassuolo. The performance took place on 2 December 1587 to celebrate the entrance of the ruler of Sassuolo, Marco Pio di Savoia, and Clelia Farnese, the illegitimate daughter of Cardinal Alessandro Farnese, who had been married on 2 August in Caprarola, the seat of Cardinal Farnese's court.[77] Marco Pio was keenly devoted to the arts and himself an active poet with a fondness for the pastoral mode.[78]

The 1587 production of *Il sacrificio* is important for our purposes here not only for the experience that it gave Guarini in the staging of large-scale spectacle, but also for its giving witness to the early artistic collaboration between Guarini and Giovan Battista Aleotti, the principal architect and engineer at the Ferrarese court—a collaboration that would resume in 1592 with the preparations in Mantua of *Il pastor fido*. For the 1587 performance, Guarini fitted Beccari's play with a new prologue tailored specifically for the Sassuolo wedding, along with a set of four *intermedi* with mythical themes.[79] Aleotti was responsible for the set designs for both the play and *intermedi*, making this the earliest known example of Aleotti's work in stage machinery. The performance also again included the Ferrarese comic actor Giovan Battista Verato, whose name would appear the following year as the title of the first published defense of *Il pastor fido* against Denores.

According to the anonymous account, news of the Sassuolo event and its "sumptuous display" seemed to have gotten around, drawing an impressive crowd that included even Barbara Sanseverino.[80] The spectators are said to have been astonished by Aleotti's sets and scenic effects, which included a forked, running river, five trees whose trunks opened to reveal five singing nymphs (the sisters of Phaethon), a Mount Parnassus rising from the stage, and a Temple of Pan modeled on the Pantheon of Rome. The chronicler also describes a substantial amount of music in the production, both in the *intermedi* and at the ends of acts, which involved the use of *musica interiore*— or musicians placed backstage or in the wings—to accompany the onstage singing, and which seems to have taken the form primarily of multi-voice madrigals.[81] The audience was particularly struck by this use of song, as the record recounts of the third *intermedio*:

> Now, as she sang, the music responded with an echo wonderful to hear. I did not note the song because, out of my amazement, I was seized by

such new novelty, and the brevity of time forbade it. Let it suffice [to say] that it was most beautiful and most ornate, and made such a miraculous sight that the spectators regretted that, when the song finished, they were deprived so quickly of seeing such fair and noble young girls that seemed new angels.[82]

The event seems to bear the influences of Ferrarese court entertainment and spectacle, particularly in the display of virtuosic female singers, which raises the question of whether Alfonso d'Este lent other forces from his court to help with the performance, along with his poet and architect.

Guarini, however, did not remain in the service of the Duke of Ferrara for much longer. Tired of his treatment by Alfonso d'Este, he left the city suddenly and on very bad terms in June 1588. This may have seemed like a good move at the time, but the jealousy and wrath of his former patron would ensure that this would not be an easy transition for the poet. Rather, the following years found Guarini venturing between numerous Italian cities—most importantly Florence, Turin, Mantua, Rome, and Padua—in search of stable, yet agreeable, employment. The first place that he approached with strong ambitions of gaining a position was the court of Grand Duke Ferdinando de' Medici in Florence, where plans were well underway for the sumptuous ducal wedding of the following year.

Guarini arrived in Florence as a guest of one of the major figures in the preparations for those entertainments, the humanist Count Giovanni de' Bardi, who had collaborated with Buontalenti in 1586 for the *intermedi* of his own *L'amico fido*, and who in 1588–89 would join forces with Buontalenti and many others for the spectacles of the grand-ducal wedding. As a testament to the watchful eye of Guarini's former patron, the most significant records of this visit survive in the letters of Annibale Cortile, the Ferrarese ambassador to Florence, who recounted Guarini's actions and intentions—as well as the reactions of Ferdinando de' Medici—in detail to Duke Alfonso. On 25 June 1588, Cortile wrote to the duke with information he had gleaned from the poet himself, stating:

> The said Guarini came to accompany me to the carriage and told me how he had left your service, and that he had come to present [*appresentare*] his Pastoral to the grand duke, who, after having used many courteous words, gave it to Signor Abbate del Monte... Cavalier Guarino [*sic*] is staying in a little house, as was arranged for him by Signor Giovanni de' Bardi, which has only two or three rooms...[83]

Guarini, however, had bigger hopes than simply to gain Grand Duke Ferdinando's praise for the pastoral. For in a letter of November 1588 to the Florentine poet and patron Giovan Battista Strozzi (Il Giovane), Guarini, now at the Villa Guarina, closes by asking, "What is the thought there of my Pastoral: will it be performed [*rappresenterà*] or not?"[84] The grand duke, in fact, had expressed interest in staging *Il pastor fido* as far back as February 1588, even delegating two men, Francesco Paciotto and, once again, Bernardo Buontalenti, to the task of preparing the spectacle and machinery.[85] Evidently, and unfortunately for Guarini, his work was pushed aside in favor of Girolamo Bargagli's *La pellegrina*. Indeed, according to Cortile's account, Guarini's manuscript of the tragicomedy was literally passed on by the grand duke to Abbate (soon Cardinal) Francesco Maria del Monte, who must have done little with it by way of a performance.

After a brief sojourn in Turin at the service of Carlo Emanuele in September and October of 1588, Guarini moved for months between Padua, Venice, and the Villa Guarina. During this time, the play at last came to print, in December 1589 (though dated 1590) by the Venetian press of Giovanni Battista Bonfadino, followed swiftly thereafter in 1590 by editions from Ferrara (Baldini and Mamarello) and Mantua (Osanna). Guarini evidently felt an urgency to relinquish the work to the press, for defective copies had already left his control and were seeping into circulation. Seeking a privilege to print the work—where, he does not say, but presumably in Florence—the poet turned again to Bardi in Florence, writing on 19 August 1589 from Padua that "copies of [the play] are going around (dear God) as cripples, wounded by a thousand errors, so that it cries to me for mercy. Nor can I, as its father, defer any longer to give it help."[86]

Mantuan Efforts of the Early 1590s

It was not until two years after the play's publication, in November 1591, that Guarini received Chieppio's request for his "Egloga Pastorale" on behalf of Duke Vincenzo Gonzaga. The records surrounding this assertive and exceptionally protracted staging attempt are extensive and have been discussed in detail in several studies, first and foremost that of Alessandro d'Ancona.[87] Therefore, rather than recount the numerous letters between Guarini, Chieppio, Vincenzo, and others, it is most profitable for our purposes here to focus on the various vicissitudes and difficulties of the preparations and the personnel involved in it.

The idea to stage *Il pastor fido* at the Mantuan court appears to have originated to some extent with Agnese Argotta, the Marchesana of Grana, who, as we have seen, was part of the circle of Barbara Sanservino and may have had the chance to hear Guarini's reading of the play in Guastalla.[88] Having stepped into Sanseverino's shoes as a mistress of Duke Vincenzo since about 1587, Argotta established residence in Mantua at the Palazzo del Te, where, as Iain Fenlon describes, she seems to have "cultivated a small academy of her own principally devoted to the arts of versification and music."[89] Argotta it appears, took charge of delegating some of the individuals to oversee the production of Guarini's tragicomedy, while the ducal secretary Chieppio acted as the principal liaison on the ground.

The first signs of problems in the preparations surface at the very start. In a dispatch of 26 November 1591 informing Duke Vincenzo of Guarini's decision to take part in the production, Chieppio describes the present disorder of the rehearsals. To begin, there was the general ineptness of the cast: the actors were obstinate, frequently missing rehearsals and forgetting a "good number of verses." Even more urgently, "that youth who does the part of Amarilli—a very long part—is deemed by all incapable due to *la mutazione della voce*."[90] Chieppio's next remark shows his serious concern for the effort altogether and how it might reflect on the court as well as the play, all for good reason:

> Beyond that, there are some parts that, in truth, need much study in order to conform [*corrispondere*] to the success of the company, and to the dignity of the work and of the place where it will be performed [*converrà recitare*].[91]

Chieppio's letter also reveals several decisions that had already been made pertaining to personnel. Firstly, two composers at the Gonzaga court, Giaches de Wert and Francesco Rovigo, were solicited to compose music for the work, none of which, it seems, survives. In addition, Chieppio informs the duke that, "with the consent of his father, *il Campagnolo* has been called from Ferrara, without whom—he holding the part of Silvio—the others will be able to rehearse badly." Whereas Evangelista Campagnolo was a singer of the Mantuan court who apparently had strayed to Ferrara (as Mantuan musicians seemed wont to do), the Mantuan preparations, in turn, relied from the outset on Ferrarese forces for important roles. In the coming months, as additional problems and delays took hold, Guarini and Campagnolo would be joined by another prominent figure in Ferrarese theatrical life, Guarini's colleague from the Sassuolo production of *Il sacrificio*, Aleotti.

Lastly, Chieppo reports that Isacchino Massarano—the Jewish dancing master and acting teacher as well as a talented soprano, lutenist, and choreographer of Mantua—had been "again entrusted ... with the care of the *balletto della Cieca*."[92] As seen earlier with Guarini's description of the scene's conception, the *Gioco della cieca* seems frequently to have been singled out from the rest of the play in its preparations for print and for the stage. This is understandable, given its demanding and distinctive use of choreography, music, and unusual verse lengths, all interspersed with dialogue. The practice of treating the *Gioco* separately from the surrounding play reached its fullest extent in 1595, when it was fashioned as a free-standing *ballo* with music and choreography by Emilio de' Cavalieri and with the text substantially revised by Laura Guidiccioni.[93]

By 23 December 1591, nearly one month after Chieppio's letter announcing Guarini's involvement, the poet had finally arrived, but in the meantime Isacchino had gone missing for several days, and a host of other problems continued to cripple the preparations. As Chieppio informs the duke, there are still difficulties finding an Amarilli "on account of the unbelievable scarcity of boys suitable with respect to the beauty, affect, and grace of that part."[94] Thus, in desperation, "of the three that have learned the part, the one least defective from the others will be chosen soon." In addition, the troublesome "Balletto della Cieca" still suffered from the ineptitude and obstinacy of the cast, and the absence of Isacchino had made it "necessary to begin the entire enterprise again."[95] With these and other issues looming over the projected performance at Carnival, the ducal secretary proposed the idea to defer the performance until after Easter, when the preparations would be "molto comodo di tutta la compagnia." Chieppio apparently wished to hide this idea from Guarini, but the death of Cardinal Gian Vincenzo Gonzaga on 22 December prompted Guarini himself to suggest postponing the production.

Work on the play had apparently resumed by April 1592, when Baldassare Castiglione *il giovane*—now supervisor of the production—expressed optimism to Vincenzo Gonzaga about its success, while also acknowledging the challenges of the task.[96] Guarini, at this stage, had not yet returned to Mantua from Ferrara, but as he wrote to Agnese Argotta on 24 April, he was pleased with the "giudiziosa" choice of Castiglione to oversee the venture. Argotta was apparently eager to have the poet onboard, for Guarini assured her: "I will hurry my return as much as I can."

Guarini's letter also reveals that it was by Argotta's solicitation that the poet's colleague at the Este court, Giovan Battista Aleotti, became enlisted in the Mantuan preparations. Responding to Argotta, and referring to the architect by the *soprannome* "il Perito" (the Expert), Guarini writes: "But of *Il Perito*—of whom Your Lordship writes expecting him to be with me—I have neither order nor news. I will arrange to see him, and if he will be summoned and release granted, I will bring him."[97] By 7 May, the secretary of the Duke of Ferrara formally offers to send Aleotti—now dubbed by his usual *soprannome*, "l'Argenta" (after his birthplace)—but only "for twelve or fifteen days."[98] Guarini did not arrive in Mantua, however, until nearly three weeks later (19 May), having been delayed while waiting for the formal release of Aleotti from Alfonso II. As Castiglione writes to Chieppio on 21 May 1592, the poet and architect were joined by two others from Ferrara: a page who was to play Corisca, and the actor and playwright Giovanni Donato Cuchetti, who would play two of the older male characters, Linco and Nicandro.[99]

Already by the time of Guarini and Aleotti's arrival, another notable figure had been added to the list of prominent personnel involved in the Gonzaga production: the artist and Prefect of the Ducal Fabric at the Gonzaga court from 1590 to 1591, Ippolito Andreasi (1548–1608). A student of the celebrated Giulio Romano in Mantua, Andreasi had contributed numerous works to the Gonzaga establishments, including some eighty paintings in the Palazzo del Te and Palazzo Ducale in the late 1560s, the decorations for the ceiling of Duke Guglielmo's *studiolo* and other projects in 1579–80, and in 1592 the restoration of Giovan Battista Bertani's theater in the ducal palace, which was heavily damaged by a fire in 1588, and his service for the Gonzaga continued until his death. In 1581, Andreasi also illustrated the second canto of Tasso's *Gerusalemme liberata*, and it must have been this capacity to conceive settings based on literary works that made him the choice candidate to design the scenery for *Il pastor fido*.[100]

But despite the impressive forces assigned to the preparations, serious concerns were again surfacing in the letters of Aleotti, Castiglione, and Guarini by May 1592. To begin, Chieppio complains again on 1 May about hindrances caused by the absences of performers. At that moment, for example, in addition to the delayed arrival of Guarini and Aleotti, the actors for the parts of Corisca, Mirtillo, Montano, and Linco/Nicandro, and one member of the chorus were missing. Three weeks later, rehearsals still lacked Alfonso Mauro, the actor for the part of Mirtillo—"without whom," Castiglione writes, "since it is so important a part, a worthwhile rehearsal cannot be done."[101] Even when the cast is present, however, it seems that rehearsals were still not entirely productive. Castiglione writes to Chieppio on 15 May that the performers "give me constant suffering, because I do not want to offend someone already, but they are moved so little by words and some of them even by threats."[102] To the absence of key personnel can also be added the late assignment of a boy to the central role of Amarilli. When this had finally been done in the final week of May, the actor showed little interest in his assigned part, "being too inclined toward that of Mirtillo, which he has already put to memory."[103]

Guarini echoes the others' concern about the absence of Mauro in a letter to Duke Vincenzo of 21 May, but on top of this, he restates his larger anxiety, first iterated to Vincenzo long before in January 1584, about the difficulty—even perilousness—of certain parts of the play. The poet writes:

> Meanwhile we attend vigorously to the rehearsals, but without Signor Mauro [i.e., Mirtillo] it is difficult to arrange this part of the rehearsal. He is, in the end, "Il pastor fido," and the entire thing concerns him, and especially the *ballo* and the sacrifice, which are the most perilous passages of the work. Therefore, we await him with great desire, not lacking anyone other than him. And be sure, Your Highness, that we are all united in agreement that the work will succeed, and that the lack of fortune will be counteracted by the diligence of the workers.[104]

This optimism about the potential to "ricompensare il difetto della fortuna," however, was not entirely genuine. For in a letter to Scipione Gonzaga six days before, the author expresses serious doubts about the feasibility of performing the play in June for the feast of San Giovanni Battista:

> In the meantime, I go preparing the nuptials of *Il pastor fido*, which His Highness wants to be performed this San Giovanni. And it happens

that the work in all its parts is warming up: we work on it vigorously at the theatre, on the set, on the *intermedi*, and attend to the rehearsal of the actors. I, nonetheless, have a certain concern that it should be deferred to another season.[105]

Vincenzo seems not to have been eager to risk any embarrassment to himself or to Guarini, for the production was again postponed. Guarini, as eager as ever to see his play successfully realized onstage, was understandably disappointed. In a letter to Nonio Acosta Osorio, evidently accompanied by a copy of the script, the poet wrote: "My *Pastor fido* will have another sleep, since its performance is delayed until September, in which time I will receive the favor of it being honored by your sight."[106]

September 1592, however, found Vincenzo Gonzaga in the midst of a pressing border dispute with the Duke of Parma, with Guarini serving as Vincenzo's diplomat to help resolve the issue. Preparations for the performance of *Il pastor fido* that month must have been far from Vincenzo Gonzaga's mind, for on 20 September, he dispatched Guarini to Innsbruck to meet with Archduke Ferdinand of Austria (Vincenzo's brother-in-law). Although these negotiations had ended by 15 October, Guarini did not return to Mantua until the following month, only to be dispatched to Steinach at the beginning of December.[107]

Thus, the efforts of 1592 never regained steam: nor did thoughts to resume the preparations in the spring of the following year amount to very much. Changes in the availability and suitability of many of the personnel made it "necessary to return to a new effort" rather than pick up where the previous attempt had left off: Castiglione was no longer available, having just been married; many actors had left or their voices had changed; and Guarini was seeking again to enlist the help of Aleotti from his resentful patron. But it was not so much the difficulties of the preparations that stifled this effort as it was the political situation of the time—a situation that gave Alfonso d'Este an ideal opportunity to avenge himself on his former courtier. Annoyed by Guarini's prolonged stay at the Mantuan court and jealous at the notion of his former poet and secretary serving another prince, Duke Alfonso began pressing the Gonzaga court in March 1593 to dismiss Guarini from its service. Guarini petitioned Duchess Eleonora de' Medici to intervene on his behalf, but Alfonso had considerable weight to throw behind the matter, having been designated by the Pope, the Emperor, and King of Spain as the peacemaker in resolving the Gonzaga–Farnese dispute.[108] In this capacity, Alfonso succeeded not only in having Guarini sent back from Mantua, but also in stamping out the Mantuan plans to stage *Il pastor fido* by refusing to go to Mantua in June as mediator if a performance took place.[109] When all was through, Duke Alfonso had gotten his way and peace was reached between the Gonzaga and the Farnese in June 1593, while Guarini was forced to leave Mantua in mid-July without having seen a performance of his tragicomedy.[110]

This was, in fact, the last known staging attempt that would involve Guarini directly, and following the collapses of the efforts in Mantua, Ferrara, and Turin in the 1580s, the 1591–93 Mantuan preparations were perhaps the most extensive and promising. Still there were many factors stacked against their success, including, first and foremost, the use of a very amateur cast for a stage production of such demanding scope and psychological depth. Clearly, the production would have been best entrusted to a professional troupe, such as the *Gelosi*, *Confidenti*, or *Uniti*, all of whom had close ties to the Duke of Mantua.[111] This limitation seems to have been due chiefly to Vincenzo's concern over the expense of the production, which is something that is discussed continuously in the letters between the duke, Chieppio, and Castiglione. Thus, as Lisa Sampson has pointed out, "while the staging of the play experimented with novel choreography and scenography, the acting still followed a pattern established by late fifteenth-century erudite comedies and practised more recently in pastorals in Ferrara" of being executed by a largely inexperienced cast.[112] The use of boys for lengthy, complex parts of nymphs demanded too much of the young, amateur actors, and created debilitating problems when their voices changed.[113] Along with this, as is seen time and again in the rehearsal updates, the actors were undisciplined, failing to turn up to rehearsals, refusing to follow orders, and showing difficulty in learning and executing the roles. Particularly in light of the frequent, often abrupt, changes in the personnel overseeing the rehearsals and the intricacy of such scenes as the *Gioco della cieca* and the *sacrificio* (as Guarini warned), the inconsistent attendance of the cast, especially of those in major roles, might alone have doomed the production—at least until Alfonso d'Este terminated the effort for good.

At the same time, the failure of these efforts might not have been simply a matter of bad luck for Guarini. In fact, as we shall soon see, a trail of failed productions shadowed the poet's direct involvement specifically, while the first successful efforts were those that did not involve him. There is some indication, in other words, that at least some of the blame for the play's difficult beginnings in the theater falls on Guarini, both for the rather unreasonable demands of the play itself (as both critics and supporters pointed out), but also in his seemingly clumsy handling of the courtly system. Provoking his own patron's ire while preparing the work in Mantua in the early 1590s is a clear example. It seems that Guarini's presentation of the play in Turin also provoked competition between Alfonso d'Este and the Duke of Savoy, which led to Guarini's being recalled to Ferrara before a staging of the play had reached fruition. The brokering between the two courts may have benefited the poet's employment, but only, it seems, at the expense of the play's premiere, which was left waiting in the wings in Turin as the poet returned to Ferrara.

The First (Confirmed) Productions

The failure of Duke Vincenzo's production seems to have been taken as a challenge for other courts to attempt their own stagings of the play, for after 1592, a host of other northern Italian centers began launching their own preparations, most of them with success. (In fact, if we are to believe "L'Attizzato"—the author of the second defense of *Il pastor fido*—"many cities in Italy had performed" the play already by 1591, though there is no indication of which ones.)[114] Yet despite this growing fortune of his play onstage, Guarini had no part in these productions, not even as a spectator, as news of them came from proud patrons and participants only after the performances had taken place. When he finally did have the opportunity to see his characters realized on stage—at the grand performance in Mantua in November 1598 for the Queen of Spain—it was merely as a passing visitor, not as a collaborator. This disappointment of a diplomat who had so adroitly advanced his play at three leading cultural centers was undoubtedly due to more than simply an unfavorable turn of fate. Rather, Guarini himself, as the overly zealous and proud father of a novel and well-liked work, might have overindulged in his prospects, especially given his responsibilities at the Este court, launching preparations in one court only to be yanked away by the demands of one or another patron (but usually the Duke of Ferrara), leaving nothing but loose ends and fruitless attempts in his wake. It therefore makes perfect sense that later efforts excluding Guarini would enjoy much more success, presumably benefiting from a consistent cast and crew, not to mention, perhaps, also from their distance from the ambitious and possibly fastidious demands of the playwright.

Indeed, the first documented successful performances of *Il pastor fido* took place in centers with only indirect associations with Guarini. The first of these may have taken place in the eastern city of Rimini at the same time that Guarini was occupied with the preparations in Mantua in 1592–93. The only known record of this event, however, is an undated letter from the poet to "Signor Dottor Marzini da Rimini," which begins:

> The city of Rimini, no less for its virtue than for its most noble ancientness, can bring honor to whatever deed it undertakes. And although the greatest fortune deemed that my *Pastor fido* be reputed worthy not only of the performance that will soon take place, but of the judgment of many noble minds that will make it a subject for eternity. And as this honor is infinite, so I give you all infinite thanks with the hope that you value me as apt to serve you in works of deeds, as you value me in works of words.[115]

There seems to be no reason to question whether the Rimini performance took place, but when the production occurred leaves room for some conjecture. Some indication can be found in a statement from later in Guarini's letter: "As for the costumes, I am sending you here in the adjoined writing the very ones that were ordered by me in Ferrara, and which will serve us again here, if it is performed."[116] The letter is signed from Mantua and must have been written in 1592 or 1593, this being the only staging attempt in

Mantua with which Guarini was directly involved following the Ferrarese effort of 1584–85 (for which the costumes were presumably designed).[117]

At roughly the same time, in August 1592, Guarini contacted Belisario Bulgarini—a Sienese critic and scholar of languages, who was a member of the Accademia degli Intronati and the founder and host of the Accademia degli Accesi—about some unfinished business regarding a bookseller in Siena.[118] Two years earlier, 105 copies of *Il pastor fido* had been sent to the bookseller, whose name Guarini had since forgotten, and he asked Bulgarini to find the bookshop and retrieve the money received and any unsold copies of the play.[119] The following March (1593), Guarini wrote briefly again from Mantua to Bulgarini, asking the Sienese scholar "to have the sixty-five *lire* and two *soldi* paid in Florence to Signor Bastiano de Rossi," the first secretary of the Accademia della Crusca (1582–1623), of which Guarini had been a member since 12 July 1587. That money had come from the "many volumes of *Pastor fido* sold" in Siena.[120] The play indeed had found some admirers in the Tuscan city, for in his next letter to Bulgarini—undated, but likely written shortly after the previous one of March 1593—Guarini thanks Bulgarini and other "cortesi Signori" of Siena for the performance given there of his tragicomedy, which had been fitted with a new prologue possibly written by Bulgarini himself.[121]

In addition to the Guarini–Bulgarini correspondence, two letters from the Florentine poet and scholar Roberto Titi to the prominent Sienese academician Scipione Bargagli (1540–1612) speak first of preparations, then of a recent performance of Guarini's tragicomedy. Bargagli, like Bulgarini, was a member of the Accademia degli Intronati, the group responsible for staging *La pellegrina* in Florence in 1589. In fact, it was Bargagli who, in a letter of 23 February 1587, proposed the idea to perform his late brother Girolamo's comedy for the 1589 Medici wedding, thereby ousting other works from contention, including *Il pastor fido*.[122] Now, Bargagli and the Intronati found themselves at work on their own production of Guarini's pastoral in Siena three years after its publication.

Both of Titi's letters are revealing in several ways. The first—from 27 February 1593—while substantiating the preparations to stage Guarini's work, also (as we have seen) betrays the Florentine's understanding of how the Turin effort fared. Titi writes to Bargagli:

> I know that it is not an opportune time to bother Your Lordship by giving you my letter to read, you being occupied, as I believe, by the beautiful Pastoral that is performed there... Signor Silvio Spannacchi tells me that the Pastoral is *Il pastor fido*. It will be a glory to that city to perform what had not been done on the occasion that gave beginning and birth to the poem, because I understand that it was not performed in Turin for the nuptials of that Most Serene Duke, for which it was written.[123]

The second letter of 25 March relates the news Titi had heard about the Sienese performance from Henry Wotton, an English author and diplomat traveling in Europe in 1589–94.[124] As Titi recounts:

> From Signore Wotton I learned some particulars about the spectacle of *Il pastor fido*, so that, along with what you very graciously told me of it through your [letter?], I became almost a spectator of such a beautiful performance. My conception of you other Signori Senesi is such that I believe there is no difficult thing of this type that is not rendered most easily there [in Siena]...[125]

Guarini, who suffered one of his many bouts of sickness in March 1593, had wanted to visit Siena for the first time once his health improved. As he ended his letter to Bulgarini of that month: "I am beginning to get better, thank God, with the hope of my journey to Rome, during which I could see Your Lordship as I greatly desire, and that most noble city, which I have never seen."[126] He did visit the city, but it was not until many months after the staging of *Il pastor fido*, as he was making his way to Rome to bring his young son Guarino to the Jesuit seminary. Guarini stayed for two and a half days in Siena near the start of November 1593, where he was scammed by a cunning "Vetturino di Firenze," but also—in the wake of the successful sales and production of his play—welcomed and honored by many Sienese, including Bulgarini and his family, the archbishop, and Scipione Bargagli.[127]

The hospitality of the Bulgarini family evidently continued after Guarini had become settled in Rome. There he stayed at the *rotonda* in the house of one Giovanni Casale, but he enjoyed the "gentlest nature and paternal kindness" of Bulgarini's son, Paris, who worked in the service of Cardinal Girolamo Rusticucci.[128] By the next month, Guarini was enjoying himself immensely among his company in Rome, writing to his friend Guido Coccapani on 10 December:

> I will stay here until Easter, as I am very fond of my room, and am well looked after and honored by all, and in particular by the Signori Nepoti of the Holy Cardinals. I wanted to share this with you so that you know where I find myself, so you can send me your orders, since I wholeheartedly beseech them. I assure you that I have never lived so content as I am now: being relieved of all the things that had burdened me, and living in a grand city like this, where I have conversations according to my taste, and where one sees and does great things each day.[129]

Although annoyed by the end of January by the Romans' incessant demand for his verses, Guarini returned to Rome the following December, leaving in the middle of April 1595 in order to meet Alfonso d'Este in Bologna for an attempted reconciliation.[130] During precisely these same years (1594–95), another pivotal development took place in the history of *Il pastor fido*: the publication of two madrigal books containing fifteen settings of passages from Guarini's play by the Roman composer Luca Marenzio (c.1553–99), and another, containing four settings, by Mantuan composer Giaches de Wert. These publications by two leading composers of the day seemed to open the doors for other composers to draw musical texts from the pages of *Il pastor fido*. The notion that Guarini's presence in Rome in 1593–95 inspired Marenzio's abrupt and extensive interest in the play, as scholars have suggested, is attractive and, indeed, plausible. But as we will see in later chapters, there are other factors that point toward a different source and chronology.

While Guarini was in Rome this second time, yet another opportunity to see his *tragicommedia pastorale* performed passed him by. This production, described in the accounts as quite lavish and polished, yielded two performances in the palazzo of Lodovico Zurla during Carnival in Crema.[131] The primary record of the spectacle is the *Proseguimento della storia di Crema dall' anno 1586 sino al 1664* of Ludovico Canobio, a major supporter of theatre in Crema, particularly by way of the academy he founded and directed there, the Accademia degli Immaturi.[132] Canobio's account tells us of a "boschereccio teatro" suited to the "scena di quella tragicommedia pastorale," which was constructed in the courtyard of Zurla's palazzo. In terms of the performance itself, it was carried out "with sumptuous costumes, with excellent music, and with such exquisiteness of the performers, almost all of them Cremaschi," before an audience not only of locals, but also—"by the fame of that work already praised throughout Lombardy"—of foreigners. The competition for entrance into the performance must have been fierce, and must also have been foreseen, leading the skilled military engineer Francesco Tensini of Crema to make counterfeit tickets to gain access into Zurla's palazzo, for which he was subsequently exiled from the Veneto altogether.[133]

The production in Crema, however, was not the only effort being made to bring *Il pastor fido* to the stage for Carnival in 1595, for at that time, Alfonso d'Este was also making his second and final move to perform the work of his former poet.[134] Yet this time, again, Alfonso's production was almost certainly a failure. A much more successful venture, though one of a very different nature, however, was soon underway in Florence: the *Giuoco della cieca* of Emilio de' Cavalieri and Laura Guidiccioni.[135] The composition of the Florentine *Giuoco* likely followed the same course as that of Guarini's own *Gioco della cieca* on which it was based, beginning with the choreography, then adding the music, and finally, "under the notes of that music, the poet made the words."[136] Indeed, from what contemporary sources indicate, this seems to have been the standard practice for the development of staged *balli* in Ferrara, Mantua, and Florence in the 1580s and 1590s.[137]

Guidiccioni and Cavalieri were hardly new to this procedure, nor was this the first time the two had worked together in executing it. Guidiccioni (1550–97) came to the Medici court from Lucca in December 1588, and months later, she was entrusted by Cavalieri to fit text to his choreography and music for *O che nuovo miracolo*, the final *ballo* of the 1589 *intermedi* for the grand ducal wedding.[138] Following a performance of Tasso's *Aminta* in February 1590—with music by Cavalieri (possibly to texts by Guidiccioni) and set designs and machinery by Buontalenti[139]—Guidiccioni completed her own pastoral play, *Il satiro*, which incorporated music by Cavalieri and was performed for Carnival in the Hall of Statues in the Palazzo Pitti. In December that same year, the poet and the composer–choreographer staged another pastoral play with music, *La disperatione di Fileno*, this time at the Villa Medici a Careggi—where Guidiccioni and Cavalieri had been staying—with singing by the celebrated soprano Vittoria Archilei, who had accompanied Cavalieri in the move from Rome to Florence when Ferdinando de' Medici resigned from his cardinalship to become grand duke.[140]

Thus, when the time came to prepare the *Giuoco della cieca* for its October 1595 performance, the pair had had several opportunities to try their hands at staging works of various scopes that incorporated music, choreography, acting, and verse, not to mention a pastoral setting. The performance of the *Giuoco* marked the occasion of a visit by Cardinal Montalto (Alessandro Peretti), an eminent patron of music in Rome, who came to Florence to serve as godfather in the baptism of Prince Francesco de' Medici. The work must have been well suited to Montalto's visit, for in the previous years the cardinal had been a patron of Roman composer Luca Marenzio, whose many settings of *Il pastor fido* were published immediately after his time in Montalto's service, and the following year (1596), the cardinal would make his own move to stage the play in Rome. The *Diario di etichetta* states for 29 October 1595 that there was a feast and dancing in the Palazzo Pitti in the early evening, with some "60 gentildonne" present. After this, "a *pastorella*, all in music, was performed dancing," and then, after some *confetture*, the women were given leave.[141] Nothing has been found of Cavalieri and Guidiccioni's work itself, but additional information of it survives in written accounts of two later performances by the Medici court: on 6 June 1598 for the visit of Archduke Ferdinand of Austria, in the capacity of godfather to Prince Carlo;[142] and on 5 January 1599 for Cardinals Montalto and Del Monte, Virginio Orsini, Antonio de' Medici, and Prince Cosimo II de' Medici. From these accounts we learn that the entire work was sung to music, that it lasted between one hour and an hour and a half, and that it again involved some "60 gentildonne fiorentine."

This reference to "sixty" (perhaps shorthand for "quite a few") Florentine ladies, consistent in both the accounts of 1595 and 1599, has been overlooked, but it is indeed conspicuous and may provide some insight into the final shape of the work. To begin, a letter from Bartolomeo Malaspina to Cesare d'Este, Duke of Modena, of 5 January 1599 relates that "a performance was done with shepherds and nymphs entitled *la mosca cieca*, with dances (*balli*) set to music, which lasted only an hour."[143] The play's *Gioco della cieca*, as Guarini describes it, however, was simply a "*ballo*, done by a chorus of nymphs" (ballo, fatto da un choro di Ninfe), not multiple *balli* incorporating both nymphs and shepherds—although there is one shepherd, Mirtillo, who lingers on the sidelines and inserts himself late in the game—and lasted only a fraction of a hour. Furthermore, the noted presence of a multitude of ladies for the Florentine performances who departed after the *pastorella* and *confetture* suggests that these women were not merely props to accompany the guests at dinner and in social dancing, but possibly actual participants in the *balli*.

Cavalieri and Guidiccioni's work now takes on some of the general characteristics of what we know about the Ferrarese *balletto della duchessa*—that is, a group of ladies dressed as nymphs and shepherds performing a dance with music set to a text by Guarini, which lasted about an hour.[144] These Ferrarese *balletti* were typically much smaller in size, numbering between four and twelve dancers. Cavaliere Giacomo Grana, writing from Ferrara to Cardinal Luigi d'Este on 24 January 1582, for instance, refers to a "gran baletto" that included only eight ladies and "lasted three quarters of an hour."[145] Malaspina's account of Cavalieri's work, on the other hand, refers to *balli*, not a single *ballo*. What Cavalieri and Guidiccioni's *Giuoco* entailed, therefore, might have been a series of dances utilizing various smaller ensembles of shepherds and nymphs that expanded the four-section form (and intermittent dialogue) of the danced choruses in act 3, scene 2 of Guarini's play. These changes from one dance movement to another, and from one set of participants to another, would fit precisely with the variety in aspects such as instrumentation, costume, performance forces, mode, vocal register, meter, and characters that Cavalieri sought in his works.[146] Indeed, as Warren Kirkendale attests, in Cavalieri's "pastorales, as in [the *Rappresentatione di*] *Anima e Corpo*, he would prefer to avoid monotony of unrelieved declamatory recitative, and to create variety by greater use of choruses, ensembles, and solos in the more melodic canzonetta style."[147] In all, with its grand scale, substantial length, and inclusion of shepherds as well as nymphs, the *Giuoco* of Giudiccioni and Cavalieri must have had only a faint resemblance to the game in Guarini's play between Amarilli and her nymphs that inspired it. Later musical settings of the play's *Gioco*, as we will see, tend to stick much more faithfully to Guarini's printed text, and prove more fitting for a scene within a larger theatrical drama than Guidiccioni and Cavalieri's vast *ballo*.

It seems entirely predictable given the trail of performance attempts that followed Guarini from Ferrara to Mantua, Turin, and Florence that preparations for a staging of *Il pastor fido* would spring up in Rome after the poet's visits there in the winters of 1593–94 and 1594–95. It also makes perfect sense that these preparations would be headed by Cardinal Montalto, the voracious patron of music and theater, whose visit to Florence in 1595 (and again in 1599) coincided with the performance of Cavalieri and Guidiccioni's *Giuoco*. By this time, Montalto would undoubtedly also have been at least aware of (if not directly behind) the numerous musical settings from *Il pastor fido* coming out of Rome in the mid-1590s by composers such as Marenzio and Giuseppino Cenci, who enjoyed Montalto's protection around that time.[148]

The seeds of Montalto's production of the tragicomedy seem to have been planted in preparations for the wedding celebrations of his younger brother, Michele Peretti, and Margherita della Somaglia in the spring of 1596. According to an *avviso* of 28 February 1596:

> Don Michele Peretti, who had planned to do beautiful things for his wedding, has little desire to do anything because of the death of Contestabile Colonna [his brother-in-law], although it is said that after Easter [14 April] he wants to have performed in the Sala della Cancelleria the tragicomedy of Guarini, called *Il pastor fido*, resolving to spend on the *intermedi* and other things two or three thousand *scudi*.[149]

John Walter Hill surmises that the performance was called off in the end because the symbolism of the play "could have been found unsuitable for a marriage with Margherita della Somaglia."[150] The reasons for this stem from the tangled negotiations that preceded the marriage, which included a contract for Peretti to marry Caterina Gonzaga that was negotiated and signed in Rome by Duke Vincenzo himself, only to be annulled in the summer of 1595 when the pope verified that Peretti had secretly married della Somaglia in 1588 or 1589 at the age of 11. As Hill argues, the turn of events in the play involving the annulment of Amarilli's betrothal to Silvio in favor of a marriage to Mirtillo following the revelation of Mirtillo's true parentage, might have resonated too closely with the situation between Michele Peretti and his two brides-to-be. (Yet, it could also be argued that wedding entertainments of the period often did not shy away from opportunities to convey moral and practical lessons, particularly to brides, in harsh and allegorical ways.)

Hill also reasons that, "since the performance was to have taken place shortly after Easter," Montalto and Michele Peretti must have begun their preparations well before the 28 February date of the *avviso*—even a year or more in advance—"considering the long preparations for performances of *Il pastor fido* in Ferrara, Turin, Florence, and Mantua, and the extended periods of gestation that preceded the production of Florentine intermedi and early operas."[151] Thus, Hill maintains, "we may safely conclude that the idea to perform *Il pastor fido* originated in the context of a projected Peretti–Gonzaga wedding," not a Peretti–Somiglia one.[152] But backdating the beginning of the preparations to the summer of 1595 or earlier, as Hill's reasoning implies, seems unnecessarily long. To begin, nowhere in the records does it state that the performance was to take place "shortly after Easter;" rather, the *avviso* simply indicates "dopo Pasqua." It will be remembered that in late December 1591, the projected Mantuan performance was also delayed, following the death of Gian Vincenzo Gonzaga, until "dopo Pasqua" (which in 1592 fell on 29 March), and in that case, preparations did not even resume until the middle of April. In Montalto's situation, the production was aborted only after Easter, which means that preparations might have been set to continue for some time before a projected performance.

Secondly, while Hill suggests that "Guarini himself may have helped the Peretti prepare their production when he was in Rome in winter of 1594–95," there is nothing to indicate this in Guarini's letters from Rome at the time. Thus, Guarini's presence in Rome (and other factors, to be considered later) could very well have piqued Montalto's interest in the play, which likely intensified even more in October 1595 following the Florentine *Giuoco della cieca* of Cavalieri. But from what the sources tell us, formal plans for a Roman production seem to correspond with those for a Peretti–Somaglia wedding in early 1596.

Thus, if the time range for the production is extended reasonably in either direction—say, beginning in January 1596 for a performance in late May—it would allow sufficient time for Montalto's preparations to take shape. Guarini had warned Vincenzo Gonzaga in April 1584 that the play "could not be put together in three months," as the duke had hoped, given its "novelty," its "very grand passages that need to be set to music and rehearsed repeatedly onstage," and especially the *Gioco* of the third act.[153] Some twelve years had passed since Guarini's warning, however, during which time the play had been staged at least two or three times in its entirety and brought through at least seven separate production attempts that progressed to relatively advanced stages. Montalto would surely have been aware of some of this history and of the demands of the production, and would certainly have had access to the necessary resources to carry out what he had begun. In all likelihood, he also benefited from having discussed the play in considerable detail in the intellectual circles of Rome, presumably in the company of Guarini in the previous winters, as well as from having witnessed Cavalieri and Guidiccioni's effective, large-scale rendition of the play's most difficult scene.

Hence, even if the *intermedi* for Peretti's wedding celebrations, which could be attached to any theatrical production, had been planned a long time in advance, Montalto seemed well equipped to bring *Il pastor fido* to the stage within a matter of months—or at least he might have hoped as much. Yet the question still remains as to why the production eventually fell through. It might have been cancelled out of concerns over the appropriateness of the subject matter, as Hill has suggested, but one would think in that case that the cancellation would have happened earlier—sparing, no doubt, a good deal of expense—given Montalto's familiarity with both the play and the dispute. Another possibility is that rehearsals simply came apart, which could have had nothing to do with Montalto's preparedness. As Vincenzo Gonzaga's failed staging of 1591–93 demonstrates, even a patron with close ties to Guarini's play and with the assistance of some of the most talented personnel in stage production of the day (including Guarini) had little hope of mounting a production with an unreliable and unruly cast. As Hill quite compellingly proposes, however, the vestiges of the Montalto production might in the end have been salvaged for an event of a much smaller scale outside of Rome, in the small Farnese territory of Ronciglione only a few months later, in September 1596.

The details of the circumstances in Ronciglione are recounted to Guarini by Gabriele Bombasi of Reggio d'Emilia, a member of Cardinal Odoardo Farnese's *famiglia* in Rome since 1589.[154] On 4 September 1596, Bombasi writes:

> Just the day before yesterday the Cardinal Farnese, my Lord—who because of this heat enjoys the amenities of Capraruola and the climate of this area—moved to Ronciglione, his land, with a fine company of prelates and *signori*, and with the court, where *Il pastor fido* was performed with so much excellence that the patron and we all were amazed by it, even though it was noted that the performers were *accademici*, very talented and most of them scholars and of good letters. Of that success I wanted at once to give you an account...[155]

As Bombasi relates, the rather impromptu performance had only the barest of costumes ("in habito così semplice, e quasi nuda") and stage sets, which suited the pastoral play well, for this "most beautiful *favola* has no need of pompous ornaments."[156] Bombasi and the Farnese court must have taken some pride in the fact that the small center of Ronciglione could accomplish what other, more prominent cultural centers could not. The courtier, in a statement that at once reaffirms the failure of earlier staging attempts by Alfonso d'Este and attests to the play's success in both the theatrical and literary realms, writes:

> And who would have ever believed that a *favola* of such fame, of so many characters, so grand, and so noble, so full of *giuochi di cacce*, of sacrifices, and of choruses, of a knot so intertwined, and of resolutions so unexpected and wonderful, should be performed with such delight in Ronciglione...? And it is indeed known that the Ferrarese, the Bolognese, and the Paduans, who have wanted to do it, have elected rather to contemplate its wonders through reading it than to put their dignity in peril by staging it.[157]

Just how this performance was accomplished is some mystery, for there are no apparent records of any preparations that had taken place in Ronciglione or Capraruola. Preparations were made, however, in Rome earlier the same year, and as Hill points out, it is certainly plausible that Cardinal Montalto's—or, rather, Michele Peretti's—production was simply given over to Cardinal Farnese to take with him to Capraruola, which then ended up being transferred to Ronciglione with the rest of Farnese's entourage.[158]

Odoardo Farnese, the son of Alessandro Farnese (the Duke of Parma from 1586) and Maria of Portugal, was placed under the protection of his great uncle, Cardinal Alessandro Farnese, in 1583 at the age of ten, and by 1591, promptly raised to the purple. As a part of Cardinal Alessandro Farnese's *famiglia*, there can be no doubt that the young Odoardo Farnese took part in the August 1587 wedding in Capraruola between Marco Pio di Savoia and Alessandro's illegitimate daughter Clelia, who had previously been living in Rome. It does not seem at all improbable, then, that Odoardo also attended the celebrations that followed in Sassuolo at the end of November, which included Guarini and Aleotti's production of Beccari's *Il sacrificio*, and that Odoardo even encountered Guarini himself (as well as Beccari) years before the poet's extended visits to Rome in 1593–95. This early exposure to pastoral drama in the events surrounding the Pio–Farnese wedding, whether direct or indirect, might have established an example for the cardinal's own use of pastoral drama in the summer of 1596, when he turned to Guarini's more current, now controversial contribution to the genre.

The close ties between Sassuolo and both Ferrara and the Roman Farnese following the Pio–Farnese union might offer a different explanation for the origins of the *Pastor fido* production in Ronciglione from the one proposed by Hill involving the aborted Montalto–Peretti preparations. It is known— from a letter of Ridolfo Arlotti, a former member of the Eterei—that sometime before the beginning of 1597 Marco Pio had established "una virtuosa Accademia" devoted to letters, music, and theatrical performances, and that he was currently making "grand and beautiful preparations to have Sophocles' tragedy *Oedipus Rex* performed at Carnival."[159] In Bombasi's description of the Ronciglione performance of *Pastor fido*, he notes specifically that the cast was comprised of "Accademici molto virtuosi" without giving any indication as to where these academicians came from. It could very well be that Pio's academy in Sassuolo, rather than a Roman troupe, had prepared Guarini's pastoral tragicomedy for some small-scale performance that was then brought to Ronciglione, or even that the production was made expressly for a staging before Odoardo Farnese's court during his summer respite in Capraruola.

Whatever the case, the event was evidently looked highly upon, for a repeat performance was arranged for "the arrival of many *signori*" the following Sunday.[160] While Bombasi gives no indication who these *signori* were, he does single out for Guarini two spectators from Rome who attended the initial performance: Francesco Colonna, "who was an admirer of [the play], not to mention a most attentive spectator," and Guarini's close friend, Pier Paolo Crescenzi—later the dedicatee of composer Fabio Costantini's *L'aurata Cintia armonica … di diversi eccellentissimi autori, à 1, à 2, à 3, & à 4* (Orvieto: Michel' Angelo Fei and Rinaldo Ruuli, 1622), which contains two settings of *Pastor fido* texts by Fabio's brother, Alessandro Costantini—"who came flying from Rome to Ronciglione" to catch the performance.[161]

The Mantuan Productions of 1598 and the Madrigals of Gastoldi

Not present at the performance in Ronciglione, however, was of course Guarini himself, who, after failing to carry stagings of his work through in Ferrara, Turin, and Mantua, received merely written word of the successful productions in Siena, Crema, possibly Rimini, and now Ronciglione in more recent years. To Guarini's dismay, this trend would continue into 1598, when a series of three resplendent performances of *Il pastor fido* was mounted, at long last, by Duke Vincenzo Gonzaga of Mantua. The first of these performances, as Francesco Ongarino relates on 24 June 1598 to Ercole Udine, was meant to be performed that very day, but the event was delayed several days due to a malfunction of the stage machinery.[162]

The performance, in fact, took place before Pope Clement VIII and a sizeable entourage of some twenty-seven cardinals—including the pope's nephew, the papal legate of Ferrara and the recent dedicatee of Guarini's *Rime* (1598), Pietro Aldobrandini, as well as Cardinals Montalto and Monte from Rome—and forty bishops, who had made their way to the Gonzaga court from the newly acquired papal territory of Ferrara.[163] While an anonymous chronicler details the new prologue honoring the pope and the elaborate *intermedi* depicting the courtship of Peleus and Thetis that adorned Guarini's tragicomedy for the occasion, no mention is made of the authors and composers who devised these works.[164] The report does, however, indicate the use of music in each of the *intermedi*. In the first *intermedio*, for example, Thetis sings while riding a dolphin and is answered in song by a sea god, while in the second, Peleus appears singing in a boat accompanied by "three women playing lutes and singing with wonderful sweetness, to the gentle sound of which Thetis fell asleep."[165] The third *intermedio* featured Thetis and Peleus on a "beautiful boat" with sixteen others, including virtuoso Francesco Rasi, who sang to his own accompaniment on the chitarrone and was answered by two echoes. After the final act, the worlds of Arcadia and Olympus join when the gods descend to celebrate the marriage of Mirtillo and Amarilli.[166]

Federico Follino and Gasparo Asiani had directed the rehearsals for the production, which had likely begun by at least 9 April 1598, when Annibale Chieppio in Mantua speaks of the difficult preparations of a "Comedia" in correspondence with Tullio Petrozanni in Casale and Duke Vincenzo Gonzaga.[167] Guarini was unable to attend the production, as he says himself in a letter to Duke Vincenzo of 17 June 1598: he was, in fact, detained in Ferrara not only by grief, but also by legal battles over the brutal murder of his daughter, Anna—a virtuoso singer and lutenist in the Ferrarese *concerto delle donne*—one month earlier (3 May 1598). Instead, Guarini sent his son Alessandro (who was "also very experienced in the theatre") in his place to serve the duke, a move that would lead to Alessandro's employment at the Mantuan court for several years to come.[168]

On 1 August 1598, an unnamed member of the Mantuan court was writing again in regard to a performance of *Il pastor fido*, this time to alert the Venetian Giulio Contarini of a staging that was to occur "next Sunday" for Juan Fernández de Velasquez, Duke of Frías, Constable of Castille and Leon, and Governor of Milan from 1592 to 1600. The author writes:

> I promised to advise Your Sereneness in Venice when *Il pastor fido* was to be performed here again, and being put in order as needed to perform it next Sunday with the occasion of the coming of the Signor Contestabile, I did not want to neglect to inform you...[169]

Velasquez, however, lingered in Milan for several weeks, and it was not until 1 September that Chieppio contacted Ercole Udine, the Mantuan ambassador in Venice, requesting that he notify Contarini and others of the performance the coming Sunday.[170] The Contestabile did arrive on Sunday as planned, bringing a retinue of 400. He was evidently impressed by the spectacle of the performance—so much so that later in the month a Spanish architect was sent from Milan to study the stage machinery of the Mantuan production, for Velasquez would not stop "preaching of the miracles that he had seen."[171]

Guarini understandably was not pleased at having missed the two Mantuan performances that summer, but found some solace in receiving detailed accounts of them, in knowing that it had been enjoyed by those dear to him, and in learning that it would soon be performed again.[172] As he writes to one Dottore Ferrari of Verona:

> My *Pastor fido* was already performed twice in Mantua with spectacle and success worthy of that great prince, and I could not be at my "nuptials"... It is said that it is being prepared yet a third time for the passage of the Princess of Spain. This occasion—if it is true—I do not want to escape me by any means.[173]

Guarini did indeed make it to Mantua for this third, illustrious occasion. His only surviving reference to the event—a brief note to the Duke of Mantua expressing his regret for having to leave immediately after the performance to return to Ferrara for the departure of "Nostro Signore" (presumably Pope Clement VIII)—is disappointing in its lack of any detail whatsoever about the performance.[174]

Guarini could not have been displeased with the vast scale of international publicity that this third performance brought to his work. The staging took place on Sunday, 22 November as part of the celebrations for the young Queen of Spain, Margherita of Austria, who arrived from Ferrara two days earlier with her cousin, Archduke Albert VI of Austria (himself having just married Margherita's sister-in-law, Isabella); her mother, Archduchess Maria; and a train of some 3,000. Her marriage to the newly crowned King

Phillip III (by proxy)—along with that of the archduke to Isabella, the king's half-sister—had been officiated by Pope Clement VIII one week earlier, on Sunday, 15 November 1598, in Ferrara. Presumably a large share of the guests, coming from Austria and Spain, were not able to understand Italian, so Margherita and her mother (and possibly others) were provided with a summary of the play and *intermedi* in German.[175] According to several contemporary accounts, the spectacle, held in the Castello di San Giorgio, began in the afternoon, after the baptism of Eleonora Gonzaga (with the queen and archduke as godparents), and lasted roughly eight hours—thus, delaying the queen's dinner to such a late hour that a light meal was served in the middle of the play.[176] Giovanni Battista Grillo, in his published chronicle of the occasion, wrote that in addition to the many foreign guests, the event drew, "one could almost say, all the nobility of Italy from Venice, Florence, Genoa, Verona, Brescia, and other surrounding cities to see performed the aforementioned *Pastorale*, which has borne so famous a name everywhere."[177] Giovanni Battista Vigilio's *La insalata*—a record of Mantuan events covering 1561–1602—records that Duke Vincenzo ordered that no Mantuans were to enter the theater, only "forastieri," which resulted in an outbreak of violence at the main entrance.[178] On top of this, as with the performance at Zurla's palazzo in Crema in 1595, the numbers in attendance had to be controlled through the issuing of *segni*. A letter from Federico Capilluti to the Gonzaga court written the day of the performance, for example, states that "Federico Contarini with three other Venetian gentlemen find themselves in Mantua and desire to see the *Tragicomedia*, and I understand that Your Sereneness has the charge of dispensing the *segni* to foreigners."[179]

In addition to the Queen of Spain and her family, the event may have included some very illustrious guests who, according to Vigilio, arrived the day before the performance for a hunt, along with "six thousand and more, most of them foreigners." These visitors included, once again, Cardinal Pietro Aldobrandini, "accompanied by six bishops and other prelates, cavalieri, and gentlemen," as well as the Duke of Modena, Cesare d'Este, who appeared *incognito* along with his brother Alessandro d'Este, Ferrante Gonzaga, Federico Picco, Camillo da Correggio, Camillo II Gonzaga (Count of Novellara), and "many others, most notably some cardinals and bishops, whose names will not be written for their having come *incogniti*," or unofficially.[180]

Despite the large numbers in attendance, Guarini's reluctance to express his opinion of the performance in his note to Duke Vincenzo makes one wonder if its lavishness was to his liking. Some six years earlier, for instance, when Guarini, Aleotti, and Castiglione were struggling to mount the play in Mantua, the poet seemed to hint in a letter to the duke that a respectable play should not need the adornment of *intermedi*. Guarini writes:

> It seems to me also relevant to touch on something about the *intermezzi*, which—if I should say what I feel about them—for reason and for taste,

I would advise that they be left out, since they are necessary only where there is doubt that the *favola* will be pleasing without them. But perhaps, being a spectacle of a great Prince, it could seem that it cannot be performed without this ornament. I will say that when Your Highness is resolved that they should be done, it will be necessary that you entrust the care of them to one who is not only a good architect, but a most practiced engineer...[181]

In fact—presumably to Guarini's dismay—the two principal accounts of the 1598 event, by Grillo and Vigilio, speak at great length about the astonishing *intermedi* but give no description of the play itself. Virgilio, in fact, does not even name Guarini's work, but refers to it only as "una comedia," whereas Grillo at least acknowledges its name, stating that, in the *intermedio* that began the performance, some shepherds and nymphs appeared "in costume for the *Pastor fido* (which is the name of the work performed) ... to celebrate the firm faith of the queen bride."[182] The indifference to the play is rather to be expected in the culture of court spectacle, as perhaps Guarini knew: it is fortunate that any record survives, for example, of even the title of the play performed at the festivities for the 1589 Medici wedding, whereas the *intermedi* that accompanied it are portrayed in extensive detail in the official chronicles. Those who reported the Mantuan event of 1598 apparently followed a similar tactic, and the play, at least, could be read in print.

There is no record of who devised the music and text of the *intermedi*, nor have any parts of those been identified. It is possible that the texts (or some part of them) were penned by Gasparo Asiani, who had published his own comedy, *La pronuba*, with *intermedi* in 1588, and who, along with Federico Follino, had directed the rehearsals of *Il pastor fido* in the spring of 1598. But there was no shortage of other poets in Mantua who could have supplied the verse. The stage sets and machinery were the work of the Prefect of the Ducal Fabric, Antonio Maria Viani of Cremona. Viani had entered Gonzaga service to oversee expansions of the Palazzo Ducale in 1591—hence, at the time when earlier protracted efforts were underway to stage Guarini's tragicomedy—so there is a possibility that the designs for the 1598 production relied on Aleotti's plans for the earlier failed production.[183]

The *intermedi* for the November 1598 production depicted the mythological tale of the marriage of Mercury and Philology, whose effect of cosmic peace and celebration had obvious political overtones suitable to a dynastic marriage. The tale also provided ample opportunities for awe-inspiring spectacle that included scenographic depictions of Mantua, the Elysian Fields, Mount Parnassus, and a stormy seascape, as well as the mouth of Hell with the city of Dis in flames, Fame rising atop a tower while sounding a trumpet, and the special effects of clouds, rain, thunder, and lightning. While historians have emphasized the resounding success of the production and the immense international prestige that it brought to the Gonzaga court—a perspective propagated especially by Grillo's and Vigilio's chronicles—two unofficial accounts reveal that the occasion was not devoid of some serious flaws. According to the *Diario di Santa Barbara, 1572–1602*, a mishap arising from a mechanical failure in the *intermedi* tainted the entire event: "The *comedia* was begun, which did not succeed because some ropes were cut, as a result of which several were hurt."[184] In a letter to Ercole Udine three days after the performance, ducal secretary Francesco Ongarino provides a rare reflection on the success of the play itself, specifying that it was not the tragicomedy but the *intermedi* that were the problem.[185] These candid depictions of the grand spectacle reveal not only a more realistic picture of how things unfolded, but also the vast influence of contemporary propagandist accounts, whose blindly optimistic portrayal has endured even in recent scholarship.

Although the *intermedi* themselves do not survive, Grillo describes the use of music not only in the *intermedi*, as would be expected, but also in parts of the play. Because Grillo devotes all of his attention to the *intermedi*, his only mention of the play, including its use of music, apart from the prologue, focuses on the ends of the acts that lead into the following *intermedi*. Hence, Grillo acknowledges "the *concerto* of onstage music [*musica di dentro*]" that precedes the first *intermedio*, and describes how, "after the fourth act, at the finishing of the music onstage, one heard the sound of trumpets under the stage." The conclusion of the play also witnessed the gods appearing in the sky to join the shepherds in song in celebration of the marriage.[186] Although Grillo does not say as much, the music in each of these instances likely entailed the singing of the choruses (or a portion thereof) that conclude each act of Guarini's play.

Despite the lack of descriptions about the staging of the play itself, it is certain that music was used in at least one place other than the *intermedi* and end-of-act choruses: the danced choruses of nymphs in the *Gioco della cieca* in the second scene of act 3. As we have seen—based on Guarini's 1584 letter to Vincenzo Gonzaga and his 1602 *Annotazioni*—the poet penned the verse for the *Gioco* only after "Leone" (Tolosa) completed the choreography and Luzzaschi, the music. For the 1598 occasion, however, the *Gioco* seems to have appeared in a new, Mantuan musical setting—by Gastoldi, *maestro di cappella* of the Gonzaga chapel of Santa Barbara from 1588 to 1609, whose Fourth Book of madrigals for five voices (Venice: Amadino, 1602) contains a setting of all four choruses of the *Gioco della cieca* in the form of a four-*parte* madrigal with the incipit *Cieco, Amor, non ti cred'io*. Support for this connection between Gastoldi's music and the Mantuan production comes not only from the composer's position in the Gonzaga chapel and the homophonic, dance-like character of the music, but also from the caption that introduces the cycle in the 1602 partbooks: "The *Gioco de la cieca* performed for the Queen of Spain in *Il pastor fido*."[187]

The likely origins of Gastoldi's *Cieco, Amor, non ti cred'io* as music for the stage make it unique, for aside from two small pieces by Alfonso della Viola from a 1554 production of Agostino Beccari's *Il sacrificio* in Ferrara—which might have been known to Guarini following his involvement in the 1587 staging of Beccari's play in Sassuolo—few examples of music designed for use in a play have been concretely identified (despite much speculation), even though accounts such as Grillo's tell us such music existed.[188] Gastoldi's *Gioco della cieca*, however, is but one of fifteen settings of passages from *Il pastor fido* that Gastoldi published between 1598 and 1604. Given the compelling evidence that ties his *Gioco della cieca* to the Mantuan staging, is there a possibility that any of Gastoldi's other *Pastor fido* settings also played a role in this or another stage production, either as "diegetic" music (i.e., music made and/or heard by the onstage characters), like the *Gioco*, or in some other capacity? As yet, this question has received little consideration, owing presumably to the lack of known sources linking the madrigals to any specific event or to the theater in general, and perhaps also to the lack of scholarly editions of most of Gastoldi's music. While Gastoldi's musical responses to the play's texts are given close consideration in Chapter 8, the potential theatrical role of the settings is most relevant here, in the contexts of the nature and surviving records of the 1598 Mantuan production.

The logical place to begin such an inquiry is with another portion of the play that, based on Grillo's report, seems to have involved music: the end-of-act choruses. Gastoldi published three settings of passages from the choruses of *Il pastor fido*. All three appeared in separate publications—the Third Book for five voices (1598), the Fourth Book for five voices (1602), and the *Concenti musicali* for eight voices (1604)—yet treat adjacent passages from the same chorus from the end of act 2 and, thus, together form a continuous text (see Table 2.1). Grillo's account describes music being used at precisely this point in the performance for the Queen of Spain. Grillo writes: "After the second act, with the finishing of the music, an earthquake was felt, and meanwhile the scene was changing and became entirely clouds and sea."[189] In other words, the second act ended with a musical performance that led directly to the following *intermedio*.

Musical performance of the choruses in a staged drama was, it seems, nothing out of the ordinary, and it was a practice with which Guarini must have been familiar.[190] He was involved in two theatrical productions known to have included sung choruses while composing his pastoral

Table 2.1 Gastoldi: Settings of the Act 2 Chorus of Guarini's Il *pastor fido*

Piece	Year	Voices	Verses	Mode	System	Clefs	Canto range
Ciechi mortali voi che tanta sete	1602	5	II,C: 1022–35	G-mix	*durus*	High	$g'–g''$
Ben è soave cosa	1598	5	II,C: 1036–50	G-mix	*durus*	High	$f\sharp'–g''$
Baci pur bocca curiosa e scaltra	1604	8	II,C: 1051–67	G-mix	*durus*	Low	$f'–f''$

tragicomedy in the mid-1580s: the 1585 performance of *Oedipus Rex* in Vicenza, which included music for the choruses by composer and organist of San Marco in Venice, Andrea Gabrieli, and the 1587 staging of Beccari's *Il sacrificio* in Sassuolo.[191] Even more, a contemporary critic of Guarini's play, Giovanni Pietro Malacreta, while scrutinizing the choruses ("parlo di quello, ch'è in fine degli atti") and their verisimilitude in pastoral drama, seems to assume that these choruses would have been sung when questioning whether the chorus "remains onstage for the entire performance or, having left, comes precisely between one act and the other *to sing its song*" (a cantare quella sua canzona).[192] As the openings of Virgil's *Aeneid* ("Arma verumque canto") and Dante's *Purgatorio* ("e canterò di quel secondo regeno") famously illustrate, the reference to "singing" (*cantare*) poetry need not always be literal. Yet, the practical nature of Malacreta's inquiry, and the reference here to *cantare* within a discussion of verisimilitude in a spoken play, give the impression that he may, in fact, mean actual singing.

Yet, while there may be reason to believe, based on these various accounts, that the choruses of Guarini's play were truly sung in the November 1598 performance, that Gastoldi's settings of the act 2 chorus served this purpose is another matter. Some indication of how suitable these works were for the theater might be gleaned by comparing them to another group of chorus settings that were almost certainly used onstage: Gastoldi's treatment of the *Gioco della cieca* (Table 2.2). The four sections of the *Gioco* are plainly unified in a number of ways: they are grouped together physically in the Fourth Book and labeled as successive *parti* of a single work; they utilize the same cleffing (*chiavetti*, or high clefs) and mode (G-dorian, though internal *parti* do not always begin or end on the final); and they rely predominantly on homorhythmic, declamatory texture.

The features linking the three settings from the act 2 chorus, by contrast, are not so straightforward. To begin, although the works set adjoining sections of text, comprising verses 1022–67 of the act, they appeared in three separate publications in non-chronological order (see Table 2.1). The three pieces do share a common mode—G-mixolydian—but the setting of the third section utilizes low clefs (*chiavi naturali*) and eight voices, whereas the first and second sections use high clefs and five voices.

Table 2.2 Gastoldi, *Il Gioco della cieca*, in *Il quarto libro de madrigali a cinque voci* (Venice, 1602)

Gioco della cieca (1602)	Voices	Verses	Mode	System	Clefs	Canto range
prima parte	5	III,2: 92–107	G-dor	*mollis*	High	$g'–f''$
seconda parte	5	III,2: 118–27	G-dor	*mollis*	High	$g'–f''$
terza parte	5	III,2: 137–46	G-dor	*mollis*	High	$g'–f''$
quarta parte	5	III,2: 170–89	G-dor	*mollis*	High	$g'–f''$

These discrepancies do not exclude the possibility that the works were performed one after the other at the end of the act, however. For, first, despite the contrasting clefs, the actual ranges of the four voice types in all three works are very similar, with the Canto and Tenore parts operating chiefly within their respective G octaves of the G-mixolydian mode, and the Alto and Basso centering on the respective D octaves of the collateral (plagal) mode, but extending a third or fourth lower in the third section, *Baci pur bocca curiosa e scaltra* (thus perhaps explaining the use of lower clefs in this section). Secondly, the fact that all three pieces share the same mode is a significant aspect of kinship, as G-mixolydian was not an altogether common mode for Gastoldi, particularly in these madrigal books. The relative consistency of mode and vocal ranges would have unified the separate sections of the chorus even as the ensemble was augmented from five to eight voices between the second and third pieces—perhaps as a result of the two smaller (*a5*) choruses from sections 1 and 2 merging for section 3—thus adding grandeur to the end of the chorus and act. This amplification of forces in itself might also have proven a practical strategy for transitioning from the subdued Arcadian setting of the play to the tempestuous scene of Jupiter's rejection of the marriage of Mercury and Philology in the *intermedio* that followed. In the end, there is no way to know for certain if and how these pieces might have been performed at the event, or in turn, if the music had been reworked for publication as self-contained madrigals after being used in the play, in which case the alignment of the mode, texts, and voice ranges of the three works would be a crucial indication of their former coherence.

Along with the musical, textual, and contextual connections between the three chorus settings, there are additional sources that testify to the use of Gastoldi's music in the theater, the demand for music and trained musicians for the events of November 1598, and an established practice of ensemble music in plays in Vincenzo Gonzaga's Mantua. The first source comes from the dedication of Gastoldi's *Concenti musicali* for eight voices of 1604, the book containing the last of his three settings from the act 2 chorus, *Baci pur bocca curiosa e scaltra* (see Table 2.1 above). In dedicating his new madrigals to the Mantuan prince, Francesco Gonzaga, the composer writes:

> They are (one can say) creatures of your most gracious pastimes, since the better part of them was composed by me, at your order...and was often heard in concerts in the chamber, and also publicly in the theatres with much attention by you, your father [Duke Vincenzo Gonzaga], and all of the *popolo* at the same time.[193]

The statement does not explicitly tie *Baci pur bocca curiosa e scaltra* to a stage performance of *Il pastor fido*, but it does attest that some of the works from the *Concenti musicale* had been performed "publicly in the theaters" before coming to print in 1604. Precisely what type of role these works played in the theater, however, he does not divulge.

The second document is a letter by court diplomat Francesco Ongarino from 22 November 1598, the day of the play's performance. Presumably in the hours before the event began, Ongarino wrote to the Prior of the ducal chapel of Santa Barbara:

> For the service of our duke, all the musicians that participate in the *Pastorale* will need to gather in Santa Barbara immediately after lunch. However, I beg *Vostra Paternità* to order your fathers that are in the *concerti* to appear on time.[194]

The letter reveals that the duke had requested chapel musicians not only for the day's festivities in general, but precisely to "participate in the Pastoral" (intervengono nella Pastorale). What exactly Ongarino means by "nella Pastorale" remains uncertain: is he speaking about the event as a whole, with all of its surrounding pomp, or about the play with its *intermedi*; or does he literally mean "in the pastoral"—that is, Guarini's play—itself? Further, as *maestro di cappella* of Santa Barbara, Gastoldi would presumably have had a part in preparing these musicians for the occasion, along with supplying music for their performance. Thus, with the evidence presented so far, it seems plausible that while rehearsals for the actors were being conducted in the theater, separate rehearsals were being held for musicians in Santa Barbara for some other musical dimension of the production.

Lastly, testament that Duke Vincenzo recruited composers explicitly for the purpose of providing music for the theater during Margherita of Austria's visit comes in a 1609 publication of Bernardino Bertolotti, a composer previously employed at the Ferrarese court. In dedicating his Third Book of madrigals for five voices to Duke Vincenzo's second son, Cardinal Ferdinando Gonzaga, Bertolotti writes that he had served Duke Alfonso II d'Este for twenty years until the latter's death in 1597. Then, "when the occasion came of the passage of the Queen through Mantua, I was commanded to serve the Most Serene Duke [Vincenzo Gonzaga], Your Highness's father, in the festivities and *Comedie* that were made for the recreation of the Catholic Majesty."[195] Bertolotti does not say that he had assisted in the *intermezzi* or *balli*, but specifically in "comedie," signifying theatrical works portraying "common" (rather than noble) individuals, and a label that was often applied to Guarini's tragicomedy. Bertolotti's extant output contains no settings from Guarini's play, but his Second Book of madrigals, published sometime between 1593 and 1609 (the dates of his First and Third Books), does not survive.

Indeed, two important sources inform us that the Gonzaga court under Vincenzo and his sons showed a predilection for precisely this brand of varied production that incorporated various modes of singing into a spoken play. The first comes in a letter from Muzio Manfredi to Ferrante Gonzaga of 25 August 1590, in which the poet informs the Prince of Guastalla that his *favola boscareccia*, *Le nozze di Semiramide con Memnone* is finished, save for the prologue and four "*canzonette* for the chorus, which I call *canzonette* because they will be such, being played [with instruments], sung, and danced" (canzonette del Coro, le quali chiamo canzonette, perciochè tali saranno, andando elle suonate, cantate e ballate).[196] Manfredi continues: "I made it in twenty-eight days and there are 2,735 verses, including two madrigals in two necessary places, and the final canzonetta of the farewell, which like the others will be danced, sung, and played."[197] The *canzonette* to which Manfredi refers are likely end-of-act choruses, with the "final *canzonetta* of the farewell" being that of the last act. But the *due madrigali* likely played a more integrated role in the *boscareccia* as onstage (diegetic) music—and indeed later evidence suggests as much.

The following year it was not Ferrante's court in Guastalla that sought to perform Manfredi's play, but Vincenzo Gonzaga's court in Mantua. On 20 November 1591, Manfredi sent the play to Duke Vincenzo Gonzaga accompanied by three letters addressed to the stage director Leone de' Sommi, choreographer Isacchino Massarano, and composer Giaches de Wert, all containing instructions for staging the *boscareccia*.[198] In his letter to Wert, Manfredi writes: "I believe that Your Highness [Vincenzo Gonzaga] will wish to have it performed, and I am certain that he will give you the task either of composing or of having composed the necessary music."[199] Manfredi then specifies that the music for the four "canzonette del Coro" should follow the affects of the texts, contain imitative passages, and allow for the intelligibility of the words, and that the same applies for the "ballo d'Himeneo" and the "Madrigale in laude della Dea." However, the latter work—presumably one of the "due madrigali" referred to in Manfredi's earlier letter, which, indeed, appears to have been diegetic music similar in function to that of the sacrifice scene in the 1554 production of Beccari's *Il sacrificio*—should be performed without any instruments but with some brief imitation (*fughetta*).[200] Manfredi's specifications underscore the importance of these musical and danced components of the play, as well as his confidence in the Mantuan court's ability to devise and execute them. Already by 1591, it seems the staging of a dramatic work with ensemble singing and dancing proved nothing out of the ordinary in Mantua. This is not to say, however, that such a venture did not pose its difficulties, as the fruitless struggles to prepare Guarini's *Pastor fido* and its *Gioco della cieca* in 1591–93 demonstrate.

There is still one further potential link between Vincenzo Gonzaga's 1598 production and the use of music onstage, which involves the *commedia dell'arte* troupe accused by Guarini of having leaked drafts of his play from the attempted Turin staging of 1585: the *Gelosi*, or as Guarini calls it, the "Compagnia dell'Isabellina," after one of the ensemble's central female actors, Isabella Andreini. Andreini had published her own pastoral play, *Mirtilla*, in 1588, a year before *Il pastor fido* came to print. Not only did the pastoral highlight the talents of Andreini as both actor and playwright, but it also showcased the musical capabilities of the *Gelosi* with a song contest in act 3, scene 5 between two nymphs, Mirtilla and Filli, played by Andreini and Vittoria Piisimi, both of whom would again perform in competition with one another in the 1589 celebrations in Florence for the marriage of Grand Duke Ferdinando and Christina of Lorraine.[201]

The *Gelosi* were indeed known for their musical talents, which was especially true of the principal female actors, Vincenza Armani, Piisimi, and Andreini. The troupe enjoyed frequent patronage by the Gonzaga through the late sixteenth century, and they were also greatly admired by the Hapsburgs of Austria: in fact, Archduke Albert (who had accompanied the Queen of Spain to Mantua in 1598) enlisted Isabella and Francesco Andreini to perform at the celebrations in 1599 for his own wedding to Isabella of Spain.[202] Anne MacNeil has suggested that the *Gelosi* might have been involved in the November 1598 performance of *Il pastor fido*.[203] The company was in Bologna in the summer of 1598 to perform for Archduke Ferdinand before being summoned to Mantua by Duke Vincenzo in the months before Queen Margherita's arrival. If the Gonzaga court had a multifaceted production incorporating acting, music, and dance in mind for the Queen's visit (and, perhaps, for the earlier stagings of 1598), and had requested music from composers such as Gastoldi, Bertolotti, and possibly others, a professional troupe of *comici* such as the *Gelosi* would have been capable of executing such a performance to the highest standards, and would have been a wise choice for such a momentous occasion, rather than venturing to produce the play again with an amateur cast.

Altogether, these sources and circumstances make for a compelling case that Gastoldi's chorus and *Gioco* settings had a role in the 1598 staging of *Il pastor fido*: Bertolotti and Ongarino recalling that the Gonzaga court recruited musicians specifically for a *pastorale* or *commedia* during the Queen's visit in November 1598; the possible (but unverified) involvement of a musically skilled acting troupe in the production; Gastoldi's own caption stating that his *Gioco della cieca* had been "performed for the Queen of Spain in *Il pastor fido*"; and the latter's dedication to his *Concenti musicali* attesting to his works—including the last section of the act 2 chorus—being performed "in the theaters" for the Gonzaga and "all of the *popolo*." All of these correlations together lend considerable weight to the notion that music and theater shared the stage in the Gonzaga production of *Il pastor fido*, not merely during the *intermedi*, but also diegetically in the act 3 *Gioco* and in the end-of-act choruses.

Whether Gastoldi's eleven other *Pastor fido* settings were also used in any stage performance, however, is another matter, for all of them treat lines of spoken monologues, for which there is no documented practice of sung delivery in plays from this period, let alone in the November 1598 production specifically. Yet, these madrigals might have ties to this performance in other ways, while remaining offstage and outside the theater. Indeed, traces of such a relationship come in an oblique manner from a rather unexpected source—one dealing not with music, but with the rigorous censure of

Guarini's pastoral: Malacreta's *Considerazioni intorno al Pastorfido* (1600). Amidst his disapproval of the tragicomedy for its lack of decorum and historical accountability and for its excessive length, Malacreta remarks that "the poem was (one could say) circumcised in a bad way in Mantua, in the presence of the Queen of Spain."[204] As the critic explains, "without upsetting the slightest thing at all of the story that was important, around 1,600 verses deemed indulgent [*oziosi*] were removed" for the performance, amounting to roughly one-fourth of the entire work.[205] The comments are valuable for their rare insight into the rendering of the play itself, rather than only its *intermedi*. Malacreta, moreover, must have had access—either direct or indirect—to the Mantuan rehearsals, or to actors' copies of the script, for he provides a comprehensive list of the excisions for the reader to consider.

Modern historians have proposed that at least some of these cuts might have been motivated by efforts to make the play more appropriate for the young Catholic Queen and the important clergymen in attendance. Lisa Sampson notes, for example, that "many of the more risqué parts were removed," including the elder:

> Titiro's lyric speech on girls needing to be plucked early like a rose (I,4: 157–203) ... Corisca's immoral persuasion of Amarilli to feign 'onestà' in order to pursue adulterous relationships (III,5: 50–129), her tempting of Mirtillo to take other lovers, and her almost Epicurean promotion of sensual pleasure (III,6: 96–116, 165–86, 204–26).[206]

Sampson also suggests that other omitted sections "may have been considered imprudent to present...before a royal bride-to-be and clergymen, including the pope's nephew and papal legate, Pietro Aldobrandini." These passages include Carino's speech in act 5 criticizing court life (often taken to be an autobiographical insertion by Guarini), "Nicandro's exchange with Amarilli on matters of free will" in act 4, and the recounting of a kissing game played by Amarilli and a group of nymphs in act 2.[207] Later defenders of the play offer other explanations for how and why it was shortened for the production, including that the poet himself was directed to cut the work in order to make room for the lavish set of *intermedi*.

Many of the passages in Malacreta's list of excisions were already at the time, or would become, some of the most popular texts for musical setting. The *seconda parte* of many composers' treatments of *Cruda Amarilli che col nome ancora* (I,2: 280–91) and most of *O primavera gioventù dell'anno* and *O dolcezze amarissime d'amore* (III,1: 4–22, 29–45) appear in Malacreta's list, for example, as do the better parts of *Ch'i' t'ami e t'ami più de la mia vita* (III,3: 296ff.) and *M'è più dolce il penar per Amarilli* (III,6: 930–43). The entire texts for madrigals such as *O misera Dorinda* (II,2: 438–53), *Arda pur sempre o mora* (III,6: 894–901), and *Com'è dolce il gioire* (or *Com'è soave cosa*; III,6: 979–95) were also apparently struck from the script. It seems that the qualities of these passages that made them *oziosi*—their introspection, impassioned rhetoric, elaborating imagery, sensuality, and lyricism—also made them distinctively appealing for setting as polyphonic madrigals. Altogether, these "circumcisions" comprise numerous texts treated by the most celebrated composers of the period, including four by Claudio Monteverdi and Sigismondo D'India; seven by Luca Marenzio; eight by Antonio Cifra, Philippe de Monte, and Giovanni Piccioni; and eleven by Giovanni Ghizzolo. In terms of the number of times composers turned to these omitted verses for their madrigals, however, no composer rivals the *maestro di cappella* of the Gonzaga chapel himself, Gastoldi.

Of the fifteen total *Pastor fido* settings that Gastoldi published between 1598 and 1604, all but five are based on passages allegedly cut from the Mantuan performance of November 1598 (Tables 2.3 and 2.4). Furthermore, of the five settings of passages not cited by Malacreta, one is the *Gioco della cieca* (*Cieco amor non ti cred'io*) and three are the settings of the act 2 chorus. What these four works have in common, of course, is that they all set choral portions of the play that reportedly involved music—a function that these madrigals might have fulfilled. This means that, of Gastoldi's fifteen known settings from Guarini's play, ten set verses that were cut from the 1598 performance, four set choral passages that were likely sung in that performance, and only one sets a passage that was neither cut nor choral: *O sfortunato e misero Mirtillo*, the earliest passage in the play that Gastoldi set to music (see Table 2.3). The many overlaps between the play's "circumcision" and the passages set by Gastoldi and other Mantuan composers around 1598 raise the question of whether there is any relationship—particularly any causal relationship—between them.

Table 2.3 Gastoldi's *Pastor fido* Settings (1598–1604)

Piece	Cut/ choral	Year	Verses	Final	System	Clef
O sfortunato e misero Mirtillo		1602	I,2: 525–30	A	*durus*	C1
Come in vago giardin rosa gentil	Cut	1602	I,4: 858–92	A	*durus*	G2
Tu se' pur aspro a chi t'adora	Cut	1602	II,2: 386–97	D	*durus*	C1
O misera Dorinda	Cut	1602	II,2: 438–53	G	*mollis*	C1
Ciechi mortali voi che tanta sete	Chorus	1602	II,C: 1022–35	G	*durus*	G2
Ben è soave cosa	Chorus	1598	II,C: 1036–50	G	*durus*	G2
Baci pur bocca curiosa e scaltra	Chorus	1604	II,C: 1051–67	G	*durus*	C1
Cieco amor non ti cred'io	Chorus	1602	III,2: 92–189	G	*mollis*	G2
Deh bella e cara e si soave un tempo	Cut	1602	III,3: 332–62	G	*mollis*	G2
Come assetato infermo	Cut	1602	III,6: 835–47	A	*durus*	G2
Tanto è possente amore	Cut	1602	III,6: 848–58	F	*mollis*	C1
Arda pur sempr'o mora	Cut	1602	III,6: 894–901	G	*mollis*	C1
Dimmi misero amante	Cut	1602	III,6: 914–25	A	*durus*	C1
M'è più dolce il penar per Amarilli	Cut	1598	III,6: 930–43	G	*mollis*	C1
Com'è soave cosa	Cut	1598	III,6: 983–95	F	*mollis*	C1

Table 2.4 Gastoldi's Settings of Verses from Malacreta's List of Excisions

Omitted passage	Excerpt set by Gastoldi
Act I,4: 846–92	
	Come in vago giardin rosa gentil (I,4: 858–92), Book 4
Act II,2: 387–97	
	Tu se' pur aspro a chi t'adora (II,2: 386–97), Book 4
Act II,2: 432–58	
	O misera Dorinda (II,2: 438–53), Book 4
Act III,3: 351–62	
	Deh bella e cara e si soave un tempo (III,3: 332–62), Book 4
Act III,6: 840–47	
	Come assetato infermo (III,6: 835–47), Book 4
Act III,6: 850–72	
	Tanto è possente amore (III,6: 848–58), Book 4
Act III,6: 877–901	
	Arda pur sempr'o mora (III,6: 894–901), Book 4
Act III,6: 909–29	
	Dimmi misero amante (III,6: 914–25), Book 4
Act III,6: 932–43	
	M'è più dolce il penar per Amarilli (III,6: 930–43), Book 3
Act III,6: 977–1001	
	Com'è soave cosa (III,6: 983–95), Book 3

On the one hand, the qualities that made these verses dispensable, or "oziosi," might also have made them more generically versatile, more universal, or otherwise particularly well suited to the diegetic, collaborative, self-contained context of the madrigal. In terms of their impacts on the play, the excisions listed by Malacreta typically do make sense: the narrative is maintained, and there tend not to be awkward juxtapositions of incomplete or uncoordinated thoughts. Indeed, there is some truth to Malacreta's statement that these passages were removed "without upsetting anything at all of the story that was important"—that is, aside from exhibiting the bucolic characters' refined capacity for philosophical reasoning, courtly discourse, Petrarchan lyricism, and expressive eloquence that critics so frequently faulted. The eloquent and sometimes gratuitous self-reflection and emoting in the play evidently accorded well with the madrigal and the predilections of its composers, patrons, and other readers. It seems, in effect, that dramatic superfluousness corresponded closely with lyric and madrigalian potential. This correlation might also explain why Guarini's tragicomedy generated such a greater abundance of madrigal settings as compared to tauter dramatic works, such as Tasso's *Aminta*.

On the other hand, the concentration of settings with conspicuous ties to the November 1598 production in Gastoldi's Fourth Book—"circumcised" speeches, choral passages, and the caption to the *Gioco della cieca*—indicates that the volume was significantly shaped by the illustrious event. Yet, with its inclusion of verses cut from the script, the book could hardly be considered a commemoration of the occasion, but instead seems to recognize, and even make amends for, the play's mutilation by giving its omitted passages "life" in a different, musical setting. Indeed, by designating one work—the *Gioco*—explicitly as "represented for the Queen of Spain," the book calls attention to the possibility that the other works were expressly not performed at the event, not only musically, but also as spoken texts. The stimulus for these madrigalian reparations could have come from a number of sources: the playwright, who witnessed and possibly had a hand in the work's dismemberment himself; the zealous and, perhaps, rueful patron, Vincenzo Gonzaga; the composer; or another figure familiar with the circumstances.

The resulting collection—by virtue of its ubiquitous textual source, if not also for its ties to a specific performance—is decidedly a "book" with considerable unity. Within this relatively consistent scheme, however, the one other *Pastor fido* setting stands out as an anomaly: *O sfortunato e misero Mirtillo*, which sets a monologue for Mirtillo that was left intact for the 1598 production. Yet, this work, too, could play a role in the book's event-driven theme. The madrigal sets only five verses from act 1, scene 2, which encapsulate the central conflict of the play: Mirtillo's suffering in his love for Amarilli. But the shepherd's state, as expressed in the text, can also be read as an allegory for the "sfortunato e misero" *Pastor fido*, which witnessed "many fierce enemies, so many arms and so much war" for the Mantuan performance.[208]

Numerous other settings of cut passages appeared in madrigal settings by Mantuan composers from around 1598—including two by the duke's *maestro di musica*, Pallavicino, and two by Salamone Rossi—but the conspicuous number of them from Monteverdi presents another possible instance of redress for *Il pastor fido*'s maiming. The entire *prima* and *terza parti* (save for four verses) of Monteverdi's *Ch'io t'ami, e t'ami più de la mia vita*; all but the first two lines of his *M'è più dolce il penar per Amarilli*; and the final section of his five-*parte Ecco, Silvio, colei che'n odio hai tanto* center on verses struck from the script. All three of Monteverdi's settings appeared in his Fifth Book of 1605, but *Ch'io t'ami* was completed by at least 16 November 1598—when it was heard at a concert in Ferrara—thus, less than a week before the play's performance for the Queen of Spain in Mantua.[209] Though leaving Monteverdi some two and a half months to compose the works if the "circumcision" had been carried out after the second *Pastor fido* performance in September 1598, the possibility that musical settings of cut portions of the play were expressly planned for performance in Guarini's "home" city of Ferrara days before the third Mantuan production adds a dimension of retribution to the event, wherein the madrigals effectively undercut the play using its own discarded lines. Monteverdi, too, might have found gratification in such a plot, given his lasting resentment at having been rebuffed for the position of *maestro di musica* by the Duke of Mantua two years prior. In all, however, the notion of madrigals compensating for the shortening of the play is most compelling in the case of Gastoldi, given the proportion of his settings that match Malacreta's list, and the consolidation of these works in a single book. Monteverdi, on the other hand, seems to have had other matters in mind with his arrangement of several *Pastor fido* madrigals at the opening of his Fifth Book, as we shall see.

Stagings in the Early Seventeenth Century

Whatever the fate of the *versi oziosi*, witnessing the presentation of his play in disfigured form must have been a bittersweet occasion for the poet, who had endured years of setbacks and missed opportunities before finally seeing his work on the stage. After the grand and widely flaunted spectacle of 1598, the history of performances of Guarini's tragicomedy continues much in the way it had proceeded before then: with scant documentary evidence pointing to performances at centers closely associated with Guarini— Ferrara, Mantua, and Rome—interspersed with those at other cities further afield. Along with repeat performances in 1599 of Cavalieri and Guidiccioni's *Giuoco della cieca* in Florence—where Guarini was serving as secretary for the grand duke—first for Cardinals Montalto and Del Monte, and again for Archduke Ferdinand of Austria, the play was performed that year in its entirety in Nola with a new prologue penned by the young Giambattista Marino, and (as Malacreta tells us) in Vicenza sometime before 1600, with the original prologue for the river Alfeo replaced by one for the goddess Iris.[210] The Mantuan court resurrected its November 1598 production of both the play and *intermedi* in 1600, but with pared-down machinery and its own new prologue.[211] A performance in Rome may have followed in the summer of 1600,[212] along with one around this time in the town of Clusone (near Bergamo) to honor the visiting *capitano* Giovanni Andrea Venier;[213] and the Accademia degli Intrepidi of Ferrara mounted its own production on 21 February 1602, the first confirmed performance there after nearly twenty years of fruitless efforts.[214] Sometime between 1602 and 1605 the play was also performed in a Latin translation, *Pastor fidus*, at King's College in Cambridge.[215]

Following the rapid succession of performances that stretches through the 1590s and into the early 1600s, there is a sudden lacuna in the records of the play's productions spanning nearly two decades. The next mention of any performance comes from Correggio in 1621, where a sumptuous staging with *intermedi* by Niccolò Bonasio took place in the palace of Prince Giovanni Siro.[216] Another performance followed two years later (17 December 1623) in the public theater of Bologna, which is documented as a result of the fire that erupted immediately after the play, wiping out much of the recent improvements that had been done to the building.[217] The Correggio performance is especially noteworthy for the glimpse it provides at this later point in the play's performance history of the intersection between the theatrical and musical realms under the influence of artistic patronage. For in 1613–15, Prince Giovanni Siro had obtained as *maestro di cappella* one of the most prolific composers of *Pastor fido* madrigals Giovanni Ghizzolo. Ghizzolo published over two dozen settings of texts from the play between 1608 and 1621, including seven in his Second Book for five and six voices (1614), dedicated to Giovanni Siro. It was some six years after Ghizzolo left Correggio that Giovanni Siro's staging of *Il pastor fido* took place, thus exhibiting the progression of the play from a source of lyric-like passages for music of the chamber, and from a bound text for private reading, only later to a fully realized dramatic work of the theater.

Despite the lack of documentary evidence between the 1602 Ferrara and 1621 Correggio performances, it is hard to believe that the widespread efforts to stage the play suddenly came to a halt after 1602. Rather, given the fleeting and often ambiguous nature of so many of the references to performances of the play, it is surely only a matter of time before similar accounts, intimating of additional stagings, are uncovered. The more general history of Guarini's tragicomedy during this period, however, is far from sparse. Just as the first productions were being mounted in the mid-1590s in Rimini (possibly), Siena, and Crema, the play's roots in the realm of music were gaining a fast hold with the numerous settings by two esteemed madrigal composers, Marenzio of Rome and Wert of Mantua, with a flood of composers to follow them. The play's place in the critical sphere had sputtered following the initial exchange in 1586–93 between the "Verrati" and the Paduan critic, Denores, but soon erupted anew at the turn of the century with a barrage of attacks and retaliations centered on the tragicomedy. The play, in other words, took on multiple lives through the realms of theater, literature, music, and criticism, which interacted with one another and thrived in individual ways—and not only for a brief time. As Nicolas Perella writes, "throughout the seventeenth century the *Pastor Fido* was the most widely read book of secular literature in all of Europe." It was also widely pursued for the stage, vigorously debated in print, and one of the principal sources of madrigal texts for decades on end. In the following chapter, it is to the critical realm and to the connections between one specific critical reading and a composer's early madrigal settings of the play that we shall turn.

Notes

1 The draft is held in the Biblioteca Nazionale Marciana in Venice, Codex Zanetti Italy 65 (=4782). Guarini had, in fact, used the term "tragicomedia pastorale" in a letter to Vincenzo Gonaga of 7 April 1584, before the fifth act and the choruses had been completed ("manca tutto il quinto atto et tutti i chori"), perhaps to correct the prince's reference to the work as "l'Egloga Pastorale" (discussed below). The letters appear in Alessandro d'Ancona, *Origini del teatro italiano*, 2nd ed., 3 vols. (Turin: Loescher, 1891), II, 539. Carla Molinari

acknowledges the emendation and its penmanship as Guarini's in her thorough study of the draft, "Per il 'Pastor fido' di Battista Guarini," *Studi di filologia italiana, bollettino annuale dell'Accademia della Crusca* 43 (1985): 161–238.

2 Document 2.1: Battista Guarini, *Lettere* (Venice: Ciotti, 1596), II, 50. Although undated, the letter is datable roughly to 1595 by its reference to the appearance of a French translation of the play, the first of which was *Le Berger fidèle, pastorale, de l'Italien du seigneur Baptista Guarini, chevalier* (Paris: P. Mettayer, 1595).

3 Guarini, *Lettere* (Parma: Viotti, 1595), 280; also *Opere di Battista Guarini*, ed. Marziano Guglielminetti (Turin: Unione Tipografico-Editrice, 1971), 104–05.

4 Document 2.2: Guarini, *Lettere* (1595), 284–85, also *Opere di Battista Guarini*, 107. Rossi, *Battista Guarini ed il Pastor fido: Studio biografico-critico con documenti inediti* (Turin: Loescher, 1886), 180, mistakenly has "*vaso* delle Muse," while in *Opere di Battista Guarini*, Guglielminetti has a note defining "il vago" as "l'amico." The reading in Guastalla is also mentioned in *Il Verato secondo ovvero replica dell'Attizzato accademico ferrarese, in difesa del Pastorfido, contra la seconda scrittura di Messer Giason De Nores intitolata Apologia* (Florence: Filippo Giunti, 1593); in *Delle opere del cavalier Battista Guarini*, G.A. Barotti and A. Zeno, eds., 4 vols. (Verona: Tumermani, 1737–38) [hereafter Guarini, *Opere*], III, 82.

5 See George McClure, "Women and the Politics of Play in Sixteenth-Century Italy: Torquato Tasso's Theory of Games," *Renaissance Quarterly* 61 (2008): 765–68.

6 Alfredo Zerbini, in a historical poem, describes Sanseverino as "one of the most beautiful, cultivated, and vivacious ladies of her time, idol of all the courts, inspiration of illustrious poets, among whom was Torquato Tasso, who celebrated her spirit and charm in diverse and passionate sonnets" ("La congiura di feudatàri," in *Tutte le poesie*, ed. Gino Marchi and Italo Petrolini [Parma: Luigi Battei, 1982], 12). On her patronage of Fabrizio Dentice, see John Griffiths and Dinko Fabris, eds., *Neapolitan Lute Music: Fabrizio Dentice, Giulio Severino, Giovanni Antonio Severino, Francesco Cardone* (Middleton, Wisconsin: A-R Editions, 2004), xii. Paolo Fabbri (*Monteverdi*, trans. by Tim Carter [Cambridge: Cambridge University Press, 1994], 99) proposes that she may be the *ingrata* "Barbara fierezza" in Claudio Monteverdi and Ottavio Rinuccini's *Ballo delle ingrate*.

7 See Iain Fenlon, *Music and Patronage in Sixteenth-Century Mantua*, 2 vols. (Oxford: Oxford University Press, 1980), I, 149.

8 According to a letter from Manfredi of 22 Aug. 1587, it seems that Francesco Patrizi devised the scheme for *Enone*, which Ferrante then used as a basis for his verse. See Alfredo Saviotti, "Muzio Manfredi e Battista Guarini," in *Guariniana, a proposito di una recente pubblicazione* (Pesaro, 1888), 6–7. In addition to keeping a circle of *letterati* at his small court in Guastalla, Ferrante Gonzaga was the founder of the Accademia degli Affidati in the early 1580s. It is possible, therefore, that some of the "altri ancora" in attendance at Guarini's reading were members of this academy. Giuseppe Gerbino discusses Ferrante's ties to pastoral drama through his affiliation with Muzio Manfredi and the Accademia degli Innominati in Parma, an "academy most intensely committed to the pastoral genre" that also included Guarini and Tasso, in *Music and the Myth of Arcadia*, 344–49.

9 On the Accademia degli Innominati, see Lucia Denarosi, *L'Accademia degli Innominati di Parma: Teorie letterarie e progetti di scrittura (1574–1608)* (Florence: Società Editrice Fiorentina, 2003). A list of "Accademici Olimpici" from an attendance role of 1596 includes Marenzio (under the "Absenti"), Guarini, Ferrante Gonzaga, and Angelo Ingegneri. See Bizzarini, "L'ultimo Marenzio: tipologie di committenza e di recezione," *Studi marenziani*, Piperno and Fenlon

eds. (Venice: Fondazione Ugo e Olga Levi, 2003), 67–87. Bizzarini puts forth the hypothesis that Marenzio was admitted to the Accademia on account of Count Mario Bevilacqua's recommendation between 1587 and 1592. Bevilacqua, a member of the Accademia until his death in 1593, was the dedicatee of Marenzio's *Madrigali a 4, 5, e 6* of 1587.

10 On the possible connections of Marenzio's Eighth Book to Ferrante Gonzaga, and specifically to the Accademia degli Innominati, see Gerbino, *Music and the Myth of Arcadia*, 344–51.

11 Manfredi's reference is to Horace's statement in the *Ars poetica* (v. 139)—in turn referencing *Aesop's Fables* (no. 520)—"Parturient montes, nascetur ridiculus mus" (The mountains will labor, and an absurd mouse will be born), implying that the work was not worth the tremendous effort invested in its creation. For alternative interpretations of the verse, however, see Howard Jacobson, "Horace *AP* 139: *parturient montes, nascetur ridiculus mus*," *Museum Helveticum* 64 (2007): 59–61.

12 Document 2.3: Manfredi to Ferrante Gonzaga; cited in Saviotti, "Muzio Manfredi e Battista Guarini," 9.

13 Document 2.4: Manfredi, *Lettere brevissime* (Venice: Pulciani, 1606), 262–63.

14 While no record has been found of these earlier readings in Ferrara, an indication that readings might have taken place in October 1584 exists in a letter from Count Federico Miroglio to Duke Alfonso II, in which he writes: "Guarini entertained the duchess and ladies by reading one of his comedies. Luzzasco and Fiorino [Ippolito Fiorini] come to Belvedere each day with Signora Tarquinia [Molza]" (Il Guarini ha trattenuto la Duchessa e le dame leggendo una sua commedia. Mo Luzasco e Fiorino con la Sig.ra Tarquinia vengono ogni giorno a Belvedere). Cited from Elio Durante and Anna Martellotti, *Cronistoria del Concerto delle Dame principalissime di Margherita Gonzaga d'Este* (Florence: Studio per edizioni scelte, 1979), 284.

15 See Guarini, *Lettere* (Venice: Ciotti, 1600), 50–51, 343, and 344.

16 Document 2.5: Faustino Summo, *Due discorsi: l'uno contro le tragicommedie e le pastorali, l'altro contro il Pastor Fido* (Padua: F. Bolzetta, 1600); in Guarini, *Opere*, III, 596.

17 Summo, *Due discorsi*; in Guarini, *Opere*, III, 590.

18 The verses cut for the 1598 performance are listed in Giovanni Pietro Malacreta, *Consideratoni [sic] … sopra il Pastot [sic] fido, tragicomedia pastorale del … Battista Guarini* (Vicenza: Greco, 1600), 58r–61r; reprinted in Guarini, *Opere*, IV, 70–75. On the novelty in *Il pastor fido* of displaying a woman torn between social and moral obligation and inner feelings, Nicolas Perella writes:

> After Corneille, Racine, and Metastasio, such a situation [as Amarilli's dilemma] seems commonplace. But it needs to be pointed out that the basic dramatic situation of conflict within the female heart, which was to become practically the mainspring of seventeenth-century French tragedy, received its first important dramatic and casuistical treatment in Guarini's *Pastor Fido*.
>
> ("Amarilli's Dilemma," 354)

19 "Se 'l peccar è sì dolce / E 'l non peccar sì necessario; oh troppo / imperfetta nature / che repugni a la legge; / oh troppa dura legge / che la natura offendi!" As Clive Griffiths notes of the monologue,

> For many [of the earliest critics] the ambiguities of its sentiments confirmed the existence of moral laxity which they felt characterized the whole play and which was generally held to have seriously damaged the moral health of a large section of the female Italian population.

Griffiths, "Guarini's *Il pastor fido*: A Beginning or an End for Renaissance Pastoral Drama," in *The Cultural Heritage of the Italian Renaissance*, eds. C. Griffiths and R. Hastings (Lewiston, NY: Edwin Mellen Press, 1993), 315–27.

20 It is recorded, however, that the readings included a "presentazione" for the Accademia Olimpica: see the *Atti dell'Accademia Olimpica*, Biblioteca Bertoliana, Vicenza, MSS, busta 2, fasc. 10 (L), 18 September 1584 (fol. 30v). On Guarini's time in Vicenza, including his "presentazione" of the play, see Stefano Mazzoni, *L'Olimpico di Vicenza: un teatro e la sua 'perpetua memoria'* (Florence: Le Lettere, 1998), 99. On the production of *Oedipus Rex* and its contemporary reception, see Alberto Gallo, *La prima rappresentazione al Teatro Olimpico, con i progetti e le relazioni dei contemporanei* (Milan: Il polifilo, 1973).

21 Likewise, Laura Riccò explores the relationship between Ingegneri's dramaturgy and Guarini's theories and conception of several scenes in *Il pastor fido* in *"Ben mille pastorali": l'itinerario dell'Ingegneri da Tasso a Guarini e oltre* (Rome: Bulzoni, 2004), esp. 219–49. From another angle, Guarini's time in Vicenza, as well as Guastalla, may be significant for the influence his play and readings had on Vicentine poet and playwright Madalena Campiglia and specifically her 1588 pastoral drama, *Flori, favola boscareccia* (Vicenza: Gli heredi di Perin Libraro & Tomaso Brunelli, 1588). See Virginia Cox and Lisa Sampson's introduction to Campiglia, *Flori, A Pastoral Drama: A Bilingual Edition*, ed. Virginia Cox and Lisa Sampson, trans. by Virginia Cox (Chicago, IL: University of Chicago Press, 2004), 13–14.

22 In a letter to Guarini of 9 March 1585, Giacomo Dolfin praises the off-stage singing and playing in the production by the Pellizzari sisters, Lucia and Elisabetta (given in Gallo, *La prima rappresentazione*, 33–37, at 35). Their father, Antonio Pellizzari, served the *Olimpici* as musician and custodian in 1582–87, while Lucia and Elisabetta likewise appear as salaried musicians. See also Lisa Sampson, "Actors Meet Professionals: Theatrical Activities in Late Sixteenth-Century Italian Academies," in *The Reinvention of Theatre in Sixteenth-Century Europe: Traditions, Texts, and Performance*, eds. T.F. Earle and C. Fouto (London: Routledge, 2015), 187–218, esp. 192–94. On the authorship of the two *Verrati*, see Chapter 3.

23 Likewise, in April 1589, the Pellizzari accompanied Duke Vincenzo to Ferrara, where they performed for the duke and duchess, and in May, they took part in the 1589 Florentine *intermedi* as part of Vincenzo Gonzaga's retinue. See Susan Parisi, "Ducal Patronage of Music in Mantua, 1587–1627: An Archival Study," Ph. D. diss., University of Illinois at Urbana–Champaign, 1989, 153, as well as the payroll accounts on pp. 21–36, and Fenlon, *Music and Patronage*, 128.

24 The following discussion of Scipione Gonzaga relies largely on Rossi, *Battista Guarini*, 16–21 and Iain Fenlon, "Scipione Gonzaga: A 'Poor' Cardinal in Rome," in *Music and Culture in Late Renaissance Italy* (Oxford: Oxford University Press, 2002), 93–117. In a letter to Ferrante Gonzaga following Scipione's death, sent from Mantua in March 1593, Guarini describes Scipione as a "true friend, infallible friend, companion of my studies, judge of my writings, counselor of my sufferings, support of my thoughts, aid of my needs, life of my life" (amico vero, amico infaticabile, compagno de' miei studi, giudice de miei scritti, consolatore de' miei travagli, appoggio de' miei pensieri, soccorso de' miei bisogni, vita della mia vita). Guarini, *Lettere* (1595), 162.

25 Three madrigals "di Scipion Gonzaga" appear in Paolo Clerico's Second Book *a 5* (Venice: Scotto, 1562), dedicated to Ercole Gonzaga, and his first published poem, "Son questi, in cui si spatial horrida morte," appeared in the collection *Componimenti volgari et latini* (Mantua: Osanna, 1564), published by the Accademia degli Invaghiti. See Fenlon, *Music and Culture*, 98–101.

26 The Accademia degli Elevati of Padua even employed a respected composer, Francesco Portinaro, to instruct its members. Whether Scipione had been

formally involved with the Elevati is uncertain, but, as Iain Fenlon proposes, there is a strong possibility that he at least received some training from Portinaro and the tutors that worked under him. The dedication of Portinaro's First Book of madrigals for four voices to Scipione suggests that there existed some sort of relationship between Scipione and the composer. (Fenlon, *Music and Culture*, 99–100.)

27 It is known that Tasso, by then a close friend of Scipione Gonzaga, was specifically invited to Padua to become a member of the Eterei. See Pierantonio Serassi, *La vita di Torquato Tasso*, ed. Cesare Guasti, 3rd ed., 2 vols. (Florence: Barbèra e Bianchi, 1858), I, 164. On the theory that Guarini's decision to return to Padua was prompted by Scipione, see Rossi, *Battista Guarini*, 17–19.

28 "Io sono a Padova, sicuro, & solito porto de' miei naufragi ... patria senza fastidi." Letter from Guarini (Padua) to Scipione Gonzaga of 3 September 1590; in Guarini, *Lettere* (1595), 86. The letter continues with other descriptions of Guarini's longing for the Eterei, and Scipione in particular, in Padua.

29 Document 2.6: *Il Verato secondo* (1593); in *Opere*, III, 32. Guarini also seems later to have kept Riccoboni abreast of staging attempts of *Il pastor fido*, as shown in his affectionate letter to the humanist of 19 March 1593 from Mantua. Document 2.7: Guarini, *Lettere* (1595), 243–44.

30 For the entire first statement, see Document 2.8: Guarini, *Il Verato secondo*, in *Opere* III, 32. For the second, see Document 2.9: *Il Verato secondo*; in *Opere*, III, 28.

31 Document 2.10: Guarini, *Il Verato secondo*; in *Opere*, III, 28.

32 Guarini, *Il Verato secondo*; in *Opere*, III, 28.

33 Riccoboni and Zabarella were at odds specifically on Zabarella's belief that poetry belonged to Logic expressly by virtue of its use of examples of things and actions. Both agreed, however, that pleasure and utility were principal ends of poetry. For a summary of the issues, see Bernard Weinberg, *A History of Literary Criticism in the Italian Renaissance* (Chicago, IL: University of Chicago Press, 1961), I, 21–22 and 582–83. On the marked influence of Zabrella's thought on Guarini's work, see Claudio Scarpati, "Poetica e retorica in Battista Guarini," *Studi sul Cinquecento italiano* (Milan: Università Cattolica del Sacro Cuore, 1982): 208–38.

34 Document 2.11: Guarini, *Il Verato secondo*; in *Opere*, III, 32.

35 In *Il Verato secondo*, "L'Attizzato" asks: "You were there every day with him [Guarini], everyday in the same bookshop, and you pretend not have had news of it" (eravate pur voi ancora ogni dì seco, ogni dì nella medesima libreria, e v'infingete di non averne avuto notizia?); in *Opere*, III, 32.

36 *De Gymnasio Patavino Antonii Riccoboni libri sex* (Padua: Franciscum Bolzetam, 1598), 96r–97v; cited in Scarpati, "Poetica e retorica," 218.

37 Rossi, *Battista Guarini*, 181.

38 Also among Contarini's close friends was Bernardino Baldi, abbot and balìa of Guastalla. In a letter to Guarini of 21 Nov. 1594 (Guarini, *Lettere* [1596], part 2, 69–70), Baldi recounts having heard Guarini's reading of the play in Guastalla over ten years before, and confesses his intense desire ever since to read the play. Of the other members of the audience, Baldi mentions only Ferrante Gonzaga and Barbara Sanseverino. Among Guarini's audience at Ferrante's court, Baldi seems to have been genuine in his enthusiasm for the play (Document 2.12).

39 In fact, the dialogue takes place in Contarini's home, as his *Pastor fido* readings had years earlier. The poet writes admirably of the house at *Il Segretario* (Venice: Meietti, 1594), 76.

40 Document 2.13: Guarini, *Il Verato secondo*; in *Opere*, III, 23.

41 "A' letterati delle corti d'Italia, ne anche questo, conciosicosachè [sic] tutti i Prencipi loro hanno avuto notizia del Pastorfido, e hannolo sommamente onorato, e lodato." *Il Verato secondo*; in *Opere*, III, 28.

42 Fenlon, *Music and Patronage*, 123.

43 On the history of these two ensembles, see Anthony Newcomb's *The Madrigal at Ferrara, 1579–97*, 2 vols. (Princeton, NJ: Princeton University Press, 1981), I, 7–89.

44 On the composition of the *balletto della duchessa*, see the documents presented in Kathryn Bosi, "Leone Tolosa and *Martel d'amore*: a *balletto della duchessa* discovered," *Ricercare* 17 (2005): 5–70, especially 56–60.

45 On the putative surviving repertory of the Ferrarese *concerto* of the 1580s and 1590s, see Newcomb, *Madrigal at Ferrara*, and Laurie Stras, *Women and Music in Sixteenth-Century Ferrara*, in series New Perspectives in Music History and Criticism (Cambridge: Cambridge University Press, 2018), Chapter 7 ("Musical Practices of the 1580s *Concerto*"), 241–88.

46 Among the many studies of the 1589 Florentine *intermedi*, see Robert Ketterer, "Classical Sources and Thematic Structure in the Florentine Intermedi of 1589," *Renaissance Studies* 13 (1999): 192–222; James Saslow, *The Medici Wedding of 1589: Florentine Festival as* Theatrum Mundi (New Haven, CT: Yale University Press, 1996); and Nina Treadwell, *Music and Wonder at the Medici Court: The 1589 Interludes for "La Pellegrina"* (Bloomington: Indiana University Press, 2008).

47 Rossi, *Battista Guarini*, 297.

48 Rossi, *Battista Guarini*, 297.

49 Ancona, *Origini del teatro italiano*, 539.

50 Document 2.14: Mantua, Archivio di Stato (Archivio Gonzaga), busta 1514, fasc. III, c.496 (7 April 1584).

51 On the compositional process of the *Gioco della cieca*, see Newcomb, *The Madrigal at Ferrara*, 43–46 and Fenlon, *Music and Patronage*, 151–57.

52 Guarini, *Il pastor fido, tragicommedia pastorale del molto illustre Sig. Cavaliere Battista Guarini, ora in questa XXVII impressione di curiose, & dotte Annotationi arrichito* (Venice: Ciotti, 1602), 91. Most scholars have accepted and perpetuated the assumption (seemingly stemming from Ancona's 1891 *Origini del teatro italiano*, 540) that Guarini's references to "Leone" refer to the Mantuan director–playwright Leone de' Sommi. Kathryn Bosi, however, has shown that Leone Tolosa "ebreo" proves a more compelling fit for the role, not only for his being a dancer–choreographer in Ferrara, but also for his known collaborations with Guarini in other *balletti della duchessa*. See Bosi, "Leone Tolosa and *Martel d'amore*," esp. 16–17.

53 See Document 2.14.

54 Document 2.15: Mantua, Archivio di Stato (Archivio Gonzaga), busta 1523, fasc. IV, cc. 773–74 (23 November 1591).

55 Document 2.16: Mantua, Archivio di Stato (Archivio Gonzaga), busta 2654, fasc. cc.n.n (26 November 1591); emphasis mine.

56 The editions published by the end of 1591 include those of Bonfadino (Venice, 1589/90), Baldini (Ferrara, 1590), Mamarelli (Ferrara, 1590), Osanna (Mantua, 1590), Volfeo (London, 1591), and Viani (Pavia, 1591).

57 Document 2.17: Giuseppe Campori, ed. *Lettere di scrittori italiani del secolo XVI* (Bologna: Gaetano Romagnoli, 1877), 193–94.

58 "...che non debbiano nè mostrarle, nè recitarle a persona che sia: et molto meno levarne copia: che veramente non mi assicuro di darle fuori senza questo difensivo." In Campori, *Lettere*, 194.

59 See the letter of the Ferrarese ducal secretary to Paolo Brusantini in Rossi, *Battista Guarini*, 298, also 182.

60 Amadio Ronchini, *Lettere d'uomini illustri conservate nel R. Archivio dello Stato* (Parma: Reale, 1853), vol. 1, 650; the relevant passage appears in Ancona, *Origini del teatro mantovano*, 535. See also Rossi, 182; a list of parts, preserved

in the Biblioteca Marciana, 188r, believed to form part of Guarini's letter to Ferrante is transcribed in Rossi, 298.

61 The letter is given in Ancona, *Origini del teatro mantovano*, 535–36, note 5.

62 See David Parrott, "The Mantuan Succession, 1627–31: A Sovereignty Dispute in Early Modern Europe," *English Historical Review* 112 (1997): 20–65 and Parrott and R. Oresko, "The Sovereignty of Monferrato and the Citadel of Casale as European Problems in the Early Modern Period," in Daniela Ferrari and A. Quondam, eds., *Stefano Guazzo e Casale tra Cinque e Seicento: atti del convegno di studi nel quarto centenario della morte, Casale Monferrato, 22–23 ottobre 1993* (Rome: Bulzoni, 1997), 11–86.

63 Letter of Roberto Titi, "letterato di Borgo S. Sepolcro," to Scipione Bargagli (Florence, 27 Feb. 1593), held in the Biblioteca Comunale di Siena (Incarnat. 1592, Doc. XXII). Given in Cosimo Corso, "Carteggio inedito fra Battista Guarini e Belisario Bulgarini," *Bullettino senese di storia patria* 57 (1950): 55–106, at 61.

64 Guarini formally began this post on 2 December 1585. See Rossi, *Battista Guarini*, 84–86.

65 See Pannizzari's note in Rossi, *Battista Guarini*, 185. Also Pieri, "Il 'Pastor fido'," 11; Stefano Mazzoni, *L'Olimpico di Vicenza*, 68; and Lisa Sampson, *Pastoral Drama in Early Modern Italy: The Making of a New Genre*, Italian Perspectives 15 (London: Legenda, Modern Humanities Research Association and Maney Publishing, 2006), 186.

66 Document 2.18: Letter from Guarini (Padua) to Filippo d'Este in Turin, c. 1586; in *Opere*, ed. Guglielminetti, 113–14.

67 Fenlon, *Music and Patronage*, 149 and "Music and Spectacle at the Gonzaga Court," *Proceedings of the Royal Musical Association* 103 (1976–77): 90–105, at 92. Later Fenlon states similarly:

> It would appear that the only firmly documented performance of the play before 1592 was the Turin performance of 1585, though since the work had not then been officially published it is difficult to know if the *Gioco* was included in this version.
>
> (151)

Despite this, he is correct in his statement that "there may have been no established performing tradition of the play upon which Mantuan performers of 1592 could rely," since the productions in Ferrara and Turin in the 1580s had failed (151). Judith Cohen, "Words to Dance and Music—Music to Dance and Words: The Case of the *Gioco della cieca*," *Fundamentals of Musical Language: An Interdisciplinary Approach*, ed. Mojsej Grigorevic Boroda (Bochum: Brockmeyer, 1993), 175–95, at 177, for example, accepts that "the *Pastor fido* was staged in 1584 in Ferrara ... [and] in 1585 in Turin."

68 Letter in Ancona, *Origini del teatro mantovano*, 535–36, note 5. See also Rossi, *Battista Guarini*, 182.

69 On the Duke of Savoy's gift, see Rossi, *Battista Guarini*, 184. Guarini writes to Visdomini, it seems, to refuse a request from Duke Ottavio Farnese for verses in honor of his wife, Duchess Margarita of Austria, and Prince Alessandro Farnese, due to his lack of time ("ho si poco tempo di poetare, come in ciò si richiede, che non mi posso prometter d'un verso solo"). As Guarini states, this has also kept him from finishing and publishing *Il pastor fido* (Document 2.19).

70 "Intendo che non fu *recitato* in Torino nelle nozze di quel Ser.mo Duca, per cui fu composto," Roberto Titi, "letterato di Borgo S. Sepolcro," in a letter to Scipione Bargagli (from Florence, 27 Feb. 1593): The letter is held in Biblioteca Comunale di Siena (Incarnat. 1592, Doc. XXII), given in Corso, "Carteggio inedito," 61. Canobio, in his *Proseguimento della storia di Crema dall' anno 1586 sino al 1664* (Crema: Rajnoni, 1849), likewise writes that that play "non era già

riuscito alla corte di Savoia, a contemplazione di cui era quell'opera stata composta." The relevant entry in the *Proseguimento* is given in Riccardo Truffi, "La prima rappresentazione del *Pastor fido* e il teatro a Crema nei sec. XVI e XVII," *Rassegna bibliografica della letteratura italiana* 8 (1900): 330–35, at 331.

71 Rossi, *Battista Guarini*, 183–85. See also Document 2.20.

72 Guarini's concern over retaining authorial control of the printed text of his work seems to anticipate the attitude around 1600 of Ben Jonson, who, as David Scott Kastan writes, "labored to rescue his plays from the theatrical conditions in which they were produced, seeking to make available for readers a play text of which he could be said in some exact sense to be its 'author'." See Kastan, *Shakespeare and the Book* (Cambridge: Cambridge University Press, 2001), 17. For an informative survey of the perceptions and functions of print in Shakespearean theatre, see the first chapter of Kastan's *Shakespeare and the Book*, "From Playhouse to Printing Press; or, Making a Good Impression" (14–49).

73 Guarini, *Lettere* (1595), 314.

74 *Il Verato secondo*, in Guarini, *Opere*, III, 25.

75 *Il Verato secondo*, in Guarini, *Opere*, III, 29–32. Guarini writes:

> Will it be more likely, then, that you took the idea of pastoral tragicomedy from one never seen, but heard only recited by memory by *commedianti dalla gazzetta* than from the *Pastor fido*, most celebrated in all of Venice, in all of Padua, in all of Italy?
>
> (Document 2.21: *Opere*, III, 31)

76 "...l'esser servidor vecchio, & segretario nuovo, percioche le cose van molto male, quando la fatica succede in luogo del premio;" in Guarini, *Lettere* (1595), 166.

77 Details of the Sassuolo wedding are preserved in an anonymous contemporary account, which is presented, with analysis, in Armando Fabio Ivaldi, *Le nozze Pio–Farnese e gli apparati teatrali di Sassuolo del 1587: studio su una rappresentazione del primo dramma pastorale italiano, con intermezzi di G.B. Guarini* (Genoa: Erga, 1974), 7–47. See also Enzo Cioni, "Feste e spettacoli a Sassuolo nell'età barocca," in *Musica, teatro, nazione dall'Emilia all'Europa nel Seicento* (Modena: Aedes Muratoriana, 1982), 27–44, especially 27–33. The marriage was apparently not the first choice for either of the pair. Clelia Farnese had been widowed only two years earlier by her first husband, the Roman patrician Giorgio Cesarini, and showed considerable reluctance to marry again and isolate herself from the brilliant and familiar culture of Rome. Marco Pio, on the other hand, had originally hoped to marry none other than the famed Countess of Sala, Barbara Sanseverino, but she refused, calling him a "man of sad nature" (uomo di trista indole) in a letter to the Duke of Parma, Alessandro Farnese (24 April 1587). See Amadio Ronchini, "Vita della contessa Barbara Sanseverini," in *Atti e memorie delle RR. Deputazioni di Storia Patria per le provincie modenesi e parmensi* (Modena: Carlo Vincenzi, 1863), I, 47.

78 An inventory of Pio's personal library records "poesie da finirsi" and "frag-menti della pastorale di S.E.," all lost. There are also accounts of an unknown "Ecloga pastorale" performed by Pio in 1588. See Cioni, "Feste e spettacoli a Sassuolo," 28.

79 As Ivaldi shows, the texts for the Sassuolo *intermedi* survive in the Biblioteca Ariostea in Ferrara (cod. ferr. 156, T. I, fols. 18rff) and are transcribed by Rossi (*Battista Guarini*, 311–13), who suggests wrongly that these texts derive from the 1598 Mantuan performance of *Il pastor fido* (*Le nozze Pio–Farnese*, 35–36).

80 The account reads: "Tratto da la fama del sontuoso apparato fatto fare da quel Signore, per far recitare in questa occasione, Il Sacrificio Favola Pastorale del Sig. Agostino Beccari ferrarese." Ivaldi, *Le nozze Pio–Farnese*, 7.

81   A manuscript in the Biblioteca Ariostea di Ferrara (Codice Ferrarese 156, t. I c., fol. 18r) describes the use of *musica interiore* in the third *intermedio* to accompany the Muses onstage pretending to play their instruments: "Intorno al monte [Parnaso] siano disposte le Muse con gli stromenti loro et faccian veduta di sonare et la musica interiore sia quella che faccia l'armonia." Quoted in Ivaldi, *Le nozze Pio–Farnese*, 74–75, note 74. The anonymous account describes music at the end of acts preceding the following *intermedi*. For example: "At the conclusion of the first act began the sweetest harmony of songs and music, after which appeared the first *intermedio*" (Finito il primo Atto, cominciò una suavissima armonia di canti, e suoni, la quale finita apparve il primo Intermedio; see *ibid.*, 11). Orazio Vecchi documents the festivities—including the performance of Beccari's pastoral and its intermedii—in his *terza rime* poem, "Come suol ch'alla patria fa ritorno." See Lodovico Frati, ed., *Rime inedite del cinquecento* (Bologna: Romagnoli-dall'Aqua, 1918), 176–87.

82   Document 2.22: anonymous account, as given in Ivaldi, *Le nozze Pio–Farnese*, 13.

83   Letter from the Archivio di Stato di Modena, Cancelleria Ducale, Oratori Estensi a Firenze; as quoted in Rossi, *Battista Guarini*, 94, note 3. Cortile wrote to Duke Alfonso again at the end of Guarini's visit (2 July 1588) with mostly the same information (see Document 2.23).

84   "Qui farei fine, ma vò prima ottener una grazia da V.S. & questa è di saper per mezzo suo quel, che costì si crede della mia Pastorale. Si rappresenterà ella ò nò?" In Guarini, *Lettere* (1600), 217. An undated letter sent from Padua reveals that, after reading one of Strozzi's sonnets, he thought to send "one of his *Pastorfidi*" (presumably meaning one of many copies). See Guarini, *Lettere* (1600), 352–53.

85   See Ancona, *Origini del teatro italiano*, 561, note 5.

86   The full statement appears in Document 2.24: Guarini, *Lettere* (1600), 135–36.

87   See especially Chapter 8 of Ancona's *Origini del teatro italiano*, "La rappresentazione del *Pastor fido* a Mantova," 535–75.

88   On the interest to stage the play in Mantua in 1592, Fenlon claims: "It is entirely typical of Vincenzo Gonzaga's extrovert brand of artistic patronage that it was soon after the play's first publication, when it had already become thoroughly controversial, that plans were laid to produce it in Mantua." While the controversial aspect of play may indeed have helped its publicity, it must not be forgotten that Vincenzo showed intense interest in staging the play as early as 1584. It also remains uncertain how much of an influence Agnese Argotta had in instigating the production, in which case the motivations behind it may have been very different.

89   Fenlon, *Music and Patronage*, 149.

90   Document 2.25: Mantua, Archivio di Stato (Archivio Gonzaga), busta 2654, fasc. cc.n.n.

91   Document 2.25.

92   "Ho incaricato di nuovo a Isachino hebreo la cura del balletto *della Cieca*" (*ibid.*). On Isacchino's role at the Gonzaga court, see Fenlon, *Music and Patronage*, 41–42. The dancing master was likely also quite wealthy and well established in courtly circles: As Eduard Burnbaum notes, on 13 January 1594, Isacchino held a ball at his house, which was attended by Vincenzo Gonzaga with Annibale and Alfonso Gonzaga, all *incognito* and "accompanied by a bevy of ladies and gentlemen" (*Jewish Musicians at the Court of the Mantuan Dukes (1542–1628)*, ed. Judith Cohen [Tel-Aviv: Tel-Aviv University, 1978], 15–16). Chieppio's remark that he had "again entrusted" (incaricato di nuovo) Isacchino with the task of preparing the *Gioco* is rather puzzling. The only previous attempt to stage *Il pastor fido* at the Mantua court was in 1584, which only amounted to Guarini's denial to send Vincenzo a draft of the play. The phrase "incaricato di

nuovo" could mean "newly entrusted," or simply refer to the fact that Chieppio had entrusted Isacchino with other *balli* in the past.

93 On Cavalieri and Guidiccioni's *Giuoco*, see Warren Kirkendale, *Emilio de' Cavalieri, "Gentiluomo romano": His Life and Letters, his Role as Superintendent, of all the Art at the Medici Court, and His Musical Compositions* (Florence: Olschki, 2001), 185–212.

94 Document 2.26: Mantua, Archivio di Stato (Archivio Gonzaga), busta 2654, fasc. cc.n.n.

95 The passage is translated in Newcomb, *The Madrigal at Ferrara*, 44:

> The *balletto della cieca* is giving us difficulty, since some of those who have already rehearsed it, as I understand it, in the presence of Your Highness are now gone, some are sick, and some have become so obstinate in not wanting to take part that, after the absence of Isacchino [Massarano] for a few days, it was necessary to begin the entire enterprise again. And the difficulty has been found to be greater in trying to incorporate it skillfully into the tragicomedy. The ballet has four parts—besides the exit—and they are all different: four madrigals must be sung and the speeches of *Amarillide*, *Mirtillo*, and *Corisca* must be inserted between them, all of which can be integrated only with the greatest difficulty into the same scene.

96 Mantua, Archivio di Stato (Archivio Gonzaga), busta 2657, fasc. I, c. 9 (18 April 1592).

97 The letter, unknown to Ancona, is printed in Guarini, *Opere*, ed. Guglielminetti, 133–34: "Ma del perito, che Vostra Signoria illustrissima mi scrive aspettarsi con esso meco, non ho nè ordine nè novella; farò opera di vederlo, e se sarà intimato e licenziato, il condurrò" (134). As Stefano Mazzoni believes (*L'Olimpico di Vicenza*, 71–72), Guarini's description of the necessary talents to stage the play in a letter to Duke Vincenzo from Mantua, 14 April 1592 refers to Aleotti (Document 2.27).

98 Modena, Archivio di Stato (Archivio per Materie), busta 1, cc.n.n. (7 May 1592).

99 Mantua, Archivio di Stato (Archivio Gonzaga), busta 2657, cc.n.n. (21 May 1592).

100 The first mention of Andreasi's enlistment in the preparations appears in a 1 May 1592 letter from Chieppio: "As for the set, I understand that there is a design of it made by Ippolito Andreasi, seen by the Most Serene Highness, and it pleased him, and it was made with the pleasure of Guarini" (cited in Ancona, *Origini del teatro italiano*, 549).

101 "I Recitanti cominciano a fare il debito, nè vi manca se non il Signor Mauro, senza il quale, che è la parte così importante, non si può far prova che vaglia." Mantua, Archivio di Stato (Archivio Gonzaga), busta 2657, cc.n.n.

102 "...ma questi recitanti et dal Ballino mi danno un continuo et estremo travaglio, perchè non vorrei già disgustare alcuno, ma poco si movono per parole et anco menaccie qualchun di loro..." Mantua, Archivio di Stato (Archivio Gonzaga), busta 2657, cc.n.n. (15 May 1592). The letter contains a list of the actors and dancers for the planned performance.

103 "Ma il poveretto non si sapeva disporre a questa parte, per essere troppo inclinator a quella di Mirtillo, che di già aveva a memoria." Mantua, Archivio di Stato (Archivio Gonzaga), busta 2657, c.n.n. (25 May 1592).

104 Document 2.28: Mantua, Archivio di Stato (Archivio Gonzaga), busta 2656, fasc. I, cc. 10–11.

105 Document 2.29: Guarini, *Lettere* (1596), I, 168. See also Guarini's letter to Vincenzo Gonzaga, in which the poet lists a series of matters that remain to be resolved concerning the play, its intermedi, and its prologue (Guarini, *Lettere* [1596], 83–85). Rossi assigns the letter tenably to April 1592.

106 Guarini, *Lettere* 1595, 102. The letter is undated, but surely pertains to the circumstances in Mantua in late May or June of 1592. On the delay of the 1592 staging, see also Ivaldi, *Le nozze Pio–Farnese*, 57.

107 See, for example, Guarini's letter to Belisario Bulgarini (from Spruch, 2 Nov. 1592): "...per dirne il vero chi penserebbe mai che hora fossi tra l'alpi di Germania?" *Lettere* (1595), 153.

108 See Rossi, *Battista Guarini*, 109–10 and 228.

109 It is amidst these events that Guarini wrote to his friend in Padua, Riccoboni, about the uncertainty of the performance of his play (Document 2.30: Guarini, *Lettere* [1595], 243–44). On the dating of this letter, see Rossi, *Battista Guarini*, 228, note 2.

110 Guarini, too, would eventually find his own way to avenge himself against his former master, but only posthumously in May 1598, when he dedicated his first collection of *Rime* (Venice: Ciotti, 1598) to Cardinal Pietro Aldobrandini, who was then in charge of the Papal annexation of the Este territory following Duke Alfonso d'Este's death without issue. Thus, the title page of the *Rime* boldly announces Aldobrandini's new title, "Vicario Generale in Temporale et Spirituale nella Città et Ducato di Ferrara." While the dedication proper is signed by the printer, Giovanni Battista Ciotti, Guarini penned the sonnet "in lode & esaltatione di esso Illustrissimo, & Reverendissimo Signor Cardinale Aldobrandini" that immediately follows the dedication.

111 For an overview of *commedia dell'arte* troupes in the late Cinquecento, see Oliver Crick and John Rudlin, *Commedia dell'arte: A Handbook for Troupes* (New York: Routledge, 2001).

112 Sampson, "Guarini's *Pastor fido*," 81. Sampson gives the examples of the Ferrarese productions of Giraldi's *Egle* (1545) and Argenti's *Lo sfortunato* (1567), which relied on university students for their casts.

113 On the use of women for female parts onstage, see Richard Andrews, "L'attrice e la cantante fra Cinquecento e Seicento: la presenza femminile in palcoscenico," in *Teatro e musica: écriture vocale et scénique*, Actes du Colloque, 17–19 February 1998 (Toulouse: Presses Universitaires du Mirail, 1999), 27–43.

114 Document 2.31: Guarini, *Il Verato secondo*, in *Opere*, III, 383. The treatise was published in 1593, though allegedly completed by 1591. A detailed examination of the public debate surrounding *Il pastor fido* and pastoral tragicomedy is the subject of the following chapter.

115 Document 2.32: Guarini, *Lettere* (1595), 99–100.

116 "Quanto a gli habiti le mando nella qui annessa scrittura que' medesimi che da me furono ordinati à Ferrara, & de' quali ci serviremo eziandio qui, se si rappresenterà." Guarini, *Lettere* (1595), 100–101. Presumably what Guarini sent were verbal descriptions or drawings, and not the costumes themselves.

117 See also Ancona, *Origini del teatro italiano*, 562–63, who deduces the same dating of the letter.

118 Bellisario Bulgarini of Siena (1539–1619) entered the debates surrounding Dante's *Divina Commedia*—in support of Dante—and Aristotelian poetics in c.1576 (*Alcune considerazioni sopra'l discorso di M. Giacopo Mazzoni, fatto in difesa della Comedia di Dante*, published in 1583), and later in his *Repliche alle Risposte del sig. Orazio Capponi* (dated Siena 1579, published 1585), where he argues that poetry is not a part of moral philosophy but an instrument of it, and criticizes Dante for the lack of verisimilitude and unity in his work. The exchange between Bulgarini, Mazzoni, Capponi, Lelio Marretti, and Alessandro Carriero represents a shift of the debates in the 1570s and 1580s from Florence to Siena and Padua. See Weinberg, *History of Literary Criticism*, I, 18–21, 598–99, and II, 853–65.

119 Letter given in Corso, "Carteggio inedito," 84–85.

120 Document 2.33: Corso, "Carteggio inedito," 86.

121 In Corso, "Carteggio inedito," 86–87; see also 61–64 on the Siena performance.

122 On Scipione Bargagli, see A. Marenduzzo, "Notizie intorno a Scipione Bargagli," *Bulletino senese di storia patria* 7 (1900): 325–47.

123 Document 2.34: Corso, "Carteggio inedito," 105.

124 Wotton would also much later become a central character of Oscar Wilde's *The Picture of Dorian Gray* (1890).

125 Document 2.35: Corso, "Carteggio inedito,"105.

126 Document 2.36: Corso, "Carteggio inedito," 87.

127 See Guarini's letter to Bulgarini of 6 November 1593 in Corso, "Carteggio inedito," 87–89, which relates his bad experience with the Florentine coachman. Also, on his visit to Siena, see Corso, 64–65.

128 "Noi siamo spesso insieme il Signor Paris et io et egli continua di favorirmi secondo la sua gentilissima natura et paterna benignità." See Guarini's letter to Bulgarini of 28 November 1593 in Corso, "Carteggio inedito," 89.

129 Document 2.37: Giuseppe Campori, *Lettere di scrittori italiani*, 206–07.

130 See Guarini's letter to Bulgarini of 22 January 1594 (Document 2.38).

131 The date of the Crema performance is given wrongly by Ancona, and many after him, as 1596. See Corso, "Carteggio inedito," 61–62 and Truffi, "La prima rappresentazione del Pastor fido," 330–35. Corso mistakenly gives Zurla's name as Federico, instead of Ludovico. For the mistaken dating of 1596, which derives from Guarini's *Lettere* of 1596 (letter of 15 March 1596, II, 58–59), see Ancona, *Origini del teatro italiano*, 563 and Rossi, *Battista Guarini*, 228. The year 1595 is given by Canobio's *Proseguimento* and Giuseppe Racchetti, *Genealogie delle famiglie nobili cremasche* (codex in Biblioteca civica di Crema), in the preface and life of Zurla, as cited in Truffi, "La prima rappresentazione," 331.

132 Canobio's *Proseguimento* was not published until 1849, in Crema by Rajnoni; the 1595 account of the performance of *Il pastor fido* is also given in Truffi, "La prima rappresentazione," 331–2. On Canobio, see Truffi, 332, which references the manuscript account of Cesare Francesco Tintori, *Memorie patrie*, in the Biblioteca del Seminario di Crema, vol. 10, chapter entitled "Memorie dell'Accademia canobiana, sotto il titolo degli Immaturi; Feste teatrali celebrate su le patrie scene in varii tempi da nobili e cittadini cremaschi sotto la direzzione di Lodovico Canobio istitutore di detta accademia." See also Guarini's letter of thanks to Zurla of 15 March 1596, a full year after the event. As Canobio supports: "così nel seguito anno 1596 rispose egli [Guarini] al Zurla, ringraziandolo ... come nelle lettere di lui si legge" (Truffi, 331).

133 Tensini then enjoyed great success at the courts of Milan, the king of Spain, and Emperor Rodolfo II, where he worked as a military engineer. He published his celebrated *La fortificatione, guardia, difesa ed espugnatione delle fortezze, esperimentata in diverse guerre* in 1624. See Truffi, "La prima rappresentazione," 332, referencing the account of Cesare Francesco Tintori, *Memorie patrie*, vol. 10, "Memorie dell'Accademia canobiana."

134 One faint reference to the preparations comes in Guarini's letter from Venice, 4 December 1595, to Marfisa d'Este: "L'havermi Vostra Eccellenza scritto una lettera si cortese per occasione di que' pochi avvertimenti, che le mandai per la rappresentazione del Pastorfido, è stato anzi un tacito ammonirmi di quello, ch'io dovea fare, che un debbito ringraziarmi di quel che ho fatto"; *Lettere* (1596), II, 59–60.

135 For an excellent overview of the Florentine *Giuoco*, see Angelo Solerti, "Laura Guidiccioni Lucchesini ed Emilio de' Cavalieri," *Rivista musicale italiana* 9 (1902): 797ff and Warren Kirkendale's *Emilio de' Cavalieri*, 201–12. Kirkendale is inaccurate, however, in his assertion that "no stage performance [of Guarini's play] was forthcoming until Cavalieri's *Cieca* of 1595. It has been overlooked that

this represents the first recorded performance of any part of *Il pastor fido*." As we have seen, the play had already been performed in Siena and Crema, and possibly also in Rimini, before the premier of Cavalieri's *Giuoco* in October 1595.

136 See Guarini, *Il pastor fido* (1602), 91; also published in *Annotazioni sopra "Il pastor fido"* (Verona: Giovanni Tumermani, 1737); facsimile in *La questione del "Pastor fido"*, in series La scena e l'ombra: collana di testi e studi teatrali 2 (Rome: Vecchiarelli, 1997), 54. Cavalieri and Guidiccioni followed this same order of composition, dance–music–text, in their collaboration for the final *ballo* of the Florentine *intermedi* of 1589. Cristofano Malvezzi's 1591 publication of the *intermedi* states, "le parole furno fatte dopo l'aria del ballo, dalla Sig. Laura Lucchesini de Guidiccioni," *Intermedii et concerti, fatti per la commedia rappresentata in Firenze nelle nozze del Serenissimo Don Ferdinando Medici, e Madama Christiana Gran Duchi di Toscana* (Venice: Vincenti, 1591); for a modern edition, see *Les fêtes du mariage de Ferdinand de Médicis et de Christine de Lorraine*, ed. D. P. Walker (Paris: Éditions du Centre national de la recherche scientifique, 1963), lvi–lviii and 140–54.

137 See, for example, Fenlon, *Music and Patronage*, 151–57 and Bosi, "Leone Tolosa and *Martel d'amore*."

138 In Malvezzi's 1591 print of the *intermedi*, Cavalieri's *ballo* for the sixth *intermedio* bears the title: "La Musica de questo ballo, & il ballo stesso fù del Sig. Laura Lucchesini de' Guidiccioni gentildonna principalissima della città di Lucca ornata di rarissime qualità e virtù." *Nono parte. Intermedii et concerti fatti per la commedia rappresentata in Firenze.*

139 On Cavalieri's and Guidiccioni's collaborations and their role in the development of dramatic music, see Laura Riccò, *"Ben mille pastorali"* and *Dalla zampogna all'aurea cetra: egloghe, pastorali, favole in musica* (Rome: Bulzoni, 2015).

140 Both *Il satiro* and *Fileno* are lost. See Warren Kirkendale, "L'opera in musica prima del Peri: le pastorali perdute di Laura Guidiccioni ed Emilio de' Cavalieri," in *Firenze e la Toscana dei Medici nell'Europa del Cinquecento*, 3 vols. (Florence: Olschki, 1983), II, 365–95.

141 Document 2.39: *Storia di etichetta di Toscana dal 1589 al 1612* (Archivio di Stato di Firenze, Guardaroba medicea, Diari di etichetta), II, 62; also cited, with other accounts of the event, in Solerti, "Laura Guidiccioni Lucchesini ed Emilio de' Cavalieri: I primi tentativi del melodramma," *Revista musicale italiana* IX (1902): 797–823, at 814. See also Kirkendale, *Emilio de' Cavalieri*, 193.

142 See Kirkendale, *Emilio de' Cavalieri*, 192–93.

143 The relevant portion of the letter is given in Kirkendale, *Emilio de' Cavalieri*, 193.

144 On the *Balletti della duchessa*, see Katherine Bosi's "Leone Tolosa and *Martel d'Amore*," especially 12–16. Accounts of the Ferrarese dances sent from the Florentine ambassador in Ferrara to the Grand Duke of Tuscany specifically note that half of the ladies "dressed in short clothes, because in contrast to the others, they were dressed as men" (14). Letters sent from Ferrara to Cardinal Luigi d'Este in Rome describe the roles similarly.

145 Given in Bosi, "Leone Tolosa and *Martel d'amore*," 15 and 58.

146 See Alessandro Guidotti's preface to Cavalieri's *Rappresentatione di anima, et di corpo* (Rome: Nicolò Mutij, 1600); also in Murray Bradshaw, ed. (Middleton, WI: American Institute of Musicology, 2007), 7–9.

147 Kirkendale, *Emilio de' Cavalieri*, 212.

148 On Cenci's settings of *Il pastor fido* and Montalto's patronage, see John Walter Hill, *Roman Monody, Cantata, and Opera from the Circles around Cardinal Montalto*, 2 vols. (Oxford: Clarendon Press, 1997), I, 235–57. Hill raises the possibility that the recitational settings from the play by Cenci and other composers in Montalto's circle may even have their origins in the planned performance of 1596.

149 I-Rvat, Urb.Lat.1064, fol.122r; given in James Chater, "Musical Patronage in Rome at the Turn of the Seventeenth Century: The Case of Cardinal Montalto," *Studi musicali* 16 (1987): 179–227, at 207.

150 Hill, *Roman Monody*, 241.

151 Hill, *Roman Monody*, 239.

152 Hill, *Roman Monody*, 240.

153 Mantua, Archivio di Stato (Archivio Gonzaga), busta 1514, fasc. III, c. 496 (7 April 1584); see above, note 50. It is possible, however, that Guarini was exaggerating about the time frame for his own benefit, in order to secure longer employment in Mantua.

154 On the correspondence between Guarini and Bambasi, see Ancona, *Origini del teatro italiano*, 564; also Margherita Fratarcangeli, "Gabriele Bombasi: Un letterato tra Annibale Carracci e Odoardo Farnese," *Paragone Arte* 48 (1997): 112–30. Bombasi was also a member from 1580 of the Accademia degli Innominati in Parma, which included Tasso and Guarini.

155 The letter appears in Ancona, *Origini del teatro italiano*, 563–64.

156 Ancona, *Origini del teatro italiano*, 564–65.

157 Ancona, *Origini del teatro italiano*, 564.

158 Hill writes:

> Under the circumstances I can suggest only one explanation for the apparent ease with which Cardinal Farnese was able to produce a well-rehearsed performance of *Il pastor fido* without advance planning: the production was the fruit of the long and elaborate preparations made by Cardinal Montalto and his brother, preparations that would have gone to waste once their festive performance was cancelled.
>
> (*Roman Monody*, 256–57)

Hill deduces that "the performers had come from Rome to Caprarola along with the cardinal and his household only a few days earlier" (*Roman Monody*, 256), but I can find no verification that the performers came from Rome or that they were part of his entourage, although both are certainly possibilities.

159 See Ivaldi, *Le nozze Pio–Farnese*, 25, 71 n. 51, which quotes two letters referring to Marco Pio-Savoia's "virtuosa Accademia." Letter of Ridolfo Arlotti, 24 January 1597, to then-Cardinal Alessandro d'Este: "Il Signor Marco a Sassuolo, dove ha fondato una virtuosa Accademia, fa grandi et belli preparamenti per fare che si reciti a carnovale l'Edipo Tiranno Tragedia di Sofocle." Also, a letter by Arlotti of 6 February 1597: "A Sassuolo miracoli. Oltre alla Tragedia che scrissi [*Epido tiranno* di Sofocle], preparano un'Anellata, una Quintanata et una Barriera con inventione di certo Castello. Ballano di più in Rocca il giovedì e la domenica che alla Ducale."

160 John Walter Hill surmises that "a little later, the performance had to be repeated for other noblemen and prelates who came out from Rome to marvel at the apparently unplanned celebration" (*Roman Monody*, 256). I can find no evidence, however, that the "molti signori" who arrived for the Sunday restaging came from Rome, that they traveled to Capraruola specifically "to marvel at" the staging of Guarini's play, or that they were precisely "noblemen and prelates."

161 Bombasi's letter at this point reads: "Il sig[nore] Francesco Colonna, che ne fu ammiratore, non che spettatore attentissimo, la saluta caramente. Et il suo Monsignor Crescentio, che se ne venne di Roma a Ronciglione volando, le bacia le mani." Quoted in Ancona, *Origini del teatro italiano*, 565. On the friendship between Guarini and Crescenzi, see Rossi, *Battista Guarini*, 113.

162 Document 2.40: Mantua, Archivio di Stato (Archivio Gonzaga), busta 2675, cc. n.n. Ancona notes that the staging probably amounted to "a type of first run in

front of a few privileged spectators" ("consistere soltanto in una specie di prima prova fatta dinnanzi a pochi e privilegiati spettatori" [*Origini del teatro italiano*, 566]). If this was the case, it was indeed a lavish "prima prova," not to mention that a court would presumably not show a "dress rehearsal" to a pope.

163 See Paolo Marni's letter to Aberdale Manerbio of 17 June 1598, announcing the arrival of Montalto and Monte, in Mantua, Archivio di Stato, busta 475, fasc. 12, cc. 587–88.

164 The *intermedi* are described in the anonymous *Intermedi fatti nella Pastorale del Cav.re Guarino in Mantova del mese di giugno 1598*, Perugia, Biblioteca Comunale Augusta, Ms. 1307, 98–99, given in Susan Parisi, "Ducal Patronage of Music in Mantua," 188, note 80. The courtship of Peleus and Thetus was a typical subject of wedding entertainments, but there is no indication of a prominent marriage in Mantua in June 1598.

165 See Document 2.41: *Intermedi fatti nella Pastorale del Cav.re Guarino*; cited in Parisi, "Ducal Patronage," 188, note 80.

166 "...quivi ["sopra una belissima Nave"] era il Rasi con il Chitarrone che cantò mirabiliss[amen]te, a cui rispondavano duo Echo con meravigliosa eccellenza." Given in Parisi, "Ducal Patronage," 188, note 80.

167 Chieppio writes to Vincenzo Gonzaga that "we go attending to the business of the *Comedia* with all diligence, but all of these undertakings at the start are finding some difficulties, which cannot be overcome without a little time" (Si va attendendo al negotio della Comedia con ogni diligenza, ma tutte queste imprese nel principio trovano delle difficultà, che non si possono superare se non con un poco di tempo; Mantua, Archivio di Stato [Archivio Gonzaga], busta 2674, cc.n.n. [9 April 1598]). According to another letter from Gasparo Asiani in Mantua to an anonymous recipient, the difficulties of the production persisted into the following month. Asiani, on 7 May 1598, writes: "The constant rehearsal of this *comedia* and the many difficulties that are surfacing, which are almost unsurmountable, leave me no time to give you account of some trifles [*menucie*] that I would like to be able to take care of without bothering you"— these "menucie" being payment concerns for "le opere et lavorieri della comedia" (Il continuo esercizio di questa comedia et le molte difficoltà che quasi insuperabili tuttavia si vanno scuoprendo, a quali vorrei puoter sodisfare senza fastidirla; Mantua, Archivio di Stato [Archivio Gonzaga], busta 2674, cc.n.n.). Parisi identifies the references to a "comedia" in all three of these letters with *Il pastor fido* ("Ducal Patronage," 188, note 79).

168 Mantua, Archivio di Stato (Archivio Gonzaga), busta 1261, cc. n.n. See also the poet's letter to his son—undated, but estimated by Rossi to date from the summer of 1598, likely around the time of his letter to Vincenzo Gonzaga—in which he describes his plans for a prologue and four *intermedi* depicting "le quattro musiche del mondo: l'una della terra, la seconda del Mare, la terza dell'Aria et la quarta del Cielo" (cited in Rossi, *Battista Guarini*, 311).

169 Document 2.42: Mantua, Archivio di Stato (Archivio Gonzaga), busta 2247, c.n.n.

170 Mantua, Archivio di Stato (Archivio Gonzaga), busta 2675, cc.n.n. (1 September 1598).

171 Chieppio notes, however, that the visitor will see little, because the set has been dismantled and new machinery was being prepared for the third performance of Guarini's work. See Document 2.43: Mantua, Archivio di Stato (Archivio Gonzaga), busta 2674, c.n.n. Velasquez was indeed an avid patron of theatrical productions, and as Gustavia Yvonne Kendall notes, he "hosted most of the important and highly noted state spectacles of Cinquecento Milan." On 18 July 1599, Velasquez was at least present at a presentation in Milan of a *festa a*

ballo for the visit of Archduke Albert and Archduchess Isabella of Austria (see below). Kendall, "Theatre, dance and music in late Cinquecento Milan," *Early Music* 32 (2004): 74–95, especially p. 80.

172　"Il che se m'habbia spiacciuto, il lascio a considerare a V.S., la quale, poichè vi si è trovata, e me ne dà così minuto ragguaglio, confesso veramente che mi ha mitigato in gran parte il mio dispiacere, confidandomi che sia stato veduto et gustato in mia vece da chi è da me tanto amato e stimato." The "loved and esteemed" viewer who saw it in Guarini's place may refer to his son, Alessandro. The letter appears in Ancona, *Origini del teatro italiano*, 569.

173　*Ibid.*

174　Mantua, Archivio di Stato (Archivio Gonzaga), busta 2674, c.n.n. (23 November 1598).

175　Ferrante Persia, in his *Relatione de' ricevimenti fatti in Mantova alla Maestà della Regina di Spagna dal Serenissimo Signor Duca, l'Anno MDXCVIII del mese di Novembre* (Mantua: Camerale, 1598; repr. Ferrara: Baldini, 1598; found in Venice, Biblioteca Nazionale Marchiana, Misc. 425.14), states that "si era preparata una compendiosa tradottione in lingua Alemanna di quanto fú recitato, & rappresentato, ch fú loro data nel principiare dell'opera, legata in due libretti separatamente" (fol. A4v). Perhaps it is no coincidence that the first Spanish translation of the play appeared in 1602, only four years after this performance for a number of illustrious Spanish spectators, although, at the same time, this version seems to have followed a trend of international editions and translations of the play, including the 1591 London (Volfeo) edition, and French (1593) and English (1601/02) translations. See also below, Chapter 3, note 68.

176　Franz Christoph Khevenhiller, *Annales Ferdinandei* (Leipzig, 1724), vol. 5, 1884–85, states that "è durata otto ore" and "nel corso di questa è stata servita una superba colazione, fornita di ogni lusso," while the *Diario di Santa Barbara 1572–1602* (Mantua, Archivio Storico Diocesano) relates that it "finì alle 6 hore"—likely connoting six hours after sunset, so the play would have finished around 10:00pm. Ferrante Persia, *Relatione de' ricevimenti fatti in Mantova*, writes:

> perchè la cena doveva essere alquanto tarda, al mezzo della favola si fece una sontuosa collatione, con rinfrescamenti in gran copia a Sua Maestà et a gl'altri Prencipi, et Dame, che erano presenti in grandissimo numero. Finito questo trattenimento alle sette hore dopo la commedia Sua Maestà havendo cenato si ritirò alle sue stanze.
>
> (8)

See Licia Mari, ed., "L'ingresso a Mantova di Margherita d'Asburgo e la rappresentazione de *Il pastor fido*," in Umberto Artioli and Cristina Grazioni, ed., *I Gonzaga e l'Impero: Itinerari dello spettacolo, con una selezione di materiali dall'Archivio informatico Herla (1560–1630)* (Florence: Le Lettere, 2005), 379–98, at 382 and 385.

177　"...quasi si può dire tutta la nobilità d'Italia concorsa da Venetia, Firenze, Genova, Verona, Brescia & altre città circonvicine, per vedere rapresentare la detta Pastorale che portava così celebre nome per ogni parte..." Giovanni Battista Grillo, *Breve trattato di quanto successe alla maestà della regina D. Margarita d'Austria N.S.* (Naples: Appresso Costantino Vitale, 1604), 30–57, at 55.

178　Document 2.44: Vigilio, *La insalata: cronaca Mantovana dal 1561 al 1602*, 42r–v; in D. Ferrari and C. Mozzarelli, eds. (Mantua: Arcari, 1992), 89.

179　Document 2.45: Mantua, Archivio di Stato, Archivio Gonzaga, busta 2764, c.n.n (22 November 1598).

180　Document 2.46: Vigilio, *La insalata*, 41v.

181　Document 2.47: Guarini, *Lettere* (1596), part 1, 85.

182 Document 2.48: Grillo, *Breve trattato*, 42; also repr. in Achille Neri, "Gli 'Intermezzi' del 'Pastor fido'," *Giornale storico della letteratura italiana* 11 (1888): 405–15, at 407.

183 See Mazzoni, *L'Olimpico di Vicenza*, 72–73. The plates of the 1602 Ciotti edition of *Il pastor fido* possibly show Aleotti's designs for this production, as proposed in Adriano Cavicchi, "La scenografia dell'Aminta nella tradizione scenografica pastorale Ferrarese del secolo XVI," Maria Teresa Muraro, ed., *Studi sul teatro veneto fra rinascimento ed età barocca* (Florence: Olschki, 1971), 53–72, especially 63–69. Cavicchi draws further evidence of Aleotti's influence on (or even direct involvement in) the 1598 production through his association with the Accademia degli Intrepidi, which, Cavicchi proposes, may be symbolized in the figure of Alfeo, who delivers the play's prologue. In 1599, Viani was sent to Milan to oversee the spectacles of a pastoral play staged for the wedding of Archduke Alberto and Archduchess Isabella of Austria. See the various letters between Milan and Mantua, cited in Ancona, *Origini del teatro italiano*, II, 572–75 and above, notes 97–99.

184 *Diario di Santa Barbara 1572–1602*, 774, in the Archivio Storico Diocesano, Mantua; quoted in Mari, "L'ingresso a Mantova," 386.

185 "La pastorale che si recitò Dom.ca sera riuscì bene, ma non gl'intermedi, per i disordini che seguirono, come dai Nobili Veneti che là viderò intenderà, con mio gran disgusto" (25 November 1598). Archivio di Stato, Mantua, Archivio Gonzaga, busta 2675. See also Mari, ed., "L'ingresso a Mantova," 387. Ercole Udine was a poet and academician, who published a translation in *ottava rima* of Virgil's *Aeneid* (Venice: Ciotti, 1597) and his own epic poem, *La psiche* (Venice: Ciotti, 1599). Tasso dedicated his sonnet *Quel, che là dove i verdi paschi inonda* "ad Ercole Udine traduttore di Virgilio."

186 Document 2.49: Grillo, *Breve trattato*. The use of music in *Pastor fido*, based on Grillo's account, is discussed also in Gary Tomlinson, *Monteverdi and the End of the Renaissance* (Oxford: Clarendon, 1987), 114–15: "The descriptions of all but one of the *intermedi* begin with locutions like "Dopo il secondo atto nel finir della musica," suggesting that the choruses ending the acts of *Il pastor fido* were sung" (115).

187 "Il Gioco de la cieca rapresentato alla Regina di Spagna nel Pastor Fido," in Gastoldi, *Il quarto libro de' madrigali a cinque voci* (Venice: Amadino, 1602), 6. See also Cavicchi, "Teatro monteverdiano e la tradizione teatrale Ferrarese," in R. Monterosso, ed., *Claudio Monteverdi e il suo tempo* (Verona: Valdonega, 1969), 139–56, at 149–50 and Newcomb, *The Madrigal at Ferrara*, 45–46. As discussed in Chapter 8, Gastoldi had a widespread reputation as a composer of dance music. His *Balletti a cinque voci con li suoi versi per cantare, sonare, & ballare* (Venice: Amadino, 1591), which was dedicated to the Duke of Mantua, for example, had been reprinted some thirty times by the middle of the seventeenth century.

188 In the sacrifice scene (act 3, scene 3) of Beccari's play, the priest sings three invocations to the accompaniment of a *lira*, which are followed by responses from a four-part chorus of shepherds. The final *canzone* of act 5 also consists of a four-part, largely homophonic chorus. See Henry Kaufmann, "Music for a *favola pastorale* (1554)," in Edward Clinkscale and Claire Brook, eds., *A Musical Offering: Essays in Honor of Martin Bernstein* (New York: Pendragon Press, 1977), 163–82 and Jessie Ann Owens, "Music in the Early Ferrarese Pastoral: A Study of Beccari's *Il sacrificio*," in *Il teatro italiano del rinascimento* (Milan: Edizioni di Comunità, 1980), 583–601. Beccari evidently composed music for many Ferrarese play productions, including Giraldi's *Orbecche* (1541), Lollio's *Aretusa*, and Argenti's *Lo Sfortunato* (1567), none of which survives. See, for example, Document 2.50: Preface to Alberto Lollio, *Aretusa, comedia pastorale* (Ferrara: Valente Panizza Mantoano, 1564). For a general history of purported

music and dance for the stage in Renaissance Italy, including the particularly rich tradition thereof in Ferrara reaching back at least to the late fifteenth century, see Nino Pirotta and Elena Povoledo *Music and Theater from Poliziano to Monteverdi*, trans. by Karen Eales, in series Cambridge Studies in Music (Cambridge: Cambridge University Press, 1982).

189 "Dopo il secondo atto nel finir della musica, si sentì il terremoto, et fra tanto la scena mutandosi, divenne tutta nuvoli et mare" (Grillo, *Breve trattato*, 46).

190 In his *Della poesia rappresentativa & del modo di rappresentare le favole sceniche* (Ferrara: Baldini, 1598), Angelo Ingegneri—the poet, playwright, and theorist with whom Guarini worked on the 1585 staging of *Oedipus Rex* in Vicenza—discusses the use of sung choruses in staged drama, arguing that, while necessary in tragedy, choruses prove optional for comedy and pastoral plays. For pastorals, he advises the playwright to put "at the end of each act this word, *Choro*, and put a song to be sung there. But one might find other occasions at which to introduce them, for example, celebrations, weddings, dances, games, *freschi*, sport, or other similar entertainments" (see 17–27, at 23). Ingegneri signed the dedication to Cesare D'Este, Duke of Modena, in Ferrara on 8 August 1598. Earlier in the 1590s, the poet served in Rome at the household of Cardinal Cinzio Aldobrandini, alongside Guarini, Tasso, and composer Luca Marenzio. On Ingegneri's oblique role in the *Pastor fido* debates, see Chapter 3.

191 Andrea Gabieli set four end-of-act choruses from *Oedipus Rex* to music in homophonic style ranging from one to six voices. For an overview of the production and an edition of Gabrieli's music, see Leo Schrade, *La Représentation d'Edipo Tiranno au Teatro Olimpico* (Paris: Centre national de la recherché scientifique, 1960). Details of the Sassuolo wedding are preserved in an anonymous contemporary account, which is presented, with analysis, in Ivaldi, *Le nozze Pio–Farnese*, 7–47. In addition to the music of the *intermedi*, the anonymous chronicler at Sassuolo also describes music at the ends of acts preceding each *intermedi*. For example: "At the conclusion of the first act began the sweetest harmony of songs and music, after which appeared the first *intermedio*" (*ibid.*, 11).

192 Document 2.51: Malacreta, *Considerazione intorno al Pastorfido*; in Guarini, *Opere*, IV, 120. Malacreta, on the one hand, doubts the verisimilitude of having the chorus leave and return in this way ("ognuna dà cagione di dubitare di poca verisimilitudine, e convenevolezza"), but on the other, "if the chorus comes to sing each time the act is finished, this too seems to be done with little or no verisimilitude" (Ma se il coro viene a cantare ogn'ora, che si è finito l'atto, questo ancora con poco o nullo verisimile pare farsi). Moreover, the lack of knowledge he shows here and elsewhere in his criticism about how the play was to be executed stresses that he had not seen it performed onstage, either in Mantua in November 1598 or at another staging, and in turn reinforces the second-hand nature of his information regarding the abridgment of the play (see below).

193 Document 2.52: Gastoldi, *Concenti musicali con le sue sinfonie a otto voci* (Venice: Amadino, 1604).

194 Document 2.53: Mantua, Archivio di Stato (Archivio Gonzaga), busta 2674, c.n.n. (22 November 1598).

195 Document 2.54: Bertolotti, dedication of *Il terzo libro de madrigali a cinque voci* (Venice: Amadino, 1609).

196 The letter is quoted in Alfredo Saviotti, "Muzio Manfredi e Battista Guarini," 8.

197 "L'ho fatta in 28 giorni e son 2735 versi, fra' quali sono due madrigali in due luoghi necessari, e la canzonetta ultima del Comiato, che come l'altre andrà balata, cantata e suonata." Quoted in Saviotti, "Muzio Manfredi e Battista Guarini," 8.

198 See Manfredi, *Lettere brevissime*, letters 322–24 (pp. 266–69).

199 "Credo che S.A. vorrà farlo rappresentare: E sò certo, che à V.S. darà il carico ò di comporre, ò di far comporre le musiche, che in esso bisognano;" Manfredi, *Lettere brevissime*, 268. See also Ancona, *Origini del teatro italiano*, 424–25.

200 Document 2.55: Manfredi, *Lettere brevissime*, 268. On Manfredi's, Guarini's, and Ingegneri's varying conceptions of the roles of music, song, and dance in stage drama, see Kirkendale, *Emilio de' Cavalieri*, 201–11 and Riccò, *'Ben mille pastorali'*, 276–86.

201 See Anne MacNeil, *Women and Music of the Commedia dell'Arte in the Late Sixteenth Century* (Oxford: Oxford University Press, 2003), 36–46. MacNeil reasons that the music of the contest likely took the form of a madrigal-like composition for four parts, similar to Merulo's music for the 1574 production of Frangipani's *Tragedia*.

202 See "Cronologia dei testi drammatici e degli eventi spettacoli relative alla città di Milano," in *La scena della gloria: Drammaturgia e spettacolo a Milano in età spagnola*, ed. A. Cascetta and R. Carpani (Milan: Vita e Pensiero, 1995), 731–54.

203 MacNeil also raises the possibility that Monteverdi played a role in the event in *Women and Music of the Commedia dell'Arte*, 82–83.

204 "In Mantova alla presenza della Serenissima Regina d'Ispagna fu questa poema (si può dire) di una mala maniera circonciso"; Malacreta, *Considerationi ... sopra il Pastor fido*, folio 57v; in Guarini, *Opere*, IV, 70.

205 "Senza punto sconcertare cosa pur minima della favola, che importante fosse, gli si levarono versi intorno al numero di 1600, stimati oziosi." Malacreta, *Considerationi ... sopra il Pastor fido*, fol. 57v; Guarini, *Opere*, IV, 70.

206 Sampson, "Guarini's *Pastor fido*," 73.

207 Sampson, "Guarini's *Pastor fido*," 73.

208 The opening lines of the madrigal read: "O unfortunate and miserable Mirtillo / so many fierce enemies, / so many arms and so much war / against a dying heart?" I am grateful to Tim Carter for suggesting this potential connection between the madrigal text and the shortening of the play to my attention. For the complete text and analysis, see Chapter 8.

209 The 1598 performance of several of Monteverdi's forthcoming madrigals is documented in Giovanni Maria Artusi's *L'Artusi, overo Delle imperfettioni della moderna musica ragionamenti dui* (Venice: Vincenti, 1600), fols. 39r–v; translated by Oliver Strunk in *Source Readings in Music History* (New York: Norton, 1998), 526–27. Artusi's account and subsequent criticism of the madrigals are given closer consideration in Chapter 6 and elsewhere below.

210 On the Nola performance, see references in Nicolas Perella, *The Critical Fortune of Battista Guarini's "Il pastor fido"* (Florence: Olschki, 1973), 36. On the staging at Vicenza, Malacreta writes: "E in Vicenza appunto mia patria, dovendosi rappresentar, fu levato il prologo di Alfeo, e sopposta la persona d'Iride, che disse cose del tutto varie, e diverse da quelle di Alfeo" (in Guarini, *Opere*, IV, 42).

211 Alessandro Guarini's letter to Duke Vincenzo, 11 June 1599, alluding to the inclusion of an updated prologue to the play survives in the Archivio di Stato, Mantua (Archivio Gonzaga), busta 2677, c. 349 (11 June 1599); see also the letters cited in Parisi, "Ducal Patronage," 205, note 141.

212 See Rossi, *Battista Guarini*, 233, who cites as evidence an unpublished letter from Guarini to Crescenzi, 23 June 1600.

213 A reworking of Guarini's prologue by Niccolò Averara, which is delivered by the river Serio in Clusone, survives in Matteo Bordogna, *Raccolta di poesie di diversi* (Bergamo: Comin Ventura, 1602), also dedicated to Venier. See Rossi, *Battista Guarini*, 234.

214 As Rossi notes, "on 23 February 1602, il Magnanini [of the academy] wrote to Guarini that the Accademia Intrepidi believed the poet would have come to

Ferrara to attend 'alla rappresentazione d'esso *Pastor Fido* fatta l'altr'ieri qui in Ferr[ar]a'" (*Battista Guarini*, 233).

215 Two manuscript copies of *Pastor fidus* survive in Cambridge: Trinity College, MS R.3.37 and Cambridge Univeresity Library, MS Ff.2.9. On the Latin translation, in the context of the influence of *Il pastor fido* on early seventeenth-century English drama, see Raphael Lyne, "English Guarini: Recognition and Reception," *Yearbook of English Studies* 36 (2006): 90–102.

216 Rossi writes: "Nel 1621 il *Pastor Fido* veniva pure recitato in Correggio, con grandissima pompa, nel palazzo del principe Siro, con intramezzi di Niccolò Bonasio" (*Battista Guarini*, 235).

217 See Ricci, *Il vecchio teatro del pubblico in Bologna (1547–1788)*, in *Atti e Memorie della Regia Deputazione di storia patri per le province di Romagna*, Series 3, vol. 2 (1884): 409, which states:

> Quella nuova forma data al *teatro della Sala* non durò gran tempo, chè la sera del 17 dicembre 1623, finita la rappresentazione del *Pastor fido* del Guarini, prese fuoco e in brevissimo tempo tutte le fatiche del signor Giovanni Gabriele Giudotti dileguarono in fumo e in faville.

References

Accademici degli Eterei. *Rime degli Accademici Eterei.* Venice: Comin da Trino, 1567.

Artusi, Giovanni Maria. *L'Artusi, overo Delle imperfettioni della moderna musica ragionamenti dui.* Venice: Vincenti, 1600. Trans. by Oliver Strunk in *Source Readings in Music History.* New York: Norton, 1998.

Bizzarini, Marco. "L'ultimo Marenzio: tipologie di committenza e di recezione." In *Studi marenziani*, eds. F. Piperno and I. Fenlon, 67–87. Venice: Fondazione Ugo e Olga Levi, 2003.

Bosi, Kathryn. "Leone Tolosa and *Martel d'amore*: a *balletto della duchessa* discovered." *Recercare* 17 (2005): 5–70.

Burnbaum, Eduard. *Jewish Musicians at the Court of the Mantuan Dukes (1542–1628).* Ed. Judith Cohen. Tel-Aviv: Tel-Aviv University, 1978.

Campiglia, Madalena. *Flori, favola boscareccia.* Vicenza: Gli heredi di Perin Libraro & Tomaso Brunelli, 1588. Trans. by Virginia Cox as *Flori, A Pastoral Drama: A Bilingual Edition*, eds. Virginia Cox and Lisa Sampson. Chicago, IL: University of Chicago Press, 2004.

Campori, Giuseppe, ed. *Lettere di scrittori italiani del secolo XVI.* Bologna: Gaetano Romagnoli, 1877.

Cavicchi, Adriano. "La scenografia dell'Aminta nella tradizione scenografica pastorale Ferrarese del secolo XVI." In *Studi sul teatro veneto fra rinascimento ed età barocca*, ed. Maria Teresa Muraro, 53–72. Florence: Olschki, 1971.

———. "Teatro monteverdiano e la tradizione teatrale Ferrarese." In *Claudio Monteverdi e il suo tempo*, ed. R. Monterosso, 139–56. Verona: Valdonega, 1969.

Chater, James. "Musical Patronage in Rome at the Turn of the Seventeenth Century: The Case of Cardinal Montalto." *Studi musicali* 16 (1987): 179–227.

Cioni, Enzo. "Feste e spettacoli a Sassuolo nell'età barocca." In *Musica, teatro, nazione dall'Emilia all'Europa nel Seicento*, 27–44. Modena: Aedes Muratoriana, 1982.

Cohen, Judith. "Words to Dance and Music—Music to Dance and Words: The Case of the *Gioco della cieca.*" In *Fundamentals of Musical Language: An Interdisciplinary Approach*, ed. Mojsej Grigorevic Boroda, 175–95. Bochum: Brockmeyer, 1993.

Corso, Cosimo. "Carteggio inedito fra Battista Guarini e Belisario Bulgarini." *Bullettino senese di storia patria* 57 (1950): 55–106.

Crick, Oliver and John Rudlin. *Commedia dell'arte: A Handbook for Troupes.* New York: Routledge, 2001.

D'Ancona, Alessandro. *Origini del teatro italiano.* 2nd ed. 3 vols. Turin: Loescher, 1891.

Denarosi, Lucia. *L'Accademia degli Innominati di Parma: Teorie letterarie e progetti di scrittura (1574–1608).* Florence: Società Editrice Fiorentina, 2003.

Durante, Elio and Anna Martellotti. *Cronistoria del Concerto delle Dame principalissime di Margherita Gonzaga d'Este.* Florence: Studio per edizioni scelte, 1979.

Fabbri, Paolo. *Monteverdi.* Trans. by Tim Carter. Cambridge: Cambridge University Press, 1994.

Fenlon, Iain. "Scipione Gonzaga: A 'Poor' Cardinal in Rome." In *Music and Culture in Late Renaissance Italy,* 93–117. Oxford: Oxford University Press, 2002.

———. *Music and Patronage in Sixteenth-Century Mantua.* 2 vols. Oxford: Oxford University Press, 1980.

———. "Music and Spectacle at the Gonzaga Court." *Proceedings of the Royal Musical Association* 103 (1976–77): 90–105.

Fratarcangeli, Margherita. "Gabriele Bombasi: Un letterato tra Annibale Carracci e Odoardo Farnese." *Paragone Arte* 48 (1997): 112–30.

Gallo, Alberto. *La prima rappresentazione al Teatro Olimpico, con i progetti e le relazioni dei contemporanei.* Milan: Il polifilo, 1973.

Gerbino, Giuseppe. *Music and the Myth of Arcadia in Renaissance Italy.* Cambridge: Cambridge University Press, 2009.

Griffiths, Clive. "Guarini's *Il pastor fido*: A Beginning or an End for Renaissance Pastoral Drama." In *The Cultural Heritage of the Italian Renaissance,* eds. C. Griffiths and R. Hastings, 315–27. Lewiston, NY: Edwin Mellen Press, 1993.

Grillo, Giovanni Battista. *Breve trattato di quanto successe alla maestà della regina D. Margarita d'Austria N.S.* Naples: Appresso Costantino Vitale, 1604.

Guarini, Battista. *Opere di Battista Guarini.* Ed. Marziano Guglielminetti. Turin: Unione Tipografico-Editrice, 1971.

———. *Delle opere del cavalier Battista Guarini.* Eds. G.A. Barotti and A. Zeno. 4 vols. Verona: Tumermani, 1737–38.

———. *Annotazioni sopra "Il pastor fido".* Verona: Giovanni Tumermani, 1737. Facsimile in *La questione del "Pastor fido."* In series La scena e l'ombra: collana di testi e studi teatrali 2. Rome: Vecchiarelli, 1997.

———. *Il pastor fido, tragicommedia pastorale del molto Illustre Cavaliere Battista Guarini, ora in questa XX impressione di curiose e dotte Annotationi arrichito.* Venice: Ciotti, 1602.

———. *Lettere.* Venice: Ciotti, 1600.

———. *Lettere.* Venice: Ciotti, 1596.

———. *Lettere.* Parma: Viotti, 1595.

———. *Il Segretario.* Venice: Meietti, 1594.

———[?]. *Il Verato secondo, ovvero replica dell'Attizzato accademico ferrarese, in difesa del Pastorfido, contra la seconda scrittura di Messer Giason De Nores intitolata Apologia.* Florence: Filippo Giunti, 1593.

———[?]. *Il Verrato ovvero difesa di quanto ha scritto M. Giason Denores contra le tragicomedie, et le pastorali, in un suo discorso di poesia.* Ferrara: Alfonso Carassa, 1588.

Hill, John Walter. *Roman Monody, Cantata, and Opera from the Circles around Cardinal Montalto*, 2 vols. Oxford: Clarendon Press, 1997.

Ingegneri, Angelo. *Della poesia rappresentativa & del modo di rappresentare le favole sceniche*. Ferrara: Baldini, 1598.

Ivaldi, Armando Fabio. *Le nozze Pio–Farnese e gli apparati teatrali di Sassuolo del 1587: Studio su una rapresentazione del primo dramma pastorale italiano, con inter-mezzi di G.B. Guarini*. Genoa: Erga, 1974.

Jacobson, Howard. "Horace *AP* 139: parturient montes, nascetur ridiculus mus." *Museum Helveticum* 64 (2007): 59–61.

Kastan, David Scott. *Shakespeare and the Book*. Cambridge: Cambridge University Press, 2001.

Kaufmann, Henry. "Music for a *favola pastorale* (1554)." In *A Musical Offering: Essays in Honor of Martin Bernstein*, eds. E. Clinkscale and C. Brook, 163–82. New York: Pendragon Press, 1977.

Kendall, Gustavia Yvonne. "Theatre, Dance and Music in Late Cinquecento Milan." *Early Music* 32 (2004): 74–95.

Kirkendale, Warren. *Emilio de' Cavalieri, "Gentiluomo romano": His Life and Letters, His Role as Superintendent of All the Art at the Medici Court, and His Musical Compositions*. Florence: Olschki, 2001.

———. "L'opera in musica prima del Peri: le pastorali perdute di Laura Guidic-cioni ed Emilio de' Cavalieri." In *Firenze e la Toscana dei Medici nell'Europa del Cinquecento*, II, 365–95. Florence: Olschki, 1983.

Lyne, Raphael. "English Guarini: Recognition and Reception." *Yearbook of English Studies* 36 (2006): 90–102.

MacNeil, Anne. *Women and Music of the Commedia dell'Arte in the Late Sixteenth Century*. Oxford: Oxford University Press, 2003.

Malacreta, Giovanni Pietro. *Consideratoni [sic] ... sopra il Pastot [sic] fido, tragicomedia pastorale del ... Battista Guarini*. Vicenza: Greco, 1600.

Manfredi, Muzio. *Lettere brevissime*. Venice: Pulciani, 1606.

Mari, Licia, ed. "L'ingresso a Mantova di Margherita d'Asburgo e la rappresentazi-one de *Il pastor fido*." In *I Gonzaga e l'Impero: Itinerari dello spettacolo, con una selezione di materiali dall'Archivio informatico Herla (1560–1630)*, eds. U. Artioli and C. Grazioni, 379–98. Florence: Le Lettere, 2005.

Mazzoni, Stefano. *L'Olimpico di Vicenza: un teatro e la sua 'perpetua memoria.'* Florence: Le Lettere, 1998.

McClure, George. "Women and the Politics of Play in Sixteenth-Century Italy: Torquato Tasso's Theory of Games." *Renaissance Quarterly* 61 (2008): 765–68.

Molinari, Carla. "Per il 'Pastor fido' di Battista Guarini." *Studi di filologia italiana, bollettino annuale dell'Accademia della Crusca* 43 (1985): 161–238.

Monteverdi, Claudio. *Scherzi musicali a tre voci*. Venice: Amadino, 1607.

———. *Quinto libro di madrigali a cinque voci*. Venice: Amadino, 1605.

Neri, Achille. "Gli 'Intermezzi' del 'Pastor fido'." *Giornale storico della letteratura italiana* 11 (1888): 405–15.

Newcomb, Anthony. *The Madrigal at Ferrara, 1579–97*. 2 vols. Princeton, NJ: Princeton University Press, 1981.

Owens, Jessie Ann. "Music in the Early Ferrarese Pastoral: A Study of Beccari's *Il sacrificio*." In *Il teatro italiano del rinascimento*, ed. M. de Panizza Lorch, 583–601. Milan: Edizioni di Comunità, 1980.

Parisi, Susan. "Ducal Patronage of Music in Mantua, 1587–1627: An Archival Study." Ph. D. diss., University of Illinois at Urbana–Champaign, 1989.

Parrott, David. "The Mantuan Succession, 1627–31: A Sovereignty Dispute in Early Modern Europe." *English Historical Review* 112 (1997): 20–65

Perella, Nicolas. *The Critical Fortune of Battista Guarini's "Il pastor fido."* Florence: Olschki, 1973.

————. "Amarilli's Dilemma: The *Pastor fido* and Some English Authors." *Comparative Literature* 12 (1960): 348–59.

Persia, Ferrante. *Relatione de' ricevimenti fatti in Mantova alla Maestà della Regina di Spagna dal Serenissimo Signor Duca, l'Anno MDXCVIII del mese di Novembre.* Mantua: Camerale, 1598; repr. Ferrara: Baldini, 1598.

Pirotta, Nino and Elena Povoledo. *Music and Theater from Poliziano to Monteverdi.* Trans. by Karen Eales. In series Cambridge Studies in Music. Cambridge: Cambridge University Press, 1982.

Riccò, Laura. *Dalla zampogna all'aurea cetra: egloghe, pastorali, favole in musica.* Rome: Bulzoni, 2015.

————. *"Ben mille pastorali": l'itinerario dell'Ingegneri da Tasso a Guarini e oltre.* Rome: Bulzoni, 2004.

Rossi, Vittorio. *Battista Guarini ed il Pastor fido: Studio biografico-critico con documenti inediti.* Turin: Loescher, 1886.

Sampson, Lisa. *Pastoral Drama in Early Modern Italy: The Making of a New Genre.* In series Italian Perspectives 15. London: Legenda, Modern Humanities Research Association and Maney Publishing, 2006.

Saviotti, Alfredo. *Guariniana, a proposito di una recente pubblicazione.* Pesaro: Federici, 1888.

Scarpati, Claudio. "Poetica e retorica in Battista Guarini." In *Scarpati, Studi sul Cinquecento italiano*, 208–38. Milan: Università Cattolica del Sacro Cuore, 1982.

Schrade, Leo. *La Représentation d'Edipo Tiranno au Teatro Olimpico.* Paris: Centre national de la recherché scientifique, 1960.

Stras, Laurie. *Women and Music in Sixteenth-Century Ferrara.* In series New Perspectives in Music History and Criticism. Cambridge: Cambridge University Press, 2018.

Summo, Faustino. *Due discorsi: l'uno contro le tragicommedie e le pastorali, l'altro contro il Pastor Fido.* Padua: F. Bolzetta, 1600.

Tomlinson, Gary. *Monteverdi and the End of the Renaissance.* Oxford: Clarendon, 1987.

Treadwell, Nina. *Music and Wonder at the Medici Court: The 1589 Interludes for 'La Pellegrina.'* Bloomington: Indiana University Press, 2008.

Truffi, Riccardo. "La prima rappresentazione del *Pastor fido* e il teatro a Crema nei sec. XVI e XVII." *Rassegna bibliografica della letteratura italiana* 8 (1900): 330–35.

Vigilio, Giovanni Battista. *La insalata: cronaca Mantovana dal 1561 al 1602.* Eds. D. Ferrari and C. Mozzarelli. Mantua: Arcari, 1992.

Weinberg, Bernard. *A History of Literary Criticism in the Italian Renaissance.* 2 vols. Chicago, IL: University of Chicago Press, 1961.

3 From Poetic Monster to *Raccolta di madrigali*

The *Pastor fido* Debate, 1586–1602

In changing the label of his *Pastor fido* from "favola pastorale" to "tragicomedia pastorale" on his sketch of 1585, Guarini was undoubtedly well aware of the ongoing polemics in literary theory and poetics and the backlash that his title would provoke. This is especially likely given the poet's involvement that year in the production of Sophocles' *Oedipus Rex* by the Accademia Olimpica in Vicenza, which was in many ways an outgrowth of the scholarly and critical focus in recent years on Horatian and Aristotelian theories of poetics. As we have seen, a year earlier, Guarini had given a "presentazione" of his unfinished play for the academy, which included among its members two prominent figures from his 1584 readings in Guastalla, Ferrante Gonzaga and Muzio Manfredi. But the poet's closest encounter with the contemporary literary debates did not come in Vicenza or Guastalla, but in the city that had remained most dear to him since his early years as a student and as a member of the Accademia degli Eterei (1564–67), and where he spent much of his time in the mid-1580s discussing and giving readings of his new pastoral play: Padua.

Perhaps more than any other center in late-Cinquecento Italy, Padua represented the nucleus of the foremost critical debates surrounding such literary cornerstones as Dante's *Divina commedia*, Ariosto's *Orlando furioso*, Sperone Speroni's *Canace e Macareo*, and Tasso's *Gerusalemme liberata*. The critics and poets involved relied heavily upon the writings of Aristotle, Plato, Horace, Homer, Virgil, Petrarch, and other masters in their criticisms; the *Pastor fido* debate was no different. Bernard Weinberg views the controversy over Guarini's tragicomedy as the last in this line of important literary quarrels of the sixteenth century. But *Il pastor fido* also represented an important break from the past—a starting point for a new era—not only in poetics and theater, through the poet's assertion of creative license and public taste over long-standing theoretical and civic demands and of a new means of poetic purgation through a synthesis of tragedy and comedy, but also in music, through its slightly later association with a similar confrontation between theoretical propriety and artistic innovation in the dispute between theorist Giovanni Maria Artusi and composer Claudio Monteverdi.

DOI: 10.4324/9781315463056-4

There has been a vast amount of literature devoted to the *Pastor fido* debates; the attention it has continued to attract seems to have been anticipated—and, perhaps, fostered—by Guarini himself, who compiled the initial defenses of the play (the two *Verrati*), along with his own extensive annotations, into a single, elaborately decorated authoritative edition of the tragicomedy in 1602.[1] Even before this, Guarini issued a separate synopsis of the two vindications of tragicomedy by the Moderns, "Il Verrato" and "L'Attizzato" (both commonly believed to be Guarini himself), against Giasone Denores, representing the conservative Aristotelians, in the *Compendio della poesia tragicomica tratto dai duo Verati*, compiled by the poet in 1599 but only published in 1601 (Venice, Ciotti). Although many of the principal documents of the controversy have appeared in more recent editions, modern analyses of the polemic (particularly in music scholarship) have tended to be limited in scope and to derive from a shared set of earlier, influential synopses—most notably Vittorio Rossi's *Battista Guarini ed il Pastor fido* (1886), Allan Gilbert's *Literary Criticism: Plato to Dryden* (1940), Weinberg's *History of Literary Criticism in the Italian Renaissance* (1961), and Nicolas Perella's *The Critical Fortune of Battista Guarini's 'Il pastor fido'* (1973)—and to focus on the four initial exchanges between Denores, "Il Verrato," and "L'Attizzato."[2] This reliance on selected secondary sources and translations has led on the one hand to a perpetuation of specific arguments, excerpts, and citations of the dispute, and on the other to a neglect of many strands and details, some of considerable interest and importance, including with respect to the play's expanding influence in the realms of music, literature, and lyric poetry.

The present study, therefore, is based on a detailed reading of the eleven original pamphlets of the debate, issued between 1586 and 1602. The objective of this analysis is to provide a general overview of the chief issues at stake, focusing especially on those aspects that relate most to the play's lyric and sensual qualities and stylized poetic language, and to its immediate appeal and success in the realm of music. Moreover, the critical pamphlets yield insight into the play's intricate stage history and suggest an unexpected source of the first *Pastor fido* madrigals, all of which seems to have eluded modern scholarship. Chapter 4 will then situate the beginnings of the play's history as an enduring source of madrigal texts in the contexts of Italian courts and patrons, considering general trends across the history of the *Pastor fido* madrigal from 1580 to 1640 and variant readings of early textual and musical sources.

The present investigation will begin in Padua, for it is here more than anywhere else that the seeds of confrontation were prepared in the intellectual circles of earlier decades and prodded in the poet's readings of the mid-1580s. And, I will argue, it is also here that the kernel was laid that would soon give rise to a rampant flowering of musical works lasting well into the seventeenth century, stimulated by the madrigals of Luca Marenzio and Giaches de Wert in the mid-1590s. The discussions of Aristotelian philosophy that dominated much of the debates in the second half of the sixteenth century were indebted largely to the work of Francesco Robortello (1516–67), a professor of philosophy, rhetoric, and classics at the university in Padua, whose translation and commentary of the *Poetics* was highly influential for late-Renaissance humanists. Robortello's style of conservative interpretation of Aristotle's works came to characterize the Paduan Studio through the end of the Cinquecento, as it was taken up (and often reconsidered) by later generations of professors at the university, including Jacopo Zabarella, Antonio Riccoboni, Giasone Denores, Faustino Summo, and Paolo Beni—all participants in the early discussions and polemic that enveloped Guarini's work. As a consequence, the debate can be divided largely into two main schools: the Ancients, who stood for a more doctrinaire and conservative reading of Aristotle and the classics; and the Moderns, who—interpreting Aristotle more liberally—believed that poetry was only effective when it appealed to modern audiences and therefore should be allowed to change.

In the second published defense of the play, *Il Verato secondo* (1593), L'Attizzato ("the incited one")—ostensibly Guarini himself—gives some indication of both the support and hostility that surrounded the poet and the play in the intense academic environment of Padua, specifically in the bookshop of Paolo Meietti and the home of Jacopo Zabarella. Guarini gave readings of his tragicomedy in both places, and it was in Meietti's bookshop that the poet discussed his work with "the excellent Riccoboni, most honored reader in that Studio [i.e., the university], in the presence of many others."[3] Among these "many others" was, of course, Giasone Denores, professor of moral philosophy at the university and the first detractor of the play, who provokes Guarini into violating one of the cardinal rules of "pamphlet wars" by condemning Denores explicitly as "a scandalous slanderer, who with invidious and dishonest manners consciously sought to offend the work of a friend, in the capacity of which it was introduced to him."[4] Thus commenced the "controversia Iasonis Denores habita cum Baptista Guarino equite," as Riccoboni terms it in his *De Gymnasio Patavino* of 1598. Riccoboni perhaps did not foresee that in the years after 1598 the controversy would see a second outbreak, expanding well beyond Denores and Guarini (if indeed the latter was the author of the two *Verrati*) as other humanists and critics from Padua and elsewhere joined the fray. This analysis will end with a confrontation between the Paduan Studio and a largely neglected but uniquely intriguing treatise from Verona dedicated to the Duke of Mantua that casts new uncertainty on well-established assumptions about the play, the debate, and the tragicomedy's early associations with poetic and musical madrigals—including the authorship of the two *Verrati*, the circumstances of the play's 1598 "circumcision," and the transferral of certain "lyric" speeches from play to poetic and musical madrigal (or vice versa).

The First Wave of Debate: Denores and the Two "Verrati," 1586–93

The first attack from Denores came in his *Discorso...intorno à que' principii, cause, et accrescimenti, che la comedia, la tragedia, et il poema heroico ricevono dalla philosophia morale, e civile, e da' governatori delle republiche* of 1586.[5] Denores—adhering to the "rules" of critical etiquette—does not single out *Il pastor fido* by name: the pamphlet is, in fact, little more than a general discourse on the utility of three principal genres of poetry—epic, comedy, and tragedy—for the *res publica*. But (as Verrato would be quick to point out) the play is strongly implied by references to a *tragicommedia pastorale*—of which, Verrato claims, *Il pastor fido* is the only contemporary example—and by the fact that Denores was a regular visitor to Meietti's bookshop, where Guarini and others read and conversed about the play. The contentious discussion of pastoral tragicomedy occupies only the final few leaves of the *Discorso*, but therein Denores set the tenor for much of the debate that followed, condemning Guarini's exemplar of the genre for its lack of verisimilitude, unity, and decorum; its mixture of the distinct classical genres of tragedy and comedy; and, most of all, its failure to serve an accepted utilitarian end—specifically that of providing catharsis and moral instruction to its audience for the purpose of bettering society—while at the same time condoning Tasso's *favola pastorale* of 1573, *Aminta*.

Denores points to the sophisticated language, manners, and deviousness of the pastoral characters as a principal cause for the lack of verisimilitude in the unnamed *tragicommedia*. The Arcadian nymphs and shepherds, as peasants, were traditionally conceived as simplistic, innocent, and unrefined, and hence "are capable of neither the ridiculous [for comedy], nor equally of the terrible and miserable" for tragedy.[6] Such characters belong, rather, in the small-scale confines of the eclogue, which is short (rarely more than one hour), set in the countryside, and suitable for *feste* and banquets and for entertainment while setting the tables. But now, Denores charges, poets have afforded these eclogues much more:

> the scope of comedy and tragedy, with five acts, without proportion, without propriety, without verisimilitude, attributing to shepherds high reasonings, speeches on celestial matters, wise conceits, and most grave judgments that are hardly suitable for princes and philosophers, not noticing, however, their being in the woods and in the groves, and not in the palaces and academies.[7]

Denores's comparison of pastoral tragicomedy to an immoderate eclogue must surely have antagonized Guarini, for his correspondence with Vincenzo Gonzaga and other diplomats of the Mantuan court in 1584–85 clearly shows his determination to dissociate his work from that label. Even more, because Denores considered the primary purpose of dramatic poetry (precisely, tragedy and comedy) to be the instruction of an urban public—or perhaps *re*public, given the pamphlet's provenance in the Veneto—the rural setting of Arcadia and the rustic concerns and habits of its inhabitants seemed to bear little relevance to contemporary urban audiences. As Denores saw it, pastoral poetry may actually have the negative effect of enticing readers to abandon the city for the simpler, more tranquil life of the countryside, whereas urban societies promised much greater potential for human achievement.[8]

Of greatest concern to Denores and his later followers, however, was the issue of the play's genre and what objectives this unsanctioned hybrid could fulfill in terms of public benefit. In its conflation of the two distinct and opposing classical genres of comedy and tragedy, and the further mixing of these with the pastoral mode typical of bucolics, *Il pastor fido*, Denores maintained, was "outside of the principles ... and rules of moral and civil philosophy," and hence could not conceivably provide any improvement to those living in the city.[9] If this were not true, Denores and later critics argued, then Aristotle would surely have included tragicomedy and the pastoral in his discussion of poetic *mimesis* and catharsis in the *Poetics*. Instead, Aristotle deals only with the dramatic, or imitative, genres of tragedy and (in the lost, second part of the *Poetics*) comedy, along with the narrative (diegetic) genre of heroic poetry, or epic. As the Paduan philosopher explains, tragedy, by imitating the actions of noble and illustrious personages, seeks to purge audiences of terror and compassion, preparing them for the harsh scenarios of the battlefield and demonstrating the miserable fate of tyranny; whereas comedy, by imitating the deeds of private, common individuals, relieves spectators of melancholy caused by the travails of daily life.[10] Through these purgative effects, Denores argues, the essential purpose of poetic *mimesis* is "to introduce virtue into the souls of the spectators, of the listeners, for the shared benefit of a well-ordered Republic."[11] Pastoral tragicomedy, with its confused mixture of tragic and comic actions of lowly characters within a rural setting, he alleges, does just the opposite.

Moreover, this juxtaposition of disparate elements from conflicting genres would demand that

> the plot of tragicomedy [should] necessarily not be simple, but double, contrary to what is required, comprising in itself two plots directly opposed: one of private individuals [i.e., comic], which by its nature must end in happiness; and the other, of illustrious persons [i.e., tragic], which by its nature must end in adverse circumstances.[12]

Such duplicity conflicts with the fundamental Aristotelian requirement of unity. Decades later, in 1627, Denores's sentiments with regard to plot would continue to echo in the criticism of Benedetto Fioretti, who argues that Guarini's play is

> a poetic monster, so huge and deformed that centaurs, hippogriffs and chimaeras are comparatively graceful and charming...fit to bring a

blush to the cheek of the muse, a disgrace to poetry, a mixture of ingredients in themselves discordant, inimical and incompatible.[13]

A rebuttal to Denores's criticism came in 1588 under the title *Il Verrato, ovvero Difesa di quanto ha scritto M[esser] Giason Denores contra le tragicomedie, et le pastorali, in un suo discorso di poesia.* Signed "Il Verrato"—the celebrated Ferrarese actor who worked alongside Guarini in Vicenza (1585) and Sassuolo (1587) and would pass away in 1589—the pamphlet has been universally ascribed to Guarini himself, despite the poet's public silence on the matter. But while Guarini seems to have been reluctant to reveal his authorship in print, it has been claimed that he had done so for at least one reader. In an unpublished letter to Francesco Maria II della Rovere, Duke of Urbino, written shortly after *Il pastor fido* came to press, the poet wrote:

> I am sending Your Highness my legitimate daughter [i.e., the play], which it pleases me so much to call my *favola*, now published by me... And because I have been told that Your Highness has not seen the Apologia written by me about this type of poem, and since writings of curious things do not at all displease you, I am pleased to send you this as well.[14]

Scholars since the nineteenth century have accepted this equivocal reference to an apologia as verification of Guarini's authorship of both this defense and the *Verato secondo.* As later participants in the polemic will make clear, however, there may be reason to question this attribution, and thus, here, the author will be identified simply by this pseudonym.

Il Verrato—published by Alfonso Carassa in Ferrara, and thereby, perhaps, aligning it with a cultured court mileau apart from the severe scholastic orbit of Padua—bears a dedication to the two Venetian gentlemen, Jacopo Contarini and Francesco Vendramini, who had hosted the poet's readings of the play in 1585.[15] Citing the works of Aristotle, Theocritus, Plautus, Virgil, Petrarch, Boccaccio, Ariosto, and many others for support, the author deals systematically in turn with each of Denores's charges against the play, as well as his claims about Aristotle's demands of poetry in general. In the defense, the author goes beyond arguing merely for the legitimacy of the new genre of tragicomedy: he claims that it is, in fact, superior to the classical genres in its appeal and relevance to contemporary audiences. In doing so, Verrato refutes Denores and the conservatives' reading of the *Poetics* not by taking a stance against Aristotle, but by pointing out the often adaptable and notoriously inconclusive nature of the Philosopher's theories. Not only is the *Poetics* fragmentary in its physical form, failing to deal at all with dithyrambic poetry alongside dramatic and epic verse, but, Verrato argues, it is also selective in its scope, treating only those genres paramount in Aristotle's own day: namely, tragedy, comedy, and epic. The author continues by distinguishing those basic elements of dramatic verse that are universal and fixed—imitation, verisimilitude, verse, limited scope, recognition, reversal, and so forth—from those that are open to adaptation. Tragedy and comedy, the poet asserts, no longer appeal to modern audiences, the former being excessive in its calamity and terror, and the latter having "come to such boredom and contempt that, if it is not accompanied by the marvels of the *intramezzi*, there is no longer anyone today who can stand it."[16] In order to remain relevant through the changes of time, poetry must utilize its intrinsic adaptability and expand through the development of new genres—a notion that, the author points out, is never explicitly denied by Aristotle.

Having demonstrated an inherent flexibility in Aristotle's poetics and the necessity of such flexibility for maintaining relevance and taste for a modern audience, Verrato explains that tragicomedy is not a conflation of tragedy and comedy, as Denores claimed, but a new and distinct genre altogether that upholds the universal principles of dramatic poetry (verisimilitude, unity, decorum, and so forth) while incorporating aspects of both ancient genres:

> From the one [tragedy] it takes the illustrious persons and not the actions; the verisimilar plot, but not true; the moved affections, but blunted; delight, not sorrow; danger, not death; and from the other [comedy], the moderate laughter, modest pleasure, the false knot, the happy reversal, and above all, comic order...[17]

Part of this merging of tragedy and comedy, of course, involved the mixing of both high and low, illustrious and common personages, to which Denores had objected, particularly in an Arcadian setting. But, Verrato argues, characters of both sorts may indeed be combined in a single plot, as illustrated in one of the author's chief examples from antiquity, Sophocles' *Oedipus Rex* (which would have been fresh on the minds of both Guarini and the true Verato in 1588).[18] Furthermore, Verrato refutes Denores's claims that peasants are all good and simple by their nature, and that there is no hierarchy among them. Citing examples from Virgil and Theocritus, the author contends that shepherds may be simple or noble, have the capacity for wisdom and governance, and at the same time need not be uniformly virtuous and chaste and unsusceptible to corruption. Shepherds, he writes, "are also men like us, and have anger and lust like all others, and in them are the affects of ire, hate, love, jealousy, fear, hope, envy, joy, sorrow, and, in sum, of every other disturbance of the mind no less than city-dwellers have."[19] Later, Verrato goes so far as to cite the prophets and patriarchs of the Old Testament, including Abraham, Isaac, Moses, and David, as models of exalted shepherds, ultimately turning to Jesus as signifying "the profession of a good shepherd," and, thus, the potential hierarchy and diversity of pastoral personages.[20]

Along with his clarification of tragicomedy's status as a discrete genre, Verrato contests Denores's requirement that poetry impart moral and civil instruction, asserting that this new genre also carries a benefit of its own to contemporary audiences. He does this by distinguishing the instrumental, or inherent, end of poetry from the architectonic end that results from it. The instrumental end of tragedy, therefore, is the imitation of misfortune, which, as its architectonic end, purges the spectator's soul homeopathically of excess fear and compassion, whereas comedy, through the instrumental end of imitating the actions of private individuals and moving the audience to laughter, purges the soul allopathically of sorrow and melancholy.[21] But the types of catharsis provided by comedy and tragedy, the author asserts, are no longer relevant in contemporary society, since comedy itself is no longer desirable, and the purgation of terror and pity is accomplished by Scripture—a tool lacking in ancient society, whose own pagan gods were, in fact, principal instigators of the terror-inducing events of tragedy.[22] Verrato's argument, therefore, turns the tables on Guarini's critics, responding to their accusations of heresy against Aristotelian orthodoxy by implying that they, in effect, have privileged classical authority over Scripture.

Tragicomedy has its own instrumental end (tragedy tempered by moderation and laughter), but an architectonic effect similar to that of comedy (in prior times, when it was still effective):

> to imitate onstage an action that is fictional and mixed of all those tragic and comic parts that, with verisimilitude and decorum, can come together properly in a single dramatic form, for the end of purging with delight the sadness of the listeners.[23]

This purpose of delighting audiences—of *movere* (moving) with affect and rhetoric—rendered through a hybrid plot with danger averted for a happy ending, is pertinent to modern citizens as well as to the present-day poet, whose role is not to instruct on good, moral behavior, but to please, leaving audiences in turn with a tempered disposition.[24] (As L'Attizzato would famously contend of poetry in the later *Verato Secondo*, "its end is not to imitate the good, but to imitate well, whether the morals be good or bad."[25]) At the same time, however, Verato explains that the tragic aspect of the plot has an additional *utile* of a homeopathic and ethical purgation of fear and pity not through terror and actual death, as in true tragedy, but through danger, or potential but avoided death (as seen in the narrowly averted executions of both Amarilli and Mirtillo).[26] Such mixing of comedy and tragedy also has precedent in the works of ancient drama, such as the *Amphitryon* of Plautus, which proves more comic, and the satyr play *Cyclops* of Euripides, which proves more tragic.

The author also finds in antiquity examples of the need for poetic forms to adapt to the changing demands of the public. Since all audiences do not share a need for the purgation of terror, tragedy has changed over time, from more playful beginnings to graver episodes, and even (as in Euripides) incorporating satyrs. Verrato concludes:

> And this is the true reason for the differences and grades that characterize the more or less tragic plays, for the poets, seeing the diverse

tastes of the spectators, sometimes composed plays with happy endings in order to relieve that bitterness...[For] most listeners go to public performances for recreation, and not to weep and make themselves sad.[27]

Comedy, too, had changed over the centuries, with the laughter becoming "more or less dissolute, making the plot more or less comic." He refers to the Old Comedies in the manners of Aristophanes and Menander as "sfacciatissime meretrici," or brazen harlots—the very label that would be applied to "modern" music, and specifically to Monteverdi's theoretically defiant *Pastor fido* settings, in 1603—in contrast to "the most chaste and venerable women [Matrone]" of the New Comedy of Plautus and Terence.[28] Even Horace condoned "gravitas mixed with playfulness" ("la gravità mischiar co'l giuoco"), as seen in the satyr play. Thus, Verrato asks, "why would the mixture of tragicomedy be an indecorous composition bereft of art and judgment?"[29] This capacity of poetic forms to evolve gives the author grounds to explain that the eclogue, too, has changed, being ennobled by Aeschylus and Sophocles from its beginnings as trivial entertainment and "simple songs chanted by drunkards" to the ranks of tragedy and comedy.[30] Likewise, the pastoral was elevated as the Muses "grafted tragedy onto the trunk of the dithyramb, and onto the stamen [they grafted] comedy; then, into their most fertile garden, [they] planted the tiny sprig of eclogue," from which blossomed the noble pastoral.[31]

Il Verrato, therefore, sets out four principal points of contention with the rigid reading of the *Poetics* championed by Denores: that the creation of new genres such as tragicomedy was not only legitimate, but necessary; that tragicomedy had its own roots in classical poetry; that certain aspects of Aristotelian theory were universal and fixed, while others could be adapted over time; and that poetry is not bound to any moral or didactic obligation—its primary purpose is not to instruct through the example of its characters, but to delight its listeners, thereby relieving them of melancholy (through laughter) and fear (through scarcely averted peril). He also defends the pastoral as a viable dramatic mode alongside tragedy and comedy in the types of plot and characters that it could support: the rustic setting, in effect, posed few limitations in terms of language, action, scope, and gravity.

As customary in pamphlet wars, the same views from both sides are largely reiterated in the next round of debate between critic and supporter (again, masked by a pseudonym). Still, whereas the series of exchanges has become known in scholarship collectively as the "*Pastor fido* debate," Denores, in his *Apologia contra l'auttor del Verrato* (1590), again makes no mention of *Il pastor fido* by name or any specific aspect of it.[32] In fact, he denies outright that his criticisms were aimed at any existing work at all, but rather claims that they merely reflected his "opinion on a general, universal matter in defense of Aristotle." The Paduan philosopher declares that he has "never seen, nor read, nor heard performed that very poem that was approved and lauded by Your Most Illustrious Lordships"—a denial that L'Attizato would later forcefully challenge.[33]

A noteworthy argument of the critic's new rebuttal is his more vigorous rejection of the eclogue as a source for dramatic poetry—namely, the pastoral. Denores restates his dismissal of both the eclogue and pastoral on the grounds that they confer no benefit to urban dwellers, but rather threaten to entice them to move to the countryside. He further admonishes the eclogue in its new guise for its unwieldy scope, profuse and ornamented lyricism, and lack of decorum: while the eclogue is certainly permitted to expand, Denores objects to the idea that it could evolve into another genre, as Verrato had proposed. The critic writes:

> If it is born an eclogue, it continues to grow as an eclogue and is always called an eclogue. But being born an eclogue, in growing it cannot become a comedy or tragedy, or in its virility become an epic. Who has ever seen born a lamb that then, in its development, changes into a horse, and in its stature reaches the size of an elephant?[34]

Denores was, in fact, correct in his judgment that an overgrown eclogue "is always called an eclogue," given the repeated uses of the label—seemingly to Guarini's displeasure—for *Il pastor fido*. New to Denores's argument, however, is the reasoning that Aristotle intentionally excludes specific types of poetry because they fail to comply with his fundamental principles of poetics. Aristotle, he explains:

> excludes from future poetry hymns, *nomoi*, and dithyrambs because they do not contain an action that progresses either from fortune to failure, or from failure to prosperity, and because they do not have scope within a fixed time; and Priapic poems, because they are imperfect, dishonest, and no longer used; and the *citaristica* and those of flutes because they imitate not with words, but with poetic meter or harmony, or with gestures and sound; and eclogues because they do not contain a complete action or a change of fortune, and because they are games, preludes, scenes [*disposizioni*], and *presercitamenti* rather than truly complete poetic compositions.[35]

A rebuttal to Denores's *Apologia* came in *Il Verato secondo*, purportedly written in 1591, but, for reasons unknown to the author, not published until 1593.[36] The pamphlet bears a dedication to Vincenzo Gonzaga, praising the duke for his attention to staging the work—albeit unsuccessfully, as would soon become evident—and for his generous protection of both the poet and the play.[37] The author identifies himself only as "l'Attizzato Accademico Ferrarese," for the original author, Verrato, had died. In the prefatory letter to his "benigni lettori," the author explains that with Denores's own death in 1590, some may deem a rebuttal inappropriate—as indeed it was by critical etiquette—but it should be remembered that Denores had done the same to Verrato by issuing his *Apologia* after the latter's death. Moreover,

L'Attizzato explains that he writes not against the Paduan critic himself, but to the living readers "against the doctrine of Denores, which lives in his letters," and with the aim of defending the honor of one who was offended undeservedly—that is, of course, Guarini.

The author's disclaimer for attacking a dead man is warranted, for the tone of the debate changes considerably between the empirical and dispassionate *Verrato* and the spiteful *Verato secondo*. Indeed, living up to the moniker L'Attizzato, or "the incited one," the author is scathing in his rebuke of the *Apologia* and in his personal attacks on Denores. The treatise is the first in the debate to identify *Il pastor fido* by name, not only in its title (*Il Verato secondo…in difesa del Pastor fido*), but also throughout the defense, with brief but frequent references to the tragicomedy, most often simply with a terse statement such as "come nel Pastorfido si vede…" (as one sees in *Il pastor fido*). The chief focus of the protracted and unrelenting pamphlet, however, centers on disproving Denores's *Apologia* issue by issue, statement by statement, singling out a multitude of faults in the moral philosopher's own rebuttal against Verrato—from his false reasonings, simple reiterations of earlier arguments from the 1586 *Discorso* (often nearly verbatim), and failure to address particular matters, to his misrepresentations of Verrato's statements and contortion of Aristotelian doctrine. The sardonic tenor of the text is made clear from the very start with the claim that Denores's *Apologia* is itself a tragicomedy:

> More malicious and less intelligent than ever, Messer Jason de Nores, with his second invective, masked with the guise of Apology—which instead deserves the name Alogia [i.e., dysfunctional speech]—goes mixing comic lies with tragic quarrels against the author of *Il pastor fido*. He has indeed, against his intentions, composed one of those tragicomedies that, as marvelous mixtures, he furnishes with repeated attacks and vain torment.[38]

Denores, like so many scholars after him, ascribed *Il Verrato* to Guarini, in spite of the denials of Verrato, L'Attizzato, and Guarini.[39] But L'Attizzato refutes this attribution up front, charging Denores with attacking a poet who never offended him or even defended himself against the Paduan professor's initial attack.

The *Verato secondo* comprises four parts: (1) a disclosure of "the artifice… of the sophistic Apologista"; (2) a defense of "the modesty of Verrato against the immodesty of Denores"; (3) proof that "the poem defended by Verrato is well defended and poorly accused"; and (4) attestation that "the poem mixed of parts tragic and comic, called *tragicommedia* by the author of *Il pastor fido*, is a legitimate poem according to Aristotle."[40]

The first part of the defense scrutinizes Denores's tactic in the *Apologia* of casting himself as being on the defensive—when, the author claims, he was the attacker—and accuses the philosopher of altering his statements and arguments from the 1586 *Discorso* when quoting them in the *Apologia*—a charge raised repeatedly throughout the *Verato secondo*. The second part, devoted to "treating the immodesty" of Guarini's detractor, aims to undercut Denores on three fronts: his betrayal of Guarini as a friend, the unlikelihood that the Paduan critic could have had access to a legitimate text of *Il pastor fido* before attacking it in 1586, and finally, by weighing the professor's character against that of Verrato and Guarini. Linking the critic's betrayal of Guarini to the civic, utilitarian demands of his own poetic theory, L'Attizzato frames Denores as one of "those who give the first move in dissolving friendship—that is, that divine chain with which human life and companionship are conserved, and from which springs the happy state of Republics."[41] Denores, in other words, becomes the embodiment of precisely what he makes *Il pastor fido* out to be: a bane to well-ordered society.

As discussed earlier with respect to the performance history of the play in the 1580s, L'Attizzato criticizes Denores for attacking a work he claims never to have "seen, nor read, nor heard performed," which leads L'Attizzato to assert that by 1586 (the year of Denores's *Discorso*) the play was "still neither printed, nor performed, being still in the hand of the author."[42] This being the case, the author then asks where Denores might have encountered other specimens of pastoral tragicomedy: in the bookshops of Venice, in the bookshop of Paolo Meitti in Padua, or through the circles of Paduan literati, such as Zabarella and Riccoboni? In other words, in the places frequented by Denores, where *Il pastor fido* was known, discussed, "many times read and reread" by the poet, and "most highly lauded" by the listeners in the mid-1580s. Even more, if Denores truly never had examined *Il pastor fido*, as he maintains, how could he criticize the genre and unity of pastoral tragicomedy, of which *Il pastor fido* was the only modern example?[43]

But Denores had allegedly encountered another tragicomedy, not through a written text, but through *commedianti*, a class of performers disparaged by the professor—and, as we have seen, feared by the poet for their leaking of corrupt copies of his play from the Turin production. L'Attizzato seizes upon the notion that Denores had founded his writings and applications of Aristotelian theory on such dubious sources, mocking:

> From *commedianti dalla gazzetta* (good Lord!) Messer Jasone has taken the idea of such *favole*. From *commedianti dalla gazzetta* he has undertaken defending (what insult!) the great Aristotle. Through *commedianti dalla gazzetta* he has composed his poetics, his discourses. [...] Will it be more likely, then, that you took the idea of pastoral tragicomedy from one never seen, but only heard recited from memory by *commedianti dalla gazzetta*, than from the *Pastor fido*, most celebrated in all of Venice, in all of Padua, in all of Italy?[44]

L'Attizzato then redoubles his assault, first by attacking Denores's character, then with a series of direct blows that brand the critic "a beast," "an ignoramus, and a maligner," and berate him for his own personal invectives against Verrato, when Verrato had merely disapproved of Denores' reasonings and work.[45] L'Attizzato frames the author, "Il Verrato," as the actual Verato, the Ferrarese actor, rather than a pseudonym, and defends him as "a man of good, of honor, considered by all the world a good citizen of his homeland," whereas Denores does not merit the titles "Illustrissimo" and "Signore" that grace the rest of the "Illustrissima casa Nores."[46]

The third part of the pamphlet—devoted to "demonstrating that the *Poema* which Verrato defended is well defended by him and poorly accused by Denores"—occupies nearly three-fourths of its length and represents a substantial recapitulation and reinforcement of the major points of the debate: that Aristotle never intended to limit poetry to three principal genres; that the aim of poetry is not to uphold the laws of moral and civil philosophy, but to imitate well; and that tragicomedy is composed not of distinct tragic and comic plots, but of a single plot that unifies and tempers the two. The author is likewise careful to secure credit for Guarini for his dramaturgical innovations, while at the same time placing him in a lineage of esteemed masters and declaiming the new hybrid form on the title page of the work. The poet himself would later ensure this legacy with the lavish 1602 Ciotti edition, which combined a synopsis of the two defenses and new *Annotazioni* with the play itself. Composer Claudio Monteverdi would employ a similar tactic in defending several of his *Pastor fido* musical settings in print in 1605 and 1607 by staking a claim for the term *seconda pratica* to denote his progressive approach to text-setting, while also framing himself as the heir of Cipriano de Rore, Marc'Antonio Ingegneri, Giaches de Wert, Luca Marenzio, and other acknowledged masters who advanced this new practice.[47]

Of particular relevance to the play's ingress into the realm of music in this part of *Il Verato secondo* is the considerable amount of attention devoted to Guarini's use of shepherds and the pastoral mode in a full-scale dramatic work. The topic arises first as L'Attizzato points out the essential flaw of Denores's criticism of using shepherds onstage—hence, as models of good citizenry for the populace—which is that urban citizens innately have more vices than shepherds, which should (by Denores's standards) make pastoral characters, in fact, better subjects for the stage. Rather than object to the pastoral, one might expect Denores to see such plays as beneficial to the republic, for "by the light of nature," shepherds seek goodness, kindness, and religion. Moreover, "the first men of the Jews were—and were called— shepherds," as were such eminent historical personages as Romulus, Remus, and Moses.[48]

The author soon turns his attention to the objections of "the Apologist of false name" to the uses of "parlar figurato" (metaphorical speech) and "ornamenti de' poeti lirici" (ornaments of lyric poetry) in pastoral drama. Although he "could discuss this inane and frivolous opposition at length, citing innumerable authorities from the Greek and Latin writers," the author need only turn to the *Poetics* and *Rhetoric* "of Aristotle, the sole master of all others," for whom metaphor and ornaments are, quite simply, basic aspects of poetry, and specifically of dramatic poetry.[49] To Denores' claim that Aristotle "does not take aim at metaphors and ornaments as such, but as lyrics, which are improper and poorly suited to dramatic poetry," L'Attizzato challenges the critic "to show us which ornaments are lyric, and which are dramatic, and how they are different."[50]

The discussion of language and ornaments leads to the author's distinction of "two manners of lyric poetry": "one florid, grand, agitated, excited, full of gravitas," which is the manner of Pindar and Horace, "the other graceful, delicate, calm, full of seemliness, full of beauty, which is that of Anacreon," as well as Catullus, Petrarch, and Giovanni della Casa.[51] The association with Petrarch seems to be the aim of this delineation of lyric style, as the author states: "I will not deny the ornamental lyrics in *Il pastor fido*, if one means with the style, metaphors, voice, and verse resembling those of Petrarch and of his followers"; after all, "who should one imitate if not the purest and most noble writer that our language has known?"[52] As we will see, purity of language was indeed a foremost concern for Guarini: he sought input specifically on such matters when sending a late draft of the play to the Florentine Accademia della Crusca, a group devoted to codifying the Tuscan vernacular and purging it of contaminations and improprieties. The connection of Guarini's dramatic style with the style of Petrarch, too, highlights well the play's imminent role in Italian music, as it would assume a place alongside Petrarch's *Canzoniere* as one of the foremost sources of lyric verse for polyphonic madrigals.

On the questions of the artful style and sophisticated rhetoric of Guarini's dramatic language—qualities intimately tied to the play's burgeoning relationship with music and specifically the madrigal—L'Attizzato responds with scrupulous detail:

> Given, then, the distinction of these two styles [those of Pindar and Anacreon], if our opponent speaks of the grand [style], I say this is utterly false, since if one found in *Il pastor fido* such ornaments, being elaborate and forceful, they would not be suitable to the verisimilitude of who is speaking. Yet they are appropriate to one who lauds, celebrates, or prays, or one who, taken by a great furor, seeks to amplify, illustrate, and carry to the heavens the subject of which he speaks. In *Il pastor fido*, the verse is not pompous; it is not clamorous, not dithyrambic. Its episodes are not long, not terse, not complex, not harsh, not difficult to understand without rereading them many times. Its metaphors are taken from meaningful *topoi*, from *topoi* not distant, from pertinent *topoi*. Its locution is pure, but not base; familiar, but not vulgar; figurative, not enigmatic; elegant, not affected; grand, not inflated; affectionate, not weak. And so, to conclude in a single word, as it is not far from ordinary speech, so it is also not close to that of the plebes. It is not so elaborate

that the setting abhors it, nor so vulgar that the audience despises it, but one can perform it without annoyance, and read it without strain.[53]

"Is *Il pastor fido* not set in Arcadia?" L'Attizzato asks. "It is no marvel, then, if the shepherds of Arcadia, being most noble, embellish their reasonings with poetic elegance, being more than any other nation friends of the Muses."[54] Such lofty verse, therefore, is entirely fitting—that is, verisimilar—for the shepherds of Arcadia, who were raised as poet–musicians. Citing Polybius, the author writes:

> That all Arcadians were poets; that their principal study, their prin-
> cipal endeavor was music; that they learned it as children; that their
> laws bound them to learn it; that the choruses of their children were
> accustomed to celebrating with song the praises of their heroes, their
> gods; that in this profession they had as teachers the most renowned
> musicians of Greece; that they spent all their life, all their activity in
> song and in verse; so that to know little of anything else other than being
> a good musician was not the slightest insult.[55]

The author immediately bolsters this stance on poetic, musical shepherds by calling on the example of two additional masters:

> If Theocritus and Virgil at times made country folk, out of habit, speak
> so nobly, why is it not right for us to make Priests and Heroes speak
> ornately, when their profession—by both custom and law—was nothing
> but music and poetry?[56]

Armed with the authority of Polybius, Theocritus, and Virgil, L'Attizzato embarks on a lengthy exegesis of Verrato's argument that pastoral drama grew out of the eclogue—a discussion that yields the first direct reference to the events of *Il pastor fido* in the debate, as the author cites the exchange between Silvio and Dorinda in act 4, scene 9, after Silvio inadvertently wounds Dorinda with an arrow, as an example of an eclogue adorned by a dramatic context.[57] By grounding the association between music, lyric verse, and Arcadian life in ancient practice, Guarini's advocate explicitly backs the use of shepherds and the pastoral mode in a tragicomic drama, but he implicitly does much more: he validates the incorporation of music into performances of *Il pastor fido*—or any pastoral play—presumably in "diegetic" fashion (i.e., as part of the onstage action), as in the *Gioco della cieca* and end-of-act choruses, when the characters onstage break into song.[58] Not only were music, metaphors, ornamented speech, and other qualities of lyric poetry acceptable in a pastoral drama, but they could also enhance the verisimilitude and decorum of such a work by allowing Arcadians to behave as they realistically would by nature. Music and lyricism in a work like *Il pastor fido*, in other words, should be expected, not rebuked.

In the fourth and final part of *Il Verato secondo*, the author sets out to demonstrate "that the poem, mixed of tragic and comic parts, is poetry according to Aristotle."[59] The discussion centers first on celebrated examples of "new species derived from the fount of poetic nature, taught to us by the Philosopher," including Dante's *commedia*, Petrarch's *trionfo*, and Ariosto's *romanzo*—all of which (like Guarini's *tragicommedia pastorale*) arose after Aristotle's *Poetics* and supplemented his three principal genres.[60] Focus then turns toward the crucial argument over unity in the plot of a work composed of both tragic and comic elements. The issue prompts the second (and last) discussion of specific details in *Il pastor fido*. To counter Denores' accusation that the plot is necessarily double and lacking unity, the author explains that all events revolve around and serve the central plot involving Amarilli and Mirtillo. The removal of any aspect of the story or any character would destroy the chain of occurrences that leads ultimately to the *lieto fine*.[61]

The discussion of the plot of *Il pastor fido*, as grand an undertaking as it might seem, is conspicuously brief, as though the author only reluctantly brings the work, at long last, directly into the critical spotlight (perhaps because it was shaky ground for an argument). In all, the number of pages devoted to the discussion of the work's plot—as opposed to the superficial references to its title that are so common—could likely be counted on one hand. Here, after a mere two pages, L'Attizzato abruptly shifts the focus to Euripides' tragedy *Hecuba*, then toward the debate surrounding Ariosto's *Orlando furioso* and other sundry topics before concluding the pamphlet.

By the time *Il Verato secondo* was issued in 1593, the play had already appeared in nine Italian editions from printers in Ferrara, Venice, Mantua, Pavia, Tours, and London, as well as in its first French translation, *Le Berger fidelle: pastorale* (Tours, 1593). Indeed, L'Attizzato's claim that the play "lives [and] pleases, praised, loved, and read" ("vive, piace, lodato, amato, e letto") proves accurate and telling in its emphasis on readers ("letto") rather than spectators ("visto" or "udito").[62] The disfavor shown by Denores and other conservative critics, in other words, seems to have done little to discourage the public's demand for the play—at least in print—both in Italy and abroad.

How much the critical debate between Denores and the play's supporters influenced the discussion and reception of the work in Italian courts and academies is difficult to ascertain, but its effect could not have been entirely unfavorable. While the general public showed keen interest in the work as a literary and theatrical text, intellectual, courtly, and academic circles might have found additional cause to scrutinize it and weigh both sides of the polemic, only increasing the play's readership as a whole. At least this is the impression one gathers not only from the steadily growing number of editions issued across Italy and Europe, but also from the sudden trend that enveloped Italian secular music from the mid-1590s through the 1640s, as composers of all statures included settings of *Pastor fido* texts in collections dedicated to patrons, both secular and ecclesiastical, across the peninsula and north of the Alps. The critical disfavor, therefore, seems to have done little to discourage the interest of composers, their patrons, and their readers.

One charge that Denores introduced in his second attack proves particularly germane to the play's relatively seamless transition into the realm of music: that of its "putting into the mouths of shepherds certain metaphorical speech with ornaments of lyric poets"[63]—a quality that, the Paduan critic argued, is entirely inappropriate in a theatrical work, for it belonged to the lower art of dithyrambic poetry. Writing in 1590, Denores would not have been aware that within ten years the play's lyricism would be so eagerly embraced not only by silent readers, but also by composers and performers and presumably their noble, learned, and ecclesiastical patrons and audiences. But the critic might have witnessed the trend in its formative beginnings, which saw variant passages from the tragicomedy set to music by Luca Marenzio (1587), Annibale Coma (1588), Philippe de Monte (1590), and others. To put this in perspective, the number of known musical settings with textual ties to *Il pastor fido* by 1590 already surpassed that of Tasso's pastoral play, *Aminta*, which was first performed in 1573 and published in 1580 (Cremona: Cristoforo Draconi).

By the time *Il Verato secondo* came to press in 1593, musical settings from Guarini's work had continued to appear in steady succession (Table 3.1). As James Chater has pointed out, however, the majority of these works, including those published after the play came to print, seem to have taken their texts not from the play itself, but from variant poems that circulated independently potentially before being incorporated into the play.[64] Given the rapid appeal of *Pastor fido* texts to madrigal composers in these early years, the charge of lyricism would seem difficult to repudiate; hence, L'Attizzato did the very opposite: he embraced and rationalized its lyricism as not only fitting, but essential to an Arcadian setting. The notion that certain of the play's speeches had actually derived from preexisting autonomous lyric poems, however, was an offense that Denores had overlooked, but that later critics would seize upon.

Table 3.1 Earliest Known *Il pastor fido* Settings

1584–85(?)	L. Luzzaschi	Music for *Il gioco della cieca* (lost) and possibly two madrigals published in 1601	
1587	L. Marenzio	*O che soave e non inteso bacio*[65]	*IV a 6*
1588	A. Coma	*Non sospirar, cor mio, non sospirare*	*II a 4*
1590	P. de Monte	*O d'aspido più sorda e più fugace*	*XIV a 5*
1591	L. Leoni	*Quell'augellin che canta*	*Bella Clori*
1592	C. Monteverdi	*O primavera, gioventù de l'anno*[66]	*III a 5*
1592–93	Wert, Rovigo, and Massarano	Music for a planned performance in Mantua	
1593	G. Belli	*Ah, dolente partita*	*III a 6*
1593	P. de Monte	*Non son, come a te pare*	*XVI a 5*

The Second Wave of Debate, 1600–01

The controversy surrounding the play, of course, did not end in 1593 with *Il Verato secondo*, but rather changed hands to a new pack of contenders. Denores by this time had died, and although Guarini in the coming years produced his *Compendio* (1599, pub. 1601) and the *Annotazioni* for the voluminous 1602 Ciotti edition, he did not (re)engage directly in the debate. This may have been due to the fact that in this second round of debate that ensued around 1600 other voices came to the defense of both tragicomedy and Guarini's work in particular. These proponents, however, did not outnumber the multitude of voices inveighing against the play.

Though couched in the role of running commentary on the work, and not in critical defense, Guarini's *Annotazioni sopra Il pastor fido* continue the tactics of the earlier defenses of invoking a host of literary models and authorities from antiquity (Aristotle, Plato, Virgil, Dante, Cicero, Ovid, Catullus, Homer, Anacreon, and others) to more contemporary times (including Petrarch, Boccaccio, Sannazaro, Tasso, Ariosto, and Guarini himself) in support of the play. The exegesis guides the reader through the entirety of the plot, proceeding nearly verse by verse with intertextual references and interpretative explanations, beginning with the very title, *Il pastor fido*—a reference to the protagonist, Mirtillo—which, the poet explains, was inspired by Petrarch and, like Petrarch's *Canzoniere*, shows the main character in the end as a virtuous model of love and faith.[67] These references might be seen as the poet's implicit effort to insinuate his place within a lineage of venerable writers, whose tradition—the author reassures us—finds new vigor and purpose in the novel genre of pastoral tragicomedy. Guarini's alignment of his work morally and thematically—if not stylistically and rhetorically—with Petrarch, moreover, may be revealing, as if conceding to some extent that the work is not entirely in keeping with dramatic poetry, and therefore embracing its affinity to Petrarch as an exemplar of its lyrical, rhetorical vein. The *Annotazioni* have also proven an important historical document: we have already encountered, for example, Guarini's description of the genesis of the *Gioco della cieca* that seems to defy the trope in late-Cinquecento scholarship of *musica per poesia* by subordinating the text to the choreography and music in the compositional process.

Despite the labored effort of the *Annotazioni* to buttress the play with elucidation and authority and offer a definitive, yet indirect, *risposta* to its critics, Guarini could not have been too troubled at this point over the acceptance of the work by the general, public readership. By the time of the 1602 Ciotti edition, the total number of editions of the play in Italy alone had climbed to at least twenty, with some forty more issued in the following century. Also in 1602, translations in English and Spanish followed the 1593 edition in French,[68] and in 1609, the text appeared in a bilingual edition for French/Italian language instruction.[69] Indeed, by Nicolas Perella's judgment, "throughout the seventeenth century, the *Pastor Fido* was the most widely read book of secular literature in all of Europe."[70] In this case, the fact that the work had garnered a number of vocal adversaries in learned corners is hardly a surprise.

While more meticulous in citing the faults of Guarini's tragicomedy, the second wave of attacks primarily builds on the arguments of Denores rather than raising new issues of their own. Unlike Denores, however, these later critics would have seen firsthand the play's growing appeal in the realms of literature, theater, and music, as the number of madrigal settings soared around the turn of the century. The play's lyricism, sensuality, rhetorical elegance, and abundance of emotive, self-contained monologues seemed to invite this conversion into music, as excerpts from its scenes could be transplanted directly from their theatrical, mimetic context into the diegetic (narrative) multi-voice setting of the madrigal with little or no need for revision, as if they were lyric poems. For although a handful of musical settings connected to the play had appeared by 1593, a pivotal change took place the following years, when Luca Marenzio published four *Pastor fido* settings in his Sixth Book of madrigals for five voices (1594) and twelve more (one composed by Antonio Bicci) in his Seventh Book (1595), and Giaches de Wert issued four in his Eleventh Book (1595). Thereafter, madrigal collections containing multiple *Pastor fido* settings began to appear, and by 1600, composers were devoting entire books to settings from the play, even advertising the fact with titles that referred overtly to the pastoral, its scenes, and its characters—such as *La cieca* of Gabriele Fattorini (1598) and Marsilio Casentini (1609); *Il pastor fido* of Monte (1600), Giovanni Piccioni (1602), and Giovanni Nicolò Mezzogorri (1617); *Corisca* of Biasio Tomasi (1613); and *L'Amarillide* of Scipione Cerreto (1621). As James Chater has described it, in terms of the musical history of Guarini's tragicomedy, "the first ten years [1584–94] turns out to contain a mere trickle of texts, suddenly swelling into a flood in the 1594–95 settings of Wert and Marenzio."[71]

Marenzio's and Wert's books of 1595 also signal a marked shift in the relationship of the musical settings to the play by identifying the play's characters for the first time by name. Philippe de Monte's 1591 setting of the variant *O d'aspido più sorda e più fugace*, for example, is very different from an interpretative and referential standpoint from Marenzio's and Wert's 1595 settings of that same speech from act 1, scene 2, but beginning with the line *Cruda Amarilli, che col nome ancora*. Such explicit references to a named character strengthen the music's ties to both the play and the specific scenarios of its plot and personas, thus heightening the potential for intertextual reading and expanding the interpretative scope of the madrigals.

In all, despite the pastoral's rocky beginnings in the theatrical and critical realms, it apparently encountered no such difficulty as a printed, literary text for reading or musical setting. It is understandable given this trajectory of the play's musical history through the 1590s why critics after Denores so ardently and consistently condemned it for its lyrical quality and apparent cross-fertilization with poetic madrigals, even alluding directly to its currency in the realm of music. The first critic in this renewed exchange,

Faustino Summo—a student of Denores and a lecturer of logic at the university in Padua (cited in Chapter 2 for his comments on the play's appeal to women readers)—for example, writes in his *Discorsi poetici* (1600):

> The style of this writer is (as Signor Denores had rightly judged) entirely lyric, and badly suited to dramatic composition, given that if one removed only a few parts—where the style is too relaxed and beyond the bounds of decorum, and often irrelevant and contrary to verisimilitude—the rest is suitable only for singing of love to the sound of the kithara. [...] And indeed, such a style would well befit *sonettini*, *canzonette*, and *madrigaletti*, in which the author is well experienced.[72]

In criticizing Guarini's improper, licentious use of the kiss in scenes such as the recounted "kissing game" between Amarilli and her nymphs (act 2, scene 6), the *Gioco della cieca* (act 3, scene 2), and the passage containing "O che soave e non inteso bacio" (act 5, scene 8), set by Marenzio in 1587, Summo also raises concerns about Guarini's reputation as a lyric poet and his capacity to compose in a style suitable to dramatic poetry. He even goes so far as to accuse the poet of recycling many of his "laudable *madrigaletti* composed earlier on the subject of the kiss" for use in the play, essentially "pulling them out of their first native soil, where they were kept, flowering, beautiful, and bright, and ruining them by transplanting them in a strange new site." This, Summo argues, only shows Guarini to be "a man of little talent and judgment," who resorts to reusing poems out of a "povertà d'invenzione."[73] Summo concludes that, with his lyrical and sensuous Petrarchan style, "it seems the author has designed to do nothing other than show himself as fair and lascivious...in order to earn the hearts and favors of beautiful and courteous Ladies and pretty, elegant youths."[74] There may indeed have been grounds for Summo's suspicion—or, perhaps, envy—given Guarini's letter from around 1595 to Pietro Duodo boasting that "*Il pastor fido* has become the delights of those beautiful and never adequately exalted and revered Ladies of France."[75]

In June that year (1600), in his *Considerationi sopra Il pastor fido*—a work we had encountered earlier for its description of the "circumcision of the Faithful Shepherd" for the November 1598 performance in Mantua—Giovanni Pietro Malacreta condemned the tragicomedy on many counts, weighing it not only against examples of antiquity, but also against Tasso's *Aminta*, thereby calling attention to the close kinship between the two Ferrarese plays that the two *Verrati* conspicuously skirted.[76] Malacreta also takes issue with the tragicomedy's viability as dramatic verse owing to the abundance of reflective, lyric-like passages suitable to a volume of *rime* when he writes:

> I leave to one side how satisfied the judicious spectator or reader might be when, believing that he hears a true imitation of someone in despair, he hears a senseless collection of madrigals.[77]

Though Malacreta does not explain why madrigal-like speeches are inappropriate as a vehicle for conveying despair, or how such a speech differs from "vera imitazione," presumably what troubled him was the sheer volume of monologues that could function just as well outside the play (as autonomous, lyric poems) as within it (as the imitated speech of their specific characters), as well as possibly the mannered, unverisimilar linguistic style. These sentiments resonated well into the Seicento, as critics repeatedly compared the style and language of the play to those of poetic madrigals. In his *Proginnasmi poetici* (c.1627), for instance, Benedetto Fioretti dubs the tragicomedy a "filza di madrigali amorosi" (string of amorous madrigals), and N. Villani writes in 1631 that "you could gather from this tale nearly sixty madrigals"—a judgment that was, in fact, a sizeable underestimate.[78] Malacreta goes one step further, however, by criticizing Guarini's tendency to lapse into a lyric, madrigalian style in his attempts to "imitate the affects well," then citing specific examples of poetic "madrigals" that spring from Guarini's efforts to "imitate desperate Mirtillo." Indeed, Malacreta's examples include many speeches that by 1600 were already circulating independently as polyphonic madrigals, and that were to become some of the most widely set passages of the era, including "Cruda Amarilli, che col nome ancora," "Ah dolente partita," "Udite, lagrimosi," and "M'è più dolce il penar per Amarilli."[79] This fact may indeed have influenced Malacreta's judgment and selections. But whether even these self-contained musical settings truly shed their identities as components of the play and became "raccolte di madrigali" or retained some degree of interpretative ties to the plot (now in the form of reported speech of their given characters) is another matter—one that will be explored more closely in the analytical chapters that follow.

A rebuttal against Malacreta quickly followed in September 1600, in the *Risposta alle considerazioni o dubbi dell'eccellentissimo signor dottor Malacreta…sopra il Pastorfido* (Venice: Paolo Ugolino, 1600) of Paolo Beni, a lecturer in humanities at the university in Padua. Beni's defense deals with Malacreta's attack issue by issue, focusing on topics ranging from the play's genre and verisimilitude to the poet's freedom to invent plots, characters, customs, and actions, rather than adhering to historical accuracy. Beni's appreciation of the work's poetic language and lyricism, meanwhile, is widely apparent. In his address to the readers at the outset, Beni claims:

> In *Il pastor fido* is found something quite outstanding and rare; this, without doubt, is the grandeur and gracefulness of the verse, which, accompanied by the sharpness and charm of the conceits, renders the poem the most famous of this sort that has perhaps been heard or read to this day.[80]

Also, the lyrical style, Beni (like L'Attizzato) contends, is entirely in keeping with the pastoral setting, owing to Arcadians' propensity for music, as many examples from antiquity support.[81] Beni continues by dismissing one of the earliest complaints raised by Denores: that of the play's alleged inability to carry out the purgative effects of either comedy or tragedy. Beni explains that, while

> delighting the ears and filling the hearts with such grace of conceits and sweetness of rhyme and verse, it tempers and enlivens the souls...improving the behavior of the listeners by rendering them more cautious and prudent, and, in a word, more harmonious and wise.[82]

Another defense of the play came also from Paduan circles the following year—Giovanni Savio's *Apologia...in difesa del Pastor fido tragicomedia pastorale*—which advocated a more liberal understanding of Aristotelian poetics.[83] As the author admits in his opening letter to the readers, Paolo Beni had beaten him to the press with his response to Malacreta, published some five months earlier in August 1600. But Savio claims that his own work was written by September 1600 (though published on 1 February 1601), and he has many considerations to add to the fray. By this time, Guarini had been in Florence for nearly two years in the service of the Grand Duke, Ferdinando de' Medici—a patron who, as we have seen, had shown great interest in the play. Consequently, Savio dedicates his *Apologia* to Grand Duke Ferdinando, explaining that he defends *Il pastor fido* on Guarini's behalf so that the poet ("suo secretario") could devote more time to his service.

Savio was evidently an active participant in Paduan intellectual discussions of the work and the issues surrounding it. As he states at the opening, having found himself "in a circle of gentlemen where this subject is debated, and with some, by the reasoning of these Signori [Summo, Malacreta, and Ingegneri], having fallen into the opinion that there are many imperfections in *Il pastor fido*," he feels compelled to defend the play against its detractors.[84] Hence, he begins by ridiculing previous critics' motivations for entering "quella famosissima controversia": Summo, he contends, criticized the work "simply to defend his friend, Signor Jasone [Denores]," and Malacreta, only "to exercise his mind and pen and provoke others to write."[85]

Savio divides his *Apologia* into three parts, the first dealing with the genre of tragicomedy in general, the second focusing specifically on aspects of Guarini's plot singled out for disparagement (unity of plot being the foremost issue), and the last examining all aspects of the play ("Pastor fido disteso"), with much attention devoted to the components of *dispositio* and *elocutio*.[86] Just as this second wave of critics relies heavily on the initial arguments of Denores, Savio's defense is largely indebted to the earlier retaliations of the two *Verrati*, which is made apparent by repeated references to L'Attizzato, such as "the point is clarified by l'Attizzato" ("il ponto vien chiarito dall'Attizzato"), "as l'Attizzato says well" ("come bene dichiara l'Attizzato"), and "all of this has already been noted by l'Attizzato" ("tutto questo ha notato anco l'Attizzato").

What is most interesting about Savio's writing for our purposes, then, is not so much its critical stance, but the insight it provides into how vastly divergent the play's public reception was from its reception by certain vehement academics. As Savio describes it, the play enjoyed immense favor among its general readership, in spite of those few critics attempting to derail Guarini's success. In the opening letter to the reader, he writes hyperbolically:

> *Il pastor fido*, by Signor Cavaliere Battista Guarino, being at this point lauded and accepted not only by every nation, but by people of all types, is also now bitterly censured, after having been embraced by all the world, beyond that disputation made against it by Signor Jasone de Nores, of good memory.[87]

Savio seems to imply that the play's public appeal only stoked renewed opposition from scholastic corners, which might explain the sudden onslaught of pamphlets issued around 1600, after the initial bout of the controversy had cooled for several years. One might suspect that these later critics, while undoubtedly primed by other recent literary quarrels and discussions thereof among academic circles, sought to capitalize to some extent on the play's current fashionability by linking themselves to it—albeit as adversaries—as a means of exposure (a strategy that, as this study demonstrates, seems to have worked in their favor).

In the end, Savio's ultimate vindication of the play is twofold, echoing the fundamental arguments from the two *Verrati*: that tragicomedy is a valid genre with ancient roots, and that it benefits the public through delight.[88] The difference now, however, is that Savio has witnessed the play's effects on its audience of readers and, therefore, can attest to the effectiveness of both its instrumental and architectonic ends. As the author writes toward the end of the first part of his *Apologia*:

> Now, with such grand commotion and applause from so many cities, so many provinces, so many kingdoms that praise *Il pastor fido*, how does one hear the jeers of four or six who might condemn it? How does one not clearly see that tragicomedies are rational, good works? [...] It is not the invention of Signor Cavaliere [Guarini]; no, tragicomedy is an ancient poem.[89]

In the second part of his defense enter two issues of particular interest: the refutation of several criticisms made by Angelo Ingegneri (Guarini's former colleague in the preparations of *Oedipus Rex* in Vicenza in the early 1580s), and the justification for the alleged truncation of the play for the November 1598 performance in Mantua. Ingegneri has been cast in recent literature chiefly as a proponent for *Il pastor fido*, owing to his support—highlighted in Weinberg's synopsis of the debate—of pastoral and tragicomedy, which he claims (like the *Verrati*) are preferable in modern times to both tragedy and comedy.[90] Savio acknowledges Ingegneri's support of the play's genre, but he nevertheless takes issue with Ingegneri's criticisms of Guarini's pastoral indirectly through judgments about the appropriate scope and casting of such a work. In his *Della poesia rappresentativa e del modo di rappresentare le favole sceniche* (1598), Ingegneri states generally that a pastoral play should not exceed 2,500 verses and twelve characters in order to be manageably staged and enjoyed by spectators. *Il pastor fido* far exceeds both of these parameters, with more than 6,000 verses and no fewer than eighteen characters (apart from the choruses).[91] By comparison, Tasso's *Aminta* has some 2,000 lines and nine individual roles.

Savio has two lines of defense for Guarini's massive work. First, he argues plainly that "one cannot consider something prolix that pleases, but rather that which creates boredom and annoyance."[92] He counters Ingegneri's claim about the limited number of personages by asserting that the larger number of characters in Guarini's play may, in fact, "help our cause":

> For such performances can only be attempted by *persone grandi*, who with authority assemble a large cast, whose stage is able to match the reputation of this work and this author. Precisely so was *Il pastor fido* performed in Savoy with royal pomp, in Venice many times (but always by figures of great standing), and chosen many times by the Most Serene [Duke] of Mantua, and in particular, the last time, when it was performed for the Queen of Spain with extraordinary splendor.[93]

Savio's statement, of course, underscores our lack of knowledge about early performances of the tragicomedy, for not only does he cite a performance "con pompa reale" at the Savoy court in Turin—for which there is dubious evidence—but he also attests to multiple stagings being carried out in Venice under private patronage before February 1601 (the date of his *Apologia*), for which there is presently no known record. In fact, aside from the private readings of 1585, there is no information regarding any performances of the play in Venice through the mid-seventeenth century.

Savio also provides another perspective on the possible motivations behind the play's supposed "circumcision" in Mantua. Based on his testimony, the work was shortened not directly due to its own excessive length, as Malacreta had charged, but to make room for the lavish and lengthy *intermedi*. Even more, Savio alleges that the poet himself carried out these excisions:

> It will be said of me, perhaps, that I am contrary in my opinion to the author himself, who as if believing the poem to be prolix, greatly truncated it when it was performed for the Queen of Spain on her passage through Mantua. I respond that Signor Cavaliere [Guarini] did that to shorten it somewhat, with the *intermedi* being so lengthy, not because

he judged it better to present the *favola* in this form before Her Majesty. And to prove this, *Il pastor fido*, when reprinted after this occasion, does not have a single verse less than the other impressions, nor have I yet seen anyone who has omitted those verses based on this example, despite having the opportunity to know which had been left out in Mantua.[94]

By rebutting the notion that the poet deemed "it better to present the *favola*" in curtailed form to the queen, while also calling attention to the fact that it was restored to its complete form for the later print, Savio implicitly also refutes the accusation that the play had to be cut in order to purge its improprieties.

The critic continues his denunciation of the play's truncation and Ingegneri's theories, as well as earlier critics' remarks about the play being filled with recycled madrigals, in the third part of the *Apologia*, which presents a scene-by-scene response to the attacks against the tragicomedy. Nothing, Savio argues, could be removed from the script without doing it harm, and in shortening it himself, Guarini, in fact, omitted "some of the most beautiful things to demonstrate that it was impossible to alter this rare composition without ruining it."[95] With this presumption, Savio in effect alleges that Guarini deliberately sabotaged the Mantuan performance precisely to prove that the play would suffer from any revision. Yet, despite the work's diminished state, the poet could be "assured that there was no one in the theater who had not read (and reread) *Il pastor fido*" beforehand, given its widespread fame, and that the performance would only motivate everyone to reread it yet again.

Savio then calls attention to many of the struck passages to demonstrate their indispensability. Of the speech by Titiro (Amarilli's father) to Montano (Silvio's father) from act 1, scene 4, expressing his concern for his daughter's betrothal to Silvio—a passage that contains the verses of Gastoldi's *Come in vago giardin rosa gentile*—for example, Savio asserts:

> But I must not forget to point out that from the verse "E che la mia fin qui l'obbligo solo" through "Titiro, fa buon core" an abrupt jump was made in Mantua. Yet one will see how necessary this part is, since, with Montano having said that time will reveal the Oracle's truth, Titiro would not have been able to open his mouth any more if he had not been aggravated and damaged by this false expectation, wherefore it was necessary to give the justification for his so great urgency and haste: for the former, that it is a peril that the young girl who has been promised a marriage faces disorder; and for the latter, his conclusion that "Thus she loses beauty, if the fire lasts / and losing the season, loses prospect."[96]

The missing verses, he continues, also prove necessary in order for Montano's following response to Titiro's lecture to be fully understood. But sometimes it is simply for their elegant *concetti* that verses should have remained, as in a passage from act 4, scene 9 between Dorinda and Silvio—set notably to music by Marenzio, Monteverdi, and D'India—which "for its *vaghezza* does not deserve to be truncated," and the second and fourth shepherds' choruses in act 4, scene 6, which "were cut in Mantua, despite being most useful and graceful *canzoni*."[97] Savio's allegation about the poet's own part in cutting the play is taken up again by the pastoral's next public proponent.

Savio broaches the issue of the play's madrigalian passages when his run-down arrives at the start of act 3—a fitting place, considering the number of musical settings from Mirtillo's opening monologue of the act that had appeared by 1601. The opening passage itself, "O primavera gioventù de l'anno," had already been set by Wert (1595), Felice Anerio (1598), Gioseffo Biffi (1598), and Monte (1599), and in varied form by Monteverdi (1592) and Luzzaschi (1601), and settings from later scenes in the third act, such as *Ah, dolente partita* (III, 3), *O Mirtillo, Mirtillo anima mia* (III, 4), and *Udite, lagrimosi* (III, 6), proved even more numerous. Savio, referring to poetic madrigals, addresses the subject:

> At the beginning of this third act…it will be very pertinent to say two words about the madrigals beginning with a speech by Mirtillo, with which [the act] is full, according to the Signori Oppositori, in whose case (to say it bluntly) I do not know either why they call these [passages] in *Il pastor fido* madrigals, or if they are, why they would want to banish them. I would gladly hear from them why it constitutes a madrigal—if for the *concetto* or for the rhyme.[98]

Savio dismisses the possibility that either rhyme or *concetti*, or the topic of love, could distinguish a madrigal within dramatic poetry, for then nearly all versed works would be "madrigals"—recalling L'Attizzato's challenge for Denores to distinguish the lyric conceits from the dramatic ones. Moreover, Savio contends that "the so-called madrigals are necessary for showing the affections and for moving the audience more sweetly, and they are useful for enticing [the audience] and making it receptive."[99] Near the end of the *Apologia*, Savio returns to the issue one last time to refute Summo's accusation that Guarini, "out of a lack of invention (*diserto d'invenzione*)… had more than once transplanted madrigals into *Il pastor fido* with poor results [*cattivo frutto*]." Savio, continuing the gardening metaphors, counters:

> The inspired and abundant skill of Signor Cavaliero [Guarini] is very well known by all the world; and those who have read his writings would know, too, if ever he made use of a *concetto* more than once. But if he had transplanted them, he would have made them flourish and produce the strongest, excellent roots.[100]

Savio, however, does not include *lettori* or *uditori* of polyphonic madrigals, who might have heard or sung certain passages before they appeared in print in the contexts of the play, nor does he acknowledge the variant readings of several speeches that had appeared in poetic anthologies from northern Italy—most notably the *Rime di diversi celebri poeti dell'età nostra* (Bergamo: Cosimo Ventura, 1587) assembled by Giovanni Battista Licino and the *Della nova scelta di rime di diversi eccellenti scrittori del[l]'età nostra* (Casalmaggiore: Antonio Guerino, 1590) compiled by Benedetto Varoli. Yet, by the standards of musical treatments, Savio seems to have been right in claiming that Guarini would improve on his *madrigaletti* by grafting them into the play, for these variant readings from poetic anthologies fell largely into disuse in the musical realm as they were overtaken by the corresponding passages from *Il pastor fido.*

Several of these questions are given further consideration in the last major document in the *Pastor fido* debate from this time: Orlando Pescetti's *Difesa del Pastorfido tragicomedia pastorale,* which followed closely on the heels of Savio's in 1601. (The dedication is signed 1 April 1601, precisely two months after that of Savio's *Apologia.*[101]) Pescetti, a known dramatist in his own right, acknowledges being beaten to Guarini's defense, but he assures the reader that, "although many times we [Savio and Pescetti] correspond, in some [ways] we are different—and perhaps it will happen that in some of these I will observe the truth better than he."[102] Unlike most other participants in the debate, Pescetti writes not from Padua, but Verona, and he dedicates the *Difesa* to one of the play's most enduring supporters, Duke Vincenzo Gonzaga, as L'Attizzato had his *Verato secondo.* Like Savio, however, Pescetti does not approve of the purported decision to abridge the play for the recent Mantuan production, and he does not refrain from making his opinion known to the duke. Pescetti states outright in the dedication that Guarini spoiled the play "in order to obey your Serene Highness, who wanted to shorten it in order to give space to the *intramezzi,* with which he wanted to honor Her Majesty, the Queen of Spain."[103] As a result, Pescetti wants to demonstrate (as Savio had recently done) that the cuts "were made only for your satisfaction, and not because those verses that were removed are superfluous," as Malacreta had alleged.

Pescetti divides his defense into four parts, each devoted to a particular attack: parts one and two respond to the eleventh and twelfth essays of Summo's *Discorsi poetici,* respectively; part three to Malacreta's *Considerationi;* and part four to Beni's *Risposta alle considerazioni o dubbi.* Although, as Pescetti admits, there are many points that overlap between his discussion and Savio's, there are several remarks of interest to the history of the play and the surrounding critical debate. In his response to Summo, for example— after refuting the latter's criticisms of the play's genre, language, and decorum and reproving his reliance on (and misuse of) Denores—Pescetti disputes the notion that the authors of the two *Verrati* are Guarini. He asks:

> But from where do you gather what you say of Cavaliere Guarini, since he has never moved, spoken, or opened his mouth, despite the many stings and bites that you all have given him? Where did you, or Denores, find proof that the *Verati* were his works?[104]

Soon after, he raises the issue again:

> L'Attizzato denies that Verrato was invented by the author of *Il pastor fido*. What did you respond? Nothing. Why, then, do you return simply to say what Denores had said before, without proving it first?[105]

Pescetti's attempt to put the issue to rest, however, was to no avail, for to this day it has continued to be accepted that Guarini penned both *Verrati* himself.

Like many others before him, Pescetti also stresses the play's appeal to a wide readership, singling out certain important supporters. Reverend Monsignor Francesco Ricalchi, for example, is reported to have defended the legitimacy of tragicomedy and the quality of *Il pastor fido* in a lecture before the Accademia Filarmonica in Verona (the source of several *Pastor fido* settings in the 1610s); and Luigi Lollini, Bishop of Cividale, praises the play in a letter of 16 June 1600 to dispel Summo's claim that he disapproved of the work ("for him to censure a work so approved as the *Pastorale* of Signor Guarini, which I likewise honor as much as I hold in ire the indiscreet manner of that doctor [Summo]").[106]

In testifying to the play's appeal to numerous audiences—"princes, cardinals, bishops, and abbots," the "principal academies," cities, "many noble circles in Venice and Padua"—Pescetti also alludes to performances "by almost all the cities and academies in Italy," including "by the Florentine nation with grand magnificence and splendor."[107] As we have seen, the only known performances in Florence by 1601 were the stagings of Emilio de' Cavalieri and Laura Guidiccioni's *Giuoco della cieca* in 1595, 1598, and 1599, although the play was considered (but ultimately rejected) for the 1589 festivities for the wedding of Grand Duke Ferdinando and Christina of Lorraine. Although we cannot be certain how much to trust Pescetti's testimony, given his own agenda and patent (but commonplace) propensity for hyperbole, remarks such as this do, at least, suggest that the play enjoyed a richer performance history in the 1590s than the known records convey.

When he turns to Malacreta, Pescetti likewise takes issue with the Vicentine's deduction that the play was abridged in Mantua because it was full of *versi oziosi*. His defense is similar to Savio's from a few months earlier: it was for the expansive *intermedi*, and not a consequence of the play's own qualities. But rather than citing editions of the play as evidence that it was not excessively long, he cites the other stagings of the work, in its complete form, in Mantua only months before. Pescetti addresses Malacreta:

> And who told you that those verses were removed for the reason that you say? If this were so, would that Prince [Vincenzo Gonzaga] not have removed them also the first and second times that the poem was performed, since he would have known as much the first and second times as the third that those [verses] were redundant [*oziosi*]. And the same

would have been done in other cities and academies that have done the poem the same honor... I would bet ten against one that it was done for no other reason than because that generous and magnanimous Prince, wanting to perform it with the *intermedi* in order to better display his splendor, and to honor more that personage for whom it was performed; and finding those [*intermedi*] perhaps longer than the verses that were removed would have allowed, it was necessary to maim and mangle [the play] in that way so that the spectacle would not be too long—which, I believe, that most prudent Prince would not have done without displeasure.[108]

The author is clearly seeking to strike a diplomatic balance between condemning not only Malacreta's judgment, but also the decision to "maim and mangle" ("mutilarlo, e stuparlo") the play in Mantua, while at the same time praising the "prince" (Vincenzo Gonzaga), who likely had the final say about how the production was executed. The *intermedi* were needed to show the duke's magnificence and to honor the Queen of Spain, yet their inclusion meant the disfigurement of Guarini's work, which, in turn, could only have displeased the duke. Pescetti was surely aware of Vincenzo Gonzaga's regard for the play, given his dedication of the *Difesa* to him. He would also have needed to handle his cards carefully, for, as a letter of 14 April 1601 between Mantuan court diplomats Agostino Giusti and Giovan Battista Guerrieri reveals, only two weeks after signing the dedication, the Veronese playwright traveled to Mantua in the hope of presenting his *Difesa* to the duke in person.[109]

Although there is no direct verification of Duke Vincenzo's wish to involve Guarini in the revision of his script in the case of *Il pastor fido*, there is record of similar excisions being made to the poet's older comedy, *L'idropica*, for the lavish celebrations for the marriage of Prince Francesco Gonzaga and the Infanta Margherita of Savoy on 28 May 1608. A letter from Federico Follino to the duke on 24 November 1605 relates a plan to stage the comedy, but hints at the same sorts of problems that had plagued rehearsals of *Il pastor fido* in the early 1590s, stating simply that the comedy proves "very difficult to stage," and that a comedy by Tasso was being considered instead.[110] The plans were apparently abandoned, but Duke Vincenzo turned his attention again to *L'idropica* in late 1607, which prompted Guarini to write to the duke asking to revise the text before copies were given out to the actors.[111] The duke responded on 14 November 1607, asking the poet not only to emend the work, but also to shorten it for the performance, presumably to accommodate the elaborate *intermedi* that would adorn it with an assortment of mythological scenes and a final *balletto*, with texts by Gabrielo Chiabrera set to music by Monteverdi, Salamone Rossi, Marco da Gagliano, and other Mantuan composers. Guarini willingly reduced the script, sending a new, shortened version to Duke Vincenzo on 1 December 1607, nearly six months before the performance.[112]

Evidence, therefore, exists of Duke Vincenzo's directing Guarini to cut one of his plays for a high-profile event involving *intermedi*, and specifically for a dynastic wedding, even though no records are known of this arrangement being made for the November 1598 performance of *Il pastor fido*. In fact, Guarini's letter of that year to Dottore Ferrari in Verona, in which he acknowledges the earlier performances in Mantua of 1598, seems to indicate that he was scarcely aware of the approaching November production ("It is said that it is being prepared yet a third time..."), and hence would not, at that point, have been involved in revising the script for it. It is feasible, though, that the excisions were made on relatively short notice, for, unlike the staging of *L'idropica*, which was newly prepared (and hence required that revisions be made months in advance), the actors and stage crew would already have been familiar with *Il pastor fido* leading up to the November production and might have been able to incorporate late changes to the script.

The bigger question, however, is whether Guarini's advocates, Savio and Pescetti, can be taken at their word, as neither writer had any direct, documented connection with Guarini, the November 1598 staging, or the Mantuan court (save for Pescetti's visit to Mantua only after his *Difesa* was printed). In fact, the credibility of Pescetti's testimony, and his knowledge of matters surrounding the play and the fate of its texts, would soon be called into question in a rebuttal from his opponent, Summo, as will be seen. Yet, as it stands, Pescetti's account lends weight to the scenario raised in the previous chapter that Mantuan composers set so many of the verses cut from the November 1598 performance precisely either because their "redundancy" also made them suitable for the self-contained madrigal, or because these composers (most notably Gastoldi) or their duke sought to atone for the play's dismemberment by setting some of the omitted lines to music. Moreover, whether or not that "most prudent Prince," Vincenzo Gonzaga, had truly been displeased by the so-called maiming of the play, or Pescetti only assumes as much to shield his dedicatee from criticism for having allowed the "circumcision" to happen, the outpouring around 1600 of Mantuan settings of these eliminated passages—some of them, such as *Cruda Amarilli* and *M'è più dolce il penar*, in multiple treatments—attests not only to their aptness as madrigal texts, but also to their appeal at the Mantuan court, if not to the demands of the duke himself.

In response to Summo's accusation that *Il pastor fido* was filled with "lodevoli madrigaletti altre volte composti in soggetto di baci" ("laudable little madrigals composed earlier on the subject of kisses"), Pescetti asserts that this is not the case: that at least some of these (poetic) *madrigaletti*, in fact, originated in the play and were extracted only later specifically for musical setting. This practice, Pescetti writes, can be traced to Guarini's former patron, the late Duke of Ferrara:

And here, indeed, is a mix of lies, since the *madriali de' baci*—or to put it better, the *madriale de' baci*, for one reads only one in the print—was extracted from *Il pastor fido*, like many others, at the bidding of Duke Alfonso for music, and not from the book of *madriali* transferred to *Il pastor fido*. And that this is the truth, see that *Il pastor fido* was printed by the directive of the author, and these [*Rime*] without his knowledge by the printer after the death of the duke.[113]

Though nearly all participants in the debate refer to music generally as a part of Arcadian life, Pescetti is exceptional in his association of the play with contemporary courtly musical practice. His statement implies that opponents' perception of the play as a "senseless gathering of madrigals" stemmed ultimately from the work's infiltration into the musical realm at Duke Alfonso's behest, whereby certain passages took on independent existences as detached poetic madrigals, not the other way around. Whereas earlier critics were seemingly unaware of this practice and, Pescetti suggests, only saw that these excerpts appeared in poetic collections as madrigals, Pescetti explains that this transition happened by way of musical settings—that is, passages were "extracted from *Il pastor fido*...for music," then consequently assumed lives as independent poems. Pescetti was seemingly unaware—or was conveniently forgetting—that multiple passages from the play had appeared much earlier as independent *rime*.

This and other claims appearing in Pescetti's *Difesa* prompted an immediate response from Summo: a newly written "replica dell'istesso autore alla difesa del detto *Pastor fido*, pubblicata sotto nome di Orlando Pescetti," which he appended to the second printing of his *Due discorsi* issued the very same year (1601).[114] The *Replica* has been neglected by nearly all modern studies, despite the often compelling twists and unique allegations it contributes to various aspects of the *Pastor fido* debates. Of greatest relevance here is Summo's deduction regarding the authorship of the two *Verrati*. Evidently provoked by Pescetti's claim that Guarini had "never moved, spoken, or opened his mouth, despite the many stings and bites" he received, and by his questioning why Summo overlooks L'Attizzato's denial that Verrato is Guarini and "returns to say what Denores had said before"—namely, that Guarini penned the response to Denores—Summo investigates the matter further. Describing to the reader his encounter with Pescetti's *Difesa*, Summo writes:

> I took it and read it. Finally, having considered it from top to bottom, inside and out, consulted with many friends most experienced in the style of modern writers, and compared it with diligence to other works of this man, we discussed it and all concluded that this work was produced by that single hand from which also came *i Verrati* and *gli Attizzati*. To make such a judgment, we were compelled by the same phrase, the same curses, the same hyperbolic exaltations of *Il pastor fido*, and of its author, with many other things that it contained, not understood, known, or able to be imagined by anyone but him. [...] But whether [Guarini] is or is not the

true author of the work, but [rather] Pescetti—the name under which he appears—to Pescetti I intend to direct my argument.[115]

Summo and his learned circle in Padua, in other words, believe that a single author composed *Il Verrato, Il Verato secondo*, and Pescetti's *Difesa*, and that this author might be Guarini. As Summo states it, "L'Attizzato is your machination; you are the accusers, the witnesses, and the judges."

In leaving open the possibility that Guarini stood behind all three documents, Summo shows his lack of awareness of Pescetti's anticipated visit to Mantua to present his *Difesa* in person to Vincenzo Gonzaga, as documented in Agostino Giusti's letter of April 1601. If the three defenses were indeed all composed by the same hand, then Pescetti must also be a potential candidate. The notion of Pescetti's authorship of the *Verrati* is in some ways compelling, particularly in light of the Veronese playwright's personal interest in pastoral drama. Indeed, his own *favola boschereccia, La regia pastorella*, came to print in 1589, in the midst of the dispute between Il Verrato and Denores over pastoral tragicomedy and only months before the publication of *Il pastor fido*. The attribution of the three defenses based on style and commonalities of language and perhaps even orthography, though beyond the scope of this study, warrants further investigation.

Summo also responds directly to Pescetti's claim that "madrigals" were taken out of *Il pastor fido* for use as poetic and musical madrigals, rather than the other way around, as Summo and other earlier critics had contended. Summo's reasoning is straightforward:

> The *madrigale de' baci* was, you say, extracted from *Il pastor fido*, like many other [passages], at the bidding of Duke Alfonso for his music, and not transplanted into *Il pastor fido* from a book of madrigals. And [you say] it is true that *Il pastor fido* was printed many years before the madrigals, and that [the play] was printed by the author's order, but these [madrigals] without his knowing by the printer after the duke's death. And so it seems to you that you have convinced me of lies.
>
> But I remember that at the time *Il pastor fido* was printed, I found in the bookshop of Paolo Meietti a volume of *rime di diversi*, in which there were the *madrigali di baci* by Signor Cavalier Guarini, and it was printed some years earlier. So I inquired about it to the said Messer Paolo [Meietti], who remembers it well and will testify whenever necessary, because I do not remember the date the volume was printed, nor who compiled it. I am certain that this is true, because I saw them and read them.[116]

Summo is no doubt referring to the anthology *Rime di diversi celebri poeti dell'età nostra* compiled by Licino and published in Bergamo in 1587. The volume included the so-called *madrigale de' baci*, or "O che soave e non intero bacio"—a variant of Ergasto's speech celebrating the union of

Mirtillo and Amarilli in act 5, scene 8—which had appeared in musical setting in Marenzio's Fourth Book of madrigals for six voices that same year
(discussed in the next chapter). Summo's account, therefore, may very well
be accurate, although it does not resolve the question of whether the *madrigale de' baci* originated in the play or as a separate poem, but simply that
the latter version appeared first in print. Regrettably, nor does Summo's
recollection from Meietti's shop shed any additional light on Pescetti's claim
that musical settings were the means by which passages from the play took
on independent existences as lyrical poems, for this practice could have occurred at the Ferrarese court at any point during the play's development.

The exchange between Pescetti and Summo in 1600–01 highlights the
extent to which the play had taken root in the theoretically and socially
separate spheres of versed drama for the stage and lyric poetry for both private reading and sung madrigals in the chamber. But composers' treatments
of these passages traversed the rigid boundaries between these realms not
functionally or generically, by dragging the madrigal onstage or making it in
some sense dramatic or representational (i.e., mimetic), but interpretatively,
by harnessing the intertextual dimensions of the texts to convey aspects of
the external plot that lie beyond the boundaries of the madrigal text itself,
and doing so diegetically—in the narrative framework of reported speech.
Moreover, despite critics' dissatisfaction with the play and expectations of
its theatrical failure, the work found modest success onstage in the decades
after its publication, while its provocative composite genre, pastoral setting,
rhetorical elegance, and surplus of introspective monologues only bolstered
its enduring influence in music, in print, and as an exemplar of early modern
pastoral drama. Thus, as it turned out, the play's gravest fault in detractors'
eyes—its versatility in genre, style, readership, and realization—proved to
be one of its greatest assets.

Notes

1 The full title of the 1602 Ciotti edition reads: *Il pastor fido, tragicommedia pastorale…ora in questa XXVII impressione di curiose, e dotte Annotationi arricchito,
e di bellissime figure in rame ornato. Con un Compendio di Poesia tratto da i duo
Verati, con la giunta d'altre cose notabili per opera del medesimo S. Cavaliere.*
References to the *Compendio* are from Guarini, *Opere*, III, 385–469. All references to the documents of the debate will also use this edition.

2 In addition to Weinberg's thorough account of the debate in *A History of
Literary Criticism*, II, 1074–1105; Rossi's *Battista Guarini ed il Pastor Fido*, 238–
51; and Perella's *The Critical Fortune of Battista Guarini's 'Il pastor fido'*; see
Lisa Sampson, *Pastoral Drama in Early Modern Italy*, 129–68 and Matthew Tre-
herne, "The Difficult Emergence of Pastoral Tragicomedy: Guarini's *Il pastor
fido* and Its Critical Reception in Italy, 1586–601," in *Early Modern Tragedy*, ed.
Subha Mukherji and Raphael Lyne (Woodbridge: D.S. Brewer, 2007), 28–42.
Many English-language discussions of the debate, moreover, rely chiefly on the
abridged translation of Guarini's *Compendio* in Allan Gilbert, *Literary Criticism: Plato to Dryden* (1940; repr. Detroit: Wayne State University Press, 1962),
504–33. Numerous studies have examined the effects of Guarini's dramaturgy

and the theoretical debates over tragicomedy on Shakespearean and early seventeenth-century English drama. See especially Frank Humphrey Ristine, *English Tragicomedy, Its Origin and History* (New York: Columbia University Press, 1910), esp. 35–44; Louis George Clubb, *Italian Drama in Shakespeare's Time* (New Haven, CT: Yale Univ. Press, 1989); G.K. Hunter, "Italian Tragicomedy on the English Stage," *Renaissance Drama* 6 (1973): 123–48; Robert Henke, "'The Winter's Tale' and Guarinian Dramaturgy," *Comparative Drama* 27 (1993): 197–217; and Raphael Lyne, "English Guarini: Recognition and Reception," *Yearbook of English Studies* 36: 90–102.

3 "...all'Eccellente Riccobono Lettore onoratissimo in quello studio, in presenza di molti altri," *Il Verato secondo*; in Guarini, *Opere*, III, 28.

4 Document 3.1: *Il Verato secondo*; in Guarini, *Opere*, III, 32.

5 Giason Denores, *Discorso...intorno à que' principii, cause, et accrescimenti, che la comedia, la tragedia, et il poema heroico ricevono dalla philosophia morale, e civile, e da' governatori delle republiche* (Padua: Paulo Meieto, 1586); in Guarini, *Opere*, II, 149–206.

6 "Ma le persone de' pastori, essendo una specie de' contadini, verisimilmente non sono capaci de' ridicoli... Nè sono capaci parimente del terribile, e del miserabile." Denores, *Discorso*, in Guarini, *Opere*, II, 203.

7 Document 3.2: Denores, *Discorso*; in Guarini, *Opere*, II, 204. Some twenty years later, English poet and playwright Ben Jonson expressed a similar concern, stating that "Guarini, in his *Pastor Fido*, kept not decorum, in making Shepherds speak as well as himself could." *Ben Jonson's Conversations with Wm. Drummond of Hawthornden* [1619], ed. R.F. Patterson (London: Blackie and Son, 1923), 7; quoted in Nicolas Perella, "Amarilli's Dilemma: The *Pastor fido* and Some English Authors," *Comparative Literature* 12 (1960): 348–59, at 349.

8 Denores writes: "Perciocchè se egli si costituisce la favola pastoral col principio turbolento, e col fine prospero, questo è un tacito invitar gli uomini a lasciar le città, ed a innamorarsi della vita contadinesca..." (*Discorso*; in Guarini, *Opere*, II, 202).

9 Document 3.3: Denores, *Discorso*, in Guarini, *Opere*, II, 201–2.

10 See Denores, *Discorso*, in Guarini, *Opere*, II, 155–71.

11 This appears in *Poetica di Iason Denores* (Padua, 1588); cited in Giuseppe Toffanin, *La fine dell'umanesimo* (Milan: Fratelli Bocca, 1920), 146. The full statement reads: "Sarà dunque la poesia imitazione di qualche azione umana meravigliosa, compita e convenevolmente grande, o rappresentando, o narrando...per introdurre virtù negli animi degli spettatori, degli uditori, ad beneficio comune di una ben ordinate Repubblica."

12 Document 3.4: Denores, *Discorso*, in Guarini, *Opere*, II, 201–2.

13 Fioretti (under pseudonym Udeno Nisieli), *Proginnasmi poetici di Udeno Nisieli* (Florence: Pier Cecconcelli, 1627), III, 130; quoted in Benedetto Croce, *Aesthetic as Science of Expression and General Linguistic*, trans. Douglas Ainslie, 2nd ed. (London: MacMillan, 1922), 441.

14 Document 3.5: Pietro Odescalchi, "Lettere inedite del cavalier Battista Guarini al Duca di Urbino," *Giornale arcadico di scienze, lettere, ed arti* 6 (1820): 101–109, at 103. The letter here is dated Venice, 8 December 1584, the year of which must be incorrect, given that the play was printed by the end of December 1589.

15 Guarini [?], *Il Verrato ovvero difesa di quanto ha scritto M. Giason Denores contra le tragicomedie, et le pastorali, in un suo discorso di poesia* (Ferrara: Alfonso Carassa, 1588); reprinted in Guarini, *Opere*, II, 211–308.

16 Document 3.6: *Il Verrato*, in Guarini, *Opere*, II, 262. As is often the case, the passage is slightly altered in the later *Compendio*, specifying at the end that "non è più alcuno che sofferire oggi la possa" (420). Guarini is especially candid in his disparagement of modern comedies in the prologue to his own work in

the genre, *La Idropica*, where he writes that after its "beginning and perfection by the divine Ariosto," comedy has been not only starved of sustenance, but

> much more miserable still by becoming a roving public harlot, giving herself for the cheapest price to the mercy of the sort of men that make merchandise of her...in such a way that, where she used to most modest and pleasing, with the customs of a lady, today she is artless, lawless, and without decorum, filled only with confusion and unbridled license.
>
> (Guarini, *La Idropica* [Venice: Ciotti, 1613])

Gregorio de' Monti's opening letter to the readers, however, states that the play was finished by the end of 1583 and presented to Vincenzo Gonzaga, who sought to perform it. It then disappeared for nearly twenty years, and upon its recovery, was staged for the wedding celebrations of Prince Francesco Gonzaga and Margherita of Savoy in May 1608, as discussed below.

17 Document 3.7: *Il Verrato*, in Guarini, *Opere*, II, 244.
18 See *Il Verrato*, in *Opere*, II, 240–41. Verrato also cites as a model for the play's label Plautus' *Amphitryon*, which the ancient writer specifically termed a "tragicomedy" (see *Opere* II, 267–69). On the referential reworking of the tragic father–son recognition and reversal from *Oedipus Rex* in *Il pastor fido*, see Elisabetta Selmi, *Classici e Moderni nell'officina del 'Pastor 'Fido'* (Alessandria: Orso, 2001), 89–120.
19 Document 3.8: *Il Verrato*, in Guarini, *Opere*, II, 286.
20 Document 3.9: *Il Verrato*, in Guarini, *Opere*, II, 301–02.
21 See *Il Verrato*, in Guarini, *Opere*, II, 245–50.
22 See Document 3.10: *Il Verrato*, in Guarini, Opere, II, 262.
23 Document 3.11: *Il Verrato*, in Guarini, *Opere*, II, 262.
24 Document 3.12: *Il Verrato*, in Guarini, *Opere*, II, 263–64.
25 *Il Verato secondo*, 66; in Guarini, *Opere*, III, 83.
26 See Federico Schneider's detailed analysis of the cathartic ends of the play in *Pastoral Drama and Healing in Early Modern Italy* (Burlington, VT: Ashgate, 2010), esp. Chapter 1, "The Art of Purging" (13–65).
27 Document 3.13: *Il Verrato*, in Guarini, *Opere*, II, 260.
28 "Le quali tutte secondo i tempi loro furono buone, se ben le prime parevano sfacciatissime meretrici, e le seconde castissime, e venerande Matrone..." *Il Verrato*, in Guarini, *Opere*, II, 261. Likewise, the Bolognese theorist Artusi contrasts the virtuous music of nuns with the depraved and corrupting music of the *Moderni*: "Ma come l'ha conservata casta, se corrompendola, egli la fa diventare come una sfacciata meretrice?" *Seconda parte dell'Artusi ovvero delle imperfettioni della moderna musica* (Venice: Vincenti, 1603), 38.
29 Document 3.14: *Il Verrato*, in Guarini, *Opere*, II, 266.
30 Document 3.15: *Il Verrato*, in Guarini, *Opere*, II, 295–96.
31 Document 3.16: *Il Verrato*, in Guarini, *Opere*, II, 297.
32 Denores, *Apologia contra l'autor del verato...di quanto ha egli detto in un suo Discorso delle Tragicommedie, e delle Pastorali* (Padua: Paolo Meietti, 1590), in Guarini, *Opere*, II, 309–75. The treatise was dedicated again to the Venetian noblemen, Jacopo Contarini and Francesco Vendramini, also the dedicatees of *Il Verrato*. Denores takes issue with Verrato having dedicated his work to the Paduan critic's "most honored patrons and protectors," arguing that Verrato should have consulted them first before publishing his counterattack, for, he argues, they would have defended Denores—especially Contarini, given their common origins in Cyprus (see Guarini, *Opere*, II, 327–30).
33 Document 3.17: Denores, *Apologia*, in Guarini, *Opere*, II, 330–31, and Document 3.18: *ibid.*, 311.
34 Document 3.19: Denores, *Apologia*, in Guarini, *Opere*, II, 367.

35 Document 3.20: Denores, *Apologia*, in Guarini, *Opere*, II, 337. The statement
   seems to draw from Plato's discussion of hymns, paeans, and dithyrambs with
   respect to music in *Laws* (700a–701c); trans. in Piero Weiss and Richard Taruskin, *Music in the Western World: A History in Documents*, 2nd ed. (Belmont,
   CA: Thomson Schirmer, 2008), 5–6.
36 "Certissima cosa è che, fin del novantuno, questa opera fu finita, e tanto basti
   per dichiarare, che la lunghezza non è venuta da me: il qual non entro a dirne il
   perchè..." Prefatory letter "a benigni lettori" of *Il Verato secondo*, in Guarini,
   Opere, III, 1–384. The author uses the spelling "Verato" throughout, despite the
   form "Verrato" used in the earlier defense.
37 Document 3.21: *Il Verato secondo*, in Guarini, *Opere*, III, dedication (unnumbered).
38 Document 3.22: *Il Verato secondo*, in *Opere*, III, 1.
39 L'Attizzato writes:

> If you wanted, according to your nature, to bite him who offended you, why
> do you not vomit your venom against Verrato? Why infest the author of *Il
> pastor fido*, who does not want a quarrel, who speaks not, who is not moved,
> who suffers, who does not care to be forgiven? Will you say the same that he
> says: that the author of *Il pastor fido* is different from the author of *Il Verato*?
> [...] If Your Nores has the opinion that the author of *Il pastor fido* had written
> the work of Il Verato, why do you not speak with the said author? Why did
> you not direct your second invective solely toward him? And if you wrote
> against Il Verato, why do you not leave the author of *Il pastor fido* alone, if he
> did not offend you?
>   (Document 3.23: *Il Verato secondo*, in Guarini, *Opere*, III, 272–73)

   I have changed the author's references to Denores from third to second person
   in my translation.
40 Document 3.24: *Il Verato secondo*, in Guarini, *Opere*, III, 5.
41 "...quelli che danno il primo moto del dissolvere l'amicizia, ch'è quel divino vin-
   colo, con cui l'umana vita e compagnia si conserva, e onde nasce il felice stato
   delle Repubbliche" (*Il Verato secondo*, in *Opere*, III, 20).
42 "Non basta a dire non l'ho veduta, nè letta, nè sentita rappresentare: e chi nol
   sa, non essendo ancor nè stampata, nè recitata? essendo essa ancora in man
   dell'Autore?" (*Il Verato secondo*, in *Opere*, III, 25).
43 L'Attizzato writes:

> Fine reasoning: 'I have never examined *Il pastor fido*, but I have said indeed
> that *favole* made in such a way are monsters, therefore I have not spoken of
> *Il pastor fido*.' Is this not a subtle argument? [...] What blunders are these:
> 'I have not examined all the parts of *Il pastor fido*, therefore it is not unified'?
>   (Document 3.25: *Il Verato secondo*, in Guarini, *Opere*, III, 25)

   L'Attizzato raises the issue again in the second part of the pamphlet, stating:

> Was your [Denores's] defense not based on the point that you had never seen,
> nor read, *Il pastor fido*, and that in your first invective you could not have
> meant this one? Now what do you say? When your second [invective] was
> published, was the work of your friend not printed? Now can you deny hav-
> ing noticed it?
>   (Document 3.26: *ibid.*, 272)

44 Document 3.27: *Il Verato secondo*, in Guarini, *Opere*, III, 29–31.
45 Document 3.28: *Il Verato secondo*, in Guarini, *Opere*, III, 33.
46 See Guarini, *Il Verato secondo*, in *Opere*, III, 32–44. Of the actor, L'Attizzato
   writes:

Il Verato, student of the Most Illustrious Bentivogli, disciple of the great Ariosto, Ercole Bentivoglio, Giovanbattista Giraldi, who has taught the good and proper use of the stage to modern poets. Lastly, Il Verato, whose sepulcher was deemed worthy by Torquato Tasso to be honored before he died with a beautiful sonnet, which one can read in [Tasso's] *Rime.*

(Document 3.29: *ibid.*, 44)

47 See Monteverdi's letter to the *studiosi lettori* at the end of his *Quinto libro de madrigali a cinque voci* (Venice: Ricciardo Amadino, 1605) and Giulio Cesare Monteverdi, *Dichiaratione*, appended to the end of Claudio Monteverdi's *Scherzi musicali a tre voci* (Venice: Amadino, 1607); trans. in Oliver Strunk, *Source Readings in Music History* (New York, 1998), 540.
48 See *Il Verato secondo*, in Guarini, *Opere*, III, 253–57.
49 Document 3.30: *Il Verato secondo*, in Guarini, *Opere*, III, 300–01.
50 Document 3.31: *Il Verato secondo*, in Guarini, *Opere*, III, 301.
51 Document 3.32: *Il Verato secondo*, in Guarini, *Opere*, III, 302.
52 Document 3.33: *Il Verato secondo*, in Guarini, *Opere*, III, 304. On the relevance of Petrarchan style, language, and themes in *Il pastor fido*, see Nicolas Perella, "Heroic Virtue and Love in the Pastor Fido," *Atti del Real Istituto veneto di Scienze, Lettere ed Arti* 132 (1973–74): 658–706, esp. 702–6, and Claudio Scarpati, "Poetica e retorica in Battista Guarini," *Studi sul Cinquecento italiano* (Milan: Vita e Pensiero, 1982), 201–38.
53 Document 3.34: *Il Verato secondo*, in Guarini, *Opere*, III, 303–04.
   Clive Griffiths' summary of more recent scholars' disparaging comparisons of *Il pastor fido* to Tasso's *Aminta* echoes the sentiments of many early critics. For example:

It has...frequently been asserted that, in his determination to best Tasso, Guarini generally strives after an affect which seems to elude him. [...] There is in Tasso's language a lightness of touch, a simplicity which lacks nothing in its power of evocation and which when compared with some of Guarini's lines makes them appear forced and pedestrian. In *Il pastor fido*, some of the worst aspects of *seicentismo* are already apparent in poetic conceits which simply collapse through their own weight and lose all effect through over-elaboration. In Guarini's drama there is also a frequently excessive indulgence in word-play and repetition...

Yet, for Griffiths, Guarini's achievement lies most in giving "expression to his characters' innermost yearning for freedom, for control of their own destinies." See Griffiths, "Guarini's *Il pastor fido*," 315–27.
54 *Il Verato secondo*, in Guarini, *Opere*, III, 305. Verrato likewise draws comparisons to the stylized elegance of Sperone's poetic language, which was also a subject of intense critical debate in the mid-Cinquecento; see Weinberg, *A History of Literary Criticism*, II, 912–53. Schneider holds that

Guarini fully exploits the whole gamut of Petrarchan poetic/rhetorical devices not for mere artfulness' sake, but rather in order to obtain a specific therapeutic result: the temperament of affects through the arousal of moral affects according to the tenets of tragicomic aesthetics.

(*Pastoral Drama and Healing*, 107–08)

Schneider also argues that the sensuality of the play transcends the mere physical and erotic by merging with the spiritual in a Petrarchan manner, thus acting as "a pedagogic strategy aimed at teaching a much more complex lesson on love" (101).

55 Document 3.35: *Il Verato secondo*, in Guarini, *Opere*, III, 305–06.
56 Document 3.36: *Il Verato secondo*, in Guarini, *Opere*, III, 306.
57 L'Attizzato writes:

> It would please me to draw one of them [an eclogue] from *Il pastor fido*, since (if I am not mistaken) it would be very fitting to take the ninth scene of act four, in which Silvio—out of pity for Dorinda, whom he had inadvertently wounded—becomes her lover, not by narration, but through dialogue [*negozio*]. If it were separated from the entire body of the play [*favola*], what else would it be than an eclogue of the dramatic genus? Now one adds to it the episodes, the actors, the set, and the other particulars that are proper to the dramatic genus and that Aristotle says were added to a tragic poem: will a full-formed pastoral play not be made from a little eclogue?
>
> (Document 3.37: *Il Verato secondo*, in Guarini, *Opere*, III, 312)

58 For a compelling critique of the term "diegetic music," see Stefano Castelvecchi, "On 'Diegesis' and 'Diegetic': Words and Concepts," *Journal of the American Musicological Society* 73 (2020): 149–71. Castelvecchi proposes the terms "mimetic" and "endogenous" music as possible replacements for "diegetic," or music "originating from within" the plot.
59 "Resta la quarta, e ultima, nella quale vi ho promesso di far vedere, come farò, che il poema, misto di parti tragiche, e comiche, è poesia di Aristotile" (*Il Verato secondo*, in Guarini, *Opere*, III, 338–9).
60 *Il Verato secondo*, in Guarini, *Opere*, III, 339.
61 See *Il Verato secondo*, in Guarini, *Opere*, III, 358–60.
62 *Il Verato secondo*, in Guarini, *Opere*, III, 384. L'Attizzato stresses the statement by putting it in uppercase, reading in its entirety: "Messer Jasone [Denores]. IL PASTORFIDO al vostro, E all'altrui dispetto, VIVE, PIACE, LODATO, AMATO, E LETTO."
63 "mettendo in bocca de' pastori alle volte certi parlari figurati con ornamenti de' poeti Lirici" (Denores, *Apologia*, in Guarini, *Opere*, II, 323). This entire passage is nearly identical to that of Denores' *Discorso* (p. 204), cited in note 7 above, only with the comparison to "poeti Lirici" newly added. See also Perella, *The Critical Fortune*, 15.
64 James Chater, "'Un pasticcio di madrigaletti'?: The Early Musical Fortune of *Il pastor fido*," in *Guarini: la musica, i musicisti*, ed. A. Pompilio (Lucca: Libreria Musicale Italiana Editrice, 1997), 139–55.
65 Marenzio's *O che soave e non inteso bacio* appeared in his Fourth Book for six voices, dated 20 December 1586 in the dedication. The text had never before appeared in print. When it was included the following year in the anthology *Rime di diversi celebri poeti dell'età nostra nuovamente e poste in luca*, ed. Giovanni Battista Licino (Bergamo: Comino Ventura e compagni, 1587, 191; hereafter referred to as Ventura), the poem took a much different form from the versions of the madrigal and of earlier extant drafts of the play, with the incipit "O che soave e non intero bacio," rather than "inteso bacio," as in the madrigal. The poem also appeared in the 1590 anthology *Della nova scelta di rime di diversi eccellenti scrittori de l'età nostra parte prima* (ed. Benedetto Varoli [Casalmaggiore: Antonio Guerino e compagno, 1590], 42), but with differences from the Ventura edition, and it appeared again in shortened form in Guarini's *Rime* of 1598 (Venice: G.B. Ciotti, 1598, fol. 93v) with the abbreviated incipit, "O che soave bacio." For descriptions of the various sources, the differences between them, and further discussion of a possible genealogy of the poem, see James Chater, "Un pasticcio di madrigaletti," 142 and 144–46; and Elio Durante and Anna Martellotti, "Il Cavalier Guarini e il concerto delle dame," in *Guarini: la musica, i musicisti*, 91–127, at 113–14. As James Chater has pointed out,

Marenzio's text most closely resembles that of the play (V,8: 1424–51), which was then circulating only in manuscript form. In the play, the first line of the passage again reads "O che soave e non intero bacio," and there are various other divergences between the play and the text of Marenzio's madrigal. As Chater notes, there are indications that an earlier form of this text—possibly even that of Marenzio's work—existed independently of the play, and that this autonomous poetic madrigal then served as the source for the passage in the fifth act of *Il pastor fido* ("Un pasticcio di madrigaletti," 145–46).

66 Monteverdi's text is substantially shorter than the corresponding passage in the play and agrees most closely with a variant form published a few months after *Il pastor fido* in Varoli's anthology *Della nova scelta di rime*, 78. On Monteverdi's madrigal and its relationship to Wert's and Luzzaschi's settings of the passage, see Chapter 6.

67 Document 3.38: Guarini, *Il pastor fido* (1602), 6r. See also Nicholas Perella, "Heroic Virtue," 658–706 and, on the pervasive role of Petrarch in the *Annotazioni*, Carla Molinari, "La parte del Guarini nel Commento al *Pastor fido*," *Schifanoia* 15/16 (1996): 141–50.

68 The play appeared in France as *Le Berger fidelle, pastorale*, trans. Roland Brisset (Tours: Jamet Mettayer, 1593)—which is the first illustrated version, with its inclusion of five woodcuts—in England as *Il pastor fido: or The faithfull Shepheard*, trans. anon. (London: Thomas Creede, 1602); and in Spain as *El pastor fido*, trans. Cristòbal Suàrez de Figueroa (Naples: Tarquinio Longo, 1602). An Italian edition of Guarini's work together with Tasso's *Aminta* had already appeared in England by 1591 (London: Giovanni Volfeo). The play's enduring appeal internationally is attested by the new translations that continued to appear through the seventeenth century, including into Dutch (c.1653), German (c.1672), and Swedish (c.1696), and in prose German in 1697 or 1699; these editions, however, lack precise publication dates. A fascinating reworking of the play as *El Pastor fido* (Madrid: Andres Garcia de la Iglesia, 1657), first performed in 1654 or 1656, arose through a collaboration between three celebrated Spanish Baroque poets, Antonio Solìs de Rivadeneira, Antonio Coello, and Pedro Calderòn de la Barca, each of whom composed one of the work's three acts. This "comedia famosa" uses many of the same characters from Guarini's play as well as new ones and adds newly interpolated scenarios. Calderòn also wrote an allegorical *auto sacramental* titled *El pastor Fido* for performance in 1678 for Corpus Christi in Madrid, which was only published in 1701 in an unauthorized edition (Barcelona: Sebastiàn de Cormellas), then in c. 1714 in an edition with no imprint. See Calderòn, *El pastor Fido*, ed. Fernando Plata Parga, in Autos Sacramentales Completos de Calderòn, vol. 40 (Kassel: Reichenberger, 2003).

69 Guarini, *Il pastor fido, Le Berger Fidelle*, trans. Roland Brisset (Paris: Guillemot, 1609). The subtitle reads: "Presented in Italian and French for the use of those who wish to learn the two languages."

70 Perella, *The Critical Fortune*, 6.

71 Chater, "Un pasticcio di madrigaletti," 150.

72 Document 3.39: Summo, *Due discorsi*; in Guarini, *Opere*, III, 595–96.

73 Document 3.41: Summo, *Due discorsi*; in Guarini, *Opere*, III, 591.

74 Document 3.42: Summo, *Due discorsi*; in Guarini, *Opere*, III, 596.

75 Guarini, *Lettere* (1596), II, 50; discussed above in Chapter 2.

76 Guarini likewise avoids mention of *Aminta* in his *Annotazioni*, despite the copious number of literary models, both modern and ancient, that he invokes. On the relationship between the two pastoral dramas and Guarini's attempt to downplay it, see Vincenzo Quercio, "La lezione dell'*Aminta* e il *Pastor fido*," *Studi seicenteschi* 43 (2002): 119–60 and Sampson, *Pastoral Drama in Early*

Modern Italy, and on their relationship in the contexts of Ferrarese pastoral drama, see Selmi, *Classici e moderni*, 141–78.

77 "Lascio quanto pago resti lo spettatore giudicioso, o il lettore, mentre credendo sentire una vera imitazione di un disperato, sente una dissipita raccolta di madrigali." Giovanni Pietro Malacreta, *Considerazioni intorno al Il pastor fido*; in Guarini, *Opere*, IV, 102. It is notable how Malacreta takes specific care to address Guarini's reader as both "spettore" and "lettore," showing perhaps his consciousness of the play's widespread readership as a printed text.

78 "potrai coglier da questa favola una sessantina di madrigaletti." In N. Villani, *Considerazioni di messer Fagiano sopra la seconda parte dell'Occhiale del Cav. Stigliani* (Venice, 1631), 569–574. See also Nisiely (Benedetto Fioretti), *Proginnasmi poetici*, III (prog. 51), 132. Both are quoted in Perella, *The Critical Fortune*, 35.

79 Malacreta, *Considerazioni intorno al Pastor fido*; in Guarini, *Opere*, IV, 102–105.

80 Document 3.43: Paolo Beni, *Risposta alla considerazioni*; in Guarini, *Opere*, IV, 126.

81 See Beni, *Risposta alla considerazioni*; in Guarini, *Opere*, IV, 182–85 and 281–85.

82 Document 3.44: Beni, *Risposta alla considerazioni*; in Guarini, *Opere*, IV, 127. For more on Beni's stance in favor of *Il pastor fido*, particularly of his backing of the poet's right to invent, rather than rely steadfastly on historical truth, see Weinberg, *A History of Literary Criticism*, 1097.

83 Giovanni Savio, *Apologia di Gio[vanni] Savio venetiano in difesa del Pastor fido, tragicomedia pastorale del molto illust[re] Sig[nor] Cavalier Battista Guarino dalle oppositioni fattegli da gl' eccell[entissimi] Sig[nori] Faustino Summo, Gio[vanni] Pietro Malacreta, & Angelo Ingegnero* (Venice: Horatio Larducci, 1601); in Guarini, *Opere*, IV, 301–643.

84 Document 3.45: Savio, *Apologia ... in difesa del Pastor fido*, in Guarini; *Opere*, IV, 308.

85 Savio, *Apologia ... in difesa del Pastor fido*; in Guarini, *Opere*, IV, 308.

86 The subtitle of the pamphlet states, *Apologia...divisa in tre parti: nella prima, si ragiona della Tragicommedia in universale, nella seconda, della favola del Pastor Fido, nella terza, del Pastor Fido disteso"* (Savio, *Apologia...in difesa del Pastor fido*; in Guarini, *Opere*, IV, 300).

87 Document 3.46: Savio, *Apologia...in difesa del Pastor fido*; in Guarini, *Opere*, IV, 307.

88 Savio finds an example for tragicomedy in Aristotle's mention of tragedy with a *lieto fine*. See Document 3.47: Savio, *Apologia...in difesa del Pastor fido*, in Guarini, *Opere*, IV, 341–42. He continues by drawing further parallels between tragicomedy and the *Poema Satirico* ("Il Satirico, che è in fine quello, che noi chiamiamo Tragicomico, contiene il Pastorale, dunque con ragione si sarà Tragicomedia pastorale" [350]).

89 Document 3.48: Savio, *Apologia...in difesa del Pastor fido*; in Guarini, *Opere*, IV, 346.

90 Angelo Ingegneri, *Della poesia rappresentativa*. The work is dedicated to the illegitimate heir of the "Serenissima, & sempre gloriosissima Casa da Este," Don Cesare d'Este, Duke of Modena and Reggio. For a summary of Ingegneri's treatise, see Weinberg, *A History of Literary Criticism*, 1090–93.

91 As Ingegneri writes:

> Reason convinces us of this, since the performance with all the choruses or even the interludes must not last more than three and a half or four hours; and that performance which comes to five hours, no matter how delightful it may be, will not avoid the tedium of many of the auditors.
>
> (translated in Weinberg, *A History of Literary Criticism*, 1092)

As the accounts of the 1598 festivities in Mantua report, the staging of *Il pastor fido* grossly exceeded these limitations. The play also overtly flouts Ingegneri's reasoning that "soliloquies, long or short, should generally be avoided," in the process providing an abundance of reflective verse for madrigalists.

92 Savio, *Apologia...in difesa del Pastor fido*; in Guarini, *Opere*, IV, 362. The page numbering through the 360s in the *Opere* is incorrect, showing 390s, evidently owing to the upside-down placement of the character "6." In addition to the total number of verses, Ingegneri argues that individual scenes should be no longer than 100 verses each, to which Savio responds by citing numerous examples of longer scenes from the ancients, which were made even longer in performance through the incorporation of music and dance (381–83).

93 Document 3.49: Savio, *Apologia...in difesa del Pastor fido*; in Guarini, *Opere*, IV, 362–63.

94 Document 3.50: Savio, *Apologia...in difesa del Pastor fido*; in Guarini, *Opere*, IV, 379.

95 Document 3.51: Savio, *Apologia...in difesa del Pastor fido*; in Guarini, *Opere*, IV, 433.

96 Document 3.52: Savio, *Apologia...in difesa del Pastor fido*; in Guarini, *Opere*, IV, 475.

97 "...se bene si tacque in Mantova con quel concetto...il quale per la sua vaghezza non merita di esser troncato," Savio, *Apologia...in difesa del Pastor fido*; in Guarini, *Opere*, IV, 594; "Il Coro de i pastori cinque volte parla, ma la seconda, e la quarta furono recise in Mantova, se bene sono utilissime, e leggiadrissime canzoni" (581).

98 Document 3.53: Savio, *Apologia...in difesa del Pastor fido*; in Guarini, *Opere*, IV, 516–17.

99 "i madrigali così chiamati sono necessari per mostrare gli affetti, e per più dolcemente commovere il Teatro, e sono attrattivi ad allettarlo, e farselo benevolo." Savio, *Apologia...in difesa del Pastor fido*; in Guarini, *Opere*, IV, 519.

100 Document 3.54: Savio, *Apologia...in difesa del Pastor fido*; in Guarini, *Opere*, IV, 628.

101 Orlando Pescetti, *Difesa del Pastorfido tragicomedia pastorale...da quanto gli è stato scritto contro da gli Eccellentiss[imi] SS. Faustin Summo, e Gio. Pietro Malacreta, con una breve risoluzione de' dubbi del molto Rev. Sig. D. Pagolo Beni* (Verona: Angelo Tamo, 1601). Pescetti's work does not appear in Guarini's *Opere*; thus, citations refer to the 1601 Tamo edition.

102 "...se bene siamo in molte cose conformi...in alcune però siamo differenti: e forse avverrà, che in alcune di queste io avrò meglio la verità scrota di lui..." Pescetti, *Difesa del Pastorfido*, second introductory letter "al benigno lettore." Pescetti's own *Il Cesare* (Verona, 1594), dedicated to Duke Alfonso II d'Este, has been compellingly cited as a model for Shakespeare's *Julius Caesar*; see, for example, Alex Boecker, *A Probable Source of Shakespeare's Julius Caesar* (London: Forgotten Books, 1913). Five years earlier, he had also published a *favola boschereccia*, entitled *La regia pastorella* (Verona: Girolamo Discepolo, 1589), which put him squarely into the tradition of pastoral drama cultivated by Tasso and Guarini.

103 Document 3.55: Pescetti, *Difesa del Pastorfido*, dedication.

104 Document 3.56: Pescetti, *Difesa del Pastorfido*, 4.

105 "L'Attizzato niega, che'l Verato sia stato introdutto dall'Autore del Pastorfido. Voi che gli rispondete? Nulla. Perche dunque tornate à dire quel, che prima avea detto il Nores, senza provarlo innanzi?" (Pescetti, *Difesa del Pastorfido*, 7).

106 Documents 3.57 (Pescetti, *Difesa del Pastorfido*, 2) and 3.58 (8–9, where Lollini's letter is cited at length).

107 Document 3.59: Pescetti, *Difesa del Pastorfido*, 103–104.

108 Document 3.60: Pescetti, *Difesa del Pastor fido*, 179.
109 Giusti requests that Guerrieri meet Pescetti and arrange for his meeting with Duke Vincenzo Gonzaga. See Mantua, Archivio di Stato (Archivio Gonzaga), busta 1533, fasc. III, fols. 390–91.
110 Mantua, Archivio di Stato (Archivio Gonzaga), busta 2702, fasc. III, doc. 6.
111 Letter of Guarini to Duke Vincenzo Gonzaga (20 October 1607); in Mantua, Archivio di Stato (Archivio Gonzaga), busta 1539, fasc. III, fol. 472.
112 See Mantua, Archivio di Stato (Archivio Gonzaga), busta 2268, c. n. n.; b. 1539, fasc. III, fol. 513; and b. 1539, fasc. III, fol. 520. Additional documents show that, to assist in overcoming the reported difficulties of staging the work, the Mantuan court sought the help of Gregorio Monti, who had worked with Guarini to stage *L'Idropica* in Venice. See the letters between Udine, Chieppio, and Alessandro Striggio in Mantua, Archivio di Stato, b. 1539, fasc. I, fol. 171 and b. 1265, cc.n.n.
113 Document 3.61: Pescetti, *Difesa del Pastorfido*, 94. James Chater was presumably unaware of Pescetti's defense of these lyric episodes when he asserted that "neither Guarini nor his supporters attempted to refute the charge of self-borrowing" from his lyric poetry, and therefore deduced that "we may be reasonably sure that the madrigal [*O che soave e non inteso bacio*]...served as the source for this part of Ergasto's speech, rather than the other way around" ("Un pasticcio di madrigaletti," 146).
114 Faustino Summo, *Due discorsi, l'uno contra le Tragicomedie et moderne pastorali, l'altro particolarmente contra il Pastor Fido dell'Ill.re Sig. Cav. B.G. Con una replica dell'istesso autore alla difesa del detto P.F., pubblicata sotto nome di Orlando Pescetti et insieme una risposta del medesimo in difesa del metro nelle poesie e nei poemi, contro il parere del molto Rev. Sig. Paolo Beni* (Venice: Francesco Bolzetta, 1601).
115 Document 3.62: Summo, *Due discorsi ... con una replica*, 1–2.
116 Document 3.63: Summo, *Due discorsi ... con una replica*, 60.

Reference List

Artusi, Giovanni Maria. *Seconda parte dell'Artusi ovvero delle imperfettioni della moderna musica*. Venice: Vincenti, 1603.

Beni, Paolo. *Risposta alle considerazioni o dubbi dell'eccellentissimo signor dottor Malacreta...sopra il Pastorfido*. Venice: Paolo Ugolino, 1600.

Castelvecchi, Stefano. "On 'Diegesis' and 'Diegetic': Words and Concepts." *Journal of the American Musicological Society* 73 (2020): 149–71.

Chater, James. "'Un pasticcio di madrigaletti'?: The Early Musical Fortune of Il pastor fido." In *Guarini: la musica, i musicisti*, ed. A. Pompilio, 139–55. Lucca: Libreria Musicale Italiana Editrice, 1997.

Clubb, Louis George. *Italian Drama in Shakespeare's Time*. New Haven, CT: Yale University Press, 1989.

Croce, Benedetto. *Aesthetic as Science of Expression and General Linguistic*. Trans. by Douglas Ainslie. 2nd ed. London: MacMillan, 1922.

Denores, Giason. *Apologia contra l'autor del verato...di quanto ha egli detto in un suo Discorso delle Tragicommedie, e delle Pastorali*. Padua: Paolo Meietti, 1590.

———. *Discorso...intorno à que' principii, cause, et accrescimenti, che la comedia, la tragedia, et il poema heroico ricevono dalla philosophia morale, e civile, e da' governatori delle republiche*. Padua: Paulo Meieto, 1586.

Durante, Elio and Anna Martellotti. "Il Cavalier Guarini e il concerto delle dame." In *Guarini: la musica, i musicisti*, ed. A. Pompilio, 91–127. Lucca: Libreria Musicale Italiana Editrice, 1997.

Gilbert, Allan. *Literary Criticism: Plato to Dryden.* 1940; repr. Detroit: Wayne State University Press, 1962.

Griffiths, Clive. "Guarini's Il pastor fido: A Beginning or an End for Renaissance Pastoral Drama." In *The Cultural Heritage of the Italian Renaissance*, eds. C. Griffiths and R. Hastings, 315–27. Lewiston, NY: Edwin Mellen Press, 1993.

Guarini, Battista. *Delle opere del cavalier Battista Guarini.* Eds. G.A. Barotti and A. Zeno. 4 vols. (Verona: Tumermani, 1737 and 1738).

———. *La Idropica.* Venice: Ciotti, 1613.

———. *Il pastor fido, Le Berger Fidelle.* Trans. by Roland Brisset. Paris: Guillemot, 1609.

———. *Il pastor fido, tragicommedia pastorale del molto Illustre Cavaliere Battista Guarini, ora in questa XX impressione di curiose e dotte Annotationi arrichito.* Venice: Ciotti, 1602.

———. *Rime.* Venice: G.B. Ciotti, 1598.

——— [?]. *Il Verato secondo, ovvero replica dell'Attizzato accademico ferrarese, in difesa del Pastorfido, contra la seconda scrittura di Messer Giason De Nores intitolata Apologia.* Florence: Filippo Giunti, 1593.

———. *Le Berger fidelle, pastorale.* Trans. by Roland Brisset. Tours: Jamet Mettayer, 1593.

——— [?]. *Il Verrato ovvero difesa di quanto ha scritto M. Giason Denores contra le tragicomedie, et le pastorali, in un suo discorso di poesia.* Ferrara: Alfonso Carassa, 1588.

Henke, Robert. "'The Winter's Tale' and Guarinian Dramaturgy." *Comparative Drama* 27 (1993): 197–217.

Hunter, G. K. "Italian Tragicomedy on the English Stage." *Renaissance Drama* 6 (1973): 123–48.

Ingegneri, Angelo. *Della poesia rappresentativa e del modo di rappresentare le favole sceniche.* Ferrara: Vittorio Baldini, 1598.

Licino, Giovanni Battista, ed. *Rime di diversi celebri poeti dell'età nostra nuovamente e poste in luca.* Bergamo: Comino Ventura e compagni, 1587.

Lyne, Raphael. "English Guarini: Recognition and Reception." *Yearbook of English Studies* 36: 90–102.

Malacreta, Giovanni Pietro. *Consideratoni [sic] ... sopra il Pastot [sic] fido, tragicomedia pastorale del ... Battista Guarini.* Vicenza: Greco, 1600.

Molinari, Carla. "La parte del Guarini nel Commento al Pastor fido." *Schifanoia* 15/16 (1996): 141–50.

Odescalchi, Pietro. "Lettere inedite del cavalier Battista Guarini al Duca di Urbino." *Giornale arcadico di scienze, lettere, ed arti* 6 (1820): 101–109.

Perella, Nicolas. "Heroic Virtue and Love in the Pastor Fido." *Atti del Real Istituto veneto di Scienze, Lettere ed Arti* 132 (1973–74): 658–706.

———. *The Critical Fortune of Battista Guarini's "Il pastor fido."* Florence: Olschki, 1973.

———. "Amarilli's Dilemma: The Pastor fido and Some English Authors." *Comparative Literature* 12 (1960): 348–59.

Pescetti, Orlando. *Difesa del Pastorfido tragicomedia pastorale...da quanto gli è stato scritto contro da gli Eccellentiss[imi] SS. Faustin Summo, e Gio. Pietro Malacreta, con una breve risoluzione de' dubbi del molto.* Rev. Sig. D. Pagolo Beni. Verona: Angelo Tamo, 1601.

Quercio, Vincenzo. "La lezione dell'Aminta e il Pastor fido." *Studi seicenteschi* 43 (2002): 119–60.

Ristine, Frank Humphrey. *English Tragicomedy, Its Origin and History.* New York: Columbia University Press, 1910.

Rossi, Vittorio. *Battista Guarini ed il Pastor fido: Studio biografico-critico con documenti inediti.* Turin: Loescher, 1886.

Sampson, Lisa. *Pastoral Drama in Early Modern Italy: The Making of a New Genre.* Italian Perspectives 15. London: Legenda, Modern Humanities Research Association and Maney Publishing, 2006.

Savio, Giovanni. *Apologia di Gio[vanni] Savio venetiano in difesa del Pastor fido, tragicomedia pastorale del molto illust[re] Sig[nor] Cavalier Battista Guarino dalle oppositioni fattegli da gl' eccell[entissimi] Sig[nori] Faustino Summo, Gio[vanni] Pietro Malacreta, & Angelo Ingegnero.* Venice: Horatio Larducci, 1601.

Scarpati, Claudio. *Studi sul Cinquecento italiano.* Milan: Vita e Pensiero, 1982.

Schneider, Federico. *Pastoral Drama and Healing in Early Modern Italy.* Burlington, VT: Ashgate, 2010.

Selmi, Elisabetta. *Classici e Moderni nell'officina del 'Pastor Fido.'* Alessandria: Orso, 2001.

Strunk, Oliver. *Source Readings in Music History.* New York: Norton, 1998.

Summo, Faustino. *Due discorsi, l'uno contra le Tragicomedie et moderne pastorali, l'altro particolarmente contra il Pastor Fido dell'Ill.re Sig. Cav. B.G. Con una replica dell'istesso autore alla difesa del detto P.F., pubblicata sotto nome di Orlando Pescetti et insieme una risposta del medesimo in difesa del metro nelle poesie e nei poemi, contro il parere del molto Rev. Sig. Paolo Beni.* Venice: Francesco Bolzetta, 1601.

———. *Due discorsi: l'uno contro le tragicommedie e le pastorali, l'altro contro il Pastor Fido.* Padua: F. Bolzetta, 1600.

Taruskin, Richard. *Music in the Western World: A History in Documents.* 2nd ed. Belmont, CA: Thomson Schirmer, 2008.

Toffanin, Giuseppe. *La fine dell'umanesimo.* Milan: Fratelli Bocca, 1920.

Varoli, Benedetto, ed. *Della nova scelta di rime di diversi eccellenti scrittori de l'età nostra parte prima.* Casalmaggiore: Antonio Guerino e compagno, 1590.

Weinberg, Bernard. *A History of Literary Criticism in the Italian Renaissance.* 2 vols. Chicago, IL: University of Chicago Press, 1961.

4 Marenzio, Guarini, and the Origins of the *Pastor fido* Madrigal

Marenzio's "O fido, o caro Aminta" (1595): An Introduction to Some Textual Conflicts

Upon hearing the opening exclamation "O fido, o caro Aminta" ("O faithful, o dear Aminta") of Marenzio's madrigal, a listener familiar with Guarini's *Pastor fido* might struggle at first to remember where the text belongs in the play. When the madrigal later identifies Amarilli as Aminta's beloved, one might question whether the text belongs in the play at all, for Aminta is not an actual enacted character in the drama but part of Arcadian history referenced by other characters. Amarilli, on the other hand, is the play's female protagonist, who secretly loves the "faithful shepherd" Mirtillo, not Aminta. From this clue alone, it becomes clear that the madrigal has created a setting and a set of relationships distinct from what exists in Guarini's Arcadia. This transition from play to madrigal—from dramatic plot to self-contained lyric—and Marenzio's treatment of the passage in his music exemplify a number of key issues in the play's musical history pertaining to poetic genre, voice, intertextuality, interpretative reading, and musical structure. For reasons we shall see, the madrigal also provides a fitting place to begin this evaluation of the play's textual sources and the early chronology of the *Pastor fido* madrigal.

O fido, o caro Aminta appeared in Marenzio's Seventh Book (Venice: Angelo Gardano, 1595) and sets a passage from the dialogue in act 1, scene 2 between Mirtillo and his companion Ergasto. The scene is well known in music scholarship for the famous lament with which it opens, Mirtillo's entrance monologue, "Cruda Amarilli, che col nome ancora," which appeared in musical settings by Monte in 1590 (as *O d'aspido più sorda e più fugace*), Marenzio and Wert in 1595, and dozens of composers thereafter. After Mirtillo (a newcomer to Arcadia) bemoans the beauty and coldness of his beloved Amarilli, Ergasto relates a tale from Arcadia's past that has placed Amarilli's fate—and marriage—in the hands of an oracle, thus leaving her torn between personal desire (her hidden love for Mirtillo) and divine and social duty (her arranged marriage to Silvio to ensure Arcadia's welfare). With its implications in the love between the two central characters,

DOI: 10.4324/9781315463056-5

Ergasto's tale proves vital for the backdrop of the play's main tragicomic plot (see Figure I.1).

The story involves the brave and faithful Aminta, priest of the goddess Diana, who falls in love with Lucrina—as Ergasto describes her, "a nymph wondrously graceful and beautiful, but wondrously false and vain" (ninfa leggiadra a maraviglia e bella, ma senza fede a maraviglia e vana). Once betrayed and rejected by Lucrina, Aminta prays to Diana to take vengeance upon Arcadia. It is believed, then, that the goddess struck Arcadia with her bow, wreaking incurable sickness on its people. According to the oracle (cited piecemeal by various characters throughout the play), the goddess's wrath could only be placated when Lucrina, or another citizen brave enough to stand in her place, was sacrificed at Aminta's hand—the sacrificial ritual that serves as the tragic foundation of the play. In the last moment before killing Lucrina, however, Aminta turns the blade on himself to spare both his beloved and Arcadia. Through this deed, Aminta became a model of ideal faith and love for future generations, while Lucrina became the embodiment of inconstancy and deceit, and of the bad fortune that unchaste actions may bring to all citizens.

The tale continues that Lucrina, moved by Aminta's selfless act, was overcome by a sudden love for the priest. In Aminta's final moments, Lucrina proclaimed her love, drew the blade from Aminta's breast, and turned it upon herself to join him in death. Ergasto's narration of Lucrina's final words and suicide appears nearly in its entirety in Marenzio's setting:

Disse piangendo: "O fido, o forte Aminta,	She said, weeping, "O faithful, o dear Aminta,
O troppo tardi conosciuto amante,	o lover known too late,
Che m'hai data, morendo, e vita e morte,	who has given me, dying, both life and death,
Se fù colpa il lasciarti, ecco l'ammendo	if it was a fault to leave you, now I amend it
Con l'unir teco eternamente l'alma."	in uniting my soul with you eternally."
E questo detto, il ferro stesso ancora	And this said, the same blade, still
Nel caro sangue tiepido e vermiglio	warm and red with the dear blood,
Tratto dal morto e tardi amato petto,	she drew from the dead and late-loved chest,
Il suo petto trafisse, e sopra Aminta,	and stabbed her own breast, and upon Aminta,
Che morto ancor non era e sentì forse	who was not yet dead and felt perhaps
Quel colpo, in braccio si lasciò cadere.	that blow, let herself fall into his arms.
Tal fine hebber gli amanti, à tal miseria	Such an end had the lovers, and such misery
Troppo amor, e perfidia ambidue trasse.	did too much love and faithlessness bring them both.

At the start of the play, Arcadia finds itself still in the grips of Diana's curse, requiring the yearly sacrifice of a virgin to avoid calamity. An oracle has revealed, however, that the curse can be lifted once and for all by the marriage of two citizens of divine heritage. Hence, it has been arranged that Amarilli, a descendent of Pan, will marry Silvio, a descendent of Hercules, who cares only for hunting. Despite this betrothal and its importance to Arcadia, Mirtillo remains steadfast in his pursuit of Amarilli's heart.

As Guarini acknowledges in his *Annotazioni* to the play, the origins of the Aminta tale lie not in his Arcadia, but in Pausanias's history of ancient Greece.[1] In Pausanias's version, the tale involves Coresus, a priest of Dionysus, who falls in love with the maiden Callirhoë. Pausanias explains:

> But the love of Coresus for Callirhoë was equaled by the maiden's hatred of him. When the maiden refused to change her mind, in spite of the many prayers and promises of Coresus, he then went as a suppliant to the image of Dionysus. The god listened to the prayer of his priest, and the Calydonians at once became raving as though through drink, and they were out of their minds when death overtook them. So, they appealed to the oracle of Dodona....[2]

As in the Aminta tale, Coresus also "slew himself in place of Callirhoë," but Pausanias's Callirhoë cuts her throat later at the spring of Calydor, whereas Guarini's Lucrina more poignantly pierces her breast and falls directly into the arms of the dying Aminta. Through this patent borrowing, the history of Guarini's Arcadia is intertwined with that of ancient Greece, and Guarini's shepherds and nymphs—criticized so severely for their excess of *civiltà*—become inextricably bound to the citizens of antiquity. The Pausanias reference ensures that these are not simple, rustic shepherds conventional to sixteenth-century pastoral, but sophisticated and virtuous individuals.[3]

The passage set by Marenzio represents the climax of the tale—the moment when Lucrina's heart is moved by Aminta's ultimate act of devotion (which threatens to be reenacted by Mirtillo later in the play). The story demonstrates considerable generic versatility, shifting from Pausanias's historical narrative to Guarini's pastoral tragicomedy (where it also forms part of the recounted past), and then to the lyric (narrative) madrigal. As part of Arcadians' (and Greeks') shared history, Ergasto's speech seems perfectly suited to the collective, narrative voice of the polyphonic madrigal, which draws no distinction between the individual "I" and the communal "we." In the play, Ergasto's role as spokesman for his community is highlighted by his preface to the story: "Ti narrerò de le miserie *nostre*" ("I will tell you of *our* miseries"). Although this line, with its insinuated first-person plural perspective, is not included in Marenzio's madrigal, it very well could be. Instead, this diegetic framework is implied, and the madrigal begins directly with the reported speech of the female beloved, before shifting to the underlying narrative voice (represented by Ergasto in the play) in line 6:

Text of Marenzio's madrigal	*Guarini,* Il pastor fido *(I, 2)*
1 "O fido, o caro Aminta, O troppo tardi conosciuto amante, Che m'hai dato, morendo, e vita e morte, Se fù colpa il lasciarti, ecco l'amendo 5 Con l'unir teco eternamente l'alma." E questo detto la bell'Amarilli, Il ferro stesso ancora Nel caro sangue tepido e vermiglio, Tratto dal mort'e tardi amato petto, 10 Il suo petto trafisse e sopr'Aminta, Che mort'ancor non era, e sentì forse Quel colpo, in braccio si lasciò cadere. Tal fine hebber gli sfortunati amanti.	[Disse piangendo:] "O fido, o forte Aminta, O troppo tardi conosciuto amante, Che m'hai data, morendo, e vita e morte, Se fù colpa il lasciarti, ecco l'ammendo Con l'unir teco eternamente l'alma." E questo detto, il ferro stesso ancora Nel caro sangue tiepido e vermiglio Tratto dal morto e tardi amato petto, Il suo petto trafisse, e sopra Aminta, Che morto ancor non era e sentì forse Quel colpo, in braccio si lasciò cadere. Tal fine hebber gli amanti, à tal miseria Troppo amor, e perfidia ambidue trasse.

There are three conspicuous discrepancies between the madrigal text and the play: the substitution of "caro" for "forte" in verse 1, the addition of Amarilli's name—in the phrase "la bell'Amarilli"—in verse 6, and the removal of the last verse and a half of Ergasto's speech and interpolation of "sfortunati" to fill out the final hendecasyllabic verse. The madrigal text proves straightforward and autonomous: there is no Arcadian curse attached to it, no intervention of a goddess, and—owing to the removal of "perfidia" and the final verse—no explicit infidelity. Amarilli simply makes amends for the fault of leaving Aminta. Even more, the insertion of Amarilli into the scene further weakens the intertextual ties to the plot, for in the play, Amarilli neither speaks to nor loves the ill-fated Aminta, nor could she even if she wished, as Aminta had lived generations ago. Even more, the characters of Guarini's play, including Amarilli, are all fortunate enough to elude death, as any reader who has made it through the weighty text (or a performance) would know. From the passage alone, the reader only learns that Aminta has died to save Amarilli, who, realizing her love for Aminta, then kills herself, too.

While these blatant differences between the madrigal text and the play have evoked multiple interpretations in the literature on Marenzio's *Pastor fido* settings and his Seventh Book, there is another, subtler class of disparities that has gone entirely unnoticed. These variants involve not the addition, deletion, or replacement of words, names, and phrases, but subtler details in the spellings, conjugations, and other orthographical features of individual words. Even more, whereas analyses of this and other madrigal texts have relied almost exclusively on the 1602 Ciotti edition of Guarini's play (and rarely the 1589 Bonfadino *princeps*), the significance of these seemingly trifling discrepancies comes to light only when all extant sources of the tragicomedy of c.1584–95, both manuscript and print, are considered.

A comparison of readings of *O fido, o caro Aminta* from these sources, for example, shows the following:

Marenzio's madrigal	*Manuscripts (pre-1586)*	*Printed editions (1589–95)*
1 O fido o caro Aminta	...o fido, o forte Aminta,	...o fido, o forte Aminta,
O troppo tardi conosciuto amante		
Che m'hai dato morendo e vita e morte	...data/dato/datta	...data
Se fù colpa il lasciarti ecco l'amendo	Se fu fallo ...l'ammendo	...l'ammendo
5 Con l'unir teco eternamente l'alma		
E questo detto la bell'Amarilli		E, questo detto, il ferro
Il ferro stesso ancora	E, questo detto, il ferro	stesso, ancora
Nel caro sangue tepido e vermiglio	stesso, ancora	... tiepido/tepido
Tratto dal morto e tardi amato petto	...tepido	
10 Il suo petto trafisse e sopra Aminta		
Che mort'ancor non era e senti forse	Che ancor morto non...	
Quel colpo in braccio si lasciò cadere		
Tal fine hebber gli sfortunati amanti.	Tal fine ebber gli amanti, à tal miseria	Tal fine ebber gli amanti, à tal miseria
	Vanitate/Troppo amor e perfidia ambidue/ambedue trasse	Troppo amor, e perfidia ambodue/ambidue/ ambedue trasse

In addition to the three major differences already noted—"caro"/"forte" (v. 1), "la bell'Amarilli" (vv. 6–7), and "sfortunati amanti" (v. 13)—a number of small-scale disparities emerge. The manuscripts contain three versions of the madrigal's "dato" (v. 3), whereas all of the printed editions read "data." The manuscripts also read "fu fallo" in place of "fu colpa" in verse 4, and invert the word order of "Che mort'ancor" in verse 11, while the madrigal text and editions all agree. More minutely, the madrigal text conflicts with all *Pastor fido* sources in its spelling of "amendo" (v. 4) and with certain printed editions (but no manuscripts) at "tepido" (v. 8).

Altogether, the variations offer an array of contrasting correlations: in some instances, the madrigal matches certain manuscripts and no editions, or all manuscripts and some editions, or no manuscripts and some (or all) editions. And, of course, there are places where the madrigal's reading proves unique—"caro" in verse 1 and "amendo" in verse 4, for example. Although it might seem unlikely that a strong connection could be found between the madrigal text and any of these sources, the text of Marenzio's work does, in fact, align closely with one distinctive yet intangible source: a lost draft of the play, the vestiges of which survive in other contemporary sources. This correlation between a missing manuscript and the madrigal text, however, does not stop here, with this single work, but encompasses the greater share of Marenzio's *Pastor fido* settings. The potential implications of these seemingly tedious textual details are extensive, impacting not only the accepted dating of Marenzio's textual source and his madrigals, but also the broader chronology of the early *Pastor fido* madrigal as a whole. These details and their consequences unfold through the course of this chapter, with its exploration of the ties between Marenzio, Guarini, and Cardinal Scipione Gonzaga in Rome, and an unexpected connection of all three figures—along with Marenzio's madrigals—to a Florentine academy and an ongoing crusade to salvage the Tuscan vernacular from linguistic impurities. The harrowing scene between Aminta and Amarilli/Lucrina, meanwhile, will return at the start of the next chapter, with the close study of Marenzio's musical treatment of its changes in voice and genre, its phonetic allusions and deictic devices, and its complex intertextuality extending to both Guarini's play and the madrigal's own context in Marenzio's Seventh Book.

Marenzio and His Patrons in Rome

What is especially noteworthy of Pescetti's description in the *Difesa del Pastorfido* (1601) of the practice of extracting texts from the play for musical setting is his attribution of the custom to Duke Alfonso II d'Este. For although the duke was well known for his zealous patronage of poetry, music, and dance, and for his ardent demand of Guarini's verse in particular, equally well known are his efforts to conceal the artistic products of his court from the outside world.[4] In all, of the nearly 400 musical settings from *Il pastor fido* of 1590–1640, the majority came not from composers in or associated with Ferrara, but from Rome (47 known settings) and Mantua (43), followed at a distance by Naples (27), Prague (23), and Florence (23), as shown in Figure 4.1.[5] From Ferrara—which Pescetti claimed to be the fount of the *Pastor fido* madrigal, and which was indeed the birthplace of the play itself—we have only two settings: one published by the foremost composer of Duke Alfonso II's court, Luzzasco Luzzaschi in 1601—four years after the duke's death, but composed during the years of the *concerto delle donne* (c1580–97)—and a single setting from 1615 by Alessandro Grandi, who was *maestro di cappella* at the Accademia dello Spirito Santo in 1610–15 before taking the same role at the cathedral in Ferrara.[6] If what Pescetti tells us is true about Alfonso d'Este requesting musical settings of the play, these works presumably suffered the same fate as much of the music, documents, and other cultural products of the Este court in the last part of the sixteenth century, which were either destroyed or never recorded in the duke's attempts to maintain secrecy, or lost or damaged in the precarious transfer of the ducal court to Modena by the ousted illegitimate heir, Cesare d'Este, in 1598.

Thus, although the vibrant artistic environment of Ferrara might seem the most probable breeding ground for the *Pastor fido* madrigal in its earliest years, there are very few sources indicating as much. Instead, it is a composer from Rome, Marenzio, who stands at the forefront of the trend,

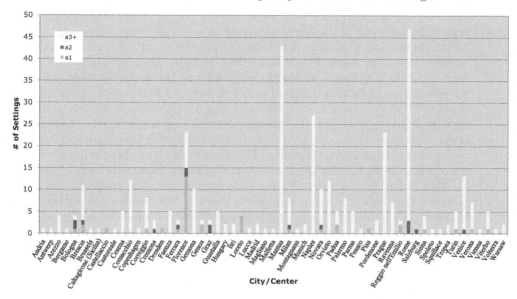

Figure 4.1 Origins of *Pastor fido* Settings, 1587–1627, Based on Composers' Positions

followed close behind by the *maestro di musica* of Mantua, Wert.[7] Nevertheless, despite spending nearly his entire active career (1580–99) in Rome,
Marenzio's connections with Ferrara remained strong, albeit indirect,
throughout his life and showed lasting impacts on his music and employment. The early part of his career, for example, was spent in the service
of Duke Alfonso d'Este's brother, Cardinal Luigi d'Este (1538–86), who divided his time between Rome and the Villa d'Este in Tivoli.[8]

Documents reveal that Luigi d'Este showed considerable interest in the
artistic happenings and developments at his brother's court in Ferrara
through the 1570s–80s, as he was kept abreast of performances by the duke's
concerto and *balletto delle donne* through correspondence with Ferrarese in-
siders. Hence, on 26 July 1581, the Ferrarese *cavaliere* Giacomo Grana informed the cardinal of a visit to the Este court by a Polish gentleman, "for
whose pleasure the duke presented *la musica di quelle signore*, who grow
better every day."[9] On 7 February of the following year, Grana wrote to
Luigi d'Este again, stating that "in the evening...was presented the *musica
delle dame* of the duchess; the same was done yesterday evening in the apartments of the Duchess of Urbino, where I was able to enjoy it."[10] A letter
from Cardinal d'Este to Marenzio of 9 September 1582, relating that "some
gentlewomen desire that you should set to music the enclosed madrigal,"
suggests that Marenzio might even have composed music for Duke Alfonso's famous *concerto*.[11] Indeed, verse by Ferrarese poets, particularly Tasso
and Guarini, figures prominently in Marenzio's output during this time and
continued to do so throughout his career. Luigi d'Este's fascination with the
artistic happenings of Duke Alfonso's court was given a fitting close when,

following the cardinal's death on 30 December 1586, Guarini gave a funeral oration in his honor at the Ferrarese chapel.

But Marenzio's focus on verse from the secretive and guarded court of Alfonso d'Este in the mid- and late 1580s seems to have sprung not only from the duke's brother—who was clearly well aware of the duke's jealous nature—but also from a different cardinal from a family of close artistic rivals. For in the summer of 1586, as Luigi d'Este's health was showing signs of decline, Marenzio had already entered negotiations with another court with close ties to *Il pastor fido* in the hope of finding new employment: the court of Duke Guglielmo Gonzaga in Mantua. Mediating these negotiations in Rome was Guarini's close friend and former colleague from his days in Padua: the humanist, poet, composer, and soon-to-be cardinal, Scipione Gonzaga (1542–93). Scipione is perhaps best known for his close friendship with the poet Torquato Tasso and for his role in reviewing Tasso's works—most notably the *Gerusalemme liberata* for both the 1581 and 1584 editions.[12] As Iain Fenlon has pointed out, Scipione might have passed unpublished drafts of Tasso's poetry on to Marenzio in the mid-1580s, which would account for the uniqueness of many of the composer's Tasso texts.[13] Marenzio's setting of *Giunto alla tomba* from the *Gerusalemme liberata*, for instance, differs notably from other extant sources of the text. The madrigal appeared in his Fourth Book of madrigals of 1584, making it plausible that Scipione gave an intermediate draft of the text to Marenzio while preparing the 1584 edition of Tasso's epic. As seen in Chapter 2, however, Scipione was also closely acquainted with the other great poet of the Este court at the time, Guarini. Tasso, Guarini, and Scipione were all members of the Accademia degli Eterei in Padua in the mid-1560s, and all three contributed poems to the academy's *Rime* of 1567—the source of two of Marenzio's Tasso settings.[14]

It was around the same time that he was mediating negotiations between Marenzio and the Mantuan court in 1586–87 that Scipione received a draft of Guarini's *Il pastor fido*. Although the draft itself has been lost, a record of Scipione's general opinion survives in a letter to Guarini of 30 September 1587, in which he declares—perhaps foreseeing critics' reactions to its pervasive lyricism and artful style—that "if anyone can raise an objection against this marvelous work, it is its being too beautiful, in precisely the way that others might criticize a feast at which no fare is offered other than sugar and honey."[15] Testament to the close relationship between the cardinal and poet is inscribed into the play itself. In a quasi-autobiographical speech by the character Carino in act 5, scene 1, Guarini makes an oblique allusion to Scipione with the phrase "il famoso Egon di lauro adorno."[16] This reference is pointed out explicitly in the *Annotazioni* for the 1602 Ciotti edition, where Guarini expands on his homage with praise for the cardinal's poetry and leadership of the Eterei, concluding, "This lovely poem [*Il pastor fido*], before coming to print, passed through his hands, and was praised by his most noble judgment, as was the *Gerusalemme liberata* of Torquato Tasso."[17]

It was between Scipione's negotiations between Marenzio and Mantua and his comments on the draft of Guarini's play that the first known madrigal with ties to *Il pastor fido* came to print: Marenzio's *O che soave e non inteso bacio*, which appeared in the composer's Fourth Book for six voices, signed 20 December 1586, less than two weeks before the death of Cardinal Luigi d'Este. As we have seen, the version of the text in Marenzio's madrigal was the first of several variants to appear in print, and when it was included months later in Ventura's *Rime di diversi celebri poeti*, the poem took a much different form from that of the madrigal. As James Chater has observed, Marenzio's text most closely resembles that of the play, which at that time was circulating only in manuscript.[18] This raises the obvious question, then, of how Marenzio in Rome might have gotten hold of this *Pastor fido* text three years before the play's publication.

There are several indications of a possible artistic relationship between Marenzio and Scipione Gonzaga during this period, including Marenzio's dedication of a book of motets to Scipione in 1585,[19] his Tasso settings of the mid-1580s, and the correspondence involving the position at Duke Guglielmo Gonzaga's court in Mantua in 1586. It is conceivable that in 1586, Scipione also introduced Marenzio to *Il pastor fido*—or, more specifically, that he introduced Marenzio to *Il pastor fido* as a promising source of madrigal texts—and that for years, these settings served a private function before being published. For it was not until 1594 that Marenzio would again publish settings from the play. The seven intervening years brought radical changes for both Marenzio and *Il pastor fido*. For Marenzio, there came new stylistic trends heralded by the anomalous and austere *Madrigali a quattro, cinque, e sei* (1588); a nearly two-year stay in Florence to assist with preparations (notably the *intermedi*) for the 1589 Medici wedding festivities; and the publication of only a single book of madrigals between 1588 and 1594. Meanwhile, for the play, these years witnessed a string of aborted stage productions—along with at least one successful attempt—the first wave of the critical debate between Denores and the *Verrati*, and numerous editions printed in Italy and abroad.

Hence, when Marenzio published fifteen additional *Pastor fido* settings in his Sixth and Seventh Books of madrigals in 1594–95 (and two more in his Eighth Book of 1598), not only was the play steeped in controversy, but it had also probably never been seen onstage by the vast majority of its readers. This was the case as well for the circles of *letterati* that formed Marenzio's immediate audience in Rome: an audience which included not only his current patron and esteemed supporter of the arts, Cardinal Cinzio Aldobrandini; his earlier patron of 1590–93 and musical amateur, Virginio Orsini[20]; Tasso (who remained in Aldobrandini's protection in 1592–95); Cardinal Montalto; and Michele Peretti, but also during the winters of 1593–94 and 1594–95, Guarini himself. Also members of Cinzio Aldobrandini's notable *famiglia* of scholars and *letterati* in the mid-1590s were a number of prominent literary theorists who were active participants in various ongoing literary quarrels, including Angelo Ingegneri, Francesco Patrizi, and Giovanni de' Bardi di Vernio. Ingegneri, a dramatic theorist and author of *Della poesia rappresentativa* (discussed above), and Patrizi, a Platonic philosopher at the University of Ferrara (1577–92) and *Studium Urbis* in Rome (1592–97), were involved in the debates over poetic genres in the 1590s, wherein both represented the progressive views of the Moderns and defended the virtue of poetic invention and the mixing of classical genres to suit the tastes of contemporary audiences.[21] The Florentine humanist, writer, and critic Giovanni de' Bardi—known to us already for his role in the grand Florentine stage works of 1586 and 1589—was a member of Cinzio's household in Rome beginning in 1592. Bardi knew Guarini personally from the poet's visit to Florence in June 1588 to promote (unsuccessfully) the staging of his tragicomedy for the 1589 wedding celebrations, and Ingegneri's interactions with the poet extend back at least to their theatrical collaborations in Vicenza in 1583–85. Bardi, Ingegneri, and Patrizi would certainly have been familiar with *Il pastor fido* and the surrounding polemic by the mid-1590s, and Bardi's and Ingegneri's support for the work could well have been nurtured further in the intellectual milieu and daily discussions of Cinzio Aldobrandini's *ridotto*, and by Guarini's residence there in 1593–95.[22]

This dynamic cultural environment in Rome would have ensured that Marenzio's new *Pastor fido* madrigals were performed before an audience with profound familiarity with, and presumably respect for, Guarini's work. Both his Sixth and Seventh Books were, after all, dedicated to central figures within this Roman circle: Marenzio's patron, Cinzio Aldobrandini, was himself the dedicatee of the Sixth Book, and the Seventh Book bears a dedication to Diego de Campo, a personal valet to the reigning Pope Clement VIII, Ippolito Aldobrandini (Cinzio Aldobrandini's uncle), and a canon of Santa Maria Maggiore in Rome.[23]

Scholars have surmised that Marenzio's settings, like the planned Montalto–Peretti staging of the play, were products of the composer's direct interactions with Guarini in Rome during this period,[24] although it seems equally plausible that he composed the works before the poet's sojourns and any discussions of the play these visits might have generated. Thus, *Il pastor fido* might have been the focus not only of deliberations and spoken readings among Cinzio's circle, but also, through Marenzio's madrigals, of sung performances of specific close readings that enhanced the texts with the added interpretative and affective dimensions of music. It might be said, therefore, that Marenzio's *Pastor fido* madrigals, on the one hand, fulfilled a special function for contemporary audiences in Rome and elsewhere: they offered affective, musical renderings of speeches envisioned for the stage, yet evidently troublesome and costly to mount as a dramatic work—passages ostensibly meant to be seen and heard through actors' representations, and not simply read, silently or aloud, from the page. There was indeed interest among Marenzio's Roman patrons to experience the play through performance, as would be manifest in the efforts by Michele Peretti and Cardinal

Montalto in 1596 to mount a full-scale production with *intermedi*. At the same time, however, Marenzio's madrigals intimate more fundamentally the play's already prominent reputation as a text for reading—silently, aloud, and in song—even more than for the stage. Guarini's initial readings and correspondence from readers hint early on of this robust non-theatrical role. The long history of musical settings, editions, and translations testifies to its enduring fertility as verse to be read and sung in intimate and private quarters.

Marenzio's madrigals highlighted *Il pastor fido* for the first time as a rich source of musical texts to more than simply this close group of Roman *letterati*, nobles, and ecclesiastics, but to the wider spheres of madrigal composers, music patrons, and consumers of madrigal prints. While the inception of this musical–textual trend is significant in itself in the history of late-Renaissance and early-Baroque music, what makes it even more noteworthy is the novelty in the tradition of the Italian madrigal of utilizing a dramatic text for such a purpose. While the musical settings of Marenzio and his Mantuan contemporary, Wert, came at a time when *Il pastor fido* was still very much at the center of discussions and staging efforts in the major Italian courts, academies, and intellectual circles, later composers may have seen the play principally in this more literary light, as a trove of lyric reflections and a text for reading—that is, as "una dissipita raccolta di madrigali" (a dissolute gathering of madrigals)—rather than as an integral dramatic work, which is precisely how Malacreta, Summo, and other opponents portrayed it. This transition from play to musical–poetic madrigal would likely have been made ever easier, given Guarini's already well-established reputation as a lyric poet and expressly as an author of musical texts.

Guarini and the Lyric Madrigal

Having served as a court secretary for Duke Alfonso d'Este since 1567, Guarini took over the position of court poet in 1579 after Tasso was committed to the Ospedale di Sant'Anna.[25] Well before assuming this post, however, Guarini was extremely active as a poet for the Ferrarese court, with his verses playing a major part in fulfilling Alfonso d'Este's voracious demand for poetry for music, dance, and theatrical events. As we saw in Chapter 2, several sonnets by Guarini appeared alongside those of other respected poets (including Tasso and Scipione Gonzaga) as early as 1567 in the *Rime degli Accademici Eterei*, which promptly made their way into composers' hands, beginning in 1569 with the madrigal settings of Giulio Fiesco, and his verse continued to appear in poetic anthologies and, starting in 1598, editions of his own *Rime*.[26]

While a *cavaliere* at the Ferrarese court in the 1570s and 1580s, Guarini was also given the task of writing poetry expressly for composers of Duke Alfonso's esteemed *concerto delle donne*. The first edition of his *Rime* of 1598 (dedicated to Cinzio Aldobrandini's brother, Cardinal Pietro Aldobrandini) contains an immense body of lyric poetry and some of the most widely set madrigal texts of the late Cinquecento and early Seicento, such as *Ardo sì, ma non t'amo* (61 settings, 1585–1678), *Lasso perché mi fuggi* (32 settings, c1582–1675), *Occhi un tempo mia vita* (28 settings, 1588–1668), *Tirsi morir volea* (27 settings, 1578–1633), *O come è gran martire* (25 settings, 1582–1622), and the *Canzon de' baci* (*Baci soavi e cari*; 17 settings, 1581–1640).[27] His lyric verse is characterized by its epigrammatic and sometimes erotic wit, clever wordplay, labyrinthine syntax, and penetrating explorations of the many forms, facets, and circumstances of love, as well as its skillful use of word sound and rhetorical devices such as metaphor, oxymoron, hyperbole, and anaphora—in other words, the more profane, sensual side of Petrarchan lyricism, and the very same qualities that fill the speeches of *Il pastor fido*.

Two examples—one a poetic madrigal published in the *Rime* of 1598, the other a speech by Mirtillo from the play—illustrate some of the aspects of kinship between Guarini's lyric and dramatic verse:

1	Ite, amari sospiri,	Go, bitter sighs,
	A la bella cagion del morir mio,	to the fair cause of my dying
	E dite: O troppo di pietate ignuda,	and say: "O woman too bereft of pity,
	S'havete pur desio	if indeed you wish
5	Di lungamente conservarvi cruda,	to remain cruel for so long,
	Allentate il rigore,	ease your severity,
	Che quel meschin si more,	for that wretched one is dying,
	E darà tosto fin co'l suo morire,	and his death will quickly bring an end
	A la durezza vostra, al suo languire.	to your harshness, to his languishing."

1	Udite, lagrimosi	Hear, mournful
	Spirti d'Averno, udite	spirits of Avernus, hear
	Nova sorte di pena, e di tormento.	of a new sort of pain and torment.
	Mirate crudo affetto	Witness cruel affection
5	In sembiante pietoso.	in a merciful guise.
	La mia Donna crudel più de l'Inferno,	My lady, crueler than the Inferno,
	Perch'una sola morte	because one single death
	Non può far sazia la sua ingorda voglia,	cannot satisfy her greedy desire—
	E la mia vita è quasi	and my life is almost
10	Una perpetua morte,	a perpetual death—
	Mi comanda ch'io viva,	commands me to live,
	Perché la vita mia	so that my life
	Di mille morti il dì ricetto sia.	is the refuge of a thousand deaths a day.

Both texts were set first by Marenzio—*Ite, amari sospiri* in his Eighth Book (1598) and *Udite, lagrimosi* in his Sixth Book (1594)—and inspired numerous other musical treatments thereafter: seventeen in total for *Ite, amari sospiri*, and twenty-one for *Udite, lagrimosi*. Both texts likewise show a (male) speaker appealing to pneumatic forces (sighs and spirits) for relief from a cruel beloved, beginning with commands: "Ite" (Go) and "Udite" (Hear). They then proceed with a rich lexicon of descriptions of the lady's vindictiveness ("amari," "di pietate ignuda," "cruda," "durezza," "crudo affetto," "ingorda voglia") and with alliteration rooted in the consonance *M* ("morir," "mio," "meschin," "mirate," "mille," and so forth) before ending with a rhyming couplet. Both passages also cater especially well to euphemistic readings based on the conventional use of death ("morte") as a metaphor for sexual release. In this erotic light, the lovers suffer not from rejection, but from the "insatiable desires" ("ingorda voglia") of their amorous partners. This interpretation is enhanced further by the speakers' appeals in both cases to airy, spirit-like substances similar in nature to their own animate spirits, given the contemporary conception—following ancient humoral theory—of spirit as a vaporous substance that departed the body in one of two principal ways: through death or orgasm ("death").[28]

A key distinction between the two texts is the shift of perspective in *Ite, amari sospiri*—from the lover's opening appeal, to the imagined speech he wishes his sighs to deliver—whereas the speaker of *Udite, lagrimosi* merely complains to the spirits in his own voice throughout. From a composer's standpoint, *Ite, amari sospiri*—like *O fido, o caro Aminta*, with its shift from Amarilli/Lucrina's reported speech to narrative voice—offers a wider range of interpretative options and challenges than the single-voice text. But this change of perspective is hardly indicative of poetic source, as both the *Rime* and speeches from *Il pastor fido* encompass a range of approaches to voice, perspective, and address.

In all, presented in this manner, *in vacuo*, the second text, *Udite, lagrimosi*—Mirtillo's monologue from the opening of act 3, scene 6—gives no clear indication that it belongs to a larger dramatic work.[29] In fact, the two texts could conceivably be used interchangeably at this position in the play without upsetting anything in terms of sentiment, meaning, or dramatic function. This *in vacuo* scenario, however, does not reflect the "real-world" cultural environments from which these musical settings arose: environments that included not only aristocratic, ecclesiastical, and cultured circles such as the Mantuan court and the Roman households of Cinzio Aldobrandini, Cardinal Montalto, and Virginio Orsini that were notably well acquainted with Guarini's tragicomedy through readings, stage performances, and musical settings, but also a substantial, largely tacit popular readership that drove the play's many reprints, translations, and musical settings across Italy and north of the Alps. Indeed, a crucial distinction between these two poetic sources—*Rime* versus play—that has been often overlooked in the music scholarship is precisely that, despite their universality and lyric-like language, the texts and speaking personas from *Il pastor fido* are part of a broader, specific narrative—a larger work—and therefore offer the potential for strongly intertextual readings that draw on the backstories, present circumstances, and known future of the external plot. The madrigal, in turn, has the capacity to realize these implicit exterior dimensions of its texts by drawing references, internally and externally, to other musical and textual moments, and, thereby, evoking affects, concepts, and characters that lie beyond the immediate and literal text. This propensity for intertextuality represents one crucial aspect of the madrigal's innate means of discourse.

Scholars have attributed the scarcity of musical settings of *Il pastor fido* prior to 1594 to the difficulty of rendering texts from a theatrical work in the lyric setting of the madrigal. James Chater, for instance, maintains that "the idea of setting to music speeches from a play... posed a challenge composers were not yet ready to meet."[30] As we have seen, however, this seems an unlikely explanation, given the play's often criticized episodes of madrigalian lyricism and reflection, not to mention the facility with which composers of diverse standing and from all corners of Europe handled its passages once the practice was underway. Excerpts from the play were, in fact, so well suited to transplantation into the madrigal that, whereas the texts of the earliest musical settings of 1584–92 tend to deviate from extant sources of the tragicomedy and to conform most closely to variant readings published in poetic anthologies, settings that appeared after the play's publication typically adhere closely to the printed text. Differences that do occur in these post-1589 settings are generally superficial, such as the altering of first or last lines to create rhymes or to make the text syntactically or grammatically self-sufficient, and the substitution of named characters from the play with generic pastoral names (Tirsi, Filli, Clori, and the like) or metonymic phrases, such as "mio cor" and "anima mia."

In this respect, *Il pastor fido* gives the impression of being a ready-made source of madrigal texts, its passages conducive to both madrigalian (diegetic) and theatrical (dramatic) contexts with little or no modification. Despite theorists' complaints about its mixed genre, lack of verisimilitude, and overabundance of length and lofty rhetoric, the versatility in terms of readership and function that these and other features afforded proved an asset for its continued and varied relevance. The issue of genre—play versus lyric poem, imitated speech by a character onstage versus collective reading in a private chamber—thus evidently had little to do with composers' slightly delayed interest in the work (if, indeed, there was such a delay, and not simply a delay of their works' publication). Nor did the play suffer from lack of exposure or availability, given its early promotion by the playwright, circulation in manuscripts, and preparations for the stage even before its appearance in print. Rather, it seems, on the face of it, that the growing trend of *Pastor fido* madrigals formed part of a larger, more general vogue of setting Guarini texts to music that grew steadily from the late 1560s through the 1590s and surged dramatically around the turn of the century (Table 4.1 and Figure 4.2).[31] From this viewpoint, *Il pastor fido* served as but an additional source of verse by a poet who had already been gaining increasing attention from madrigal composers and patrons for decades before the play's publication, and whose texts were poised to experience a boom in musical treatments—strengthened by the popularity of the new tragicomedy and by the publication of the 1598 *Rime*—around 1600 and the decades that followed.

Table 4.1 Settings of Guarini's *Rime* and *Il pastor fido*, 1568–1631

	Rime	*Il pastor fido*	*Total*
1568			0
1569	4		4
1570			0
1571	1		1
1572			0
1573			0
1574	1		1
1575	1		1
1576	1		1
1577			0
1578	1		1
1579	1		1
1580	26		26
1581	4		4
1582	7		7
1583	8		8
1584	6		6
1585	46		46
1586	26		26
1587	26	1	27
1588	21	1	22
1589	9		9
1590	28	1	29
1591	17	1	18
1592	22	1	23
1593	11	2	13
1594	11	4	15
1595	10	17	27
1596	19	1	20
1597	19	6	25
1598	15	16	31
1599	23	10	33
1600	51	25	76
1601	28	6	34
1602	39	29	68
1603	25	4	29
1604	44	7	51
1605	32	17	49
1606	41	7	48
1607	39	4	43
1608	50	18	68
1609	56	14	70
1610	25	5	30
1611	38	18	56
1612	37	12	49
1613	30	14	44
1614	36	25	61

(Continued)

Table 4.1 Continued

	Rime	*Il pastor fido*	*Total*
1615	40	7	47
1616	39	10	49
1617	62	30	92
1618	12	6	18
1619	36	8	44
1620	26	2	28
1621	26	27	53
1622	24	5	29
1623	12	10	22
1624	4	3	7
1625	9	2	11
1626	17	8	25
1627	11	0	11
1628	5		5
1629	20		20
1630	3		3
1631	2		2

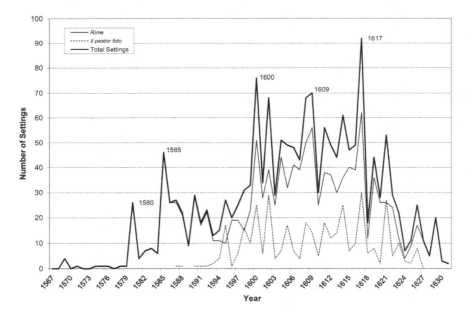

Figure 4.2 Settings of Guarini's *Rime* and *Il pastor fido*, 1567–1631

As Table 4.1 and Figure 4.2 show, through the 1580s, there is a considerable rise in the number of Guarini settings from the lyric poems alone as compared to prior decades. After the 1590s, which saw the publication of the play, *Rime*, and many *Pastor fido* settings of Marenzio, Wert, and others, the total volume of Guarini settings increased markedly, maintaining its highest overall levels in 1600–23 and peaking at seventy-six in 1600 and ninety-two in 1617. Yet, while the number of settings stemming solely from *Il pastor fido* (represented by the dotted line in Figure 4.2) consistently supplements the total Guarini settings after 1594, the play remains largely overshadowed by the *Rime* as a textual source. In fact, in only three instances does the number of *Pastor fido* madrigals exceed settings of the *Rime*, and only one of these bears a significant difference: in both 1598 and 1621, *Il pastor fido* edges out the *Rime* by only one setting, while in 1595—owing to Marenzio's and Wert's books of that year—the settings from *Il pastor fido* surpass those of the *Rime* by seven.[32] According to these figures, then, the Guarini vogue centered chiefly on his lyric verse, while the play appears to have been swept along with it later and secondarily, offering composers additional supply, variety, and, perhaps, novelty, while functioning essentially as a lyric source. But these figures alone, although informative, do not paint a full picture.

To begin, considering that there were over twice as many options of madrigal texts from the *Rime* (192) as from *Il pastor fido* (85), the ratio of *Pastor fido* to *Rime* settings adjusted to scale is roughly 4:5 (80%) in 1590–1631. This relative perspective alone paints a very different picture from what the raw numbers in Figure 4.2 convey: while the *Rime* provided more than double the number of madrigal texts as the play, those texts drew, on average, only 20% more settings. Moreover, by the time the play was published on the cusp of 1590, independent poems by Guarini had been circulating in print for over two decades—since the *Rime degli Accademici Eterei* of 1567. Despite the extra decades of exposure for many of the *Rime* poems, the most frequently set texts from both sources received similar numbers of treatments overall: both have five texts with twenty or more settings, and two with more than thirty treatments.[33]

Second, the large number of *Rime* settings from the 1580s is inflated greatly by a handful of idiosyncratic collections devoted largely or entirely to Guarini settings, including twenty-six *Rime* settings in the manuscript Mus.F.1358 from the Biblioteca Estense di Modena, estimated by Vassalli and Pompilio to date from 1580 to 1582, which were never published[34]; thirty-one settings of Guarini's *Ardo sì, ma non t'amo* commissioned for the Bavarian volume *Sdegnosi ardori: musica di diversi auttori, sopra un istesso soggetto di parole* of 1585 (Munich: Adam Berg)[35]; and eleven settings in Philippe de Monte's Eleventh Book (1586). Eleven other treatments of *Ardo sì, ma non t'amo* boost the totals for 1586–91. Thus, the onset of the upsurge in *Rime* madrigals resembles that of the *Pastor fido* madrigal in general character, with sporadic peaks generated by exceptional Guarini-rich collections in the early years, followed soon after by a more consistent outpouring from a greater variety of sources.

While these considerations of scale and trajectory show the musical appeal of both sources to be much more balanced than what the sheer numbers imply, the foremost origins of settings in the late 1590s and 1600s also suggest that *Il pastor fido* was not merely "swept along" secondarily with the

Rime, but rather instrumental in driving the growing trend of Guarini settings. For it was in the cultural centers brimming with ambitions to stage the tragicomedy in the 1590s, particularly Rome and Mantua, that the heaviest outpourings of Guarini settings took shape during this same period: some 114 madrigals—54 from *Il pastor fido*, 60 from the *Rime*—from Rome (Marenzio) and Mantua (Wert, Gastoldi, Pallavicino, Rossi, and Monteverdi) between 1594 and c.1600 (although some appeared later in print). The enthusiastic embrace of Guarini's work seems to have proliferated from there, as composers elsewhere followed suit by issuing books that combined passages from the play with *Rime* by Guarini and other poets, and occasionally devoted books entirely to the tragicomedy. As later chapters will show, Marenzio's madrigals played a distinctive influential role in this early stage of the Guarini vogue, including in Mantua, both in the texts he set (and their singular variants) and in the ways he treated them.

Although the discrete poetic genres of *Rime* and pastoral play might seem to invite discrete compositional techniques, particularly in light of the more verisimilar, representational possibilities of solo song around 1600, a comparison of the proportion of settings from the two sources for solo voice (Figure 4.3) reveals little difference in the way composers treated them in terms of vocal/instrumental forces. Although the peaks in solo settings from *Il pastor fido* often exceed those for the *Rime*, the average proportions of monodies through the most prolific years (1600–27) are reasonably close: 12.4% for the *Rime* and 14% for the play. The proportion of *a1* settings for *Il pastor fido*, then, remains relatively low overall and does not increase over time in response to the proliferation of monody and *musica rappresentativa*. Furthermore, whereas the graph shows the proportions of *a1* settings from the *Rime* rising sharply after the play fell out of fashion as a musical source in 1627, the total number of *Rime* settings in those years was relatively low: hence, while 83% of settings in 1633 were *a1*, this amounted to only five out of six total settings from that year. These trends reinforce the idea that composers viewed (and continued to view) their madrigal settings of Guarini's tragicomedy in a narrative framework—as impassioned retellings or readings of the characters' words—and bypassed the opportunity for enhanced realism and enactment of soloistic means.

Of the composers who took interest in Guarini's play, it comes as no surprise that the exceptionally prolific kapellmeister of the imperial court in Prague, Philippe de Monte, stands among the first with his *O d'aspido più sorda e più fugace* of 1590 and *Non son, come a te pare* of 1593 (see Table 3.1). For Monte bore the Guarini standard in the north throughout much of his long and prolific career, becoming the second known composer (behind Giulio Fiesco of Ferrara) ever to publish a Guarini setting in 1571 with his treatment of *Hor che'l mio vivo sole* from the *Rime degli Academici Eterei* (1567),[36] among the first to include multiple Guarini settings in a single madrigal book, and possibly the most committed composer of Guarini madrigals with over fifty settings between 1586 and 1600. As Table 4.2 shows, Monte's Eleventh (1586), Twelfth (1587), and Fifteenth (1592) Books yielded twenty-five settings from Guarini's *Rime*, followed in 1593 by one *Pastor fido* madrigal included with two *Rime* settings in his Sixteenth Book.[37] The tide then turns sharply in the other direction, with Monte's *La fiammetta* (1599) and *Musica sopra il pastor fido* (1600) producing far more settings from *Il pastor fido* (21) than from the *Rime* (2).

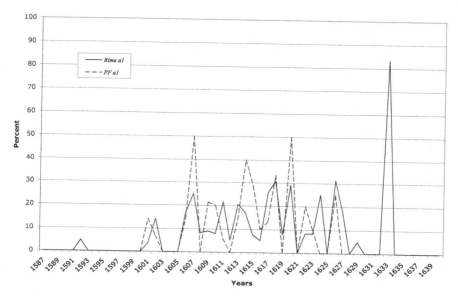

Figure 4.3 Proportions of *Pastor fido* and *Rime* Settings for Solo Voice, 1587–1640

Table 4.2 Madrigal Books with a Large Presence of Guarini Texts, 1586–1605[38]

Year	Composer	Book	Rime	Il pastor fido	Total
1586	Monte	*XI a 5*	10		10
1587	Monte	*XII a 5*	5		5
1588	Pallavicino	*IV a 5*	5		5
1590	dalla Casa	*II a 5*	6		6
1592	Monte	*XV a 5*	10		10
1592	Monteverdi	*III a 5*	8	1	9
1593	Monte	*XVI a 5*	2	1	3
1594	Marenzio	*VI a 5*		4	4
1595	Marenzio	*VII a 5*		12	12
1595	Wert	*XI a 5*		4	4
1596	Masnelli	*II a 5*	5		5
1597	Savioli	*II a 5*	8	1	9
1598	Marenzio	*VIII a 5*	2	2	4
1598	Gastoldi	*III a 5*	1	3	4
1599	Marenzio	*IX a 5*	3		3

(*Continued*)

Table 4.2 Continued

Year	Composer	Book	Rime	Il pastor fido	Total
1599	Monte	*La fiammetta*	1	7	8
1599	Capilupi	*I a 5*	7		7
1600	Pallavicino	*VI a 5*	11	3	14
1600	Monte	*Il pastor fido*	1	14	15
1600	Arnoni	*I a 6*	9		9
1600	Rossi	*I a 5*	11	2	13
1600	Savioli	*III a 5*	6		6
1601	Bargnani	*I a 5*	3	5	8
1601	Luzzaschi	*Musiche a 1–3*	7	1	8
1601	Stivori	*Concenti musicali*	5		5
1601	Verso	*II a 6*	5		5
1602	Piccioni	*Il pastor fido*	1	12	13
1602	Gastoldi	*IV a 5*	1	10	11
1602	Pecci	*Musica a 5*	6		6
1603	Monteverdi	*IV a 5*	8	2	10
1603	Pecci	*Canzonette I a 3*	6		6
1604	Priuli	*I a 5*	7	2	9
1604	Pallavicino	*VII a 5*	7		7
1604	Gastoldi	*Concenti musicali*	6	1	7
1604	Caletti	*I a 5*	6		6
1605	Monteverdi	*V a 5*	5	5	10
1605	Orlandi	*III a 5*	6		6
1605	Cifra	*Book I a 5*	2	5	7

Whereas Chater ascribes the scarcity of *Pastor fido* madrigals before 1594 to composers' reluctance to set texts from a theatrical source, the numbers suggest rather that Guarini texts in general became increasingly more fashionable toward and following the end of the Cinquecento—principally in settings for polyphonic madrigals—and that *Pastor fido* settings simply followed this trend. The early transition of the tragicomedy from a theatrical to a literary, lyric, and musical tradition, then, might have been facilitated just as much by Guarini's already established and growing reputation as a lyric poet as by the play's inherent qualities. Both of these factors undoubtedly fostered composers' and patrons' embrace of the play effectively as a quasi-lyric source. The same, indeed, might be said of the growing tendency of later critics to chastise the work for its lyric qualities: Guarini's standing as a lyric poet, the ornamented style and metaphorical language of the verse, and the numerous reflective monologues all came under scrutiny just as the play was being turned by composers literally into a "raccolta di madrigali," like his *Rime*, giving critics all the more reason to refute its viability as a dramatic work by Aristotelian standards.

In short, as Guarini's poetry came under increasing demand in the late Cinquecento and early Seicento, madrigal composers appear to have sought additional Guarini texts regardless of their origins. *Il pastor fido*, then, came at a time when several factors were working in favor of its acceptance into the musical realm: (1) Guarini's repute as a lyric poet; (2) the lyric tendencies of many of the play's speeches that made them easy to extract (if some of them had not begun as lyric poems in the first place); and (3) stylistic qualities of Guarini's dramatic verse that made it particularly akin to the contemporary poetic madrigal. Furthermore, although the *Pastor fido* vogue had theoretically opened the door for the use of other theatrical texts in the madrigal, no such fashion came about. Rather, alongside the surge of madrigal settings of Guarini texts in the early to mid-seventeenth century, a similar trend took hold of setting the lyric texts of Neapolitan poet Giambattista Marino as madrigals, both polyphonic and for accompanied solo voice or duet, while dramatic texts were fashioned expressly for settings in the new *stile rappresentativo* as early opera.[39]

The uniqueness of the role *Il pastor fido* played in the polyphonic madrigal becomes especially pronounced through comparison with another pastoral play from Ferrara by a poet also known for his lyric verse: Tasso's *Aminta*. (In fact, the two plays appeared together as early as 1591 in a single London edition by Giovanni Volfeo.) While *Aminta* was performed onstage for the first time in 1573, was published in 1580, and remained a fashionable work for the stage and for readers for decades to come, it never secured the interest of madrigal composers in the way that *Il pastor fido* did—even when accounting for the fact that Guarini's play is more than three times longer than Tasso's (Figure 4.4).[40] Nor was the number of *Aminta* settings noticeably affected by the infiltration of *Il pastor fido* into the madrigal tradition. Even adding together the settings of Tasso's sizeable epic *Gerusalemme liberata* (1581) and those of his *Aminta* (shown by the dashed line in Figure 4.3) has little effect on the outcome: settings of Guarini's play far outnumber those of Tasso's epic and dramatic works combined. A comparison of settings from both poets' *Rime* yields similar results: madrigal composers preferred the witty, impassioned, and often epigrammatic texts of Guarini to the more sensuous, melic verse of Tasso. At the same time, while *Aminta* likewise continued to find enormous demand at the press—at least twenty-four Italian editions had appeared by 1600, with some thirty more by the 1630s—and success on the stage, it never attracted the level of critical attention that enveloped *Il pastor fido*, owing likely to its taut and integrated form, modest scale and lyricism, and more restrained use of the sorts of lengthy, eloquent, *oziosi* monologues that garnish Guarini's work—not to mention its avoidance of the label *tragicommedia pastorale*.

Yet, while composers readily drew from both Guarini's dramatic and lyric sources for polyphonic setting, whether they treated these texts in the same manner is another matter. For, indeed, composers often seem to reflect aspects of the broader dramatic contexts in their renderings of the play's

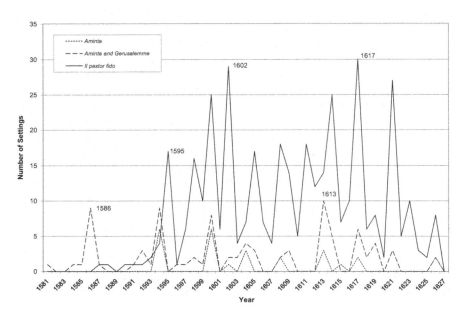

Figure 4.4 Settings of *Il pastor fido* versus Tasso's *Aminta* and *Gerusalemme liberata*, 1581–1627

speeches—not only by juxtaposing in their madrigal books passages that are contiguous in the play or that relate to one another in discernible ways, but also by exploring and projecting "behind the scenes" of the texts and their speaking personas, as later analyses will show. This intertextual approach suggests that it was not simply the lyricism, expressiveness, and rhetoric of the play's speeches that appealed to composers and their audiences, but also the personas and scenarios that develop throughout its plot. The extracted texts may prove universal enough to pose as autonomous poems, but they are also enriched by the added dimensions of the characters, situations, and background of the play. This intertextuality, in turn, broadened the interpretative potential of the madrigal and offered composers and readers enhanced opportunities to play with multiple contrasting—sometimes even antithetical—readings.

A vivid illustration of this dual dimensionality comes in the speech *Com'è dolce il gioire*. In isolation—and deceptively in the play—the passage reads as compassionate advice to a despairing shepherd to find another, more affectionate lover and forget the cruel, unattainable Amarilli. Like *Ite, amari sospiri* above, the speech is divided rhetorically between an opening statement (how sweet it would be for you to have an adoring lover, unlike the cruel Amarilli) followed by reported speech (the imagined words of this ideal lover).[41] In their settings of the passage—both of which insert the generic name Tirsi in place of Mirtillo as addressee—Marenzio (1595) and Salamone Rossi (c.1600) incorporate expansive modal–structural conflicts and networks of musical–textual allusions to insinuate that the true nature of the speech (based on the play) is not what it seems, but instead part of a scheme by the cunning Corisca to win the shepherd's heàrt for herself while maligning her rival, Amarilli. The referential and structural–expressive strategies, therefore, enable the two madrigals to convey what the text itself does not: that the imagined, adoring *donna* (third person) and the unnamed speaker (Corisca in the play) are, in fact, one and the same. Yet, the madrigals also do not exclude a straightforward, superficial reading of the text. Rather, by combining the portrayal of this subtle subtext at deeper and larger-scale levels with a more overt rendering of the outward sense of the text on the musical foreground, the madrigals support readings of the passage in both ways: as independent of and in association with the contexts of the play. The question of how the texts' transition from mimetic enactment (of a character in the play) to diegetic retelling (of the character's words in the polyphonic madrigal) proves fundamental to the *Pastor fido* madrigal and to what it can tell us about modes of reading in (and of) the madrigal at large.

Marenzio's Guarini Settings, 1580–99

As we have seen, Marenzio's and Wert's madrigal books of 1594 and 1595 represent a turning point in an emergent compositional trend of showing a strong inclination toward Guarini's texts. What is significant and unique about Marenzio's and Wert's books, however, is not only the number of *Pastor fido* texts they include, but also their concentration exclusively upon texts from the play without using any from Guarini's *Rime*—a practice that would not be repeated until Giovanni Mezzogorri's *Il pastor fido armonico* in 1617 and Scipione Cerreto's *L'Amarillide a tre voci* in 1621.[42] With their marked spotlighting of the play, still in its nascent phase as a musical text, Marenzio and Wert ushered in Guarini's pastoral tragicomedy as a viable and fertile source of madrigal texts alongside the poet's *Rime*, and likewise set a strong precedent for which passages to choose. Seven of the eight most commonly set speeches from *Il pastor fido* through 1605 appear in the books of Marenzio and Wert—although not all of them for their first time in musical setting—and many times the precise excerpts and textual variants from the two composers' settings resurface in later works as well, revealing the possible influences that the poetic choices—and, as we will see, the musical responses—of both composers had on the later tradition.[43] Thereafter, the stage was set for Guarini's verses, both theatrical and lyric, to inundate music books for decades to follow, in a variety of guises, but always with a decided preference for the traditional polyphonic madrigal.

In keeping with his continued and multifarious (albeit indirect) ties with Ferrara, the *Pastor fido* settings do not represent the beginning of Marenzio's interest in the texts of Duke Alfonso d'Este's court poet. He turned regularly to Guarini's verse from the very outset of his career (Table 4.3) and no doubt played an important role in bringing the poet to the center of the madrigalian tradition well before doing so specifically for his pastoral tragicomedy. Marenzio's First Book of madrigals (1580), which brought forth his celebrated rendering of the immensely fashionable Guarini text, *Tirsi morir volea*, was the eighth known music print ever to include a Guarini madrigal. Through his career, Marenzio published thirty-five Guarini settings, handily more than of any other poet, including Petrarch (29), Tasso (27), and Sannazaro (26). While these settings draw nearly equally from Guarini's theatrical and lyric sources—eighteen have ties to *Il pastor fido* and seventeen exist only as independent poems—Marenzio's focus on the play in the 1590s marks a drastic change in his interest in the poet, as well as in his approach to musical–textual expression in the madrigal, as we will see.

While Marenzio's texts—particularly those of the Seventh Book—occasionally deviate from printed versions of the play, these versions were, as Chater describes, "considered exemplary enough to be reused by several later composers"—including, conspicuously, composers at Vincenzo Gonzaga's court in Mantua around 1598.[46] The reappearance of these variant texts implies not only that Marenzio's texts might have been viewed as being in certain ways better suited to the self-contained madrigal than the corresponding passages in the play—or that they were simply more readily accessible to later composers and patrons—but also that Marenzio's settings remained active in the madrigalian tradition to such an extent that they, rather than the play itself, came to function as the direct textual source for subsequent settings of these texts. This practice goes against the broader tendency of later *Pastor fido* settings to conform more to the play than settings of the 1590s had, possibly owing to the growing circulation of the printed text.

Table 4.3 Marenzio's Early Guarini Settings, 1580–94

1580	I a 5	*Tirsi morir volea*
1582	III a 5	*Oimè se tanto amate*
		Sì presso a voi, mio foco
		O dolce anima mia, dunque è pur vero
1585	V a 5	*Oimè l'antica fiamma*
1585	III a 6	*Donò Cinzia a Damone*[44]
1587	IV a 6	*Dice la mia bellissima Licori*
		O che soave e non inteso bacio (*Pf*)
		Lasso perché mi fuggi
1591	V a 6	*Baci soavi e cari*
1594	VI a 5	*Ah, dolente partita* (*Pf*)
		Udite, lagrimosi (*Pf*)
		Deh, Tirsi, Tirsi, anima mia, perdona[45] (*Pf*)
		Anima cruda sì, ma però bella (*Pf*)

Table 4.4 *Marenzio's Variant Pastor fido Texts That Reappear in Later Settings*

Text	Composer	Publication
Care mie selve, a Dio	Lucretio Ruffulo	*III a 5* (1612)
	Anonymous	Raffaelo Rontani's *Musiche I* (1614)
Com'è dolce il gioire, o vago/caro Tirsi	Salamone Rossi	*I a 4* (c.1600, pub. 1614)
Cruda Amarilli, che col nome ancora	Benedetto Pallavicino	*VI a 5* (1600)
Deh, dolce anima mia (Antonio Bicci)	B. Pallavicino	*VI a 5* (1600)
Deh Satiro, mio gentil, non far più strazio	G. B. Boschetti	*I a 5* (1613)
Deh, poi ch'era ne' fati ch'i' dovessi	Sigismondo D'India	*IV a 5* (1616)
O dolcezze amarissime d'amore	Salamone Rossi	*I a 4* (c.1600, pub. 1614)
Ombrose e care selve	Giovanni Ghizzolo	*Madrigali et arie II a 1–2* (1610)
	S. D'India	*III a 5* (1615)
Quell'augellin che canta	S. D'India	*III a 5* (1615)
Tirsi mio, caro Tirsi	Salamone Rossi	*I a 5* (1600)
	Giovanni Francesco Anerio	*II a 5–6* (1608)
	G. Ghizzolo	*Madrigali et arie II a 1–2* (1610)
	G. Ghizzolo	*II a 5* (1614)

Table 4.4 lists the known settings by later composers of variant *Pastor fido* texts that first appeared in Marenzio's books. The text of Florentine composer Antonio Bicci's *Deh, dolce anima mia*, included in Marenzio's Seventh Book, for example, shows several departures from the play; in fact, the entire first verse and a half of the madrigal's text appear to be newly added. All of its discrepancies reappear precisely in the 1600 setting of the same passage by Benedetto Pallavicino, then *maestro di musica* of the Gonzaga court. Similarly, the variant reading of the final verse (along with the bipartite division of the text) of Marenzio's *Care mie selve, a Dio* resurfaces in Lucretio Ruffulo's Third Book of 1612 and in an anonymous madrigal of 1614.

The most compelling indication that Marenzio's madrigal books served as textual sources for later composers involves the two final works in the Seventh Book: *Tirsi mio, caro Tirsi* and *Ombrose e care selve*. The former (discussed in detail in Chapter 8) significantly alters the scenario of the text from the padre–figlia (father/priest–daughter) relationship of the play—specifically Amarilli's pleading for her life to the priest Nicandro in act 4, scene 5—to that of the pastoral lovers "Tirsi" and "Filli." Hence, Amarilli's opening cry, "Padre mio, caro padre" (My father, dear father), in the play becomes "Tirsi mio, caro Tirsi" (My Tirsi, dear Tirsi) in Marenzio's madrigal.[47] The setting also omits verse 3, "Padre d'unica figlia" ("father of a single daughter"), which clearly does not suit the new Tirsi–Filli relation-ship of the madrigal, and replaces the last three lines referring to Amarilli's wedding-turned-execution with verses begging for compassion from Filli's deserting lover. These same modifications reappear in the settings of Salam-one Rossi (1600), Giovanni Francesco Anerio (1608), and Giovanni Ghiz-zolo (1610 and 1614). Similarly, in the final madrigal of the Seventh Book, the five-syllable opening line in *Il pastor fido* (V,8), "Selve beate," is expanded to a full *settenario*, "Ombrose e care selve," and the final verse of the play, "De' duo beati amanti," becomes "d'Amarilli e di Tirsi / aventurosi amanti"—a reading that clearly confounds its relationship with the play by pairing Am-arilli with Tirsi, and that returns in Ghizzolo's *Madrigali et arie II a 1–2* (1610) and D'India's Third Book (1615).

Marenzio's settings of Guarini's *Rime*, by comparison, seldom show such prominent modifications from the printed sources. Scholars have suggested that the *Pastor fido* texts were altered specifically to make them more self-suf-ficient, to dissociate them from the particular circumstances of the play and, in turn, make them more universally applicable—in effect, more generically lyric—by replacing or omitting character names and redirecting the focus toward broader themes of love and love-suffering. While this rationale cer-tainly holds true in the case of the priest/nymph scenario so atypical of a madrigal, or in instances where the boundaries of an open-ended passage are sutured closed grammatically, the substituting of generic pastoral names for character names is a more complicated matter. For such name changes tend not to affect the text formally or grammatically, and the fact that such modifications also occur occasionally in non-*Pastor fido* settings—as with the replacement of Licori and Batto by Cinzia and Damone in Marenzio's 1585 setting of Guarini's poem "Donò Licori a Batto" (Table 4.3)—raises the possibility that they served another function, such as referencing an in-dividual or patron by a pastoral/academic *soprannome* (Virginio Orsini, for example, went by Tirsi in his pastoral-themed society, the Shepherds of the Tiber Valley),[48] or out of a preference for certain word sounds. Yet, while such changes may have little interpretative impact on a generic lyric poem, in the case of *Il pastor fido*, where they pertain to "actual" (specific) perso-nas, such variations complicate and potentially sever the text's ties to its speaker and the play. But even these revisions of names might have carried some aspect of literary, madrigalian fun by prompting—and challenging—readers acquainted with the play to rationalize the madrigal text with its former contexts and speaker.

The notion that madrigal composers turned to, or even preferred, Maren-zio's madrigal books (particularly the Seventh Book) as textual sources over the play is bolstered further by instances where several of Marenzio's vari-ant texts resurface in a single book by a later composer—as in Pallavicino's settings of *Deh, dolce anima mia* and *Cruda Amarilli, che col nome ancora* in his Sixth Book (1600)[49]; Rossi's *Com'è dolce il gioire* and *Tirsi mio, caro Tirsi* in his First Book *a4* (c.1600); Ghizzolo's *Tirsi mio, caro Tirsi* and *Ombrose e care selve* in his *Madrigali et arie II* (1610); and D'India's *Quell'augellin che canta* and *Ombrose e care selve* in his Third Book (1615; see Table 4.4). The fact that Marenzio's Seventh Book (1595) underwent six additional printings between 1600 and 1632 in Italy and north of the Alps attests that the volume maintained widespread currency through the early decades of the Seicento and would have been accessible to later composers and other readers.[50] But in addition to its sheer availability and apparent appeal among readers, the notion that there was something distinctive about Marenzio's approaches to the texts that gave them exceptional weight, esteem, or some air of authority as musical–textual models for later composers and their patrons is a theme that will continue through the chapters to come.[51]

Guarini's Drafts and Salviati's Lost Manuscript

The accepted narrative of Marenzio's *Pastor fido* madrigals holds that they sprang from the ardent cultural milieu of Cinzio Aldobrandini's *ridotto* and Guarini's visits to the Vatican in 1593–95, and that the texts, while drawn from the published play, were altered to distance them from the particular circumstances of the plot (by substituting names, for instance), and to make them more semantically, formally, or grammatically autonomous— for example, by replacing the opening conjunctions "Ma" or "E" with the exclamation "Deh"; the adjective "nerborute" (stocky, referring to Satiro's knees) with the more becoming "belle, care" (beautiful, dear); or the ending couplet "figla"–"sera" with the routine rhyme "sorte"–"morte." Moreover, while scholars routinely note the divergences of Marenzio's *Pastor fido* texts from printed editions of the play, their accounts remain for the most part limited to the most noticeable and outwardly substantial discrepancies, including the addition, substitution, or removal of words and verses, such as those cited above. Seemingly minor variations, such as variant spellings, are generally overlooked entirely. Furthermore, these studies tend to compare Marenzio's texts to the more accessible and authoritative 1602 Ciotti edition of *Il pastor fido*, rather than to the numerous earlier editions that are contemporary with the madrigals.

Yet, as suggested earlier, it has perhaps been altogether too hastily assumed that the source of Marenzio's *Pastor fido* texts was a printed edition at all, and that the madrigals correspond with circumstances in Rome around the time in which they were published. (Marenzio's dedication to the Sixth Book, for example, was signed in Rome, 1 January 1594, precisely during Guarini's first sojourn in Cinzio Aldobrandini's household.) Appendix A shows the texts of Marenzio's *Pastor fido* madrigals, with conflicting readings that appear in editions of the play from 1590–95 and (for reference) 1602 shown in the right column.[52] In the middle column appear variant readings that arise in the four surviving drafts of the play: two complete drafts bound together in the Biblioteca Nazionale Marciana in Venice, MS 4782, Zanetti It. 65 (referred to here as M1 and M2, following Rossi); a full manuscript held in the Biblioteca Comunale Ariostea in Ferrara, Classe I.H. (referred to as F); and a clean, finely penned copy in the Biblioteca Nazionale in Turin, N.IV.26 (referred to as T).[53] The Turin draft was largely destroyed in a fire in 1904; only the second half of the manuscript remains intact (beginning with act 3, scene 5), yet with the outer edges of the remaining pages substantially burned.[54] Along with these sources, between the M1 and M2 drafts in the Marciana manuscript sits an assortment of folios of varying sizes and origins containing sketches and reworkings of numerous passages and scenes (mostly from act 5), as well as outlines of scenes, cast lists, and some writings not related to the play.[55] Although all of these manuscripts predate the earliest known musical settings of *Il pastor fido*, they are, as it turns out, exceptionally useful for tracing the origins of some of these works.

In their detailed analyses of these early drafts, Vittorio Rossi and Carla Molinari concur that the order of composition went from M1 through F and T to M2. Some disagreement, however, has surrounded the scribal source of the Marciana (Venice) and Ariostea (Ferrara) drafts. Based on the script of the M1 copy, Rossi considers it primarily the work of copyists and, hence, contests Giovanni Andrea Barotti's 1739 assessment deeming the entire manuscript—the copy of the play as well as the extensive revisions written between the verses and in the margins—to be in Guarini's hand, aside from a portion of scene 3 and all of scenes 5–9 of the third act, which he judged to be in the hands of various copyists.[56] Despite this, Rossi considers "the entire copy to have the authority of an autograph, since even in the parts written by others, Guarini corrected it in his own hand."[57] Molinari, in turn, refutes Rossi's judgment of the handwriting, supporting Barotti's initial reasoning that the manuscript, both the main script and corrections, is in the author's hand, aside from the sections of act 3 cited by Barotti.[58] The three analysts hold to the very same opinions of the M2 draft: based on the script and the multitude of errors, Rossi challenges Barotti's view that it is an autograph, while Molinari supports Barotti's assessment based on closer scrutiny.[59]

The debate over the Ferrara draft follows a rather different course, beginning in the late nineteenth century with a divide between scholars who denied Guarini's penmanship and those (all with ties to the Biblioteca Ariostea itself) who stood adamantly behind it. The argument against Guarini's authorship was put forward first by Luigi Napoleone Cittadella, then director of the Biblioteca Ariostea, in his *I Guarini, famiglia nobile ferrarese* (1870), and later supported by Rossi and Molinari. One year after Rossi's 1886 biography, the new director of the Ariostea, Aldo Gennari—without acknowledging his predecessor's assessment to the contrary—issued a defense of the draft's autograph status based on similarities in penmanship between the manuscript and the poet's letters held by the library.[60] Gennari found support in Giuseppe Antonelli's *Indice dei manoscritti della civica biblioteca di Ferrara* from just two years prior (1884), which claims that "one of the most precious codices presently in our library is certainly this one of Guarini that is autograph and finely copied."[61]

It seems reasonable in judging the authorship of these sources to follow the findings of the most scrupulous of all these studies—that of Molinari—and consider the Marciana manuscripts almost entirely autograph, and the Ferrara and Turin drafts non-autograph copies. Furthermore, letters by Guarini and others regarding the progress of the play in the mid-1580s, along with the development of the text itself toward its printed form, has made it possible to date the manuscripts with some degree of certainty. We know, for example, that Guarini began writing act 5 in February 1584, and that acts 1–4 were completed by April of that year, when Vincenzo Gonzaga expressed his wish to stage the play for his wedding celebrations. Act 5, however, was not finished until 6 January 1585, when it was sent to the Duke of Ferrara for the failed staging attempt for Carnival. This progress, particularly of act 5, is visible in the M1 draft, dating the draft precisely to this time frame in 1584–85. The Ferrara and Turin drafts were copied before September 1585, when the play—with its prologue, but without the choruses—was presented to its dedicatee, Carlo Emanuele I, in Turin. By tracing the development of the opening verses between the two drafts—the Turin manuscript still fully intact at that time—Rossi shows the Ariostea draft to fall between those of M1 and Turin.[62] M2 represents the latest surviving complete manuscript, deriving from the period between September 1585 (the *terminus ante quem* for F and T) and 14 July 1586, when the poet sent a draft of the tragicomedy to Lionardo Salviati for comment. The latest extant pre-publication sources—three sketches dealing with the first and second scenes of act 1—survive in the complex middle portion of the Marciana codex (examined in detail by Molinari).

The texts of Marenzio's madrigals occupy their own position within this lineage of drafts and, eventually, printed editions of the play. While the madrigal texts generally adhere more closely to the 1590 edition than to the revised edition of 1602, an even closer association can be found in a source from several years earlier: the draft sent by Guarini to Lionardo Salviati for evaluation in July 1586. Salviati, a Florentine philologist, playwright, and poet, was, like Guarini, an active participant in the literary debates of the late Cinquecento. Yet, while Guarini was concerned chiefly with the issues of dramatic poetry relevant to his own work, Salviati's critical writings of the 1580s deal primarily with matters surrounding epic poetry and form an integral part of the earlier quarrels over Dante's *Divina commedia*, Ariosto's *Orlando furioso*, and Tasso's *Gerusalemme liberata*. In these writings, Salviati stands alongside the Moderns in calling for a more liberal interpretation of Aristotle's *Poetics* and in underscoring the importance of invention, imitation, and verisimilitude in poetry—a view that leads to his denunciation of Tasso's *Gerusalemme liberata* for its unimaginative retelling of history in verse form.[63] As "Il Verrato" would do only three years later, Salviati also uses Aristotle as the basis for his argument that the ultimate end of poetry is pleasure, not moral instruction or civic benefit, as claimed by the Ancients of the Paduan Studio.[64] Many of Salviati's pamphlets were published under his academic pseudonym, L'Infarinato, or "The Floured One," on behalf of the Florentine Accademia della Crusca, which Salviati and others founded in 1583 with the aim of purifying, codifying, and preserving the Tuscan vernacular.[65] These linguistic and theoretical perspectives prove central to his appraisal of *Il pastor fido*.

At the very time that he corresponded with Guarini over his tragicomedy in 1586, Salviati had begun taking steps to establish ties with the Este court in the hope of gaining employment in Ferrara. This contact with the poet proved instrumental in the Florentine's securing a post as secretary for Duke Alfonso II by the end of that year.[66] The following January, Salviati delivered a funeral oration in Florence for Marenzio's Roman patron, Cardinal Luigi d'Este (as Guarini had done in Ferrara that same month) before transferring to Ferrara to serve in the Este court.[67] It is therefore of little surprise that Salviati's critical writings anticipate many of the fundamental, forward-looking ideas that formed the basis of Guarini's formulation of tragicomedy, and that would later appear in Guarini's *Annotazioni*, given the presence of both the poet and Salviati in Ferrara between March 1587 and Guarini's departure from Este service in June 1588.

In addition to his involvement in the literary debates, Salviati was a major figure in continuing the reforms of the Tuscan vernacular instigated by scholar and poet Pietro Bembo in the early Cinquecento. In his *Degli avvertimenti della lingua sopra il Decamerone* (1584), a study of Boccaccio's language in the *Decameron*, Salviati argues that Quattrocento humanists contaminated the Tuscan dialect—once perfected by the "Three Crowns" of the previous century, Dante, Petrarch, and Boccaccio—by introducing unnatural Latinisms and other linguistic impurities. Poets, Salviati urges, should look to the language of the Tuscan Trecento as an exemplar, and he likewise cites Bembo's *Prose della volgar lingua* (1525) and Ariosto's *Orlando furioso* (1532) as modern examples of a pure and perfect linguistic style. In the same treatise, Salviati also finds opportunity to praise Guarini, known at the time almost exclusively for his lyric poetry and courtly prose, referring to the poet's writings as the "delights of the *belle lettere* of our time" ("delizie delle belle lettere dei nostri tempi").

Guarini would undoubtedly have been aware of Salviati's views on poetry and linguistics when he sought the philologist's evaluation of his newly finished play in mid-1586. Certainly he respected Salviati's authority, for all of Salviati's suggested revisions were later incorporated into the play. Correspondence between the two began in early 1586, and as a sign of Salviati's interest in Ferrarese employment, it seems to have been initiated by the Florentine: writing on 26 April 1586, Salviati relates to Guarini that he often hears of "your kindness, your goodness, your valor, your wisdom, your learning, your talent and rarest courtesy" (la sua gentilezza, la sua bontà, il suo valore, il suo senno, la sua dottrina, il suo ingegno e la rarissima cortesia), and that "your most exquisite *Pastorale* through all of Italy is praised by the most lauded tongues of this century."[68] Evidently

Guarini's efforts to publicize the work were proving effective, for the printing and first staging of the play were still years away. On May 22, Guarini broached the idea of sending a draft of his *tragicommedia pastorale* to Salviati in Florence:

> Yet even before I had provided a copy [of the pastoral], which is already finished, I thought of sending it into your hands to secure that benefit of which I can assure myself from your intelligence and generosity.[69]

Salviati responded on 14 June 1586, inviting Guarini to send a copy of the play,[70] which Guarini did one month later, asking the philologist to review it harshly, "with the eye of a severe master," and to observe "every part of it, but especially the language, that it not be filthy with 'Lombardisms'." At the same time, the Ferrarese poet safeguards himself against L'Infarinato's discerning judgment by declaring—clearly with false modesty—his inexperience in writing verse, adding:

> And so that you may tell me your opinion with utmost freedom, know that this is the work of a person who does not claim to be a poet, but only writes verses for his own leisure and diversion from other studies of greater importance, and who will no less willingly give to the flames than to the presses any poems of his that are not good—and who does not deem them good if they are not excellent.[71]

Numerous scholars have attempted to link Salviati's draft, which would postdate the M2 copy, to the Ariostea manuscript of the play. Barotti did this first in his *Difesa* of 1739, and Antonelli repeated the error in 1884, even though Cittadella had shown it to be false years earlier (1870).[72] Not only does the Ariostea manuscript lack the prologue—which Salviati certainly had in 1586, for he reviews it—but the pagination and verses do not match Salviati's references. Rossi, by contrast, maintains that Salviati's copy "is represented, save for some small differences, by the Turin manuscript."[73] But Molinari brings us even closer to the draft sent to the philologist, showing a precise correspondence between Salviati's annotations and a fragment found in the middle section of the Marciana codex. The remnants—bound in what Molinari labels the A2 portion of the manuscript (fols. 143r–147v) that immediately follows the M1 draft—comprise only the first five folios of the draft, yet the verses align precisely with Salviati's references.[74]

Salviati's *Annotazioni* and the Texts of Marenzio's Madrigals

Although the draft of the play sent to Salviati has been lost (apart from the five pages in the Marciana codex), the response that Salviati sent to Guarini on 8 October 1586 survives in the Biblioteca Ariostea in Ferrara. This correspondence consists of three documents: an introductory letter; a general commentary "dalla favola del *Pastor Fido*," which assesses the work's plot, characters, verisimilitude, and structure; and the academician's complete "Annotazioni"—a scene-by-scene list of detailed observations on matters of grammar, style, *suono* (word sound), and other minute, orthographical matters. These documents are, in fact, entirely sufficient for understanding the Florentine's assessment on their own, without the 1586 draft on which they are based, and have been studied and transcribed in several publications beginning in 1873.[75]

In his discussion "dalla favola del *Pastor fido*," Salviati addresses many of the same issues that would prove central to the imminent attacks on the play.[76] His foremost concern, he states, is the unruly length, considering that audiences would presumably be watching the work in the theatre and not reading it in print:

> The main concern that I have about this poem is the long span that it would take to perform it. Although what Aristotle seems to determine does not pertain to the *Arte poetica*, it is necessary for us to consider whether we wish [our works] to be not simply read, but seen in the theater, where these spectacles should be. As delightful and magnificent as one might wish, I do not believe that the spectators can stay more than four hours without regret and annoyance. Thus, I fear that our tragicomedy would occupy at least six hours.[77]

Guarini apparently viewed the work's function differently, since it was never shortened for publication; in fact, it would soon grow even longer with the addition of the choruses to acts 1–4. As it turned out, the overwhelming majority of the play's audience would indeed be made up of *lettori*, not true *spettatori*, since successful stagings would remain (by what surviving records indicate) rather scarce.

Salviati's detailed *Annotazioni* strongly reflect his concern for the reform of the Tuscan vernacular and the influence of Pietro Bembo's theoretical writings, as they turn consistently to the authority of the "Tre Corone" of Italian verse: Dante, Petrarch, and Boccaccio (though Bembo relied chiefly on the latter two). The majority of his observations concern the phonetics of individual words, the sonority of specific word-pairings, syntax, and painstaking matters of orthography. Certain stock statements relating to "suono" in particular pervade the *Annotazioni*, such as "fuggirei questo suono" (I would avoid this sound), "mi noia l'orecchio" (this bothers my ear), "mi par di sentire asprezza e percotimento" (to me this sounds harsh and beaten), "credo mal suono" (a bad sound, I believe), and simply "aspro" (harsh).

Suggestions for the respelling or replacement of individual words—generally owing to problems of orthography, syntax, or context (especially with regard to *suono*)—form the bulk of Salviati's observations and betray the humanist's agenda of literary reform. In the first note to act 1, scene 1, for example, Salviati writes of Guarini's use of the term "nume": "I do not recall if this was used by the Ancients, nor with this offense, who would want to follow the Moderns in this regard."[78] Advice to respell or replace a given word generally comes in one of three forms: the old word followed by the new word (*"risco, rischio"*); the old and new words separated by "per" (*"volse*, per *volle"*); or an explanation of why the word should be altered (*"Tant'osi*, I would finish *tant'* and write *tanto osi* to avoid the sound of *tantosi*, without, I believe, requiring any direct rule of orthography, as I think I have said in my books"),[79] or often, "error di penna," assuming that Guarini or a copyist simply made a mistake. On occasion, Salviati refers to his own forthcoming *Vocabolario* ("la dirò nel Vocabolario"), a linguistic treatise presenting the complete Tuscan lexicon as sanctioned by the Accademia della Crusca.[80] Thus, while Guarini's tragicomedy stood on shaky ground in terms of its impending critical reception, Salviati's revisions ensured that the work met the strictest standards linguistically and orthographically—at least from a Tuscan perspective.

Although Salviati's observations were made between 14 July and 8 October 1586 and were, for the most part, incorporated into the play by the 1589/90 edition, only rarely do the texts of Marenzio's *Pastor fido* settings reflect Salviati's suggested revisions. The table in Appendix A provides a comparison of all extant print and manuscript sources of *Il pastor fido* through 1595 with the texts of Marenzio's madrigals. As the Appendix shows, the madrigal texts correspond most consistently with a hypothetical version of the play that had not yet undergone Salviati's corrections—that is, one situated between M2 and the draft sent to the Florentine philologist on 14 July 1586—suggesting that the passages set by Marenzio originated in a source from mid-1586. The variations that distinguish Marenzio's texts from the passages edited by Salviati come in the form not of conflicting verses or even words, but of seemingly incidental disparities in spelling and conjugation, for it is precisely such details that occupied Salviati most.

In *Deh poi ch'era ne' fati ch'i' dovessi*, the first piece of Marenzio's Seventh Book, for example, the final word reads "mori" in the 1595 partbooks, which conflicts with "muori" of the 1590 and subsequent editions of *Il pastor fido*. The 1586 draft of the tragicomedy sent to Salviati, however, must also have read "mori," which prompted Salviati to note: "for *mori*, use *muori*, and for the thousand others of this usage, I have said what I think in my *Avvertimenti*."[81] "Mori" was accordingly emended by the time the play came to print, yet it stands in the text of Marenzio's madrigal.

Similarly, the reading "avventuroso" in 1590 and subsequent editions of the pastoral appears as "aventuroso" in both Salviati's comments and earlier manuscripts, as well as in Marenzio's *O dolcezze amarissime d'amore*. This, too, was emended on Salviati's suggestion. On the use of "aventuroso" in act 2, scene 1, Salviati notes: *"aventuroso, avventuroso*, and likewise always below."[82] The same is true for the conflicting reading of "tepido" (in *O fido, o caro Aminta*) with "tiepido": the madrigal agrees with all of the manuscript sources, including the 1586 draft evaluated by Salviati, yet conflicts with most printed editions of the play, which seem to have followed the philologist's observation: "*tepido*, I believe that it should be written *tiepido*, as it is pronounced."[83]

The modification of the verb conjugation "vedesti" to "vedessi" in the passage containing *O Mirtillo, Mirtillo anima mia* (III,4) proves a more complicated case. Salviati's annotation at this point reads simply "*Se vedesti, se vedessi*," and in response to Guarini's use of "vedesti" earlier in the text, the humanist surmises that it must be an "error of the pen, needing to say *vedessi*."[84] Yet Salviati's advised revision of the word does not appear in the 1590 Bonfadino and Mamerelli editions, presumably by mistake, nor does it appear in the 1592 Senese, 1594 Senese, 1594 Baldini, or 1595 Bianco prints, all of which (like the madrigal) retain "vedesti" here. Curiously, however, the change to "vedessi" was incorporated into several other editions, including 1590 Baldini, 1591 Volfeo, and 1591 Viani, before eventually forming part of the authoritative 1602 Ciotti print. Since in this case, the majority of the printed editions essentially duplicate the "unrevised" readings of the 1586 Salviati draft (as preserved in his comments back to Guarini) and the surviving manuscripts in having "vedesti," the madrigal text of *O Mirtillo, Mirtillo anima mia* agrees with all manuscript sources as well as some editions, while conflicting with other printed sources and Salviati's revision.

This comparison of Salviati's orthographical corrections and the texts of Marenzio's settings reveals so far that the madrigals agree in all cases with the (conjectural) 1586 draft sent to the Florentine academician, rather than with the typically revised readings of the printed editions—a correlation that suggests that Marenzio's madrigal texts might have come from a source of the play dating from 1586 or earlier. There are, however, two other types of cases to consider, one of which is dubious, and the other, seemingly at odds with this correspondence between Marenzio's works and the 1586 source. The first, dubious case pertains to the use of "chieggio" in the madrigal *Se tu, dolce mio ben, mi saettasti*, published in Marenzio's Eighth Book (1598). Salviati's annotation for this passage in act 4, scene 9 suggests a change from *chiedo*—what appears in the versions of M1, F, T, and evidently the 1586 Salviati draft—to *cheggio, chieggo,* or *chieggio*, the latter of which appears in M2 and ends up in Marenzio's madrigal. Salviati's comment reads: "If Your Lordship does not have the authority (which I, to myself, have not lent), of this word I would say *chieggio, chieggo,* or *cheggio*."[85] Guarini's use of "chiedo" at this point in M1 and F contrasts with his use of *cheggio* (M1) and *chieggio* (F) in act 2, scene 6 of these same drafts, neither of which were problematic to Salviati. Likewise, Marenzio's setting of this latter passage in act 2 as *Deh, Tirsi, mio gentil, non far più stratio*, also in the Eighth Book, reads *chieggio*, as in F. M2, on the other hand, reads *chieggio* in both instances (act 2 and act 4), like Marenzio's madrigals, while the prints vary between *chieggio* and *cheggio*.[86]

It is not out of the question, however, that Marenzio's madrigals at one time agreed with Salviati's draft—that is, reading *chieggio* in *Deh, Tirsi, mio gentil, non far più stratio* (II,6) but *chiedo* in *Se tu, dolce mio ben, mi saettasti* (IV,9). Given that these are the only *Pastor fido* settings in Maren-zio's Eighth Book and both contain the first-person form of *chiedere* (to ask), one might posit that at some point before coming to press, a decision was made to standardize the spelling between the two instances of the verb. Since *Deh, Tirsi, mio gentil* (no. 10) comes before *Se tu, dolce mio ben* (no. 15) in the book's ordering, its form ("chieggio") might have been selected for both works—a form that also happens to concur with Salviati's suggested revision of *chiedo* in act 4, scene 9. Both madrigals' texts, therefore, read "chieggio" and align with Salviati's preferences, meaning at the same time that *Se tu, dolce mio ben* no longer corresponds with the 1586 draft.

There is another possible explanation for the disagreement between the madrigal and the 1586 draft, however, that relates to that of the second, more blatant type of disparity. The passage containing the text of Maren-zio's *O fido, o caro Aminta* in act 1, scene 2 contains the verse "Se fu fallo il lasciarti ecco l'ammendo" in all of the manuscript sources, including the draft reviewed by Salviati. The Florentine humanist evidently objected to the unbecoming word pairing "fu fallo," for he advised: *"fu fallo. I would avoid this suono."*[87] Considering the correspondence between Marenzio's madrigal texts and the pre-revised forms of the *Pastor fido* excerpts, one might expect the composer's setting of *O fido, o caro Aminta* also to read "fu fallo," but in fact, it bears the revised word pairing that shows up in all printed editions: "fu colpa." An explanation for this disagreement between madrigal and draft—as well as for that of *chieggio/chiedo* in *Se tu, dolce mio ben, mi saettasti*—may lie in the intellectual environment in which these madrigals were likely performed in the early to mid-1590s.

Guarini, as will be remembered, was a visitor at the household of Maren-zio's patron, Cinzio Aldobrandini, in the winters of 1593–94 and 1594–95, the very years in which the majority of the composer's *Pastor fido* madrigals came to press, raising the possibility that these settings played some part in discus-sions of Guarini's new tragicomedy among Cardinal Aldobrandini's intellec-tual circle, with the poet in attendance. Several members of this group, such as Angelo Ingegneri, Francesco Patrizi, Giovanni de' Bardi, and Cardinal Montalto, were likely already familiar with Guarini's work, either through their own personal connections to the poet and play, or through their involve-ment in the ongoing controversy surrounding it (which by this point included the first four exchanges between Denores, Verrato, and L'Attizzato).

While such an exceptionally informed audience might understandably have failed to recognize the singers' performance of "comanda" instead of "com-manda," "mori" in place of "muori," or "tepido" in place of "tiepido," even if following along with the respective passages in the play, the sounding of "fu fallo" instead of "fu colpa," or "chiedo" instead of "chieggio" would surely have caught their attention. It is only in these two, most audible cases that the texts of Marenzio's madrigals agree with the printed editions rather than the 1586 Salviati draft, whereas the smaller, less aurally discernible variants prove faithful to the lost draft, not the editions. This clear-cut division in the correlations of the madrigal texts according to audibility could indicate that the more pronounced discrepancies between musical work and printed play were identified through musical performance, not through visual inspection of the musical works, thereby allowing the less conspicuous discrepancies to slip by unnoticed. These more audible variants might then have been emended to accord with the printed text of the play before the madrigals themselves came to print in 1594–98, while the more minor (less audible) variants remained, reflecting an earlier reading of the play that predates Salviati's corrections. The milieu of Cinzio Aldobrandini's household in 1593–95 Rome, with the composer, the poet, and an audience of scholars and literati (including several with expertise in theater and poetics) in attendance, offered precisely the type of scenario that would have fostered active discourse between authors, listeners, and musical readings, and potentially have prompted the revision of the madrigal texts, thus bringing the performance (musical) text in line with the printed (dramatic) text in instances where they were aurally at odds, but not when they were indiscernible.

This hypothesis of the madrigal texts agreeing with the printed editions when substantial variations (such as entire words or phrases) are concerned, but with a pre-publication draft for more minor discrepancies (such as spelling) also holds true in instances not involving Salviati's *Annotazioni*. In more explicit cases, where words or considerable parts of verses conflict between various sources, Marenzio's madrigals agree at all times with the editions. In cases involving spelling and other minor variants, however, the madrigals correspond overwhelmingly (ten out of thirteen times) with the manuscripts. Hence, where the manuscripts pair "caldi" and "caldamente" in Corisca's lines "A i tuoi caldi sospiri / Caldamente sospiri" (III, 6), Marenzio's *Com'è dolce il gioire* reads "dolci" and "dolcemente," like the printed versions of the play. Likewise, in *Deh, poi ch'era ne' fati*, the madrigal agrees with the printed texts in reading "Da lei che n'è cagion gradita fosse," as opposed to the manuscripts' "Da colei che la fà gradita fosse." In a case similar to that of *chiedo/chieggio*, the text of Marenzio's *Ah, dolente partita* conjugates the verb *morire* (to die) as "moia," which conflicts with "mora" of the M1 and M2 drafts and "viva" of the Ariostea draft (F), but concurs with all printed editions. Also, the soft *g* of "stringe" and "stringi" in all of the extant manuscript versions of act 3, scene 4 stand prominently apart phonetically from "strigne" and "strigni" of the 1590–95 print sources and Marenzio's *O Mirtillo*. In these clearly audible cases, then, the madrigals concur with the printed texts.

With less audible cases involving variant spellings, on the other hand, the madrigals coincide most often with the manuscript sources. For example, "satia" in *Udite, lagrimosi* agrees with the drafts, thus diverging from "sazia" of the prints; and "morò" in *Cruda Amarilli* and "amar" in *O Mirtillo* agree with the two later drafts, F and M2, while contrasting with "morrò" and "amor" of the editions. In a case very similar to *satia/sazia*, "stratio" in both *Arda pur sempre o mora* and *Deh, Tirsi, mio gentil, non far più stratio* follows the manuscripts, whereas all but one of the printed sources of the play read "strazio."[88]

The seemingly minor disparities between the texts of Marenzio's *Pastor fido* settings and published versions of the play, therefore, align the madrigals most compellingly with a textual source that predates Salviati's *Annotazioni*, which were sent to Guarini in October 1586. There are, of course, some (but few) instances where the music disagrees with the manuscript or print sources, or with both, for which there is no reference by Salviati.[89] In such cases, it is impossible to know exactly how the text appeared at the time of Salviati's draft. Nevertheless, when a correlation does exist, here, too, the musical texts show a marked distinction between imperceptible and clearly audible variants, the former aligning chiefly with the drafts, and the latter with the printed texts. In other words, the madrigal texts seem to follow a 1586 reading of *Il pastor fido*, except when a departure from the published play would have been discernible in performance.

The *Pastor fido* settings of Marenzio's Mantuan contemporary, Giaches de Wert, also published in 1595, show no such consistency in their adherence to either printed or pre-publication sources (see Appendix B). Wert published only four settings from the play, all in 1595, so the sample size for comparison is substantially more limited than for the seventeen settings of Marenzio, even considering the expansiveness of Wert's five-part treatment from act 3, scene 1, *O primavera, gioventù de l'anno*. Moreover, the excerpts set in these four madrigals coincide with only two comments by Salviati. The text of Wert's *Udite, lagrimosi* is nearly identical to that of Marenzio's setting published a year earlier. Both read "satia," like the manuscripts, as opposed to "sazia" of the prints (except 1595 Bianchi), and both retain "comanda," which Salviati had deemed inferior to "commanda" (as it appears in all 1590–95 editions).

In *O primavera* (Table 4.5)—the major part of which comprises the text of Marenzio's *O dolcezze amarissime d'amore* from the same year—the phrase "aventurosi dì" conflicts with all known sources. Whereas the drafts of the tragicomedy read "aventuroso dì" and the prints—following Salviati's counsel—read "avventuroso dì," Wert's madrigal deploys the plural of what Salviati would consider the improper form—an alteration permitted by the invariable singular/plural noun "dì" (day). One edition, 1594 Baldini, agrees with Wert's madrigal in its use of the plural, but presents it in the form sanctioned by Salviati: "avventurosi." In fact, the 1594 Baldini edition corresponds with a number of variants in this part of Wert's text, including the use of "Ho" for the exclamation "O"—thereby changing the meaning of Guarini's phrase "O lungamente sospirato in vano / Avventuroso dì"—and "doppo" in place of "dopo." All of these forms conflict with the text set by Marenzio, as does the inclusion in Wert's setting of several intermediate verses omitted in Marenzio's work.

As discussed earlier, a letter to Duke Vincenzo Gonzaga from the ducal secretary, Annibale Chieppio, of November 1591 implies that Wert had been charged with providing music for the production of *Il pastor fido* currently

Table 4.5 Texts of Wert's and Marenzio's Settings of Act 3, Scene 1 (as They Appear in the Partbooks)

Wert (1595)	*Marenzio (1595)*
O Primavera gioventu de l'anno	
Bella madre de fiori	
D'herbe novelle e di novelli amori	
Tu torni ben ma teco	
non tornano i sereni	
e fortunati dì de le miei gioie	
Tu torni ben tu torni	
Ma teco altro non torna	
Che del perduto mio caro thesoro	
La rimembranza misera e dolente	
Tu quella se tu quella	
Ch'eri pur dianzi si vezzosa e bella	
Ma non son io già quel ch'un tempo fui	
Si caro à gl'occhi altrui	
[Seconda parte]	
O dolcezz'amarissime d'Amore	O dolcezz'amarissime d'amore
Quanto è piu duro perdervi che mai	Quant'è piu duro perdervi che mai
Non v'haver ò provate ò possedute	Non v'haver ò provate ò possedute
Come saria l'amar felice stato	Come saria l'amar felice stato
Se'l già goduto ben non si perdesse	Se'l già goduto ben non si perdesse
O quand'egli si perde	O quand'egli si perde
Ogni memoria ancora	Ogni memoria ancora
Del dileguato ben si dileguasse.	Del dileguato ben si dileguasse
[Terza parte]	
Ma se le mie speranze hoggi non sono	Ma se le mie speranz'hoggi non sono
Com'è l'usato lor di fragil vetro	Come l'usato lor di fragil vetro
O se maggior del vero	//
Non fa la speme il desiar soverchio	//
Qui pur vedrò colei	Qui pur vedrò colei
Ch'è'l sol de gl'occhi miei	Ch'è'l sol de gl'occhi miei.[90]
[Quarta parte]	
E s'altri non m'inganna	//
Qui pur vedrolla al suon de miei sospiri	Qui pur vedroll'al suon de miei sospiri
Fermar il pie fugace	Fermar il piè fugace[91]
Qui pur da le dolcezze	Qui pur da le dolcezze
Di quel bel volto havrà soave cibo	Di quel bel volt'havrà soave cibo
Nel suo longo digiun l'avida vista	Nel suo lungo digiun l'avida vista
Qui pur vedrò quell'empia	Qui pur vedrò quell'empia
Girar in verso me le luci altere	Girar inverso me le luci altere
Se non dolci almen fere	Se non dolci almen fere
E se non carche d'amorosa gioia	E se non carche d'amorosa gioia
Si crude almen ch'io moia	Si crud'almen ch'i moia
[Quinta parte]	
Ho lungamente sospirato in vano	O lungamente sospirato in vano
Aventurosi dì / Se doppo tanti	Aventuroso dì, se dopo tanti
foschi giorni di pianti	Foschi giorni di pianti
Tu mi concedi Amor di veder hoggi	Tu mi concedi Amor di veder hoggi
Ne begl'occhi di lei	Ne begl'occhi di lei
Girar sereno il sol de gl'occhi miei.	Girar sereno il sol de gl'occhi miei.

being rehearsed in Mantua.[92] Chieppio gives no indication of what type of music was expected of the composer, or what function this music was to serve. Historians have surmised that the four *Pastor fido* settings published in Wert's Eleventh Book might have originated as part of the 1591–93 stage preparations. A comparison of the texts of Wert's settings with sources of the play from 1585 to 1595 sheds little light on the question, except to rule out the use of a source from before July 1586. Relative to Marenzio's settings, however, Wert's texts prove truer to the printed editions, particularly the Baldini edition of 1594, published in nearby Ferrara. Nevertheless, it remains plausible that Wert took his texts from a second-generation source, such as actors' parts, which might explain the occasional, patent deviations from the printed texts of the play—for example, the numerous disparities in *O primavera* that appear in no other extant source, including "thesoro," "longo," and "aventurosi dì."

The large number of *Pastor fido* settings published by Marenzio in 1594–98, however, provides a more compelling case for a potential source and date of the Roman composer's texts. For, of all the sources at hand—the drafts of 1584–86 and printed editions of 1590–95—the texts of Marenzio's madrigals stand most closely in agreement with the lost draft of July 1586 on which Salviati commented—that is, with the stage in the play's genesis just prior to the incorporation of the philologist's revisions. It seems unlikely that Marenzio would have acquired a copy of *Il pastor fido* directly from Guarini or Salviati around 1586, for there is no evidence of a direct connection to either at this time.[93] We know for certain, however, of one other manuscript of the play from late 1586 or early 1587 that has not survived: the copy sent to, and revised by, Scipione Gonzaga, which was presumably the same or very similar to the text given to Salviati.[94]

Scipione Gonzaga and Marenzio's *Pastor fido* Settings

The intersection of these various factors concerning Marenzio's *Pastor fido* madrigals—the agreement of his texts most consistently with the 1586 draft, his association with Scipione Gonzaga in the 1580s and 1590s, and Scipione's possession of an early draft of the play around this same time—opens the doors to alternative scenarios to the long-standing view that Marenzio composed these works under Cinzio Aldobrandini's roof, and for his intellectual gatherings there, in the mid-1590s, including the possibility that the settings arose through the mediation of Scipione Gonzaga. It is conceivable, for instance, that sometime between 1587 and 1593, Marenzio received an early draft of the play from Scipione Gonzaga or acquired it upon the cardinal's death in January 1593, and used this source as the basis for his madrigals in the mid-1590s, possibly in anticipation of Guarini's visit to Cinzio's *ridotto*.

Alternatively, it cannot be ruled out that Marenzio, in fact, composed the madrigals using Scipione's 1586–87 draft before the cardinal's death in 1593—possibly as early as the late 1580s, or in the early 1590s, while residing at the palace of the young pastoral-loving and esteemed patron of music and poetry, the Duke of Bracciano, Virginio Orsini (1572–1615)[95]—and waited to publish the settings because they remained in some sense in Scipione's ownership.[96] The madrigals could then still have formed part of the gatherings in Rome of 1593–95, where they piqued and complemented discussion of Guarini's new and controversial work, and, in turn, underwent slight modifications to bring them audibly into accord with the published play. As mentioned earlier, Scipione Gonzaga seems to have played a similar role in Marenzio's Tasso settings of 1581–84, the texts of which contain variants with no known source—some of the works, in fact, appeared in print even before the poetic texts themselves were published—suggesting that perhaps Marenzio had access to unique readings of the *Gerusalemme liberata* and the poet's *Rime*.[97] A likely source of these texts, Fenlon explains, is Scipione Gonzaga, who maintained close contact with Tasso during this period and played a crucial role in editing his work.

Lending support to Scipione's involvement in Marenzio's Guarini settings are several documents indicating that after assisting Marenzio in negotiating employment in Mantua, the cardinal also set to work finding employment for Guarini in Rome in 1590–91, just prior to the poet's sojourn in Mantua for the 1591–92 stage preparations of *Il pastor fido*. It will be remembered that after leaving his post under Duke Alfonso d'Este in June 1588, the poet, though disillusioned by his time as a courtier in Ferrara, began seeking employment elsewhere, turning first to Florence and Turin in 1588, then living itinerantly between Venice, Padua, and the Villa Guarina before being summoned to Mantua by Duke Vincenzo in late 1591. Through these uncertain years, as the poet returned repeatedly to the environs and vivid memories of the late Accademia degli Eterei in Padua, correspondence between Guarini and Scipione intensified. Following the exchange over *Il pastor fido* in 1586–88, Guarini wrote on 13 June 1588 to inform Scipione of his having left Alfonso d'Este's service, perfunctorily reaffirming his unfailing devotion to the cardinal.[98] In what hints of a subtle plea for employment, the poet assures Scipione that, "in whatever state my fortune may turn me, you should hold me for that same servant that I always was to you."[99] On 3 September 1590, Guarini wrote from Padua ("the secure and familiar port of my shipwrecks") to express his longing for both Scipione and the "albergo Etereo." Again, the poet iterates his fond thoughts of Scipione's supervision, possibly suggesting his desire to join the cardinal in Rome, as he states:

> I return to myself, who in the times of the Eterei used to have the greatest pleasure from two things: your presence and your orders. Now that distance has taken me away, I pray that these at least you will not take from me, since serving you is for me like seeing you.[100]

Scipione's reply of 27 January 1591 is equally rich in compliments and nostalgia, as the cardinal assures his long-time friend:

you should believe that in all your needs, I would always avail myself most liberally of your courtesy; but with the same confidence I also wish that you avail yourself of me, since my wish to involve myself in any matter that serves you is not at all slighter than the grandest esteem I know [is held] of your virtue.[101]

All of this, indeed, could be taken as token praise and necessary formalities of courtly rhetoric, but the affection and mutual regard between the two Eterei was undeniably genuine. Moreover, Guarini's repeated affirmations of his readiness to serve Scipione and be near him seem to be more than rhetorical. This is made clearer in a letter of 20 November 1591. As the poet formulated plans to bring his son Guarino to Rome to enter the Seminario dei Gesuiti—the motivation that would bring the poet to Cinzio Aldobrandini's circle in 1593–95—he conveyed his aspirations to find a patron in Rome and remain there for the rest of his life. Even more, it appears that Scipione was assisting in this search, for Guarini writes:

> Considering that I am not yet so old or so infirm that I cannot exercise that talent that God is pleased to give me, and as it seems to do me harm, living uselessly these years, that by nature's path I could live there [in Rome] for the benefit of my house, and my son [Guarino], whose inclination to the priesthood I would like to assist as much as I can, I have considered relying on a patron, through whom I hope to attain my ends. And so Your Most Illustrious and Most Reverend Lordship petitioned to help find me a match in Rome, where I might gladly work and finish my life, when I have the luxury of pursuing honorably my modest hopes. Whatever the case, I do not know how to live idly, nor would I ever want death to find me with my hands in my belt, if I survive my elderly years [years of Nestor]. And when I bring forth no other fruit, I would be near Your Most Illustrious and Reverend Lordship, and be able to enjoy this, and serve you.[102]

After Scipione's death in January 1593, Guarini might have found himself needing to take a more active role in courting potential patrons in Rome, thus leading to his extended visits there the following winters. When Scipione was still available to negotiate for Guarini, as he had for Marenzio in 1586, however, one practical, yet subtle, tactic for showcasing the poet's work to potential patrons would have been through musical settings and performances of his verse. Scipione was well acquainted with both Marenzio and Guarini, and reportedly fond of their work. While the notion of his prompting the union of both artists' talents through madrigal settings of *Il pastor fido* is in itself entirely plausible—especially so given the strong associations between Marenzio's madrigal texts and the lost draft of Guarini's play—the cardinal's would-be efforts to find a post for Guarini in Rome would have provided an added impetus for the settings.

These concurrences open up the possibility that the madrigals were designed not to meet the desires of Cinzio Aldobrandini's circle to experience excerpts of the tragicomedy in performance, as scholars have proposed—though the works might have served this purpose later—but as "calling cards" for Guarini in Rome, promoting his pastoral play to a cultured audience through the discerning musical renderings of an esteemed and well-connected Roman composer at Scipione Gonzaga's bidding in the late 1580s or early 1590s. The notional ties between Marenzio and Guarini through Scipione, therefore, present two new plausible time frames for the composition of Marenzio's *Pastor fido* settings: after Scipione Gonzaga had acquired the draft of the play from Guarini in late 1586 or early 1587, or while the cardinal might have been helping the poet find employment in Rome in 1590–93.

This alterative chronology of Marenzio's madrigals based on their textual correlations with a pre-publication draft of the play could greatly alter our understanding of the genesis of Marenzio's music, his interest in the tragicomedy, and the trajectory of the *Pastor fido* tradition altogether. No longer would his settings seem to coincide with Guarini's presence among the *letterati* of Cinzio Aldobrandini in 1593–95, but rather with his interactions with Scipione Gonzaga in the years before. This scenario could give historians reason to reconsider the composer's already influential role and position in the tradition of *Pastor fido* madrigals, as his settings could possibly antedate the earliest settings based soundly on the printed play of Leoni (1591), Belli (1593), and Wert (1595), all of whom set passages also set by Marenzio, but that Marenzio only published in 1594–98.

Notes

1 Guarini writes:

> This tragic tale is taken in full from Pausanias except for the names, which have been changed. But the rest is all the same: the loving priest, the unfaithful nymph, the priest who prays for the vengeance of his goddess, the plague which is delivered, the oracle consulted, the response that the same nymph must be sacrificed—or some other for her—and be sacrificed by the hand of the priest who loves her...

Document 4.1: Guarini, *Il pastor fido* (1602), 30v. The tale derives from Pausanias, *Description of Greece*, trans. by W.H.S. Jones, 6 vols. (London: William Heinemann, 1918), vol. 3, Book 7, Chapter 21, 1–5.

2 Pausanias, *Description of Greece*, vol. 3, Book 7, Ch. 21, 1–2.

3 The nobility of Aminta offers a clear example: Pausanias inscribes the status of the tale's protagonist as a model of exceptional morality in ancient Greece when he writes, "He thus proved in deed that his love was more genuine than that of any other man we know" (*Description of Greece*, 4–5).

4 See, for example, Newcomb, *The Madrigal at Ferrara*, I, Chapter 4 ("Musical Practice within the 'Musica Secreta'"), 53–89.

5 Here and throughout this study, multi-*parte* madrigals are counted as one work. Hence, for example, Gastoldi's four-part setting of the *Gioco della cieca* (*Cieco*

amor non ti cred'io) is considered one work, as is his one-*parte* madrigal, *Com'è soave cosa*.

6 James Chater (presumably unaware of Pescetti's statement) observes:

> Even Luzzaschi showed scant interest in the play as a source of madrigals, while settings by Ferrarese giants such as Gesualdo and Fontanelli are conspicuously lacking. The reason for this scarcity and for the alterations of many of the first lines [of early *Pastor fido* settings] may perhaps be sought in the need to elude identification at a time when Alfonso II was still smarting at what he regarded as Guarini's treachery in presenting his pastorale to the Duke of Savoy in 1585...
>
> ("Un pasticcio di madrigaletti," 150–51)

Chater, however, notes the numerous settings with Ferrarese connections, particularly those of Monteverdi's Fourth and Fifth Books (1603 and 1605), discussed in Chapters 6 and 7. The subtitle of Luzzaschi's *Madrigali per cantare et sonare a uno, doi, e tre soprani* (Rome: Verovio, 1601) states that the contents served "per la musica del già Serenissimo Duca Alfonso d'Este," and the dedication elaborates on this function. See, for example, the dedication and introduction in Luzzaschi, *Madrigali*, ed. Elio Durante and Anna Martellotti (Florence: Studio per edizioni scelte, 1980). Another, three-voice madrigal in this collection begins with a well-known verse from *Il pastor fido*, "O dolcezze amarissime d'Amore," but as Chater notes, the remainder of the text comes from Guarini's poem *Questo è pure il mio core*. Interestingly, however, this opening line is the verse that, in the play, immediately follows the passage set in *O primavera gioventù dell'anno* earlier in Luzzaschi's book.

7 As James Chater writes,

> it seems clear that interest in the play among composers was stimulated in Rome by the interest taken by Cardinal Montalto c. 1594–96 and by the performance in Ronciglione under the auspices of Cardinal Odoardo Farnese and in Mantua by the rehearsals and performances in 1591–92 and 1598.
>
> ("Un pasticcio di madrigaletti," 153, note 72)

As we will see below, however, interest in the play as a source of madrigal texts in Rome might have begun considerably earlier and have been motivated by different circumstances.

8 For a detailed account of Luigi d'Este's musical establishment and his patronage of Marenzio, see Marco Bizzarini, "Marenzio and Cardinal Luigi d'Este," *Early Music* 27 (1999): 518–32. Here Bizzarini writes,

> none of Marenzio's later protectors or patrons—not the Grand Duke of Tuscany, Ferdinando I de' Medici, nor Cardinal Cinzio Aldobrandini-Passeri, nor Pope Clement VIII, nor Sigismund III, King of Poland (to cite only a few)—would have such obvious influence on his career and creative output.
>
> (519)

9 Durante and Martellotti, *Cronistoria*, 143–44 (A33); passage trans. in Newcomb, *Madrigal at Ferrara*, 10 and Appendix V, Document 3a.

10 Newcomb, *Madrigal at Ferrara*, 10–11 and App. V, Document 3b.

11 The letter is cited in Steven Ledbetter, "Luca Marenzio: New Biographical Findings," Ph.D. diss., New York University (1971), 162 and discussed in Newcomb, *The Madrigal at Ferrara*, I, 206 and Bizzarini, "Marenzio and Cardinal Luigi d'Este," 527.

12 Tasso first sent drafts of the *Liberata* to Scipione in 1575 for criticism, before it was published by Baldini in Ferrara in 1581—what is considered today to be the most authoritative version of the poem. Scipione later edited the work for

the 1584 Osanna edition from Mantua. He was also the dedicatee of Tasso's *Discorsi dell'arte poetica e del poema-eroico*, written in the 1560s yet published in 1586.

13 See Iain Fenlon's "Cardinal Scipione Gonzaga (1542–93): 'Quel padrone confidentissimo'," *Journal of the Royal Musical Association* 113/2 (1988): 223–49.

14 From the Accademia degli Eterei's *Rime degli Accademici Eterei* (Venice: Comin da Trino, 1567). Marenzio set Tasso's *Padre del cielo* in his *Madrigali spirituali* of 1584 and *Su l'ampia fronte* in his Third Book of madrigals for six voices of 1585. The 1588 reprint of the *Rime* (Ferrara: Baldini) was dedicated to Scipione Gonzaga, the academy's founder.

15 Document 4.2: Guarini, *Lettere* (1595), 226. Guarini replied on 8 March 1588, briefly thanking Scipione for the "cortese diligenza" with which he examined the poem. See *Lettere* (1595), 178–79. In Summo's response to Pescetti, appended to the second edition of his *Due discorsi*, he cites Scipione's statement as evidence of the cardinal's criticism veiled in hyperbolic praise (Document 4.3: Summo, *Due discorsi ... con una replica*, 6).

16 The full passage in the play (V,1: 92–101) reads:

> There, the famous Egon adorned with laurel
> I saw, with scarlet and with virtue, such that
> he resembled Apollo himself; thus I, devoted,
> consecrated the lyre and heart to his name.
> And in that realm where glory resides,
> it would have suffered me well to have at last
> arrived at that end to which my heart aspired,
> the heavens having made me happy on earth;
> such a master, such a guardian
> of my happiness it had made me.
>
> (Document 4.4)

17 Document 4.5: Guarini, *Il pastor fido* (1602), 197v.

18 In the play, the first line of the passage again reads "O che soave e non intero bacio." As Chater argues, there are indications that an earlier form of the text—possibly even that of Marenzio's work—existed independently of the play, and that this autonomous poetic madrigal then served as the source for the passage in the fifth act of *Il pastor fido* ("Un pasticcio di madrigaletti," 145–46).

19 Marenzio, *Motecta festorum totius anni...liber primus* (Rome: Gardano, 1585). Scipione had been appointed Patriarch of Jerusalem that year by Pope Sixtus V (Felice Peretti) and was raised to cardinal two years later.

20 On Orsini's avid patronage of musicians and poets, particularly in Rome in 1589–94, see Valerio Morucci, "Poets and musicians in the Roman–Florentine circle of Virginio Orsini, Duke of Bracciano (1572–1615)," *Early Music* 43 (2015): 53–61 and note 48 below.

21 Further suggestion of a connection between Guarini, Marenzio, and Ingegneri lies in the artists' membership in the Accademia Olimpia of Vicenza beginning sometime before 1596. A list of "Academici Olimpici" from an attendance role of 1596 includes Marenzio (under the "Absenti"), Guarini, Ferrante Gonzaga (dedicatee of Marenzio's *Book VIII a 5*), and Ingegneri. The list is reproduced in Marco Bizzarini, "L'ultimo Marenzio: tipologie di committenza e di recezione," in *Studi marenziani*, eds. Piperno and Fenlon (Venice: Fondazione Ugo e Olga Levi, 2003), 67–87. Bizzarini puts forth the hypothesis that Marenzio was admitted to the Accademia on account of Count Mario Bevilacqua's recommendation between 1587 and 1592. Bevilacqua, a member of the Accademia until his death in 1593, was the dedicatee of Marenzio's *Madrigali a 4, 5, e 6* of 1588.

Patrizi's writings are primarily concerned with challenging Aristotle's *Poetics*, but this consequently leads him to favor Guarini's tragicomedy and Ariosto's *Orlando furioso*, while opposing particularly the poetic style and theories of Tasso. His principal works include a series of volumes under the title *Della poetica di Francesco Patrici*, published in 1586–88, and his *Parere in difesa dell'Ariosto* of 1585. Patrizi served as chair of philosophy at the University of Ferrara (1577–92) before being invited to Rome by Pope Clement VIII. On his critical writings, see Weinberg, *History of Literary Criticism*, II, esp. 765–86, 997–1000, and 1024–25.

22 Cinzio Aldobranini's secretary and biographer, Guido Bentivoglio, writes that the cardinal's academic circle met every morning for seventeen years. On Aldobrandini's circle and support of Tasso in the 1590s, see Ludwig Pastor, *History of the Popes from the Close of the Middle Ages*, ed. Ralph Francis Kerr, 40 vols. (London: Kegan Paul, Trench, Trubner, & Co., 1933), vol. 24, 451–66.

23 The dedication of the Seventh Book states: "Al molto illustre et reverendissimo signor mio patron osservandiss. Il signor Don Diego de Campo, Intimo Cameriere participante, & assistente di N[ostro] Sig[nor]." It continues by referring to "the affection which Your Reverence has shown in always favoring my works with the courtesy of listening to them willingly, as if with kindness to praise them beyond their merit." Translated in the introduction to Patricia Myers's edition of Marenzio, *The Secular Works* (New York: Broude Brothers, 1980), vol. 14 (*Il settimo libro de' madrigali a cinque voci*) xviii. As James Chater points out, De Campo evidently had a strong interest in music, and, as indicated in the Sistine Chapel diaries for 1594 and 1596, was in charge of conveying the Pope's instructions to the Papal choir. See Chater, "Luca Marenzio: New Documents, New Observations," *Music and Letters* 64 (1983): 2–11, at 7, n. 25. De Campo is also the dedicatee of Philippe de Monte's Sixteenth Book for five voices of 1593. Here De Campo is referred to as "Protonotario Apostolico, Canonico di S[anta] M[aria] Maggiore..., Camarier secreto di sua Santità." The dedication is reprinted in Brian Mann, *The Secular Madrigals of Filippo di Monte, 1521–1603*, in series Studies in Musicology, no. 64 (Ann Arbor, MI: UMI Research Press, 1983), 449–50.

As Sigismondo Sigismondi, a Ferrarese academician, describes in his *Prattica cortegiana morale, et economica* (Ferrara: Baldini, 1604), a *cameriero secreto* (personal valet) is typically dear to their patron not only for their long and capable service, but also for their generosity, trustworthiness, and other virtues of character, and in turn, these *camerieri* often "have the [direct] ear of their Padrone" (86–89). In addition to De Campo's genuine appreciation of Marenzio's music, then, the dedication to the Pope's *cameriero secreto* might also reflect the composer's political concerns and motivations, given—based on his imminent transferral to Poland—the apparent precariousess of his position in the Vatican. I am grateful to Laurie Nussdorfer for bringing Sigismondi's book to my attention.

24 See, for example, Patricia Myers, Introduction to Marenzio, *The Secular Works*, vol. 14, xx; Laura Macy, "The Late Madrigals of Luca Marenzio: Studies in the Interactions of Music, Literature, and Patronage at the End of the Sixteenth Century," Ph.D. diss., University of North Carolina at Chapel Hill, 1991, 92–101; and Massimo Ossi, "Monteverdi, Marenzio, and Battista Guarini's 'Cruda Amarilli'," *Music and Letters* 89 (2008): 311–36.

25 On Tasso's biography, a useful place to begin is Angelo Solerti's seminal *Vita di Torquato Tasso*, 3 vols. (Turin: Loescher, 1895), and in English, C.P. Brand, *Torquato Tasso: A Study of the Poet and of his Contribution to English Literature* (Cambridge: Cambridge University Press, 1965).

26 Giulio Fiesco, in his *Musica Nova* of 1569, includes at least four Guarini texts, three of which are from the *Rime degli Accademici Eterei: Da qual porta d'Averno*

apristi l'ale, Fede a cui fatto ho del mio core un tempio, and *Or che'l mio viva sole altrove splende. S'armi pur d'ira in voi turbato ed empio* was included in Guarini's 1598 *Rime.* It is possible, if not likely, however, that the other twenty-five texts in the volume are also by Guarini, although they have not been identified in any other source. Fiesco's dedication to Lucretia and Eleonora d'Este, sisters of Alfonso II, Duke of Ferrara, states that he composed the works on Guarini's request.

27 *Tirsi morir volea* and *Baci soavi e cari* were erroneously included in Tasso's *Rime,* parte I (Venice: Aldo Manuzio, 1581) but later appeared in Guarini's 1598 *Rime.* For a complete list of known settings of Guarini's poetry, see Antonio Vassalli and Angelo Pompilio, "Indice delle rime di Battista Guarini poste in musica," in *Guarini: la musica, i musicisti,* 185–225.

28 For an explication of the *morire* metaphor in sixteenth-century poetry and music, see Laura Macy, "Speaking of Sex: Metaphor and Performance in the Italian Madrigal," *Journal of Musicology* 14 (1996): 1–45; also Galen's *On Semen,* trans. Phillip De Lacy (Berlin: Akademie Verlag, 1992); *On the Natural Faculties,* trans. Arthur John Brock (Cambridge, MA: Harvard University Press, 1991); and *On the Usefulness of the Parts,* trans. Margaret Tallmadge May, 2 vols. (Ithaca, NY: Cornell University Press, 1968); David J. Furley and J.S. Wilkie, *Galen: On Respiration and the Arteries* (Princeton, NJ: Princeton University Press, 1984); as well as Aristotle's *Generation of Animals,* trans. A.L. Peck (Cambridge, MA: Harvard University Press, 1990).

29 For a detailed study of settings of *Udite, lagrimosi* from 1594 to 1611, focusing on Lucia Quinciani's idiosyncratic solo rendering of 1611, see Seth Coluzzi, "Monody in Verona and Rome: Marc'Antonio Negri's *Affetti amorosi...libro secondo* (1611) and the Curious Case of Lucia Quinciani's *Udite, lagrimosi,*" *Studi musicali* 12 (2021): 7–54.

30 Chater, "Un pasticcio di madrigaletti," 152.

31 The information for Table 4.1 and Figure 4.2 was assembled using the invaluable resources of James Chater's *"Il pastor fido* and Music: A Bibliography," in *Guarini: la musica, i musicisti,* 157–83; Antoni Vassalli and Angelo Pompilio, "Indice delle rime di Battista Guarini poste in musica," in *ibid.,* 185–225; Emil Vogel, Alfred Einstein, François Lesure, and Claudio Sartori, *Bibliografia della musica italiana vocale profana pubblicata dal 1500 al 1700* (Staderini: Minkoff, 1977); and Emil Vogel, *Bibliothek der gedruckten weltlichen Vocalmusik Italiens aus den Jahren 1500–1700,* 2 vols. (Hildesheim: Olms, 1962), II; which were supplemented by new research.

32 The catalyst for the play's unusual edge over the *Rime* in 1621 is the nineteen *Pastor fido* settings in Scipione Cerreto's *L'Amarillide III a 3*—an atypically high number in the context of this data, even when compared to Marenzio's Seventh Book and the *Pastor fido* books of Monte and Piccioni, which contain fourteen and twelve settings, respectively. Ghizzolo's Third Book of that year contributes an additional six settings.

33 The most widely set *Rime* text, *Ardo sì, ma non t'amo,* appeared in sixty-one known treatments—considerably more than the thirty-seven settings of *Ah, dolente partita,* the most frequently set *Pastor fido* text—but this figure is magnified greatly by the thirty-one treatments of this text that make up the Bavarian collection *Sdegnosi ardori* (1585), discussed in the next paragraph.

34 Vassalli and Pompillo, "Indice delle rime di Battista Guarini," 186.

35 George Schuetze includes ninety-five settings of Guarini's *Ardo sì, ma non t'amo* and related texts—including Tasso's *Ardi e gela à tua voglia,* which was sometimes paired with Guarini's poem in *proposta* (Guarini)–*risposta* (Tasso) arrangement—in *Settings of "Ardo sì" and its Related Texts,* in series Recent Researches in the Music of the Renaissance (Madison, WI: A-R Editions, 1990), 78–81. Vassalli and Pompilio fail to account for the thirty-one settings in the

Sdegnosi ardori (except those that appear elsewhere) in their "Indice delle rime di Battista Guarini."

36 See note 26 above.

37 The case of Monte's Guarini settings refutes somewhat Brian Mann's opinion that the composer was "a follower rather than a trend-setter, in literary as well as in musical matters," as his settings of both the *Rime* and the play stand at the front of the curve of the Guarini madrigal vogue. Mann, however, is right in terms of Monte's sudden absorption in Guarini's texts, when he states: "Monte's attitude towards *Il Pastor Fido* is typical of his lifelong habits; he is not one for half-measures, and when his interest in a poet's work is aroused…he explores it thoroughly." See Mann's *The Secular Madrigals of Filippo di Monte*, 59–60.

38 In most cases the list shows books containing five or more Guarini settings. For sparser years toward the earlier end of the *Pastor fido* trend (before 1600), books containing the largest number of Guarini texts are shown.

39 Giambattista Marino's *Rime* appeared in the same year and from the same publisher as the revised, authoritative edition of *Il pastor fido* (Venice: Ciotti, 1602) and was revised in 1614 as *La lira, rime del Cavalier Marino*. For indices of seventeenth-century settings of Marino's verses organized by composer and by incipit, see Roger Simon and D. Gidrol, "Appunti sulle relazioni tra l'opera poetica di G.B. Marino e la musica del suo tempo," *Studi secenteschi* 14 (1973), 81–188.

40 The evidence presented here challenges the claims of several theater historians that Tasso's play, as Umberto Bosco describes it, "inspired a great many composers that clothed it with notes" (*Saggi sul rinascimento italiano* [Florence: Le Monnier, 1970], 154). Although speaking more about the musicality of Tasso's verse than specifically of musical settings thereof, Raeffaello Ramat similarly writes, "*L'Aminta* è infatti un'opera lirica, opera musicale; e il miglior suo musico, fra quanti la rivestirono in parte o interamente di note, è il Tasso medesimo; ché le sue parole son già musica" ("*L'Aminta*," in *Per la storia dello stile rinascimentale*, vol. 42 of series *Biblioteca di cultura contemporanea* [Messina: D'Anna, 1953], 119–51, at 125).

41 For the full text of *Com'è dolce il gioire*, see Chapter 8, p. 413.

42 Before the books of Mezzogorri and Ceretto, which draw texts exclusively from *Il pastor fido* without any from the *Rime*, Monte comes close in 1599, setting seven play texts and one *Rime* text in his *La fiammetta*, and in 1600, setting fourteen play texts and one *Rime* text in his *Musica sopra il pastor fido*. In 1602, Giovanni Piccioni includes twelve play texts and one *Rime* text in his *Il pastor fido musicale*, and Gastoldi includes ten from the play and one from the *Rime* in his Fourth Book.

43 See Chater, "Un pasticcio di madrigaletti," 154 for a table of the "ten most frequently set texts" from the play through 1605.

44 Guarini's text, published in the 1587 Ventura anthology *Rime di diversi celebri poeti* along with "O che soave e non intero bacio," begins "Donò Licori a Batto" (196).

45 This verse in the play reads "E tu, Mirtillo, anima mia, perdona" (III,4: 539).

46 Chater, "Un pasticcio di madrigaletti," 153. Most of Philippe de Monte's many *Pastor fido* settings also show considerable, unique modifications to the play's texts, but these readings do not reappear in later musical settings.

47 On the transition of this passage from play to madrigal, see Seth Coluzzi, "*Tirsi mio, caro Tirsi: Il pastor fido* and the Roman Madrigal," in Calcagno, ed., *Perspectives on Luca Marenzio's Secular Music*, in series *Epitome musical* (Turnhout, Belgium: Brepols, 2014), 51–73 and Gerbino, *Music and the Myth of Arcadia*, 352–55.

48 On Orsini's associations with the Pastori della Valle Tiberna and the hypothesis that Orsini and his wife, Flavia Peretti (sister of Cardinal Montalto), are inscribed in Marenzio's Sixth Book of madrigals through their pastoral aliases,

Tirsi and Clori, see James Chater, "Fonti poetiche per i madrigali di Luca Marenzio," *Rivista italiana di musicologia* 13 (1978): 60–103, at 77 and Gerbino, *Music and the Myth of Arcadia*, 361–64.

49　Pallavicino's *Cruda Amarilli, che col nome ancora* also adheres to Marenzio's bipartite division of the text, such that the *prima parte* includes verses 272–279, the *seconda parte*, verses 280–291. See Chapter 8 below.

50　Later editions of the Seventh Book were published in 1600 and 1609 by Angelo Gardano, and in 1609 by Girolamo Scotto. In 1601, Paul Kauffmann in Nuremberg published a complete edition of Marenzio's five-voice madrigals. The Sixth, Seventh, Eighth, and Ninth Books were published together as a single collection in 1609 and 1632 by Pierre Phalèse (Antwerp).

51　On the influence of Roman composers, including Marenzio, on music in Verona around 1610, see Coluzzi, "Monody in Verona and Rome," 23–54.

52　Appendices appear in the Support Material for this book. The textual differences shown in Appendix A do not take into account variant uses of punctuation (except where it impinges upon versification or the sense of the passage) and contractions. Spaces within any given madrigal text indicate divisions of the text into two or more *parti* or, when text appears in the right-hand column adjacent to the blank, verses from the play that are omitted.

53　For a description of the three manuscripts and their contents, see Vittorio Rossi, *Battista Guarini ed 'Il pastor fido'*, 189–223.

54　See Angelo Giaccaria, "Identificazione di manoscritti italiani frammentari nella Biblioteca Nazionale Torino," *Giornale storico della letteratura italiana* 164 (1987): 206–18, at 214; also, Chater, "Un pasticcio madrigaletti," 141–42.

55　Carla Molinari describes the contents of the Marciana manuscript in her thorough and invaluable study of the early sources of the play, "Per il *Pastorfido* di Battista Guarini." Access to the Turin copy, however, was limited at the time of Molinari's work, as the manuscript was deemed irrecoverable; it was partially restored soon after (see p. 164, note 3).

56　Giovanni Andrea Barotti, *Difesa degli scrittori Ferraresi, composta dal dottor Giovannandrea Barotti da quanto ha pubblicato contro di loro l'autore delle Osservazioni al terzo libro dell' 'Eloquenza italiana' di Monsignor Giusto Fontanini* (Venice: S. Occhi, 1739), 81; Rossi, *Guarini ed Il pastor fido*, 190.

57　"...la copia intera ha valore di autografo, perchè anche nelle parti scritte da altri il Guarini fece di suo pugno le correzioni" (Rossi, *Guarini ed Il pastor fido*, 190).

58　Molinari, "Per il *Pastorfido*," 166–67, note 3.

59　Barotti, *Difesa degli scrittori Ferraresi*, 82; Rossi, *Guarini ed Il pastor fido*, 191; Molinari, "Per il *Pastorfido*," 167, note 3.

60　Aldo Gennari, "Il pastor fido di G. B. Guarini," *Il bibliofilo* 8 (1887): 35–36.

61　Giuseppe Antonelli, *Indice dei manoscritti della civica biblioteca di Ferrara* (Ferrara: A. Taddei, 1884), 23–28, at 23.

62　Rossi, *Guarini ed Il pastor fido*, 217–19. Rossi also outlines the development of act 5, scene 8 at pp. 219–21.

63　In his *Degli Accademici della Crusca difesa dell'Orlando furioso dell'Ariosto contra'l dialogo dell'epica poesia di Cammillo Pellegrino* (Florence: Domenico Manzani, 1584), for example, Salviati writes:

> The poet is not a poet without invention; therefore, if he writes history, or upon a story already written by another, he loses his being completely.... Imitation and invention are one and the same things as far as the plot is concerned.
> (p. 13; translated in Weinberg, *History of Literary Criticism*, 1005)

64　As Salviati succinctly states, "Aristotle...says that when the poem has pleased, the poet has achieved his end" (*Difesa*, 11v; trans. Weinberg, *History of Literary Criticism*, 1006).

65 The Academy included among its members the humanist, critic, and future member of Cinzio Aldobrandini's *famiglia*, Giovanni de' Bardi, who was invited to Rome to serve as *maestro di camera* to Pope Clement VIII (Cinzio Aldobrandini's uncle) beginning in 1592, a position that he held until returning to Florence in 1605 following the election of Pope Paul V. As we have seen, Bardi played an important role in devising *intermedi* for the Medici in the 1580s and hosted Guarini during the poet's visit to Florence in 1588.

66 See Peter M. Brown, *Lionardo Salviati: A Critical Biography* (Oxford: Oxford University Press, 1974), 199–200.

67 Lionardo Salviati, *Orazione delle lodi di don Luigi d'Este fatta dal cavalier Lionardo Salviati nella morte di quel signore* (Florence: Antonio Padovani, 1587). See also Rossi, *Guarini ed Il pastor fido*, 88. Salviati's funeral orations eulogize some of the most illustrious figures of the time in Florence, including Michelangelo Buonarroti (1564) and Grand Duke Cosimo I de' Medici (1574), and later in Ferrara, Duke Alfonso II d'Este (1597).

68 Document 4.6: Guarini, *Lettere* (1595), 50. A summary of these correspondences also appears in Rossi, *Battista Guarini*, 185–187.

69 Document 4.7: Guarini, *Lettere* (1595), 54. The letter is erroneously dated 6 February 1586 in the *Lettere*, but corrected by Rossi, *Battista Guarini*, 186.

70 Document 4.8: Guarini, *Lettere* (1600), 348.

71 Document 4.9: Guarini, *Lettere* (1595), 58–59.

72 See Barotti, *Difesa degli scrittori Ferraresi*, I, 84; Antonelli, *Indice dei manoscritti*, I, 23; and Cittadella, *I Guarini, famiglia nobile*, 81–82.

73 Rossi, *Guarini ed Il pastor fido*, 210–12, at 210.

74 Molinari, "Per il *Pastor fido*," 221–23.

75 Salviati's annotations to act 1 alone were published in *Prose inedited del Cav. Leonardo Salviati*, ed. Luigi Manzoni (Bologna: G. Romagnoli, 1873). Salviati's letter of 8 October and a small portion of his annotations are given in Rossi, *Battista Guarini*, 299–300 and 304–305. The letter and annotations are transcribed in full in "Le annotazioni al *Pastor fido* di Lionardo Salviati," in *Poeti estensi del Rinascimento: con due appendici*, ed. Silvio Pasquazi (Florence: Felice Lemonnier, 1966), 209–33 and Deanna Battaglin, "Leonardo Salviati e le 'Osservazioni al Pastor fido' del Guarini," *Atti e memorie dell'Accademia Patavina di scienze, lettere, ed arti* 77 (1964–65): 249–84. For a discussion of Guarini's literary style and various changes made in drafts of the play that reflect the development of this style, see Deanna Battaglin's "Il linguaggio tragicomico del Guarini e l'elaborazione del *Pastor fido*," in *Lingua e strutture del teatro italiano del rinascimento* (Padua: Liviana Editrice, 1970), 291–353.

76 The first criticism, Denores' *Discorso...intorno à que' principii, cause, et accrescimenti*, also appeared in 1586. Although the letter of dedication is not dated, it seems likely that the pamphlet appeared after Salviati's comments on *Il pastor fido*, given that no mention is made of any public criticism in the Guarini–Salviati correspondence. Hence, Salviati, in truth, provides the first substantial criticism of the play, albeit an amicable and as yet private one.

77 Document 4.10: Salviati, "Annotazioni al *Pastor fido*," 213.

78 "Fac[cia 3] verso 18. *nume*. Non mi ricordo, che sia usato dagli antichi; nè per questo danno chi in ciò volesse seguire i moderni" (Salviati, "Annotazioni al *Pastor fido*," 214).

79 "Fac[cia] 102 ver[so] 4. *Tant'osi*, finirei il *tant'* e scriverei *tanto osi*, per cacciar via quell suono di *tantosi*, senza che così richiede, credo, diretta regola d'ortografia, come nei miei libri penso aver detto" (Salviati, "Annotazioni al *Pastor fido*," 223).

80 The volume was left incomplete upon Salviati's death in 1589 and later formed the basis of the first dictionary of the Italian language, published by the Accademia della Crusca in 1612 under the title *Vocabolario degli Accademici della*

Crusca (Venice: Giovanni Alberti, 1612). The importance of Salviati's work in the making of the *Vocabolario* is acknowledged in the volume's introduction, which references the philologist's *Avvertimenti della lingua* and his commentary on Boccaccio's *Decameron* while stating more genereally:

> As for rules, precepts, and grammatical details, this not being the place to deal with them appropriately, we refer to that written on the subject by Cavalier Lionardo Salviati, whom we have sometimes cited in his *Avvertimenti della lingua*, as in the case of accented sounds. And the same can be said of *particelle* [e.g. pronouns], signs of case, and the like.
>
> (Document 4.11)

81 "Fac. 13. ver. 3. Di *mori*, per *muori*, e di mille altri di questa fatta ho detto ne' miei *Avvertimenti* quel ch'io ne senta" ("Annotazioni al *Pastor fido*," 215).

82 "Fac. 49. ver. 21. *Aventuroso, avventuroso*, e così sempre di sotto" (in "Annotazioni al *Pastor fido*," 219).

83 "Fac. 18. ver. 14. *tepido*, stimo che si debba scriver *tiepido*, come si pronunzia…" (in "Annotazioni al *Pastor Fido*," 216). The spelling "tepido" of the manuscripts and madrigal, however, resurfaces in three editions: those from Senese of 1592 and 1594, and Baldini of 1594. See Appendix A.

84 "Fac. 105. ver. 13. *Se vedesti, se vedessi*" ("Annotazione al *Pastor Fido*," 223); and later: "Fac. 6. ver. 15. *vedesti*, dee esser error di penna, dovendo dir *vedessi*" (215).

85 "Fac. 189 ver. 18: Se V.S. non ha autorità (che io per me non l'ho presta), di queste voci direi *chieggio, chieggo, o cheggio*" ("Le Annotazione al *Pastor Fido*," 229).

86 The 1592 Senese, 1594 Senese, and 1595 Bianchi editions contain "chieggio," while the 1590 Baldini, 1590 Bonfadino, 1590 Mamarelli, 1591 Volfeo, and 1594 Baldini prints read "cheggio."

87 "Fac. 18 ver. 11. *fu fallo*. Fuggerei questo suono qui" ("Le Annotazione al *Pastor Fido*," 216).

88 In the passage containing *Arda pur sempre o mora*, all of the manuscripts contain "stratio" (like the madrigal), and all of the printed editions but one (1595 Bianco) read "strazio." In the excerpt containing *Deh, Tirsi, mio gentil, non far più stratio*, M1 has "strazio," which was changed in the later drafts (F and M2) to "stratio" (the spelling of Marenzio's madrigal); the 1594 Senese edition is the only print to retain "stratio," while all other editions have "strazio."

89 Examples of unique readings in the madrigal texts—at least as compared to extant versions of the play, and excluding instances where the madrigal texts are explicitly reworked—are infrequent and include "fusti" in *Se tu, dolce mio ben* (where all known sources read "fosti") and "amendo" in *O fido, o caro Aminta* (conflicting with "ammendo"). "Esiglio" in *Arda pur sempre o mora* is rather exceptional, as it agrees only with M1, while the other manuscripts and all but one of the 1590–95 editions read "essiglio." (The 1595 Bianchi edition has "essilio.") The term occurs, in fact, in the same verse that also contains "stratio" ("Stratio pene tormenti esiglio e morte"). While the printed editions of 1590–95 all vary with the madrigal in this verse—all read "strazio" and essiglio," but the 1595 Bianchi print, which has "stratio" and "essilio"—the manuscript M1 is true to the madrigal text. F, T, and M2 agree in their readings of "stratio" but differ at "essiglio." Although it is not uncommon for one or more of the printed editions to be at odds with the others, the 1595 edition from the firm of Antonio Bianchi in Turin is the only print to do this with noticeable regularity, which might raise questions about Bianchi's source text (bearing in mind the circulation in Turin of corrupted copies of the play by the "Compagnia dell'Isabellina"), variations in dialect, or the hurriedness of Bianchi's effort to bring the popular work to market.

90 This verse sometimes appears as "Che'l sol de gl'occhi miei" when repeated in some of the parts.

91 "Piè" appears both with and without the accent in the partbooks.

92 "It still remains to hear the music ordered from the Most Serene Giaches and Rovigo, whom I will solicit according to the need" ("Restano ancora a far sentire le musiche loro ordinate, li SS.ri Giaches et Rovigo, i quali solecitarò secondo il bisogno"); Ancona, *Origini del teatro italiano*, II, 543.

93 As noted above, Salviati served Duke Alfonso d'Este in Ferrara in 1587–88 before returning to Florence in the summer of 1588. Marenzio and Salviati, thus, would have been in Florence together in 1588–89—and joined in June–July 1588 by Guarini—but the possibility of a 1586-stage draft passing from either the philologist or the poet to Marenzio seems unlikely given Salviati's gravely ill state and the proximity at that point of the play's publication (and, hence, its more advanced stage). Nevertheless, the possibility of some interaction between the three men in Florence cannot be ruled out.

94 As Scipione indicates in his response to Guarini of 30 September 1587, suggestions for revisions to the tragicomedy not only by him, but also by a learned friend were to follow:

> Soon I will send Your Lordship annotations of some small things that I have been considering for [the play], but I protest that I have done this to serve you, on your request, and not because the poem requires correction, and because I hope to be able to say something that will add to the beauty of the work, rather than diminish it. A most kind man, a dearest friend of mine, of great intellect and very learned, has done the same (but not with the intention that you should see his writing) ...
>
> (Document 4.12: Guarini, *Lettere* [1595], 227)

95 It is hypothesized that Marenzio entered Orsini's court in Rome after returning from Florence, by January 1590, and remained there until at least 1593, when he likely joined Cinzio Aldobrandini's *famiglia*, although there are conflicting theories about the dates and Marenzio's residence during this period. A letter from one Venturi to Virginio Orsini of 22 July 1593 requests the use of rooms in the duke's palace formerly occupied by Marenzio, suggesting that the composer had relocated to Cinzio's apartments in the Vatican by that time. The letter is given in Steven Ledbetter, *Luca Marenzio: New Biographical Findings*, doc. 95. See also Bizzarini, *Luca Marenzio: The Career of a Musician between the Renaissance and the Counter-Reformation*, trans. James Chater (Aldershot: Ashgate, 2003), 187–192, and Morucci, "Poets and musicians," 53–61.

96 Bizzarini and Chater have shown that in March–June 1588 Marenzio fulfilled a commission to set at least two passages from another pastoral drama: *Flori*, by Vicentine poetess Maddalena Campiglia ("Flori, Olympia and the Temple of Venus: Luca Marenzio's 'Tour' of the Veneto in 1588," *Studi musicali* 5 [2014]: 137–73). The music has been lost, but Campiglia's instructions indicate that the settings were to be short and scored for four or five voices.

97 Fenlon, "Cardinal Scipione Gonzaga," 243–48.

98 Guarini, *Lettere* (1595), 171.

99 "...così in qualunque stato la mia fortuna mi giri, habbia ella à tenermi per quel medesimo servidore, che le fui sempre." Guarini, *Lettere* (1595), 171.

100 Document 4.13: Guarini, *Lettere* (1595), 88–89.

101 Document 4.14: Guarini, *Lettere* (1595), 90–91.

102 Document 4.15: Guarini, *Lettere* (1595), 268. The letter recounts an earlier letter to Scipione that had been lost.

References

Accademia della Crusca. *Vocabolario degli Accademici della Crusca.* Venice: Giovanni Alberti, 1612.

Accademici degli Eterei. *Rime degli Accademici Eterei.* Venice: Comin da Trino, 1567.

Antonelli, Giuseppe. *Indice dei manoscritti della civica biblioteca di Ferrara.* Ferrara: A. Taddei, 1884.

Barotti, Giovanni Andrea. *Difesa degli scrittori Ferraresi, composta dal dottor Giovannandrea Barotti da quanto ha pubblicato contro di loro l'autore delle Osservazioni al terzo libro dell' 'Eloquenza italiana' di Monsignor Giusto Fontanini.* Venice: S. Occhi, 1739.

Battaglin, Deanna. "Il linguaggio tragicomico del Guarini e l'elaborazione del *Pastor fido.*" In *Lingua e strutture del teatro italiano del rinascimento*, 291–353. Padua: Liviana Editrice, 1970.

———. "Leonardo Salviati e le 'Osservazioni al Pastor fido' del Guarini." *Atti e memorie dell'Accademia Patavina di scienze, lettere, ed arti* 77 (1964–65): 249–84.

Bizzarini, Marco. *Luca Marenzio: The Career of a Musician between the Renaissance and the Counter-Reformation.* Trans. by James Chater. Aldershot: Ashgate, 2003.

———. "L'ultimo Marenzio: tipologie di committenza e di recezione." In *Studi marenziani*, eds. Piperno and Fenlon, 67–87. Venice: Fondazione Ugo e Olga Levi, 2003.

———. "Marenzio and Cardinal Luigi d'Este." *Early Music* 27 (1999): 518–32.

Bizzarini, Marco and James Chater. "Flori, Olympia and the Temple of Venus: Luca Marenzio's 'Tour' of the Veneto in 1588." *Studi musicali* 5 (2014): 137–73.

Bosco, Umberto. *Saggi sul rinascimento italiano.* Florence: Le Monnier, 1970.

Brand, C.P. *Torquato Tasso: A Study of the Poet and of his Contribution to English Literature.* Cambridge: Cambridge University Press, 1965.

Brown, Peter M. *Lionardo Salviati: A Critical Biography.* Oxford: Oxford University Press, 1974.

Chater, James. "*Il pastor fido* and Music: A Bibliography." In *Guarini: la musica, i musicisti*, ed. A. Pompilio, 157–83. Lucca: Libreria Musicale Italiana Editrice, 1997.

———. "'Un pasticcio di madrigaletti'?: The Early Musical Fortune of *Il pastor fido.*" In *Guarini: la musica, i musicisti*, ed. A. Pompilio, 139–55. Lucca: Libreria Musicale Italiana Editrice, 1997.

———. "Luca Marenzio: New Documents, New Observations." *Music and Letters* 64 (1983): 2–11.

———. "Fonti poetiche per i madrigali di Luca Marenzio." *Rivista italiana di musicologia* 13 (1978): 60–103.

Coluzzi, Seth. "Monody in Verona and Rome: Marc'Antonio Negri's *Affetti amorosi...libro secondo* (1611) and the Curious Case of Lucia Quinciani's *Udite, lagrimosi.*" *Studi musicali* 12 (2021): 7–54.

———. "Tirsi mio, caro Tirsi: *Il pastor fido* and the Roman Madrigal." In *Perspectives on Luca Marenzio's Secular Music*, ed. M. Calcagno, 51–73. In series *Epitome musical*. Turnhout: Brepols, 2014.

D'Ancona, Alessandro. *Origini del teatro italiano.* 2nd ed. 3 vols. Turin: Loescher, 1891.

Denores, Giason. *Discorso...intorno à que' principii, cause, et accrescimenti, che la comedia, la tragedia, et il poema heroico ricevono dalla philosophia morale, e civile, e da' governatori delle republiche.* Padua: Paulo Meieto, 1586.

Durante, Elio and Anna Martellotti. *Cronistoria del Concerto delle Dame principalissime di Margherita Gonzaga d'Este.* Florence: Studio per edizioni scelte, 1979.

Fenlon, Iain. "Cardinal Scipione Gonzaga (1542–93): 'Quel padrone confidentis-simo'." *Journal of the Royal Musical Association* 113/2 (1988): 223–249.

Furley, David J. and James S. Wilkie. *Galen: On Respiration and the Arteries.* Princeton, NJ: Princeton University Press, 1984.

Galen. *On Semen.* Trans. by Phillip De Lacy. Berlin: Akademie Verlag, 1992.

———. *On the Natural Faculties.* Trans. by Arthur John Brock. Cambridge, MA: Harvard University Press, 1991.

———. *On the Usefulness of the Parts.* Trans. by Margaret Tallmadge May. 2 vols. Ithaca, NY: Cornell University Press, 1968.

Gerbino, Giuseppe. *Music and the Myth of Arcadia in Renaissance Italy.* Cambridge: Cambridge University Press, 2009.

Giaccaria, Angelo. "Identificazione di manoscritti italiani frammentari nella Biblioteca Nazionale Torino." *Giornale storico della letteratura italiana* 164 (1987): 206–18.

Guarini, Battista. *Il pastor fido, tragicommedia pastorale del molto Illustre Cavaliere Battista Guarini, ora in questa XX impressione di curiose e dotte Annotationi arricchito.* Venice: Ciotti, 1602.

———. *Lettere.* Venice: Ciotti, 1600.

———. *Lettere.* Parma: Viotti, 1595.

Ledbetter, Steven. "Luca Marenzio: New Biographical Findings." Ph.D. diss., New York University, 1971.

Luzzaschi, Luzzasco. *Madrigali per cantare et sonare a uno, doi, e tre soprani.* Rome: Verovio, 1601. Eds. Elio Durante and Anna Martellotti. Florence: Studio per edizioni scelte, 1980.

Macy, Laura. "Speaking of Sex: Metaphor and Performance in the Italian Madrigal." *Journal of Musicology* 14 (1996): 1–45.

———. "The Late Madrigals of Luca Marenzio: Studies in the Interactions of Music, Literature, and Patronage at the End of the Sixteenth Century." Ph.D. diss., University of North Carolina at Chapel Hill, 1991.

Mann, Brian. *The Secular Madrigals of Filippo di Monte, 1521–1603.* In series Studies in Musicology, no. 64. Ann Arbor, MI: UMI Research Press, 1983.

Marenzio, Luca. *Il settimo libro de' madrigali a cinque voci.* Venice: Gardano, 1595. Ed. Patricia Myers in Marenzio, *The Secular Works.* Vol. 14. New York: Broude Bros., 1980.

———. *Motecta festorum totius anni…liber primus.* Rome: Gardano, 1585.

Marino, Giambattista. *La lira, rime del Cavalier Marino.* Venice: Ciotti, 1613.

———. *Rime.* Venice: Ciotti, 1602.

Molinari, Carla. "Per il 'Pastor fido' di Battista Guarini." *Studi di filologia italiana, bollettino annuale dell'Accademia della Crusca* 43 (1985): 161–238.

Morucci, Valerio. "Poets and musicians in the Roman–Florentine circle of Virginio Orsini, Duke of Bracciano (1572–1615)." *Early Music* 43 (2015): 53–61.

Newcomb, Anthony. *The Madrigal at Ferrara, 1579–97.* 2 vols. Princeton, NJ: Princeton University Press, 1981.

Ossi, Massimo. "Monteverdi, Marenzio, and Battista Guarini's 'Cruda Amarilli'." *Music and Letters* 89 (2008): 311–36.

Pastor, Ludwig. *History of the Popes from the Close of the Middle Ages.* Ed. Ralph Francis Kerr. 40 vols. London: Kegan Paul, Trench, Trubner, & Co., 1933.

Pausanias. *Description of Greece.* Trans. by W.H.S. Jones. 6 vols. London: William Heinemann, 1918.

Ramat, Raeffaello. *Per la storia dello stile rinascimentale.* In series Biblioteca di cultura contemporanea 42. Messina: D'Anna, 1953.

Rossi, Vittorio. *Battista Guarini ed il Pastor fido: Studio biografico-critico con documenti inediti.* Turin: Loescher, 1886.

Salviati, Lionardo. "Le annotazioni al *Pastor fido* di Leonardo Salviati." In *Poeti estensi del Rinascimento: con due appendici,* ed. Silvio Pasquazi, 209–33. Florence: Felice Lemonnier, 1966.

―――. *Prose inedited del Cav. Leonardo Salviati.* Ed. Luigi Manzoni. Bologna: G. Romagnoli, 1873.

―――. *Orazione delle lodi di don Luigi d'Este fatta dal cavalier Lionardo Salviati nella morte di quel signore.* Florence: Antonio Padovani, 1587.

―――. *Degli Accademici della Crusca difesa dell'Orlando furioso dell'Ariosto contra'l dialogo dell'epica poesia di Cammillo Pellegrino.* Florence: Domenico Manzani, 1584.

Schuetze, George, ed. *Settings of "Ardo sì" and its Related Texts.* In series Recent Researches in the Music of the Renaissance. Madison, WI: A-R Editions, 1990.

Simon, Roger and D. Gidrol. "Appunti sulle relazioni tra l'opera poetica di G.B. Marino e la musica del suo tempo." *Studi secenteschi* 14 (1973), 81–188.

Solerti, Angelo. *Vita di Torquato Tasso.* 3 vols. Turin: Loescher, 1895.

Summo, Faustino. *Due discorsi, l'uno contra le Tragicomedie et moderne pastorali, l'altro particolarmente contra il Pastor Fido dell'Ill.re Sig. Cav. B.G. Con una replica dell'istesso autore alla difesa del detto P.F., pubblicata sotto nome di Orlando Pescetti et insieme una risposta del medesimo in difesa del metro nelle poesie e nei poemi, contro il parere del molto Rev. Sig. Paolo Beni.* Venice: Francesco Bolzetta, 1601.

Tasso, Torquato. *Rime.* Venice: Aldo Manuzio, 1581.

Vassalli, Antonio and Angelo Pompilio. "Indice delle rime di Battista Guarini poste in musica." In *Guarini: la musica, i musicisti,* ed. A. Pompilio, 185–225. Lucca: Libreria Musicale Italiana Editrice, 1997.

Vogel, Emil. *Bibliothek der gedruckten weltlichen Vocalmusik Italiens aus den Jahren 1500–1700.* 2 vols. Hildesheim: Olms, 1962.

Vogel, Emil, Alfred Einstein, François Lesure, and Claudio Sartori. *Bibliografia della musica italiana vocale profana pubblicata dal 1500 al 1700.* Staderini: Minkoff, 1977.

Weinberg, Bernard. *A History of Literary Criticism in the Italian Renaissance.* 2 vols. Chicago, IL: University of Chicago Press, 1961.

5 Beyond the Theater in Rome and Mantua

The Settings of Marenzio and Wert

Pescetti's affirmation that the nexus between musical madrigal and play sat at the court of Alfonso II d'Este in Ferrara, if true, suggests that a cornerstone of the body of *Pastor fido* madrigals no longer exists. In its place lie the first major sources of musical renderings from the play that survive today: the madrigal books of Marenzio and Wert. Although preceded in print by a handful of isolated settings (see Table 3.1), these books served as foundations not only in the example they set of drawing multiple excerpts from the troublesome stage work, but also in the specific passages on which they focused. The works of both composers appeared in print in 1594–95, but as we have seen, their texts leave open the possibility that they were composed earlier—as early as 1586 for Marenzio's settings, and most likely after the publication of the play (1590) for Wert's. Opportunely for the sake of comparative study, all four of Mirtillo's speeches set by Wert were also set by Marenzio, although the boundaries of these passages do not always correspond. Whereas both composers' settings of *Ah, dolente partita* (III,3) and *Udite, lagrimosi* (III,6) match precisely in terms of the texts, Wert's treatment of the opening of act 3, *O primavera gioventù*, extends well beyond the scope of Marenzio's setting of the same speech in *O dolcezze amarissime d'amore* (see Table 4.5), and Marenzio's reading of *Cruda Amarilli* (I,2) is five verses longer than Wert's setting.

The two composers' approaches to text-setting generally stand very much apart, possibly reflecting their contrasting environments in Rome and Mantua, but also their differing priorities as readers. The scholarly literature has tended to paint these differences with a broad and hackneyed brush, with Marenzio preferring pastoral texts, the lighter style of the canzonetta, and pictorial depictions of the word, and Wert inclined toward weightier texts, juxtapositions of counterpoint and speech-like declamation, and the portrayal of the overall sense of the poem. The analysis of their settings from *Il pastor fido* here will present more varied pictures of both composers, with their focuses shifting between the narrow and far-reaching, the playful and profound. The results reveal a very different perspective of the two composers from that of earlier studies—Wert's readings being dictated strongly by formal and rhythmic qualities of the verse, and Marenzio's, by rhetorical

DOI: 10.4324/9781315463056-6

features and overarching sentiment and trajectory. These differences are amplified by the sheer contrasts in the composers' handling of mode, harmony, and large-scale structure.

This comparison looks deeply at the composers' treatments of *Cruda Amarilli* and more broadly at their settings from act 3 of the play. The inquiry will begin, however, by returning to the scene of the dying Aminta and Lucrina-turned-Amarilli rendered in Marenzio's *O fido, o caro Aminta*. The piece had introduced some issues of textual variants in Marenzio's *Pastor fido* settings in the previous chapter; here, the madrigal's meticulous rendering of the scene offers a launching point for the study of musical renderings of the play.

Marenzio's *O fido, o caro Aminta*: The Integration of Text and Music

Marenzio's madrigal is one of only two known settings of Ergasto's tale: some twenty-one years later (1616), in his *Terzo libro de' madrigali a 5*, Claudio Pari of Palermo set a much longer portion of the speech, beginning with Aminta's self-sacrifice fifteen lines earlier (*Strinse intrepido Aminta il sacro ferro*) and ending at the penultimate verse of Marenzio's madrigal text.[1] Only the Canto and Basso partbooks of Pari's work survive, but they are enough to confirm that the text does not follow the variants of Marenzio's setting. Instead, Pari's madrigal adheres closely to printed editions of the play but incorporates its own modifications. Whereas Marenzio's work had inserted Amarilli in the place of Lucrina, Pari's replaces Lucrina with another name from *Il pastor fido*, Dorinda—a striking substitution given Dorinda's role as a model of constancy and natural love, the very antithesis of Aminta's unfaithful beloved. Moreover, while Marenzio's madrigal had lessened its attachment to the play by curtailing the final verse and its reference to perfidy ("Troppo amor, e perfidia ambidue trasse"), Pari's piece achieves the same effect by also omitting this verse and by cutting another line that identifies Aminta as "sacerdote" (priest).

The surviving outer parts show the remarkable diversity of Pari's work, supporting the book's claim that its contents are "made out of many styles and new inventions never used by anyone, and with much demand for imitation, attention to counterpoint, and imitation of the words."[2] In other words, the 1616 setting is unequivocally madrigalian in the traditional, polyphonic sense, presenting the text through a multitude of styles, textures, and voicings, even abstaining from the use of basso continuo (which by this time had become common, even in multi-voice settings). Marenzio's setting from decades earlier likewise draws on a multitude of tactics to render Ergasto's tale and Lucrina-turned-Amarilli's reported speech within it. The work exemplifies the composer's strategies for delineating a change of poetic voice (from Amarilli to narrator) through texture, structure, and modal character, and for complementing musically details of word sound, referentiality, and affect in Guarini's verse. The text, as Marenzio set it, reads:

1 "O fido, o caro **Aminta**,
   O troppo tardi conosciuto **amante**,
   Che m'hai dato, morendo, e vit**a e morte**,
   Se fù colpa il lasciarti, ecco l'**amendo**
5 Con l'unir teco etern**a**mente l'alma."
   E questo detto la bell'Amarilli,
   Il ferro stesso ancora
   Nel caro sangue tepido e vermiglio,
   Tratto dal mort'e tardi amato petto,
10 Il suo petto **trafisse** e sopr'**Aminta**,
   Che mort'ancor non era, e sentì forse
   Quel colpo, in braccio si lasciò cadere.
   Tal fine hebber gli sfortunati **amanti**.
	"Oh faithful, oh dear Aminta,
	oh lover known too late,
	who has given me, dying, both life and death,
	if it was a fault to leave you, now I amend it
	in uniting my soul with you eternally."
	And this said, the fair Amarilli,
	the same blade still
	warm and red with the dear blood,
	she drew from the dead and late-loved chest,
	and stabbed her own breast, and upon Aminta,
	who was not yet dead and felt perhaps
	that blow, let herself fall into his arms.
	Such an end had the unfortunate lovers.

The madrigal text is divided rhetorically into two parts, the first containing Amarilli's avowal in direct speech (verses 1–5), and the second, the narrator's (Ergasto's) description of her ensuing suicide and collapse into the dying Aminta's arms (verses 6–13). The music mirrors this bipartite division on multiple levels. Most straightforwardly, Amarilli's words are set primarily in full-voiced homophonic declamation. The narrative continuation yields a sudden shift to reduced texture that gradually builds, beginning with the three uppermost voices for verses 6–8 (mm. 31–41), adding the Quinto in verses 9–10 (mm. 42–52), then the Basso at "e sopr'Aminta" at the end of v. 10. Apart from intermittent staggering and rhythmic displacements of one or more voices, the second section also proceeds chiefly in declamation, the major exception being the description of Amarilli's collapse ("si lasciò cadere") in verse 12. As we shall see, Marenzio also marks the change of poetic voice at the end of Amarilli's speech with corresponding shifts in the background structure and in the intervallic/modal features on the foreground.

The madrigal uses *cantus mollis* (one-flat system) with high clefs and A final. These parameters, plus the prominence of the modal $\hat{4}$ (D) and $\hat{6}$ (F) as cadential and non-cadential points of arrival, strongly suggest the phrygian mode on A. But the true modal nature of *O fido, o caro Aminta*, while assuredly "on A," is not so straightforward as to be gleaned from system and cadence plan alone. For as the work progresses—from Amarilli's words to the narrator's—the role of B♮ diminishes, making it increasingly clear that B♭ is the true second degree, and A-dorian, the madrigal's true mode.

The initial phrase, "O fido, o caro Aminta" (mm. 1–6), sets out the key musical–textual ideas of the piece, all of which hinge on the name Aminta. The most prominent of these is the semitone figure that pervades the Canto's phrase, which rises *e″–f″* with "*O fido*," then forms a neighboring motion a step lower (*d″–e♭″–d″*) for "o caro Aminta" (Example 5.1). Underlying these coupled semitone gestures is a string of falling fifths in the Basso—*a–d–g–c*—which then bounces back to *g* to end the phrase. Although advancing in plaintively "slow" rhythms of semibreves and minims, the harmonic motion of the phrase remains active, never rearticulating the same harmony and progressing disjunctly through fifth-related sonorities. Yet across the phrase as a whole, four of the five voices move only a single step, while the Tenore—moving primarily in offset fifths with the Basso—traverses a sixth.

The c–G gesture that ends the verse could be interpreted as either a non-cadential approach to G from the fifth below or a *clausula in mi* (phrygian cadence) to D, with the basic M6–octave cadential motion in the Canto and Quinto. Considering the text, however, the closing gesture may more profitably be viewed as comprising three parts rather than two: hence, the three syllables of "Aminta," which form a neighboring-like phonetic motion around the assonance *A* (*a–i–a*), are rendered musically in neighboring motions around a G sonority (G–c–G) and with the motivic semitone (*d″–e♭″–d″*) in the Canto, and other alternating motions in three of the four lower voices. As the continuation of Marenzio's reading reveals, there is

Example 5.1 Marenzio, *O fido, o caro Aminta*, mm. 1–12

significance behind this musical depiction of the aural character of Aminta's name.

As the semitone figure and motion by fifths at "Aminta" set out the basic musical motives to follow, the name Aminta represents a textual focal point that reappears in various phonetic allusions. These "Aminta" echoes create a web of sonic references to the male beloved, linking later moments in the passage to the opening exclamation "Aminta" and ensuring the name's ubiquitous presence before its literal restatement in verse 10. Thereafter, the phonic echoes resume.

These "Aminta" echoes employ different combinations of the basic vowel and consonant phonemes of the name, but always maintain their proper arrangement syllabically:

1	2	3
a	*i*	*a*
	m/n	t

These phonemes generate seven "Aminta" echoes after the literal pronouncement of the name in verse 1:

Verse	1	2	3
1	**A**	**min**	**ta**
2	A	man	te
3	(vi)ta e	mor	te
4	A	men	do
5	(eter)na	men	te
9	A	ma	to
10	Tra	fis	se
	A	**min**	**ta**
13	A	man	ti

Amarilli's speech (vv. 1–5), permeated by echoes of Aminta's name, remains fixed on Aminta as second person. She addresses Aminta using both direct and indirect object pronouns, *ti* and *te*, and the second-person verb form "hai," in addition to his name and "amante." Additional pronominal signifiers are woven throughout her speech not as actual pronouns, but as sounds embedded within words, pointing fixatedly toward the second person:

O fido, o caro Aminta,
O troppo tardi conosciuto ama**nte**,
Che m'hai dato, morendo, e vita e mor**te**,
Se fu colpa il lasciar**ti**, ecco l'amendo
Con l'unir **te**co **e**ternam**ente** l'alma.

When the perspective of the narrator(s) begins in verse 6, such embedded second-person signifiers become nearly absent. However, the syllables *ti* and *te* in the first part of the text gain added emphasis in Marenzio's treatment.

"Amante" (lover), at the end of verse 2, represents a threefold reference to Amarilli's faithful lover as the first "Aminta" echo, a direct reference to Aminta, and the first embedded pronoun ("aman*te*"). The madrigal bolsters the connections between "Aminta" and "amante" not only through similar settings of the words themselves, but also through correlations in the musical phrases in which they occur (mm. 1–12; Example 5.1). Both phrases descend by step between their opening and closing sonorities—A to G in verse 1, E♭ to D in verse 2—and conclude with bouncing fifth motions (G–c–G and D–g–D) that contain *clausulae in mi* between the Canto and Quinto. In place of the interlocking semitone motion of verse 1, the Canto's motion across verse 2 counters the overall descent from E♭ to D sonorities by projecting an ascent from G to A—only this is composed out as a descending minor seventh, *g″* to *a′*. Together, the contrary stepwise motion between the Basso and Canto across the verse expands and superimposes two essential elements from verse 1: the Basso's overall descent from *a* to *g* in mm. 1–6 is now reversed and stretched out across the Canto's range as *g″–a′*, and the Canto's *e♭″–d″* at "A*minta*" is now projected across verse 2 in the Basso's *e♭–d*.

The momentum of the Canto toward A, which ends in the *b♭–a′* semitone of "*aman*te," governs the setting of verse 2 and its concluding D–g–D harmonic motion (mm. 10–12). This approach to A, in fact, encompasses verses 1–2 together, imparting a deeper-level stepwise descent from *e″* to *a′* in mm. 1–12 (Example 5.2).[3] The second phrase, therefore, serves as both a complement and a structural continuation of the first phrase: both begin with the exclamation "O," share the same general harmonic contour (motion

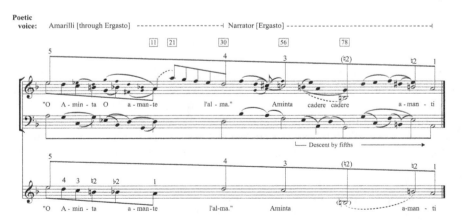

Example 5.2 Marenzio, *O fido, o caro Aminta*, Structural Analysis

by fifths), and end with references to Aminta. The strength of this first echo symbolizes the proximity of Aminta both temporally (in the text and music) and spatially (to Amarilli): Amarilli has just confessed her newly realized love while weeping his name, which he—"who was not yet dead"—hears before dying.

Amarilli/Lucrina's transformation in this passage from cold and disloyal to compassionate and penitent becomes realized in the madrigal's exposition of mode. This structural expression takes root in verses 1–2, whose parallel textual–motivic construction forms a unified expansion of the primary background pitch, e''. Here, the middleground $e''-a'$ descent passes through both forms of $\hat{2}$, B-*mi* and B-*fa*, and highlights the basic conflict of the work: whether B♭ (as the system indicates) or B♮ is the true modal $\hat{2}$ (Example 5.2). Thus, the confirmation of the mode's identity hinges on the resolution of this B♮/B♭ opposition. This identity grows clearer as the work progresses and, in the end, remarkably contradicts what the $b\flat-a'$ ending of mm. 1–11 and the *cantus-mollis* system suggest. The madrigal, like Amarilli/Lucrina, therefore, seems to transform, shedding its illusory *cantus mollis* increasingly after the beloved's speech to reveal a true *durus* nature, and in turn, emerging from its A-phrygian façade to show its A-dorian interior.

The second pronominal signifier, "mor*te*," also coincides with a musical–textual echo of "Aminta," now less vivid with the increasing temporal distance. Here, the words "vi*ta e morte*" evoke Aminta's name phonetically while recalling elements of its earlier musical setting: paired semibreves with semitone motion in the Canto, this time in the form of two ascents, e''–f''–$f\sharp''$. This twofold reference arises in Amarilli's juxtaposition of life and death, representing the fated precipice at which the lovers have been united through Aminta's selfless act—namely, offering his own life in Amarilli/ Lucrina's place. In this light, the first two echoes—"amante" and "vita e morte"—inscribe Aminta's name at two crucial moments: Amarilli's realization of her love (calling Aminta "lover"), and her resolution to join Aminta—in a characteristically paradoxical madrigalian way—in a death full of life.

The next pronominal indicator of Aminta, "lasciar*ti*" (leave *you*, v. 4), does not coincide with an echo, but elicits a salient deictic (gestural) response in the music to reinforce its referential role. Buried in the middle of the verse and in an elision with the subsequent word, "ecco," the moment seems to leave little opportunity for enunciation in a musical setting. Precisely at this elision, however, the Canto leaps a major sixth from c'' to its highest pitch in the piece, a'' (m. 21), supported by an unusual D_3^6 sonority (Example 5.3). With this striking figure, the madrigal counters the syllable's weak position in the verse and tactus, not only calling attention to "ti" (the dying Aminta, and the one abandoned by the speaker), but also gesturing outwardly toward him as a musical–textual deictic.[4]

a) Measures 18–30

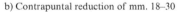

b) Contrapuntal reduction of mm. 18–30

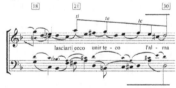

Example 5.3 Marenzio, *O fido, o caro Aminta*

In verse 5, the pronoun "*teco*" (m. 24)—a loose phonic pun on "-ti ecco" from the line before—is distinguished rhythmically as a semibreve sur-rounded by syllables of lesser durations (Example 5.3). Like "lasciarti," the syllable elicits a salient rise in the Canto and a $^6_3$ sonority: this time to *g″* above a marked G^6_3. The coordinated use of register and $^6_3$ sonorities—a voicing that stands out for its instability and infrequency—allows the mad-rigal to underscore and, in effect, act out the personal deictics at "lasciar*ti ecco*" and "*teco*." The association of these syllables extends even beyond their references to the second person, high tessituras,[5] and $^6_3$ sonorities: both show the Canto an octave apart from the Alto, emphasizing Amarilli's reaching outwardly toward Aminta. Moreover, the madrigal accentuates both references with chromatically raised pitches in the Basso that stand a perfect fifth apart from one another (F♯ and B), thereby projecting between them the very interval linked to "Aminta" in verse 1 (G–c–G), the "amante" echo (D–G–D), and other "Aminta" gestures later in the piece. The coordination of "lasciar*ti ecc*o" and "*teco*" as deictic gestures (and phonic puns) distinguishes also their connection on a deeper, middleground level as the initial pitches of a stepwise a''–d'' descent, the completion of which articulates the end of Amarilli's speech, as well as the first change in the madrigal's background structure: the motion from $\hat{5}$, e'', to $\hat{4}$, d'' (Example 5.3b).

In the syllables preceding this new background pitch (d''), "eternamente" brings about the final, attenuated "Aminta" echo of Amarilli's speech along with two concealed pronominal signifiers, none of which is overlooked in Marenzio's setting. The final two syllables, "eterna*mente*" (mm. 26–27), are delivered rhythmically very much like those of "A*minta*" in mm. 5–6, with homophonic semibreves disrupted by the Tenore's delay of the last syllable. The semitone motion carried by the Canto at "Aminta," "amante," and "morte" now occurs in both outer voices, obscuring the underlying perfect-fifth harmonic motion (also associated with Aminta) with the use of a $\frac{6}{3}$ sonority on the penultimate syllable (m. 26). The delay of the Tenore at "-te" further accentuates the second-person reference by reiterating the syllable while it is sustained in the other voices. With this setting, the notion of *eternità* is imbued with musical and phonic allusions to Aminta, insinuating the outcome of Amarilli's actions in bringing her together with Aminta forever in death. Structurally, again, the second-person reference *te* continues the middleground a''–d'' descent by articulating f'' (see Example 5.3b). The first three steps of this descent, a''–g''–f'', therefore, convey the syllables *ti–te–te* referring to Aminta as addressee. The final step, e''–d'', coincides with the two syllables of Amarilli's last word, "l'alma," generating a prominent cadence on D in support of the background d''. Verses 4–5, then, carry out an inverted function to verses 1–2: whereas the latter expanded the background e'' with which they began, the former prefigure the background d'' with which they end (see Example 5.2).

The transition from Amarilli's reported words to the narrator's voice prompts marked shifts from full-voice to pared-down texture, from e'' to d'' as governing structural degree, and from the chiefly *durus* setting of vv. 3–5 to the *mollis* realm of v. 6, announced with the sonorities d–B♭⁶–E♭. The text refers explicitly to the preceding speech from the new perspective of the narrator(s)—"E questo detto, la bell'Amarilli"—and the remainder of the tale proceeds in past tense. The setting of the first four verses of the second section (vv. 6–9) maintains a subdued tone and focuses primarily, it seems, on recounting the events expediently in homophonic declamation with slower harmonic rhythm and mostly conjunct motion. There is little in the way of affective and arresting displays, as found in the impassioned opening speech.[6] Likewise, the new structural state maintaining d'' for the beginning of the narrator's speech is palpable in the focus on that pitch on the musical surface, particularly in the uppermost voice, and in the underlying support of cadences, verse-endings, and sonorities on D and B♭.

In setting the scene for the tale's tragic end, the narrator begins in verse 6 by speaking solely of Amarilli as subject. Verses 7–8 then vividly describe the blade and blood, while verse 9 reveals that Amarilli had pulled the blade from Aminta's breast. It is not until verse 10 that Amarilli performs any true action (Example 5.4). The madrigal splits the *endecasillabo*—a line typically of eleven syllables with a defining stress on the tenth syllable—into two parts: Amarilli's suicide ("Il suo petto trafisse") and collapse onto Aminta ("e sopra Aminta"). The action that ended Amarilli's mortal life and began her eternal one with Aminta (*trafiggere*) produces the first definitive cadence on the modal final so far in the madrigal (mm. 50–52): a *clausula in mi* on A elaborated by a poignant semitone upper neighbor. This assertive arrival, overlaid with semitone motion in the Canto, links the moment of Amarilli's death to the musical–textual moments when her love for Aminta was born: the opening A sonority at "O" and the semitone motion and *clausula in mi* of "Aminta" (mm. 4–6). It now becomes evident why A has been used so

Example 5.4 Marenzio, *O fido, o caro Aminta*, mm. 46–57

sparingly to this point as both a sonority and cadential goal: to preserve its function as an evocation of union—a union with the modal final, as well as of the lovers. Along with this, the slightest whisper of Aminta's name resounds assonantly in "trafisse."

The second part of verse 10 (mm. 53–57), "e sopra Aminta," brings Amarilli literally, musically, and structurally upon Aminta with a return to the homophonic declamation, uninterrupted descents by fifth of verse 1, and the next background motion from d'' down to c''—with the structural pitch maintained through all three syllables of *Aminta*. Here, the fifths motion leads from D to F (and ultimately to B♭ with the start of the next verse), conveying at once the contradictory images of Amarilli's collapse and "sopra" (upon) as the overall motion of the phrase in terms of pitch space is a *rise* from a D to an F sonority. In a sense, Amarilli has descended into death (and physically onto Aminta's body), yet is elevated to a life awakened in love. For the second time in the madrigal, Aminta's name sounds explicitly, retaining the same short–long–long (minim–semibreve–semibreve) rhythmic character as the original statement but without any lagging voices. This statement retains only the first half of its original motivic construction in the Canto and Basso: a rising semitone (e''–f'') above a rising fourth (c–f) between the first two syllables of "*Amin*ta." Now that it is the narrator, not Amarilli, speaking Aminta's name as part of the distant past, the musical allusion has correspondingly grown fainter.

Amarilli's death is drawn out even further in verses 11–12 with the delay of her collapse from verse 10 by relative clauses (similar to those in verses 7–9), which reveal that Aminta is still alive to feel Amarilli fall upon him. The madrigal responds by forging its way briskly in declamation from B♭ to the *durus* realm of E major (mm. 58–63). The fleeting pleasure of this corporeal union, however, quickly gives way to Amarilli's mortal *cadere* and, in response, a series of cascading musical phrases for the conclusion of verse 12, "in braccio si lasciò cadere" (into his arms she let herself fall). This phrase, in fact, imparts the second and final action of the tale, which, like the first action ("trafisse"), brings a shift to imitative polyphony, this time extending for sixteen measures (mm. 63–78). It is in this passage that the madrigal's subtle use of musical and phonic references breaks open into a barrage of motivic gestures. The imitative subject for "si lasciò cadere" comprises a descending octave divided arithmetically into P5 plus P4; the falling fifth, however, is expanded by an intervening semitone neighbor note that incorporates a pathetic m6 descending leap into the phrase (Example 5.5). By introducing the semitone neighbor into an underlying P5 harmonic motion (A–D–A), the madrigal embeds a musical allusion to Aminta in the depiction of Amarilli's collapse through the conflation of both "Aminta" motives (Example 5.6).

Through the repetition of the phrase in imitation, "Aminta" literally lies at the heart of Amarilli's death—or of the madrigal's reading of Amarilli's death—symbolizing with the joining of musical references and text the eternal union of the "sfortunati amanti."

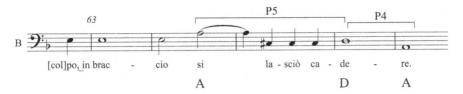

Example 5.5 Marenzio, *O fido, o caro Aminta*, "si lasciò cadere"

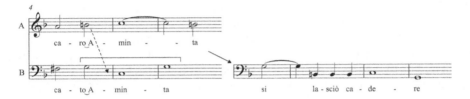

Example 5.6 O fido, o caro Aminta, Linear Conflation of "Aminta" Motives

The merging of "Aminta" motives and Amarilli's death also takes shape on the larger scale. Through the course of these cascading points of imitation, we are led again through a chain of descending fifths, expanded contrapuntally to drive from E to G in mm. 63–78 (see Example 5.2). This sustained non-cadential close on G at the end of verse 12, while marking the end of life for Amarilli and Aminta, does not mark the end of the madrigal. Instead, the arrival delivers the penultimate pitch of the modal structure, *b-mi*, the culmination of this long, contrapuntal unfolding of motivic descents. The background pitch defies what the madrigal's *cantus-mollis* parameter seemed to infer, for it is unequivocally the second degree of the A-dorian mode (B-*mi*), not that of A-phrygian (B-*fa*).

After one last appearance of B♭ (mm. 79–80), the descent by fifths accelerates, driving from G all the way to the terminal A cadence—G–C–F–B-*mi*–E–A—in plaintive, "slow" declamatory rhythms reminiscent of verse 1 (see Example 5.2). (The *mi contra fa* from F to B is averted by the Basso's filling-in of the diminished fifth.) B♭ and the *mollis* (F) hexachord play no part whatsoever in the final ten measures of the madrigal, as this terminal cadential drive lies entirely in the natural and *durus* realms. The rearticulations of B♮ in the cadential approach and the antepenultimate B-major sonority underscore the primacy of this pitch over B♭ at this decisive stage in the work in terms of modal–structural resolution, and assure that this is not a phrygian-mode conclusion.

The long-range projection of the reconciliation and joining of Amarilli and Aminta is played out in the gradual revelation of the madrigal's true modal underpinning. The lucid background structure of *O fido, o caro Aminta* is obscured by a foreground that eludes modal affirmation until the final moments. This ambiguity stems above all from the *cantus-mollis* system, the fluid vacillation between both forms of $\hat{2}$ (B-*fa/mi*), and the lack of a clear exposition of the mode anywhere near the opening of the piece. For a reader looking at the printed music, it is clear that the madrigal finishes on A and that the Canto and Tenore reside in the A modal octave. Yet the mode-defining divisions and interval species within his A octave remain uncertain (and even misleading) at the local level, and even at deeper middleground levels the mode's identity proves ambiguous: the *diapente* descents from *e″* to *a′* through *both* b♮ and b♭ (mm. 1–11) and from *a″* to *d″* (mm. 21–30), the projected ascent through the modal octave from *a′* to *a″* (mm. 11–21), and the unfolding of the *diatessaron a′–d″* (mm. 31–41) are prominent examples. The modal obscurity that shapes the surface of *O fido, o caro Aminta*, however, is counterbalanced by a background framework that is, in fact, exceptionally stable and well-articulated. This structure consists of a *diapente* descent from *e″* to *a′*—a first-species *diapente* on A—that encompasses the entire piece and passes through the second degree of the A-dorian mode (B-*mi*), rather than that of the A-phrygian mode (B-*fa*), as the B♭ system implies. The *cantus mollis*, then, proves erroneous, even deceitful, possibly resulting from the seeming phrygian tendencies of the opening phrases (Example 5.1), or serving as a representation of the protagonist's changed heart.

Marenzio's and Wert's Readings of *Cruda Amarilli* (1595)

O fido, o caro Aminta exemplifies many key aspects of Marenzio's approach to Guarini's tragicomedy, most notably his discerning sensitivity to the semantic, formal, referential, and phonetic qualities of the text, and his use of musical form and structure for rhetorical–expressive ends. The dynamic nature of his approach, with its networks of allusions, shifting modal and tonal focus, and progressive unfolding of the mode, is a key characteristic that sets Marenzio's settings apart from the majority of Wert's treatments. Mirtillo's well-known entrance monologue that opens his exchange with Ergasto in act 1, scene 2, *Cruda Amarilli, che col nome ancora*, offers an informative comparison of the composers' aims and priorities as readers of the play's texts.

The speech was to become one of the most widely set passages from the play, generating some twenty-seven known treatments by 1626, and making it a useful touchstone with which to weigh composers' responses to one common text.[7] Marenzio's setting has maintained a prominent position in music scholarship chiefly, it seems, on account of its association with Monteverdi's celebrated rendering in his Fifth Book—published in 1605, but composed by late 1598—which became a focal point of the famed debate between Monteverdi and theorist Giovanni Maria Artusi.[8] It was in response to Artusi's attack on *Cruda Amarilli* and other madrigals of Monteverdi's Fourth (1603) and Fifth Books that the composer heralded a *seconda pratica*: a new practice in music composition, begun by Cipriano de Rore and advanced by

Ingegneri, Marenzio, Wert, Luzzaschi, and others, which "makes the words the mistress [*padrona*] of the harmony," and hence prioritizes expression of the text over theoretical decorum.[9]

Madrigal scholars have proposed so many conflicting hypotheses regarding the lineage of *Cruda Amarilli* settings branching out from Marenzio's and Wert's works that nearly every possible permutation has been represented. This comparative practice in itself is rooted primarily in Alfred Einstein's *The Italian Madrigal*, where the author traces the parentage of these madrigals to Marenzio's Seventh Book, pointing specifically to the opening of Monteverdi's setting, where the younger composer "openly paid tribute to Marenzio, thus acknowledging him as his predecessor in the *seconda prattica*."[10] Some, including James Chater, have followed suit,[11] while Gary Tomlinson, Massimo Ossi, and others ascribe more influence to Wert's work, with some designating it as the forebear of these early settings, including Marenzio's—a deduction that the textual chronology of the prior chapter challenges.[12] Aspects of these various arguments and the broader issue of pedigree will return in the course of investigating the subsequent settings of Monteverdi and Pallavicino.

Despite their differing conclusions, all of these studies consider the settings of *Cruda Amarilli* as belonging to a unified tradition in which composers could challenge, salute, and join their predecessors—especially, in its early stage, Marenzio and Wert, and later, with his growing "modern" (dis)repute, Monteverdi.[13] Though informative in their comparisons, these earlier studies have focused overwhelmingly on features at the superficial level of the music, such as the treatment of individual phrases or words in terms of texture, rhythm, and melodic contour. One aspect of the settings that has received little consideration—indeed, that has scarcely been mentioned at all in the literature—is, in fact, one of the most essential components of the music: mode.[14] The analyses here will extend these earlier studies of *Cruda Amarilli* readings by exploring more closely the interactions of text and music at all levels of structure in the earliest settings of Marenzio and Wert, and in later chapters, by expanding the investigation to the settings of Wert's successors at the Mantuan *cappella* that came shortly after them.

The speech itself, when removed from the play, bears the features of a typical Cinquecento lyric in the pastoral vein: an unnamed male speaker bemoans his rejection by his beloved (Amarilli) in the form of a direct (I–you) address.[15] Although delivered in the company of Ergasto in the play (where it prompts the latter's retelling of the Aminta–Lucrina tale of *O fido, o caro Aminta*), on its own, the text gives no indication that it is anything other than the private reflection of a conventional late-Cinquecento lyric poem: an outpouring of thoughts and passions by a universal first-person (*io*) to his absent beloved. The first section (vv. 1–8) complains of Amarilli's bitterness and deafness to her suitor's pleas. In the second section, the speaker, silenced by Amarilli's cruelty, proclaims that his suffering will be resounded in nature—by the hills, mountains, woods, springs, and winds—or if all else fails, in his death. Although lacking a regular rhyme scheme, the passage contains three rhyming couplets, which become the main formal divisions and endings for Wert's, Marenzio's, and other settings:

1	Cruda Amarilli, che col nome ancora,	Cruel Amarilli, who even with your name
	D'amar, ahi lasso, amaramente insegni;	to love, alas, you bitterly teach.
	Amarilli, del candido ligustro	Amarilli, than the white privet
	Più candida e più bella,	whiter and more fair,
5	Ma de l'aspido sordo	yet than the deaf asp,
	E più sorda e più fèra e più fugace,	deafer and fiercer and more fleeting;
	Poi che col dir t'offendo,	since in speaking I offend you,
	I' mi morrò tacendo.	I will die silently.
	Ma grideran per me le piagge e i monti	Yet for me will cry out the slopes and the mountains
10	E questa selva, a cui	and these woods, to which
	Sì spesso il tuo bel nome	so often your fair name
	Di risonar insegno.	I teach to resound.
	Per me piangendo i fonti	Weeping for me, the springs,
	E mormorando i venti,	and the winds murmuring,
15	Diranno i miei lamenti;	will tell my laments;
	Parlerà nel mio volto	in my face will speak
	La pietade e 'l dolore;	compassion and suffering;
	E se fia muta ogn'altra cosa, al fine	and if every other thing is silent, in the end
	Parlerà il mio morire,	will speak my dying,
20	E ti dirà la morte il mio martire.	and my death will tell you of my suffering.

Whereas Marenzio sets this entire passage, concluding the *prima* and *seconda parti* with the rhymed couplets at verses 7–8 ("offendo"/"tacendo") and 19–20 ("morire"/"martire"), Wert treats only the first fifteen verses, also ending the *prima parte* at the first rhymed pair (vv. 7–8), but concluding his piece with the couplet in verses 14–15 ("venti"/"lamenti"). Monteverdi, by contrast, ends his entire madrigal at verse 8, thus foregoing the elaborating nature imagery and largely redundant substance of verses 9–20 in favor of epigrammatic concision and, perhaps, sense, given that Mirtillo says in v. 8 that he will die silently. Although all later settings begin at the top of the scene ("Cruda Amarilli…"), where they conclude varies between these three endpoints: Pallavicino (1600), Giovannelli (1606), Rontani (1610), Ghizzolo (1614), Cerreto (1621), and most other composers treat the full passage set by Marenzio and uphold the same two-part division, while D'India (1606 and 1609), Saracini (1614), Pari (1616), Nauwach (1623), and others treat the briefer excerpt used by Monteverdi. Only Cifra (1621) ends at verse 15, like Wert.[16] Each of these different endpoints has its own virtues and often reflects (or perhaps elicits) composers' differing aims. Lines 1–8 impart the core subject of the speech (and play)—the speaker's (Mirtillo's) fixation on the cold Amarilli—and conclude with his resolve to die silently. Lines 9–15 contrast this inward perspective with sympathetic nature, therein granting numerous opportunities for word-painting (which Wert exploits). Lines 16–20 then turn inwardly again to add (rather superfluously) that the speaker's face will reveal his compassion and sorrow, and his silent death will show his suffering. These last lines contribute little to the meaning of the speech, but with their turn from subdued death in v. 8 to outright suffering in v. 20, they do add to its intensity—a quality that Marenzio and others harness for exceptional ends in their music.

The lament opens with a celebrated display of Guarini's wordplay capitalizing on the root *amar*. Originating in the name *Amar*illi of verse 1, the root reappears in verse 2 as the basis of "amar" and "amaramente." Thus, the beloved's name encapsulates the two sources of the lament and the qualities that define Amarilli herself: love and bitterness.[17] The interjection "ahi lasso" in verse 2 highlights the relationship of all three *amar*-based words—the beloved's name, love, and bitterness—by creating the effect that the speaker has frozen mid-word upon the beloved's name: "d'Amar… ahi lasso!" (The use of similar elisions at "d'amar" and "cru-*d'Amar*illi" strengthens the connection.) Marenzio's reading bolsters this interpretation by drawing out the second syllable, "d'a-*mar*," in declamation, then resting, as though the speaker cannot voice Amarilli's name a second time without erupting in "ahi lasso." Wert, by contrast, adheres more strictly to the versification of the text by setting verse 2 as a continuous imitative phrase. The arrival of "*amar*amente" makes the wordplay unmistakable, and in retrospect makes it clear that the drawing out of "d'a*mar*" with "ahi lasso" was not a madrigalian depiction of the speaker's breaking down mid-word, but the iambic setting of an entirely different word: "D'a*mar*, ahi lasso, *amar*amente insegni." Verse 3 presents the beloved's name again in full, hence bringing the *amar* pun full circle.

While the witty play on *amar* proves a key part of the rhetoric of Mirtillo's speech, it had no part in the earliest conceptions of the passage. In fact, based on the five surviving drafts of this scene, the figure seems to be a relatively late addition (Table 5.1). In the three earliest drafts, representing various states of the play between April 1584 and early 1586—hence, when Guarini was giving private readings in Vicenza, Padua, and Venice—the monologue proceeds directly from the opening exclamation "Cruda Amarilli mia" to

Table 5.1 Readings of *Cruda Amarilli*, 1584–95

April 1584–early 1586 *(M1, F, M2)*	*Early- to mid-1586* *(Mb)*	*Published reading* *(Marenzio, Wert,* *and editions)*
Cruda Amarilli mia	Cruda Amarilli, che col nome ancora	
Più candida e più bella	D'amar ai lasso amaramente insegni.	
Del candido ligustro	Amarilli del candido ligustro	
	Più candida, e più bella,	
Ma de l'Aspido sordo	Ma del Aspido sordo	
Più sorda e più fugace	Più sorda e più fugace	E più sorda e più
Poi che col dir t'offendo	…	fera e più fugace;
I' mi morrò tacendo		
…		

the comparison of Amarilli with the white privet, which later would become verses 3–4. Thus, the clever play on *"Amarilli"* is entirely absent—not only here, but in the play as a whole—raising the possibility that Guarini only realized the full potential of the name fortuitously, when the play was all but finished. The *amar* figure first appears in the latest partial draft of the scene (Mb), dating from before July 1586, when Guarini sent the play to Lionardo Salviati. But verse 6 ("Più sorda e più fugace") underwent further development before the play's publication. If it is true that Marenzio's madrigal text came from a source roughly contemporary with the copy given to Salviati, as discussed in Chapter 4, then Guarini must have expanded verse 6 soon after the Mb draft, before sending the play to the Florentine philologist in July 1586.

The derivatives of *amar*—love, bitterness, Amarilli—embody not only the sources of Mirtillo's suffering, but also Amarilli's own internal struggle. As anyone who knows the play (or who knows Marenzio's Seventh Book) would understand, Mirtillo's lament has two simultaneous perspectives, one explicit, based on Mirtillo's present sorrow, and another broader and implicit, deriving from later revelations in the play. At the core of this double meaning are Amarilli's twofold dual identities: to Mirtillo, she is outwardly beautiful but intrinsically cruel; to herself, she is outwardly cruel and resolved, but inwardly loving and suffering for it. The external Amarilli is the obedient daughter and citizen content with the fate of marrying Silvio to save her people, while the true Amarilli wrestles with the dichotomy between law and love, social/ethical obligation and personal desire. This dichotomy sits at the center of several of Amarilli's own monologues, including the widely set lament from act 3, scene 4, *O Mirtillo, Mirtillo anima mia*.

Although the full scope of Amarilli's strife is unknown to Mirtillo and therefore not an explicit part of his speech, Marenzio conveys these dichotomies musically through ambiguities and clashes of both mode and cadences. Whereas the uncertainty in *O fido, o caro Aminta* centered on two modes with the same final (A) but different octave species, that in *Cruda Amarilli* involves two modes within the same E-octave species but opposing finals: the E-phrygian and A-hypodorian (or hypoaeolian) modes. At its most basic level, the madrigal projects a sound E-phrygian framework, but generates ambiguity locally with cadences that persistently avoid the E final, and that, in their evasive construction, conjure the notion of equivocation that typifies the madrigal's subject, Amarilli. In the *prima parte*, cadences to the foreign goal D materialize out of thwarted preparations for the modally compliant pitch, A. At the madrigal's conclusion, a striking modification to the conventional phrygian ending renders the notions of *morte* (death), *martire* (suffering), and duality with exceptional dissonance and a preparation that falsely suggests an arrival on G, but that proves nonetheless effective as an E-phrygian resolution. At the same time, Marenzio ensures coherence at the foreground level with networks of musical–textual references that behave similarly to the "Aminta" echoes in Ergasto's tale.

The atypical handling of cadences and the relationship of these cadences to the underlying mode represent key rhetorical–expressive features in Marenzio's *Cruda Amarilli*. For the composer matches the anguished tone of Mirtillo's lament to the most doleful and idiosyncratic of modes, E-phrygian. The phrygian/hypophrygian modal pair is unique in the modal family for its cadential approach of the final from the half-step above (F–E, or *fa–mi*) rather than from below (Example 5.7a–c), and its accentuation of A ($\hat{4}$) and C ($\hat{6}$) as secondary cadence goals and melodic boundaries.[18] In fact, in Marenzio's madrigal A and C play much larger roles as sonorities and cadential centers than the final itself, which is not unusual of phrygian works. Although the intervallic structure of the basic two-part cadence to a phrygian (*mi*) final is the same as that of other finals—M6 to octave, or m3 to unison—its contrapuntal support is utterly different. Owing to the threat of *mi contra fa* between $\hat{2}$ (F) and $\hat{5}$ (B), supporting the $\hat{2}$–$\hat{1}$ (F–E) cadential motion with $\hat{5}$–$\hat{1}$ bass is not a viable option. Instead, composers reinforced the cadence with a lower voice that moved either in parallel thirds with the *clausula tenorizans*—hence $\hat{7}$–$\hat{6}$ (D–C; Example 5.7d)—or that leapt $\hat{7}$–$\hat{4}$ (D–A; Example 5.7e).

The notion that a firm cadential resolution need not coincide with a sonority based on the final—that is, that a cadence to E-*mi* may end with a sonority on C or A—stands very much at odds with more modern (tonal)

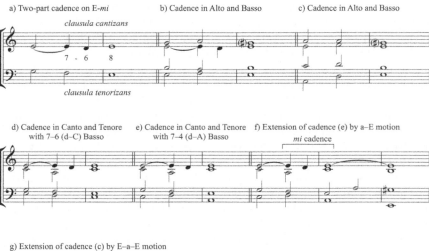

Example 5.7 Clausula in mi, or Phrygian Cadence

harmonic conceptions of cadence, and indeed has led many modern analyses of phrygian-mode works astray. This potential disparity between bass pitch and cadential final underscores the primacy of the M6–octave contrapuntal motion—whether fulfilled or evaded—over its variable consonant support, including the harmonies generated therein. Agreement between sonority and cadence goal could, however, enhance rhetorical force. For this reason, composers in the late-fifteenth and sixteenth centuries often fortified terminal cadences in phrygian pieces by sustaining the final in one or more voices and tacking on a post-cadential extension that leads from the A or C sonority at the resolution to a sonority on E—hence, a–E or C–E (Example 5.7f)—or that incorporates a longer series of sonorities that supports the final in an upper voice (namely, A, C, and E) before landing ultimately on E (Example 5.7g).[19]

Perhaps as a means to reinforce the inherently weak *mi* cadence at the end of a work, composers of the late Cinquecento began incorporating a new terminal gesture for phrygian-type pieces that proves utterly devoid of theoretical backing. This gesture foregoes the contrapuntal M6–octave motion and any stepwise motion to the final altogether in favor of a non-cadential, "plagal"-type a–E ending (Example 5.8). In place of the $\hat{2}$–$\hat{1}$ resolution, the formation incorporates a terminal $\hat{6}$–$\hat{5}$ (C–B) descent in one of the upper voices. Owing to its lack of the true cadential features by contemporary (theoretical) standards, I have termed this gesture the phrygian quasi-cadence. As the analysis will show, although entirely consonant in its standard form, the phrygian quasi-cadence undergoes an unsettling transformation in Marenzio's hands to match the agony of Mirtillo's final words.

The distinctive traits of the phrygian-type modes—such as their intervallic make-up with a diminished fifth (d5) between $\hat{5}$ and $\hat{2}$ (B–F); focus on $\hat{1}$ (E), $\hat{4}$ (A), and $\hat{6}$ (C) as cadential centers, sonorities, and melodic boundaries; and terminal a–E motion—contribute also to the unique structural behavior of phrygian-mode pieces, including at the most fundamental level. Whereas the basic framework of works in the other modes comprises a linear descent through the mode-defining species of fifth (*diapente*), $\hat{5}$–$\hat{1}$, as described in Chapter 1, phrygian-mode works project an overarching

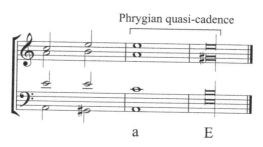

Example 5.8 Phrygian Quasi-Cadence

descent through the species of fourth (*diatessaron*) from the final ($\hat{8}$) to the fifth degree ($\hat{5}$), or E–B (Example 5.9). The customary prolongation of the final (E) through the opening—and sometimes majority—of phrygian pieces with the contrapuntal support of E, A, and C accounts for the characteristic and often-noted prominence of these pitches and sonorities on the musical surface.[20] Because the E-phrygian background descent (E–B) corresponds to the first four steps ($\hat{5}$–$\hat{2}$) of the A-dorian/hypodorian framework, the phrygian- and dorian-type modes tend to show notable (and often misleading) similarities in foreground and cadential behavior, particularly through the beginning portions of works. Perhaps the most prominent and heavy-handed misconstruals of phrygian-mode pieces in recent years come from Susan McClary's influential *Modal Subjectivities*, where she denies the mode's existence altogether in the late Cinquecento and instead reads the works mistakenly as aeolian/hypoaeolian ending on the "dominant," E. In introducing Willaert's E-phrygian *Lasso, ch'i' ardo*, for example, McClary asserts: "After music theorist Glareanus let his colleagues off the hook by proclaiming a new modal pair on A...music affiliated with phrygian—true or quasi—almost disappeared."[21] Yet, in truth, the phrygian mode remained very much alive and in use.

The opening of Marenzio's *Cruda Amarilli* (Example 5.10) clearly establishes the E modal octave divided at A and the primary background pitch, *e″* ($\hat{8}$), but leaves unconfirmed whether these features bespeak an E-phrygian or A-hypodorian framework. The composer balances this dichotomy between surface instability and deeper-level clarity by maintaining the governing E with firm contrapuntal support at the middleground level, as is customary of the phrygian structure—compare the accentuation of *e″* in the Canto throughout mm. 1–23 (Example 5.10) with the structural model of Example 5.9—while at the same time renouncing it as a cadential goal in favor not only of A, as would be expected, but also of the modal seventh, D. The opening subject contributes to the uncertainty by presenting the final as part of an ambiguous C–E third (accompanied by either G or A) that merely suggests the hegemony of A, C, or E. Thus, while continuing the consonant support of E, the initial statements of "Cruda Amarilli" and pronounced cadences on A and D seem to suggest an A-hypodorian, or even D-dorian, setting, not E-phrygian.

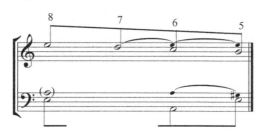

Example 5.9 Phrygian Background Structure

With the play on *amar* in verses 1–3, both phonic and descriptive allusions to Amarilli saturate the opening twenty-five measures of the piece in a fashion similar to the "Aminta" echoes at the opening of *O fido, o caro Aminta*. The madrigal highlights this recurrence of the syllables by enunciating "a-*ma(r)*" repeatedly with the volatile sixth degree (*c″*) in the topmost voice: first at "A-*ma*-rilli" (m. 7), then as a semibreve at the arrival on A at "D'a-*mar*" (m. 12). Thereafter, the impulse of 6̂ to step down to 5̂ is thwarted by the opposition between *b′* in the Canto and *c*—now an octave lower (in the Tenore and Quinto) and an unstable pitch above the Basso's E (mm. 13–14) and G (m. 16). To resist this downward 6̂–5̂ impulse and reattain the

Example 5.10 Marenzio, *Cruda Amarilli, che col nome ancora*, mm. 1–23

background e'', the Canto pronounces the final *amar-* in "a-*ma*-ramente" with the raised 6̂, *c♯''*, which pushes back upward to the final while intensifying, as a modally foreign pitch, the bitter and beloved (*amar-*) pitch/syllable association. This treatment of verses 1–3 and the *amar* pun shows Marenzio's attention to both text and large-scale musical framework in joining a crucial word sound and reference not only with a specific pitch, but also with its deeper modal–structural function: the tendency of 6̂ to descend to 5̂ amid the need to maintain 8̂, *e''*, as background pitch.

Marenzio, likewise, renders the opposing notions of *amar* (to love) and *amaramente* (bitterly) musically in a context filled with cadential contradiction. Cadences, here and throughout the work, play a major role in this portrayal. The second statement of "Cruda Amarilli" (mm. 5–9), for instance, ends in an archaic double-leading-tone cadence to D—a straightforward move *fuori di tuono* ("outside the mode") that temporarily undermines the preservation of the primary structural pitch, *e''*.[22] In its preparation, however, the cadence points plainly to an arrival on A rather than D (Example 5.11a–b). The passage even reuses two voices from the initial statement of "Cruda Amarilli" that leads to A—the Tenore and Basso from mm. 1–5 reappear in the Quinto and Canto of mm. 5–9—further insinuating another approach to that pitch, but a last-minute modification in the Canto transforms the voice from a *clausula tenorizans* to A (*b'–a'*) to a *clausula cantizans* to D (*b'–c♯''–d''*). Most deceiving of all is the Quinto's verbatim restatement of the line previously held by the Tenore, which contains the *clausula cantizans* for an A cadence (*a–g♯–a*); this time, however, the figure leads to the fifth above the cadential goal (Example 5.11b). In its conflicting impulses toward two separate goals, D and A, this anomalous cadence serves as the first contrapuntal rendering not merely of Amarilli's cruelty, but specifically the deceptive role of this cruelty (in the play) as a cover for her hidden struggle, here tied to the explicit accusation "Cruda Amarilli." The gesture prefigures other cadential subversions to come.

The continuation of verses 1–2 (mm. 10–23) resumes the larger E/A duality by returning the tonal focus securely to A, while emphasizing the E-octave boundaries and P4/P5 divisions and the structural *e''* at the top of the texture. (See especially the Canto's *b'–e''* leaps at "ahi lasso.")[23] If we recognize the cadence in m. 9 as an evaded A cadence redirected to D, all of the major cadences in mm. 1–23 lead toward—though not always to—A,

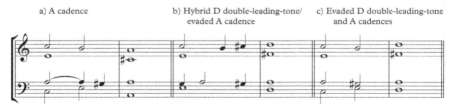

Example 5.11   Double-Leading-Tone Cadences in Marenzio's *Cruda Amarilli*

linking this rival of the modal final to the dichotomy inscribed in Amarilli's name and to her cruelty pronounced in verses 1–2. The focus on A and D as cadential goals persists as the lament continues, as does the madrigal's use of the cadential emblem of duplicity and intrinsic conflict: the double-leading-tone cadence. Moreover, the expansion of E within a context centered cadentially on A obscures the true nature of E as final across the madrigal's opening, framing it instead as A-hypodorian $\hat{5}$.[24] While the phrygian mode proves the ideal vehicle for extreme pathos, the concealed identity of the mode here conveys the crucial aspect of Mirtillo's situation in the play: Amarilli's cruelty is merely a front for her true but suppressed love for him—a front she must guard in her duty to marry Silvio and free Arcadia. Like the identity of the mode from the perspective of the listener, Mirtillo does not, and cannot, recognize the inward truth through the tumultuous exterior.

Before the question of mode is even resolved, verses 3–7 (mm. 24–47) bring about a forceful displacement at the middleground level of the governing *e″* by its lower neighbor, *d″*, and with it, a prevailing D octave (Example 5.12). The shift accompanies Mirtillo's feverish comparison of Amarilli's features to the white, fair flowers of the privet and her nature to a deaf, fierce, and fleeing snake ("Più candida e più bella...e più sorda e più fera e più fugace") that amasses tension with an ascent in the Canto from *f♯′* to a climactic *d″* at "*sordo*" (deaf), finishing with yet another double-leading-tone cadence to D. But here the arrival ricochets beyond its goal of D to G between the syllables "sor-do," so as to render the notion of Amarilli's deafness and elusiveness with a twofold display of cadential failure.

The disruptive *d″* persists until the final verse of the *prima parte*, where the background *e″* and E-octave return with Mirtillo's acceptance of a silent death. The madrigal signals the weakening role of D and the D-octave and the pivot back to A and its E-octave with yet another failed double-leading-tone cadence in mm. 46–47. This cadence resembles those earlier in the work in seeming to approach A, but the preparatory E sonority simply moves directly to D without motion through its leading-tone, *b′–d″*, thus

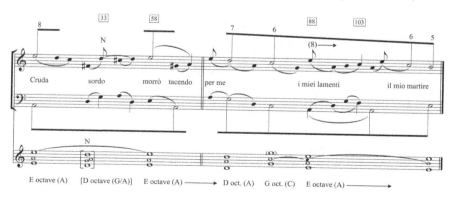

Example 5.12 Marenzio, *Cruda Amarilli*, Structural Analysis

creating a doubly evaded cadence to A and D, similar to the form shown in Example 5.11c.

Marenzio further underscores the shift in rhetoric and modal–structural context for the lengthy and convoluted parenthesis of verses 3–6 with a change in texture from imitative polyphony in vv. 1–2 to four-voice homophony. Yet the madrigal maintains continuity across these and other formal–structural divisions with a system of motivic references tied to Amarilli's character. Heeding the return of "candido" from verse 3 in its feminine form, "candida," in verse 4, the madrigal declaims both phrases with the same rhythmic figure:

This pairing grows out of the inherent accentual qualities of Guarini's verse and anchors Amarilli's relationship to the white privet flower with matching rhythms in the phrases "del candido ligustro / Più candida e più bella." Indeed, Wert and others after him seize upon this same metrical feature in their own settings of the text, using the very same rhythms (often with repeated notes for "candido"/"candida") as in Marenzio's reading. The similar treatments of this and other passages of the text, and scholars' interpretations of them, will be examined further in Chapter 7.

This "candida" accentual pattern proves an important idiomatic figure in descriptions of Amarilli in Mirtillo's speech, and Marenzio exploits its recurrences. The motive can, in fact, be traced back to "che col nome ancora" of verse 1 (m. 10) in the madrigal, where only the rhythmic aspect is present (see Example 5.10), and then to "amaramente insegni" of verse 2 (mm. 17–21), where it appears in imitation with similar melodic characteristics as at *candido/candida*. The specificity of the reference, therefore, increases as the text progresses: from a single statement of the rhythmic component at "che col nome ancora," to an imitative motive with both the rhythmic and melodic dimensions at "amaramente," and ultimately to a specific rhythmic–melodic gesture tied to complementary statements of *candido/a*. The recurring pattern, therefore, lends a clear element of surface-level unity to the *prima parte*, along with the larger-scale processes of the e''–d''–e'' neighbor motion and its associated alternation between A/D modal–cadential centers, and the text's fixation on the antithetical nature of cruel-but-beautiful Amarilli.

While the *prima parte* brought considerable turbulence to the phrygian context by way of modal equivocation, archaic and conflicted cadences, and an expansive disruption of the E modal octave, the *seconda parte* proves more resolute while still allowing for cadential and modal variety with its steady advancement through the descending steps of the E-phrygian background, e''–d''–c''–b'. The contrasts between the two *parti* underscore the differences in tone between the two sections of text—the first more rancorous and belligerent, the second forlorn and longing for expressive outlet. Hence, the *seconda parte* counterbalances the *prima* not only with its decided course toward resolution, but also by maintaining the basic E-phrygian grounding without substantial disruptions. It achieves this modal stability in the midst of structural motion by establishing the background d'' only briefly in mm. 63–67 before pushing ahead to c'', where e'' reemerges as an overlapping, subsidiary voice, and where the E-octave and its divisions at A and B prove crucial in supporting the background pitch. (Compare the madrigal's background structure in Example 5.12 with the archetypal model in Example 5.9.)

At the surface, Marenzio's *seconda parte* opens with a musical–textual motive tied to the speaker's means of self-expression. The figure originates in the *prima parte* as an imitative subject with verse 7, where it corresponds with the notion that by merely speaking the first person offends his beloved (mm. 38–48):

At the outset of the *seconda parte*, as the speaker—now silenced—proclaims that the landscape will sigh in his place (mm. 58–61), the motive returns in an extended form to suit an *endecasillabo*, but with the same rhythmic opening and with the minim-semibreve pair reversed at the pictorial leap for "piagge" (slopes):

The figure surfaces again to evoke the winds murmuring the speaker's laments in verses 14–15 (mm. 81–82):

Unlike the earlier ("candida") motivic figure, where the musical accent aligns with the stress patterns of the verse, this second figure accentuates the first syllable—thus, the conjunctions "Poi," "Ma," and "E" that would normally be weaker. This irregular stressing of these verses and their association through a common motive prioritizes their shared function of signaling rhetorical shifts (with conjunctions) over a more naturalistic enunciation.

Moreover, by correlating this motive with references to the speaker's expression ("dir," "grideran," "mormorando"), and the "candido" motive with descriptions of Amarilli, the madrigal organizes the text through its recurring themes, as *O fido, o caro Aminta* had done using musical–textual echoes of "Aminta." These and other instances of varied recurrence in the music and the text—such as the *amar-* root (verses 1–2), "candido"/"candida" (verses 3–4), five instances of "più" (verses 4–6), two statements of "per me" (verses 9 and 13), and the three rhyming couplets—lend coherence to the work in a way that fosters, rather than sacrifices, *varietà*.

The conclusion of the madrigal, while cogent on a structural scale, represents a culmination of Marenzio's cadential manipulations in rendering the closing image of death expressing the speaker's suffering ("E ti dirà la morte il mio martire"). The final cadence takes the basic form of the phrygian quasi-cadence, as expected. But in portraying Mirtillo's agony, Marenzio transforms this conventional a–E phrygian ending into a tortured formation that replaces the penultimate A-minor sonority with a jarring f♯^{o6}, thus creating, in effect, the terminal motion f♯^{o6}–E (Example 5.13). Yet Marenzio injects even more dissonance into the gesture by incorporating a 7–6 suspension (G–F♯) that resembles a *clausula cantizans* directed at G. The preparation, therefore, mimics a basic "vii^{o7-6}–I" approach to G that instead lands on E-major, with the false *clausula cantizans* (G–F♯) ending on g♯′ (the raised third of the final E sonority) and the Basso moving A–E. The result represents an amalgamation of an evaded cadence to G and a phrygian quasi-cadence to E, continuing the madrigal's expressive use of hybrid cadences that originated in the second statement of "Cruda Amarilli." Importantly, however, the altered phrygian quasi-cadence retains the $\hat{6}$–$\hat{5}$ (C–B) upper-voice motion, the essential feature for terminal resolution of the mode's background $\hat{8}$–$\hat{5}$ descent (e″–b′).

By stating the last verse four times in succession, the madrigal subjects the listener to multiple rounds of this wrenching formation at two different pitch levels, E and B, each time with a different voicing and all but the last

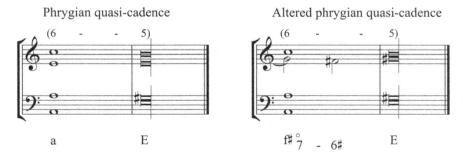

Example 5.13 Altered Form of the Phrygian Quasi-Cadence in Marenzio's *Cruda Amarilli*

evaded: E (m. 115), B (m. 123), B (m. 129), and E (m. 135). In its first appearance directed at E (mm. 113–15), for example, the feigned *clausula cantizans* (g–f♯–g♯) appears in the Basso, strengthening the impetus toward G. The evasion of g for g♯ undermines the arrival on either pitch-center, E or G, and the contrapuntal momentum pushes forward as a *cadenza fuggita* on A for the start of the next phrase (m. 116). This form of the altered quasi-cadence, with the suspension in the Basso, is especially striking in its nearly unrelenting dissonance, whereby the resolution of one jarring suspension leads only to another dissonance—a vivid aural realization of the "martire" (suffering) referenced in the text.[25]

In modifying the normative phrygian quasi-cadence, Marenzio concludes his reading in a manner that conveys both torment and large-scale resolution. The reworking of the gesture precludes the customary sustaining of E through a closing a–E motion, but it preserves the basic purpose of ushering the fundamental descent from $\hat{6}$ (c″) to $\hat{5}$ (b′). Even the ubiquitous use of the raised second degree (F♯) in the final passages does not interfere with the phrygian framework and its large-scale *diatessaron* ($\hat{8}$–$\hat{5}$) unfolding. Unlike *O fido, o caro Aminta*, where the terminal close underscores the status of the A final as *re*, not *mi*, through its use of raised $\hat{2}$ (B-*mi*) despite the *cantus-mollis* system, here the final cadence does just the opposite: the altered phrygian quasi-cadence invokes ♯$\hat{2}$ as an expressive surface inflection—as part of the deceptive cadential preparation for G—while continuing to fulfill its structural role as a phrygian ending. The conclusion demonstrates well the potential misinterpretation that could result from an analysis seeking a large-scale descent toward the final in a phrygian work, such as $\hat{5}$–$\hat{1}$ or $\hat{4}$–$\hat{1}$, since the $\hat{2}$–$\hat{1}$ resolution here leads F♯–E.

With its span of a fourth rather than a fifth, the phrygian background inherently offers less potential for structural motion than background descents of a fifth. But Marenzio offsets the reduced interval with the protracted neighboring motion between e″ and d″ in the *prima parte*. The motion to d″ acts as a false instigation of the structural descent at a deep middleground level that only reverts back to the initial state (e″) before truly advancing in the *seconda parte*. The effect, together with the steady unfolding of the background in the *seconda parte*, creates a dynamic structural process that envelops the entire madrigal. Marenzio's combination of structural animation, conflicting modes, and remote and eccentric cadences generates considerable tension that drives the piece forward and provides a fitting depiction of the speaker's agony and distress. The approach stands in sharp contrast to Wert's interpretation, where modal contrast and structural activity play little part.

Despite its use of the C-hypolydian (i.e., C-hypoionian) mode and *misura di breve*, and its generally more pictorial response to the text, Wert's treatment of Mirtillo's lament bears several conspicuous similarities to Marenzio's work, particularly in its handling of verses 1–4. Given the close proximity of the two settings in terms of publication—Wert's dedication is dated 18 August 1595, and Marenzio's, 20 October—questions of influence, referencing, and rivalry become especially intriguing, as it raises the likelihood that one composer's madrigal made its way to the other composer in some pre-publication form, whether or not through performance. Wert would have been familiar with the play at least by November 1591, when the first extant reference was made to Wert's and Rovigo's role in providing music for Duke Vincenzo Gonzaga's attempted staging of 1591–93. Hence, Wert's settings might date from well before their 1595 printing, even though the madrigals likely have no direct ties to the Mantuan production. Yet, the possibility that Marenzio's *Pastor fido* texts came from a preliminary draft of the tragicomedy dating from 1586, as discussed earlier, means that the Roman composer might still have paved the way for his Mantuan contemporary in setting *Cruda Amarilli*, even if Wert beat him to print.

As scholars have often noted, both Marenzio and Wert set the initial cry, "Cruda Amarilli," using similar descending figures in very similar rhythms (compare Examples. 5.10 and 5.14). This opening figure resurfaces in Monteverdi's setting from three years later (Example 7.1), and in many settings thereafter. In both Wert's and Marenzio's madrigals the successive entries of the voices carry out the structural function of ascending to the primary background pitch: in Marenzio's, the E-phrygian final, *e″*; in Wert's, the

Example 5.14 Wert, *Cruda Amarilli*, che col nome ancora, mm. 1–9

C-hypolydian fifth, *g"*. The voice entries in both works even begin on the same pitches, C, E, and G—that is, the only notes consonant with the initial background pitches of both works.

Despite their motivic parallels, the structural implications of these openings prove vastly different. Whereas Marenzio's handling of verses 1–2 brings only cadences on pitches other than the final and creates considerable modal uncertainty, Wert's reading does just the opposite: the cadences lead tenaciously to the C final, and Mirtillo's complaints of Amarilli's bitterness yield surface dissonances within a clear-cut modal context. Hence, Wert's opening matches three statements of "Cruda Amarilli" to three firm cadences on C (Example 5.14).[26] By the end of verse 2 (m. 23), there have been five cadences to C and a non-cadential verse-ending on E (m. 11)—by most theoretical accounts a primary cadence tone of the C-hypolydian mode. The cadential focus on the final continues in subsequent verses until the last line of the *prima parte*, "I' mi morrò tacendo," where a torrent of chromatic descents shifts the focus toward G while maintaining that degree as a fixed background pitch (*g"*). The saturation of the musical space contrapuntally with references to the speaker's self ("i' mi") and his death ("morrò") renders the text in a manner that seems antithetical its meaning. While the speaker concedes that he shall die silently, the five voices reiterate and superimpose the words in a frenzied barrage, as though insisting that the speaker's voice be heard while foretelling his silent death.[27]

The most explicit instances of word-painting in Wert's setting come at the opening of the *seconda parte*. For verse 9, the composer renders the slopes and mountains through an imitative phrase that first descends in skips through a twelfth for "piagge," then leaps upward a tenth at "monti" (Example 5.15). Wert likewise turns to pictorial techniques for "fugace" (mm. 30–31) and "mormorando" (mm. 63–70).

In terms of structure, Wert's *seconda parte* continues the static state of the *prima parte* by rearticulating the primary background *g"* at the start and maintaining it until the final three measures of the piece with a context secured firmly on C modally and cadentially. Accordingly, the melodic outlines for verses 9–15 accentuate the C and G octaves and their divisions, with C, G, and sometimes F stressed invariably as the basis of sonorities. All of the prominent cadences lead to C. The pictorial rendering of the slopes and mountains of verse 9, for example, consists entirely of the pitches C, G, and E in all voices, with *g"* maintained continuously in the Canto and Quinto (both sopranos) or at a lower register (Examples 5.15 and 5.16). The penultimate verse, "E mormorando i venti" (mm. 63–70), in most instances yields straightforward ascents through the C and G octaves, therein articulating the fifths C–G and F–C and reaffirming the background *g"* in the Canto and Quinto parts. Exploration of contrasting tonal or modal regions plays no part in Wert's reading, for instead the conditions of modal, harmonic, and ultimately structural stasis create a seemingly paradoxical musical effect of

Example 5.15 Wert, *Cruda Amarilli*, mm. 51–58

atemporality, of fundamental invariability and motionlessness, akin to a state of lyric reflection.

In contrast to Marenzio's *Cruda Amarilli* and *O fido, o caro Aminta*, where the modal framework unfolds gradually and involves disruptions and changing modal contexts for expression, *varietà*, and structural support, Wert's *Cruda Amarilli* sustains the primary background pitch, g'', through nearly the entire piece before unfolding the full structural descent, $g''-c''$, in the final breves (Example 5.16). The emphasis of Wert's reading lies not in the progressive expansion of the modal framework and the expressivity and tension-driven expectation therein, for the piece is nearly devoid of modal, cadential, and at times even harmonic variation. Instead, the madrigal's expressive means concentrate on the surface level, by way of immediate delivery, particularly through contrasts in register and rhythmic phrasing, and by the affective use of counterpoint and chromaticism.[28] Greater cadential and modal variety might even detract from Wert's direct and often unpretentious presentation of the verse.

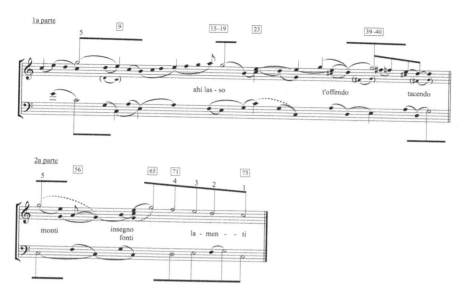

Example 5.16 Wert, *Cruda Amarilli*, Structural Analysis

   The performance environment in which the work arose might have had some impact on its design and methods. At the Mantuan court in the early 1590s, where the duke maintained a *concerto delle donne* modeled on that of Ferrara, the experience of vocal polyphony in performance would have been complemented by the talent—not to mention beauty—of the women performing the three upper voices. Moreover, the cadential and modal consistency and constricted harmonic rhythm and breadth of the madrigal might have afforded more opportunities for improvisation and gesture. Whereas the unexpected cadential turns, modal digressions, and animated structure of Marenzio's setting build notable tension and, indeed, display his technical virtuosity in portraying at once the speaker's suffering and his beloved's cruel and conflicted nature, Wert's work places more emphasis on performance— the intertwining chromaticism, the sweeping spans of pictorial leaps and runs, and the upper reaches of the voices, particularly the sopranos with their continual highlighting of the prolonged structural pitch, *g″*.
   Despite their many correspondences, both subtle and pronounced, the two madrigals, thus, convey very different perspectives of Mirtillo's well-known speech. Although Marenzio has sometimes been stereotyped as a composer inclined toward "picturesque" renderings of words and phrases, as compared to Wert's focus on the overall sense and mood of the text, their settings of *Cruda Amarilli* show the very opposite.[29] Wert's attention here lies consistently on individual images, while Marenzio more frequently eschews word-painting in favor of farther-reaching portrayals of overarching

sentiments and the inner complexities of the characters that often extend beyond the literal speech. Subtle images take shape on occasion in Marenzio's reading—the brief runs in the upper voices for "fugace" and the paired semibreves and breves for "monti"—but many more invitations (such as "fonti," "mormorando," "venti," and "muta") are passed over. Instead, on the smaller scale, the Roman composer focuses on Guarini's wordplay, comparatives, recurrent rhythmic figures, and deixis, while also looking beyond the musical text itself, to Amarilli's true nature as it is revealed through later acts of the play, showing her to be much more than a fair and bitter flower. Thus, Marenzio's reading recognizes the text as more than an isolated lyric poem.

Three Settings from Act 3

Several of the basic findings from the analyses of the two *Cruda Amarilli* settings apply to Marenzio's and Wert's other *Pastor fido* settings as well. Marenzio's readings tend to traverse a range of contrasting yet coordinated modalities and textures while forming networks of musical–textual motives and highlighting rhetorical features of the text, such as assonance, puns, and phonic allusions. The modal framework most often unfolds incrementally across the piece in a dynamic process that encompasses extended periods of modal–structural conflict, disruption, and ambiguity, and intensifies the anticipation of large-scale closure. As with the portrayal of Amarilli's hidden struggle in *Cruda Amarilli*, Marenzio's depictions seem many times to read beyond the given madrigal text to render broader dimensions its subjects, personas, and scenarios through the musical interplay of foreground and larger-scale structure, of surface and subtext. Wert's settings tend to favor one predominant texture—homorhythmic declamation or imitation—while juxtaposing different combinations of voices and at times superimposing two or more poetic lines (with their associated musical phrases) contrapuntally. Structurally, most of Wert's settings (with the exception of *Udite, lagrimosi*) remain fixed in their opening structural state, maintaining the initial background pitch until the very last measures and rarely venturing beyond the principal cadence points and melodic boundaries of the mode. This structural approach is unusual within the broader repertory of late-Renaissance polyphony, where modal–structural tensions prove an integral aspect of large-scale syntax, rhetoric, and affect. Thus, whereas Marenzio most often matches the portrayal of the text to the varied pacing and contexts of the background descent and a versatile, reference-filled foreground, Wert's focus rests more on speech rhythms and the harmonies, textures, and voice groupings joined to them, while the modal background acts as a suspended uniform backdrop.[30] This emphasis in Wert's *Pastor fido* madrigals on surface-level elocution results in a reading focused most on the immediate affective state and on realizing the isolated reflective moment of the speech, rather than the more comprehensive, intertextually informed rendering of the characters and their motivations seen in Marenzio's works.

These contrasting approaches to modal structure and the play's texts—Wert's prioritization of elocution and direct import using a suspended structure, and Marenzio's rendering of dramatic development and intertextual subtexts with an animated background—yield two distinct temporal effects. Both of these principal structural types—dynamic or steadily advancing versus static or atemporal—take the same essential shape at the most basic level: a stepwise descent through one of the mode-defining species of perfect consonances—typically the *diapente* or, in phrygian works, the *diatessaron*. The distinction, however, lies in the pacing of this underlying framework— the distribution of its steps—across the length of a work. In a temporally dynamic structure, like that of Marenzio's *Cruda Amarilli*, some or all of the initial steps ($\hat{5}$–$\hat{2}$ or, in phrygian, $\hat{8}$–$\hat{6}$) unfold incrementally through the course of the piece. Like the conflict in a dramatic work or the first quatrain of a sonnet, the early instigation of this descent drives the piece forward with its inherent instability and demand for resolution, conveying an effect of structural–temporal progression (Example 5.17a). There may be temporary diversions, superficial and middleground descents, and local-level resolutions through the course of this expanding structure—like the completions of verses in a sonnet or scenes in a play—but these events serve as but subsidiary components of one larger integrated, end-driven process.

Rather than advance through the steps of this background progressively through a work, many of Wert's later madrigals—including his *Pastor fido* settings—suspend the structure in its initial state, waiting until the final moments to descend hastily toward closure (Example 5.17b). Thus, in place of a dynamic, phased unfolding across a piece, as typically occurs in this repertory, many of Wert's late madrigals project an unmoving, consistent state that dwells on the primary background pitch, withholding any sense of departure and any impetus toward resolution. The effect is one of structural stasis, of atemporality. These steady frameworks, thus, seem to suspend the

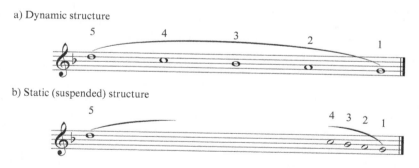

a) Dynamic structure

b) Static (suspended) structure

Example 5.17 Modal Structure: Dynamic vs. Static (Suspended)

piece in time, rendering the text as an isolated moment analogous to that of a lyric poem, a reflective monologue, or a visual illustration—such as those in the woodcuts for the 1602 Ciotti edition of Guarini's play. In terms of its teleological unfolding, then, the music has neither departed nor arrived in any fundamental way, until the final phrase or verse of text and its perfunctory (and obligatory) act of structural closure. With both effects of structural time, whether freezing it or coordinating its movement with the features and stages of the music and text, Wert and Marenzio invite the listener and performers into the frame, the "picture," of the speaker's world, allowing them to explore inside it, to experience it vicariously, while contemplating all manner of things from various perspectives.

The structural–interpretative strategies of their *Pastor fido* settings stand at odds with the general representation of the two composers in modern scholarship. For example, in a comparison of their handlings of texts from Tasso's *Gerusalemme liberata*, Jessie Ann Owens offers the dictum that "Marenzio is most interested in the texts' 'conceits', while Wert works with the 'concept' or idea."[31] Yet *Cruda Amarilli* shows Wert dealing more with "conceits" than his Roman contemporary, who probes more deeply into the characters' states. Wert's other *Pastor fido* settings behave similarly. As for attention to the overarching idea of the text, it would be difficult to nominate one composer over the other, their means of expression being so different.

Several aspects of Wert's later style—declamative texture, natural speech rhythms, and repeated and sustained sonorities—have led some scholars to label his works "dramatic," "dramatizations," and even "dramas," insinuating a direct representation or enactment of the speaking persona in a mimetic (quasi-operatic) manner.[32] The madrigal, of course, cannot be truly "dramatic," or mimetic, in a generic sense, or "empower performers to become in effect flesh-and-blood characters," given its inherently diegetic nature and, hence, its manner of presenting its texts as cooperative readings or retellings in a narrative, third-person perspective, as if prefacing *Cruda Amarilli* with an understood statement, "Thus, Mirtillo lamented: 'Cruda Amarilli...'"[33] The association of Wert's madrigals with the "dramatic" proves especially problematic given what we have seen of the composer's accustomed treatment of large-scale structure in response to texts specifically dramatic in origin. With their unvarying backgrounds and restricted harmonic and cadential spheres, these madrigals underscore the lyric quality not only of the madrigal's subjects, but also of the play's extracted monologues by mimicking, in the innately temporal medium of music, a timeless state of lyric reflection. His settings, then, transform speeches of Guarini's play not into "miniature dramas" or "stylized dramatizations" set in the here-and-now, but into collective (diegetic) recounts—collaborative narrations—of a moment from the past, in the (Arcadian) then-and-there. In so doing, Wert's works demonstrate precisely the lyrical, madrigalian potential of the play's monologues at which critics took aim. This effect of musical–structural atemporality, moreover, stands in direct contrast to the digressions, oppositions, and end-directed thrust that characterize the dynamic processes of Marenzio's readings.

Marenzio's attention to large-scale expressive strategies, referential ties, and intertextual reading seems at times to reach beyond the individual work and its given text to the madrigal book as a whole. Numerous scholars have pointed to consistencies in general mood, compositional style, subject matter, and textual source as evidence of overarching unity in several of Marenzio's books. Richard Freedman, for example, has argued compellingly that the idiosyncratically grave tone, archaic *misura di breve*, and weighty texts (dominated by Petrarch and Sannazaro) that typify the *Madrigali a 4, 5, e 6* of 1588 mark it as a "cyclic collection" with a clear "artistic program," the aesthetics of which cater to "the specialized tastes" of the book's dedicatee, Count Mario Bevilacqua, and his *ridotto* at the Accademia Filarmonica of Verona.[34] James Haar later built on Freedman's analysis by presenting persuasive evidence that the collection might instead have been designed for the austere predilections of the Duke of Mantua, Guglielmo Gonzaga, from whom (it will be remembered) Marenzio was seeking employment in mid-1586, and whose death in 1587 prompted the composer to redirect his dedication toward Bevilacqua and Verona.[35] Likewise, with its prevalence of Tasso's and Guarini's pastoral verse and the characters Tirsi and Clori, the Sixth Book may also convey an allegorical narrative linked to the composer's patron in the early 1590s, Virginio Orsini, and his wife, Flavia Peretti, who adopted the sobriquets Tirsi and Clori as members of a pastoral-themed society of Roman literati, led by Orsini himself, known as the Shepherds of the Tiber Valley.[36]

The Seventh Book, too, has piqued the interest of madrigal scholars for its nearly chronological ordering of twelve passages from *Il pastor fido* and incorporation of non-*Pastor fido* texts in ways that can be read as a unified narrative (Table 5.2). Patricia Myers set the tone for these later assessments by deeming the book a "cycle" that conveys "the same succession of emotional states which Guarini's play elicited by means of sudden twists of plot and the rapid reversal of fortune."[37] Myers concludes that "the meaningful order in which the Guarini texts are arranged and the non-Guarini texts are integrated suggests, therefore, that the arrangement of pieces is not at all accidental."[38] More recently, Massimo Ossi has argued that Marenzio, in fact, "creates a more coherent organization for this madrigal book than Myers recognizes," one that "follows a rhetorical, rather than dramatic, plan."[39]

Such organizational schemes work in conjunction with the strict grouping of the pieces in both books by cleffing and system—primarily cleffing, then secondarily system, in the Sixth Book, and the reverse in the Seventh Book—a format favored by the Venetian printing firm of Angelo Gardano. Any deliberate ordering of the pieces according to narrative, by the composer or someone else, then, would also have needed to incorporate within that narrative an ordering by musical parameters, so that in the end, sequence of pieces would create consistent system–clef groupings. The fact

Table 5.2 Marenzio, Seventh Book of Madrigals (1595), Contents

	Title	Textual source	System	Clefs	Final
1.	Deh, poi ch'era ne' fati ch'i' dovessi	Guarini: *Pastor fido* (I,2)	durus	standard (C1)	A
2.	Quell'augellin, che canta	Guarini: *Pastor fido* (I,1)	durus	standard	G
3.	Cruda Amarilli, che col nome ancora	Guarini: *Pastor fido* (I,2)	durus	standard	E
4.	O disaventurosa acerba sorte	Bembo: *Alma cortese*	durus	standard	B
5.	Al lume de le stelle	Tasso: *Rime e prose*	durus	high (G2)	A
6.	Ami, Tirsi, e me 'l nieghi	Anon.	durus	high	A
7.	O dolcezz'amarissime d'amore	Guarini: *Pastor fido* (III,1)	durus	high	C
8.	Sospir nato di fuoco	Anon.	durus	high	E
9.	Arda pur sempre, o mora	Guarini: *Pastor fido* (III,6)	mollis	high	F
10.	Questi vaghi concenti	Anon.	mollis	high	G
11.	O fido, o caro Aminta	Guarini: *Pastor fido* (I,2)	mollis [?]	high	A
12.	O Mirtillo, Mirtillo, anima mia	Guarini: *Pastor fido* (III,4)	mollis	high	C
13.	Deh, dolce anima mia (by A. Bicci)	Guarini: *Pastor fido* (III,3)	mollis	standard	G
14.	Com'è dolce il gioire, o vago Tirsi	Guarini: *Pastor fido* (III,6)	mollis	standard	G
15.	Care mie selve, a Dio	Guarini: *Pastor fido* (IV,5)	mollis	standard	D
16.	Tirsi mio, caro Tirsi	Guarini: *Pastor fido* (IV,5)	mollis	standard	D
17.	Ombrose e care selve	Guarini: *Pastor fido* (V,8)	mollis	standard	F

that most arguments for a planned organization in the Seventh Book are based chiefly on musical texts that are innately related through their pastoral theme and (in most cases) common source might raise questions about objective standards for what constitutes a unified "book" or narrative and, conversely, about confirmation bias in studies aiming to prove such coherence or "book-like" status. Moreover, such pursuits of "bookhood" may simply betray the partialities of modern conceptions of reading.

At the same time, as I have argued elsewhere, the true identity of *O fido, o caro Aminta* (No. 11) as A-dorian (aeolian), not A-phrygian, discussed above, suggests that the madrigal was wrongly cast in the *cantus mollis* (B♭) system, presumably owing to its early A-phrygian tendencies and, in turn, a broader misunderstanding of its mode, likely by the printer or compiler.[40] A "correction" of its system to *cantus durus* and high clefs (*chiavette*) would then shift the piece upward as far as No. 5, alongside the other A-final, *cantus-durus*, high-clef works (shown by the arrow in Table 5.2). This revised ordering would adhere much more closely to the chronology of *Il pastor fido*, as all of the settings would be arranged by act, with non-*Pastor fido* settings intermixed within each group, and no longer with an anomalous act-one setting positioned among treatments from act 3.

Wert's *Pastor fido* settings, also issued by Angelo Gardano, do not appear in chronological order in the Eleventh Book. Instead, as Table 5.3 shows, the book is also arranged by clef and system, as expected, apart from no. 11—a setting of the anonymous text *Anima del cor mio* in *cantus durus* and standard clefs (*chiavi naturali*) that sits anomalously between the *mollis* and *durus* high-clef (G2) groups. Although the pieces do not show any outward signs of being ordered beyond these parameters, a closer inspection of the music reveals that after the primary factor of cleffing, the works are arranged by modal factors: first by transposition level, and secondarily by modal (numerical) sequence. Each clef group, therefore, leads from pieces transposed downward (hence, in *cantus mollis*), then untransposed *(cantus durus)*, and finally those transposed upward (also *cantus durus*). It is notable that the irregularly placed *Anima del cor mio* (no. 11) is a phrygian-mode work: for, like Marenzio's misclassified *O fido, o caro Aminta* (also no. 11 in its book), it betrays the idiosyncrasy and distinctive (mis)treatment of phrygian-type pieces even in the late sixteenth century. Yet, whereas Marenzio's A-dorian work appears in the wrong position in its book as a result of being cast in an improper system, Wert's E-phrygian madrigal is labeled correctly but situated among pieces with a blatantly different cleffing, rather than alongside its kindred E-phrygian piece: the *Pastor fido* setting, *Udite, lagrimosi* (No. 6). One potential explanation for this peculiar placement could be that Wert (or the compiler of his book) desired a work in an untransposed mode to complete the cycle of modal–transposition levels for the high-clef (G2) group, and there being no high-clef pieces in an untransposed mode, one with low clefs was inserted. Whether other, extra-musical factors could have played a part in the book's organization and the madrigal's peculiar placement, however, warrants further consideration.

Wert's four *Pastor fido* settings are dispersed throughout the book according to these objective factors. Even the two settings that open the book, *Ah, dolente partita* and *O primavera gioventù*, are reversed from their order in the play, despite sharing the same parameters (*cantus mollis* with standard clefs) and mode, meaning they could appear in either order. Clearly chronology in the play was not a priority in the ordering of the book—a factor that reinforces the lyric, self-contained nature of Wert's settings. The placement of *Ah, dolente partita* at the front of the book, meanwhile, could be a response to a real-world "parting"—perhaps, given the potential *terminus post quem* of Wert's *Pastor fido* settings of 1590, even the dismissal of Wert's lover, the *virtuosa* singer Tarquinia Molza, from the Ferrarese court in late 1589, following the discovery of their unseemly, long-term affair.

Table 5.3 Wert, Eleventh Book of Madrigals (1595), Contents

	Title	Textual source	System	Clef	Final
1	Ah, dolente partita	Guarini: Pastor fido (III,3)	mollis	standard	G
2	O primavera, gioventù dell'anno	Guarini: Pastor fido (III,1)	mollis	standard	G
3	Ahi come soffrirò dolce mia vita	Anon.	mollis	standard	G
4	Ancor che l'alto mio nobil pensiero	Anon.	mollis	standard	G
5	Scherza nel canto e piace	Cesare Rinaldi, Rime	durus	standard	D
6	Udite, lagrimosi	Guarini: Pastor fido (III,6)	durus	standard	E
7	Poi che vuole il ben mio	Anon.	durus	standard	G
8	Voi nemico crudele	Anon.	durus	standard	A
9	Ahi lass' ogn' hor veggio io	Anon.	mollis	high	G
10	Felice l'alma che per voi respira	Luigi Tansillo, Rime	mollis	high	G
11	Anima del cor mio	Anon.	durus	standard	E
12	Cruda Amarilli, che col nome ancora	Guarini: Pastor fido (I,2)	durus	high	C
13	Amor se non consenti	Anon.	durus	high	C
14	Che fai alma (Dialogo a7)	Anon.	mollis	high	G

All of Wert's *Pastor fido* settings come from Mirtillo's speeches in different contexts: *Cruda Amarilli* from his dialogue with Ergasto in act 1, and the three remaining settings from act 3. The third act represents a turning point in the drama, where Mirtillo and Amarilli's tumultuous encounter in the *Gioco della cieca* (III,2) opens the door for Corisca's nearly fatal scheme to frame Amarilli as an unfaithful bride-to-be and, in turn, win Mirtillo for herself. Wert's settings reflect the three principal stages of the act from Mirtillo's perspective: his private anticipation of Amarilli's arrival (*O primavera*), the final words from his humiliating exchange with her (*Ah, dolente partita*), and his desperate lament—unknowingly overheard by Corisca—following the event (*Udite, lagrimosi*). The three texts, therefore, offer lyric-like snapshots of the protagonist's emotional state at each of these stages, and Wert sets these portrayals accordingly, with suspended, atemporal structures and his accustomed means of foreground text-setting.

One of these means, the contrapuntal superimposition of poetic lines and their associated musical subjects, represents a hallmark of Wert's output of the 1580s–90s. The technique acts as a musical response to the coupling of interdependent poetic lines with rhyme, although the device sometimes appears without the presence of rhyme. Alfred Einstein labeled the technique *contrapposto* after the practice in classical and Renaissance sculpture of depicting the human figure with its weight shifted to one foot, causing the shoulders and arms to sit off axis from the hips and legs. The effect in the visual arts, seen in monumental works such as Alexandros of Antioch's *Venus de Milo* and Michelangelo's *David*, creates an impression of movement latent in relaxation. In the late madrigal—specifically in the hands of Wert and other madrigalists around the turn of the seventeenth century—*contrapposto* often precipitates a buildup of momentum as a new musical–poetic line merges with and gradually eclipses the line before it, driving ultimately to an assertive cadence.

Despite the potential semantic and affective motivations for combining poetic lines in this way, Wert's use of *contrapposto* seems to serve more as a formalistic approach to textual scheme than an expressive or interpretative response to the content. In other words, where rhyming couplets appear in the text, Wert is likely to set them in *contrapposto*, irrespective of their substance. The device occurs routinely at the ends of works and of internal *parti*, where rhyming couplets also commonly appear, particularly in settings of *versi sciolti* (free verse), such as Guarini's play.[41] In *Cruda Amarilli* and *Udite, lagrimosi*, Wert sets every rhyming couplet in *contrapposto*, and in *Ah, dolente partita*, whose eight-line text contains three rhyming couplets, Wert superimposes two of them. In the play, as in poetic madrigals, such rhymed verse-pairs generally complement one another or even show grammatical or semantic interdependence. Although the verses would sound one after the other in a spoken reading of the poem, on the page the silent reader experiences the verses in various spatial and temporal arrays: not only in succession—one followed by the other—but also together (one above the other), and likely even recursively by circling back to the previous line after reading the later one. In *Ah, dolente partita*—Mirtillo's impassioned *partenza* to Amarilli at the end of act 3, scene 3—Guarini presses these ocular acrobatics to a frenzied pace with a flurry of rhymed couplets in predominantly short (*settenari*) verses:

Ah, dolente **partita**,	Oh, painful parting!
Ah, fin de la mia **vita**.	Oh, end of my life!
Da te parto, e non moro?	I part from you and do not die?
E pur io provo la pena de la morte,	Yet I feel the pain of death
E sento nel **partire**	and in parting feel
Un vivace **morire**,	a living death
Che da vita al **dolore**,	that gives life to pain,
Per far che moia immortalmente il **core**.	so that my heart dies eternally.

Through *contrapposto*, the madrigal mimics this manner of visual reading from the page by presenting the lines in succession, as one verse gradually gives way to its successor, in superimposition, as the two verses align vertically in counterpoint, and recursively, as the verses recur in alternation within and between the voices—thus, for a period, seeming to dispense with any notion of temporal–spatial arrangement. Concepts coupled by rhyme and meaning in Guarini's text—*vital/partita* and *core/dolore* in *Ah, dolente partita*; *t'offendo/tacendo* and *venti/lamenti* in *Cruda Amarilli*; and *mia/sia* in *Udite, lagrimosi*—therefore, find expanded dimensions and, hence, new spatial and temporal relationships in Wert's music.

There are several instances, however, where Wert does not deploy *contrapposto* for rhymed couplets. In *Ah, dolente partita*, for example, the middle couplet (*partire/morire*, vv. 5–6) sounds in blocks of staggered declamation with no overlapping of verses. The motivation here may be formalistic and aesthetic—Wert sets the opening and closing couplets in extended *contrapposto*, but favors concision and variety for the middle one—as well as semantic—to draw focus to the oxymoron "un vivace morire" (a living death) in verse 6 with the greater clarity of homophonic texture. The rhymed couplets in *Cruda Amarilli* and *Udite, lagrimosi* all mark the ends of *parti* and pieces, and likewise undergo paired contrapuntal treatment.

The five-*parte O primavera* illustrates well how the placement of rhymed verse-pairs influences Wert's formal strategies and use of *contrapposto*, as well as his means of unifying an expansive span of music and text on various levels. The madrigal treats the larger share of Mirtillo's monologue of act 3, scene 1, where the shepherd—heeding Ergasto's advice—waits in hiding for Amarilli, Corisca, and a band of nymphs to arrive and play the *Gioco della cieca* (game of blind man's buff). Alone, the speaker laments in turn to spring, love, and the day itself that has brought him "here," while revealing the mix of optimism and despair he faces in that moment. Wert's madrigal text, with translation, reads as follows (with verses also set in Marenzio's *O dolcezze amarissime d'amore* in italics):

1ᵃ parte

1	O primavera, gioventù de l'anno,	O spring, youth of the year,
	Bella madre di fiori,	fair mother of flowers,
	D'herbe novelle e di novelli amori,	of fresh grass and new loves,
	Tu torni ben, ma teco	indeed, you return, but with you
5	Non tornano i sereni	do not return the serene
	E fortunati dì de le miei gioie;	and happy days of my joy.
	Tu torni ben, tu torni,	Indeed, you return, you return,
	Ma teco altro non torna	but with you returns none else
	Che del perduto mio caro thesoro	than the miserable and painful memories
10	La rimembranza misera e dolente.	of my dear lost treasure.
	Tu quella se', tu quella	You are the one, you
	Ch'eri pur dianzi sì vezzosa e bella;	who was before so fair and lovely;
	Ma non son io già quel ch'un tempo fui	but I am no longer what I once was,
	Sì caro a gl'occhi altrui.	so dear to another's eyes.

2ᵃ parte

15	O dolcezze amarissime d'amore,	O most bitter sweetness of love,
	Quanto è più duro perdervi, che mai	how much harder it is to lose you, than
	Non v'haver o provate o possedute.	never to have tasted or possessed you.
	Come saria l'amar felice stato,	How happy love would be
	Se'l già goduto ben non si perdesse;	if the already enjoyed goodness were not lost;
20	O quand'egli si perde,	or when it is lost,
	Ogni memoria ancora	each memory, too,
	Del dileguato ben si dileguasse.	of the vanished goodness were vanished.

3ᵃ parte

Ma, se le mie speranz'hoggi non sono,	But if my hopes are not today,
Com'è l'usato lor, di fragil vetro,	as is their custom, of fragile glass,
25 O se maggior del vero	or if hope does not make
Non fa la speme il desiar soverchio,	overwhelming desire greater than the truth,
Qui pur vedrò colei	here yet I will see her
Ch'è'l sol degl'occhi miei.	who is the sun of my eyes.

4ᵃ parte

E s'altri non m'inganna,	And if others do not deceive me,
30 Qui pur vedroll'al suon de' miei sospiri	Here yet I will see her, to the sound of my sighs,
Fermar il piè fugace.	halt her fleeing foot.
Qui pur da le dolcezze	Here yet, from the sweetness
Di quel bel volto havrà soave cibo	of that fair face, splendid food
Nel suo lungo digiun l'avida vista;	in its long fast my eager sight will have;
35 Qui pur vedrò quell'empia	here yet I will see that pitiless one
Girar inverso me le luci altère,	turn toward me her proud eyes,
Se non dolci, almen fère,	if not sweet, then fierce,
E se non carche d'amorosa gioia,	and if not full of loving joy,
Sì crude almen ch'i' moia.	so cruel that at least I may die.

5ᵃ parte

40 O lungamente sospirato invano	O long desired in vain
Aventuroso dì, se dopo tanti	Fortunate day, if after so many
Foschi giorni di pianti,	dismal days of weeping,
Tu mi concedi, Amor, di veder hoggi	you allow me today, Love, to see
Ne' begli occhi di lei	in her beautiful eyes
45 Girar sereno il sol degl'occhi miei.	the sun of my eyes turn serenely.

[Lines following in the play]

Ma qui mandommi Ergasto, ove mi disse	But here Ergasto led me, where he told me
ch'esser doveano insieme	Corisca and the fairest Amarilli
Corisca e la bellissima Amarilli	would be together
per fare il gioco de la cieca; e pure	to play the Gioco della Cieca; and yet
qui non veggio altra cieca	here I see no other blind thing
che la mia cieca voglia...	than my own blind desire...

The passage works perfectly well as a self-contained lament—if an exceptionally long one—lacking any reference to specific events or characters in Guarini's play. In fact, the excerpts set by Wert and Marenzio end just before Mirtillo refers to the three characters involved in luring him to his waiting place: Ergasto, Corisca, and Amarilli (given after the madrigal text above).

There are eight rhyming couplets in the forty-five-line passage, four of which coincide with the ends of *parti*. Wert sets three of these closing couplets in *contrapposto*: *colei/miei* in the *terza parte*, *gioia/moia* in the *quarta parte*, and *lei/miei* in the *quinta* (final) *parte*. The *prima parte* also ends in rhyming verses, but Wert forgoes the opportunity to superimpose them and instead repeats the last line alone in succinct imitative phrases. From a formal perspective, it seems logical that Wert would approach the end of the *prima parte* in this way, for the less substantial contrapuntal preparation provides adequate closure but reserves the more climactic and rhetorically forceful endings with extended *contrapposto* for the later *parti*. Within this layout, the *seconda parte* stands apart for its lack of a closing rhyme yet its superimposition of the three last unrhymed verses nonetheless. While the endings of these verses (*perde/ancora/dileguasse*) lack unity in word sound, the effect of juggling them together in prolonged counterpoint underscores the emotional struggle that together they express: the chronic aching to let go of a bygone love ("Or when [love] is lost, [if] every memory, too…were vanished"). With its three-line *contrapposto*, Wert's setting evokes the undying memories and enduring pain of lost love in the persistent refusal to yield and the resulting obstruction to closure of the penultimate and antepenultimate verses as they cycle in cascading fashion. This ending, with three grammatically rather ungainly lines, in turn, creates a formal division before the rhetorical shift with a forceful "Ma" to begin the *terza parte* and its more optimistic prospects.

The extended contrapuntal drive of *contrapposto* gives the ending of the *seconda parte* more force than that of the *prima parte*, yet the absence of a closing rhyme makes it weaker than the three endings that follow it. The increasing rhetorical strength of the endings across the five *parti* adds a sense of direction to a piece that—like Wert's *Cruda Amarilli*—nevertheless remains anchored in its opening structural state until the final moments of its exceptional length (see Example 5.18). The madrigal's surface makes this constant background context clear. Each of the five *parti* begins and ends on a G sonority and maintains the primary structural pitch—the G-hypodorian $\hat{5}$, d''—audibly and contrapuntally through melodic boundaries, as well as harmonies and cadences centered principally on G, B♭, and D. (There are also infrequent cadences to F, and one cadence to A-*mi* in the *quinta parte* that comes as an affective response to "pianti.") The background d'' appears saliently at the top of the texture throughout the madrigal, at times slipping into an inner voice or the bass before resurfacing on top. Any diversions from this primary pitch are short-lived—namely, middleground diminutions of the background d''—and the madrigal promptly restores its more fundamental opening state, as though nothing has passed but a number of words. Indeed, this structural paralysis in Wert's music again conjures an effect of arrested time, which is precisely the state that the text reveals, whether in the play specifically—as Mirtillo surveys his emotions in the seemingly endless moments before Amarilli's arrival—or as a universal reflective poem.

Three integral components of this middleground expansion of d'' are the rapid *diapente* descents at a lower register, $d'-g$ ($\hat{5}-\hat{1}$), that precede the final cadences of the first three *parti* (shown in Example 5.18). Each of these *parti*, therefore, is at once self-contained tonally—by beginning with and ending cadentially on the G final—yet also inconclusive, in having gone nowhere structurally and lacking true large-scale closure. (Wert's *Cruda Amarilli*, by comparison, has a middleground $\hat{5}-\hat{2}$ descent, $g''-d''$, with a cadence on the modal $\hat{5}$, G, to end its *prima parte*, which marks it clearly as structurally open.) By excluding a similar closing $\hat{5}-\hat{1}$ descent in the *quarta parte*, Wert

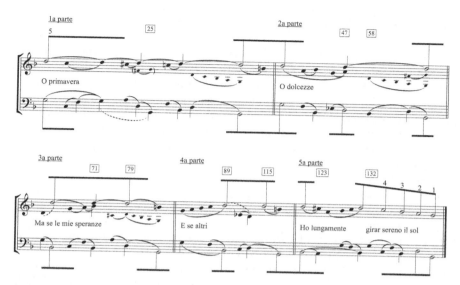

Example 5.18 Wert, *O primavera gioventù dell'anno*, Large-Scale Structure

further weakens the conclusiveness of its ending, thus maintaining momentum into the final *parte* and accentuating the weight of its (and the madrigal's) terminal cadence.

At the large-scale level, the madrigal remains fixed in its opening position, supporting *d″* as fundamental pitch, until—after some nine to ten minutes (nearly 140 breves) of structural stasis—the full G-hypodorian framework unfolds in the last moments. This effect of protracted structural suspense conveys a remarkable rendering of the "long delay of fear and anxiety that shades my heart" ("Questa lunga dimora / Di paura e d'affanno il cor m'ingombra"), as Mirtillo describes it shortly after the madrigal text breaks off. A "lunga dimora" is certainly an apt summarization of Wert's madrigal from a modal–structural perspective.

Wert's partitioning of the text works in conjunction with the musical–structural parallels between various *parti*. Hence, *parti* 1, 2, and 5 begin "O" (though written "Ho" in the partbooks for the *quinta parte*), and *parti* 3 and 4 commence with conjunctions—"Ma se le mie speranze" and "E s'altri non m'inganna." *Parti* 1, 3, and 5 likewise end with common references to "gl'occhi," while in *parti* 3 and 5, this correspondence expands to the entire closing phrase, "il sol degl'occhi miei" (the sun of my eyes)—a parallelism that Marenzio also exploits in his setting. All five *parti* additionally share an overarching textural design wherein an extended contrapuntal ending—either in *contrapposto* or (in the *prima parte*) imitation based on a single verse—contrasts with the chiefly declamatory delivery that precedes it. This broad formal–textural scheme of progressing from prevailing homophonic recitation to a contrapuntal ending—along with the sheer length of the text—might explain the composer's unusual restraint in setting rhymed verse-pairs (particularly internal ones) to *contrapposto* in this madrigal, when he so readily does so in his other *Pastor fido* settings and elsewhere in the Eleventh Book. Wert's formalistic perspective likewise applies to his treatment of the lines individually and his demarcation of verse-endings even in cases of awkward enjambment.

Altogether, as in *Cruda Amarilli*, Wert's static structural approach in *O primavera* captures the effect of atemporal reflection of Mirtillo's mono- logue and its new lyric guise, while the restrained modal, cadential, and harmonic scope brings the focus to the surface of the music and its varied means of heightened elocution, which range from phrase-level variations in rhythmic pacing, voice groupings, offset voices, sonority, and texture, to immediate responses to individual words through tactics such as chromatic inflections ("misera e dolente" and "dolcezze amarissime"), deviant sonor- ities ("tanti foschi"), and word-painting: for example, undulating runs at "gioie" (joy) and "girar" (turn); sprightly rhythms at "amorosa gioa" (lov- ing joy); a plaintive A-*mi* cadence at "pianti" (weeping); and the three-part succession long rhythms–rest–*fusae* roulades for "fermar il piè fugace" (halt her fleeting foot). A seeming limitation of this portrayal, however, involves the aspect of verisimilitude: that the madrigal in performance cannot simu- late the solitary speaker in a literal or semi-realistic manner, as a solo enact- ment of the character could, whether in spoken or sung drama. Instead, the work acts as a collaborative recounting of Mirtillo's words in naturalistic speech rhythms by way of an ensemble of voices as reader–narrators, which evokes the speaker's affective state(s) for both performers and listeners to experience vicariously amid the illusion of suspended time in the unmoving musical structure. Thus, removed from the temporal currents and specific events of a dramatic plot, the spoken words of Guarini's character become timeless and universal—elements of a shared past—capable of being spo- ken, read, or sung by anyone and everyone.

Marenzio takes a different approach to the text, deploying a dynamic structure to effect a phased unfolding of the C-hypolydian background. This dispersal of the individual steps of the large-scale descent parses the text into contrasting stages shaped by the governing background pitch, contextual mode, and tonal–cadential centricity, as well as the resulting (and other) foreground features. As opposed to the extended lyric-like sta- sis of Wert's *O primavera*, the fluctuating contexts, tension-driven expec- tation, and foreground clashes of Marenzio's setting create a multi-tiered rendering of the speaker's unrest as it materializes through the course of the speech.

As Marenzio's *O fido, o caro Aminta* excluded the reference to faithless- ness in the final line of the play ("perfidia ambidue trasse"), *O dolcezze am- arissime d'amore*, too, omits explicit allusions to external factors of the play that might compromise its universality—namely, the unnamed speaker's

(Mirtillo's) concern that others have deceived him (v. 29) and the naming of Ergasto, Corisca, and Amarilli immediately following the passage. At the same time, the exclusion of vv. 25–26 reduces the occurrences of the assonance *O* at verse beginnings and endings, but also the elaborative redundancy of these lines. Altogether, the omissions make the speech more direct and strengthen its internal associations by bringing them into closer proximity, such as the linking of "vetro" and "vedrò" in vv. 24 and 27 and the parallel openings "Qui pur"—one of which, through the omission of v. 29, begins Marenzio's *seconda parte*.

Marenzio begins his madrigal not with Mirtillo's address to spring ("O primavera"), but fifteen verses later, with his cry to bittersweet love, thereby evoking the *amar* puns from the start of *Cruda Amarilli* with the lines "O dolcezze *amar*issime d'*amore*" and "Come saria l'*amar* felice stato." The madrigal depicts the oxymoronic image of love's "dolcezze amarissime" (most bitter sweetness) with the bold harmonic motions, chromaticism, and dizzying modal uncertainty of its opening sonorities: C–E–b–G^6–d–A^6 (mm. 1–9). This striking early turn toward distant sharp sonorities establishes the association between the notion of sweetness (*dolce*) and the *durus* (sharp) realm that returns saliently later in the piece, when "dolcezze" (mm. 95–96) yields the sonorities D–B, and "se non dolci, almen fère" (mm. 114–20) turns from an evaded G cadence to another unorthodox, dizzying passage that leads f♯^{6}–B^7–E$_4^6$...–f♯^{7}–G$_{♯7}^9$–A$^{6♯−5}$ before closing on D. Wert takes the very opposite approach to *dolce*, matching each occurrence with *mollis* (flatward) turns: for example, alternating G-major and C-minor sonorities at "dolcezze amarissime" (mm. 37–39), motion from G-minor to E♭ and B♭ at "Qui pur da le dolcezze" (mm. 95–97), and repeated B♭ cadences at "Se non dolci" (mm. 104–108).

Equally striking at the surface level of Marenzio's setting are the dissonances, many of which lack proper preparation or resolution. A prominent (though contrapuntally "correct") example is the cluster of "wicked" inverted and seventh sonorities at the end of "Qui pur vedrò quell'empia" that form the succession d–G$_5^6$–C–D$_2^4$–G^6 (mm. 107–10). Incidental augmented sonorities occasionally arise in Marenzio's output as part of cadential approaches, typically as a result of a ♭6–5 suspension or neighboring motion 5–♭6–5 over a pre-cadential ("V") sonority. In *O dolcezze amarissime*, however, these augmented sonorities arise in one instance without such preparation (and without proper resolution) as part of a pre-cadential approach (mm. 55–56), as expected, but in another instance outside of any cadential motion (mm. 25–27), where a dissonant *f″* preempts the coming D-minor by sounding above an A-major sonority. These highly dissonant formations seem to have caught the attention of Marenzio's Mantuan contemporary, Benedetto Pallavicino, who, as we shall see, uses them for expressive purposes in his own *Pastor fido* settings and other madrigals of 1600.

Operating beneath these pronounced dissonances, *durus* shifts, and other foreground features is the end-directed impulse of the C-hypolydian *diapente* descent, *g"–c"*. Like his *Cruda Amarilli*, Marenzio's *O dolcezze amarissime* expands the primary structural degree, *g"*, across the entire *prima parte*, but generates tension and forward thrust through its displacement by a middleground upper neighbor, *a"* (see Example 5.19). The disruption engenders a clear change of mode in mm. 43–61 from C-hypolydian (occupying a G octave) to D-hypodorian (occupying an A octave), which carries with it the accentuation of the new, foreign boundaries and cadence pitches, D and A. This modal–structural digression, moreover, aligns precisely with the speaker's admission of his habitual self-doubt in vv. 23–24 ("But if my hopes are not today of fragile glass, as is their custom...") and subsides with a restoration of *g"* and the true mode at the more optimistic projection that ends the *prima parte*: "Here yet I will see her, who is the sun of my eyes" (mm. 61–68). At this moment, four of the five voices articulate the reinstated $\hat{5}$ (in varying registers) with upward leaps that link the structural pitch to the beloved sun (*sol*) and to a solmization pun that sets "ch'è'l sol" in most instances as *re–sol* (D–G). The image of the "sun" is even evoked pictorially on the page—as an example of *Augenmusik* (eye-music)—with the setting of "sol" in most cases as a high semibreve (sometimes dotted). The Canto highlights the shift here from the A octave (centered on D) back to the G octave (centered locally on G) by supplanting the leap *a'–d"* immediately with *d"–g"* in mm. 61–62.

Marenzio presents the final verse twice at the end of the *prima parte*, with both statements leading to the cofinal, G—an unusual design given that most endings with paired statements of verse, including those of Marenzio, cadence first on the fifth above (or in some cases below) and then on the local final. When the very same verse-ending ("il sol degl'occhi miei") returns at

Example 5.19 Marenzio, *O dolcezze amarissime d'amore*, Structural Analysis

the end of the madrigal, Marenzio again depicts "sol" in symbolic semibreves and hexachordally as *sol*, first in homophony with a G sonority—where G and D both represent *sol* in the C and G hexachords, respectively (mm. 154–55)—then contrapuntally with leaps to g' and g'' in the uppermost voices. The cadential planning and general texture of this conclusion further reinforce the textual parallels between the two endings by again stating the closing phrase twice in counterpoint: first *a4* without the Basso, then with all voices, both times leading to the same cadential goal, this time the final, C. Marenzio, like Wert, therefore, recognizes the rhetorical parallels in Guarini's verse as opportunities to create formal, structural, and referential symmetries in his music, and, in turn, to integrate his reading intimately with the text.

Many of the general features of Marenzio's and Wert's settings of *Cruda Amarilli* and act 3, scene 1 apply to their other *Pastor fido* settings as well. These approaches—Wert's temporal–structural stasis, and Marenzio's restive, reference-filled designs—highlight different qualities of Guarini's verse: Wert, the accentual patterns, imagery, and exploration of a unifying mood or sentiment; Marenzio, the poet's integrated wordplay, rhetorical–formal escalation toward a culminating conceit, and the steady revelation of the internal struggles and motivations of his characters.

In terms of their priorities as readers, Wert in most cases takes a more formalistic approach, privileging the integrity of the versification over semantic and grammatical units, while Marenzio more often observes sense and syntax over form. Hence, in verses 1–2 of *Cruda Amarilli* ("che col nome ancora / d'amar, ahi lasso..."), Wert breaks the musical phrases according to the line break, whereas Marenzio follows the grammatical phrasing by overriding Guarini's lineation and enjambment ("che col nome ancora d'amar / ahi lasso..."). Later in the madrigal, Wert emphasizes the break between the enjambed lines 10–11 ("E questa selva a cui / Si spesso il tuo bel nome") with a non-cadential pause and rests in all voices, whereas Marenzio again downplays the enjambment with continuous motion through the line break in three of the five voices. Yet, in spite of his reimposition of the grammatical unit across the line break, Marenzio nevertheless preserves the *settenario* meter of verse 10 by setting the final word, "cui," as two syllables, rather than as a diphthong.

Marenzio does the very same thing in *O dolcezze amarissime* as well. Verses 16–17 of the scene read "Quanto è più duro perdervi, che mai / Non v'haver o provate o possedute" (see the *O primavera* text above). A grammatical break clearly separates "perdervi" and "che mai" in verse 16, and the latter phrase continues in verse 17 as an enjambment. Wert marks the text's line-ending at "mai" with a *mi* cadence, followed by rests in his *O primavera*. But Marenzio partitions his musical–textual phrases according to syntax, not lineation—to the effect "Quanto è più duro perdervi, / che mai non..."—while again keeping the syllable count intact by dividing "mai" into two syllables. In setting the consecutive enjambments in vv. 40–42 of the same text, both composers take the same approach of following the line break at vv.

40–41, but inserting a break in the middle of v. 41 in order to splice the enjambment of vv. 41–42 into a single phrase. The musical settings, therefore, stress the phrasing "O lungamente sospirato invano / Avventuroso dì / se dopo tanti foschi giorni"—which, in fact, agrees grammatically with Wert's (mis)reading of the initial "O" as "Ho," making "sospirato" a past participle (rather than an adjective). Finally, verses 3–4 of *Ah, dolente partita* ("Da te parto e non moro? E pur i' provo / La pena de la morte") again show both composers dismissing line breaks in order to follow syntax. The splitting of the synalepha (merging of two syllables) at the end of the first, seven-syllable hemistich, "moro? E," however, creates a twelve-syllable line out of the hendecasyllabic verse 3 and shifts its distinctive tenth-syllable accent to the eleventh syllable. While Wert does the latter, thereby upsetting the poetic meter, Marenzio again shows concern for upholding the integrity of the *endecasillabo*, even while breaking from the play's versification, by omitting "E" altogether, thus reading "Da te parto e non moro? / Pur i' provo."

My purposes in enumerating these various responses to line breaks, enjambments, and syllable count in Guarini's verse is not only to emphasize the composers' differing priorities regarding poetic form (lineation and meter) and grammatical phrasing, but also, more importantly, to show how these priorities reflect their broader modes of presenting the text. Wert's preference for demarcating verses rather than grammatical divisions, for example, enhances the effect of his *Pastor fido* madrigals as sounded visualizations of the page. Just as *contrapposto* mimics the ocular act of reading by superimposing the verses vertically and interchanging them linearly, and the static structures and natural speech rhythms create an effect of lyric reflection or a stationary vignette, Wert's adherence to the written versification likewise accentuates the formal, visual qualities of the verse. Marenzio shows no such deference to formal layout when the sense and phrasing of the text are at stake, leading him more often to split the play's verses and fuse its enjambments. Yet, while the Roman composer's concern for the semantic over the formal follows in line with his attention to matching musical and textual rhetoric, he nevertheless upholds the defined meter of individual verses, even when the boundaries of these verses are redrawn in the musical phrases. Meanwhile, the successive tensions and teleological drive of his dynamic structures animate the text and its speaking persona in their exploration of affective states, impulses, and struggles (and of the poem's linguistic gambits and subtexts) as a process of performative and exegetical reading.

The impacts of Marenzio's and Wert's settings in the next stages of the *Pastor fido* madrigal run broad and deep, ranging from their texts and variants to their manners of rendering and presenting the works in their madrigal books. Indeed, the impressive wave of settings that follows from Mantua in the late 1590s and early 1600s bears these influences in subtle and prominent ways, from their handling of mode, structure, texture, and textual–motivic references, to their approaches to intertextuality within and between musical and textual works. Moreover, several of these later composers have likewise been crudely typecast, and their works, unfairly represented in modern scholarship, with Monteverdi, for example, installed at a prominent junction in the tired teleology leading from madrigal to opera and from modality to tonality, and Gastoldi lodged in a niche of "light" dance-type music owing to his immensely popular collections of *balletti*. The close consideration of their *Pastor fido* settings, however, reveals other technical and interpretative dimensions of these composers and their Manuan contemporaries, while also shedding new light on the legacies and importance of Guarini's tragicomedy and Marenzio's and Wert's works in the late-Renaissance madrigal. The next chapter turns to Monteverdi, where we will see that important achievements of his *Pastor fido* settings lie not only in their expressive reach and bold departures from theoretical norms, but also in their affective and playful use of the madrigal as a means of discourse, and in his distinctive handling of two vital frameworks that have been downplayed in most modern analyses: modality and the polyphonic fabric.

Notes

1 Claudio Pari, *Il terzo libro de' madrigali a cinque voci* (Palermo: Giovanni Battista Maringo, 1616). The print is dated 1616 on the title page, but Pari's dedication is signed 2 January 1617 (Palermo). The madrigal, with its opening reference to Aminta's blade ("ferro"), may be an allusion to the book's dedicatee, Berardo Ferro of Sicily. On the compelling links between Pari's Third Book and Monteverdi's Fifth Book, see Chapter 7 below.

2 "Fatti con più sorte di stile, & inventioni nove da nessuno usate; e con obligo grande di fughe, osservatione del contrapunto, & imitatione delle parole" (Pari, *Terzo libro*, title page).

3 This e''–a' structural motion lends support to the interpretation of the conclusion of verse 2 as a *clausula in mi* on A, where the Basso does not support the cadential goal, but instead upholds the association of "amante" with "Aminta" with a rising-fifth motion.

4 A deictic may function as a personal ("I" or "you," for example), temporal ("now," "then"), or spatial ("here," "there") gesture, and may indicate either distally (outwardly) or proximally (inwardly). Mauro Calcagno has explored the use of deictics in Monteverdi's operas in his *From Madrigal to Opera*, Chapters 4–6.

5 Meier notes that "if we consider the musical ranges of soprano melodies, we in fact discover that a soprano ascending to a'' is unusual even late in the sixteenth century—and even in a mode that intrinsically requires this ascent," such as the A-dorian mode here. Meier, *The Modes of Classical Vocal Polyphony*, 73–74.

6 Even the echo "amato" (mm. 44–45) is given little emphasis, though vestiges of the "Aminta" motives survive—the a–d' ascending fourth of the Tenore (a weakened, inverted echo of the earlier fifths), the neighboring semitone motion e'–f'–e' of the Quinto, and the rhythmic delay of a single voice for the last syllable. Once again, this "Aminta" echo contains a *clausula in mi* between the Canto and an inner voice—this time leading to E—which is undermined by the contrapuntal support. This vague reminiscence marks the first reference to Aminta by the narrator, which comes in the form of the metonym "tardi amato petto."

7 For this reason, James Chater titled his study of *Cruda Amarilli* settings "'Cruda Amarilli': A Cross-Section of the Italian Madrigal," *Musical Times* 116 (1975): 231–34.

8 For a background on the debate, see Claude Palisca, "The Artusi–Monteverdi Controversy," *The New Monteverdi Companion*, eds. D. Arnold and N. Fortune (London: Faber, 1985), 127–58. Examining in closer detail the rhetoric, cultural setting, and politics of the controversy are Tim Carter's "Artusi, Monteverdi, and the Poetics of Modern Music," *Musical Humanism and its Legacy: Essays in Honor of Claude V. Palisca*, eds. N.K. Baker and B.R. Hanning (Stuyvesant, NY: Pendragon Press, 1992), 171–94 and Susanne Cusick's "Gendering Modern Music: Thoughts on the Monteverdi–Artusi Controversy," *Journal of the American Musicological Society* 46 (1993): 1–25.

9 Monteverdi's pronouncement of a "second practice" appeared first in a postscript (to the "studiosi lettori") to his Fifth Book of madrigals (1605), which was glossed in Giulio Cesare Monteverdi's *Dichiaratione* appended to the end of Claudio Monteverdi's *Scherzi musicali* (1607); trans. in Oliver Strunk, *Source Readings*, 540. See Chapter 5.

10 Alfred Einstein, *The Italian Madrigal*, II, 678–79. Einstein also cites the similarities of the opening phrases and the treatments of verses 3–4 ("del candido ligustro / Più candida e più bella") in the two madrigals, yet emphasizes the contrasting stylistic currents from which the two settings arose:

> The similarities are as characteristic as the differences, and it is more characteristic that while Monteverdi rests his a cappella composition on a bass which will soon become a basso continuo, Marenzio remains within the stylistic limits of his more refined and nobler century, a century of vocality.
>
> (680)

11 Chater, "Cruda Amarilli," 233–34. Chater notes, for example, that "there is plenty of evidence that Pallavicino was influenced by [Marenzio]," including: the opening phrase, "i' mi morrò" (where Pallavicino inverts Marenzio's setting), the rhythm at "Amarilli del candido ... bella" and "e se fia muta ogn'altra cosa al fine," the openings of the *seconde parti*, and "la pietade" (233). Chater concludes that it was more than anything Marenzio's "flexible, expressive declamation which left its mark on Pallavicino, as his rhythmic borrowings show." On Pallavicino's setting, see Chapter 8.

12 Gary Tomlinson, for example, entertains that "Wert may even have initiated the rivalry" in setting common *Pastor fido* passages in the mid- to late-1590s, in *Monteverdi and the End of the Renaissance*, 117. Ossi builds on Tomlinson's hypothesis by stressing the possibility "that when he travelled to Rome in 1593 Guarini may have taken some of Wert's madrigals with him, including *Cruda Amarilli*," and, in turn, "the unlikelihood that Marenzio's setting might have been brought to Wert's attention in Mantua in the 1590s" ("Monteverdi, Marenzio, and Battista Guarini's 'Cruda Amarilli'," *Music and Letters* 89 [2008]: 311–36, at 331). Ossi notes that Wert, too, might have had access to unpublished drafts of the play in the 1580s during the composer's frequent visits to Ferrara, but does not account for discrepancies between extant drafts of the play from that period and the texts of Wert's madrigals, including especially *Cruda Amarilli*, where several passages are lacking from all pre-publication versions (discussed below).

13 Charles S. Brauner, for example, writes: "Monteverdi's setting of this text is similar to those of Wert, Marenzio, and Pallavicino, in what looks like a four-way competition. However, unlike the others, he made of the opening, drooping line a recurring, unifying motif." Brauner, "The *Seconda Pratica*, or the Imperfections of the Composer's Voice," in Nancy K. Baker and Barbara Hanning, eds. *Musical Humanism and its Legacy: Essays in Honor of Claude V. Palisca*, Festschrift Series No. 11 (Stuyvesant, NY: Pendragon Press, 1992), 195–212, at 208.

14 Einstein and Chater, for instance, fail even to acknowledge the mode of each setting, while Ossi cites only the final and system—or in the case of Marenzio's

work, simply that it ends "ambiguously on a plagal cadence to E major" ("Monteverdi, Marenzio, and Battista Guarini's 'Cruda Amarilli'," 320).

15 Regarding the suitability of the passage to the lyric tradition, Chater writes: "Indeed the speech, in its treatment of generalized, universal emotion ["unfulfilled desire"], has a feeling of being self-contained. For what it tells us of Mirtillo, it could have come from any pastoral drama. His predicament is sufficiently generalized and universal for him to be considered a stock Arcadian character expressing stock literary emotions" ("'Cruda Amarilli': A Cross-Section," 231).

16 Monte's earlier (1590) setting of a highly variant form of the text begins with a version of verse 5, "O d'aspido più sorda e più fugace," and ends with the analogue of verse 20, "Vi dirò il mio martire."

17 As early as 1601, Guarini's proponent Savio praised the wordplay of these verses in his *Apologia...in difesa del Pastor fido,* comparing the descriptions of Amarilli later in the passage to Virgil's *Eclogues,* and Mirtillo's doleful silence to the myth of Pan and Syrinx. He asserts that the passage is essential to the play and should not have been cut from the November 1598 performance in Mantua (Guarini, *Opere,* IV, 439).

18 $\hat{6}$ (C) represents the reciting pitch of the E-phrygian mode, and $\hat{4}$ (A), the reciting pitch of the collateral E-hypophrygian mode. Both pitches, however, play prominent roles in both modes melodically, cadentially, and harmonically, but typically with greater influence given to A ($\hat{4}$).

19 In his *Musica Poetica* (1606), German theorist Joachim Burmeister terms this manner of extension of a final cadence by sustaining the final with changing (yet supporting) sonorities *supplementum:* "the elaboration of a final pitch in a stationary voice," whereby "the various pitches in the other voices, which are united in harmony with it, create consonances with it" (Chapter 9). See Burmeister, *Musical Poetics,* 151.

20 On the phrygian mode, its cadential forms, and its background structure, see Seth Coluzzi, "Black Sheep: The Phrygian Mode and a Misplaced Madrigal in Marenzio's Seventh Book (1595)," *Journal of Musicology* 30 (2013): 129–79.

21 Susan McClary, *Modal Subjectivities,* 97–98. See also the works cited in Coluzzi, "Black Sheep," esp. 129–30.

22 Chater devotes considerable attention to Marenzio's use of this archaic form of cadence:

> In none of the settings under discussion is there anything comparable to the harmonic refinement at the cadence... Although justified by the contrapuntal movement of the voices, it is a highly individual and unexpected gesture. Other composers resort to the simpler expedient of dissonance. Thus, Wert starts boldly with an unprepared 4th between the leading voices; Monteverdi uses accented dissonances; and Pallavicino and d'India start with an identical A/B♭ clash on the first entry. Only Marenzio matches Guarini's virtuosity with real ingenuity.
>
> ("'Cruda Amarilli': A Cross-Section," 231–33)

23 The *amar* in "amaramente" even incorporates a musical pun by evoking the second statement and double-leading-tone cadence of "Cruda Amarilli" in mm. 8–9 with an evaded double-leading-tone cadence to D with the very same voicing in mm. 18–19.

24 In terms of the fundamental structures of the two modes, both interpretations are equally viable at this stage: E appears poised to descend either a *diapente* to A ($\hat{5}$–$\hat{1}$) or a *diatessaron* to B ($\hat{8}$–$\hat{5}$) across the work. The ambiguity created generally by the opening expansion of E in phrygian-mode works like this one, with the customary prevalence of A and C as cadential goals and sonorities, represents the crux of the A-aeolian/E-phrygian dilemma in

Renaissance and present-day modal theory and analysis. Phrygian works that appear to affirm A as final in their openings (as Marenzio's madrigal does) eventually conclude on E—often with the a–E phrygian quasi-cadence—thereby misleading analysts into regarding them as A-aeolian (or A-dorian) pieces that end on 5̂ with an anachronistic "half cadence." Peter Bergquist, in his analysis of Agricola's phrygian-mode *Allez mon cueur*, for instance, determines that "it is definitely in some combination of aeolian and minor modes," relegating the final twelve bars leading to E as a "coda" that is "appended to the main harmonic movements of the piece" (Bergquist, "Mode and Polyphony around 1500: Theory and Practice," *The Music Forum* 1 [1967]: 99–161). See also McClary's *Modal Subjectivities*, particularly her analyses of *mi*-final works, including Verdelot's *Sì soave è l'inganna* and *O dolce notte* (44–53), Willaert's *Lasso ch'i' ardo* (95–100), and Marenzio's *Tirsi morir volea* (138–43), all of which McClary views as A-final works with endings on the "dominant."

25 Alfred Einstein uses this setting of the final verse as an illustration of the "harmonic intensity" characteristic of the Seventh Book as a whole. Einstein writes:

> These are progressions and suspensions of the most unusual sort, yet they are logical; they are not hatched out on one of those 'chromatic' or 'enharmonic' keyed instruments that had existed since Vicentino or Zarlino, but conceived in a pure and completely vocal idiom.
>
> (*The Italian Madrigal*, II, 678–79)

26 The cadence in mm. 8–9 has been perpetually mis-transcribed and, consequently, misinterpreted following an error in Carol MacClintock and Melvin Bernstein's edition of the work, which has an F in the Basso of m. 8 (Giaches de Wert, *L'undecimo libro de' madrigali a cinque voci*, in C. MacClintock and M. Bernstein, eds., *Opera omnia*, vol. 12 [Münster: American Institute of Musicology, 1972], 43). The resulting sonority—a "V_2^4" leading to C—would indeed be extraordinary, but the 1595 Basso partbook clearly shows a dotted breve on G, not F, moving directly to C. The same error occurs again in m. 16 of MacClintock and Bernstein's edition of the piece—creating a b°$_4^6$ in place of a G sonority leading to C^6—and yet again in their edition of *Che fai alma?*, the last madrigal of Wert's Eleventh Book, where the Basso's cadence F–B♭ appears as E♭–B♭, again yielding an erroneous "V_2^4–I."

27 Wert turns routinely to chromatic imitative counterpoint for setting doleful expressions. In *Ecco ch'un altra volta* from his Ninth Book (1588), for example, the mention of "lagrime" (tears) in the final verse brings chromatic descents through a minor third from 1̂ (F) and 5̂ (C). *Mia benigna fortuna*, also from the Ninth Book, contrasts the beginning and end of the verse "Ma di menar tutta mia vita in pianto" (but to lead all my life in tears) with a line that rises and falls chromatically. His *Pastor fido* setting *O primavera gioventù dell'anno* (1595) deploys the same tactic as *Ecco ch'un altra volta*, descending in chromatic thirds at "misera e dolente" (miserable and painful). The device recalls Giuseppe Caimo's setting of "a pianger volta" in his *E se tu riva udisti alcuna volta* from some thirty years earlier (1564). See Einstein, *The Italian Madrigal*, II, 562–63.

28 In his discussion of the "Cruda Amarilli" tradition, Chater compares this focus on the images of the text in Wert's setting to Marenzio's captivation of the overall affect:

> The prevailing somber mood [of Marenzio's setting with two tenori] precludes any attempt to depict nature in such vivid tones as Wert's. His mountains rise, but not very steeply; his forests and winds are surprisingly muted. But his 'ahi lasso' (bar 13) is more dissonant, while his emphasis on

'piangendo' and 'lamenti' reveals his concern for the profounder emotions, as opposed to Wert's interest in the physical world.

("'Cruda Amarilli': A Cross-Section," 234)

29 In comparing the two composers' settings of Tasso's *Giunto alla tomba*, Einstein writes: "Marenzio outbids Wert but does not outdo him. He is no dramatist; what matters to him as a virtuoso is picturesque description... He is less concerned with emotion than with artifice—one might almost say, with dexterity" (*The Italian Madrigal*, II, 683). Jessie Ann Owens, after comparing their settings of Guarini's *Vezzosi augelli in fra le verdi fronde* and Tasso's *Giunto alla tomba*, concludes: "In effect, Marenzio reads the words, Wert the poem" ("Marenzio and Wert Read Tasso: A Study in Contrasting Aesthetics," *Early Music* 27 [1999]: 555–74).

30 Gary Tomlinson traces this use of recitational homophony, syllabic text-setting, and harmonic and textural variety in Wert's later work to his earlier Ariosto settings, whose techniques seem to derive from oral traditions for reciting epic poetry, such as *arie per cantar ottave*. See Tomlinson, *Monteverdi and the End of the Renaissance*, 60–67.

31 Owens, "Marenzio and Wert Read Tasso," 569.

32 Of Wert's *Vezzosi augelli in fra le verdi fronde* (1586)—a setting from Tasso's *Gerusalemme liberata*—for instance, Owens writes that "the repetitions and the combinations of phrases transform the text from something that could be narrated by a single reader into a miniature drama" ("Marenzio and Wert Read Tasso," 561). To contrast this effect of a "miniature drama" in *Vezzosi augelli*, Owens cites Howard Mayer Brown's assessment of another setting from Tasso's epic, Wert's *Giunto alla tomba, ove al suo spirto vivo* (1581), where Brown distinguishes the it in depicting the character Tancredi's "overwhelming grief," Wert "does not offer a direct dramatization of the scene, because he was working with a polyphonic network of voices," but instead creates "a stylized dramatization of Tancredi's emotional state." Howard Mayer Brown, "Genre, Harmony, and Rhetoric in the Late Sixteenth-Century Italian Madrigal," in J.R. Brink and W.F. Gentrup, eds., *Renaissance Culture in Context: Theory and Practice* (Brookfield, VT: Ashgate, 1993), 198–225, at 200. Though Brown seems to remain mindful of the lyric nature of the madrigal, using the phrase "polyphonic network of voices" in the general sense of having multiple voices, Owens evidently took the phrase as referring specifically to imitative texture. Hence, Owens responds to Brown by stating that, indeed, "in *Vezzosi augelli* Wert can 'offer a direct dramatization of the scene' by creating musical *personae*" ("Marenzio and Wert Read Tasso," 563), each of which is rendered by a specific grouping of voices in homorhythmic (i.e., non-imitative) texture.

33 In addressing settings of dialogic and theatrical, rather than single-speaker lyric, texts, Calcagno proposes that in such works, "composers were able to empower performers to become in effect flesh-and-blood characters, not merely conveyors of 'readings' or 'exegeses'" (*From Madrigal to Opera*, 101).

34 Richard Freedman, "Marenzio's *Madrigali a quattro, cinque et sei voci* of 1588: A Newly-Revealed Madrigal Cycle and Its Intellectual Context," *Journal of Musicology* 13 (1995): 318–54.

35 James Haar, "The *Madrigali a quattro, cinque et sei voci* of 1588: Marenzio's 'maniera assai differente dalla passata'," in Mauro Calcagno, ed., *Perspectives on Luca Marenzio's Secular Music*, in series *Epitome musical* (Turnhout: Brepols, 2014), 31–49.

36 See James Chater, "Fonti poetiche" and Gerbino, *Music and the Myth*, 361–64, cited in Chapter 4, note 48 above.

37 Myers, Introduction to Luca Marenzio, *Il settimo libro de' madrigali a cinque voci (1595)*, in Patricia Myers, ed., *Marenzio, the Secular Works*, vol. 14 (New York: Broude Bros., 1980), xiv–xv.
38 Myers, Introduction to Marenzio, *Il settimo libro*, xxiii.
39 Ossi, "Monteverdi, Marenzio, and Battista Guarini's 'Cruda Amarilli'," 332–33.
40 See Coluzzi, "Black Sheep," 162–79.
41 James Chater notes that a primary reason for modifying verses in the early settings from the play, "apart from dependence on earlier sources, would appear to be a perceived need to create a greater incidence of rhyme." In the texts favored by later composers, including Wert, Marenzio, and Monteverdi, however, rhyme is generally less prevalent, though the concluding rhymed couplet remains a widespread feature, whether these couplets derive from the play itself or from alternative versions or modifications. See Chater, "Un pasticcio di madrigaletti," esp. 151–53.

References

Bergquist, Peter. "Mode and Polyphony around 1500: Theory and Practice." *The Music Forum* 1 (1967): 99–161.

Brauner, Charles. "The *Seconda Pratica*, or the Imperfections of the Composer's Voice." In *Musical Humanism and its Legacy: Essays in Honor of Claude V. Palisca*, eds. Nancy K. Baker and Barbara Hanning, 195–212. Stuyvesant, NY: Pendragon Press, 1992.

Brown, Howard Mayer. "Genre, Harmony, and Rhetoric in the Late Sixteenth-Century Italian Madrigal." In *Renaissance Culture in Context: Theory and Practice*, eds. J.R. Brink and W.F. Gentrup, 198–225. Brookfield, VT: Ashgate, 1993.

Burmeister, Joachim. *Musica poetica*. Rostock: Stephan Myliander, 1606. Trans. by Benito Rivera as *Musical Poetics*. New Haven, CT: Yale University Press, 1993.

Calcagno, Mauro. *From Madrigal to Opera: Monteverdi's Staging of the Self*. Berkeley: University of California Press, 2012.

Carter, Tim. "Artusi, Monteverdi, and the Poetics of Modern Music." In *Musical Humanism and its Legacy: Essays in Honor of Claude V. Palisca*, eds. N.K. Baker and B.R. Hanning, 171–94. Stuyvesant, NY: Pendragon Press, 1992.

Chater, James. "Fonti poetiche per i madrigali di Luca Marenzio." *Rivista italiana di musicologia* 13 (1978): 60–103.

———. "'Cruda Amarilli': A Cross-Section of the Italian Madrigal." *Musical Times* 116 (1975): 231–34.

Coluzzi, Seth. "Black Sheep: The Phrygian Mode and a Misplaced Madrigal in Marenzio's Seventh Book (1595)." *Journal of Musicology* 30 (2013): 129–79.

Cusick, Susanne. "Gendering Modern Music: Thoughts on the Monteverdi–Artusi Controversy." *Journal of the American Musicological Society* 46 (1993): 1–25.

Einstein, Alfred. *The Italian Madrigal*. Trans. by A.H. Krappe, R.H. Sessions, and O. Strunk. 3 vols. Princeton, NJ: Princeton University Press, 1949.

Freedman, Richard. "Marenzio's *Madrigali a quattro, cinque et sei voci* of 1588: A Newly-Revealed Madrigal Cycle and Its Intellectual Context." *Journal of Musicology* 13 (1995): 318–54.

Gerbino, Giuseppe. *Music and the Myth of Arcadia in Renaissance Italy*. Cambridge: Cambridge University Press, 2009.

Guarini, Battista. *Delle opere del cavalier Battista Guarini.* Eds. G.A. Barotti and A. Zeno. 4 vols. Verona: Tumermani, 1737–38.

Haar, James. "The *Madrigali a quattro, cinque et sei voci* of 1588: Marenzio's 'maniera assai differente dalla passata'." In *Perspectives on Luca Marenzio's Secular Music,* ed. Mauro Calcagno, 31–49. In series *Epitome musical.* Turnhout: Brepols, 2014.

Marenzio, Luca. *Il settimo libro de' madrigali a cinque voci.* Venice: Gardano, 1595. Ed. by Patricia Myers in *Marenzio, the Secular Works.* Vol. 14. New York: Broude Brothers, 1980.

McClary, Susan. *Modal Subjectivities: Self-Fashioning in the Italian Madrigal.* Berkeley: University of California Press, 2004.

Meier, Bernhard. *The Modes of Classical Vocal Polyphony, Described According to the Sources.* Trans. by Ellen Beebe. New York: Broude Brothers, 1988.

Monteverdi, Claudio. *Scherzi musicali a tre voci.* Venice: Amadino, 1607.

Ossi, Massimo. "Monteverdi, Marenzio, and Battista Guarini's 'Cruda Amarilli'." *Music and Letters* 89 (2008): 311–36.

Owens, Jessie Ann. "Marenzio and Wert Read Tasso: A Study in Contrasting Aesthetics." *Early Music* 27 (1999): 555–74.

Palisca, Claude. "The Artusi–Monteverdi Controversy." In *The New Monteverdi Companion,* eds. D. Arnold and N. Fortune, 127–58. London: Faber, 1985.

Pari, Claudio. *Il terzo libro de' madrigali a cinque voci.* Palermo: Giovanni Battista Maringo, 1616.

Strunk, Oliver. *Source Readings in Music History.* New York: Norton, 1998.

Tomlinson, Gary. *Monteverdi and the End of the Renaissance.* Oxford: Clarendon, 1987.

Wert, Giaches de. *L'undecimo libro de' madrigali a cinque voci.* Venice: Gardano, 1595. Eds. Carol MacClintock and Melvin Bernstein in Wert, *Opera omnia.* Vol. 12. Münster: American Institute of Musicology, 1972.

6 "Ahi, lasso!"

Monteverdi, *Il pastor fido*, and a New, Mantuan Controversy

Monteverdi's *Pastor fido* settings stand amidst a historic transition in the composer's career. Like Marenzio's settings, their publication followed a lengthy fallow period in Monteverdi's output of five-voice madrigals, yet most of the pieces can be securely dated to the late 1590s, some five to seven years prior to their appearance in print in the Fourth (1603) and Fifth (1605) Books. The works mark Monteverdi's earliest experiments in applying instrumental forces to the polyphonic madrigal and the overtly transgressive techniques of the *seconda pratica*, coincide with his earliest writing for accompanied solo voice at the end of the Fifth Book, and stand at the cusp of his venture into truly dramatic music with the 1607 opera *L'Orfeo*. All of these aspects of his career—together with the apparent evidence of early tonal, harmonic, and dramatic thinking in his madrigals, including especially the *Pastor fido* settings—are part of the commonplace narratives of Western music history and Monteverdi's contributions therein.

This and the following chapter, however, paint a rather different portrait of the influential composer—as one who is still forward-looking, to be sure, yet also grounded firmly in the systems of mode and counterpoint in which he was trained, who embraced and developed the techniques of his predecessors, most notably Marenzio and Wert, in ways that have not been fully recognized in his approaches to both individual works and the interconnections between them. The *Pastor fido* settings, in other words, show Monteverdi as a transformative figure who worked within the traditions of the lyric madrigal and modal polyphony, rather than breaking decisively out of them. At the same time, while the famous critical debate between the composer, Bolognese theorist Giovanni Maria Artusi, and others paralleled the second wave of the polemic over Guarini's play around 1600 and exposed similar resistance to "modern" theoretical and ideological views in music, it also brought new visibility to the play in the musical realm as a source of madrigal texts. The stern Artusi, after all, withheld the name of the imprudent composer from his initial attacks, but he notably did identify the author and textual source of all but one of the offensive madrigals: Guarini's *Pastor fido*. Albeit inadvertently, Monteverdi and Artusi—along with Denores, Summo, Malacreto, and other literary critics—therefore,

DOI: 10.4324/9781315463056-7

furthered Guarini's task of publicizing the tragicomedy among different audiences and on a grand scale. There is no indication that even this "bad" publicity did any harm to the play's marketability as a printed text or in the madrigal.

These two chapters peer between the cracks in the extensive literature on Monteverdi's *Pastor fido* settings to reveal new dimensions of the composer's compositional strategies, the Monteverdi–Artusi debate, and the Fourth and Fifth Books of madrigals. Through this analysis, the music and surrounding documents serve as snapshots of Monteverdi's activities at the Mantuan court around 1600 not only as a composer, but also as an instrumentalist—as a performer of the *viola bastarda*. Chapter 8, in turn, looks beyond Monteverdi to the undervalued settings of his Mantuan contemporaries, Pallavicino, Gastoldi, and Rossi, to situate Monteverdi's works within a broader Mantuan enterprise of providing sophisticated musical–textual readings of the tragicomedy that show at once notable innovation and individuality in their technical–expressive means, but also clear indebtedness to *Pastor fido* settings that came before—most importantly those from Rome of Marenzio, rather than from Mantua itself.

Monteverdi's Early and Variant Readings, 1592–1603

As with most of the earliest *Pastor fido* settings, Monteverdi's first engagements with texts tied to the play involve variant readings. The texts of both his *O primavera gioventù dell'anno* (Third Book, 1592) and *Quell'augellin che canta* (Fourth Book, 1603) generally follow the versions published in Varoli's *Della nova scelta di rime* (1590). In the case of *O primavera*, Varoli's reading condenses the fourteen-line passage of the play to nine verses and contains minor internal discrepancies:

Monteverdi, Book 3 (1592) [and Varoli, p. 78]	Guarini, Il pastor fido (III,1)
1 O Primavera gioventù de l'anno, 　Bella madre de' fiori, 　D'herbe novelle, e di novelli amori, 　Tu ben, lasso, ritorni, 5 Ma senza i cari giorni 　De le speranze mie.	1 O primavera gioventù de l'anno 　Bella madre de fiori, 　D'erbe novella, e di novelli amori: 　Tu torni ben, ma teco 5 Non tornano i sereni 　E fortunati dì de le miei gioie; 　Tu torni ben, tu torni, 　Ma teco altro non torna, 　Che del perduto mio caro thesoro 10 La rimembranza misera e dolente.
Tu ben sei quella, Ch'eri pur dianzi sì vezzosa e bella, Ma non son io quel che già un tempo fui, Si caro à gli occhi altrui.[1]	Tu quella sè, tu quella, Ch'eri pur dianzi sì vezzosa e bella. Ma non son'io già quel ch'un tempo fui Sì caro à gli occhi altrui.

Luzzaschi published a setting of this same (Varoli) reading for solo soprano in his *Madrigali per cantare et sonare a 1–3* (Rome: Simone Verovio, 1601), but notes in the book's title page and dedication (to Cardinal Pietro Aldobrandini) that the pieces were composed "for the music of the late Most Serene Alfonso d'Este" and "sung by those most Illustrious Ladies," the duke's "musica di Dame." They existed, then, at least prior to the duke's death in October 1597. Chater has reasoned that Varoli's version of the text and Luzzaschi's setting could date from as early as 1585, based on the fact that the change at verse 12 from "che fosti" to "ch'eri pur" appears in the M2 manuscript.[2] Chater is mistaken, however; for all the manuscript sources read "che fosti," while "ch'eri pur" enters the text only by the 1589 print. The change, therefore, must have occurred at some point between 1585 (M2) and 1589 (the first edition), meaning that 1589 is the only reliable *terminus post quem* for both Varoli's reading and Luzzaschi's madrigal.

Monteverdi's *O primavera* appeared in print three years before Wert's setting of a much longer passage that adheres to the play (discussed above). Yet the younger composer's work nevertheless betrays influences of techniques Wert had tested in earlier madrigals before applying them rigorously in his *Pastor fido* settings and elsewhere in the Eleventh Book—namely the integration of *contrapposto* within a static modal–structural framework. In fact, the piece strongly calls to mind Wert's *Ah, dolente partita* in the prevailing deployment of *contrapposto* and confined modal and harmonic sphere for a concise and rhyme-filled text.[3] Monteverdi sets six of the nine verses in *contrapposto*, using the technique to divide the first six lines into two tercets: verses 1–3 (mm. 1–28) and 4–6 (mm. 28–49). Each tercet combines a rhymed pair with one unrhymed verse and comprises a distinct semantic unit: an appeal to spring ("O Primavera...") followed by the first full clause ("Tu ben, lasso, ritorni...") that sets out the first Petrarchan contrast between the cyclicity of nature (exterior) and the lover's changed and hopeless state (interior). Thus, the impressive opening triple *contrapposto* is, indeed, a marked display of contrapuntal skill, but it is one that issues from and enhances the text.

In Monteverdi's setting, each verse corresponds in most instances to a distinct musical subject that highlights key pitches of the underlying F-lydian mode.[4] Verse 1, for example, yields octave ascents from F and C; verse 2, P5 ascents to A and C; and verse 3, sloping arches of a P4 outlining F–C–F or C–G–C. The second *contrapposto* tercet reinforces the mode and the sustained background $\hat{5}$, c'', with similar melodic outlining, while also accentuating a distinctive feature of Varoli's version of the text: its exchange of the three repetitions of "Tu torni ben" in *Il pastor fido* for two statements of "Tu ben" (verses 4 and 6). First, Monteverdi gives greater formal emphasis to the phrase by dividing the single verse 6 in Varoli, "De le speranze mie, tu ben sei quella," into two separate musical–textual phrases, the first ("De le speranze mie") included with verse 4 in the *contrapposto* episode, and the second ("Tu ben sei quella") isolated outside of it. Then, by superimposing verses 4–6 temporally and spatially in *contrapposto*, the madrigal brings verse 4 ("Tu ben, lasso, ritorni") closer to the related and newly distinguished phrase, "Tu ben sei quella," that begins the next section of text. Their new proximity in the music—only four breves apart—underscores the rhetorical parallelism (*anaphora*), as does the rearticulated dissonant suspensions at "Tu ben *sei.*" This example shows Monteverdi's attention to rhetorical and semantic details of Guarini's verse, and his willingness early on to modify the text through musical phrasing in order to match his own interpretive priorities.[5] This liberal approach to the verse stands at odds with Wert's general deference to poetic form and is a practice that will resurface elsewhere in Monteverdi's *Pastor fido* settings.

The consistent F-lydian grounding and melodic and cadential focus on the principal modal boundaries F, A-*mi*, and C throughout the extensive contrapuntal treatment of verses 1–6 and varied setting of verses 7–8 preserve the static fundamental *c″* until the last four measures of the piece (mm. 80–84), where the background falls precipitously to the final, *f*. Meanwhile, through the sustained background and polyphonic texture, rhythm becomes a crucial means of expressive contrast at three key points in the setting. First, a pronounced change in rhythmic character accentuates the affective shift from the sprightly *fusae* (eighth notes), "youthful spring," and "new loves" of the first *contrapposto* (vv. 1–3), to the slower, measured steps for spring's despairing return "without the dear days of my hopes" in the second (vv. 4–6). A similar rhythmic shift reflects the change from spring's "fair and beautiful" nature of the past (v. 7), set with animated rhythms and melismas at "bella," to the speaker's changed, dejected self (v. 8), presented with plodding minims and semiminims. This dichotomy is also given emphasis in the text through the various forms in close proximity of the verb *essere* (to be): from the imperfect for spring's former hope—"ch'*eri* pur dianzi" (that you *were* before)—to the speaker's own present state—"ma non *son* io" (but I *am* not)—contrasted, in turn, with what he was in the past—"quel che già un tempo *fui*" (what I once *was*).

Whereas the expansive (forty-five-line) excerpt from the scene set by Wert presents a variety of subjects (spring, love, hope, the awaited beloved), the succinct Varoli reading treated by Monteverdi focuses more intently on aspects of time: spring, the cyclicity of the days and seasons, aging, and loss of the past. Monteverdi's madrigal, in turn, explores these contrasting perspectives of time through temporal contrasts on different levels of the music, from surface rhythms and melodic contour to large-scale structure. The *contrapposto* opening (mm. 1–28), for example, renders the dichotomy between the cyclicity of the seasons—with combined subjects that fall (verse 1) and rise (verse 2)—and time's seeming standstill for both spring (in its eternal youth) and Mirtillo (in anticipation of Amarilli)—through the perpetual support of background *c″*. This cyclical balance continues in verses 4–6 as steady descents in semibreves and minims for "Tu ben lasso" counter the stepwise M9 ascents at "Ma senza i cari giorni de le speranze" (mm. 28–49). The notion of spring—the "fair mother of flowers" (Bella madre di fiori)—as rejuvenation likewise takes shape in the cadential elisions that result as the words "Bella madre" enter at or just before the moment of arrival. (See, for example, the elided cadences to A-*mi* in mm. 5 and 20 and to C in m. 16.) Meanwhile, on the broader scale, the distinction between the lively rhythms and continuous contrapuntal motion at the surface and the sustained background evoke the disparity in the text between interior and exterior, between the speaker's agitated mind and the calm passage of time in nature.

Monteverdi's setting of the elder Linco's lesson to Silvio about the natural ways of love from act 1, scene 2, *Quell'augellin che canta*, appeared in his Fourth Book of 1603, after a gap of eleven years since the Third Book. The text appears to represent an intermediate point between Monteverdi's use of independent poems published by Varoli (like *O primavera*) and passages plainly drawn from Guarini's play. As James Chater observes, the madrigal text seems to conflate readings of both sources: whereas verses 1–7 follow the play, verses 8–11 resemble the variant poem from Varoli's edition (entitled *Dolce canoro, e garulo Augelletto*), only changing the pronouns in vv. 8–9 from second to third person.[6] The madrigal's reading (like the Varoli poem), therefore, omits several lines from the play and tacks a rhyming couplet onto the end. The penultimate line, in fact, may contain a subtle reference to the compiler of the poetic anthology, Benedetto Varoli, thus reading: "For you are *Benedetto* [blessed], loving, kind, fair little bird."

Monteverdi, Fourth Book (1603)	*Guarini,* Il pastor fido *(act 1, scene 2)*
1 Quel Augellin, che canta	Quell'augellin, che canta
Sì dolcemente e lascivetto vola	Sì dolcemente e lascivetto vola
Hor da l'habete al faggio	Hor da l'abete al faggio
Et hor dal faggio al mirto.	Et hor dal faggio al mirto.
5 S'havesse humano spirto,	S'havesse humano spirto,
Direbb', "Ardo d'amor, ardo d'amore."	Direbbe, "Ardo d'amor, ardo d'amore."
Ma ben arde nel core	Ma ben arde nel core
E chiama il suo desio	E parla in sua favella,
Che li rispond', "Ardo d'amor anch'io	Sì che l'intende il suo dolce desio.
10 Che sii tu benedetto	Et odi a punto, Silvio,
Amoroso gentil vago augelletto.	Il suo dolce desio
	Che gli risponde, "Ardo d'amor anch'io."

Gary Tomlinson has argued that the madrigal looks back stylistically to the composer's previous books of the early 1590s, with its "predilection for slowly descending basslines supporting melismas in the voices above."[7] But Monteverdi's treatment also evokes influences from more recent *Pastor fido* settings of both Marenzio and Wert—the former in the extended opening trio and canzonetta-like texture of his 1595 setting of the same text, and the latter in the chiefly homophonic setting, choice of mode (G-hypodorian), and metrical and textural distinction of the Tenore from the other voices in his 1595 *O primavera*. In fact, Monteverdi's pronounced singling out of the Tenore by anticipating the homophonic block of other voices in its entrances in verses 5–8 strongly recalls Wert's approach at various points in *O primavera* (see especially the *prima parte*). The technique seems to highlight the Tenore's provisional role as narrator—or at least, as leading narrator—precisely as the text turns to the subjunctive and conditional to distinguish the bird from the human realm (if he had a human spirit, he would say...). Perhaps in response to the ingenuous simplicity of the passage, the madrigal contains no evaded cadences, only full cadences and non-cadential endings—the latter often involving motion from a G-minor sonority, such as g–D and g–F.

While the most striking features of the madrigal—such as the prominent and recurring high-voice trio; frequent roulades depicting the bird's singing, flying, and passion; and the generally spirited mood evoked by the lively rhythms and fifth-based harmonic motion—seem to place it in the vein of "light," pastoral music, the piece also conveys an undertone of pathos particularly in the numerous half-step motions. These *fa–mi* gestures surface first in the non-cadential endings mentioned above in the opening trio: the ironically somber g–D motion with $b\flat$–a' in the Canto at "dolcemente" (sweetly) and the very same motion again at "faggio" (beech tree). The Tenore gives this phrygian-like sobriety greater prominence at its solitary recitation of verse 5, "S'havesse humano spirto" (if he had a human spirit), with the motion d'–$e\flat$–d', which the Canto then echoes an octave above. Similar phrygian-like gestures appear later—such as the g–D ending, again with $b\flat$–a' Canto, at "arde nel core" (it burns in his heart) and the pair of A-*mi* cadences at "benedetto" (blessed)—altogether giving the piece a plaintive subtext perhaps rooted in the empathic conjecture "if he had a human spirit," or even suggesting the speaker's longing for a love as natural and pure as that of the *augelletti*. The madrigal, therefore, is indeed light and florid, providing a prime showcase for a trio of gifted singers such as the *concerti di donne* of the Gonzaga and Este courts. But it also hints of a greater profundity—of a reading that looks beyond the image of the loving birds to imagine a pang of discontent in the poetic voice.

At the same time, the text itself presents numerous opportunities for a composer to play with aspects of voice and perspective—especially in the madrigal and Varoli versions, which include not only the narrator's voice and the hypothetical speech of the birds ("Ardo d'amor..."), but also a closing couplet that addresses the male bird directly as second person ("Che sii tu benedetto"). Whereas Monteverdi evokes the image of a bird "that sings so sweetly and gleefully flies" throughout (particularly in the upper trio) with lively rhythms and melismas, he downplays the changes of voice from narrator to birds in vv. 6 and 9 by assimilating them texturally and grammatically into the preceding lines, without any break between narrator and bird, perhaps to highlight the fact (emphasized in the text) that birds simply cannot "speak," and that it is the narrator merely speaking for them.

Monteverdi does respond, however, to the change of address in the final couplet, as the narrator turns from describing the male bird to addressing him directly. The piece comes to a full cadence at the end of verse 9, as if taking a moment to turn physically toward the bird, then proceeds to the plaintive assurance that "you are blessed," followed by extended flourishes—the most florid in the piece, and the only ones to engage all four upper voices—that convey "vago" in its various senses: fair, wandering, and amorous.

Ah, dolente partita—the opening piece in the Fourth Book—shows the beginnings of Monteverdi's full integration of his distinctive expressive and innovatory daring with the textural and structural techniques of Marenzio and Wert for a text that agrees fully with the play. The work first appeared in Paul Kaufmann's *Fiori del giardino di diversi eccellentissimi autori* (Nuremburg, 1597) along with three other Monteverdi madrigals that had already appeared in print—in the composer's Second (1590) and Third (1592) Books. It therefore represents Monteverdi's first published and earliest known setting of a true *Pastor fido* text (given in Chapter 5 above).

The madrigal proves a *tour de force* in expressive counterpoint that expands the use of *contrapposto* from Wert's setting—where four of the eight lines are superimposed—to all of the verses but one, verse 5 ("E sento nel partire"). The result is a tumult of interweaving poetic lines and their associated melodic subjects that conveys the death-like pain and emotional confusion that the speaker confronts. This contrapuntal approach also accentuates the careful rhetoric of the speech that combines *oxymoron* in the paradoxical notion of "vivace morire" (living death), *anaphora* ("Ah"), and a concentration of rhymes and short, *settenari* verses that heightens the visual/formal pace of the verse and the sense of desperation. The text also includes a rich infusion of the consonances *P*, *M*, and *V* rooted in the basic concepts of *partire*, *morire*, and *vita*. The two hendecasyllabic verses (4 and 8) alone seem to revel in this device, with the final line broadening this unity of word-sound to the linguistic root by embedding "morte" from verse 4 in "im*mort*almente." This poetic virtuosity—together with the universal relevance of anguish at parting, the eloquence and gender neutrality of the speaking voice, and the autonomous versatility of the speech—no doubt contributed the passage's immense popularity in the musical realm, where it generated at least thirty-seven settings, more than any other text from the play, over a span of fifty years (1593–1643).

Monteverdi's repetitions and repositioning of the verses through *contrapposto* enhance this rhetorical richness by recreating musically the experience of visualizing the verses on the page and cycling back and forth, up and down, within and between the lines, as seen in Wert's setting of this and other *Pastor fido* texts. The treatment of verses 1–4 (Example 6.1) alone occupies the opening fifty-six measures (semibreves) and prolongs the primary structural pitch, e'' ($\hat{5}$ of the work's A-dorian framework), through the three-part E-*mi* cadence that concludes the section (m. 56; Example 6.2). This structural degree maintains a commanding presence and strong contrapuntal support on the foreground of this expansive opening, including in the unison *e″* in the upper voices with which the madrigal begins ("Ah, dolente partita") and in the scalar descents through the E octave and its component fifth and fourth (E–A/A–E) in various voices for verses 1–2.

In contrast to the depiction of different perspectives of time in the static background and changing surface features of *O primavera, Ah, dolente partita* renders the antithetical notion of a "living death" (un vivace morire)

Example 6.1 Monteverdi, *Ah, dolente partita,* mm. 1–15

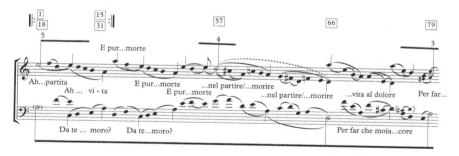

Example 6.2 Monteverdi, *Ah, dolente partita,* Structural Analysis (mm. 1–79)

with opposing surface images and impulses conveyed by an insistent background unfolding that proves more in keeping with Marenzio's dynamic structures than with the arrested temporal states common to Wert's works. The opening *contrapposto* (Example 6.1) illustrates Monteverdi's affective use of counterpoint, word-painting, and dissonance on a more local level: the madrigal (and, hence, the Fourth Book as a whole) begins with the Canto and Quinto declaiming the initial cry on a unison e'' ($\hat{5}$), when the Canto steps away by a half-step, sounding f'' against e'' and instigating a pair of dissonant 2–3 suspensions at "dolen*te partita*." This "painful parting" of the voices grows in distance, as the Quinto hovers around e'' and the Canto careens down the octave to e' with the reference to death in verse 2.[8] Verse 3, then, counters this mortal cry, rising with its antithesis ("non moro"), and in the process, thwarting several cadences that punctuate the end of verse 2 (mm. 15 and 25, for example). Measures 18–31 restate this opening in amplified form, now with four to five voices and adding the fourth verse that (in most cases) hovers on the A final before descending a P4 for the second mention of death ("la pena de la morte"). With this interweaving of poetic verses and musical subjects and the continual support of the primary $\hat{5}$ (e''), the opening *contrapposto* gives simultaneous expression to the converging effects of death, life, and painful parting that the speaker endures.

The next mention of "partire" in verse 5 (Example 6.2) evokes the notion of separation at a deeper level, as the modal background departs decisively from e'' to d''. This verse also introduces a new textural terrain of homophonic declamation for two statements of verses 5–6. This relatively brief interlude of homophonic texture otherwise foreign to the work (mm. 57–66) plays a crucial role in the madrigal's overarching scheme, for the transposition down a P5 between restatements of verses 5–6—shifting from cadences on D and A to G and D—brings about a complete octave linear descent from the new structural pitch, d'' ($\hat{4}$), to the lower register. The transition from background e'' to d'' is made explicit on the musical surface when e'', tied to the weak conjunction "e" (m. 56), is reduced from structural pitch to prefatory upper neighbor to d'' ("sento nel"); through the subsequent projection of the new structural pitch to the octave below, $d''-d'$ (mm. 54–66); and in the reorientation toward D and A as cadence goals and melodic boundaries. In terms of the text, this modal–structural shift casts the poem's reiteration of its basic premise in verses 5–6—the feeling of death that comes with parting—in a wholly new D-centered (hypodorian) context. The return of verse 6, now attached to verse 7 in a new musical guise of *parlando* rhythms and in counterpoint with verse 8 (mm. 66–83), reinforces this shift, with straightforward fifth descents toward the new background pitch, A–D, in the Canto and Quinto.

The joining of the *settenari* verses 6–7 to form a continuous fourteen-syllable phrase lends greater gravitas to the despairing end of the text and provides more balance to the *endecasyllabo* verse 8 for the final expansive episode of double-subject counterpoint (mm. 65–96). Unlike the modal–structural stasis that typifies Wert's contrapuntal combinations, the concluding *contrapposto* here drives the madrigal's fundamental structure through its remaining three steps, from d'' ($\hat{4}$) through $c''–b'–a'$ ($\hat{3}–\hat{2}–\hat{1}$). Along with the contrasting rhythmic (temporal) character of the two contrapuntal subjects—the lively rhythms of vv. 6–7 juxtaposed with the steady minims of verse 8—the melodic subject of the latter incorporates two illicit diminished-fourth leaps (usually F–C♯ and C–G♯) to the words "Per far che moia," evoking the pangs of death-like parting and foreshadowing the offensive linear dissonances that would catch Artusi's ear one year after the madrigal's appearance in 1597.

Yet, beneath the second half of this closing section is a single, protracted statement of the final verse in longer rhythms in the Basso (mm. 80–96) that leads first to a pre-cadential E lasting six semibreves in support of the background modal $\hat{2}$ (b'), followed by a sustained and repeating A that accompanies the fundamental resolution to the final, a' (mm. 89–96). The terminal background $\hat{2}–\hat{1}$, therefore, coincides with the E–A cadence in mm. 88–89, where the structural upper voice migrates from the Canto's pre-cadential b' to the Quinto's resolution to a', while the Canto overlaps the structural voice with $c\sharp''$. The remaining seven measures act as a coda, with all four upper voices restating verse 8 while sharing the role of maintaining the background a' until the final measure, passing it from Quinto (m. 89) to Canto (m. 90) to Tenore (mm. 90–91) to Alto (mm. 91–92), until the Quinto sustains it to the end (mm. 93–96). This drawn-out conclusion, embodied most in the Basso's slow-moving delivery of the final verse and restatements of "il core," offers a fitting rendering of the eternally dying heart of the wounded speaker.

Monteverdi's merging in the madrigal of the Wertian approach of *contrapposto* with deep-level motion of a dynamic structure more customary of Marenzio (as seen in the latter's setting of the same text in the collateral mode, A-hypodorian) extends the instability of the surface-level dissonances to the large scale. This "structural dissonance" of the advancing background descent presses the piece forward, conveying the urgency voiced in the text in the anticipation of long-range resolution. Whereas the text, as an isolated private reflection in the manner of a lyric poem, affords no true resolution to the speaker's despair, the madrigal fulfills its own demand for closure as a self-contained work. Yet, as the earliest datable piece of the Fourth and Fifth Books, it also shows subtle hints of Monteverdi's incendiary contrapuntal transgressions to come, not only in the d4 leaps at "che moia" in verse 8, but also in the downward leaps away from the raised "leading tones" (*subsemitonii modi*) in the Canto at "E sento nel *partire*" (mm. 56–63)—truly an agonizing "parting" for a theoretical stalwart such as Artusi. This musical license is mirrored in Monteverdi's formal reshaping of the text, where his reconfiguration of the closing verses—from 7+7+11 syllables to 14+11—alters the formal balance of Guarini's verse, giving greater weight and seriousness to the final couplet and contrapuntal episode.[9]

The first madrigal criticized by the Bolognese theorist to appear in print, *Anima mia, perdona,* stands alongside *Ah, dolente partita* in the Fourth Book in its close adherence to *Il pastor fido,* as compared to the variant reading of *Quell'augellin che canta.* The madrigal also offers a fitting transition between Monteverdi's Fourth and Fifth Books for its combined display of several key tactics deployed in the later book—including its *Pastor fido* settings—and that play a major role in Monteverdi's future compositional language, including in his approach to the *stile rappresentativo.* These strategies include (1) the manipulation of the text, (2) surface and structural voice exchanges, (3) transposed restatements of textual–musical phrases, (4) the use of motives and motivic networks for musical–textual unity and referential effect, (5) attention to the spatial presentation of the text, and, of course, (6) a provocative disregard for proper dissonant treatment. As we shall see, the opening words alone, "Anima mia, perdona," encapsulate all six of these strategies, while introducing the fundamental concern of the text: the speaker's plea for forgiveness ("perdona") for having hurt her beloved.

The madrigal text, in Monteverdi's formal setting, compares to that of the play as follows:

	Monteverdi, *Fourth Book (1603)*	Guarini, *Il pastor fido*
	1ª parte	
1	Anima mia, perdona	E tu, Mirtillo, anima mia, perdona
	A chi t'è cruda sol	A chi t'è cruda sol dove pietosa
	Dove pietosa esser non può;	Esser non può; perdona a questa, solo
	Perdona a questa,	
5	Nei detti e nel sembiante	Nei detti e nel sembiante
	Riggida tua nemica,	Rigida tua nemica, ma nel core
	Ma nel core	
	Pietosissima amante;	Pietosissima amante;
	E se pur hai desio di vendicarti,	E se pur hai desio di vendicarti;
10	Deh, qual vendett' haver puoi tu maggiore	Deh, qual vendetta aver puoi tu maggiore
	Del tuo proprio dolore?	Del tuo proprio dolore?
	2ª parte	
	Che se tu se' il cor mio,	Che se tu se' 'l cor mio,
	Come se' pur mal grado	Come se' pur malgrado
	Del ciel e de la terra,	Del cielo e de la terra,
15	Qual' hor piangi e sospiri,	Qualhor piagni e sospiri,
	Quelle lagrime tue son il mio sangue,	Quelle lagrime tue sono il mio sangue,
	Quei sospir il mio spirto	Que' sospiri il mio spirto e quelle pene
	E quelle pen'e quel dolor che senti,	E quel dolor, che senti,
	Son miei, non tuoi, tormenti.[10]	Son miei, non tuoi, tormenti.
		(III,4: 539–55)

The passage follows the lines of *O Mirtillo* in Amarilli's monologue in act 3, scene 4, where she reveals her forbidden love for Mirtillo and her remorse for her cruelty toward him, unaware that the scheming Corisca is listening nearby. Monteverdi's setting is the fourth of twelve treatments of the text, most of which—including Monteverdi's—modify the opening line, "E tu, Mirtillo, anima mia, perdona" (And you, Mirtillo, my love, forgive), to do away with its initial conjunction, pronoun, and, in many cases, its specific character reference. The first setting of the passage by Marenzio (1594), for example, begins "Deh, Tirsi, Tirsi, anima mia, perdona." The reading set by Monteverdi omits the first hemistich of verse 1 ("E tu, Mirtillo") altogether, thereby severing any explicit references to the play's personas and shortening the opening line from eleven to seven syllables. This reading reappears in later settings by Gemonese composer Marsilio Casentini (*La cieca IV a 5,* 1609) and Giovan Paolo Costa of Genoa (Second Book, 1614).

Monteverdi's formal treatment of the speech shows his growing propensity to manipulate Guarini's verse for purposes of elocution, expression, and verisimilitude. In verses 1–4, for example, the repetitions and insertions of "perdona" and restatements of verse 2, "A chi t'è cruda sol," cause the key words "perdona" and "cruda" to fill the opening twenty-two measures of the music, to the effect:

> Anima mia, perdona, perdona
> A chi t'è cruda sol, perdona, perdona,
> A chi t'è cruda sol, perdona,
> A chi t'è cruda sol
> Dove pietosa esser non può,
> Dove pietosa esser non può,
> Perdona a questa,
> Perdona a questa...

These four lines in the madrigal, furthermore, represent a rearrangement of only three lines in the play. Likewise, in the *seconda parte*, the madrigal alters Guarini's lineation by detaching the last three words of the *endecasillabo* "Quei sospiri il mio spirto, e quelle pene" (v. 17) and attaching them to the following *settenario*, "E quel dolor che senti," thereby grouping together the textual parallelism ("E quelle pen'e quel dolor") in a single verse 18 and, as in *Ah, dolente partita*, shifting the greater formal and rhetorical weight of the longer verse-length toward the end of the text. Monteverdi treats this new continuous verse as a single imitative subject that, combined with the "torments" of the final line, simulates the lovers' "pains" and "sorrow" with dissonant suspensions that grow increasingly piercing as the texture expands from two to five voices.

The opening utterance, "Anima mia, perdona," by itself combines all six of the key techniques listed above, while also anchoring the madrigal performatively and interpretatively securely in a multi-voice context. The most crucial of these tactics, voice exchange, involves transferring linear motion or a structural line between voices—especially between the two sopranos (Canto and Quinto)—to create a single composite line out of multiple voices.[11] The technique is also often tied directly to the work's notorious instances of improper dissonance treatment. A voice exchange or register transfer that separates a dissonance from its resolution is (as Artusi articulates) ineffective. Thus, Amarilli's bitterness—realized famously with illicit dissonances in Monteverdi's *Cruda Amarilli*—also takes shape through prohibited dissonances here in the setting of Amarilli's own words.

In mm. 1–3, the Canto's initial repeated *d″*—the primary tone of the work's G-hypodorian structure—becomes a rearticulated dissonance as the Basso descends to *e♭* (Example 6.3). Rather than resolve the dissonance properly by step, the Canto leaps down a P5 to *g′*, while the Quinto pronounces the resolution to *c″*. The exchanged suspension, *d″–c″*, in turn, represents the cadential preparation (*clausula cantizans*) for a phrygian close on D-*mi*. Rather than resolve *c″* upward to *d″*, as expected, while the Basso descends *e♭–d*, however, now the Quinto leaps away a dissonant d4 (*c″–f♯′*) at the cadential arrival and transfers its resolution (D) to the Alto an octave below. The effect of the opening three measures, then, is a sounding upper voice that migrates Canto (*d″*)–Quinto (*c″*)–Canto (*a′*), while the underlying D–C–D linear motion of the *clausula cantizans* moves downward through the voices from Canto (*d″*) to Quinto (*c″*) to Alto (*d′*).[12] The following phrase, "perdona / A chi t'è cruda sol" (mm. 4–6), exchanges the upper parts again, while the Tenore restates the Basso's "Anima mia, perdona" phrase a P5 higher, leading to an analogous A-*mi* cadence. The same "Anima mia, perdona" gesture returns (slightly reworked) at "quei sospir il mio spirto" in the *seconda parte* (mm. 93–95), thereby echoing the opening measures and their association with "perdona" before the closing verses.

Monteverdi, it seems, is playing games with the singers, whereby one jumps in to cover the other's contrapuntal misstep. But this gesture, with its continuation, also has interpretative significance. For, while the enlivened homophonic texture emphasizes the outer voices in these and similar passages,

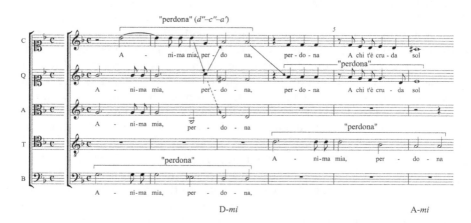

Example 6.3 Monteverdi, *Anima mia, perdona*, mm. 1–6

the voice exchanges and crossings assure that the uppermost-sounding voice and the more imperative linear motion (D–C–D, for example) actually comprise multiple voice parts. This effect of a "composite voice" comes at a contrapuntal cost: for maintaining the uppermost line in one voice alone would have avoided awkward voice-leading, such as the improper transferal of a resolution at the Canto's leap in m. 2, and the Quinto's d4 leap in mm. 2–3. From the standpoint of readership, the voice exchange seems to preclude the association of any individual voice part with the speaking subject of the text, whether regarded as Amarilli or—now devoid of its initial address to Mirtillo—a generic *io.*

Susan McClary reads this opening differently. Associating the Canto with Amarilli herself—and misconstruing the initial phrygian close on D in tonal terms as a "half cadence" in G—McClary writes: "The Canto begins forthrightly enough, outlining in her first inter[v]al the boundaries of the G *diapente* before deflecting back up to A for a half cadence."[13] It should be pointed out, however, that the G-hypodorian "Self" is not evident in the Canto alone, for the crucial missing pitches of the G–D fifth—C, and most importantly B♭—are articulated by another voice, the Quinto, while the Basso and Alto accentuate the G–D boundaries with even more clarity than the Canto. The madrigal's "subjectivity" in a modal–contrapuntal reading such as McClary's, then, might more aptly be considered a shared one between many or all voices, or, if one is intent on viewing the upper voice as speaker, between two voices (Canto and Quinto), as the analysis here shows.

The tactic of a composite voice is used repeatedly in the two other *Pastor fido* settings of the Fourth Book—*Quel' augellin che canta* and *Ah, dolente partita*—but contrasts with Monteverdi's common, compartmentalized approach in other earlier and contemporaneous works of moving the upper voices in parallel motion, often in thirds, with few crossings. For example, the opening of the following piece in the Fourth Book, *Luci serene e chiare* (Example 6.4), has many similarities to the beginning of *Anima mia, perdona*: an initial outlining of key interval species framed by longer note values, the same scoring for two sopranos in standard cleffing, and a pronounced abandoned dissonance in the Canto—a leap away from a M9, *c″*, at "Voi m'incendete" (m. 9). Yet the Canto here is positioned consistently as the higher voice—not only at the opening, but nearly throughout the piece—while the Quinto moves chiefly in thirds beneath it. This treatment—with the Quinto always ducking out of the Canto's way—enables the association of one singer with one contrapuntal line, which is precisely what the interwoven lines of *Anima mia, perdona* prevent.

A later example from Monteverdi's 1614 reworking of the *Lamento d'Arianna*—an extended recitative from his opera *L'Arianna* (1608)—for five-voice madrigal shows a similar approach to *Luci serene e chiare* in its compartmentalization of the voice parts, again in five-voice setting with two sopranos. Here, the Canto predominates overall, while the Quinto again remains generally below it, in a supportive role, often in parallel thirds (with

Example 6.4 Monteverdi, *Luci serene e chiare*, mm. 1–10

the exception of passages in imitation), as shown in Example 6.5. The setting, therefore, seems to facilitate a reading that maintains a link between
a single voice part (Canto) and the speaking persona of the dramatic work
(Arianna)—that is, at least in the opening three *parti*. Notably, as the piece
progresses, the Canto and Quinto are used more interchangeably. In the
fourth and final *parte*, the two voices begin to cross one another repeatedly
so as to create—out of Arianna's original solo part—first, a composite, static
upper voice in rapid declamation in mm. 6–8 (Example 6.6). Then, in the
work's final phrase and terminal cadence, the Canto recedes entirely beneath
the Quinto to end the madrigal as supporting voice (Example 6.7). The voice
of "Arianna," therefore, becomes increasingly shared, more polyphonic,
from beginning to end, thus seeming to portray musically the conceptual
transition from dramatic and representational (or enacted) to lyric and narrational (or communal). Note also that the Quinto's gesture in the final cadence represents a reworking of two cadences from the *prima parte* where the
Canto served as upper voice (mm. 5–8 and 30–34). Thus, the Quinto, by the
end, has essentially commandeered the Canto's role. This process can be read

affectively, as if the speaker, Arianna (ostensibly associated with the Canto), falters or even falls to pieces before the end of the lament, and the other voices come forth to take "her" place. But it also illustrates the pliable and collective rendering of the poetic voice in the madrigal, as the emphasis shifts from one

Example 6.5 Monteverdi, *Lasciatemi morire* (1614), mm. 1–8

Example 6.6 Monteverdi, *Lasciatemi morire* (1614), *quarta parte*, mm. 1–8

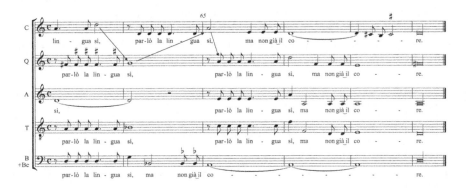

Example 6.7 Monteverdi, *Lasciatemi morire* (1614), *quarta parte*, mm. 63–68

or another voice part to many, and without an unconditional association between speaking persona and any individual singer.

Whereas some of the offensive dissonances in *Anima mia, perdona* resolve, but do so improperly—such as the transfer of the Canto's *d''* (M7) to the Quinto's *c''* (M6) in m. 2—others show no attention at all to resolution. In response to the speaker's reference to her beloved's suffering in verse 11 ("Del tuo proprio dolore"), for instance, the Canto first merely rearticulates a m7 suspension at "*pro*-prio" (m. 54). In its restatement at the end of the *prima parte* (Example 6.8), however, the phrase is intensified with full-voice texture and rearticulated dissonant m7s at both "*pro*-prio" and "*do*-lore" (mm. 65–68), the latter of which does not resolve but repeats until the sonority changes beneath it. Whereas Artusi made no mention of the transferred resolutions in the madrigal's opening (Example 6.3)—presumably because they do not stand out aurally—he did cite the reemphasized sevenths here at "proprio dolore." His only other complaint from *Anima mia, perdona* targets the final phrase of the madrigal, "non tuoi tormenti," which again evokes the notion of suffering ("torments") using an improperly prepared m7.[14] This time, however, the dissonant C is retained through voice exchange in the penultimate D sonority, resulting in a "V[7]"-type approach to the terminal G cadence.

Yet, this notorious incorporation of a m7 in the terminal cadence does not come unprepared, so to speak, on a broader scale (Example 6.9). Rather, Monteverdi introduces the interval gradually at cadences through the extended setting of the final couplet, allowing the m7 to transform from an unprepared but resolved dissonance (*c''* leading into the G cadences of mm. 103–04 and 108–09, and *f'* in the G–C cadence at mm. 119–20) to a sustained and seemingly integral part of the final two cadential preparations: A–D (mm. 125–26) and D–g (mm. 129–30). Even between these last two cadences, the seventh increases in duration and prominence, first appearing in an

Example 6.8 Monteverdi, *Anima mia, perdona,* mm. 64–68

inner voice (Alto) and occupying only the second half of the pre-cadential sonority (mm. 124–25), then being transferred from the Alto to the Canto between both halves of the preparation (mm. 128–29). What appear to the modern ear to be true "dominant-seventh" sonorities, however, prove evocative contrapuntal renderings of the torments of Amarilli and Mirtillo's forbidden love, with sevenths resulting from improper diminutions of the basic late-sixteenth-century cadence structure.

The setting of "Del ciel e de la terra" (mm. 84–85) also foreshadows techniques that Artusi criticizes in the later Fifth Book—namely in *Cruda Amarilli*—but here they go unmentioned. The voices deliver the verse homorhythmically in *fusae* (eighth notes) with numerous fleeting but blatantly illicit dissonances, including seconds between Canto and Quinto, and between Canto and Tenore. Artusi notes that modern composers rationalize such passages "from perceiving that in instruments [such discords] do not much offend the ear because of the quickness of the movement."[15] The theorist, however, sees this deception—the veiling of improper voice leading from the ear and intellect through the quickness of the passage—as an example of modern music's "sensuous excess that corrupts the senses."

The transposed restatement of phrases, either varied or (less often) unchanged, was by no means new to Monteverdi's music in *Anima mia, perdona.* But the madrigal shows the technique's growing prevalence and centrality as a rhetorical and structural device. The most common transposition levels in the Fourth and Fifth Books are the P4 and P5. Some scholars have interpreted such motions in tonal terms—for example, as phrase-level progressions between "dominant" (or "subdominant") and "tonic." Eric Chafe, for example, views transposition by fifth in Monteverdi's works at

Example 6.9 Monteverdi, *Anima mia, perdona*, mm. 103–20

times as an "expansion of the dominant–tonic idea to the phrase level," which is, in turn, an offshoot of Dahlhaus's theory that regards cadential centers as "component keys" [*Teiltonarten*] that likewise form hierarchical relationships of "tonic," "dominant," and "subdominant" within a work.[16] This anachronistic harmonic reading, however, often disregards more fundamental linear processes in Monteverdi's music that these restatements and, more tellingly, their modifications carry, and that prove more in keeping with a compositional approach rooted in counterpoint, as contemporary writings reflect.

The setting of verse 3 ("Dove pietosa esser non può") in mm. 13–19 of the *prima parte* offers a clear example. Between its two statements, the verse shifts down a P5: from a three-voice phrase moving A–F, to a five-voice phrase moving D–B♭. Despite the transposition by P5, this overarching harmonic scheme (A–F then D–B♭) is awkward from a tonal perspective, with its immediate shift from F-major to D-major sonorities between the two statements. From a linear, contrapuntal perspective, however, the function of these coupled phrases is straightforward: the realization of a stepwise m7 ascent in the upper voice from *e'* to *d''*, the prevailing structural pitch (indicated by the dashed slur in Example 6.10). The downward transposition by P5, in other words, proves secondary to the scalar climb and the consequent rearticulation of background *d''* at its apex—all of which serves as part of a middleground upper-neighbor expansion displaced by an octave (*d''–e'–d''*). As we shall see, though, despite the common portrayal of Monteverdi's music as harmonically, even tonally, directed, transposition—as well as more local harmonic motion—most often serves a deeper linear end, even though the linear process may be obscured and prolonged by diminution, voice exchanges, register transfer, and other devices.

Along with its composite upper voice and blatantly mistreated dissonances, the opening measures of *Anima mia, perdona* also introduce a three-note motive that proves central to the madrigal's projection of long-range musical and referential unity through its basis in "perdona"—the expression of remorse that motivates the speech. This "perdona" motive takes shape in the uppermost sounding "voice" formed by the Canto and Quinto: *d''–c''–a'* (Example 6.11). Below it, the Basso simultaneously presents the motive

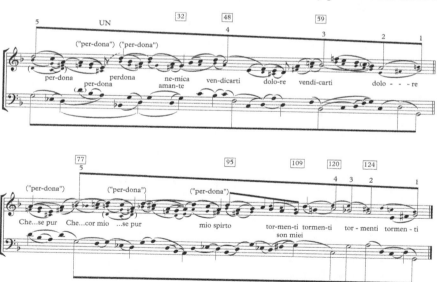

Example 6.10 Monteverdi, *Anima mia, perdona*, Structural Analysis

(slightly varied) a fifth lower: *g–e♭–d.* This basic gesture—a descending P4 divided into second-plus-third (or vice-versa)—returns numerous times later in the piece, serving as a musical recollection or mnemonic of the key notion of *perdona,* the plea for forgiveness. Monteverdi's insertion of "perdona" again with verse 2 ("A chi t'è cruda sol") yields the motive in an elaborated form, first outlining *a′–g′–e′* (Quinto, mm. 4–6), then in its original form, *d″–c″–a′* (Canto, mm. 10–12). The literal return of the word in verse 4 ("Perdona a questa") evokes further statements of the "perdona" motive, now in the Basso's inverted form from mm. 1–3—namely *d″–b♭–a′* (mm. 19–22).[17]

Despite the literal absence of "perdona" thereafter in the text, the music continues to resound Amarilli's plea for forgiveness through repeated statements of the motive (labeled in parenthesis in the structural sketch in

Example 6.11 Monteverdi, *Anima mia, perdona,* "Perdona" Motive

Example 6.10). In the *seconda parte,* Monteverdi's running together of verses 12–13 ends with a slightly embellished a'–g'–e' at "cor mio / Come se' pur" (mm. 72–74; Example 6.11), followed by its transposition up a fourth to d''–c''–a' (mm. 80–82). These occurrences highlight the gesture at the end of the musical phrases (evaded cadences on A-*mi* and D-*mi,* respectively) and affirm its continued relevance throughout the text and music. Finally, the reworking of the opening appeal ("Anima mia, perdona") at "quei sospir il mio spirto" (mm. 93–95) echoes "perdona" a final time before the protracted setting of the closing verses (Example 6.10).

After developing the sentiment of remorse for seventeen verses and some ninety-five measures, the final couplet of the text acts as a culmination of the speaker's compassion in its declaration that the beloved's (Mirtillo's) pain and suffering "son miei, non tuoi, tormenti" (are my, not your, torments). Monteverdi's treatment of these lines occupies the last thirty-five measures—over one-third—of the two-*parte* piece and centers on the graphic depiction of the first- and second-person pronouns of the final line, "miei, non tuoi," as signifiers of identity and as temporal–spatial deictics that gesture inwardly ("my") or outwardly ("your").[18]

In the context of the play, whether spoken or read, the closing line has the effect of joining the lovers who remain separated physically (and by law) by presenting them in close proximity verbally (temporally) and visually (spatially) on the page, and thereby conveying their desired union in Amarilli's mind. The madrigal, however, reverses this effect and instead uses this phrase to accentuate the lovers' seemingly hopeless separation by splitting "son *miei*" and "non *tuoi*" with rests, often of considerable duration. This distancing reaches its greatest lengths in mm. 106–17, where the Basso divides the pronouns by ten measures, and the Tenore, by five (Example 6.9). Along with this temporal (linear) separation, Monteverdi accentuates their isolation further by distancing the pronouns intervallically (vertically) with leaps of a P4, P5, M6, or octave between them. The verse also brings an unusual shift for a G-hypodorian piece to C as tonal center in mm. 118–20, which grows out of the persistent appearance of B♮ at "non tuoi" (mm. 113–18). The passage as a whole, therefore, is set apart modally and cadentially from the rest of the work. Altogether, through these different scales of temporal, intervallic, and modal isolation, readers of the madrigal hear and see the tormenting chasm between speaker ("miei") and beloved ("tuoi").[19] The accentuation of the foreign pitch-center C, with c'' in the uppermost voice, moreover, also serves the essential structural role of activating the mode's background $\hat{4}$ and instigating the fundamental descent toward the madrigal's end. This background structure in itself, however, brings its own idiosyncrasies at the scale of musical–cultural convention, as we shall see.

As Example 6.10 shows, the "perdona" motive is also closely tied to the expansion of background $\hat{5}$ (d'') in the openings of both *parti.* Despite its unorthodox voice leading, the madrigal provides a fairly conventional example of the G-hypodorian mode on most accounts, from vocal ranges and melodic boundaries to the cadential plan and overarching structure. Yet, while the frequent $d''-a'$ *diatessaron* motion of the "perdona" motive reinforces the background d'', it also leads to a conspicuous absence of cadences on the G final through the madrigal's opening. Instead, the cadences in mm. 1–27 center exclusively on pitches that support the motive's ending on A (or in one instance E)—namely D, A, and F, with one cadence to B♭ where the motive appears (intervallically reordered) in the Basso, $e♭–c–B♭$ (m. 18). The first G cadence does not arrive until m. 32, nearly halfway through the *prima parte*. The avoidance of G as a cadential goal and in the recurring motion $d''-a'$ $(\hat{5}-\hat{2})$, rather than $d''-g'$ $(\hat{5}-\hat{1})$, of the central motive heightens the sense of modal–cadential yearning to mirror the expressions of longing of the text. Meanwhile, on the broader, intertextual scale, this denial of the natural and necessary modal–cadential endpoint perhaps also hints of Amarilli's painful suppression of her true and predestined desire.

Though conventional in its general handling of the G-hypodorian mode, *Anima mia, perdona* is exceptional in its treatment of the two-*parte* madrigal form. For the *prima parte* not only ends with an assertive cadence on the G final instead of the more customary $\hat{5}$ (D), but it also carries out a complete, self-contained projection of the G-hypodorian framework, $d''-g'$. The individual steps of this basic descent, in fact, are as clearly defined, broadly spaced, and soundly supported as one would find in the dynamic structural expansion of a complete Marenzio madrigal. The decisive events in this structure include the forceful cadential move to F in m. 48 to establish the background c'' $(\hat{4})$, and another to B♭ in m. 59 to affirm the fundamental $b♭'$ $(\hat{3})$. Both structural pitches, in turn, occur with the same phrase of text, "E se pur hai desio di vendicarti." Although Monteverdi transposes the phrase down a P5 between mm. 46–48 and 57–59 as part of a transposed restatement of the last three verses, his revoicing of this restatement revises its structural function to establish the new structural pitch, B♭, rather than f', the fifth below c'', as an exact transposition would have done. (The strategy, therefore, offers another consequential example of the contrapuntal and structural implications of Monteverdi's use of transposed restatement.) The doubled articulation of $b♭'$ in the two sopranos further supports the pitch's structural status. The terminal cadence, furthermore, distinguishes the definitive $\hat{2}-\hat{1}$ descent with marked dissonance involving the background $\hat{2}$ (a'), first in its arrival (where it serves as the resolution of the reemphasized 7–6 suspension at "proprio"), then in its repetition (as a M7 above the Basso's antepenultimate B).

My reason for explaining the structural details of the *prima parte* is not only to demonstrate that it is self-contained and independently complete, but also to raise the possibility that *Anima mia, perdona* was once a single-*parte* madrigal, with the *seconda parte* added later, or that the full madrigal was designed so that the *seconda parte* was optional. Indeed, the *prima parte* is self-sufficient in terms of its text, with the *seconda parte* merely reaffirming its message of compassion (though not so elegantly), and it even concludes with the rhyming couplet *maggiore/dolore*—one of only two rhymed verse-pairs in the passage.[20]

Yet, in its published two-*parte* form, Monteverdi's work bears several marked similarities to Marenzio's two-*parte* treatment of the same passage as *Deh, Tirsi, Tirsi, anima mia, perdona* (1594). The appearance of Monteverdi's setting in the 1597 anthology *Fiori del giardino* means that Monteverdi composed his work no more than three years after the publication of Marenzio's Sixth Book. Marenzio sets the text more succinctly, without the numerous repetitions of "perdona" and of full verses toward the opening of the text, and like Monteverdi, largely in homophonic declamation: his full setting amounts to 101 measures, as compared to Monteverdi's 130 measures. As seen in his other *Pastor fido* settings, the Roman composer also explores a greater range of cadential centers and modal contexts—for example, affording considerable prominence to D, the fourth degree, in the *prima parte* of his A-hypodorian setting—and thereby generates more tension at the structural level.

Their most notable similarities, however, come at the ends of both *parti* and in their structural designs. Like Monteverdi, Marenzio ends his *prima parte* on an unusual pitch for the underlying A-hypodorian mode: the antagonizing and foreign fourth degree, D, as opposed to the more customary cofinal, E. This D-centricity—and with it, the prolongation of the background $\hat{4}$, d''—continues well into the *seconda parte*, which is a striking departure from the conventional retention of the primary background pitch (typically $\hat{5}$) into the *seconda parte* in bipartite works. The *seconda parte*—again like Monteverdi's setting—then incorporates an exceptional dissonance for "tormenti" (torments) in the final cadence: an unprepared minor sixth, C, above the pre-cadential E-major sonorities in both statements of the final verse leading to the A final (mm. 94 and 99–100; Example 6.12). The deviant pitch creates the effect of an E-augmented sonority that shifts to a conventional E sonority before moving to the cadential goal, A.

While the two settings of the passage differ in many outward ways, they both end their *parti* with anomalous cadences: the *prime parti* with arrivals on atypical pitches (the fourth degree in Marenzio's case, the final in Monteverdi's), and the *seconde parti* with aberrant dissonances in the cadential preparation (a virtual augmented sonority and a "dominant-seventh"). Marenzio, likewise, does not overlook the poignant contrast of the two deictic pronouns in the final lines—"son *miei*, non *tuoi* tormenti"—but distinguishes and isolates them, not only, like Monteverdi, with rests and large leaps between "miei" and "tuoi," but also registrally, with leaps that soar to the peaks of the voices' registers first for "miei" (see the Basso, Quinto, and Canto in mm. 91–92), then for "tuoi" (Alto in m. 92 and Canto in m. 97). The two composers also exploit the large-scale tensions and directed drive of dynamic-type structures, although the closed nature of both *parti* in Monteverdi's work defuses this anticipation at the work's midpoint and, hence, lacks the continuously mounting restlessness and impulse of Marenzio's design.

Example 6.12 Marenzio, *Deh, Tirsi, Tirsi, anima mia, perdona,* mm. 85–101

Although Marenzio unifies his setting with motives—such as "Tirsi, an-ima mia" (*prima parte*) and "Qual hor piagni" (*seconda parte*)—these ges-tures are limited in scope to their own respective *parti* and seem to lack the semantic and structural significance of Monteverdi's "perdona" motive. We have seen, however, that Marenzio uses motives in such structural–expressive ways in other works, as in his setting of *Cruda Amarilli,* where the effect of "echoing" the beloved's name musically resembles Monteverdi's technique of recalling "perdona" across Amarilli's own lament. Likewise, Marenzio's stunning transformation of the standard a–E phrygian ending in *Cruda Amarilli* to evoke Mirtillo's *martire* (suffering) also looks ahead to Monteverdi's own striking modification of the standard D–G ending in rendering the *tormenti* Amarilli feels in response to Mirtillo's anguish.

The imprints of Marenzio's techniques show strongly in Monteverdi's *An-ima mia, perdona,* his first published setting distinctly from Guarini's play. Yet Monteverdi's own setting of *Cruda Amarilli,* while equally offensive by theoretical standards, shows signs of Marenzio's influence that are more subtle, more deeply integrated, and melded with the techniques of Wert, along with the more blatant, surface-level resemblances between all three settings that countless studies have emphasized. The work also attracted more critical attention in its day by expanding Monteverdi's theoretical provocations beyond dissonance treatment to more elusive aspects of large-scale unity involving cadence plan and mode. Both *Anima mia, perdona* and *Cruda Amarilli* appeared in print amidst the crossfire of the debates over "modern music" that they purportedly exemplified. But *Cruda Amarilli* sits more squarely at the center of the controversy for its position at the head of the Fifth Book of madrigals, where Monteverdi issued his first public statement on the attacks against his music.

The Monteverdi–Artusi Debate: Musical and Extramusical Provocations

Artusi's *L'Artusi, ovvero delle imperfettioni della moderna musica* (Venice: Vincenti, 1600) issues a critique of modern music (and modern music-making) embedded within a survey of theoretical teachings on issues of tuning, performance practice, counterpoint, and mode ranging from antiquity to the present day. The treatise takes the form of a dialogue between two presumably fictitious interlocutors—Vario (a musical authority and a servant of Cardinal Pompeo Arigoni) and Luca (a servant in the retinue Archduke Albert VII of Austria)—in Ferrara in November 1598 for the combined nuptials of Albert VII (to Isabella Clara Eugenia) and Margherita of Austria (by proxy to the King of Spain). The discussion centers on two musical events held on 16 November 1598: a concert by the "universally celebrated" ensemble of nuns at the convent of San Vito, and a performance of "certi Madrigali nuovi" at the home of the young musical virtuoso Antonio Goretti later the same day.[21] In the *primo ragionamento,* devoted to San Vito, Vario praises the nuns' performance for its unity and sweet harmony while combining the forces of wind, brass, and string instruments with voices. Such agreement in an ensemble, Vario remarks, is exceptional for the time, owing to the lack of a common tuning system and to the general challenges of coordination and balance between performers. Most of the remainder of the *ragionamento* considers issues of temperament and performance practice for the joining of instruments and voices, taking aim especially at the positions on these topics of the fellow Bolognese theorist Ercole Bottrigari.

In the *secondo ragionamento,* the impressionable Luca questions Vario about the confounding new madrigals he heard performed (and repeated) at Goretti's house the previous evening. In attendance, Luca tells us, were Luzzasco Luzzaschi and Ippolito Fiorini—both eminent musicians from the recently disbanded court of Alfonso II d'Este with close ties to the *concerto delle donne*—along with "many noble spirits learned in music."[22] These "madrigali nuovi," Luca contends, "transgress the good rules founded partly on experience (the Mother of all things), partly on reflection of Nature, and partly on proven example." Instead, these works "introduce new rules, new modes, and new manners of speech that were harsh and displeasing to hear" so as to constitute "deformations of the nature and propriety of proper Harmony."[23] Yet Luca also admits to their allure. The servant then presents the wise Vario with brief *passaggi*, or "snippets," from the madrigals, devoid of text, that he had jotted down and asks for Vario's thoughts.

Luca's and Vario's perspectives seem to represent the dichotomy between visceral (sensual) experience and reasoned judgment that Artusi himself, as a man of the Church (a canon regular) and a devoted pupil of Zarlino, underwent upon hearing (and seeing) the madrigals performed in 1598 Ferrara. His sense of vulnerability therein to the irrational, corrupt, and emasculating effects of modern music, along with the compositional improprieties in themselves, no doubt contributed to the severity of his reproach and rhetoric, and to his associations of the works with unnatural creatures and audacious prostitutes. The theorist never mentions Monteverdi by name, but the offensive *passaggi* he cites come from madrigals that appeared later in the composer's Fourth and Fifth Books.[24] Artusi criticizes Monteverdi's music on two main fronts: voice-leading infractions (including dissonance treatment) and modal incoherence. Whereas the former are straightforward and objective, being based on the systematic rules of counterpoint, Artusi's accusations relating to mode are far more debatable and subjective, given the lack of consistent and clear-cut parameters for acceptable levels of modal mixture—not to mention the shortcomings of modal principles more generally—in Renaissance theory.

Over the course of the debate, Artusi singles out five of Monteverdi's madrigals to make his case, including examples in score notation for some, while denoting others simply by textual incipit. In *L'Artusi* (1600), he cites *Anima mia, perdona* for its disregard for contrapuntal norms, *O Mirtillo* for its modal "impertinence," and *Cruda Amarilli*—the theorist's foremost example—for its numerous violations from both categories. In *La seconda parte dell'Artusi overo Delle imperfettioni della moderna musica* (Venice: Giacomo Vincenti, 1603), the theorist responds to two letters defending Monteverdi's works and modern music more generally by one L'Ottuso Accademico, whose identity remains unknown.[25] Here, Artusi expands on his earlier denunciations of Monteverdi's music (still withholding the composer's name) citing two additional examples—*Era l'anima mia* and *Ecco, Silvio, colei che 'n odio hai tanto*—for their "novel" yet illicit melodic progressions (namely a diminished fourth), mistreatment of sharped and flatted pitches, and awkward text-setting (discussed in the next chapter). All of these offensive pieces but one, *Era l'anima mia*, set texts from Guarini's tragicomedy, likewise dubbed "modern" and "monstrous" by its own critics.

For Artusi, the dangers of modern music, and of Monteverdi's music specifically, reached beyond unpleasant sound: its indecorous techniques threatened to undermine generations of collective progress toward musical perfection. At Goretti's house in 1598, the Bolognese canon believed he had witnessed firsthand an assault on the principled work of past composers and theorists by a school of "nuovi Inventori" who defiled these standards out of vanity and for the sake of sensual gratification.[26] The theorist's concerns, therefore, proved as much ethical as they were pragmatic.[27]

The effects of modern music were also threatening to the unwitting listener in more immediate ways. Much of the listener's enjoyment of these novel improprieties, Artusi writes, results from the deception of the senses ("in senso ingannato dal sensibile")—that is, from the failure of the sense of hearing to judge the sounds properly before conveying them to the intellect.[28] The fallibility of hearing—an indirect sense for which the stimulus (sound) is mediated by air—leaves both the mind and soul susceptible to the corrupting, effeminizing forces of modern music. Thus, Artusi's branding Monteverdi's works as vain, monstrous, chimeras, and so forth evokes not only their base, unruly nature, but also their capacity to weaken and taint one's moral and intellectual disposition by beguiling the senses. The theorist's comparison of modern music later—in his *Discorso secondo musicale* (1608), published under the pseudonym Antonio Braccino da Todi—to a "sfacciata meretrice" (brazen harlot) underscores the belief in music's "capacity to change man inwardly, that is, the passions and the ways of the soul," through seduction and sensual gratification, and with an end of shaming and rendering its subject impotent.[29]

Monteverdi's first and only direct response to Artusi appeared not in his next volume, the Fourth Book of 1603, but on the back page of his Fifth Book of 1605, in a brief letter addressed to the "studiosi lettori." That the composer responded personally to criticism of his music, and that he did so in the volume in which these works were published, is noteworthy, even in spite of the fact that the letter is primarily a promise of more substantive explanations to come. The letter makes four basic points: (1) that Monteverdi is Artusi's unnamed target, and the madrigals he is publishing include some of the allegedly offensive passages; (2) that the composer is presently too busy serving the Duke of Mantua to reply more extensively; (3) that readers can be assured that his compositions accord with the principles of a "second practice" (*seconda pratica*), which is distinct from the manner taught by Zarlino in its treatment of dissonances and consonances, yet equally rational; and (4) that the term *seconda pratica* is Monteverdi's own.[30] Monteverdi concludes by appealing to his readers in the meantime to "believe that the modern composer builds on foundations of truth."[31]

Monteverdi claims to have written a full treatise on this new approach to composition, which, he promises, "as soon as it is rewritten, will be published bearing the name *Seconda pratica, overo Perfettione della moderna musica.*" The treatise never appeared; in fact, Monteverdi's correspondence with Giovanni Battista Doni in the early 1630s reveals that the composer still only planned to write such a text.[32] A substantial elaboration of Monteverdi's terse defense, however, appeared in 1607 in the form of a *Dichiaratione della lettera stampata nel Quinto libro de suoi Madrigali* penned by the composer's brother, Giulio Cesare, and appended to the final pages of Monteverdi's *Scherzi musicali a tre voci* (Venice: Amadino, 1607). It is in justifying his brother's works against Artusi's rigid standards that Giulio Cesare proclaims the influential doctrine of the *seconda pratica*: the new practice, begun by Rore and passed by Ingegneri, Marenzio, Wert, and "other *signori* of this Heroic school" into Monteverdi's hands, which, following Plato, "considers the harmony commanded, and not commanding, and makes the oration mistress [*signora*] of the harmony."[33]

Artusi's criticisms are based strongly on theoretical and practical precedents. In the *Dichiaratione*, however, Giulio Cesare does not refute Artusi on strict theoretical grounds: he was perhaps well aware that his opponent's criticisms were mostly valid in this respect. The rationale behind Monteverdi's aberrant compositional means seems, rather, to be primarily aesthetic and affective, which leads Giulio Cesare to do his best to vindicate them in novel, if at times oblique, ways. His defense hinges chiefly on two principal arguments: (1) that Monteverdi's offences are, in fact, justified by the demands of the text (which Artusi omitted from his printed examples of the music and from his analysis); and (2) that composers of the highest stature preceded Monteverdi in these same offences yet were not subjected to the same scrutiny and censure. He bolsters this latter defense with examples from these earlier masters, including several names esteemed (and cited as models) by Artusi, such as Willaert, Cipriano de Rore, and Artusi's own teacher, Zarlino. Crucial to Giulio Cesare's argument is the drawing of a clear distinction between two separate practices—an older *Prima pratica* ("that which considers the harmony...not servant, but mistress of the oration") exemplified by the works of Ockeghem, Josquin, Willaert, Zarlino, and others; and the *Seconda practica*, championed by Rore, Wert, Marenzio, and Luzzaschi—and the accusation that Artusi only recognizes the first of the two.

While the contrapuntal infractions of Monteverdi's music are incontrovertible by late-sixteenth-century standards,[34] other, external factors might also have made the composer especially susceptible to Artusi's attack, such as the setting and participants of the performance in Ferrara, Monteverdi's reputation as an instrumentalist, and poetic texts drawn from a dissolute, "modern" Ferrarese play. On the face of it, Artusi's strategy of concealing the composer's identity and situating his dialogue in Ferrara suggests that his principal objective lay in criticizing "modern music" at large, while perhaps secondarily associating its degenerate techniques with the hedonistic musical practices and culture of the defunct Este court. Yet, by targeting Monteverdi's music and associating it with Ferrara, Artusi obliquely paints contemporary Mantuan music also as flawed and corrupting—indeed, as "modern" and Ferrarese-like—while upholding an air of judiciousness by concealing the composer's identity and framing his criticisms in theoretical terms (albeit laced with passionate rhetoric and disparaging metaphors). Vincenzo Gonzaga's Mantua was, after all, in many respects an offspring of the profligate cultural life of 1580s–90s Ferrara. The bold and relatively green composer from Mantua provided Artusi with an ideal face of modern music not only for his compositional audacity, but also for his patron and place of employment. More decorous and established composers hired under the pious Guglielmo Gonzaga, such as Wert and Gastoldi, by contrast, became models of compositional decorum, of ingenuity tempered by reason, alongside Willaert, Rore, Palestrina, Lasso, Monte, and others in *L'Artusi,* in opposition to Monteverdi's undisciplined creations.

Margherita of Austria's passage between these northern centers—with the Pope's retinue in Ferrara and Vincenzo Gonzaga's court in Mantua—brought these rivals head to head in their displays of spectacle and entertainment, including, of course, theater and music. It was only days after leaving Ferrara that Margherita, on 22 November 1598, witnessed the stage production of *Il pastor fido* during her five-day visit to Mantua, where Duke Vincenzo showed no restraint in flaunting the skill and splendor of the court and duchy under his rule. The festivities surrounding the queen's sojourn—for which the staging of the play with *intermedi* was a centerpiece—provided Vincenzo with a prime opportunity to upstage Ferrara in its new guise as a papal territory while bolstering political ties with the powers of Spain and the House of Hapsburg on a prominent international stage. In Ferrara, by contrast, the young queen and her entourage had been treated to a morality play performed in Latin by students of the Jesuit college, as well as to a performance by members of Alfonso d'Este's now-dissolved *concerto delle donne.*[35]

From Artusi's perspective as an official of the Church—*L'Artusi* was, in fact, dedicated to Cardinal Pompeo Arrigoni, a Roman inquisitor with close ties to the pope—Monteverdi and his music would have stood directly in the middle of this political and ideological conflict between the secular courts of northern Italy, with their extravagant and modern tastes, and the conservative-minded Pope Clement VIII and post-Tridentine convictions. Even more, the 1598 performance of Monteverdi's madrigals took place in the residence of a known supporter of this modern music and its illicit mixing of distinct *genera* of pitch relations—Artusi explicitly notes that an "instrument made according to the intervals of [progressive composer–theorist] Don Nicola Vicentino is found in this city in the hands of Antonio Goretti," the host of the concert[36]—and involved prominent members of the late Duke of Ferrara's court. On top of this, all of the offensive madrigals were settings of verse by the former Este court poet and ducal secretary, Guarini—hence, of texts with overtly Ferrarese origins.[37] In this shifting, competitive environment during the papal annexation of Ferrara, the performance of Monteverdi's *Pastor fido* settings might even have been perceived—and not without reason—as an advertisement for the Mantuan performance of the play the following week, and hence as an artistic infiltration by the Gonzaga court into the pope's own celebrations for the new Queen of Spain, as well as for himself, as sovereign of Ferrara. Thus, the whole affair at Goretti's home has the air of a show of resistance by the Ferrarese and Mantuan courts against the Church's control.[38] Amidst all the enmity, both theoretical and political, it is no wonder that Monteverdi's madrigals, when finally coming to print in the Fourth and Fifth Books, appeared under the "protection" of the Ferrarese Accademia degli Intrepidi (of which Goretti was a member) and Vincenzo Gonzaga, respectively.[39]

Another possible factor in the theorist's singular aim at Monteverdi's works has less to do with the music itself or with political matters than it does with the critic's encounter with the music in performance. Before addressing the theoretical failings of Monteverdi's madrigals, Artusi sets the scene at Goretti's gathering with a commentary on the visual, physical dimension of the music he is about to condemn on theoretical terms:

> They [modern composers] do not even think of looking at the volumes of Boethius. But if you would know what they say, they are content to know how to string their notes together after their fashion and to teach the singers to sing their compositions, accompanying themselves with many movements of the body, and in the end they [the singers] let themselves go to such an extent that they seem to be actually dying—this is the perfection of their music.[40]

Given what we know about Renaissance conceptions of the body and the spirit, founded on principles of Aristotelian and Galenic theories of heat and the humors, the "dying" ("muoiano") that the singers, in Artusi's eyes, appear to bring upon themselves is likely not a literal, tragic death, but one of intense sensual arousal fueled by their movements and vocalizing that parallels the effects of sexual stimulation.[41] The physical display that accompanied the performance apparently exceeded what the principled theorist would have considered appropriate: his rhetoric of the singers letting themselves go ("si lasciano andare") suggests an improper lack of restraint, a level of looseness so great that—so Artusi believes—they could actually reach (or be reaching) the point of "dying" ("paia apunto che muoiano"). Such a display would surely have been offensive, perhaps even more so than any breaches of theoretical order that were taking place at the same time in the music.[42] As if the gestures of the performers and the *impertinentie* of the music were not enough, the possibility that the Ferrarese performance included women singers, perhaps even members of the renowned *concerto delle donne* of the late Duke Alfonso II, would have made the canon's exposure to modern music seem all the more outrageous, possibly outright threatening to his own moral fortitude.[43] Artusi's admonishment, after all, came at a time when post-Tridentine policies in the Church reflect considerable mistrust in music-making by women, even virtuous and cloistered ones. In fact, even the talented nuns of San Vito praised by Artusi for their exemplary music were stifled by severe constraints by the time *L'Artusi* appeared in print: for in 1599 the bishop of Ferrara, Giovanni Fontana, issued new ordinances for the convents of Ferrara that included enclosure of the nuns and harsh restrictions on their musical activity.[44]

Artusi's assault on Monteverdi's works, therefore, may have originated more as a *defensive* retaliation for what he perceived to be an initial assault by modern music through the animated bodies and voices of its performers—perhaps of women performers—rather than as an *offensive* launched specifically on a theoretical front. At the performance of Monteverdi's madrigals, whether by women or not, the chamber at Goretti's house would have been filled with impassioned voices that moved the bodies and souls of their listeners sympathetically, threatening to animate them, too, to the point of "actually dying."

A third additional factor that may have directed Artusi's attack toward Monteverdi's works is, of course, their textual source. For the indecorous performance of modern music at Goretti's house featured settings of a text condemned in recent years by the conservative critic and moral philosopher Denores on the counts of (among other things) immorality, sensuality, formal irregularity, and disregard for classical authority. There is no question that Artusi identified Monteverdi's music with the play, for in *L'Artusi* he introduces one example not only by the text's incipit, but also by its author and source: "le parole del Madrigale dicessero, ò Mirtillo, dal Guerino tolte nel Pastor Fido" (the words of the madrigal said, *O Mirtillo*, of Guarini, taken from *Il pastor fido*).[45] With the combination of modern music, impassioned performance, and a scandalous text by a poet known for his licentious verse—his *Tirsi morir volea* is but one well-known example, not to mention the numerous indecorous and scandalous moments from the play—there was much more to be concerned about at the gathering in Goretti's house than merely dissonance treatment and mode.[46]

That Artusi acknowledges the source of the musical texts is exceptional. Unlike the operas that would appear in the following years—where the libretto and librettist often overshadowed the music at the printing press and in attribution—madrigal prints rarely acknowledged the authors of their poetic texts.[47] In *L'Artusi*, the theorist omits the texts from the musical excerpts (*passaggi*) that he provides—a point that the Monteverdis highlight as evidence of Artusi's disregard for textual considerations—while calling attention nonetheless to their source and author. As a rare record of an informed contemporary reader of Monteverdi's *Pastor fido* settings, Artusi's attribution shows that he recognized the textual source of the music and deemed it relevant enough to name in his published dialogue.

Artusi does not reveal his own judgments of the play, aside from a general remark in the "Second Artusi" on its affective power, nor does he reference its public reputation or the critical debate that surrounded it. Yet, even if he did have objections to the work, he may have had good reason to curb them in favor of a terse compliment, given how closely intertwined the play, its author, and its musical settings had become with the Aldobrandini family and other high-ranking Church officials in the 1590s. As we have seen, this same period brought Guarini's visits to Rome (1593–95), Marenzio's settings of *Il pastor fido* while serving Cinzio Aldobrandini (1594–95), Cardinal Montalto and Michele Peretti's projected staging in 1596, and the Ronciglione performance by Cardinal Farnese, also in 1596. Whatever Artusi might have felt toward the irreverent tragicomedy, the approval it garnered from prestigious corners of the Church is unmistakable.

In his constant appeal to the authorities of antiquity and past generations to condemn the practices of the Moderni, Artusi represents for modern music very much what Denores in his attacks on *Il pastor fido* was a decade earlier for modern drama. For the Paduan critic, for instance, the fundamental purpose of poetry is "to introduce virtue into the souls of the spectators, of the listeners, for the shared benefit of a well-ordered Republic," as Aristotelian theory prescribes,[48] whereas *Il pastor fido*, he alleges, does just the opposite. Artusi similarly insists that Monteverdi's music threatens the integrity of its listeners by engendering "nothing else than the sensuous excess which corrupts the sense"[49]—a trait that later leads to Artusi's vivid comparison of modern music to a "sfacciata meretrice," denoting a class of woman that operated outside contemporary norms of chastity, silence, and obedience, and whose craft was contingent upon arousing and pleasing the senses.[50] One can imagine this same label being applied to the female characters of Guarini's play condemned by critics for their moral wavering between duty and desire (Amarilli) and their ridicule of constancy (Corisca), not to mention to the play itself, with its professed end of delight rather than instruction and moderation.

The parallels between the debates over modern drama and music extend beyond fundamental principles of technique, utility, and ethics also to the rhetoric and metaphors wielded by both factions. A major front in both confrontations, for example, proved the grotesque and unreasonable mixture of disparate components and manners in the offensive works. For Artusi, this mixture involved the three genera of tetrachords—diatonic, chromatic, and enharmonic—on the local scale, and the modes on the larger scale. Similarly, Denores and other conservative critics denounced various types of incongruous mixture in Guarini's work—generic (tragedy with comedy), stylistic (dramatic with lyrical), social/contextual (urban with pastoral), and rhetorical/intellectual (simple with sophisticated)—which deprived the work of unity, utility, and verisimilitude.[51] These appalling combinations led to Denores's characterization of the play as a "composizion mostruosa" (monstrous composition), and to Artusi's depictions of Monteverdi's music as "a monster," "deformations of nature,"[52] a "brazen whore," and a "chimera"—a monster formed from the parts of various beasts, as well as something that deceives. The theorist's charge that the music "introduces new rules, new modes, and new turns of phrase" likewise encapsulates the faults Denores saw in Guarini's work.[53]

Similar parallels surround the effect of delight for listeners and readers, although the poet and composer themselves differed in how they valued this merit. Whereas Guarini's justification for "modern drama" (in the form of pastoral tragicomedy) hinged on its aim to delight contemporary audiences, Monteverdi defends his madrigals wholly on the grounds of expression and the authority of the text, not delight *per se* as a specific end. Yet Artusi's charge that modern music charms the listener through the faculty of hearing evokes the notion of delight devoid of any intent of moral improvement—thus, a type of hedonistic pleasure—that Guarini similarly ascribed to *Il pastor fido* and advocated for pastoral tragicomedy in general. Guarini, of course, saw delight as an asset and a necessary development for dramatic poetry—for classical tragedy and comedy no longer appealed to modern audiences, and their cathartic ends were no longer relevant—whereas Artusi (like Denores and other detractors of *Il pastor fido*) frames it as a form of deceit and seduction.

Later commentaries, however, specifically point to delight as a virtue of Monteverdi's *seconda pratica*, as witnessed some fifty years later in the *Breve discorso sopra la musica moderna* (Warsaw: Pietro Elert, 1649) by the choirmaster at the royal court in Warsaw, Marco Scacchi. As Scacchi declares, "The world has reason to be indebted to modern composers for bringing harmonic delight [*dilettatione Armonica*] to the representation of words with their new musical accompaniments."[54] Following Monteverdi's distinction between an old practice that privileges theoretical propriety and a modern one that prioritizes textual expression, Scacchi advocates for this newer style by invoking *dilettare* as a key criterion for judgment:

> We already know that the aim of music is to delight. All honored theorists and practitioners have labored to demonstrate this goal of delectation. Therefore, if these modern compositions, insofar as regards style, give greater pleasure than the ancient, it does not seem to me to be a case for abandoning it.[55]

Going against Artusi's insistence that reason must prevail over the fallible senses, Scacchi deems hearing the "principale istromento per giudicare la Musica."[56] In his opening letter "to the prudent reader," Scacchi makes his opposition to the long-deceased theorist and his followers in theoretical orthodoxy clear and even mocks Artusi's claim that the "new method of composing" merely creates "castles in the air, chimeras founded on sand," when he writes:

> Perhaps they believe that modern music is founded on sand, or deprived of rules and principles? But whoever induces himself to believe this is making a mistake and shows himself to lack instruction on the profession. It explains why such [musicians] do not turn out to be very capable in this *Seconda Prattica Musicale*, which has as its end to ravish listeners by expressing a text in a way different from what our first ancient professors did...[57]

Scacchi's rhetoric brings to mind not only Guarini's call for a break from classical poetics to gratify modern readers, but in describing the power of these new techniques to "ravish listeners" (rapire gl'Ascoltanti), also Artusi's

descriptions of the sensual effects of modern music and of the bodily movements of the entranced ("dying") singers at Goretti's house. Scacchi's treatise,
coming from Warsaw in 1649, attests to the enduring and far-reaching influences of the Artusi–Monteverdi debate and of the notion of a *seconda pratica*
in music that emerged in the late-Cinquento Italian madrigal and was for-
malized in defense of settings of *Il pastor fido* at the start of the new century.

Guarini and Monteverdi both also seem to have attracted additional
criticism owing to their reputations as practitioners in their crafts: Guarini as a lyric poet, Monteverdi as an instrumentalist—namely in the highly
improvised manner of the *viola bastarda*. For Guarini, the charges of excessive lyricism and Petrarchan style were subsidiary to the fundamental issues
of genre and utility. But for Monteverdi, his identity as an instrumentalist
seems to have been a crucial factor in the debate with Artusi—one that
stood at the forefront of his accuser's mind and weighed considerably in the
allegations against modern music, yet also one that has been largely overlooked in the scholarship on the debate.

This perspective of instrumental practice likewise represents a central
component of the Fifth Book of madrigals, not only in its inclusion, for
the first time in Monteverdi's output, of both optional and required instrumental accompaniment, but also as a manifest part of Monteverdi's compositional approach and, as we shall see, his response to Artusi. Unlike the
Pastor fido settings of the Third and Fourth Books, those of the Fifth Book
remain distinctly true to the play in their texts and make this relationship
explicit by presenting character names in the opening lines of six madrigals
and *parti* thereof, and in many more instances internally. It is here in the
Fifth Book that Monteverdi demonstrates most compellingly that he, like
Artusi, was aware of the theatrical source of his madrigal texts by reflecting these intertextual ties through compositional and organizational techniques that expand on those of Marenzio's *Pastor fido* settings from no more
than three years earlier.

Notes

1
  1 O Spring, youth of the year,
      fair mother of flowers,
      of fresh grass and new loves,
      you return, alas,
      but without the dear days
  5 of my hopes. You, indeed, are that one
      who before was so fair and lovely,
      but I am no longer what I once was,
      so dear to another's eyes.
  2 James Chater, "Un pasticcio di madrigaletti," 143–44.
  3 Denis Arnold's emphasis of the different prevailing textures of the two com-
     posers' settings of *O primavera*—Wert's "recitative-like" homophony ver-
     sus Monteverdi's contrapuntal "permutations of motif, phrase, and voice

combinations"—overlooks more general similarities of texture and structural technique between the two composers—as seen in the comparison noted here between Monteverdi's *O primavera* and Wert's *Ah, dolente partita,* the texts of which are more akin in their concision and proportion of rhymed verses than the two versions of *O primavera*—as well as their contrasting formal approaches to the verse, discussed below. See Denis Arnold, *Monteverdi* [1967], in series Master Musicians, ed. Stanley Sadie (Oxford: Oxford University Press, 1990), 57.

4 *O primavera* blurs the lines considerably between the authentic and plagal form of the F-lydian mode, as the opening subjects of the mode-bearing voices alone make apparent: while the Tenore's prominent solo statement "O primavera" outlines the F modal octave, the subject appears in the Quinto (mm. 3–5) and in the Canto (mm. 12–14) first in the C octave. The Alto spans both of these ranges. All five voices, however, have what contemporary theorists consider "superfluous" ranges that encompass the authentic and plagal ranges, which favors the designation F-lydian. Altogether, these expansive ranges stem from Monteverdi's use of lengthy, sinuous contrapuntal lines, particularly for the lengthy, lyrical hendecasyllabic verses.

5 While agreeing with Tomlinson's reading that the madrigal's opening "expressed in music the semantic richness of Guarini's texts, its significant antitheses and balances, while respecting its syntactic structure through simultaneous (or near-simultaneous) presentation of the phrases that make up each of its grammatical periods," my reading of its formal manipulations of the text contradicts Tomlinson's judgment that the madrigal shows "fidelity to the sense and structure of the text," which may reflect an inclination to see *seconda pratica* principles in the composer's early works. Tomlinson also does not connect Monteverdi's "combinatory contrapuntal techniques" (i.e., *contrapposto*) to Wert. See Tomlinson's analysis of the text, with its Petrarchan antithesis of lover and nature, in *Monteverdi and the End of the Renaissance,* 78–80.

6 Chater, "Un pasticcio di madrigaletti," 147–48.

7 Tomlinson, *Monteverdi and the End of the Renaissance,* 95.

8 Lorenzo Bianconi relates this musical "parting" from a unison in Monteverdi's work to Marenzio's similar (but less pronounced) tactic in *Parto da voi, mio sole* (Third Book *a6,* 1585). See Bianconi's comparison of *Ah, dolente partita* settings, focusing on contrapuntal features of the settings of Achille Falcone (1603) and Monteverdi, in "*Ah dolente partita*: espressione ed artificio," *Studi musicali* 3 (1974): 105–30.

9 Christophe Georis provides a rigorous analysis of Monteverdi's textual manipulations in *Claudio Monteverdi "letterato" ou les métamorphoses du texte* (Paris: Honoré Champion, 2013). On *Ah, dolente partite* and its textual and thematic connections to other pieces in Monteverdi's Fourth Book, see pages 165–66 and 170–72.

10 The translation reads:

1 My soul, forgive
   the woman who is only cruel to you
   because she cannot be compassionate;
   forgive this one who
5 in her words and in her appearance
   is your rigid enemy,
   but who in her heart
   is your most compassionate lover.
   And if still you desire to avenge yourself,
10 ah, what better revenge can you have
   than your own suffering.

   For if you are my heart,
   as you truly are, in spite
   of heaven and the earth,
15 whenever you weep and sigh,
   those tears of yours are my
      blood,
   those sighs, my spirit,
   and those pains and sorrow that
      you feel
   are my, not your, torments.

11 Tim Carter examines the structural and modal behavior of *Anima mia, perdona,* specifically calling attention to the madrigal's use of registral transfer, in "'An Air New and Grateful to the Ear': The Concept of 'Aria' in Late Renaissance and Early Baroque Italy," *Music Analysis* 12 (1993): 127–145.

12 In evoking the speaker's own cruelness in the second verse ("A chi t'è cruda"; mm. 9–10), Monteverdi again transfers the stepwise motion from a dissonance to an inner voice. This time the Alto leaps away from *d'*, a M9 against the Basso's *c*, to *a*, while the Tenore picks up the linear ascent an octave lower, *e*–*f♯* (thus still failing to resolve the dissonance properly downward).

13 McClary, *Modal Subjectivities,* 176.

14 These two citations from *Anima mia, perdona* are Artusi's examples 8 and 9 in *L'Artusi,* fol. 40r.

15 *L'Artusi,* fol. 43v; cited in Claude Palisca, "The Artusi–Monteverdi Controversy," in D. Arnold and N. Fortune, eds., *The New Monteverdi Companion* (London: Faber, 1985), 127–58, at 85.

16 Chafe, *Monteverdi's Tonal Language,* 65. See also Carl Dahlhaus's analysis of Monteverdi's *O Mirtillo* and *Ecco, Silvio* in *Studies on the Origin of Harmonic Tonality,* 289–307.

17 McClary, focusing on the Canto as an embodiment of the passage's speaker in the play (Amarilli), ignores the Quinto's lead (and structural priority) over the Canto in the first of the two statements of this phrase in mm. 19–20 and misrepresents the *d''*–*a' diatessaron* (and motivic) descent as a "direct *diapente*." McClary's full assertion reads: "From the authoritative position of the upper boundary, D, she [Amarilli/Canto] traces her most direct *diapente* [*sic*?] descent yet in mm. 21–22" (*Modal Subjectivities,* 177).

18 On deictics and Monteverdi's treatment of such terms in his dramatic works, see Mauro Calcagno, "'Imitar col canto chi parla': Monteverdi and the Creation of a Language for Musical Theater," *Journal of the American Musicological Society* 55 (2002): 383–431.

19 This reading of the madrigal's separation of the lovers through their pronouns stands in direct opposition to McClary's reading in *Modal Subjectivities,* where the author (now equating not just the Canto, but the ensemble as a whole to the speaker) writes that Amarilli

> finally voices—though only with exquisite struggle—the fantasy of mutually acknowledged and shared love pangs that blossoms only at the end of the *seconda parte.* In her concluding section, we witness a simulation of their love fully consumed, even if poor Mirtillo has no knowledge of (much less share in!) the much-desired event.
>
> (176)

While I agree that the ending emphasizes love pangs, I would argue that it renders the lovers' seemingly inevitable isolation in this suffering, not their longed-for union.

20 All of the eleven other treatments of the text divide it into multiple *parti*—most of them setting the same verses as Monteverdi (and as Marenzio before him)— except for Gioseffo Apolloni of Arezzo, who ends his complete, single-*parte* setting (Book 1 a 4, 1600) at Monteverdi's line 8 ("Pietosissima amante").

21 Artusi, *L'Artusi,* fols. 1v and 39r.

22 Artusi, *L'Artusi,* fol. 39r. Based on Guarini's known activities in Ferrara and Mantua during the Queen's visits, it is plausible that he also attended the performance of Monteverdi's madrigals at Goretti's house. As discussed in Chapter 2, Guarini reports having attended the staging of *Il pastor fido* for the Queen in Mantua on 22 November and needing to return promptly afterward to Ferrara.

23 Artusi, *L'Artusi,* fol. 39v.
24 There is no evidence that Monteverdi was present himself or even in Ferrara at the time, but this performance demonstrates that his music was circulating in manuscript among Ferrarese circles. The scholarly literature on the Artusi–Monteverdi debate is extensive. For a summary of the documents and principal arguments, see Palisca, "The Artusi–Monteverdi Controversy." For more focused analyses of specific terms and facets of the debate, see, for example, Tim Carter, "'E in rileggendo poi le proprie note': Monteverdi Responds to Artusi?," *Renaissance Studies* 26 (2012): 138–55; Seth Coluzzi, "'Se vedesti qui dentro': Monteverdi's *O Mirtillo, Mirtillo anima mia* and Artusi's Offence," *Music and Letters* 94 (2013): 1–37; Suzanne Cusick, "Gendering Modern Music"; Chadwick Jenkins, "Giovanni Maria Artusi and the Ethics of Musical Science," *Acta Musicologica* 81 (2009): 75–97; and Massimo Ossi, *Divining the Oracle: Monteverdi's "Seconda prattica"* (Chicago, IL: University of Chicago Press, 2003), especially Chapter 1 ("The Public Debate").
25 Palisca explores several possibilities for L'Ottuso's identity—an invention by Artusi, the theorist Ercole Bottrigari, a Ferrarese or Mantuan composer-academic, or Monteverdi's brother, Giulio Cesare—in "The Artusi–Monteverdi Controversy," 66–69.
26 On the "novelties"—or unconventional dissonances—in modern music, Luca states:

> I believe truly that this way of composing is a vanity, a chimera, and indeed careless…because I see that in the conducting [*modulare*] of the parts, they use certain intervals that are difficult and far from good voice-leading, which the composer should surely avoid.
>
> (*L'Artusi,* fol. 48r)

Also: "So it is not allowed of anyone who strings together a tune to deprave, corrupt, and introduce new manners of composition with principles founded on sand" (fol. 42v).
27 Chadwick Jenkins examines the ethical dimensions of Artusi's criticism in "Giovanni Maria Artusi and the Ethics of Musical Science."
28 *L'Artusi,* fols. 10v–12r and 43r, and *Seconda parte dell'Artusi,* 47. On direct and indirect sensation, see also Ossi, *Divining the Oracle,* 43–45.
29 Antonio Braccino da Todi, *Discorso secondo musicale* (Venice: Vincenti, 1608), 4–5.
30 Artusi already knew of Monteverdi's conception of a *seconda pratica* in 1603, for he mocks the term in the Second Artusi (p. 33): "This Second Practice, which may in all truth be said to be the dregs of the First" (trans. in Strunk, *Source Readings,* 542). The composer, therefore, likely felt an urgent need to claim it publicly as his own.
31 Monteverdi, *Il quinto libro de madrigali a cinque voci* (Venice: Amadino, 1605), n.p.
32 In a letter to Doni of 22 October 1633, Monteverdi expresses his intentions of still writing a treatise explaining this new compositional approach, founded on Plato's three-part division of music (*melodia*) into oration, harmony, and rhythm (*oratione, harmonia, rithmo*), now with the title *Melodia overo seconda pratica musica* (Monteverdi, *Lettere, dediche e prefazioni,* ed. Domenico de' Paoli [Rome: De Santis, 1973], 321). Ossi also describes the Doni–Monteverdi correspondence and the latter's integration of ancient theory, particularly Plato and Aristotle, into his own musical thought in *Divining the Oracle,* 189–210.
33 Giulio Cesare Monteverdi, *Dichiaratione* appended to the end of Claudio Monteverdi's *Scherzi musicali* (1607); trans. in Strunk, *Source Readings,* 540. On the previous page, Giulio Cesare refers to *oratione* as "padrona." Both "signora" and "padrona" are typically translated as "mistress" and generally connote the authoritative, "commanding" component of music. While both terms agree

with the feminine "oratione"—as well as "harmonia," the *padrona/signora* of the *prima pratica*—Cusick has explored the potential implications of gendered rhetoric in the debate in "Gendering Modern Music."

34   On Artusi's more debatable criticisms pertaining to mode in Monteverdi's works, see Coluzzi, "'Se vedesti qui dentro': Monteverdi's *O Mirtillo, Mirtillo anima mia* and Artusi's Offence."

35   On the morality play, see Bonner Mitchell, *1598: A Year of Pageantry in Late Renaissance Ferrara* (Binghamton, NY: Medieval & Renaissance Texts and Studies, 1990), 41–42. Play productions by the Jesuit order were strictly regulated by the three editions of the *Ratio Studiorum* (1586, 1591, 1599). The 1599 edition specifically proscribed extravagant *intermedi* as well as any trace of femininity in the plays:

> The subject of tragedies and comedies, which must not be given except in Latin and on very rare occasions, ought to be sacred and pious; and nothing should be introduced between the acts which is not in Latin and is not becoming; nor is a feminine role nor feminine attire to be introduced.

Rule 13 of the Rector, trans. in Edward A. Fitzpatrick, *St. Ignatius and the "Ratio Studiorum"* (New York: McGraw-Hill, 1933), 140. On the concert by Livia d'Arco, Laura Pepperara, and others from the Ferrarese court, see note 43 below.

36   "Istromento fatto secondo la diuisione di Don Nicola Vicentino...si ritroua in questa Città nelle mani del Signor Antonio Goretti," *L'Artusi,* fol. 15v. See also Vicentino's *Antica musica* (1555); trans. as *Ancient Music Adapted to Modern Practice.*

37   Gary Tomlinson writes that "Vincenzo Gonzaga surely was Guarini's most ardent admirer among the rulers of Italy, nurturing throughout the 1590s a plan to stage his huge tragicomedy" (*Monteverdi and the End of the Renaissance,* 73). The poet's dedication of the impressive, revised 1602 edition of *Il pastor fido* to Vincenzo Gonzaga acknowledges the duke's admiration and support. On the flip side, however, the dedication of the 1598 Ciotti edition of Guarini's *Rime* to Cardinal Pietro Aldobrandini suggests that there was no exigent need for high-ranking officials of the church to show enmity toward the poet, even while Aldobrandini managed the Papal takeover of the poet's former court. This apparent perception of court artists, to a certain extent, as politically neutral suggests that political factors might have had little influence on Artusi's selective aim at Monteverdi as well.

38   As Tim Carter explains, at the scene in Goretti's house,

> the stage appears set for a smaller version of an ideological conflict—courtiers against churchmen—that had been played out in broader political terms in Ferrara since the early 1590s, but was exacerbated still more by the events of 1597–98.
>
> ("Monteverdi Responds to Artusi?," 142)

39   As Monteverdi suggests, the Fourth Book would have been dedicated to Alfonso d'Este if it had not been for the duke's death. The dedication of the Fifth Book to Vincenzo Gonzaga specifically mentions that under the duke's protection "they will live forever in spite of those tongues that seek to bring death to the works of others" (vivranno eterna vita ad onta di quelle lingue, che cercano di dar morte all'opere altrui). See Ossi, *Divining the Oracle,* 32–34. Ossi ("Monteverdi, Marenzio, and Battista Guarini's 'Cruda Amarilli'") makes the credible argument that in his Fifth Book Monteverdi makes a deliberate effort to align himself not only with Ferrara through his extensive use of Guarini's texts, but also with Marenzio by setting many of the same texts as the older composer and by modeling the structure of his 1605 book on that of Marenzio's Seventh Book.

40

> Luca. [Perfettione della Musica d' alcuni Moderni, qual sia.] Manco stimano, di vedere li Cartoni di Boetio; ma che di sapere ciò che dicono, a loro basta di

sapere insfilzare quelle Solfe, a modo loro, et insegnare di Cantare alli cantanti, le loro Cantilene con molti mouimenti del corpo, accompagnando la
voce con quei moti, et nel fine si lasciano andare di maniera, che paia apunto
che muoiano, et questa è la perfettione della loro Musica.

L'Artusi, fol. 43r; translated in the 1960 edition of Strunk, *Source Readings,* 402.
The passage is omitted from the 1998 edition of Strunk's *Source Readings,* 534.

41 On the *morire* metaphor in sixteenth-century poetry and music, see Chapter 4,
note 28 above.

42 Brauner, in his letter concerning Cusick's "Gendering Modern Music," acknowledges the important role that sexuality might have played in Artusi's attack.
Brauner writes:

Artusi too seems to have perceived this sexuality [in Monteverdi's music],
to his horror, in the 'wild, eye-rolling, body-distorting gestures' of the performers and in the music itself... Artusi does not oppose male and female but
instead the chaste and unchaste. He reveals a dislike—a fear, even—not of
the female but of sexuality.

(*Journal of the American Musicological Society* 47 [1994]: 550–54, at 553–54)

43 The festivities of November 1598 included the last known performance by members of the *concerto* in the wake of Estense rule. In a letter of 17 November 1598,
the Estense ambassador to Rome, Girolamo Giglioli, recounts a private performance by two members of the *concerto,* Livia d'Arco and Laura Pevarara, for
Queen Margherita that took place on 15 November. The *donne* performed with
Fiorini and Luzzaschi, both of whom (Artusi reports) also participated in the
16 November performance of Monteverdi's music at Goretti's house. A portion
of Giglioli's letter is quoted in Elio Durante and Anna Marellotti, *Cronistoria,*
209; see pp. 92–94 for more on the festivities surrounding the 1598 wedding. On
the private performance for Margherita of Austria, see also Anthony Newcomb,
The Madrigal at Ferrara, I, 184. The potential impacts of Artusi's encounter with
Monteverdi's madrigal through performance are explored more fully in Coluzzi
"'Se vedesti qui dentro': Monteverdi's *O Mirtillo.*"

44 Giovanni Fontana, *Constitutioni, et ordinationi generali appartenenti alle monache, publicate d'ordine di Monsig. Reverendiss. Vescovo di Ferrara, l'Anno MDX-
CIX* (Ferrara: Baldini, 1599); see also Jane Bowers, "The Emergence of Women
Composers in Italy, 1566–1700," in *Women Making Music: The Western Art Tradition, 1150–1950,* eds. Jane Bowers and Judith Tick (Urbana: University of Illinois
Press, 1986), 116–67, at 142. Laurie Stras provides a discerning account of the
dynamics of music-making by women in Ferrara during Queen Margherita's visit,
including the concerts by the nuns of San Vito, by the *concerto delle donne,* and at
Goretti's house, in *Women and Music in Sixteenth-Century Ferrara,* 311–20.

45 Artusi, *L'Artusi,* fol. 54v.

46 It must be noted, however, that Artusi does nod favorably toward Guarini and
his play in the *Seconda parte dell'Artusi,* by naming them alongside Petrarch as
examples of the capacity of poetry to convey affects and passions from author to
reader. Artusi writes:

Io rispondo questa Voce havere in se diversi sensi, & significati, & perciò
può torsi come passione d'animo, & eccone lo essempio del Signor Cavaliero
Guerini nel Pastor fido, come gli affetti tuoi son fatti miei; alcune volte per
desiderio, si come il Petrarca.

(*Seconda parte dell'Artusi,* part 1, 17)

47 An important exception is certain madrigal collections of settings by various
composers unified by textual theme, but even here, poetic authorship is only seldom acknowledged. Gaetano Gaspari's compilation *Madrigali pastorali...a sei
voci intitolati "Il bon bacio"* (Venice: Angelo Gardano, 1594), for example, gives

the names of the poet and composer at the start of each work, yet *Il lauro secco* (Ferrara: Baldini, 1582)—a collection commemorating the virtuosic singer-lutenist Laura Pepperara of the *concerto delle donne*—includes the poems independently on facing pages with the musical settings, and denotes the composers by name but not the poets. Likewise, *Sdegnosi ardosi* (Munich: Adam Berg, 1585) contains thirty-one settings of a single text, "Ardo, sì, ma non t'amo," but fails to credit the poem's author.

48 This appears in *Poetica di Iason Denores* (Padua: Paolo Meietto, 1588); cited in Giuseppe Toffanin, *La fine dell'umanesimo,* 146. The full statement reads: "Sarà dunque la poesia imitazione di qualche azione umana meravigliosa, compita e convenevolmente grande, o rappresentando, o narrando...per introdurre virtù negli animi degli spettatori, degli uditori, ad beneficio comune di una ben ordinata Repubblica."

49 "...altro non è, che lo Eccellente sensibile, che corrompe il senso" (*L'Artusi,* fol. 43r; trans. in Strunk, *Source Readings,* 534). Artusi continues by comparing Monteverdi's madrigals (and all modern music) to "a tumult of sounds, a confusion of absurdities, an assemblage of imperfections," which is the product of ignorance (fol. 43v; trans. in Strunk, *Source Readings,* 534). As Suzanne Cusick maintains, through his calculated use of gendered rhetoric and references, Artusi implies that modern music is more than displeasing to the ears in its flouting of theoretical propriety: it threatens to "feminize its listeners and creators" ("Gendering Modern Music," 10).

50 *Seconda parte dell'Artusi,* part 1, 38.

51 Denores writes: "Now being tragicomedy and pastoral, the one in itself a monstrous composition, and the other without a useful end, and for this without merit, and both contrary to the principles of moral philosophy..." (Ora essendo la tragicommedia, e la pastorale, l'una per se, come composizion mostruosa; e l'altra senza fine utile, e perciò come non convenevole, anzi ambedue contrarie a' Principii de' Filosofi morali). Giason Denores, *Discorso...intorno a que' principi* (1586), 240; this statement reappears nearly verbatim in the critic's *Apologia contra l'autor del verato* (1590), 323.

52 The accusation occurs in Antonio Braccino da Todi, *Discorso secondo musicale,* where the theorist claims that in spite of the good teaching of Ingegneri, and instead of "making a good and beautiful composition," the composer "farà un mostro, e queste sono di quelle cose che l'Artusi ha dimostrato che sono deformi dalla natura, dell'arte, e dal vero fine" (10).

53 "...introduce nuove Regole, nuovi modi, et nuova frase del dire" (*L'Artusi,* fol. 39r; trans. in Strunk, *Source Readings,* 527). Artusi also applies the term specifically to the new geometrical divisions of intervals that contradict those of the ancients, and to the indiscriminate mixture of the three *genera*—diatonic, chromatic, and enharmonic—to create an unsanctioned, hybrid contrapuntal idiom analogous to Guarini's amalgamation of poetic genres. During his visit to Ferrara, Artusi evidently encountered at very close proximity an instrument designed to invoke such chimeras, the "instrument made according to the intervals of Don Nicola Vicentino" mentioned above. The presence of such an instrument was, no doubt, but one more component of modern music-making in Goretti's household that contributed to Artusi's indignation.

54 Marco Scacchi, *Breve discorso sopra la musica moderna,* A3v; adapted from Palisca's trans. in "Marco Scacchi's Defense of Modern Music (1649)," in L. Berman, ed., *Words and Music: The Scholar's View* (Cambridge, MA: Department of Music, Harvard University, 1972), 189–235, at 196.

55 Scacchi, *Breve discorso,* B4v–C1r; trans. in Palisca, "Marco Scacchi's Defense," 202.

56 Scacchi, *Breve discorso,* C1r.

57 Artusi, *L'Artusi,* fol. 39v and Scacchi, *Breve discorso,* A2v; trans. in Palisca, "Marco Scacchi's Defense," 195.

References

Arnold, Denis. *Monteverdi* [1967]. In series Master Musicians, ed. Stanley Sadie. Oxford: Oxford University Press, 1990.

Artusi, Giovanni Maria [pseud. Antonio Braccino da Todi]. *Discorso secondo musicale...Per la Dichiaratione della lettera posta ne' Scherzi musicali del sig. Claudio Monteverde.* Venice: Vincenti, 1608.

————. *Seconda parte dell'Artusi ovvero delle imperfettioni della moderna musica.* Venice: Vincenti, 1603.

————. *L'Artusi, overo Delle imperfettioni della moderna musica ragionamenti dui.* Venice: Vincenti, 1600. Selections trans. by Oliver Strunk in *Source Readings in Music History,* 526–34. New York: Norton, 1998.

Bianconi, Lorenzo. "*Ah dolente partita:* espressione ed artificio." *Studi musicali* 3 (1974): 105–30.

Bowers, Jane. "The Emergence of Women Composers in Italy, 1566–1700." In *Women Making Music: The Western Art Tradition, 1150–1950,* eds. Jane Bowers and Judith Tick, 116–67. Urbana: University of Illinois Press, 1986.

Brauner, Charles. "[Letter]." *Journal of the American Musicological Society* 47 (1994): 550–54.

Calcagno, Mauro. "'Imitar col canto chi parla': Monteverdi and the Creation of a Language for Musical Theater." *Journal of the American Musicological Society* 55 (2002): 383–431.

Carter, Tim. "'E in rileggendo poi le proprie note': Monteverdi Responds to Artusi?" *Renaissance Studies* 26 (2012): 138–55.

————. "'An Air New and Grateful to the Ear': The Concept of 'Aria' in Late Renaissance and Early Baroque Italy." *Music Analysis* 12 (1993): 127–145.

Chafe, Eric. *Monteverdi's Tonal Language.* New York: Schirmer, 1992.

Chater, James. "'Un pasticcio di madrigaletti'?: The Early Musical Fortune of *Il pastor fido.*" In *Guarini: la musica, i musicisti,* ed. A. Pompilio, 139–55. Lucca: Libreria Musicale Italiana Editrice, 1997.

Coluzzi, Seth. "'Se vedesti qui dentro': Monteverdi's *O Mirtillo, Mirtillo anima mia* and Artusi's Offence." *Music and Letters* 94 (2013): 1–37.

Cusick, Susanne. "Gendering Modern Music: Thoughts on the Monteverdi–Artusi Controversy." *Journal of the American Musicological Society* 46 (1993): 1–25.

Dahlhaus, Carl. *Studies on the Origin of Harmonic Tonality.* Trans. by Robert Gjerdingen. Princeton, NJ: Princeton University Press, 1991.

Denores, Giason. *Apologia contra l'autor del verato...di quanto ha egli detto in un suo Discorso delle Tragicommedie, e delle Pastorali.* Padua: Paolo Meietti, 1590.

————. *Poetica di Iason Denores.* Padua: Paolo Meietto, 1588.

————. *Discorso...intorno à que' principii, cause, et accrescimenti, che la comedia, la tragedia, et il poema heroico ricevono dalla philosophia morale, e civile, e da' governatori delle republiche.* Padua: Paulo Meieto, 1586.

Durante, Elio and Anna Martellotti, eds. *Le due 'scelte' napoletane.* 2 vols. Florence: Studio per edizioni scelte, 1998.

Fenlon, Iain. "Music and Spectacle at the Gonzaga Court." *Proceedings of the Royal Musical Association* 103 (1976–77): 90–105.

Fitzpatrick, Edward A. *St. Ignatius and the 'Ratio Studiorum.'* New York: McGraw-Hill, 1933.

Fontana, Giovanni. *Constitutioni, et ordinationi generali appartenenti alle monache, publicate d'ordine di Monsig. Reverendiss. Vescovo di Ferrara, l'Anno MDXCIX.* Ferrara: Baldini, 1599.

Georis, Christophe. *Claudio Monteverdi "letterato" ou les métamorphoses du texte.* Paris: Honoré Champion, 2013.

Jenkins, Chadwick. "Giovanni Maria Artusi and the Ethics of Musical Science." *Acta Musicologica* 81 (2009): 75–97.

Kaufmann, Paul, ed. *Fiori del giardino di diversi eccellentissimi autori.* Nuremburg: Kaufmann, 1597.

Luzzaschi, Luzzasco. *Madrigali per cantare et sonare a uno, doi, e tre soprani.* Rome: Verovio, 1601. Eds. Elio Durante and Anna Martellotti. Florence: Studio per edizioni scelte, 1980.

Mitchell, Bonner. *1598: A Year of Pageantry in Late Renaissance Ferrara.* Binghamton, NY: Medieval & Renaissance Texts and Studies, 1990.

Monteverdi, Claudio. *Lettere, dediche e prefazioni.* Ed. Domenico de' Paoli. Rome: De Santis, 1973.

———. *Scherzi musicali a tre voci.* Venice: Amadino, 1607.

———. *Il quinto libro de madrigali a cinque voci.* Venice: Amadino, 1605.

———. *Il quarto libro de madrigali a cinque voci.* Venice: Amadino, 1603.

Newcomb, Anthony. *The Madrigal at Ferrara, 1579–97.* 2 vols. Princeton, NJ: Princeton University Press, 1981.

Ossi, Massimo. *Divining the Oracle: Monteverdi's 'Seconda prattica.'* Chicago, IL: University of Chicago Press, 2003.

Palisca, Claude. "The Artusi–Monteverdi Controversy." In *The New Monteverdi Companion,* eds. D. Arnold and N. Fortune, 127–58. London: Faber, 1985.

Scacchi, Marco. *Breve discorso sopra la musica moderna.* Warsaw: Pietro Elert, 1649. Trans. by Claude Palisca in "Marco Scacchi's Defense of Modern Music (1649)." In *Words and Music: The Scholar's View,* ed. L. Berman, 189–235. Cambridge, MA: Department of Music, Harvard University, 1972.

Stras, Laurie. *Women and Music in Sixteenth-Century Ferrara.* In series New Perspectives in Music History and Criticism. Cambridge: Cambridge University Press, 2018.

Toffanin, Giuseppe. *La fine dell'umanesimo.* Milan: Fratelli Bocca, 1920.

Tomlinson, Gary. *Monteverdi and the End of the Renaissance.* Oxford: Clarendon, 1987.

Varoli, Benedetto, ed. *Della nova scelta di rime di diversi eccellenti scrittori de l'età nostra parte prima.* Casalmaggiore: Antonio Guerino e compagno, 1590.

Vicentino, Nicola. *L'antica musica ridotta alla moderna prattica.* Rome: Antonio Barre, 1555. Trans. by Maria Rika Maniates as *Ancient Music Adapted to Modern Practice.* New Haven, CT: Yale University Press, 1996.

7 Madrigalian Discourses in (and Beyond) Monteverdi's Fifth Book

The Fifth Book opens with Monteverdi's celebrated and provocative setting of *Cruda Amarilli*—a work that generated seven of Artusi's examples of the contrapuntal infractions in Monteverdi's music, more than any other piece.[1] The first of these offensive excerpts comes at the exclamation "ahi lasso" (alas) in the opening lines: "Cruda Amarilli, che col nome ancora / D'amar, ahi lasso, amaramente insegni" (Cruel Amarilli, who even with your name / to love—alas!—you bitterly teach).[2] After the four lower voices have begun the phrase, three of them with cascading sixteenth-note (*semifusa*) descents on "ahi," the Canto enters in m. 13 on a'' (a ninth above the Basso's g) and leaps directly to f'' (a seventh above the Basso) before resolving to e'' in a C cadence (Example 7.1). This passage—devoid of its text—served as one of Artusi's chief examples of the impertinences of "modern music" and contributed (along with the work's alleged mixing of modes) to his comparison of the madrigal to a monster formed from the disparate parts of various creatures (man, crane, swallow, and ox).[3]

Less prominent in discussions of the piece, however, is the immediate restatement of "che col nome ancora / D'amar, ahi lasso" in the three lowest voices alone in mm. 14–20 (Example 7.1). In place of the Canto's unprepared dissonance at "ahi lasso" is an extended run in the Basso that leads to another C cadence in m. 20, followed by a series of poignant (and also offensive) dissonances that mirror the bitterness of Amarilli's lesson.[4] Although largely overlooked in the scholarship, this bass run is unusual in its magnitude, its extravagance, and its placement in the bass voice not only for this madrigal or for the Fifth Book, but for all of Monteverdi's output up to this point.

Another atypical feature of the second "ahi lasso" (mm. 17–20) is the Basso's deviation from the basso continuo part published with the Fifth Book. As Example 7.2 shows, the Basso elaborates the continuo's sustained c in m. 17 with an upper-neighbor note, and fills in the leap from c to g in m. 18 with a neighbor figure and a sixteenth-note run. In all, this flourish spans a minor tenth descent (d'–B) followed by a rise of a minor sixth (B–g). In the first section of the Fifth Book, the continuo is optional and represents more of a *basso seguente*. Hence, rarely does it deviate from the lowest active

DOI: 10.4324/9781315463056-8

Example 7.1 Monteverdi, *Cruda Amarilli, che col nome ancora*, mm. 1–20

voice, apart from instances where the vocal part divides a sustained pitch to accommodate multiple syllables of text. The text here—the exclamation "ahi"—is only one syllable and semantically seems an odd fit for such an exceptional display of the Basso's virtuosity and independence.

An explanation for the anomalous gesture may lie in the relationship between the two bass parts (Example 7.2). For the voice's elaborations of the

Example 7.2 Monteverdi, *Cruda Amarilli*, Basso and Continuo, mm. 11–20

continuo line in mm. 17–18 resemble the types of figurations found in manuals for instrumental diminution around this time. The Basso's passage, in other words, seems to convey an improvisatory elaboration of the basso continuo line—a stylistic practice with which Monteverdi would have been intimately familiar, given his experience as an instrumentalist and the circumstances of his employment.

Monteverdi first entered Vincenzo Gonzaga's service in Mantua in 1590 or 1591 not primarily as a composer or music director, but as a singer and violist. As the composer recalls in the dedication of his Third Book of madrigals (1592), it was the "most noble practice of the *vivuola* that opened the fortunate door for me into [the duke's] service."[5] Monteverdi's activity as an instrumentalist, therefore, was public knowledge. In his 2002 article "Monteverdi, the Viola Bastarda Player," James Bates has proposed compellingly that Monteverdi's employment in Mantua stemmed first and foremost from Vincenzo Gonzaga's interest in creating a Ferrarese-style *concerto delle donne* and, hence, from the demand specifically for a *viola bastarda* to accompany such an ensemble.[6] Anthony Newcomb has also pointed out that in the years leading up to Monteverdi's move to Mantua, both the Mantuan and Ferrarese courts vied unsuccessfully to recruit the *viola bastarda* player of the Farnese court in Parma, Orazio Bassani della Viola.[7] Monteverdi, it seems, filled this position instead.

Years after assuming this post, viola playing still occupied a large share of Monteverdi's duties. In his letter appended to the Fifth Book of madrigals, Monteverdi explained that he could not respond at length to Artusi's criticisms because, "being in the service of this Most Serene Highness of Mantua, I am not master of the time I would require."[8] Giulio Cesare elaborated on this remark in his *Dichiaratione* two years later, explaining that the composer "finds the greater part of his time taken up, now with tourneys, now with ballets, now with comedies and various concerts, and lastly in *concertar le due Viole bastarde*."[9] Even as late as 1643, in the wake of

Monteverdi's death, Matteo Caberloti remembered the composer as a "new Orpheus with the sound of his viola, at which he had no equals."[10]

The term *viola bastarda* refers not to a specific instrument, but to a virtuosic, largely extemporaneous technique of playing a bass- or tenor-sized viola da gamba.[11] The *bastarda* style connotes a wide-ranging bass incorporating rapid divisions, often reducing multiple voices of a polyphonic texture—particularly the Basso and Tenore, but also sometimes the upper parts—to a single line. As Joëlle Morton has described it, "*bastarda* refers to a style of composition in which a bass instrument or voice is called upon to step outside its usual accompanying role, taking on a purely melodic function," and a "non-chordal, linear style."[12] The seven extant collections of *viola bastarda* music from the late sixteenth and early seventeenth centuries, moreover, are filled with wide-ranging, florid *passaggi* in the bass–tenor range that resemble the Basso's figuration at "ahi lasso" in *Cruda Amarilli*.[13]

The Basso's gesture, therefore, seems to offer a glimpse—albeit a brief one—into Monteverdi's thinking, skills, and activities outside the printed madrigal book, as a performer and improviser on the *viola bastarda*. The passage, then, also represents precisely the sort of improvisatory instrumental practices—juxtaposed in print with its unadorned form in the continuo—to which Artusi objected in vocal music. Artusi does not cite the passage in mm. 17–18, for it contains no modal or contrapuntal violation. However, referring to the offensive dissonances elsewhere in the madrigal—the Canto's striking "ahi lasso" in mm. 13–14, the Quinto's dissonantly prepared suspension (*f* over *g*) for the cadence in mm. 19–20, the consecutive sevenths and ninths at "e più fugace" (mm. 42–43), and others—Artusi accuses the composer of having devised the passages through improvising on an instrument. In instrumental performance, the theorist asserts, such incidental dissonances are admissible. But in written composition, where reason must prevail over the untrustworthy senses, such offenses have no place:

> It is known that the ear is deceived, and to this these composers, or new inventors, apply themselves with enthusiasm. They seek only to satisfy the ear and with this aim toil night and day at their instruments to hear the effect which passages so made produce. The poor fellows do not perceive that what the instruments tell them is false...[14]

Monteverdi's activity as a violist would have made him a consummate target for Artusi's purposes, for it legitimized the theorist's combined criticism of modern music and the inclusion of instrumental practices in written music. The fact that Monteverdi specialized in the *viola bastarda* might have proved all the more expedient for Artusi's potential implicit agenda, for it reinforces the ties between Monteverdi's (modern) music and the musical practices of the Ferrarese and Mantuan courts with their *concerti di donne*.

As printed manifestations of Monteverdi's instrumental "toiling," the Basso's diminutions and their placement in the already provocative opening madrigal of the collection would have dealt an immediate, concerted musical retaliation to Artusi's convictions. But their implications may extend even beyond *Cruda Amarilli*. Among the numerous theories that scholars have proposed for large-scale coherence in the Fifth Book, two, in particular, have become standard currency: first, that the book conveys a narrative loosely based on the struggles between two pairs of characters—Amarilli/Mirtillo and Dorinda/Silvio—in one of its chief textual sources, *Il pastor fido*, and second, that the opening madrigals, *Cruda Amarilli* and *O Mirtillo*, function as a pair—with Amarilli's *O Mirtillo* (III,4) responding to Mirtillo's insults and anger in *Cruda Amarilli* (I,2).[15] Scholars have also noted Monteverdi's audacity in placing the contrapuntally and modally offensive *Cruda Amarilli* at the front of the book, while responding to Artusi in prose at the end.

Yet the contents of the book may also follow another narrative, at least in part, that has little to do with the storyline of Guarini's play. For the first four madrigals of the Fifth Book, all follow the precise order in which Artusi dealt with them in his first and second published critiques of 1600 and 1603. *Cruda Amarilli* and *O Mirtillo* came under fire, in that order, in Artusi's first attack (*L'Artusi*), followed by *Era l'anima mia* and *Ecco, Silvio, colei che 'n odio hai tanto* in the *Seconda parte dell'Artusi* (Table 7.1). The one madrigal that falls outside this chronology is *Anima mia, perdona*, which the theorist mentions second in his earlier pamphlet, but which appeared in Monteverdi's Fourth Book in 1603. Notwithstanding this one omission, the opening of the Fifth Book serves as a sort of digest—a *compendio in musica*—of the offences of modern music cited by Artusi.

Table 7.1 Contents of Monteverdi's Fifth Book of Madrigals (1605)

		Madrigal	Textual source
L'Artusi (1600)	1	Cruda Amarilli, che col nome ancora	Guarini, Pastor fido (I,2)
		[Anima mia, perdona (Book 4, 1603)	Guarini, Pastor fido (III,4)]
Seconda	2	O Mirtillo, Mirtillo anima mia	Guarini, Pastor fido (III,4)
parte	3	Era l'anima mia	Guarini, Rime
dell'Artusi	4	Ecco, Silvio, colei che 'n odio hai tanto (5 parti)	Guarini, Pastor fido (IV,9)
(1603)	5	Ch'io t'ami e t'ami più de la mia vita (3 parti)	Guarini, Pastor fido (III,3)
	6	Che dar più vi poss'io	Anon.
	7	M'è più dolce il penar per Amarilli	Guarini, Pastor fido (III,6)
	8	Ahi, come a un vago sol cortese giro	Guarini, Rime
	9	Troppo ben può questo tiranno amore	Guarini, Rime
	10	Amor, se giusto sei	Anon.
	11	T'amo mia vita, la mia cara vita	Guarini, Rime
	12	E così a poco a poco	Guarini, Rime
	13	Questi vaghi concenti	Anon.

Within this digest, the placement of the Basso's peculiar *bastarda*-style display hardly seems coincidental. For the gesture serves as a musical analogue to the artist's thumbing his nose at the critic. Not only does Monteverdi begin the collection with the most offensive of his madrigals and end it with a letter acknowledging Artusi's attack, but he also includes a flagrant reference to the instrumental techniques that (Artusi claims) spawned these "offenses." As a result, the opening measures of the Fifth Book flaunt all of the monstrous features of "modern music": illicit dissonances, mixing of modes (in the challenge to the underlying G-mixolydian by C-hypolydian), and the "false passages" devised on instruments. Influences of Monteverdi's instrumental practices might also lie behind the notably narrow range of modal finals in the Fifth Book—there are only two, G and D, which correspond to the two lowest strings in standard *viola bastarda* tuning—and the anomalous change of system only four measures from the end of the *prima parte* of *Ch'io t'ami, e t'ami più de la mia vita.*[16]

Whereas Scacchi's *Breve discorso* (1649) discussed above testifies overtly to the enduring and widespread influence of Monteverdi's *seconda pratica*, the example of the Fifth Book itself likewise resonated from relatively distant corners years after its publication. Several aspects of Monteverdi's works, for example, emerge in the works of Claudio Pari (1574–1619), born in Burgundy but active in Sicily in 1598–1619. The most blatant of these references come in Pari's twelve-*parte* madrigal *Il lamento d'Arianna*, published in his Fourth Book of five-voice madrigals (Palermo, 1619). Pari's work quotes Monteverdi's own *Lamento d'Arianna* (Sixth Book, 1614) while setting the same words by Ottavio Rinuccini in the *prima parte*, and thereafter continues to reference the older composer's musical ideas, even while turning from Rinuccini's text to a translation of Ovid's telling of Arianna's abandonment.

More directly relevant to our purposes here, however, are the signs of Monteverdi's influence that appear in Pari's Third Book *a5* (1617). Roughly half of the book's contents set passages from *Il pastor fido*, but the ordering of the initial pieces follows not the play, but Monteverdi's Fifth Book.[17] It begins with the lineup of *Cruda Amarilli*, *O Mirtillo*, and *Era l'anima mia*, all of which set precisely the same passages treated by Monteverdi. Comparisons of the two composers' settings are limited by the fact that only two of the five partbooks of Pari's volume survive. Yet, while the surviving Basso partbook shows no explicit references to Monteverdi's settings, its florid melismas embellishing the cadences at "ancora," "lasso," and "sorda" in Pari's *Cruda Amarilli* may act as a nod to Monteverdi's *bastarda*-style treatment of the Basso in his setting of that text, as well as to Monteverdi as instrumentalist more generally. These parallels in the texts, ordering, and techniques of the two books could be coincidental, yet Pari's allusions to Monteverdi's *Lamento d'Arianna* two years later, in 1619, further attest to his familiarity with the Mantuan (turned Venetian) composer's music and to his willingness to display this influence in his own readings of the same texts.

As we have seen, when Monteverdi's settings of *Cruda Amarilli* and *O Mirtillo* came to print in 1605, they became part of a growing stock of treatments of these texts, including those of Monte, Marenzio, Wert, Pallavicino, and Giovanelli. Given their *terminus ante quem* of November 1598, however, only the 1595 settings of Marenzio and Wert—along with Monte's 1590 treatment of a highly variant reading of *Cruda Amarilli*—likely predate them. Further, unlike many of the early *Pastor fido* settings by Marenzio and Mantuan composers Pallavicino, Rossi, and Gastoldi that sever explicit references to the play by removing or changing the names of characters, the renderings of the Fifth Book seem to bolster their ties to the tragicomedy by remaining relatively true to its readings, retaining character names, and in several cases bearing these names in their incipits. As a result, the names of four principal characters—Amarilli, Mirtillo, Silvio, and Dorinda—appear in the book's table of contents. This intertextual approach in the 1605 book differs from the strategy of the Fourth Book, where *Anima mia, perdona* omits Mirtillo's name from the opening line ("E tu, Mirtillo, anima mia, perdona") and *Quel augellin che canta* skips three lines from the play that include a reference to Silvio. While there is no way to know to what extent contemporary readers related the madrigals to the play, we have seen that at least one listener—Artusi—recognized the connection and deemed it relevant enough to name the textual source in his critique. There are many plausible explanations for the more overt referentiality of the Fifth Book: to uphold a narrative explicitly related to the play (as many have proposed), to link the book generally to Guarini's work, and to align its "modern" sensibilities with the ideals of modern drama. It is also plausible that the contents simply reflected the tastes of the Mantuan court, a specific patron, or the composer himself.

The literature on the madrigals of the Fifth Book is vast, stretching from their role in the Artusi–Monteverdi debate and novel expressive means, to their organization as a "book," incorporation of accompanied solo voice, and purported tonal behavior. The remainder of this chapter builds on and reexamines this earlier scholarship while exploring three other central aspects of the music: modal structure and temporality in the opening readings of Mirtillo's and Amarilli's laments, *Cruda Amarilli* and *O Mirtillo*; referential and affective strategies and the rendering of separate identities in the five-*parte* multi-speaker cycle *Ecco, Silvio*; and motivic associations between separate madrigals and madrigal books and the interpretative consequences thereof.

Modal Structure and the Temporal Worlds of Mirtillo and Amarilli

The study of Marenzio's and Wert's settings of *Cruda Amarilli* in Chapter 5 revealed fundamental differences in how the two composers treated Mirtillo's lament. In addition to the contrasting lengths of their texts and differing modes, the madrigals show widely divergent strategies in terms of cadence formation and plan, modal character, and structural behavior as a determinant of large-scale tension and temporality. Whereas Wert set fifteen lines with a static C-hypolydian structure that rarely ventures beyond the mode's principal cadences, Marenzio treated twenty lines with a dynamic E-phrygian framework beset by modal conflicts and unconventional cadences. These divergent readings illuminate different sides of Guarini's text and its central personas: Wert's captures Mirtillo's unflagging love for his unattainable beloved with modal constancy and an effect of timeless lyric reflection; Marenzio's renders the shepherd's suffering state through a tumultuous foreground, while also exploring the complexity of Amarilli's persona—the dichotomy between false, cruel (but beautiful) exterior and true inward struggle—on the broader scale with a modal grounding obscured by local-level oppositions.

Monteverdi's treatment is unique among the seven *Cruda Amarilli* settings issued through 1605 for the brevity of its text—only the first eight lines of Mirtillo's speech, which constitute only the *prima parte* of all the earlier settings apart from Monte's—and for its grounding in the G-mixolydian mode. The celebrated expressive force of Monteverdi's reading, moreover, comes not only in its notorious dissonances, but also in its integration of *seconda pratica* techniques into a fusion of the two approaches to structural–temporal design that separately dominate the late madrigals of Marenzio and Wert. The madrigal reveals its structural–affective strategies at the outset. As Examples 7.1 and 7.3 illustrate, the opening cries of "Cruda Amarilli" in mm. 1–8 set out a key structural motive in the madrigal: not only the melodic components and the general shift from G to C, but also the immediate displacement of the governing d'' ($\hat{5}$) by c'' ($\hat{4}$), later supporting the upper-neighbor e'' (m. 14). This is not a fundamental motion—the instigation of the background descent from $\hat{5}$ toward $\hat{4}$—but an ephemeral challenge to the established d'' at the middleground level, like a compressed version of the ousting of e'' by d'' in the *prima parte* of Marenzio's setting.

Through its many recurrences and origins in Amarilli's name, the motive echoes Amarilli's name throughout the piece with futile motions d''–c'',

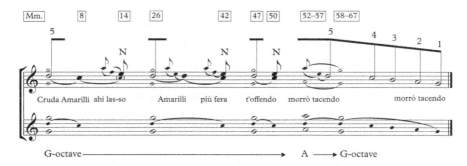

Example 7.3 Monteverdi, *Cruda Amarilli*, Structural Analysis

rendering musically Mirtillo's fixation on his beloved. Like the statements "Cruda Amarilli" in the opening measures, these echoes yield repeated shifts from G to C and displacements of the background d'' that only circle back, leading nowhere, acting instead as a structural stammer that repeatedly recalls the beloved's name. The result, then, is an arrested structure whose advancement is impeded by "Cruda Amarilli," yet also animated by these disruptive gestures at the middleground level. This portrayal complements Mirtillo's "faithful" passion that forms the basis of the play, and which receives its first direct expression here, in his opening apostrophe.

By the time we reach "ahi lasso" in verse 2 (mm. 13–14), the G modal octave with its divisions at D and C has been firmly established. As seen in Example 7.1, this second approach to C in mm. 11–14 represents the first variation of the "Cruda Amarilli" motive. While preserving the basic bass motion, the gesture is now intensified by rapid descents in the lower voices and the Canto's notorious unprepared a'', which stumbles downward through the dissonant f'', onto e'' as middleground upper neighbor. Analysts, viewing the piece in primarily vertical (harmonic) terms, have pointed to the polarity between the tonal centers G and C as the principal conflict in the madrigal, while viewing the a'' in m. 13 as a fleeting but mishandled dissonance. But it is this striking a'', with its implication of a foreign *diatessaron* species ($a''-e''$), in fact, that proves the madrigal's key obstruction—the cause of its structural faltering and enduring conflict that drives the piece forward. Thus, it also represents the key to the work's resolution on the large scale.

Susan McClary interprets the Canto's $a''-e''$ "ahi lasso" gesture as a truncated descent of a fifth from a'' to d''.[18] But this reading overlooks the crucial point that it is precisely because it arises in the G-octave context of the mixolydian mode, in a cadence directed at C, that this $a''-e''$ *diatessaron* grates against the modal framework (Example 7.3). The unresolved discord touches off a series of similarly poignant ascents to a''—all linked to Mirtillo's fixation on his beloved through "Cruda Amarilli" echoes—and sometimes impotent moves toward C as temporary modal center. Cadences to C in themselves are by no means out of place in the G-mixolydian mode: it is the reciting tone of the mode's collateral (hypomixolydian) and, in practice, a common cadence goal in both modes. But here, it is the source of these surface-level shifts toward C, in the modally conflicting descents from a'', that is distinctly unsettling, as Artusi's reaction attests.[19]

Following its first reappearance at "ahi lasso," the "Cruda Amarilli" motive resurfaces in modified form with the twofold return of Amarilli's name in mm. 26–29 (Example 7.4a). Although the texture contracts from five voices to four between the two statements, the repetition of Amarilli's name escalates nonetheless with the addition of a flourish and escape tone a'' in the Canto. The major change in this instance is that both phrases lead from C to D, meaning that they reinforce the primary background d'', rather than displace it with another structural stammer to e''/c'' (see Example 7.3). Another disruption of this faltering sort, however, comes soon after, in mm.

39–42, where the description of Amarilli's deafness and cruelty elicits a third "Cruda Amarilli" echo (Example 7.4b). Here, the motive appears in compressed form but with the original juxtaposition of G- and C-based phrases, with the latter again intensified with a leap from a'' to a dissonant f''.

Through its persistent stumbling between $\hat{5}$ and $\hat{4}$, d'' and c'', with recurring allusions to the cruel beloved, the madrigal conveys an effect of attempting to advance, but continually reverting to its original state. The structure, therefore, is effectively static, while wavering with each Amarilli echo. The G-modal octave also remains fixed until the final verse. But it is precisely this unyielding modal octave that bars the structural

a) mm. 26–29

b) mm. 39–42

Example 7.4 Monteverdi, *Cruda Amarilli*, Recurrences of the "Cruda Amarilli" Motive

unfolding. As Example 7.3 shows, from its first dissonant articulation at "ahi lasso" in m. 13, the Canto's *a″* has remained unresolved—tied to "cruda Amarilli" and the disruptive *e″* upper neighbors. The pitch's resolution at the structural level, then, requires the contextual support of its own A-octave, rather than the G-octave of the underlying mode, to allow its full descent to the background *d″*. This A-octave context finally comes at "I' mi morrò tacendo" (mm. 51–55)—Mirtillo's resolution to die silently—where the Canto climbs from *e″* to *a″* and falls not to the upper-neighbor *e″*, as before, but a full fifth to the background $\hat{5}$, *d″* (see Example 7.5). This alignment reconciles the long-standing conflict between *a″* and the G-centered framework, putting an end to the structural stammering. Thereafter, the G-octave returns and the complete background *diapente*, *d″–g′*, unfolds in the last fifteen measures, as the voices repeat Mirtillo's will to die silently.

The treatment of structure and temporality in the settings of *Cruda Amarilli* by Marenzio, Wert, and Monteverdi highlight three different aspects of the text and characters: Amarilli's doubly divided nature (cruel/beautiful, dutiful/desiring), Mirtillo's devotion, and the torment that the mere thought of "cruda Amarilli" brings to the shepherd's emotional state. Through the coordination of the madrigal's resolution of the antagonizing *a″* and background descent with the notion of a silent death at the end of the text, Monteverdi's reading likewise communicates the faithful shepherd's fidelity to his love, such that only death can shake Amarilli from his mind. This analysis, furthermore, offers an implicit, belated defense of Monteverdi's madrigal by demonstrating that its orientation toward both G and C represents not true modal mixture, as Artusi contends, but an alternation between cadential centers that complies with the normative handling in practice of the G-mixolydian framework.

Example 7.5 Monteverdi, *Cruda Amarilli*, mm. 49–55

Many analysts have read changes of texture and voicing in this and other madrigals as having some effect of representation or embodiment of the speaker's subjectivity. But, seen through the lens of the madrigal as heightened reading and not enactment (as *diegesis* rather than *mimesis*), these changes allow various voice parts—and, hence, performers—the opportunity to step forward temporarily in delivering the text, thereby taking on the role not of Mirtillo himself, as would an actor onstage, but of principal conveyor(s) of his words and his sentiments. In keeping with the shared enterprise of the madrigal and ensemble as narrator–reader, this "leading" role changes more or less frequently, and more or less manifestly through the course of the piece, falling at times on an individual voice or subgroup, and at other times shared evenly by the multiple parts, all the while drawing eyes from one angle to another, and, hence, their focus from one component voice to another.

This reading adds a new perspective to our understanding not only of this madrigal itself, but also of its potential relationship with the neighboring work in the Fifth Book, *O Mirtillo*, a setting of Amarilli's apostrophe from act 3 that also attracted considerable attention from Artusi. The passage reads:

1	O Mirtillo, Mirtillo anima mia,	O Mirtillo, Mirtillo my soul,
	Se vedesti qui dentro	if you would see what lies here
	Come sta il cor di questa	in the heart of this one
	Che chiami crudelissima Amarilli,	that you call cruelest Amarilli,
5	So ben che tu di lei	I know that you, for her,
	Quella pietà che da lei chiedi, havressi.	would feel that pity that you ask of her.
	O anime in amor troppo infelici.	Oh souls too unhappy in love.
	Che giova a te, cor mio, l'esser amato?	What good is it to you, my heart, to be loved?
	Che giova a me l'haver si caro amante?	What good is it to me to have so dear a lover?
10	Perchè, crudo destino,	Why, cruel destiny,
	Ne disunisci tu, s'Amor ne stringe?	do you separate us, if Love binds us?
	E tu, perchè ne stringi,	And you, why do you bind us,
	Se ne parte il destin, perfido Amore?[20]	if destiny parts us, deceitful Love?

The speech comes at the start of scene 4, immediately following Amarilli's harsh dismissal of Mirtillo after the *Gioco della cieca*. In the previous scene, even as Mirtillo professed his love, Amarilli not only rejects him, but scolds him and drives him away in order to guard her necessary betrothal to Silvio. Mirtillo responds with an outburst of bitter accusations that culminates in the lines of *Ah, dolente partita*. Amarilli, once alone, reacts with an outpouring of emotion, the beginning of which is the passage set by Monteverdi.

As mentioned earlier, *O Mirtillo* demonstrates more than any other madrigal in the debate that despite his rigorous scholastic approach, not all of Artusi's critical judgments rest equally soundly on their theoretical foundations. This is true especially with his appraisals relating to mode, as glimpsed already in his comparison of *Cruda Amarilli* to a hybrid beast for the prevalence of C cadences in a G-mixolydian work. In his critique of

O Mirtillo—his primary example of modal transgression—Artusi cites the madrigal's illicit mixing of modes, and most importantly, its alleged failure to begin and end in the same mode.[21] In defending the work, Giulio Cesare wisely recalls the acceptance of mixed modes by Artusi's teacher, Zarlino, in Book 4 of the *Istitutioni harmoniche* (1558).[22] But Giulio Cesare's response— like Artusi's initial criticism—has been taken as overly simplistic and unsubstantial. As Claude Palisca describes it:

> Giulio Cesare Monteverdi's gloss on his brother's letter is...naïve in replying to the first attack. He justifies the disunity of mode in *O Mirtillo* on the precedents of the mixed modes of plainchant and the mixtures of modes in compositions of Josquin, Willaert, Rore, and Alessandro Striggio the elder.[23]

But here Palisca takes only half of Giulio Cesare's defense into consideration. For in addition to the two basic defenses used elsewhere in the *Dichiaratione*—the "command" of the text and the example of Monteverdi's esteemed predecessors—the charge of modal discontinuity leads Giulio Cesare to issue a new, third premise: that the mixing of modes in his brother's work is both justified and rational when the entirety of the madrigal is taken into account—that is, when considering "not merely the portions or passages of the composition, but its whole" (cioè intorno non alle particelle o passaggi della cantilena solamente ma allo suo tutto).[24] Far from "naïve," Giulio Cesare seems to invoke a more integrated concept of modal unity than Artusi considers, and in doing so echoes the testament of many theorists before him. Zarlino, for example, explains that mode should be judged "by the whole form contained in the composition" (dalla forma tutta contenuta nella cantilena):

> It should be noted that the mode of a composition can be judged by two things: first, by the form of the entire composition, and second, by the ending of the composition, namely, by its final note. Since it is form which gives being to a thing, I would consider it reasonable to determine the mode of a composition not merely by the final note, as some have wanted, but by the whole form contained in the composition.[25]

Giulio Cesare's statement, though overlooked in recent interpretations of the debate, is significant, for it demonstrates his awareness of mode as an integrated system of expectations underlying his brother's music. His rather inchoate explication of modal unity as stemming not from the mere "details" of a composition but from "its whole" seems to demonstrate his inability to convey with words the workings of an overarching framework such as mode. Clearly, the theorists of the Renaissance faced similar difficulties as they attempted—albeit with limited success—to codify long-range tendencies they perceived in the music using such parameters as cadence plan, ambitus, melodic structure, and the beginning and ending tones of a piece. Palisca, therefore, may take matters in the wrong direction with his later claim that "Giulio Cesare's reply did not come to terms with the issue, because he lacked either the courage or conviction to proclaim the end of the tyranny of the modes."[26] Rather, Giulio Cesare's biggest weakness in the case of mode may have been his lack of a vocabulary with which to express the perception of modal structure. He—and presumably his brother—certainly showed no interest in declaring the modes dead.

Artusi's criticism of the madrigal in *L'Artusi* reads:

> I heard a madrigal not many days ago that began with the sound of the twelfth mode with B♭ [i.e., F-hypoionian]; then if I remember well, it was returned to B natural and ended in the first [mode; i.e., D-dorian]; and it seemed to me that the words of the madrigal said, *O Mirtillo*, of Guarini, taken from *Il pastor fido*; which gave me a lot to think about, nor do I know how one who has the profession of an honorable man allows himself to slip into such imperfections.[27]

Indeed, the madrigal's opening with a B♭ sonority in a *cantus-durus* context (Example 7.6) and final cadence on D, along with its variety of cadential goals, have continued to challenge analysts.[28] These features lead Carl Dahlhaus, for example, to regard the modal final—which, despite the D ending, he determines to be G in a mixolydian context—as a "first among equals" among the six pitches ("component keys") of the natural hexachord, and to deny altogether that mode has any major part in the integrated process of the work.[29] More recently, Eric Chafe has applied a similar approach of viewing cadences and non-cadential verse-endings alike (and equally) as representative of mode and, more imperatively, of hexachordal predominance, while recognizing the final of the piece more accurately as D.

While Monteverdi's work may seem to invite analysis focused on harmonic and proto-tonal features with its largely homophonic texture, frequent fifth-based patterns, and historical position on the cusp of the seventeenth century—the notional beginning of the Baroque Period—there is much to be gained from an examination based on sixteenth-century theories of counterpoint and mode (as Giulio Cesare reminds us). Recognizing the beginning of the madrigal (mm. 1–34), therefore, not as a series of arrivals on vertical sonorities—and, hence, of pitches articulated in the lowest voice[30]—but as an unfolding linear motion in the (structural) upper voice reveals that this modally unsettled rendering of the opening verses in fact forms a strongly directed stepwise ascent from $\hat{3}$ (*f'*) to $\hat{5}$ (*a'*), the first pitch of the background structure (Example 7.7), and, thus, that the work indeed begins in the D-dorian mode—the mode in which it also ends, and that which governs the madrigal's entire framework. The mode, however, remains concealed through the beginning due to the initiatory *f'-a'* ascent. While the first pitch of this structural anacrusis, *f'*, is expanded over the first

Example 7.6 Monteverdi, *O Mirtillo, Mirtillo anima mia*, mm. 1–21

two measures with the phrase "O Mirtillo"—presumably representing what Artusi considered "the sound of the twelfth mode with B♭"—the second pitch, *g'*, dominates the next three and a half verses of the text (mm. 3–29).[31]

While the general motion of this *f–a'* ascent agrees with Artusi's account that the madrigal "began with the sound of the twelfth mode with B♭" (F-hypoionian) and "was returned to B natural and ended in the first [mode]" (D-dorian), it corresponds even more closely with a later statement by the

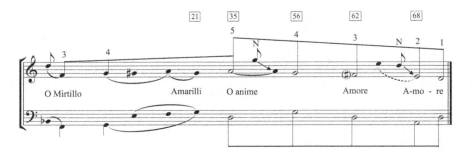

Example 7.7 Monteverdi, *O Mirtillo, Mirtillo anima mia*, Structural Analysis

Bolognese canon, published in 1605 or 1606 under the pseudonym Antonio Braccino da Todi, where his assessment of the madrigal's modal organization is revised to encompass not two modes, but three.[32] Artusi's attention to the "details or passages" of the madrigal and disregard for the larger outcome ("its whole") prompted Giulio Cesare Monteverdi's rebuttal in his *Dichiaratione* of 1607, in which he quotes the relevant passage from Artusi's otherwise lost criticism:

> If the opponent had considered the harmony of my brother's madrigal *O Mirtillo* in this light [i.e., not merely in terms of the "details or passages...but its whole"], he would not, in that discourse of his, have uttered such extravagances with regard to its mode, although it appears that he speaks generally, his words being: "*L'Artusi* has likewise explained and demonstrated the confusion introduced into composition by those who begin in one mode, follow this with another, and end with one wholly unrelated to the first and second ideas, which is like hearing the talk of a madman, who, as the saying goes, hits now the hoop and now the cask." Poor fellow, he does not perceive that, while he is posing before the world as preceptor ordinary, he falls into the error of denying the mixed modes.[33]

Artusi's description of a succession of three distinct modes is consistent with the three steps of the initial ascent (*f'–g'–a'*) and the conflicting modal centers that they seem to evoke.

At the same time, Giulio Cesare's response suggests that there is a logic behind these "mixed modes," which is perceived only when the process of the composition *as a whole* is taken into account. Indeed, whereas the ascent toward *a'*, the primary background $\hat{5}$, serves as a protracted structural anacrusis occupying roughly the first half of the piece, the second half of the madrigal responds with a firmly plotted dynamic-type descent through the D-dorian *diapente*, *a'–d'* (mm. 35–69), that rationalizes and counterbalances what had come before (Example 7.7). This two-part division into anacrusis plus structural descent comes as a direct response to the form and meaning of the text.

First, through its concealment of the mode and the instability that this causes, the opening of Monteverdi's madrigal embodies the stark disparity between surface and interior that Amarilli upheld to Mirtillo's face, but then bemoans in the initial conditional statements of her lament (verses 1–6). In particular, the prolonged elaboration of g' in mm. 3–29—the most uncertain portion of the piece in terms of the mode—renders vividly the central concern expressed at the same time in the text: Mirtillo's inability— due to Amarilli's feigned coldness—to "see what lies in the heart" of his beloved. Through this effect, the listener is kept in the dark about the inner (modal) nature of the madrigal, just as Mirtillo is unaware of Amarilli's true character. For the second section of the text, by contrast, Amarilli's turn to address love and fate ("destino") prompts a corresponding change in the music, which pivots at the return of "O" in verse 7 from the instability of the prefatory g' ($\hat{4}$) to lay out resolutely the defining steps of the D-dorian *diapente*, thereby revealing the true purpose of what had come before in the work's opening.

Apparently, the composer's structural–expressive strategies were all too effective, for Artusi's reaction to the piece bears a marked likeness to Mirtillo's harsh response to Amarilli in the previous scene of the play. Even more, whereas Mirtillo's verbal attack causes Amarilli to bemoan his failure to recognize the truth behind her feigned exterior, Artusi's attack prompts a similar complaint from the composer (through his brother) about the nature of the madrigal. Perhaps Claudio and Giulio Cesare Monteverdi had taken cues from Guarini's play, for even the rhetoric of those on the defensive is strikingly similar: for Amarilli, it is her heart that has been misunderstood ("if you could see what lies here in the heart of this one...I know that you, for her, would feel that pity that you ask of her"); for Monteverdi, it is *l'armonia* of his madrigal ("if the opponent had considered the harmony of my brother's madrigal *O Mirtillo* in this light, he would not...have uttered such extravagances with regard to its mode").[34] Due to the misapprehension of interior through exterior, both Amarilli and Monteverdi's madrigal (in presenting Amarilli's words) thwart the expectations of their audiences and are consequently subjected to injuries of their own kinds. In keeping with the autonomous structure of the madrigal, however, Monteverdi's work makes up for its seemingly wayward opening using a number of means to uphold and advance the modal structure. These include the same key tactics seen in the controversial *Anima mia, perdona* of the Fourth Book: namely, transposed and varied restatements of textual phrases, register transfer, and overlapping voices (particularly the Canto and Quinto).

With its delay of modal affirmation, Monteverdi's madrigal evokes Amarilli's abnormative, suppressed desire through abnormative modal conduct in a manner very different from, and much less pervasive than, that of Marenzio's 1595 setting of this same text. Marenzio's madrigal is likely the only *O Mirtillo* setting to precede Monteverdi's treatment, given the latter's completion date of November 1598 at the latest. (The settings of Giovanni Appolloni and Monte were completed by late 1599 and published in 1600, although there is no knowing for certain when they were composed.)[35] While Monteverdi's reading conceals the underlying mode with an evasive yet orderly opening, Marenzio's setting is troubled throughout—first by opposing modes based on C (C-hypodorian and C-hypomixolydian), then by the foreign modal final, F (Example 7.8).[36] The distinction between the two settings and the conflicts they engender might, then, be described in terms of dimension: whereas the tension of Monteverdi's madrigal plays out linearly, or temporally, with the gradual revelation of the mode's (and Amarilli's) inner nature and the resoluteness thereof over the course of Amarilli's speech, that of Marenzio's operates more spatially, or between structural levels, through the superimposition of the false and outward on the true and inward, first through a betrayal of the basic C-hypomixolydian mode from within (by the occupation of the G octave and C final by the "false" C-dorian *diapente* with E♭), and later through the opposition to the underlying mode by a foreign one (F-lydian) with a distinct final and modal octave. Both madrigals, however, render the text and these conflicts with highly dynamic structures that advance and face disruptions steadily from beginning to end.

Contrary to Artusi's unduly rigid demands of modal integrity, Monteverdi's treatment of the text, with its strongly delineated structural course, is not at all overcome by confusion when the whole ("il tutto") of the composition is taken into account. Rather, it is perhaps characterized most by the initial concealment of a modal identity that nonetheless remains steadfast and only gradually reveals itself, which is also befitting of Amarilli's state. Through the first half of the madrigal, it is as if we catch a glimpse

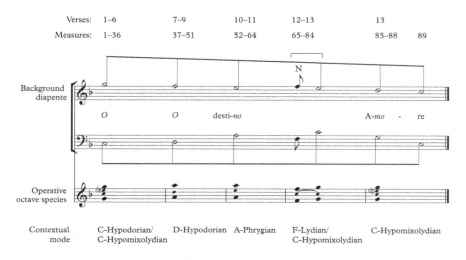

Example 7.8 Marenzio, *O Mirtillo*, Fundamental Structure

of Amarilli in the act of removing the veil of feigned indifference she had worn through her exchange with Mirtillo to expose gradually the feelings voiced in the text: the modal identity remains concealed through the initial *f–a'* ascent as the nymph addresses her absent beloved (verses 1–6), but this identity is finally laid bare as she turns to address, first, the "souls too unhappy in love" and her own heart, and, finally, the opposed forces of fate and love at the poignant exclamation, "O anime in amor troppo infelici" (verses 7–13).

Compared to Marenzio's *O Mirtillo*, a case could hardly be made that Monteverdi's modal transgressions are any more offensive; nor do these transgressions seem to exceed those of many other "mixed-mode" works that had come before, such as those of Josquin, Willaert, Rore, and Striggio cited by Giulio Cesare. In fact, despite Artusi's insistence on the improper mixing of modes, justification for the notorious opening to Monteverdi's madrigal can again be found in the theorist that Artusi held in utmost esteem: Zarlino. On the proper manner in which to begin a composition, Zarlino is rather lenient. He holds that "the true and natural initial tones" of a mode fall "on the extreme notes of the *diapente* and *diatessaron*, and on the median note which divides the *diapente* into a ditone and a semiditone"—that is, on $\hat{1}$, $\hat{3}$, and $\hat{5}$. But as Zarlino concedes without denigration, "there are many compositions that begin on other notes."[37] It should be emphasized here that Zarlino is speaking of pitches that begin a piece in the mode-bearing voices (Tenore and Canto), not of sonorities.

By these standards, Monteverdi's opening stands on firm ground: the Canto, a principal structure-bearing voice, begins pointedly on the final, *d"*, and while the first sonority is based on B♭, or $\hat{6}$ (which clearly falls under the category of "other notes"), the first cadence of the madrigal leads to the "median note which divides the *diapente*," F. In addition, through the initial ascent of mm. 1–35, the Canto and Quinto faithfully delineate the D modal octave expanded on either side by a tone (*c'–e"*). Thus, while keeping the modal framework concealed, there are still several factors that work toward establishing the context of the D-dorian mode from the outset. These factors—the establishment of the D modal octave, the initial cadence on the mediant, and the initial ascent—plus the unfolding of the D-dorian background *diapente* in the second half of the madrigal, yield the upper-voice structure:

This advancement from opening obscurity to a clearly unfolding D-dorian structure mirrors the sentiments of the text, as Amarilli reveals her hidden love for Mirtillo. It also creates an exceptionally dynamic structure, with the basic *diapente* descent preceded by a two-step anacrusis. Thus, Amarilli's confession unfolds through the course of seven structural degrees, rather than the conventional five.

O Mirtillo comes second in Monteverdi's Fifth Book, following *Cruda Amarilli*, making for an opening of exceptional turbulence in the book befitting of the central characters of Guarini's play. Scholars have indeed viewed this positioning of the two madrigals back to back as conveying the effect of Amarilli responding directly to Mirtillo's complaint about her. This reading proves compelling from the standpoint of the text—the lovers' two key monologues from separate acts of the play being brought together in Monteverdi's madrigal book—but the musical connections scholars have drawn prove more tenuous. Susan McClary, for example, regards the G-mixolydian mode of *Cruda Amarilli* as "Mirtillo's" and the D-dorian of *O Mirtillo* as "Amarilli's." Thus, McClary writes of the latter work:

> the scrolling through the circle of fifths at the beginning of this madrigal represents an agonizingly slow emergence from the position of retreat to which Mirtillo's words had driven her [in *Cruda Amarilli*]. Her articulation of G in m. 5 responds to Mirtillo on his turf, but it does not constitute her own home base, to which she can gain access only with extreme difficulty.[38]

In other words, by adopting the G centricity of *Cruda Amarilli* through much of its opening, *O Mirtillo*, in effect, shows Amarilli addressing the absent Mirtillo in his own language. McClary's reading follows Stefano La Via's detailed analysis of the two madrigals similarly as a "dialogue," but one that lasts only through the first six verses (the G-centered portion) of Amarilli's "response," while the remainder of *O Mirtillo*—beginning at "O anime in amor troppo infelici" (verse 7)—represents an "interior outburst."[39] La Via and McClary's readings of the madrigal's opening accord with the potential expressive effects of the initial f'-a' ascent in dividing the text, and the association of this opening with Amarilli's feigned "crudelissima" nature, although the more fundamental role of the ascent as an integrated part of the overall modal scheme means that it is, in fact, *part* of Amarilli's "home base," albeit a subsidiary one.

Suzanne Cusick also extends her study of gendered rhetoric in the Artusi–Monteverdi debate to a reading of the two madrigals as an interrelated pair. In Cusick's interpretation, "Mirtillo's desire," as expressed in the bold and illicit dissonances of *Cruda Amarilli*, represents "the (masculine) agent of change, while Amarilli's lament [*O Mirtillo*] becomes the (feminine) embodiment of change" by virtue of its following Mirtillo's impetus (from *Cruda Amarilli*) into the realm of modern music.[40] Cusick's construing *O Mirtillo* as "pointing the way beyond legalistic misreadings of ancient law... into new artistic territory," and as leaving the listener with "the desire to go on" after the final cadence, however, derives from her acceptance of two problematic readings discussed earlier: Palisca's depiction of (in Cusick's words) "Giulio Cesare's rather vague defense of mixed mode in *O Mirtillo*," and Dahlhaus's characterization of the madrigal's "notorious ending on an apparent half cadence."[41] Maura Calcagno, likewise, asserts that "Monteverdi indeed has Amarilli herself reply to Mirtillo ... by arranging the time events of the play to suggest a cause–effect relationship," and thereby "appropriates Guarini's voice."[42] More recently, in his detailed study of Monteverdi's textual readings, Christophe Georis looks beyond the opening pair to view the first six madrigals of the Fifth Book compellingly as projecting a three-stage succession from expressions of love in terms of death in the absence of the beloved (Nos. 1–3), through the development of love's realization in *Ecco, Silvio* (No. 4), to confessions of love in terms of life in the presence of both lovers (Nos. 5–6).[43]

The integrated view of the musical structure of *O Mirtillo* proposed here (Example 7.7) supports a different reading of the connection between the opening two madrigals that is even closer to the meaning of the text. If Amarilli is indeed trying to speak in Mirtillo's language through the subsidiary G centricity in *O Mirtillo*, as Stefano La Via and McClary propose, then she does not do a very good job at it: the strong polarity between G and C so distinctive of *Cruda Amarilli* and its G-mixolydian context is scarcely present in the G-centered opening of Amarilli's piece. The G-dominated portion of the initial ascent in *O Mirtillo*, by contrast, derives from, and is accountable to, the larger D-dorian framework—it is, in other words, subsumed into Amarilli's own expression and devoid of much of its character from *Cruda Amarilli*. This makes perfect sense, given that Amarilli has no intention to speak in the same terms as Mirtillo: whereas Mirtillo is full of vitriol and rancor in *Cruda Amarilli*, Amarilli in *O Mirtillo* speaks instead with remorse and despair. Passing through G at the opening of the piece, therefore, may be a means of alluding to Mirtillo and the G tonality of *Cruda Amarilli*, but this tonality is now presented in an entirely new light.[44]

In addition to these potential tonal references, the vastly different structural behaviors of the two madrigals also put the contrasting psychological states of the two characters in direct relief. After the suspended but stammering background of *Cruda Amarilli* realizes Mirtillo's unshakeable fixation on his cruel beloved, the steady unveiling of the true interior of *O Mirtillo* shows Amarilli baring the truth behind her cold exterior. The opposing temporal worlds of the works and their structures enhances these distinctions between characters, with Mirtillo's lament fixed in its opening state as a reflection of constancy, resolve, and perplexity, and Amarilli's confession swept through an expanded series of structural steps (and modal–cadential regions) in its climb and fall toward resolution. Whether the two works respond to one another in any direct or deliberate way will surely remain a matter of conjecture, but what they do accomplish at the start of the Fifth Book is a detailed juxtaposition of the central protagonists, their traits, and the dilemmas that drive the main plot of the play.

Interpersonal and Intertextual Dialogue in *Ecco, Silvio, colei che 'n odio hai tanto*

In *La seconda parte dell'Artusi* (1603), the Bolognese theorist brought two debates into the public eye that he had been entertaining privately in the previous years: the first part of the treatise replies to the anonymous L'Ottuso on matters relating to modern music raised in *L'Artusi*, while the second part deals primarily with defending the humanist philosopher Francesco Patrizi (a resident at Cinzio Aldobrandini's household in the mid-1590s) and his views on tetrachords, tuning, and the modes against the criticisms of theorist Ercole Bottrigari.[45] Artusi cites extensively from correspondence with L'Ottuso and from the theoretical writings of Patrizi, Bottrigari, and numerous ancient and contemporary scholars, while drawing on practical examples from Marenzio, Rore, Wert, and others. Yet, like the "First Artusi," the majority of Artusi's grievances center on the works of "Signor etc."—the theorist's pseudonym for Monteverdi. As outlined above, this second criticism adds two more Monteverdi madrigals to Artusi's hit list: *Era l'anima mia* (No. 3 in the Fifth Book) and *Ecco, Silvio, colei che 'n odio hai tanto* (No. 4 in the Fifth Book), with *Cruda Amarilli* appearing briefly again as an example of alleged modal obscurity.

The Bolognese canon gives no account of when or where he encountered *Era l'anima mia* and *Ecco, Silvio*—if it was in Ferrara in 1598, alongside Monteverdi's other madrigals cited in *L'Artusi*; through L'Ottuso's correspondence after *L'Artusi*; or from another source. Thus, while the three madrigals cited in 1600 have a secure *terminus ante quem* of November 1598, *Ecco, Silvio* and *Era l'anima mia* can only be dated with certainty to before 25 March 1603, when Artusi signed the dedication of his second pamphlet.

Unlike Artusi's detailed theoretical criticisms of Monteverdi's four other madrigals, his complaints about *Ecco, Silvio* prove more general and subjective. He cites only the madrigal's *seconda parte* (*Ma se con la pietà non è in te spenta*) in three instances. First, in part one of the treatise, he disputes L'Ottuso's claim that the work shows "novo concento," and in the second section, he observes that the opening eight measures (mm. 83–90; Example 7.9) resemble the style of a *giustiniana*—a Venetian-style canzonetta—or a *spifarata mantovana*, owing to the excessive repetitions of static sonorities.[46] The third charge comes among the theorist's list of reprehensible features of modern music, which include "povertà dell'Harmonia," excessive spacing between the voices, failure to observe the modes, and so forth. The opening of *Ma se con la pietà*, Artusi claims, illustrates the typical poor imitation of the words ("mala imitatione delle parole") that pervades modern music.

The latter criticism is a valid one, for the madrigal's square semiminim declamation of the words "la pietà non è in te spenta" proves unnatural and aligns the weak syllables "la" and "è in" with the primary stresses of the tactus, to the effect: "*la* pie*tà* non *è in* te *spen*ta" (see Example 7.9). The setting of "gentilezza e valor" ("*gen*tilezza e va*lor*") immediately after only adds to the clumsiness. The awkward elocution here is especially mystifying given

Example 7.9 Monteverdi, *Ecco, Silvio, colei che 'n odio hai tanto*, Opening of the *seconda parte* (mm. 83–90)

Monteverdi's general sensitivity to both the semantics and elocution of the text, which becomes evident just a few measures later in the naturalistic, rhythmically nimble, and expressive delivery of "Anima cruda sì, ma però bella" (mm. 94–104).

Artusi could have cited examples of improper dissonance treatment and voice leading in *Ecco, Silvio* to supplement those drawn from *Cruda Amarilli* and *Anima mia, perdona* in *L'Artusi* and from *Era l'anima mia* in the Second Artusi. The stepwise ascents through the bitter augmented fourth, B♭–E♮, at "Anima cruda sì" (mm. 94–104), for example, ignore the practices of *fa supra la*—the flatting of E as upper neighbor to D—and of avoiding linear tritones, but do so for expressive effect: to highlight the notion of "cruda," in reference to Silvio. The phrase, then, demonstrates the prioritization of *seconda pratica* principles over those of strict counterpoint—or, as Artusi would describe it, over reason and sound judgment. Likewise, Monteverdi commits offences similar to those at "e più fugace" (mm. 42–43) in *Cruda*

Amarilli—namely, consecutive and rearticulated vertical dissonances against repeated pitches—at "mia sarai" (m. 176) and "mia dura" (mm. 180 and 187–88) in the *terza parte* of *Ecco, Silvio*.

At sixty-eight verses of text and 357 semibreve measures (in Malipiero's edition), *Ecco, Silvio* was Monteverdi's longest madrigal to date in 1605 and is, by most parameters, the longest multi-voice madrigal of his entire output.[47] The madrigal is also distinctive for presenting a dialogue between two separate speaking characters, whose lines are divided between the madrigal's five *parti* in the order Dorinda–Dorinda–Silvio–Silvio–Dorinda. With this expansive scale and dialogue format, *Ecco, Silvio* posed new and distinctive challenges as a madrigal text in terms of balancing the demands of large-scale unity, continued end-directed tension, and the delineation of two separate psychological states and voices. This analysis, therefore, examines Monteverdi's strategies for handling the large-scale structure and alternations between speakers in ways that at once convey unity, distinctiveness, and the developments in the text, while pointing both forward and backward in terms of compositional technique.

The text, from act 4, scene 9, relates Silvio's transformation from callous sportsman into compassionate lover upon beholding Dorinda gravely wounded by his own arrow. The madrigal text opens with Dorinda comparing the external, physical wound from Silvio's arrow to the internal, emotional injuries caused by his persistent disdain, then continues in the *seconda parte* with her imploring Silvio to sweeten her death with the blessing, "Va' in pace, anima mia" (Go in peace, my soul). Silvio then responds in the *terza parte*, in a tone utterly different from that of the heartless hunter from earlier in the play, crying Dorinda's name, calling her "mia," and pledging to love her in life or in death. Silvio's remorse for his harsh treatment of Dorinda leads in the *quarta parte* to his kneeling before her, offering his bow and arrows, and baring his chest so she may wound him in return. Dorinda responds to this sudden change with disbelief and confusion in the final *parte*, drawing parallels now between this potential ruse and her own deception of Silvio by disguising herself as a wolf in order to follow him—the act that prompted Silvio to shoot her. In the end, Dorinda refuses the bow and chooses instead to let Silvio suffer the deeper wounds of love. As she reasons, "I know no greater revenge than to see you as a lover" ("Che vendetta maggiore / Non so bramar che di vederti amante"). The madrigal concludes with Dorinda praising the day she first loved Silvio, thus bringing the couple's union to fruition yet leaving their mortal fate unresolved. As readers of the play would know, their earthly end is fortunate, not tragic, in keeping with the nature of Guarini's new hybrid genre.

Relatively few madrigals, particularly before 1605, set texts that involve dialogue between separate speakers, and only a fraction of these dialogues come from dramatic texts. Regardless of poetic genre, composers seem to treat such dialogic texts in one of two ways in terms of texture: either they make no apparent distinction between speakers in terms of voicing, or they associate specific voices with each of the characters. The five known settings of multi-speaker passages from *Il pastor fido* and Tasso's *Aminta* that precede Monteverdi's *Ecco, Silvio* are divided between both textural approaches. Two of the works—Gabriele Fattorini's twelve-*parte* treatment of 122 lines of dialogue between Amarilli, Mirtillo, Corisca, and a chorus of nymphs from Guarini's *Gioco della cieca*, published in *La cieca: Il primo libro de madrigali a cinque voci* (Venice: Amadino, 1598), and Giovanni Piccioni's setting of Mirtillo and Corisca's dialogue from act 3, scene 6, *M'infingerò di non aver veduto*, in his *Pastor fido musicale...il sesto libro di madrigali a 5* (Venice: Vincenti, 1602)—take the former approach of treating the five-voice texture freely throughout, thus not assigning voices to characters.[48]

By contrast, in his *Novellette a sei voci* (Venice: Amadino, 1594), Simone Balsamino uses the second dialogic tactic of assigning separate voices to characters in his *Vorrò veder ciò che Tirsi avrà fatto*, a sixteen-*parte* treatment of the entire scene-length exchange between the lovesick Aminta and his companion Tirsi in act 2, scene 3 of Tasso's *Aminta*. Balsamino divides the madrigal's six voices into two groups to distinguish the parts of Tirsi (Sesto, Alto, Quinto) and Aminta (Canto, Tenore, Basso) and designates these assignments in the partbooks with the headings "Li tre Tirsi uniti" and "Li tre Aminta uniti" at the start of the first dialogic *parte*.[49] Balsamino does not maintain the Tirsi–Aminta trios through the entire cycle, but uses them typically at the beginnings of *parti* and whenever there is a change of speaker, while abandoning them for full-voice texture at the ends of the *parti* and sometimes in the middle of a character's speech.

Despite its published form, scholars have put forth various hypotheses arguing that Balsamino's work originated in a version that was entirely antiphonal, soloistic and dramaturgical, or even expressly designed as part of the 1574 staging of Tasso's play by the Della Rovere court in Pesaro.[50] In his dedication to the book, however, Balsamino seems to deter the idea that the contents were conceived as anything other than the polyphonic form in which they were published, writing that "although they are printed, they are the same as they were there [for performances in the Urbino piazza], written by hand" (se bene sono stampate, sono le medesime che erano là scritte a mano). His strategy for grappling with a dialogic text with assigned voice groups, therefore, seems to represent not a quasi-operatic technique or the vestige of a past duet or fully antiphonal setting, but a functional, semi-verisimilar way to indicate shifts between speakers that might otherwise be unclear to both performers and listeners. Moreover, Balsamino does not limit his statement to the two settings from *Aminta*—the Tirsi–Aminta dialogue and a monologue for the boorish Satiro—thus implying that it applies to all of the *Novellette*, settings of theatrical and lyric texts alike.

Balsamino's work and dedication, therefore, seem to corroborate the idea that a madrigal that sets a dramatic dialogue—even one that assigns voice groups to characters and relies heavily on homophonic declamation—need not be connected to solo song or dramatic enactment, despite historians' inclinations to see it that way. Yet, despite Balsamino's remarks, several questions relating to voice and perspective in his *Aminta* dialogue remain—questions that are also germane to Monteverdi's *Ecco, Silvio* and the *Pastor fido* madrigal at large, as well as to the present study. For example, does the text undergo some type of interpretative or generic transformation when transferred from play to madrigal? And does the madrigal present the characters' voices as direct speakers, in the here and now, in a mimetic (albeit polyphonic) fashion, or does it play the role of narrator–reader that imparts the speakers' words as part of the past, within the understood framework "Aminta said...then Tirsi said"? Or more precisely within the framework, "Balsamino says that Tasso said that Aminta and Tirsi conversed as follows"? In short, do we pretend to hear the dialogic madrigal as Aminta and Tirsi (or any other first person) speaking, or do we hear it as a collaborative reading or narration that relays and even mimics others' speech?

Uniquely revealing from these interpretative and generic standpoints are the two dialogue settings from Guarini's play in Philippe de Monte's *Musica sopra il pastor fido...libro secondo a 7* (Venice: Angelo Gardano, 1600). Both dialogues include Amarilli as interlocutor, first in her forced rejection of Mirtillo in act 3, scene 3, *Sta' cheta, anima mia*, then in her confession to Corisca of her true love for the shepherd in act 3, scene 5, *Io son vinta, Corisca, e tel confesso*. In both of these works, Monte, like Balsamino, divides the ensemble into two groups and assigns one to each of the speaking characters. He maintains these groupings strictly through the final verse of text, which is then restated by the full ensemble.

Despite this clear differentiation of speakers by voice groupings, however, the texts of Monte's works also contain interpolated phrases foreign to the play that announce each speaker in the third person. The Mirtillo–Amarilli dialogue, for example, begins (with the insertions shown in italics), "'Sta' cheta, anima mia,' / *Dicea il fido pastore*" ("Be silent, my love," *said the faithful shepherd*), followed by, "'Lasciami, traditore,' / *La ninfa rispondea*" (Leave me, you traitor, *the nymph responded*). The added phrases provide even more detail in the Amarilli–Corisca dialogue, while also supplementing the text well poetically by creating the additional rhymes *bassa/lassa* and *negare/dare*:

Play	Madrigal
AMARILLI	AMARILLI
Io son vinta, Corisca, e tel confesso	"Io son vinta," *dicea*
	Amarilli a Corisca in voce bassa
CORISCA	CORISCA
	Ed ella rispondea,
Hor che negar nol puoi, tu mel confessi.	"Hor che nol puoi negare,
	Vinta mi ti vuoi dare."
AMARILLI	AMARILLI
E ben m'avveggio, ahi lassa..."	"E ben m'avveggio, ahi lassa..."[51]

In Monte's setting, the assigned voice groups deliver the third-person interjections along with their own characters' lines, as shown in Example 7.10.

With this mixing of poetic modes (direct speech and narration), Monte's work stands apart from Balsamino's, Fattorini's, Piccioni's, and (as we
shall see) Monteverdi's settings of theatrical dialogues and takes on a form
more akin to that of Wert's setting of Guarini's erotic poem, *Tirsi morir
volea*. The text portrays a tryst between two lovers from the perspective of
a narrator, who introduces the lovers' words with phrases like, "His lovely
Nymph said...," and, "the shepherd answered her..." Wert sets the poem as
a "dialogo a 7" and distinguishes the various speakers by voice groupings in
a quasi-verisimilar manner: the narrator with lower voices and the beloved
with high voices. Toward the end of the piece, when Tirsi finally speaks,

* Reads "Ecco ti lascio" in the play.

Example 7.10 Monte, *Sta' cheta, anima mia*, mm. 1–10

however, Wert (with few other options) seems to compromise this verisimilar effect by assigning the same low-voice group reserved for the narrator to Tirsi as well. Only at the end, with the lovers' mutual fulfillment, do the voices come together (so to speak).

Monte goes one step further than Wert in undermining any notion of verisimilitude in his dialogue settings by having each voice group deliver its assigned character's lines while also introducing this character in the third person. Given that Monte's madrigals already differentiate the characters clearly by texture, the narrative insertions prove rather superfluous from a functional standpoint. Yet, this added narrative commentary was apparently important enough that it took precedence over faithfulness to the play's text and the semi-verisimilar portrayal of the speakers. So, why are the insertions there, and how do they affect the reading of Monte's works?

To begin with the latter question: most immediately, the interjections transform the musical texts from dramatic dialogues in which the characters speak directly in their own voices—from pure *mimesis*, as typical of a play—into dialogues framed in third-person narration—thus, *mimesis* embedded in *diegesis*. The variant readings, therefore, consolidate the two characters' voices within the voice of the poet/narrator, all of which the madrigals, in turn, present through the musical perspective of the composer. Rather than impose a new narrative perspective on the texts, however, the madrigals' interpolated interjections ("he said…she said") may reflect a conventional, implicit way of interpreting dialogue settings—if not the madrigal at large—in a wholly narrative perspective. In other words, the insertions ensure that listeners understand the madrigals in a specific way, perhaps the customary way, which is not as quasi-dramatic or quasi-representational realizations of the characters' voices, but as speech imparted through the polyphonic voice of the madrigal as narrator.[52]

Monte's assignment of distinct voice groups to the characters, meanwhile, invokes different aspects of the madrigal–narrator's collective voice as a means of distinguishing the speaking voices for both verisimilar effect and practical ends. Whereas the earlier settings of dramatic dialogues by Balsamino, Fattorini, and Piccioni operate entirely by this implicit narrative mode with their varied use of the ensemble (i.e., assigning voice groups to speakers), Monte's settings make this interpretative framework explicit by having the madrigals, through their textual interjections, tell us directly for whom they speak. The madrigal texts, thereby, help to rationalize the conceptual leap we make in hearing the voice of a singular *io* in an ensemble of singers, by having them state outright to the effect of, "let us tell you what Mirtillo and Amarilli [or Corisca and Amarilli] said."

By reframing the speaking voice (from characters/*mimesis* to narrator/*diegesis*) at the level of the *text*, rather than the music—for example, by changing voice–character associations mid-piece (as Monteverdi does in several of his *concertato* Marino settings in the Sixth Book)—Monte's settings seem to constrain the interpretative potential of these madrigals, not broaden it, by bridling the verse with narrative interjections.[53] Monte's strategy, thus, undercuts not only verisimilitude by combining characters and narrator in the same voices, but also free use of the full-voice texture by maintaining the three- and four-voice character groupings until the last verse. This brings us back to the first of the two questions: why did he include these textual insertions at all, given the conceptual paradoxes they create, instead of using the unmediated dialogues of the play?

One possible explanation is for instruction and interpretative clarity. Rather than leaving it to readers' judgment how to comprehend polyphonic renderings of dramatic dialogues, the madrigals tell us explicitly how to hear them—namely, as reported (narrated) speech. This strategy, in turn, may relate to Monte's immediate audience. As a cosmopolitan composer working at the Imperial court in Prague at the time, his direct readership would have comprised primarily non-Italians—thus, outsiders to the literary cultures of Italian lyric poetry and the madrigal. Monte (or the editor of his texts), therefore, might have felt a need to instruct listeners blatantly on how to read these settings. The unusual origins of their texts as dramatic dialogues might also have signaled the need for more explicit interpretative guidance.

In the larger picture, Monte's settings may offer clues to better understand how contemporary readers perceived not only settings of dialogic texts, like Wert's *Tirsi morir volea* and Balsamino's *Vorrò veder ciò che Tirsi avrà fatto,* but also conventional lyric texts with a single first-person speaker. Rather than functioning as polyphonically dressed dramaticizations or proto-recitatives wherein a single voice or voice group, or indeed the madrigal as a whole, embodies the subjectivity of the speaker(s), as many scholars have proposed,[54] Monte's examples suggest that—whether the text is a conventional lyric ("Il bianco e dolce cigno cantando more") or a dramatic monologue or dialogue ("Cruda Amarilli, che col nome ancora")—the madrigal frames the speaker's words in implicit quotation marks with the understood caption, "He/She said…," to present them through a narrative perspective. Thus, in place of representation (or true *mimesis* in an operatic sense)—speaking *as* the speaker, while entering into his or her world in the here and now—the madrigal's mode of delivery entails relating or reporting—speaking *for* the speaker—while also, through the musical setting, conjuring the individual's character, their sentiments, and their world of the (often fictional) past.[55] Monte's dialogue settings, with their explicit narrative asides, therefore, lend substantial and exceptional weight to the interpretation proposed here of the madrigal as reading/narration of its texts and the speaking voice(s) thereof, with the added interpretative factors of the nonverbal music.

In *Ecco, Silvio*, Monteverdi takes the first dialogic approach—that of Fattorini and Piccioni—by not assigning voice parts to the two speakers. In fact, for a composer who was to become so well known for his portrayals of individual personas in *stile rappresentativo* and dramatic music, it might seem puzzling that both Dorinda's and Silvio's *parti* most frequently isolate the same voice—the Tenore—from the rest of the ensemble with offset phrasing in an otherwise homorhythmic context. The madrigal's opening with Dorinda's speech (Example 7.11), for example, highlights the Alto with its anticipation of the other voices, while the Tenore remains absent through the first statement of verse 1. This absence, however, spotlights the Tenore's entrance in m. 6 to take over the Alto's role of leading the ensemble for a second iteration of verse 1. Following a polyphonic delivery of verse 2 and relatively strict homophony for verses 3–6, the Tenore emerges again ahead of the ensemble at verse 7, "Che v[u]oi tu più da lei" (What more do you want from her?).

Example 7.11 Monteverdi, *Ecco, Silvio, colei che 'n odio hai tanto*, mm. 1–18

Yet the Tenore's prominence is hardly definitive based on the *prima parte* alone, for other voices come to the fore as possible leading voices at different occasions: for instance, the Quinto at "Eccola in quella guisa" (mm. 11–15), the Canto at "Ah, garzon crudo" (mm. 34–39), and the Alto at "tu non credesti" (mm. 45–47). It is in the *seconda parte*, however, that the madrigal more emphatically distinguishes the Tenore from the rest of the ensemble by repeatedly setting it apart texturally, metrically, and textually. This accentuation begins with the opening verse and becomes especially pronounced with the offset statements of "Non mi negar ti prego" (Do not deny me, I beg you; mm. 90–97), "Non mi negar a l'ultimo sospiro" (Do not deny me at my last breath; mm. 104–09), and "con questa sola / Dolcissima parola" (with this sweetest word alone; mm. 134–42), where the Tenore anticipates the other parts and dwells on its textual phrase well after the other voices have moved on.

While it may lack verisimilitude to highlight the Tenore—a lower voice part, albeit here with a range *f–a'*—when setting Dorinda's words in the *prima* and *seconda parti*, the notion of realism becomes even more strained when the madrigal singles out the same voice for Silvio's speech in the *terza* and *quarta parti*. At Silvio's inward-gesturing statement "Pur 'mia' dirò, che mia / Sarai" (Yet "mine" I will say, for mine you will be; mm. 173–81) in the *terza parte*, for example, only after all the other voices declaim the words in strict homorhythm does the Tenore enter to deliver them separately against a new line of text in the Canto and Quinto. The Tenore's singularity increases in the *quarta parte*, as it persistently delays, anticipates, and dwells on lines while other voices function more as a group (see especially the opening, mm. 204–37).

Given the likelihood that the same singers would execute all five *parti* in performance, the textural and metrical distinction of the same voice part for Dorinda's and Silvio's lines would seemingly undermine a potential quasi-dramatic reading that associated individual subjectivities with specific voices in the ensemble. Instead, Monteverdi's dialogue setting seems to discourage such a reading—a reading that is, in any case, problematic not only in that it disregards the madrigal's inherent diegetic nature in favor of an incongruous and anachronistic aim of imitation (*mimesis*), but also in that it prioritizes metrical (temporal) displacement over other means of distinguishing voices that operate within the work.

For concurrently with its widespread temporal isolation of the Tenore, the madrigal also highlights the two upper voices through their interplay and prominence at the top of the texture. Similar to the treatment of the two sopranos as a "composite" upper voice in *Anima mia, perdona*, the Canto and Quinto in *Ecco, Silvio* frequently move in parallel thirds, cross one another, and transfer linear structural motion from one part to the other. Also especially striking are their ranges, which span the octave and a half between *d'* and *a''*, with the Canto on several occasions reaching up to an exceptional *b♭''*. As with the Tenore's metric nonconformity, the spotlighting of the Canto and Quinto as a cooperating pair occurs in both Dorinda's and Silvio's *parti*, thus thwarting any strict association between speaker, voice part, and compositional technique. The madrigal, in other words, seems to uphold the notion communicated forthrightly in Monte's dialogue settings that the individual voices form but part of a collective whole that, in turn, delivers the text from the perspective of narrator–reader, as though each *parte* opens with an implied statement "Dorinda said" or "Silvio said," even as certain component voices "step forward" at various times—or sometimes at the same time but in different ways, as in the second verse of *Il bianco e dolce cigno* (see Example I.1). Such differentiated voices remain integrally connected, and still interact, with the rest of the ensemble vocally and visually. Thus, the madrigal's true "voice"—the realization of the composer's own reading of the text—coalesces from its multiple constituent voices.

Whereas the relationships between the voice parts remain relatively consistent through the five *parti* of *Ecco, Silvio* and provide a sense of consistency across the madrigal, other aspects of the music set up a dichotomy between unity and separation that mirrors that of the characters' evolving relationship across this scene in the play. For matters are not so simple as two lovers uniting at one's impending death, as Silvio's awakening to love comes at the height of Dorinda's distress, as her faith in love wavers with doubt.

Monteverdi conveys this disparity between Silvio's new devotion and Dorinda's suspicion through marked differences in modal and cadential behavior between the characters' *parti*. Other scholars have examined the madrigal on these fronts. In their analyses of *Ecco, Silvio* in hexachordal/ harmonic terms, for example, Dahlhaus and Chafe conclude that the madrigal "sets forth both its hexachordal content and primary mode in the opening section" (mm. 1–28), which serves as "a means of establishing the one-flat hexachord as tonal 'center'."[56] Through harmonic (chordal root) motion and pitch centricity, the work, they argue, delineates its hexachordal/modal identity with such clarity that it represents "one of the most convincingly unified beginnings in either the fourth or fifth books in that respect."[57] As with their assessments of *O Mirtillo*, however, Dahlhaus and Chafe's methodology neglects several of the madrigal's integral strategies driven not simply by chordal progressions, but by the contrapuntal activity that generates these sonorities and by the modal framework that informs it. Both studies, furthermore, again fail to distinguish true cadential and non-cadential arrivals in terms of structural weight—a shortcoming that, as we will see, leads to significant mischaracterizations of the work's modal behavior and the expressive consequences thereof.

Monteverdi sets the dialogue in the G-dorian mode—one of the most straightforward of the modes owing to its tendency to conform to the prescriptions of modal theory by cadencing regularly on $\hat{1}$, $\hat{3}$, and $\hat{5}$ (as Zarlino deems proper) and outlining the intervals between the final and fifth in melodic motion. But contrary to Dahlhaus and Chafe's claim about the exceptional modal/hexachordal/tonal clarity at the opening of *Ecco, Silvio*, the setting of Dorinda's initial cries in verses 1–6 veers promptly and profoundly off course by avoiding firm cadential arrivals and the interval species expected of the G-dorian mode (Example 7.11). The work indeed begins with a G-minor sonority, yet as Dorinda enumerates the emotional wounds she has suffered, the phrases ascend by thirds to B♭, d, F, and A—all non-cadentially— supporting an upper voice ascent in parallel phrases, *d″–f″* then *f″–a″*, before arriving (by descending fifths) back at F for the first assertive cadence (m. 18).

To this point, then, the opening is characterized by a persistent avoidance of true cadences, and the first decisive arrival—at the modal 7̂, F—leaves the madrigal already in foreign territory for the G-dorian mode. In the three verses beginning "Bramastila" (you wanted her) that follow—telling Silvio that his wishes to see Dorinda wounded, as prey, and (soon) dead have been realized (verses 7–10)—the madrigal rises again by thirds, from B♭ to D to F. Before ending on F again, however, the Canto undermines the pre-cadential C sonority with a poignant *e♭″* at the self-referencing "*eccola*" (here she is) that ultimately redirects the approach from F to the final, G, for the first time in the piece (m. 28). Needless to say, this first cadence on the G final, resulting from a deflected F cadence, hardly carries the conviction expected to establish the mode after an opening marked by ambiguity and conflict. This ambiguity also encompasses the melodic behavior in all voices, which offers only oblique references to the principal boundaries between G and D.[58]

In all, to consider this "one of the most convincingly unified beginnings" of Monteverdi's madrigals from this period represents a gross misreading of the music and its expressive ends. Rather, the modal uncertainty suits not only Dorinda's panic and confusion at the start of the text, but also the passage's broader contexts as the middle portion of a tumultuous scene in the play. For the madrigal's unsettled opening thrusts the listener into the center of the scene's action, affording no time to delineating the mode and final in the customary ways. The use of non-cadential gestures for the initial arrivals on B♭ (m. 6) and F (m. 11) heightens the sense of momentum and urgency, which hardly abates even for the first cadence on the final in m. 28, where the central pitch is tied to the vision of Dorinda's impending death ("eccola morte"). Thereafter, another cadence on the final does not appear until m. 45 ("senza pietà"), following cadences on the irregular goals of C and F.

The confusion and unrest of the opening extend through all three of Dorinda's *parti* and contrast sharply with the two *parti* devoted to Silvio's speech, where his realization and avowals of love beget a tight union of musical surface and deeper structure. In Dorinda's *parti*, for example, the cadences are divided between a wide number of goals: in order of prevalence, D, G, F, C, B♭, and A. Although the modal fifth and final dominate in terms of overall frequency, cadences on F, C, and B♭ plainly prevail toward the beginnings of Dorinda's *parti*. (In the final *parte*, there is no G cadence until sixty measures in.) Silvio's *parti*, on the other hand, remain firmly rooted in the G-dorian mode throughout, as reflected in the melodic behavior and in a cadence plan that emphasizes G and D out of only four cadence pitches. The resolute modal character of Silvio's music matches the certainty of his newfound love for Dorinda, as he offers his commitment, weapons, and life to her. The regular use of E♭ (a hallmark of the G-dorian mode) for the repeated statements of "Dorinda" reinforces this stability and sets Silvio's introduction in the *terza parte* apart from Dorinda's opening in the *prima parte*, where the predominance of E♮ aligns more with the local orientation toward F than with the underlying mode (compare Examples 7.11 and 7.12).

Concurrently with these techniques of differentiating the lovers' speech, mental states, and *parti* through mode and cadential scheme, the madrigal imparts a strong sense of unity in other respects—for example, through the general prevalence of homophonic texture and the frequent isolation of the Tenore seen above. Monteverdi likewise seizes upon formal and semantic motifs of the text—rhetorical parallelisms, a focus on Dorinda as victim and beloved, and the characters' evolving relationship—to create a network of musical–textual references whose imports develop in tandem with the characters' own developments across the piece. In many instances, these referential–expressive techniques resemble those of Marenzio's *Pastor fido* settings.

Example 7.12 Monteverdi, *Ecco, Silvio*, Opening of the *terza parte* (mm. 151–60)

A straightforward example comes at the opening of the *quarta parte*, where Silvio capitulates: "Ecco, piangendo le ginocchie a terra" (Here, bending my knee to the ground"). Whereas the start of the *terza parte* (Example 7.12) emphasizes the shift of speaker from Dorinda to Silvio with its modal–cadential conformity and call to Dorinda by name, the *quarta parte* signals Silvio's physical and emotional submission to his beloved (communicated through his kneeling) and reciprocation of love ("Riverente t'adoro") not only by echoing Dorinda's initial word ("Ecco"), G-minor sonority, and four-voice declamation from "Ecco, Silvio" (Example 7.11), but also by doing so with the same voicing (*g–g′–b♭′–d″*) and delay of the Tenore with which the madrigal began. Silvio's two later "Ecco" statements, indicating his weapons ("Ecco li strali," mm. 223–24) and chest ("Eccoti il petto," mm. 256–57), also invoke G sonorities (now with B♮) and, in the first instance, the same voicing as Dorinda's "Ecco."

The madrigal deploys two other referential gestures that are farther-reaching in consequence. The first, the motion of a downward leap from a suspended high pitch, represents a salient idiomatic gesture tied expressly to Dorinda's speech in the *prima* and *ultima parti*. This "suspended-leap" figure, therefore, links the beginning and end of the piece motivically, and through its associations with the text, projects the characters' changing relationship between these points.

In its first occurrence, at "*Eccola* in quella guisa" (Here she is in that state), this gesture consists of repeated leaps downward a minor sixth from a climactic *a″* to *c♯″* between the syllables "Ec-cola" to accentuate Dorinda's impassioned inward deictic as she presents herself as victim (mm. 11–13; Example 7.11). This initial context establishes the motive's ties to Dorinda and her rhetorical (and potentially physical) self-reference. The figure reappears at "ferir, ferita" (to wound, wounded; mm. 19–20) now in a punishing M6 leap (*g″–b♭′*) to highlight Dorinda's wounded state. The return of the deictic "eccola," at "eccola morte" in mm. 26–27, elicits a third appearance of the motive, now in diminished form (*e♭′–a′*) as a marker of Dorinda's suffering.

The suspended-leap figure fades in the intermediate *parti*, surfacing only in faint intimations—as at Silvio's cries "Dorinda, ah, dirò 'mia'" in the *terza parte*, where it appears without a leap, but in otherwise similar construction in coordination with the calls to Dorinda (see Example 7.12). It then returns in its full guise, now with a falling fifth, in the final *parte*, where its import expands in reaction to Silvio's confession to encompass not Dorinda alone, but both lovers together, now unified in love. The first of these later occurrences come with Dorinda's recollections of the futility of her tears and sighs in turning Silvio's heart, hence again with inward references—"De le lagrime *mie, de′* miei sospiri" (mm. 282–83) and "in *van percosso*" (referring to Silvio's chest struck by her laments, mm. 286–87)—and then again with her questioning of Silvio's transformation, "È pur *ver che* tu spiri / E che *senti* pietate?" (Is it indeed *true that* you sigh, and that *you feel* pity?; mm. 289–99).

Through the motive's origins in Dorinda's self ("Eccola") and suffering ("ferita") in the *prima parte*, and later connection to Silvio's sighs, pity, and professed love, the madrigal insinuates what lies beyond this textual excerpt: that Dorinda's pain ("ferir") truly has transformed Silvio's once cold heart. The restatement of Dorinda's question, "È pur *ver che* tu spiri / E che *senti* pietate?" with its twofold suspended-leap figures, accentuates this musical–textual revelation.

In its last appearances, the motive makes the lovers' union explicit by joining together their pronouns ("io," "te") and the central theme of the text, "ferir" (to wound), in the question "Ferir io te?" (I wound you?), where "ferir" now applies to Silvio's, not Dorinda's, physical and emotional suffering. Through two statements of the question and its response—"te pur ferisca amore" (love instead shall wound you)—three forms of the motive drive the madrigal through an ascent, $f''-a''$, and descent, $a''-f''$, ending in an F cadence. This is the madrigal's last assertive departure from the cadential sphere of the G-dorian mode: thereafter, the cadential and non-cadential arrivals focus intently on D and G—an accord of musical surface and interior nature that mirrors the reconciliation of emotions in the scene.

While joining "io" and "te" with the musical allusion to Dorinda's self ("Eccola"), the motive's transposition from $g''-c''$ to $a''-d''$ between statements of "Ferrir io te?" also merges it with another key indicator of Dorinda: the pitch a'' itself. The pitch holds a prominent position at the start of the madrigal as the goal of the upper-voice ascent $d''-f''$, $f''-a''$, where it bridges the end of verse 1 ("...in odio hai tan*to*") with the deictic start of verse 2, "*Ec*cola," in the Canto and Quinto (Example 7.11). Its enunciation here ties it not only to Dorinda's self-reference, but also to the inception of the suspended-leap motive ($a''-c\sharp''$). As in the previous G-centered work in the Fifth Book, *Cruda Amarilli*, a'' here carries considerable salience for lying both at the upper reaches of the Canto's and Quinto's ranges and one pitch beyond the G modal octave. It represents, in other words, an expressive overreach—a strain that intensifies the modal instability by emphasizing A, rather than G, as upper melodic boundary of the collective ambitus. The pitch's reappearance soon after at "*questo* Dorin*da*?" (mm. 32–34) comes with the second assertive cadence on F, and thus couples the pitch with Dorinda's name explicitly, another inward deictic ("questo"), and the internal discord of a foreign cadence. The gesture as a whole, therefore, frames Dorinda's self-reference with the dual tension of both a'' and the pitch-center F.

The striking a'' does not appear again until the *terza parte*, precisely at the next occurrence of Dorinda's name, where it sounds repeatedly at Silvio's initial cry, "Dorin*da* ah, dirò 'mia,' *ah*, dirò mia / Se mi*a* non sei" (mm. 151–60, Example 7.12). This beginning is filled with references to the start of the madrigal. The cries of "Dorinda," for example, paraphrase the $d''-f''-a''$ ascent of Dorinda's first words, while the sonorities that support its initial climb, $d''-e\flat''-f''$ (g–c–B♭), paraphrase those of "Ecco, Silvio, colei che 'n odio hai tanto" (g–[F–d]–c–B♭).[59] Also, in its three instances at the start of Silvio's speech, a'' appears in a similar melodic ($f''-a''$) and rhythmic con-figuration as the suspended-leap figure at "Eccola," but is departed by step, rather than by leap.

Silvio's opening, therefore, represents a threefold reference: to Dorinda's "Ecco, Silvio" opening, to Dorinda herself by name, and to her pitch signi-fier, a'', which evokes both "Eccola" and "questo Dorinda" from the *prima parte*. The pitch appears elsewhere in Silvio's *parti*, tied almost exclusively to allusions to his beloved: "*v*ita" (giving Dorinda life, mm. 172–73), "Sa*rai* con la mia morte" (joining Dorinda in death, mm. 198–99), "E ti *chieggio per*-don *ma*" (asking forgiveness with the added emphasis of $b\flat''$, mm. 209–11), and several commands for Dorinda to wound him (mm. 230–53).

Like the transformation of the suspended-leap figure by the madrigal's end, the salient a'', too, adapts to the changed scenario of the scene to en-velop Silvio and Dorinda together in newly realized love. As the emotional climax of the text, the closing *parte* brings numerous ascents to a'', often in quicker rhythms than in previous occurrences, but its role of obscuring the G-dorian framework persists. The opening, for example, shows marked changes in the character of Dorinda's music, including an accelerated har-monic rhythm and for the first time in the piece, a *parte* that commences not with a G-minor sonority with d'' in the Canto, but with a unison g' in the three upper parts. This g' rises in undulating motions a full octave in the Canto to g'' at "petto." But after a brief pause on an A sonority ("Silvio"), the voice reaches above the final again to a'' as the beginning pitch of the next two verses, which lead irregularly to F and C (mm. 268–70 and 271–74). The expansion of the upper ambitus to a'' here, as in many earlier instances, displaces the G-octave context with F-lydian features.

While the madrigal text leaves Dorinda in a state of confusion, the mad-rigal brings complete resolution, perhaps pointing forward to her fortunate end in the play. As in *Cruda Amarilli*, a crucial requirement for this large-scale closure involves the reconciliation of the unruly a'' with the integral G-octave. The madrigal makes this alignment of registral upper boundary and modal octave clear between the repeated statements of the final three verses, where Dorinda's concession to praise, not seek vengeance against, Sil-vio yields a straightforward shift from an $a''-d''$ descent to $g''-d''$. Thereafter, G-dorian parameters—with E♭ supplanting E♮—prevail to the terminal G cadence, which the Canto approaches with a complete spelling out of a $g''-g'$ octave descent with the characteristic $e\flat$. The weight of this ending surpasses that of the previous four *parti*, including the more modally conforming ones devoted to Silvio's speech (both of which end on the final). With this satisfy-ing close, the madrigal seems to resolve what remains unsettled in the text: that Dorinda overcomes her disbelief and accepts Silvio's love.

Works such as this one comprising more than two *parti* pose distinct chal-lenges with the need to balance long-range tensions and direction with the demands of modal propriety and internal resolution over a long period. The beginning and ending sonorities of the five *parti* alone show Monteverdi's concern for maintaining proximity to the mode at the margins, even while challenging it elsewhere: all of the *parti* begin and end on the G final—with the conventional raised third for ending sonorities—apart from two instances that instead highlight the other principal degrees of the mode, D (end of the *prima parte*) and B♭ (beginning of the *seconda parte*). This strategy alone seems to have been enough to appease Artusi, for the critic never cites *Ecco, Silvio* for modal disorder—nor, as we have seen, do Dahlhaus and Chafe—despite the instability and ambiguity that characterize the interiors of Dorinda's *parti* and the madrigal's opening.

In approaching such an extensive text and musical structure, Monteverdi incorporates tested techniques of other composers into his own expressive and organizational strategies, as he does in *Cruda Amarilli* and *O Mirtillo*. In handling a five-*parte* work, a clear model to which Monteverdi might have turned is Wert's *O primavera*. Published in 1595, just three years before the Ferrarese performance of Monteverdi's *Pastor fido* settings, Wert's madrigal uses the same modal family (G-dorian, but the plagal form), five *parti*—all but one of them beginning and ending on the final—and a similar approach of isolating individual voices (focusing on the Tenore) in predominantly homorhythmic texture. Moreover, Wert's work calls for the same scoring of five voices with two sopranos—only in *chiavi naturali*, in keeping with the lower (plagal) form of the mode—and of course draws from the same textual source, *Il pastor fido*, but a more conventional soliloquy instead of a dialogue. The openings of the two works also show similar inclinations toward F as a temporary goal while outlining the interval D–A in the upper voice—although this motion goes downward in Wert's work, $d''-a'$ (mm. 1–5; see Example 4.18), rather than upward to the emphatic a'' in *Ecco, Silvio*. Monteverdi might also have looked to Wert's example in devising his five-*parte* structure, for at the most basic level, the structural motion of Monteverdi's madrigal behaves very much like that of *O primavera*, with a static d'' ($\hat{5}$), accentuated at the outset of nearly every *parte* and expanded through subsidiary descents, that gives way in a last-minute display of rhetorical–structural closure in the *ultima parte*. It is in the detailed processes of how Monteverdi maintains this background pitch while achieving variety and textual expression that his methods diverge notably from Wert.

Wert's madrigal, for example, adheres closely throughout to the prescribed parameters of the mode. Much of its cadential variety prioritizes degrees that uphold contrapuntal support for the background d'' and conform to the regular cadences for the mode—namely, G, B♭, and D. On a local level, this modal consistency shows in the widespread use of E♭ as the sixth degree—including for D-*mi* cadences—given the distinctive role of this pitch in the G-dorian context. The fact that E♭ plays a much more limited part in *Ecco, Silvio* indicates the contested authority of the G-dorian mode against the influences of C and F, both of which demand E♮.

This modal volatility and its resulting emphasis of E♮ underscore two important features of Monteverdi's madrigal. First, while utilizing a suspended background similar to Wert's as a means of delaying structural motion across five *parti, Ecco, Silvio* also animates this static framework with foreground disruptions similar in nature to the structural stammering of Monteverdi's *Cruda Amarilli*. In the Dorinda–Silvio dialogue, temporary displacements of the background $\hat{5}$ (*d″*) by the upper-neighbor *e″* often accompany salient gestures to the climatic and referential *a″*, while other middleground disruptions by neighbor pitches *e″* and *c″* spring from assertive moves to foreign modal and cadential centers, particularly C and F. Like *Cruda Amarilli*, then, *Ecco, Silvio* integrates aspects of Wert's (static) and Marenzio's (dynamic) structural tactics to devise an expansive framework that is at once suspended on the larger scale, and animated by diversions and diminutions at more local levels.

Secondly, as we have seen, these modal–structural disruptions correspond chiefly with Dorinda's *parti* and serve as an affective means of differentiating the characters and their affective states. Monteverdi, in other words, tailors his structural approach to the speaker of the text: Silvio's *parti* adhere more to Wert's example in their stable and unwavering state, while Dorinda's *parti* recall Marenzio's propensity to push forward from ambiguity and conflict toward clarity and resolution. Thus, while all of Monteverdi's *parti* sustain the static *d″* at the deepest level, they do so with contrasting degrees of structural defiance or unity at the middleground and foreground levels to distinguish the interior states of the two speakers.

Also akin to Wert's approach in his later madrigals is Monteverdi's nearly uniform use of three-part cadences with 5–1 bass and infrequent evasion of cadences. (There are no *cadenze fuggite*, for example, in the *prima* and *quinta parti* and few in the internal *parti*.) The relatively scarce cadences with a 2–1 bass generally coincide with specific affective or textural contexts—for instance, notions of cruelty ("Ah, garzon crudo," mm. 38–39, and "Anima cruda, sì, ma però bella," mm. 100–01), episodes of imitation with a stepwise subject (mm. 127–29), and reduced textures (mm. 147–50)—and with *mi* cadences (mm. 92–93 and 144–45).

The regularity of cadence structure in Monteverdi's *Ecco, Silvio* and other madrigals is a notable contrast from Marenzio's *Pastor fido* settings, where the diversity of cadence types serves as a means to differentiate their structural weight, finality, and expressive effect. In *Ecco, Silvio*, on the other hand, the general restraint and consistency of the cadences and texture allow the focus to fall instead on the delivery of the text (*pronuntiatio*) and set into relief moments of distinct affective, referential, and structural importance. The improperly handled dissonances toward the opening of *Cruda Amarilli* offer a striking example of this approach, but so also do the repeated *a″–c♯″* and e♭″–a′ leaps at "Eccola" (mm. 12–14 and 26–27), the subdued two-voice statements of "Va' in pace, anima mia" (mm. 141–50), and the ascending cries of "Dorinda, ah" (mm. 151–55) in *Ecco, Silvio*.

As a setting of a protracted excerpt of theatrical dialogue by a composer destined to play a decisive role in the development of opera, *Ecco, Silvio* offers a uniquely telling example of the relationship between the Italian madrigal, Guarini's play, and the potential for early dramatic thinking. For even at the opportunity to juxtapose two speaking characters, Monteverdi renders them not in a mimetic, quasi-operatic, representational, or soloistic manner, but from the perspective of a reading or retelling of the text, as if with implied captions of "she said" and "he said," like those that appear literally in Monte's dialogue settings from roughly the same period.[60] In both composers' settings, therefore, the vocal ensemble acts as a coordinated group of narrator–readers that conveys not only the meaning, affects, and words of the speakers, but also, through the expressive details of the music, aspects of their individual personas and passions, yet without embodying or enacting their subjectivities uniquely in any given part.

This distinction in genre and function between madrigal and opera, narrative and dramatic, reading and representation is essential, but it does not exclude the possibility that aspects of Monteverdi's techniques from his madrigals reappear in his later dramatic works. For *Ecco, Silvio* in particular includes various instances of superficial cadential, rhythmic, and melodic tendencies that later become key elements of Monteverdi's approach to recitative. The use of natural speech rhythms with repeated (or sustained) sonorities through the beginnings of lines, followed by quickening changes of sonorities driving toward a rhetorical/grammatical close (either cadential or non-cadential), for example, appears in both *Ecco, Silvio* and various arias and recitatives of *L'Orfeo*, including in their opening lines. Example 7.13 compares the opening used for each strophe in the Prologue for La Musica in *L'Orfeo* with the outer voices from the opening of the madrigal.

The presence of common superficial features between madrigal and opera, however, does not imply a commonality of genre and context (reading/ enactment, chamber/stage). The conceptual and performance frameworks

a) *Ecco, Silvio*, mm. 2–6 (outer voices)

b) *L'Orfeo*, Prologue, mm. 14–16

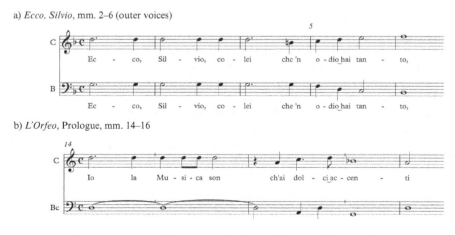

Example 7.13 Comparison of Monteverdi's *Ecco, Silvio* and *L'Orfeo* (Prologue).

of the two genres remain distinct, even when they share a common goal of rendering the inflections and expressions of impassioned speech. It seems practical, after all, that the composer would apply familiar techniques and idiomatic gestures from his madrigals to his later dramatic works. The fact that Monteverdi never set *Pastor fido* texts in a dramatic fashion—or even for solo voice, as he did various other Guarini poems, including in the Fifth Book—attests to how firmly the play remained rooted in the lyric, literary realm, as a text to be read rather than enacted, despite the availability of musical–dramatic means at the start of the Seicento.

Inter-Madrigal Motives (and Their Interpretative Consequences)

The previous analyses have shown how referential motives operate in Monteverdi's *Pastor fido* settings internally, at the level of the individual piece, and how the opening four madrigals of the Fifth Book may act collectively as a response to Artusi's criticism of these very works. Speculations of farther-reaching musical connections between separate madrigals or across an entire madrigal book in earlier scholarship, however, have often proven tenuous. There is no clear organization of pieces in the Fourth or Fifth Book by musical parameters (mode, final, cleffing, or system), for example, and hypotheses of narrative (textual) coherence in the Fifth Book generally hinge on the common origins of many of the texts in Guarini's play and on storylines that loosely trace various stages and perspectives of pastoral love that prove commonplace in lyric poetry and the madrigal repertory.

Yet, along with the types of intra-madrigal motivic references we have seen thus far—such as the "perdona," "cruda Amarilli," and "eccola" motives—and the proposed inter-madrigal narratives proposed by others, groups of pieces in the Fourth and Fifth Books are also tied together through related musical ideas. These cross-madrigal connections span both the 1603 and 1605 collections, thus adding to the unity of the two books—individually and together—and further corroborating the notion that much of the music shares a close conceptual and chronological origin.[61] From an interpretative standpoint, these recurring gestures also strengthen the potential for cross-madrigal readings by forging clear musical–textual links from one piece to another. This manner of close, rigorous reading of madrigals not only individually, but also comparatively and relationally, would require a particular type of audience and performance environment—one, for instance, of informed and perceptive readers, such as Marenzio's audiences in Rome, or of musical connoisseurs with repeated hearings of the music, as at Goretti's household in Ferrara, where Artusi evaluated Monteverdi's works. Table 7.2, for example, shows the distribution of the four motivic figures discussed here among nine madrigals from the Fourth and Fifth Books.

Most of these motivic ideas appear in prominent structural positions, such as the start of a piece or *parte*, in at least one of their occurrences.

Table 7.2 Four Inter-Madrigal Motives in Monteverdi's Fourth and Fifth Books

Motives and appearances			
"O Mirtillo"	*"Vorrei morire" (abandoned leading tone)*	*Settenario rhythm*	*Interlocking thirds*
		Quel augellin	
Cor mio, mentre vi miro			
Luci serene e chiare			
	Sì ch'io vorrei morire		
	Ah, dolente partita	*Ah, dolente partita*	
	Volgea l'anima mia		
		Cruda Amarilli	
O Mirtillo			
Ch'io t'ami	*Ch'io t'ami*	*Ch'io t'ami*	*Ch'io t'ami*
			Ecco, Silvio

The opening of *O Mirtillo* represents a notable example. Tomlinson relates this opening to "one of the most frequent and expressive gestures" of the later *Lamento d'Arianna* (1608): the leap downward of a M6 followed by a stepwise descent, as seen at "o Padre mio" and "Ah, Teseo mio." But in these instances, the leap falls on the downbeat and the entire figure unfolds over one or two sonorities, whereas the "O Mirtillo" gesture involves a sustained pitch that leaps downward after the downbeat, followed by an upper-neighbor motion, with sonorities that change with every syllable (see Example 7.6 above). Although the leap at "O Mirtillo" spans a M6, the specific interval is not crucial to the motive's referential role. Thus, when it reappears markedly later in the Fifth Book—at the opening of the *seconda parte* of *Ch'io t'ami*—it involves a P4 leap followed by upper-neighbor motion: $d''-a'-b\flat'-a'$ (Example 7.14). The sonorities, of course, vary from those at "O Mirtillo," but in both instances the upper-neighbor figure alternates between sonorities a P5 apart (D–G–D and F–C–F). Both appearances also share the rhetorical–expressive function of delivering exasperated cries from one hopeless lover to the other: Amarilli's "O Mirtillo" and Mirtillo's "Deh! bella e cara" (Oh! beautiful and dear).

In fact, in the play, the former (Amarilli's *O Mirtillo*, No. 2) comes in response to the latter (Mirtillo's *Ch'io t'ami*, No. 5), as Amarilli laments in private ("O Mirtillo") after her beloved's profession of his love ("Deh! bella e cara"). The allusion to the "O Mirtillo" gesture at the start of Amarilli's lament, then, might be seen as her echoing Mirtillo's cry ("Deh, bella e cara") from moments earlier, despite the reversed ordering of the works in Monteverdi's book. Indeed, any reader acquainted with Guarini's tragicomedy would recognize Amarilli's *O Mirtillo* as a turning point in the drama, after her skirmish with Mirtillo, when she reveals her struggle and true persona and exposes herself to Corisca's scheme. Thus, while scholars have proposed that her lament is a response to *Cruda Amarilli*—which it unquestionably is by the simple fact that it follows *Cruda Amarilli* in Monteverdi's book—it is also a response to *Ch'io t'ami*, which follows it, by virtue of its echo of the latter's "O Mirtillo" motive (an aspect of Mirtillo's musical "voice") and the circumstances of the two texts in the play. In other words, the Fifth Book may rearrange the play's speeches and juxtapose them in new, compelling ways, but it also presents them patently out of order, while also seeming to invoke (knowledge of) their chronology in the play through both text (Amarilli's central lament) and music (a motivic reference to Mirtillo's "earlier" speech).

The "O Mirtillo" reference, however, also extends beyond the sphere of *Pastor fido* settings and the Fifth Book. In *Cor mio, mentre vi miro*—a setting from Guarini's *Rime* in the Fourth Book—Monteverdi sets the parallel lines "O bellezza mortale, / O bellezza vitale" (vv. 5–6) with transposed versions of the "O Mirtillo" gesture (Example 7.15). The first "O bellezza," in fact, is identical to "O Mirtillo," only with the Tenore omitted and a different ending pitch in the Canto: $d''–f'–g'–a'$. The second "O bellezza" transposes the gesture (now with introductory rests) up a M2 to end on G (as happens with the sonorities also in the second phrase of *O Mirtillo*). Both statements also extend the correspondence to the entire first hendecasyllabic verse of *O Mirtillo* by repeating "bellezza"—hence, creating an aberrant ten-syllable line with a penultimate stress—and by presenting the latter part of the verse ("bellezza mortale/vitale") with an upper-neighbor motion in the Canto above the "O Mirtillo" Basso motion, only with a different transposition scheme between both parts of the verse in the two madrigals. The close musical parallels mirror the conspicuous textual–rhetorical parallels of the verses: "O bellezza, bellezza mortale/vitale" and "O Mirtillo, Mirtillo anima mia."

Example 7.14 Monteverdi, *Ch'io t'ami, e t'ami più della mia vita*, Opening of the *seconda parte* (mm. 49–56)

Example 7.15 Monteverdi, *Cor mio, mentre vi miro*, mm. 25–32

A variation of the gesture also arises at the repeated statements "Voi m'incendete" (You set me alight), the second line in Monteverdi's setting of Ridolfo Arlotti's poem *Luci serene e chiare* in the Fourth Book. As in *O Mirtillo* and *Cor mio, mentre vi miro*, *Luci serene e chiare* transposes an initial F-centered statement (mm. 8–10) up a M2 for a new variation of the motive leading to G (mm. 11–12). The same formations return later in the madrigal as part of the formal transposition of verses 1–3 up a tone for verses 4–6, which brings about dual statements of verse 5, "Voi mi ferite" (You wound me; mm. 26–31), with gestures now on G and A. Thus, while linking parallel expressions of the beloved's effects on the speaker (arousal and pain), the motive joins all four madrigals together through direct declarations to the second-person beloved: "O Mirtillo," "O bellezza," "Voi mi ferite," and "Deh, bella e cara" (in *Ch'io t'ami*). The gesture's distinctiveness and the clarity of these manifestations underpin these musical–textual associations.

This relationship may be useful for establishing a chronology of the works. Gary Tomlinson places *Luci serene e chiare* among the works of the Fourth Book that show a discernible Ferrarese influence—namely, through its kinship with Gesualdo's setting of the same text in his Fourth Book of 1596. If this theory is true, the madrigal could represent Monteverdi's earliest use of the "O Mirtillo" gesture. Noting the composer's similar treatment of the phrases "O Mirtillo" and "O bellezza" (in *Cor mio, mentre vi miro*), however, Tomlinson also reasons that "it is probable that *O Mirtillo*, though published later, was written before *Cor mio*."[62] Applying similar reasoning to *Luci serene e chiare* and *Ch'io t'ami*, then, it could be argued that, despite the rather general similarities that Tomlinson observes between Gesualdo's and Monteverdi's treatments of *Luci serene e chiare*, the varied use of the "O Mirtillo" gesture in both madrigals could place *Luci serene e chiare* chronologically alongside the other madrigals that make use of the figure (*O Mirtillo* and *Cor mio, mentre vi miro*), and thus among the epigrammatic,

Mantuan-style pieces of the Fourth and Fifth Books, one of which (*O Mirtillo*) dates from before November 1598.

The hook-like opening gesture of *Sì ch'io vorrei morire* represents another prominent and distinctive inter-madrigal motive—one with a strongly suggestive semantic association (Example 7.16a). The gesture as a whole comprises coupled phrases, the first of which presents the entire first verse, "Sì ch'io vorrei morire" (Yes, I would like to die), with a bassline of P4 descent–M2 rise–P5 descent, c'–g–a–d, ending in an evaded D cadence, while the second phrase recycles all but the first sonority and syllable ("Sì") to continue the M2 up–P5 down motion, d–e–A, now ending on A. In this madrigal, a third statement ("ch'io vorrei morire") restates this latter M2 up–P5 down bass pattern yet again, adding a closing return to A (A–B–E–A). This addendum strengthens the arrival on A, but it is not part of the basic motive that appears in other works. The distinguishing upper voice of each phrase, meanwhile, consists of the three components of an evaded *clausula cantizans* that leaps away from the leading tone, $\hat{8}$–$\hat{7}$–$\hat{5}$, instead of the expected $\hat{8}$–$\hat{7}$–$\hat{8}$, above the three-note bass motion ($\hat{4}$–$\hat{5}$–$\hat{1}$). In most instances, the first phrase of the motive begins with a prefatory sonority and syllable (here "Sì") that are not restated. As a whole, the two-phrase pattern carries out a linear octave descent in the upper voice, e''–e', with M3 leaps at the evaded leading tones, and, thus, serves as an expansion of the initial upper-voice pitch (e'') to the lower register.

This "vorrei morire," octave-expansion idea occurs in at least three other works in the Fourth and Fifth Books. Its appearances at "misero e privo del cor" (wretched and deprived of a heart, mm. 44–49) in *Volgea l'anima mia soavamente* (1603) and at "S'altro non mi voi dir, dimmi almen mori / E morir mi vedrai" (If nothing else you say to me, say at least, "Die," / And you will see me die; mm. 128–32 and 140–44) in *Ch'io t'ami* (1605) correspond closely with its form in *Sì ch'io vorrei morire*, including an overarching octave descent in the upper voice (Example 7.16b and c). There are other small modifications, however, in rhythm and voicing (both involve a combination of full and reduced texture, for example), and each occurs at a different pitch level: C–G (supporting a d''–d' upper-voice descent) in *Volgea l'anima*, and G–D and C–G (supporting a'–a and d''–d' descents) in *Ch'io t'ami*. Notably, in the latter, the coupled phrases of the gesture also set separate phrases of text, both of which contain references to *morire*, thus reinforcing the association with *Sì ch'io vorrei morire*. The correspondence between all three works, meanwhile, is strengthened further by the fact that the gestures are nearly exact transpositions in all of the voices.

The fourth occurrence in *Ah, dolente partita* (1597/1603) involves two separate verses—"E sento nel partire / Un vivace morire" (And I feel in parting a living death)—only the first of which uses the "vorrei morir" figure in the upper voice, while the second extends the $\hat{4}$–$\hat{5}$–$\hat{1}$ bass motion, as expected (mm. 57–66; see Example 6.2 above, labelled "...nel morire/partire..."). The twofold statement of the verse-pair yields interlocking fifth

a) *Sì ch'io vorrei morire* (mm. 1–6)

b) *Volgea l'anima mia soavamente* (mm. 44–49)

c) *Ch'io t'ami* (mm. 140–44)

Example 7.16 Three Appearances of the "Vorrei morire" Figure

descents in the upper voice, $e''-a'$ and $a'-d'$—hence, altogether, a M9 rather than an octave, owing to the inclusion of the opening syllable ("E") in the restatement. But the first statement of this syllable is prefatory not only to the motive, but also, structurally, to the onset of the background $\hat{4}$, d'', at "sento," which is then projected to the octave below ($d''-d'$) by the Canto and Alto. Once again—as in *Sì ch'io vorrei morire* and *Ch'io t'ami*—the motive coincides with statements of *morire*, thus integrating this structural moment with the cross-madrigal musical–textual figure of "death."

Tomlinson sees Monteverdi's apparent development of certain phrase-level techniques from Pallavicino's Sixth Book (1600) as reason to date *Sì ch'io vorrei morire* to after March 1600 (when Pallavicino signed the dedication of his book).[63] The recurrence of its opening motive in association with *morire* in four separate madrigals, however, could suggest either that all of these works originated in relatively close proximity—namely, around 1597, given the publication of *Ah, dolente partita* that year in the anthology *Fiori del giardino*—or that Monteverdi returned to this figure repeatedly over the course of several years, potentially expressly for expressions of *morire*.

How these cross-madrigal *morire* references might affect the interpretation of the pieces proves a more fundamental question. "Death" carries very different apparent connotations in the three pieces that present the "vorrei morire" motive with literal forms of "morire": in *Ah, dolente partita* and *Ch'io t'ami*—both from Mirtillo's response to Amarilli's rejection in act 3, scene 3—"death" denotes the anguish of love-suffering, whereas in the lyric poem *Sì ch'io vorrei morire*, "morire" functions in its euphemistic light to imply the very opposite of pain—the bliss of sexual release. The poem makes the erotic scenario unmistakable not only with its descriptions of the beloved's "bella bocca" (beautiful mouth), "cara e dolce lingua" (dear sweet tongue), and "bianco seno" (white breast), but also with its climactic reprise of the opening verse at its finish: "Deh, stringetemi fin ch'io vengo meno! / Ahi bocca, ahi baci, ahi lingua, torn'a dire: / Sì ch'io vorrei morire" (Oh, hold me until I grow faint! / Ah, mouth, ah, kisses, ah, tongue, I say again: / "Yes, I would like to die"). The madrigal matches this return of the text with a restatement of the corresponding music—the "vorrei morire" motive in its initial form (as shown in Example 7.16a).

By connecting the opposing connotations of *morire* in these three madrigals motivically, the music provides a direct conduit for the exchange and intermingling of meaning. For instance, when Mirtillo says to Amarilli with histrionic urgency in *Ch'io t'ami*, "If you say nothing else to me, say at least, 'Die,' and you will see me die," or in *Ah, dolente partita*, "And I feel in parting a living death," the listener familiar with these madrigals and the play might muse over the music's allusions to *Sì ch'io vorrei morire* and the implications of an erotic *morire* in Mirtillo's case. The music, in other words, seems to play with the interchange of *morire* between one context (sexual climax) and the other (love-suffering). Through its linking of both scenarios and their literal expressions of the term, the motive facilitates the musical–textual pun that promotes double readings even in cases where the import seems clear. Thus, while mixing the subjects of torment and eroticism in the two *Pastor fido* madrigals, *Sì ch'io vorrei morire* also acquires an added dimension of comical irony through the association of its opening and closing phrases with Mirtillo's mournful complaints in *Ah, dolente partita* and *Ch'io t'ami*.

Monteverdi's strategy of creating *morire* cross-references with conflicting connotations broadens and even complicates the readings of the madrigals in ways that might, in fact, reflect how readers already approached such texts at the time—namely, liberally and fancifully, with minds open to potential and even improbable subtexts, innuendos, intertextual references, and, of course, erotic puns. Indeed, in some instances, it is difficult to determine which sense of *morire* predominates in a lyric poem or madrigal text—that of love-suffering, sexual fulfillment, or both. This equivocality was perhaps precisely the point. As the imaginations of early modern readers flipped playfully between these different meanings, poets likewise built such interpretative ambiguity/flexibility into their verse presumably for this very purpose. As these examples from Monteverdi's madrigals show, composers could also play along in this game of crisscrossed metaphors. Likewise, in the case of Monteverdi's madrigals, the reach of this motivic–interpretative network to pieces across the Fourth and Fifth Books shows a type of referential unity and jocular exchange between madrigal books that has seldom been recognized.

The appearance of the "vorrei morire" figure again in *Volgea l'anima mia*, where it does not coincide with a literal statement of "morire," illustrates yet another facet of how a referential effect might influence a madrigal's reading (Example 7.16b). Its role here proves more ambiguous: the poem, from Guarini's *Rime*, relates the moment when the male speaker, in surrendering his heart to his affectionate beloved, experiences a bout of fear and hesitation, exclaiming, "Misero e privo / Del cor, chi mi dà vita?" (Wretched and deprived of a heart, who will give me life?). His beloved then responds "in un sospir d'amore: 'Io, che son il tuo core'" (in a sigh of love, "I, who am your heart").

The "vorrei morire" motive sounds twice precisely at the speaker's cry, "Misero e privo del cor," then three more times in a variant phrygian form for repetitions of the next phrase ("chi mi dà vita?"). The figure's ties relate this moment, on the one hand, to the anguish of Mirtillo's *Ah, dolente partita* and *Ch'io t'ami* and their expressions of mortal vulnerability at the hands of a female beloved. But on the other hand, the gesture also evokes the intimate scenario and reporting of imparted speech of *Sì ch'io vorrei morire*. Monteverdi's placement of the motive here, thus, reveals two complementary sides of the text: the speaker's fear of falling victim to the same suffering and rejection as Mirtillo, and the potential reward that his emotional wager might yield: namely, the sensual bliss of *Sì ch'io vorrei morire*. In fact, in spite of their contrasting finals (G and A) and physical separation in the Fourth Book, *Volgea l'anima mia* (No. 5) and *Sì ch'io vorrei morire* (No. 15) make a compelling pair both semantically and musically as a two-stage portrayal of burgeoning love, where the G-hypodorian expressions of vulnerability and affection in *Volgea l'anima mia* culminate in the aroused A-hypodorian declaration, "Sì ch'io vorrei morire."

Other inter-madrigal motives in Monteverdi's Fourth and Fifth Books play roles that are more pragmatic (for the sake of efficiency) than referential—stemming, for example, from scansion or the demands of counterpoint—and thus represent stock phrases to be plugged in at opportune points. Such gestures, however, can still play important roles in highlighting textual parallelisms and conveying a sense of stylistic unity, even if their simpler construction makes them less referentially compelling than weightier motives combining melodic, harmonic, rhythmic, and textual dimensions, such as the "O Mirtillo" and "vorrei morire" motives. One such example is a seven-note rhythmic figure that corresponds in most instances to a *settenario* verse with primary stresses on the second and sixth syllables, shown in Example 7.17. The pattern appears in two *Pastor fido* settings in the Fourth Book—twice in *Quel augellin che canta* and coupled with the "vorrei morire" motive at "E sento nel partire" in *Ah, dolente partita*—and several more times in two *Pastor fido* settings from the Fifth Book.

In two of its three occurrences in *Cruda Amarilli*, the pattern serves to distinguish the last seven syllables of a hendecasyllabic verse as a separate grammatical unit, thereby, in turn, playing a key role in the madrigal's semantic/formal parsing of the text. Its use at verse 3, "Amarilli, *del candido ligustro*," for instance, reinforces the parallelism with verse 4, "Più candida e più bella," where the figure appears again, while the isolation of Amarilli's name allows for its alignment with the "Cruda Amarilli" motive and disruptive upper-neighbor *a"* discussed above (see Example 7.4a). Monteverdi uses the same tactic for the opening verse by linking the exclamation "Cruda Amarilli" to its own distinct motive, and the remaining syllables ("che col nome ancora"), to a truncated *settenario* pattern (see Examples 7.1 and 7.17). This motivic division of the two phrases illustrates well Monteverdi's attention to both the formal, accentual aspects of the verse and opportunities to

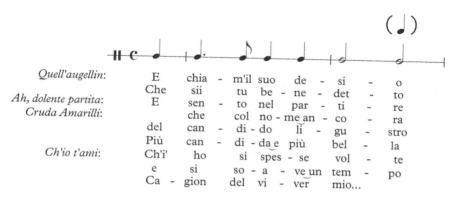

Example 7.17 Settenario Rhythm

build motivic ties between key moments of import (such as recurrences of Amarilli's name).

The *settenario* rhythm appears three more times in *Ch'io t'ami*, including at the start of the *seconda parte* (verse 9), where Monteverdi again divides an *endecasillabo* between two separate motives: the "O Mirtillo" figure for the exclamation "Deh, bella e cara," and the *settenario* rhythm for "e sì soave un tempo" (see Example 7.14). The beginning of this *parte*, therefore, joins motivic references from the first two madrigals of the Fifth Book—Amarilli's initial cry "O Mirtillo" and Mirtillo's opening line ("che col nome ancora") in *Cruda Amarilli*—to create a new cry, "Deh, bella e cara e sì soave un tempo." The voice here is Mirtillo's—addressing Amarilli after the *Gioco della cieca*—so the reuse of a recurring rhythmic pattern from *Cruda Amarilli* maintains a consistent elocutionary style, or musical "voice," between Mirtillo's two laments in the Fifth Book.

This list of recurring figures in the Fourth and Fifth Books is by no means exhaustive, but it suffices to show the effects of such gestures in establishing and bolstering musical–interpretative ties between pieces, madrigal books, and textual sources. A crucial potential consequence of these connections from the perspective of readership is the comparison and/or exchange of meaning through motivic–referential channels and their associated (but often seemingly unrelated) texts. As seen especially in the example of Amarilli's *O Mirtillo* and Mirtillo's *Ch'io t'ami*, this intertextual discourse may work with or against the chronology of *Il pastor fido* and the ordering of pieces in the collections, while also potentially shedding new light on the dating of the madrigals themselves. In a case such as the "vorrei morire" motive, the gesture's correspondence with two texts of different origins—the overtly erotic poem *Sì ch'io vorrei morire* and Mirtillo's anguished cry, *Ah, dolente partita*, after his beloved's rejection—shows the madrigal partaking in its own discursive game involving poetic conventions, interpretative interplay, and, here in the *Pastor fido* madrigal, the recontextualization of texts within entirely new scenarios. The order in which a reader encounters the pieces could also greatly affect their interpretation and their impact on the understanding of other works, which, in turn, raises the broader question of how madrigal books were conventionally regarded: as organized "texts" to be read from beginning to end, as assortments of pieces to be selected at will, or some combination of the two. Of course, there is no single definitive answer, for readings likely involved some combination of all of these scenarios, wherein individual pieces, the madrigal book(s), the specific performance or reading, and the textual source(s) all exerted their own (sometimes conflicting) influences.

Monteverdi and the Madrigal as Discourse

The madrigals of the Fourth and Fifth Books already invite a wealth of interpretations through their texts, rhetorical–expressive strategies, and internal motivic references, as well as through the connections of several works to a dramatic work, *Il pastor fido*. This analysis adds to these factors a network of cross-madrigal relationships that fosters an even broader range of possibilities than isolated readings of discrete pieces would seem to support. As Artusi's account of the musical evening in 1598 Ferrara attests, contemporary performances of Monteverdi's music brought works from both his forthcoming 1603 and 1605 books together, side by side, thus highlighting and activating the musical, as well as potential semantic, connections between them. This web of interpretative pathways would provide fertile fodder for the musings and discussions of courtly, intellectual, cultural, and recreational audiences in Mantua, Ferrara, and elsewhere in early modern Europe, not to mention of readers for centuries to come.

More fundamentally, this exploration of Monteverdi's *Pastor fido* settings underscores the exceptional extent to which these madrigals act as many-sided discourses. This interchange of ideas and influences expanded beyond that of their initial conception (bringing together music, text, and function) before the works came to print—at least by the 1598 performance in Ferrara, where several of them were performed twice for an audience of musical connoisseurs—and continued in the "ragionamento secondo" between Vario and Luca in *L'Artusi*, and thereafter in the intense debate in print for years to come between the theorist, the composer, his brother, and a variety of other known and unknown personages. The debate surely reflects only a narrow strand of the broader discourses—whether verbal, written, or sung—that enveloped the pieces in Mantua and Ferrara, at the height of both cities' fascinations with Guarini's play, and later further afield, as Scacchi's "short discourse" from 1649 Warsaw testifies.

While madrigals inherently generate continuous cycles of discourse between poet, composer, and readers (in the broadest sense of performers, listeners, and readers from the page), Monteverdi develops the genre's conventional discursive faculties in several novel ways: for example, by heightening dialogue between *parti* of an individual madrigal (*Ecco, Silvio*), between madrigals through motivic allusions, and between distinct madrigal books. Even the modal character of certain Monteverdi madrigals becomes a polemic between rival factions, as seen in *Cruda Amarilli* and *O Mirtillo*, or a collective undertaking in which multiple voices share the role of structural upper voice (*Anima mia, perdona* and *O Mirtillo*). All of these tactics work in conjunction with innate processes of polyphonic discourse. A key aspect of Monteverdi's innovative compositional approach in the Fourth and Fifth Books, then, is the expansion of the madrigal's conventional discursive scope beyond the musical–textual work itself, with the explicit engagement of other works in the same or different collections, to expose new and otherwise improbable paths of association and interpretation.

Monteverdi continued to set Guarini texts throughout his career. Yet, even as his interests turned increasingly toward dramatic music, solo song, and the *concertato* medium, he published no more settings from *Il pastor fido* after the Fifth Book. Monteverdi's treatments, however, formed part of an initial swell of *Pastor fido* madrigals that peaked in 1602, with the publication of twenty-nine settings, and that emanated conspicuously from Mantua. Chapter 8, therefore, will turn toward the readings of three of his prominent (but now lesser known) Mantuan colleagues and another important aspect of discourse that runs throughout the tradition of *Pastor fido* madrigals: the impact of earlier composers' settings on both the music and texts of later readings. As we shall see, this discourse, manifested in settings from the Gonzaga court around 1600, seems to have been dominated by the influence of one composer in particular: not Wert or Monteverdi from Mantua itself, but Marenzio from Rome. The apparent attention of these other Mantuan composers to aspects of lineage, imitation, homage, and tradition did not mean, however, that they looked staunchly to the past, that their music was conservative and backward-looking. For it is at this point in Mantua, with Monteverdi's colleagues, that the *Pastor fido* madrigal comes onstage for the first known time and accompanies the earliest known published examples of continuo and solo madrigals.

Notes

1   Artusi, *L'Artusi*, fols. 39v–40r; also, Strunk, *Source Readings*, 527–28.
2   Monteverdi sets verses 1–8 of the text shown above, p. 223. Artusi overlooks the jarring consecutive dissonances between the Canto and Basso in the opening syllables, "*Cruda Ama*rilli" (mm. 2 and 6). This poignant rendering of "cruda" results from the Basso's leap downward just as the Canto attempts to resolve (properly) its 7–6 suspension, thus creating a dissonant passing tone (m9) in place of a resolution.
3   "...Perciò vorrebbe che questa forma havesse il capo di bellissimo Giovane, il ventre di Grue, le braccia come l'ali della Rondinella, le gambe di Bue, & li piedi corrispondessero alla bellezza del capo." Artusi, *Seconda parte dell'Artusi*, 21.
4   Artusi cites the Basso's entrance on *B* beneath *d* and *f* in the Quinto and Tenore, respectively, thus creating an unprepared diminished sonority at "amaramente" (m. 21) among the madrigal's contrapuntal infractions. See *L'Artusi*, fol. 39v, example 3; also, Strunk, *Source Readings*, 528.
5   "...col nobilissimo esercitio della Vivuola che m'aperse la fortunata porta del suo servitio" (dedication to Monteverdi, *Il terzo libro de madrigali* [Venice: Ricciardo Amadino, 1592]).
6   James Bates, "Monteverdi, the viola bastarda player," in *The Italian viola da gamba: Proceedings of the International Symposium on the Italian Viola da Gamba*, ed. S. Orlando (Solignac: Ensemble baroque de Limoges, 2002), 53–70, at 62. Bates points out that "there were three generations of bastarda players associated with the Este court," which included Alfonso della Viola (1508–73), Orazio Bassano [della Viola] (c.1550–1609), and Vincenzo Bonizzi, who was employed by the Este court as an organist and *bastarda* player in the 1590s. Evidence of such singing with *viola bastarda* accompaniment in Ferrara comes from Girolamo Merenda, who describes an informal occasion in 1590 where musicians in the service of the Duchess of Urbino, Lucrezia d'Este (Alfonso II's sister), including one Giulia on the *viola bastarda*, were joined by singers from Duke of Ferrara's *concerto*. Merenda, *Vita dei signori d'Este vissuti al tempo dello scrittore. Principia col card. Ippolito I, e termina col principe Cesare, 1592*, in Ferrara, Biblioteca communale Ariostea, Coll. Antonelli 332, fols. 11r–12r.

7 Newcomb, "Bassani, Orazio," *Grove Music Online* (Oxford University Press, 2001), Accessed 9 April 2021. https://doi.org/10.1093/gmo/9781561592630.article.02229

8 "...send'io al servigio di questa Serenissima Altezza di Mantoa non son patrone di quel tempo che tal'hora mi bisognerebbe"; trans. in Strunk, *Source Readings*, 536.

9 "... (servendo a Gran Prencipe) la maggior parte del tempo si trova occupato hora in Tornei, hora in Balletti, hora in Comedie, & in varii concerti, & finalmente nello concertar le due Viole bastarde..." (Giulio Cesare Monteverdi, *Dichiaratione*).

10 "...novello Orfeo col suono della sua viola, di cui non ebbe pari," Matteo Caberloti, "Laconismo delle alte qualità di Claudio Monteverdi," in *Fiori poetici raccolti nel funerale del...signor Claudio Monteverdi*, ed. G. B. Marinoni (Venice: Miloco, 1644), 8.

11 As Thomas Binkley has described it, *bastarda* "is a performance genre in which the vocal chanson and madrigal are transformed into often brilliant instrumental solistic repertory" (Introduction to Jason Paras, *The Music for the Viola Bastarda* [Bloomington: University of Indiana Press, 1986], xi). Francesco Rognoni writes in his *Selva di varii passaggi secondo l'uso moderno, per cantare, & suonare con ogni sorte de stromenti: seconda parte* (Milan: Lomarzo, 1620): "The viola bastarda, which is the queen of all the instruments for making diminutions" ("La Viola Bastarda, qual è Regina delli altri instrumenti, per paseggiare...," 2). Paras relates the *bastara* style to "the viola da gamba's ability to shape a melodic line and to play rapid diminutions, as well as its extraordinary range, enable it to reign supreme in this soloistic Italian performance genre" (xvii).

12 Joëlle Morton, "Redefining the Viola Bastarda: A Most Spurious Subject," *The Viola Gamba Society Journal* 8 (2014): 1–64, at 56–57.

13 By comparison, there are no written-out diminutions in two contemporary madrigal books with instrumental parts by composers of Ferrarese and Mantuan circles: Salamone Rossi's First Book for five voices (Venice, 1600), which provides tablature for optional chitarrone accompaniment, and Luzzaschi's *Madrigali per cantare e sonare*, wherein the fully written-out chordal accompaniment includes only diminutions that double the upper (Canto and Alto) voices. The absence of any bass- and tenor-range diminutions in the instrumental parts of these collections highlights the florid nature and the distinctive focus on the lower range in the *bastarda* style in which Monteverdi specialized. Rossi's book is discussed in Chapter 8.

14 *L'Artusi*, fol. 42r; trans. Strunk, *Source Readings*, 532. In references to the consecutive dissonances at "e più fugace" (mm. 42–43), Artusi (through Luca) remarks that he "believes that these [dissonances] result from hearing, on instruments, that they do not offend the ear very much, owing to their rapid motion" ("...io credo che siano cavate dal sentire ne gl'Instrumenti, per il loro moto presto, che molto non offendano l'udito"); *L'Artusi*, fol. 43r; also Strunk, *Source Readings*, 533–4.

15 See, for example, Suzanne Cusick, "Gendering Modern Music," 22; Stefano La Via, "Monteverdi esegeta: rilettura di 'Cruda Amarilli/O Mirtillo'," in *Intorno a Monteverdi*, ed. M. Caraci Vela and R. Tibaldi (Lucca: LIM Editrice, 1999), 77–99; Massimo Ossi, *Divining the Oracle*, 85; and Mauro Calcagno, *From Madrigal to Opera*, 128.

16 In Seth Coluzzi, "Licks, Polemics, and the *Viola bastarda*: Unity and Defiance in Monteverdi's Fifth Book," *Early Music* 47 (2019): 333–44, I argue that the anomalous system change from *mollis* to *durus* might have been incorporated for the sake of the continuo player, to ensure that any improvised elaboration of the final cadence would match the change from B-*fa* to B-*mi* in the notated vocal parts. The extant *bastarda* repertory—and contemporary diminution manuals more broadly—shows prominent cadences to be regular sites of extensive elaboration (as the Basso's "ahi lasso" gesture in *Cruda Amarilli* demonstrates).

17 Texts from Guarini's play make up an even larger share of Claudio Pari's *Il pastor fido, secondo libro de madrigali a cinque voci* (Palermo: Maringo, 1611). The book includes three *Pastor fido* settings, two of them exceptionally lengthy: a twelve-*parte* treatment of Mirtillo's monologue from act 3, scene 8, *O crudele Amarilli*; a six-*parte* setting of Ergasto and Corisca's dialogue in act 5, scene 9, *Oh giorno pien di maraviglie! Oh giorno*; and a two-*parte* setting of Amarilli's speech of act 3, scene 7, *Bella madre d'Amore*. Only the Canto and Basso books survive.

18 McClary, *Modal Subjectivities*, 186. McClary likewise views the effect of these striking ascents to *a"* as tipping "D, the proper fifth degree, toward C as divider of the octave and would-be finale [*sic*]," rather than as instigating a discordant *a"–e"* diatessaron that, in turn, generates the C centricity.

19 Artusi cites the madrigal for having more internal cadences on the fourth degree, C (which Artusi—following Zarlino—considers to be irregular), than on the final, G, which obscures the true mode (*L'Artusi*, fol. 48v and *Seconda parte dell'Artusi*, 11). According to the strict definition of cadence as contrapuntal motion from M6 to octave, however, cadences on the final in Monteverdi's madrigal outnumber those on C or any other pitch. As the reciting pitch, or tenor, of the collateral mode, the modal fourth, C, often figures prominently in the cadential plan and melodic structure of mixolydian works as well. For Monteverdi's anonymous defender, L'Ottuso, the mode is obvious, for the madrigal begins and ends on G:

> I do not know how it could have come to the mind of [Artusi] that it is any other tone than the seventh [mixolydian], being most apparent to everyone that from the first, and then from the final notes [*corde*] one must judge the mode, and not from the median cadences.
>
> (io non so come possa cadere nell'animo a V.S. che sia d'altro tuono, che del settimo, essendo ad ogn'uno notissimo, che dalle prime, e poscia dalle finali corde si deve dar giudicio del tuono, e non dalle medie cadenze.
>
> (Quoted in *Seconda parte dell'Artusi*, 20–21)

20 The madrigal has "vedesti" in verse 2 and "havressi" in verse 6, which departs from the use of the conditional in both instances in Marenzio's setting ("vedesti" and "havresti"). While the play reads "havresti" consistently from its first printing, the form of *vedere* varies between editions. This confusion has spilled over into the modern editions of the madrigal: Gian Francesco Malipiero (Monteverdi, *Tutte le opere*, 17 vols. [Vienna: Universal, 1926–68], vol. 5, 5–8) has "vedesti" and "havressi" as in Marenzio's text, but Maria Caraci Vela (Monteverdi, *Opera omnia* [Cremona: Fondazione Claudio Monteverdi, 1970–2016], vol. , 11–15) reverses the conditional and subjunctive forms of the 1605 print ("vedessi" and "avresti"), which agrees with Myers's edition of Marenzio's setting (*The Secular Works*, vol. 14, 123–34) and certain editions of the play.

21 See *L'Artusi*, fol. 48v. The passage also appears in Harold Powers, "Monteverdi's Model for a Multimodal Madrigal," in *In cantu et in sermone: for Nino Pirotta on his 80th birthday*, ed. Fabrizio della Seta and Franco Piperno (Florence: Olschki, 1989), 185–219, at 187–88.

22 Gioseffo Zarlino writes:

> When in any of the modes set forth, whether authentic or plagal…a diapente or diatessaron used in another mode is repeated many times…the mode can be called mixed, because the diapente or the diatessaron of one mode becomes mixed with the melodic line of another.

See Zarlino, *Le istitutioni harmoniche*, Book IV, Chapter 14; trans. by Vered Cohen in *On the Modes*, 46.

23 Palisca, "The Artusi–Monteverdi Controversy," 74–75.

24 G.C. Monteverdi, *Dichiaratione*. Here Strunk (*Source Readings in Music History*, 543) has presumably misread "allo suo tutto" as "allo suo *frutto*," thus rendering the potentially problematic translation "its fruit," instead of "its whole."

25 Zarlino, *Le istitutioni harmoniche*, 336; trans. *On the Modes*, 90. The conception of mode as a unifying, ordered framework is widespread in Renaissance theory, where it is often explained using Aristotle's principle for completeness in tragedy—that it is evident in the beginning, middle, and end. In his *Liber de natura et proprietate tonorum* (1476), Tinctoris describes mode as "nothing else than the manner by which the beginning, middle, and ending of every song is arranged" (see *Concerning the Nature and Propriety of Tones*, trans. Albert Seay, 2nd ed. [Colorado Springs, 1976], Chapter 1). Frans Wiering refers to this as the "internal view" of mode—that which "considers the internal development of the music as decisive"—as opposed to the "external view," which considers mode chiefly by the final. See Frans Wiering, *The Language of the Modes: Studies in the History of Polyphonic Modality* (New York: Routledge, 2001). For an overview of Renaissance modal theory, see Meier, *The Modes of Classical Vocal Polyphony*.

26 Palisca, "The Artusi–Monteverdi Controversy," 75.

27 *L'Artusi*, fol. 48v; also quoted in Harold Powers, "Monteverdi's Model for a Multimodal Madrigal," 187–88.

28 For a complete score, see Monteverdi, *Tutte le opere*, V, 5–8 and *Opera omnia*, VI, 111–15. The following discussion draws from the more comprehensive analysis of the piece in Seth Coluzzi, "'Se vedesti qui dentro': Monteverdi's *O Mirtillo, Mirtillo anima mia* and Artusi's Offence."

29 Dahlhaus's analysis of Monteverdi's *O Mirtillo* appears in *Studies on the Origin of Harmonic Tonality*, 289–307.

30 Dahlhaus and Chafe, for example, rely heavily on the enumeration of cadential and non-cadential arrivals in the lowest voice, giving equal weight to each in their analyses of the piece in hexachordal terms.

31 The middleground g' is prolonged through neighboring motion ($g'-g\sharp'-a'-g'$) articulated by non-cadential approaches to E (m. 7), F (m. 9), A (m. 12), and C (m. 14), and through a stepwise ascent through the G octave divided at C—shared by the Canto and Quinto—that bridges the temporary departure from g' in m. 5 to its return in m. 14. Of crucial importance is the transfer of register that divides the ascent into two parts—$g'-c''$ (mm. 5–10) and $c'-g'$ (mm. 10–14)—allowing it to arrive again at G in its original register.

32 Artusi's *Discorso musicale di Antonio Braccino da Todi* has not survived; passages from it, however, are quoted in Giulio Cesare's *Dichiaratione* of 1607. While Palisca estimates that the *Discorso musicale* originated in 1606 or 1607, Massimo Ossi maintains convincingly that it "must have come on the heels of the fifth book"—that is, not long after 30 July 1605 (*Divining the Oracle*, 35), possibly after Artusi had a chance to examine the madrigal more closely in print.

33 Giulio Cesare Monteverdi, *Dichiaratione*; trans. in Strunk, *Source Readings*, 543. Also cited in Powers, "Monteverdi's Model for a Multimodal Madrigal," 189. Powers provides an illuminating examination of Monteverdi's conception of "mixed modes" by mapping Giulio Cesare's modal ascriptions for Cipriano de Rore's *Quando signor lasciaste*—a work cited in the *Dichiaratione* to validate the mixing of modes—onto the madrigal itself.

34 "Se vedesti qui dentro / Come sta il cor di questa … So ben che tu di lei / Quella pietà che da lei chiedi, havresti" (Guarini, *Il pastor fido*, III,4: 507–11); "Se havesse in tal guisa pensato l'oppositore l'armonia del madrigale *O Mirtillo* di mio fratello, non haverebbe…detto quelle esorbitanze intorno al tuono di esso" (Giulio Cesare Monteverdi, *Dichiaratione*). "Armonia" here refers to the coordination of the voices contrapuntally to form consonances and dissonances, and not to the notion of harmonic syntax of tonal music.

35 The dedication of Giovanni Appolloni's *Primo libro de madrigali a quattro voci* (Venice: Amadino, 1600) is signed Arezzo, 11 November 1599, and that of Monte's *Musica sopra il pastor fido*, Prague, 1 January 1600. Monte sets a highly variant version of the passage that begins "Anima mia dolcissima" and that, in its three *parti*, encompasses the lines set in both Monteverdi's *O Mirtillo* and *Anima mia, perdona* (and, hence, in Marenzio's *O Mirtillo* and *Deh Tirsi, Tirsi, anima mia, perdona*). Only the Canto of Appolloni's book survives, but it is enough to show that his setting of *O Mirtillo* bears several similarities to Monteverdi's setting, including its use of the D-dorian mode and its obfuscation of this mode by beginning (presumably) in the context of C before transposing the opening verses up a step to D.

36 Marenzio's affective technique of resolving the C-hypodorian/C-hypomixolydian conflict in an anomalous contrapuntal setting of verse 10, "Perché crudo destino," with the confirmation of the true modal/background $\hat{3}$ (*e''*) is discussed in Chapter 8 (and shown in Example 8.4).

37 The full passage reads:

> The true and natural initial tones of the first mode, as well as those of every other mode, are on the extreme notes of the diapente and diatessaron, and on the median note which divides the diapente into a ditone and a semiditone. Nevertheless, there are many compositions that begin on other notes, none of which I shall mention in order to be brief.
>
> (*Le istitutioni harmoniche*, Book 4, Chapter 18; trans. in *On the Modes*, 55)

38 McClary, *Modal Subjectivities*, 191.

39 La Via, "Monteverdi esegeta," esp. 89–95.

40 Cusick, "Gendering Modern Music," 22.

41 Cusick, "Gendering Modern Music," 21.

42 Calcagno, *From Madrigal to Opera*, 128.

43 Christophe Georis, *Claudio Monteverdi "letterato"*, 181–202.

44 For a closer critique of McClary's reading of referential tonality in the latter portion of *O Mirtillo*, see Seth Coluzzi, "Monteverdi's *O Mirtillo, Mirtillo anima mia* and Artusi's Offence," 25.

45 The principal texts that form the basis of the Patrizi–Bottrigari debate are Francesco Patrizi's *Della poetica, la deca istoriale* (Ferrara: Baldini, 1586), especially Book 7, "Dell'armonia compagna dell'antiche poesie," and Ercole Bottrigari's *Il Patricio, overo de' tetracordi armonici di Aristosseno* (Bologna: Benacci, 1593).

46 *Seconda parte dell'Artusi*, Part 1, 25–26, and Part 2, 5. The critic expresses the same complaints—failure to show "novo concento" and resemblance to a "Giustiniana alla Venetiana"—about *Era l'anima mia* in Part 1, 26 and 43.

47 The text of *Ecco, Silvio* is the longest set by Monteverdi in a madrigal. In terms of the music, his five-voice (plus continuo) setting of the sestina *Lagrime d'Amante al Sepolcro dell'Amata* (*Incenerite spoglie, avara tomba*) in the Sixth Book (1614) is only slightly shorter than *Ecco, Silvio* in length, despite having six *parti*, and his three-voice (plus continuo) *Gira il nemico insidioso Amore* from the Eighth Book (1638), also with six *parti*, is considerably shorter.

48 Only the Tenore partbook survives of Fattorini's *La cieca*, but the fact that this single part contains lines for all four speaking roles suggests that the setting as a whole makes no strict assignments of voice parts to characters. Fattorini, likewise, includes lines for multiple speaking characters in individual *parti*, which differs from Monteverdi's limitation of one speaker per *parte*.

49 Balsamino also highlights Aminta's drastic swings between hope and despair across the dialogue through changes between the basic F-hypolydian and foreign G-hypodorian modes. For a discussion of Balsamino's cycle, see Andrea Chegai, *Le novellette a sei voci di Simone Balsamino: Prime musiche su* Aminta *di Torquato Tasso* (1594) (Florence: Olschki, 1993), Introduction, especially 24–35

and Seth Coluzzi, "Tasso's *Aminta* and the Piazza of Urbino: Genre, Design, and the Vestiges of a Performance in Simone Balsamino's *Novellette* of 1594," in Emiliano Ricciardi, ed., *"Qual musico gentil": New Perspectives on Torquato Tasso and Early Modern Music,* in series *Epitome musical* (Turnhout: Brepols, forthcoming).

50 See, for example, Chegai, *Le novellette a sei voci*; Francesco Luisi, "'Li tre Aminta uniti': Giocchi di poesia dramma e musica verso il melodramma. Il caso singolare di Simone Balsamino e la "Camerata di Urbino"', in *Mousike: metrica ritmica e musica greca in memoria di Giovanni Comotti,* eds. B. Gentili and F. Perusino (Pisa: Istituti Editoriali e Poligrafici Internazionali, 1995), 297–347; Alfred Einstein, "Ein Madrigaldialog von 1594", *Zeitschrift der Internationalen Musik-Gesellschaft* (1913–14): 202–12; Franco Piperno, *Musiche e musicisti attorno ai Della Rovere,* in *Pesaro nell'età Della Rovere,* ed. by G. Arbizzoni and others (Venice: Marsilio, 2001), III, 375–402; and Franco Piperno, "Musiche in commedia e intermedi alla corte di Guidubaldo II Della Rovere duca di Urbino," *Recercare* 10 (1998): 151–71, esp. 165–66.

51 AMARILLI

"I am defeated," *said*
Amarilli to Corisca in a low voice.
CORISCA
And she responded,
"Now that you cannot deny it
Defeated you want to give yourself to me."
AMARILLI
"And so I notice, alas..."

52 Marenzio's *O fido, o caro Aminta,* discussed at the start of Chapters 4 and 5, offers another example of the madrigal's implicit narrative perspective made explicit, particularly for listeners aware of the text's contexts in the play, where Ergasto recounts Lucrina's final words before killing herself to join Aminta in death. Ergasto begins his speech by invoking the collective voice of Arcadia—"Ti narrerò de le miserie *nostre*" (I will tell you of *our* miseries)—and introduces Lucrina's words (set in variant form by Marenzio) with the phrase, "Disse piangendo" (She said weeping). The madrigal, therefore, acts (like Ergasto) as the communal voice of the Arcadians while retelling this tale from their collective history. The 2018 recording of the madrigal by La Pedrina (*Luca Marenzio: Il pastor fido,* directed by Francesco Saverio Padrini, Claves Records, 2018) obscures this role of the madrigal-as-narrator and Marenzio's use of the five-voice ensemble for both the imparted speech of Amarilli/Lucrina and Ergasto by realizing Lucrina's words with an accompanied (female) solo soprano, then switching to the full ensemble with a different (male) soprano beginning with the words of Ergasto/narrator, "E questo detto la bell'Amarilli" (And this said, the fair Amarilli...).

53 In his study of Monteverdi's Marino settings in his Sixth Book of 1614, Tim Carter argues that the composer varies his voicing of different speakers—both the narrator and named characters—as a way to expand the interpretative potential of both text and madrigal (Gary Tomlinson, "Beyond Drama: Monteverdi, Marino, and the Sixth Book of Madrigals [1614]," *Journal of the American Musicological Society* 69 [2016]: 1–46). This reading contrasts with the common alternative view that these madrigals perform a proto-operatic *representation* of these speakers through their assignment of solo voices to speaking characters. Monte's dialogue settings, however, do something very different from either of these processes in Monteverdi's works. With their narrative asides, the madrigals make it clear that the assigned voice groups are reading or relaying their characters' words—i.e., acting as narrator—not representing their personas, yet

both features—the verbal insertions and voice assignments—curb the works' interpretative and textural possibilities.

54 The list of studies that regard the madrigal in quasi-dramatic or representational terms and as a precursor to opera is extensive. Prominent examples, and those relevant to the present discussion, include the readings of Balsamino's *Aminta* settings by Einstein, Luisi, and Piperno cited above (note 50), as well as McClary's *Modal Subjectivities* and Calcagno's *From Madrigal to Opera* (discussed also in the Introduction). In *Monteverdi and the End of the Renaissance*, Gary Tomlinson likewise refers to the style of Monteverdi's *Pastor fido* settings directly as having "its origin as a *stile rappresentativo*, its conception as stage music" (74).

55 This narrational process, made explicit in Monte's madrigals, in fact, corresponds closely with that of the so-called madrigal comedies of Orazio Vecchi, which—as Vecchi writes in the preface to his *L'Amfiparnaso* (1597)—create "a spectacle...[that] is seen with the mind, which it enters through the ears, and not through the eyes." Vecchi's book is unified by plot and includes mostly five-voice madrigals, several of them setting dialogic texts, organized into a prologue plus three acts. For a thorough analysis of the *Amfiparnaso*, see Paul Schleuse, "'A Tale Completed in the Mind': Genre and Imitation in *L'Amfiparnaso* (1597)," *Journal of Musicology*, 29 (2012): 101–53 (at 116 and 132–44). On issues of genre, function, and poetics in Vecchi's three "madrigal comedies," see Paul Schleuse, *Singing Games in Early Modern Italy: The Music Books of Orazio Vecchi* (Bloomington: Indiana University Press, 2015), especially Chapters 3 ("Forest and Feast: The Music Book as Metaphor") and 4 ("*L'Amfiparnaso*: Picturing Theater and the Problem of the 'Madrigal Comedy'").

56 Chafe, *Monteverdi's Tonal Language*, 107; drawing on Dahlhaus, who emphasizes that the verse-endings of the opening and ending of the *prima parte* include "all the degrees of the soft hexachord," and therefore "can be understood as a complete presentation of the flat-system" (*Origin of Harmonic Tonality*, 299–302, at 301).

57 See Chafe, *Monteverdi's Tonal Language*, 107. Chafe's description that the subsequent section (mm. 28–45) comprises a "modulation downward through C, F, B♭, and E♭ to c/C and G" (107) illustrates the failure to distinguish between true cadences, non-cadential pauses, and prominent sonorities, for—following sixteenth-century criteria for cadence formation—this section includes not six cadences, but only three: F (m. 34), C (m. 39), and G (m. 45). The same inaccuracy applies to Chafe's reading that the next section (mm. 46–64) "modulates upward through B♭, F, C, and g," followed by "E♭, B♭, F, and c/C" (108), for the section truly cadences on only four of these eight pitches: F, G, B♭, and C. The misjudgment of cadences throughout Dahlhaus's and Chafe's studies leads to numerous mischaracterizations of Monteverdi's music and renderings of the text.

58 The melodic motion of the principal mode-bearing voices (Canto and Tenore), though not utterly defiant of a G-dorian context, do little to affirm the mode amidst the wayward phrase-endings and cadences through the opening. Insinuations of the modal boundaries do appear in other, less prominent voices. For example, the Alto neatly bounces from g' to d' before climbing back to $b\flat'$ in mm. 1–6, while the Quinto—moving in parallel thirds with the Canto—outlines the boundaries $b\flat'$–g'–d''.

59 In a compelling study of the generative use of schemas—conventional contrapuntal/intervallic formulas in the outer voices—in Monteverdi's Fifth Book, Peter Schubert argues that Silvio's opening cries of "Dorinda" should not be viewed as a paraphrase, or reduction, of Dorinda's opening owing to the effectively immutable nature of schemas. (As Schubert remarks, "What you see is what you get" in Renaissance music.) Whether late-Renaissance composers truly perceived schemas as fixed entities—not subject to expansion (i.e., diminution/elaboration)

or reduction—or analysts today merely select "pure," unelaborated instances of these formulas as exemplars, thereby conveying only a partial representation of their nature and functions, however, deserves further study. See Schubert, "Schemas, Splices, and Elisions in Monteverdi's Book V Madrigals," forthcoming. I thank Schubert for sharing a preliminary version of this work with me.

60 Especially interesting from these perspectives of genre, medium, and voice is Sigismondo D'India's setting of a longer passage from the Dorinda–Silvio dialogue (also including Linco) of act 4, scene 9 as a *concertato* madrigal that combines monody, polyphony, and antiphony in his Eighth Book *a5* (Rome: Giovanni Battista Robletti, 1624). Despite Glenn Watkins and John Joyce's assertion that the work "is a miniature opera scene," the mixture of various textures and voice groupings even within each character's individual speech challenges the notion of verisimilitude that the authors attribute to it and blurs any notional boundary between madrigalistic narration and truly dramatic representation. See Joyce and Watkins, "D'India, Sigismondo," *Grove Music Online* (2001); accessed 23 April 2021. https://www.oxfordmusiconline.com/grovemusic/view/10.1093/gmo/9781561592630.001.0001/omo-9781561592630-e-0000013761.

61 Tomlinson estimates the datings for the pieces in the Fourth and Fifth Books based on stylistic features in *Monteverdi and the End of the Renaissance*, 98–111.

62 Tomlinson, *Monteverdi and the End of the Renaissance*, 110. See also Gary Tomlinson, "Madrigal, Monody, and Monteverdi's 'via naturale alla immitatione'," *Journal of the American Musicological Society* 34 (1981): 60–108, at 68n.

63 Tomlinson, *Monteverdi and the End of the Renaissance*, 110–11.

References

Appolloni, Giovanni. *Primo libro de madrigali a quattro voci.* Venice: Amadino, 1600.

Artusi, Giovanni Maria. *Seconda parte dell'Artusi ovvero delle imperfettioni della moderna musica.* Venice: Vincenti, 1603.

———. *L'Artusi, overo Delle imperfettioni della moderna musica ragionamenti dui.* Venice: Vincenti, 1600. Selections translated by Oliver Strunk in *Source Readings in Music History*, 526–34. New York: Norton, 1998.

Balsamino, Simone. *Novellette a sei voci.* Venice: Amadino, 1594.

Bates, James. "Monteverdi, the viola bastarda player." In *The Italian viola da gamba: Proceedings of the International Symposium on the Italian Viola da Gamba*, ed. S. Orlando, 53–70. Solignac: Ensemble baroque de Limoges, 2002.

Bottrigari, Ercole. *Il Patricio, overo de' tetracordi armonici di Aristosseno.* Bologna: Benacci, 1593.

Caberloti, Matteo. "Laconismo delle alte qualità di Claudio Monteverdi." In *Fiori poetici raccolti nel funerale del... signor Claudio Monteverdi*, ed. G.B. Marinoni. Venice: Miloco, 1644.

Calcagno, Mauro. *From Madrigal to Opera: Monteverdi's Staging of the Self.* Berkeley: University of California Press, 2012.

Carter, Tim. "Beyond Drama: Monteverdi, Marino, and the Sixth Book of Madrigals (1614)." *Journal of the American Musicological Society* 69 (2016): 1–46.

Chafe, Eric. *Monteverdi's Tonal Language.* New York: Schirmer, 1992.

Chegai, Andrea. *Le novellette a sei voci di Simone Balsamino: Prime musiche su Aminta di Torquato Tasso (1594).* Florence: Olschki, 1993.

Coluzzi, Seth. "Tasso's *Aminta* and the Piazza of Urbino: Genre, Design, and the Vestiges of a Performance in Simone Balsamino's *Novellette* of 1594." In *Qual musico gentil"*: *New Perspectives on Torquato Tasso and Early Modern Music*. In series *Epitome musical*, ed. Emiliano Ricciardi. Turnhout: Brepols, forthcoming.

———. "Licks, Polemics, and the *Viola bastarda*: Unity and Defiance in Monteverdi's Fifth Book." *Early Music* 47 (2019): 333–44.

———. "'Se vedesti qui dentro': Monteverdi's *O Mirtillo, Mirtillo anima mia* and Artusi's Offence." *Music and Letters* 94 (2013): 1–37.

Cusick, Susanne. "Gendering Modern Music: Thoughts on the Monteverdi–Artusi Controversy." *Journal of the American Musicological Society* 46 (1993): 1–25.

Dahlhaus, Carl. *Studies on the Origin of Harmonic Tonality*. Trans. by Robert Gjerdingen. Princeton, NJ: Princeton University Press, 1991.

D'India, Sigismondo. *Ottavo libro de madrigali a cinque voci con il basso continuo*. Rome: Giovanni Battista Robletti, 1624.

Einstein, Alfred. "Ein Madrigaldialog von 1594." *Zeitschrift der Internationalen Musik-Gesellschaft* 14–15 (1913–14): 202–12.

Fattorini, Gabriele. *La cieca: Il primo libro de madrigali a cinque voci*. Venice: Amadino, 1598.

Georis, Christophe. *Claudio Monteverdi 'letterato' ou les métamorphoses du texte*. Paris: Honoré Champion, 2013.

Guarini, Battista. *Il pastor fido, tragicommedia pastorale del molto Illustre Cavaliere Battista Guarini, ora in questa XX impressione di curiose e dotte Annotationi arrichito*. Venice: Ciotti, 1602.

———. *Il pastor fido*. Venice: Bonfadino, 1589 [dated 1590].

La Via, Stefano. "Monteverdi esegeta: rilettura di 'Cruda Amarilli/O Mirtillo'." In *Intorno a Monteverdi*, eds. M. Caraci Vela and R. Tibaldi, 77–99. Lucca: LIM Editrice, 1999.

Luisi, Francesco. "'Li tre Aminta uniti': Giocchi di poesia dramma e musica verso il melodramma. Il caso singolare di Simone Balsamino e la "Camerata di Urbino." In *Mousike: metrica ritmica e musica greca in memoria di Giovanni Comotti*, eds. B. Gentili and F. Perusino, 297–347. Pisa: Istituti Editoriali e Poligrafici Internazionali, 1995.

Luzzaschi, Luzzasco. *Madrigali per cantare et sonare a uno, doi, e tre soprani*. Rome: Verovio, 1601. Eds. Elio Durante and Anna Martellotti. Florence: Studio per edizioni scelte, 1980.

Marenzio, Luca. *Il settimo libro de' madrigali a cinque voci*. Venice: Gardano, 1595. Ed. Patricia Myers in *Marenzio, the Secular Works*, vol. 14. New York: Broude Brothers, 1980.

McClary, Susan. *Modal Subjectivities: Self-Fashioning in the Italian Madrigal*. Berkeley: University of California Press, 2004.

Meier, Bernhard. *The Modes of Classical Vocal Polyphony, Described According to the Sources*. Trans. by Ellen Beebe. New York: Broude Brothers, 1988.

Merenda, Girolamo. *Vita dei signori d'Este vissuti al tempo dello scrittore. Principia col card. Ippolito I, e termina col principe Cesare, 1592*. In Ferrara, Biblioteca communale Ariostea, Coll. Antonelli 332.

Monte, Philippe de. *Musica sopra il pastor fido...libro secondo a sette voci*. Venice: Gardano, 1600.

Monteverdi, Claudio. *Tutte le opera*. Ed. Gian Francesco Malipiero. 17 vols. Vienna: Universal, 1926–68.

———. *Scherzi musicali a tre voci*. Venice: Amadino, 1607.

———. *Il quinto libro de madrigali a cinque voci*. Venice: Amadino, 1605.

―――. *Il quarto libro de madrigali a cinque voci.* Venice: Amadino, 1603.

―――. *Il terzo libro de madrigali a cinque voci.* Venice: Amadino, 1592.

Morton, Joëlle. "Redefining the Viola Bastarda: a Most Spurious Subject." *The Viola Gamba Society Journal* 8 (2014): 1–64.

Ossi, Massimo. *Divining the Oracle: Monteverdi's 'Seconda prattica.'* Chicago, IL: University of Chicago Press, 2003.

Palisca, Claude. "The Artusi–Monteverdi Controversy." In *The New Monteverdi Companion*, eds. D. Arnold and N. Fortune, 127–58. London: Faber, 1985.

Paras, Jason. *The Music for the Viola Bastarda.* Bloomington: University of Indiana Press, 1986.

Pari, Claudio. *Il pastor fido, secondo libro de madrigali a cinque voci.* Palermo: Maringo, 1611.

Patrizi, Francesco. *Della poetica, la deca istoriale.* Ferrara: Baldini, 1586.

Piccioni, Giovanni. *Pastor fido musicale…il sesto libro di madrigali a 5.* Venice: Vincenti, 1602.

Piperno, Franco. "Musiche e musicisti attorno ai Della Rovere." In *Pesaro nell'età Della Rovere*, eds. G. Arbizzoni, et al., III, 375–402. Venice: Marsilio, 2001.

―――. "Musiche in commedia e intermedi alla corte di Guidubaldo II Della Rovere duca di Urbino." *Recercare* 10 (1998): 151–71.

Powers, Harold. "Monteverdi's Model for a Multimodal Madrigal." In *In cantu et in sermone: for Nino Pirotta on his 80th birthday*, eds. Fabrizio della Seta and Franco Piperno, 185–219. Florence: Olschki, 1989.

Rognoni, Francesco. *Selva di varii passaggi secondo l'uso moderno, per cantare, & suonare con ogni sorte de stromenti: seconda parte.* Milan: Lomarzo, 1620.

Schleuse, Paul. *Singing Games in Early Modern Italy: The Music Books of Orazio Vecchi.* Bloomington: Indiana University Press, 2015.

―――. "'A Tale Completed in the Mind': Genre and Imitation in *L'Amfiparnaso* (1597)." *Journal of Musicology*, 29 (2012): 101–53.

Schubert, Peter. "Schemas, Splices, and Elisions in Monteverdi's Book V Madrigals," forthcoming.

Tomlinson, Gary. *Monteverdi and the End of the Renaissance.* Oxford: Clarendon, 1987.

―――. "Madrigal, Monody, and Monteverdi's 'via naturale alla immitatione'." *Journal of the American Musicological Society* 34 (1981): 60–108.

Wiering, Frans. *The Language of the Modes: Studies in the History of Polyphonic Modality.* New York: Routledge, 2001.

Zarlino, Gioseffo. *On the Modes.* Part four of *Le istitutioni harmoniche* (Venice, 1558). Trans. by V. Cohen, ed. C. Palisca. New Haven, CT: Yale University Press, 1983.

―――. *The Art of Counterpoint.* Part three of *Le istitutioni harmoniche* (Venice, 1558). Trans. by G. Marco and C. Palisca. New Haven, CT: Yale University Press, 1968.

8 The Settings of Pallavicino, Gastoldi, and Rossi, and the Afterglow of a Mantuan Pastoral Passion

Staging *Il pastor fido* represented a significant cultural ambition of the Mantuan court in the mid-1580s and 1590s. After the failed attempts of 1584 and 1591–93, these efforts, as we have seen, culminated in the three grand productions of 1598, with the last on 22 November for an illustrious audience of "forestieri" that included the newly crowned Queen of Spain, Margherita of Austria; her cousin, Archduke Albert VII; an entourage of some 3,000; and (as the chronicler Grillo describes it) nearly "all the nobility of Italy from Venice, Florence, Genoa, Verona, Brescia, and other surrounding cities," not to mention the poet himself.[1] These performances were followed two years later by a restaging of the tragicomedy with the same *intermedi*, but fitted with a new prologue by Guarini's son, Alessandro, glorifying the Mantuan duke and duchess.[2] Mantua's associations with the play continued to expand, however, beyond these events and the stage at large in the domain of printed music, as the court's skilled and versatile regimen of composers—Gastoldi, Pallavicino, Rossi, and Monteverdi—built on the foundations laid by Wert and Marenzio by publishing numerous *Pastor fido* madrigals and grouping most of them together in a small number of books. Altogether, this first wave of Mantuan *Pastor fido* settings composed around 1595–1600 encompasses some three dozen pieces in ten separate publications (Table 8.1), stretching from Wert's Eleventh Book (1595) to Rossi's First Book *a4* (published 1614, but likely dating from c.1600).[3]

Table 8.1 Mantuan *Pastor fido* Settings

1588	**Coma, First Book *a4***
	I,2: *Non sospirar, cor mio, non sospirare* [variant of "Non son, come a te pare"]
1592	**Monteverdi, Third Book *a5***
	III,1: *O primavera gioventù dell'anno* [variant text]
1595	**Wert, Eleventh Book *a5***
	I, 2: *Cruda Amarilli, che col nome ancora*
	III,1: *O primavera gioventù dell'anno*
	III,3: *Ah, dolente partita*
	III,6: *Udite, lagrimosi*

DOI: 10.4324/9781315463056-9

1598	**Gastoldi, Third Book** *a5*
	II,C: *Ben è soave cosa*
	III,6: *M'è più dolce il penar per Amarilli*
	III,6: *Com'è soave cosa*
1600	**Pallavicino, Sixth Book** *a5*
	I,2: *Cruda Amarilli, che col nome ancora*
	III,3: *Deh, dolce anima mia*
	III,6: *Viver io fortunato*
	Rossi, First Book *a5*
	III,6: *Udite, lagrimosi*
	IV,5: *Tirsi mio, caro Tirsi* ["Padre mio, caro padre"]
c.1600	**Rossi, First Book** *a4* [pub. 1614]
	III,1: *O dolcezze amarissime d'amore*
	III,3: *Ah, dolente partita*
	III,4: *O Mirtillo, Mirtillo anima mia*
	III,6: *Com'è dolce il gioire [o caro Tirsi]*
1602	**Gastoldi, Fourth Book** *a5*
	I,2: *Oh sfortunato e misero Mirtillo*
	I,4: *Come in vago giardin rosa gentil*
	II,2: *Tu se' pur aspro a chi t'adora, Silvio*
	II,2: *O misera Dorinda! Ov'hai tu poste*
	II,C: *Ciechi mortali, voi che tanta sete*
	III,2: *Cieco, Amor, non ti cred'io* [*Gioco delle cieca*]
	III,3: *Deh, bella e cara e sì soave un tempo*
	III,6: *Come assetato infermo*
	III,6: *Tanto è possente amore*
	III,6: *Arda pur sempre o mora*
	III,6: *Dimmi, povero amante*
1603	**Monteverdi, Fourth Book** *a5*
	I,1: *Quell' augellin che canta*
	III,3: *Ah, dolente partita*
	III,4: *Anima mia, perdona*
1604	**Gastoldi,** *Concenti musicali a8*
	II,C: *Baci pur bocca curiosa e scaltra*
1605	**Monteverdi, Fifth Book** *a5*
	I,2: *Cruda Amarilli, che col nome ancora*
	III,3: *Ch'io t'ami, e t'ami più de la mia vita*
	III,4: *O Mirtillo, Mirtillo anima mia*
	III,6: *M'è più dolce il penar per Amarilli*
	IV,9: *Ecco, Silvio, colei che 'n odio hai tanto*
1612	**Taroni, First Book** *a5*
	III,3: *Ah, dolente partita*
	III,4: *O Mirtillo, Mirtillo anima mia*
[1614	**Rossi, First Book** *a4* (c.1600)]
1619	**Basile, First Book** *a5*
	III,6: *Udite, lagrimosi*

From the perspective of readership, this body of settings proves especially illuminating for comparative study for its constant variables of timeframe, cultural center, primary patron, poet, textual source, and first-person speakers, which sets into relief the composers' individual priorities as readers and their distinctive compositional niches within the confined sphere of the Gonzaga court. These works form a varied and compelling corpus of musical readings—indeed, studies—of the play that embraces all of its principal (and some secondary) characters, four of its five acts (plus a chorus), the full range of modes, the emerging medium of accompanied solo song, and—in Gastoldi's rendering of the *Gioco della cieca* choruses—music for the stage, not to mention a multitude of structural designs and compositional strategies. Even more, the madrigals serve as meticulous records of composers' close readings of the play's speeches, from their general import and the disposition of their speakers, to details of poetic language, expression, and form. As we shall see, many of these settings—like those of Monteverdi— also act intertextually through allusions to other madrigals, textual sources, and madrigal books, including those of other composers, thereby invoking and conveying meaning beyond themselves, while potentially also revealing aspects of the interpretative processes of the composers themselves as well as their readers.

This Mantuan dimension of the *Pastor fido* madrigal centers squarely on Duke Vincenzo Gonzaga, whose close involvement with the Este court in the 1580s, before his accession to the ducal throne in 1587, undoubtedly stoked his interest in Guarini's verse and in staging the play even before its completion. Only a handful of settings from Mantuan composers appeared after Duke Vincenzo's death in February 1612, including Taroni's treatments of the fashionable texts *Ah, dolente partita* and *O Mirtillo*—although these might have been composed before the duke's death and published later in 1612—and Lelio Basile's *Udite, lagrimosi* (1619). This second, smaller wave amounted to only seven settings in 1612–19, if one includes the four settings in Rossi's First Book *a4* (1614) that, as we will see, more likely belong to the first wave of settings.

The duke's intense personal interest in the play might also explain, at least in part, why the Mantuan composers who survived him, such as Monteverdi and Taroni, never returned to *Il pastor fido* as a source of musical texts in their later careers, while they continued to draw from Guarini's *Rime*. Indeed, the sudden drop-off in Mantuan *Pastor fido* settings following those of the 1590s (published in 1595–1605) could suggest that the 1598 stagings at last satisfied Vincenzo Gonzaga's (and his court's) apparent craving for the tragicomedy. The printing of the numerous musical settings by Gastoldi, Pallavicino, Rossi, and Monteverdi in the following years, thus, may represent the afterglow of a newly quenched passion, possibly resulting from the release of works from the private sphere into the public, akin to Luzzaschi's *Madrigali* ("per la Musica del già Serenissimo Duca Alfonso d'Este) of 1601.

Of the many settings by Monteverdi's contemporaries, few have received close analytical attention, with one notable exception: Pallavicino's *Cruda Amarilli* (1600). In this case, however, it is the work's conspicuous resemblances to the settings of Wert, Marenzio, and Monteverdi more than anything that have engaged scholars' interest. This chapter, then, will begin here, with an expansion of our understanding of Pallavicino's madrigal beyond its motivic correspondences to others' works, to its distinctive and integrative realization of Amarilli's cruelty through Mirtillo's eyes in both novel and seemingly derivative ways. This exploration continues with a broader inquiry into Pallavicino's *Pastor fido* settings and his Sixth Book of madrigals, before turning to an all but overlooked, more serious side of Gastoldi, a composer known for "light" dance music, and finally to Salamone Rossi and his forceful merging of modal–structural affect, contrapuntal interplay, and idiosyncratic texts for portrayals of character, scene, and word in both polyphonic and solo guises.

Dilating Dissonances, Dynamic Structures, and Marenzian Ties in Pallavicino's Sixth Book (1600)

Pallavicino served as *maestro della musica* at the Mantuan court from 1596 until his death in 1601, and like Wert before him and Monteverdi after him, he issued his *Pastor fido* settings while holding this prominent post. Also, like Wert, Marenzio, and Monteverdi, Pallavicino's settings appeared after a considerable hiatus in the publication of five-voice madrigals—some four years for Wert, six for Marenzio, seven for Pallavicino, and eleven for Monteverdi—a fact that leaves a fair amount of room for speculation about the works' dates of conception. Thus, while it has generally been assumed that Pallavicino's and Monteverdi's works—not to mention Gastoldi's (published in 1598, 1602, and 1604) and Rossi's (1600 and 1614)—followed those of Marenzio and Wert by a sizeable margin, they could have originated in the mid-1590s, shortly after those of Marenzio and Wert.[4] Aspects of the music, meanwhile, seem to betray one fundamental tendency in this early stage of the musical tradition: that Marenzio's settings exerted a distinct influence on many of these works and acted as a common, unifying source alongside the play itself.

Pallavicino's three *Pastor fido* settings—published in his Sixth Book for five voices (Venice: Gardano, 1600)—draw from some of the most prolific scenes for musical texts: Mirtillo's *Cruda Amarilli* from act 1, scene 2; *Deh, dolce anima mia*, a striking revision of Amarilli's dismissal of Mirtillo from act 3, scene 4; and Mirtillo's *Vivrò io mai per altro amor contento*, from his speech to Corisca in act 3, scene 6 that begins "M'è più dolce il penar per Amarilli," as set by Gastoldi (1598), Monteverdi (1605), and others.[5] While showing unmistakable similarities to the settings of contemporary composers, Pallavicino's *Cruda Amarilli* also charts its own distinctive path in significant yet undervalued ways, including in its use of unorthodox contrapuntal gestures for expressive effect and its "dilation," or composing out, of fleeting but salient foreground events at a fundamental scale. This latter technique takes shape most often as an expansion of an early, isolated dissonance at deeper structural levels, where its resolution becomes crucial to the madrigal's dramatic impetus and textual reading—similar in certain respects to Monteverdi's use of the obstructive *a″* in his own *Cruda Amarilli*.[6]

This incipient germ emerges at the very start of Pallavicino's work, when the Alto's lone *a′* at "Cruda" becomes a piercing dissonance when the Tenore enters one minim later a major seventh below it with *b♭* (Example 8.1). These initial pitches thrust the piece into immediate modal disarray, for the opening *a′*, which would seem to have structural priority, could represent a number of degrees: D-dorian *la* ($\hat{5}$) against the Tenore's *fa* ($\hat{6}$), A-phrygian *mi* ($\hat{1}$) against *fa* ($\hat{2}$), or F-lydian *mi* ($\hat{3}$) against *fa* ($\hat{4}$). Yet the continuation of the opening in full-voice imitation soon establishes G as modal center with three consecutive cadences to that pitch in mm. 3, 6, and 9 (the first two *fuggite*) and with prominent use of E♭ and F♯, the customary altered sixth and seventh degrees of the G-dorian mode. It thus becomes clear that the Alto's initial *a′* is neither a consonant pitch nor a regular one to begin a G-dorian piece, but a dissonance on two levels: a major seventh against the Tenore's

Example 8.1 Pallavicino, *Cruda Amarilli*, mm. 1–11

$b\flat$, and $\hat{2}$ against the underlying mode. This large-scale tension between a' and $b\flat$, bound to the phrase "Cruda Amarilli," resonates across the entire madrigal as the central musical–textual conflict, just as "cruel Amarilli" is the motivation of Mirtillo's words.

Pallavicino distinguishes the separate roles of these opening pitches—one (a') a local dissonance with large-scale implications, the other ($b\flat$) a middleground consonance—through their opposing effects at the inception of the madrigal's background structure (Examples 8.1 and 8.2). Whereas in two instances $b\flat$ exposes a' as a dissonance—in the parallel imitative entries at mm. 1–3 (Alto and Tenore) and 4–6 (Tenore and Basso)—forcing it to descend through g' to $f\sharp'$ for evaded G cadences, the $b\flat$ likewise carries out two important early functions: descending straightforwardly $b\flat$–a–g at the foreground level to articulate the final and the identity of the mode, and instigating an initial $\hat{3}$–$\hat{5}$ middleground ascent to the primary background pitch, d'', in m. 5.

The opening "Cruda" clash resurfaces in various guises—linear and vertical, surface-level and structural—at two crucial moments later in the madrigal: the articulations of $b\flat$ and a' as $\hat{3}$ and $\hat{2}$ of the G-dorian background descent. These structural–motivic echoes inscribe Amarilli's cruelty, through musical–textual allusion, on the madrigal's core framework

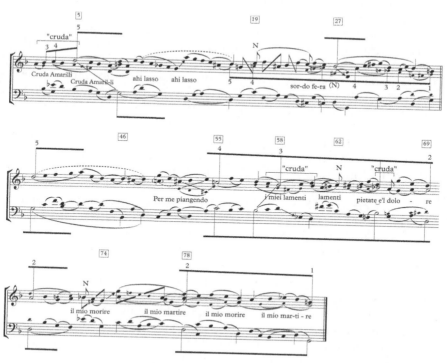

Example 8.2 Pallavicino, *Cruda Amarilli*, Structural Analysis

(labeled "cruda" in Example 8.2). The first reappearance coincides with the abrupt shift from background *c"* to *b♭*, where the expanded C sonority at "E mormorando i venti" (verse 14) drops down to B♭ at the start of "Diranno i miei lamenti" (verse 15, mm. 55–62), and the Quinto (a second tenor) pronounces the new structural pitch as a striking *b♭* at "*diran*no." As the Quinto descends to *a'* in preparation for a G cadence above the Basso's *d*, the Canto descends *d"–b♭* to create a new *a'–b♭* clash. The "cruda" dissonance turns this structural event—the instatement of background $\hat{3}$, *b♭*—into a vivid recollection of Mirtillo's initial cry, as he enumerates nature's expressions of his pain.

While this prepared G cadence gets deflected to D-*mi* in mm. 58–59, the restatement of verse 15 has the Tenore now declaiming the new background *b♭* at the peak of its range. Yet, the phrase ends in a wayward C cadence that displaces *b♭* with its upper neighbor, *c"* (m. 62). (Note how the path to this cadence renders Mirtillo's agony in a series of cross-relations—*b♭–f♯'–b♮–e♭'*—that warrants Artusi's censure for its mixture of diatonic and chromatic genera.[7]) To resolve the disruptive *c"*, Pallavicino again calls on the "cruda" dissonance at verse 17 ("La pietate e'l dolore"): this time in a linear configuration in an exceptional realization of Mirtillo's "dolore" (suffering) that places the Alto's *b♭–a'* in the context of a G-*major* sonority, thus transforming the structural *b♭* into the severest of dissonances—a chromatic semitone—against the Quinto's *b♮* and then following it with another dissonance, *a'*, a major second against both G and B (Example 8.2).

This passage is an ingenious and remarkably unusual solution to this pivotal moment in the piece. While the *b♭* serves as a pointed reemphasis of background $\hat{3}$, the verse's continuation reveals the following *a'* to be a salient anticipation of background $\hat{2}$ before its formal articulation with the D cadence at the repetition of "dolore" three semibreves later (m. 69). Pallavicino's treatment of the verse, therefore, achieves a piercing rendering of Mirtillo's pity and suffering ("pietate e dolore") by presenting the key B♭/A dissonance both vertically (between the Tenore and Basso in m. 66) and linearly (in the Alto's vain *b♭–a'* "resolution" against *b♮*). Yet, the strategy also portrays the seminal "cruda" conflict at the fundamental level, where $\hat{3}$ and $\hat{2}$ (*b♭–a'*) are presented as anomalous dissonances in what should be the most stable context of the G-dorian mode: a G sonority.

The background *a'* undergoes one last disruption by B♭ before the terminal $\hat{2}$–$\hat{1}$ resolution. The madrigal prolongs the pitch through a full initial statement of the last three verses with the support of an F sonority, which is expanded, in turn, by a middleground neighboring motion, F–g–F (mm. 71–78; see Example 8.2). This neighboring motion, however, involves an extended displacement of *a'* ($\hat{2}$) by *b♭* ($\hat{3}$), which initiates a m7 linear descent (divided by register transfer, *b♭–g'/g"–c"*) in the upper voice. This final disruption reaches its end with the forceful F cadence in m. 78, where *b♭*—as a suspended m7 in the penultimate C sonority—resolves to *a'* with the notion of death ending the speaker's agony. The pain of "cruda Amarilli," with its

A/B♭ dissonance, therefore, subsides ultimately here with the literal arrival of "morte" in the last verse.

Through the dilation of the A/B♭ dissonance from the opening syllable to the final verses, Amarilli's cruelty resounds across all levels of the madrigal. These recurrences arise primarily in the *seconda parte* to match the images in the text of nature voicing Mirtillo's sorrow and Amarilli's name with musical allusions to "Cruda Amarilli." The twofold statements of the last three verses, meanwhile, maintain the background $\hat{2}$ (a') until the final cadence, while evoking the speaker's suffering death with dissonances and cross-relations of increasing intensity. The most audacious of these include the suspended minor sixths over pre-cadential major sonorities at "morire" (mm. 73 and 82)—creating the effect of augmented sonorities similar to that of the last "Cruda Amarilli" (mm. 8–9)—and the rearticulated M9 above the antepenultimate C-minor sonority (m. 86), the resolution of which becomes a m7 in the pre-cadential D sonority.

As a whole, Pallavicino renders Mirtillo's lament with a dynamic structure that is firmly grounded in the G-dorian mode, yet that varies its cadential, melodic, and harmonic focus on the principal degrees—G, D, and B♭—with episodes dominated by the irregular pitch-centers, F and C, often as support for internal structural pitches (e.g., a', m. 78) and disruptions (e.g., e'', mm. 19–26). In many basic respects, Pallavicino's approach resembles Marenzio's handling of dynamic structures; incorporation of diverse textures, motivic references, cadence formulas, and modal/cadential regions; and, in the two-*parte* works, preservation of the primary background pitch through the *prima parte*, while disrupting it—typically by upper-neighbor motion—at the middleground level. This integration of broader formal–structural techniques with surface-level dissonances and textural changes for affect and variety shows an inherently polyphonic shaping of the text, which draws the listener's focus to particular expressive moments and from one voice or voice group to another, while conveying a vignette of Amarilli's cruelty vicariously from the shepherd's eyes.

Both Marenzio and Pallavicino also set Mirtillo's full speech, as opposed to the abbreviated passages of Wert and Monteverdi, and, like Monteverdi, fill their settings with unorthodox and sometimes jarring contrapuntal formations, only of differing varieties, owing partly to their contrasting modal characters (E-phrygian versus G-dorian). This analysis of Pallavicino's multi-level portrayal of the text, moreover, challenges Tomlinson's rather disparaging comparison of the works of Pallavicino and others to those of Monteverdi. As Tomlinson writes, Pallavicino's and others'

> rhetorical vision was...shortsighted, bound usually by the limits of a single verse or period. Their works tended...to give as a whole a fragmented, unintegrated effect especially noticeable in madrigals by Gesualdo but apparent also in pieces by Marenzio, Luzzaschi, Pallavicino, and others.[8]

The composer's structural–motivic integration of the "cruda" dissonance and the affective ramifications thereof is but one illustration of his reading beyond "the single verse or period."

To the consequential but largely overlooked features of Pallavicino's *Cruda Amarilli* should also be added discrete passages of distinctive slow-moving, sinuous counterpoint that combines prolonged sonorities, closely spaced vocal entries, and full-voice texture with suspended and linear dissonances, chromatic inflections, and little text repetition. The technique occurs, for example, at verse 13, "Per me piangendo i fonti" (mm. 51–55), where the voices enter on successive minims (some in pairs) to present the line with long rhythms, extensive semitone motion and chromaticism, and incidental dissonances (Example 8.3). While a vivid depiction of the springs' weeping in Mirtillo's place, the phrase also carries out the crucial transition from background $\hat{5}$, d''—reemphasized at the D cadence in m. 50—to $\hat{4}$, c'', which it then prolongs (primarily at the lower register, c') with a general motion in mm. 51–55 from C, through E (with c' as upper neighbor), to a non-cadential arrival on A, supporting c' in its superficially raised form, $c\sharp'$ (compare Examples 8.2 and 8.3). The next phrase, "E momorando i venti," maintains c'' through homophonic elaboration of a C sonority with the motion C–F–C–F–B♭–C (mm. 55–57), the undulations of which evoke the "murmuring" of the wind. This manner of sinuous counterpoint then returns for the exceptional rendering of "La pietate e'l dolore" (mm. 64–69), where the "cruda" dissonance reappears for the exchange of background $\hat{3}$ ($b♭'$) for $\hat{2}$ (a') in the jarring context of a G-major sonority.

The texture occurs numerous times in Pallavicino's Sixth Book and resembles an important tactic seen in Marenzio's late work, particularly in the Seventh Book. Both composers reserve the technique for moments of key textual and structural importance, often coinciding with exclamations or with references to suffering and cruelty, where the novel texture, elongated syllables, and contracted intervallic motion call increased attention to the unfolding text and intertwining voices. A passage similar to Pallavicino's "Per me piangendo," for example, occurs at Marenzio's treatment of "Perché

Example 8.3 Pallavicino, *Cruda Amarilli*, "Per me piangendo i fonti" (mm. 50–55)

Example 8.4 Marenzio, *O Mirtillo, Mirtillo anima mia*, "Perché crudo destino" (mm. 50–57)

crudo destino" (Why, cruel fate?) in *O Mirtillo* (Example 8.4). The phrase prolongs a basic A sonority in slow-moving dissonant counterpoint with chiefly semitone motion in the Canto for a tortuous rendering of "cruel fate" in Amarilli's situation. Yet, the phrase's dissonant and disorienting surface obscures its deeper, favorable role of revealing the madrigal's background $\hat{3}$, *e″*, and thereby its true modal identity after intense and continued uncertainty to this point in the piece.[9] Through this alignment of text, dissonance, and modal affirmation, Marenzio's setting portrays at once Amarilli's mistaken perception of "destino" as the source of her torment, and its true nature (revealed at the end of the play) as the force that will bring the reversal of plot and ultimately the lovers' union. This convergence of roles in a distinctive contrapuntal passage relates closely to the merging of the "cruda" dissonance and structural $\hat{3}$–$\hat{2}$ descent at "La pietate e dolore" in Pallavicino's *Cruda Amarilli*.

In his reading of Mirtillo's monologue, Pallavicino partitions the speech formally into sections of polyphony and a Mantuan (Wertian) style of homophonic declamation, infusing both with affective dissonances often reminiscent of Marenzio's techniques, but that show a greater willingness to overstep theoretical norms. In comparison to the three other *Cruda Amarilli* settings, Pallavicino turns more readily toward pictorial devices—thus, not only rapid rhythms for "fugace" and precipitous descents followed by long high notes for "le piagge e i monti," as the other settings use, but also melismatic runs at "venti" and paired semibreves as "volto" (perhaps connoting eyes or faces). All of these characteristics, in fact, apply to much of Pallavicino's Sixth Book, which on the whole betrays a basic affinity to Marenzio's Seventh Book in terms of compositional approach and musical texts, with an overwhelming focus on Guarini. Its twenty-one works include thirteen settings of Guarini (three from *Il pastor fido*) and two of Tasso, as compared to the twelve (out of seventeen) of Guarini—all from *Il pastor fido*—and one of Tasso in Marenzio's Seventh Book. Two of Pallavicino's *Pastor fido* texts also bear distinctive similarities to the specific readings of Marenzio's volume, as we shall see.

Previous comparisons of the earliest *Cruda Amarilli* settings have focused on similar melodic, rhythmic, and textural treatments of discrete phrases—such as "Cruda Amarilli," "del candido ligustro…bella," "I' mi morrò"—in order to judge the novelty, effectiveness, and influence of the works. Thus, Einstein and Chater cite Marenzio's influence on Pallavicino and Monteverdi[10]; Tomlinson declares Wert progenitor of a "family" of related *Cruda Amarilli* settings (while, like Chater, aligning Pallavicino's treatment with Marenzio)[11]; and Fabbri underscores the parallels between Pallavicino's and Monteverdi's readings and their common Mantuan declamatory style.[12] More recently, Massimo Ossi explores subtler details of the works and their cultural surroundings to challenge Chater's notion of a Marenzio–Pallavicino connection and instead (following Arnold and Fenlon) tie Pallavicino's reading primarily to Wert, and secondarily (in his use of dissonances) to Marenzio, while connecting Monteverdi's more "modern" techniques in the Fifth Book as a whole to Marenzio's Seventh Book.[13]

While the settings bear undeniable resemblances, it could also be the case that some of these parallels derive not from the influence of one setting on another, but from the intrinsic qualities of the text. Long–short–short–long–long, for example, reflects the basic scansion of the words "Cruda Amarilli," while a descent from "Cruda" observes the word's status as both the semantic and expressive focal point of verse 1 and the impetus of the entire speech. All four composers—and numerous others after them—set these words accordingly, with three of them rendering "Cruda" with improper dissonances: Wert with a bare unprepared P4, Pallavicino with a M7, and Monteverdi with a m7 moving directly to a m9. Similar text-based rationale might explain other often-cited correlations between the works. The composers' shared sensitivity to the speech rhythms and affective character of Guarini's text might, in the end, account for scholars' portrayals of the relationships between the madrigals in so many divergent ways, as if all four works had sprung from one common source. That source is, of course, the text itself.

As Marenzio's and Pallavicino's structural strategies in their *Cruda Amarilli* settings demonstrate, parallels between composers' approaches to a given text may exist on levels other than the immediate foreground. As the analysis in Example 8.2 illustrates, the *prima parte* of Pallavicino's madrigal projects a complete d''–g' descent that stretches from the reemphasized background d'' at "insegni" (m. 18) to the final G cadence (m. 38). This motion carries less weight than the fundamental line and acts as a middleground expansion of the background d''—which, at its rearticulation at "e più fugace" (mm. 27–28), acts as an upper neighbor to c'' in the more local context of this subsidiary descent. This $\hat{5}$–$\hat{1}$ motion gives a great deal of finality to the end of the *prima parte*—certainly more so than the customary *prima-parte* ending on the cofinal, D, in bipartite G-dorian works—to the extent that this *parte* alone could function convincingly as a self-contained work. The resulting single-*parte* piece would end precisely where Monteverdi's setting ends ("I' mi morrò tacendo"). Wert and Marenzio, by contrast, give no such option for closure in the *prime parti* of their works, both of which end on the secondary degrees of their respective modes: G in C-hypolydian for Wert, and A in E-phrygian for Marenzio. By engaging with Monteverdi's work on equal textual and structural footing, Pallavicino was perhaps inviting comparison with his young Cremonese rival, after having only recently bested him in the bid for Wert's former position of *maestro della musica*. Then, by continuing his setting beyond the texts of both Wert's and Monteverdi's madrigals, in an impassioned, lengthy, and highly integrated *seconda parte*, Pallavicino—at least by some parameters—outdoes them both. With such implicit vying through treatments of the same fashionable texts, these settings show the *Pastor fido* madrigal serving as its own competitive arena, just as *Il pastor fido* the stage work had done in the race for early productions.

Whatever the motivations, Monteverdi's and Pallavicino's settings provide a pair of contrasting readings of the same passage (vv. 1–8) that could be juxtaposed in performance and compared in discussion, perhaps as a way for readers at the Gonzaga court and elsewhere to relish and explore one of the play's key moments: Mirtillo's impassioned entrance. Indeed, this type of critical comparison of the two settings continues to this day. In such studies, it is the two composers' use of dissonance that scholars have generally found most noteworthy. Denis Arnold, for example, remarks that the opening of Pallavicino's madrigal is, "like Monteverdi's, a landmark in the history of harmony... In fact, Pallavicino's setting is for the most part more dissonant than Monteverdi's."[14] Despite the fact that many of these dissonances flout the contrapuntal standards to which Artusi subscribed, the theorist places Pallavicino among the virtuous composers—alongside Palestrina, Gastoldi, Giovanelli, and other "eccellenti"—whose works exemplify "valente practico" (able practice), while Giulio Cesare Monteverdi excludes him from his list of adherents of the *seconda pratica* alongside Marenzio and Wert.[15]

Pallavicino's *Cruda Amarilli* could, in fact, serve as a compendium of the violations that Artusi condemns in the works of Monteverdi, Marenzio, Wert, and others. The linear outlining of a d4 by the Alto at "E, se fia muta" ($b\flat$–$f\sharp$, m. 70) and the leap of the same interval by the Tenore at "las*so a*maramente" ($c\sharp$–f, m. 12), for instance, demonstrate what Artusi labels disparagingly as "canto accentato" (accented singing), a "nuova inventione" of modern composers, and gestures that confound the "rules founded on truth" in their mixing of diatonic and chromatic *genera*.[16] In addition to numerous unprepared dissonances, rearticulated suspensions, and descents from raised (sharp) pitches— all of which Artusi condemns in Monteverdi's works—Pallavicino also defies several teachings of Artusi's mentor, Zarlino: for example, consecutive M3s

("Parlerà il mio morire," mm. 72 and 82) and widespread false relations involving chromatic alterations, such as B-*fa*/F♯/B-*mi* at "che col nome" (mm. 9–10) and "diranno i miei lamenti" (mm. 59–61), and B-*fa*/B-*mi* at "pietate e'l dolore" (mm. 67–68).[17] This and other madrigals in the Sixth Book also use minor sevenths in several pre-cadential sonorities, as Monteverdi famously does in *Anima mia, perdona*, and *Cruda Amarilli*. Pallavicino typically handles these sevenths properly—introducing them as suspensions and resolving them 7–6–5 above a sustained bass—apart from one instance, at "e più fera" (m. 25), where the Canto rises to *f* in the pre-cadential G sonority and resolves it to *e″* at the C cadence: a patent "V⁷–I" in tonal terminology (see Example 8.2). More common as an effect of pre-cadential anguish, however, is the type of incidental "augmented" sonority that Marenzio also deploys for similar expressive purposes in his later output. Compare, for example, the latter's rendering of "destino" in *O Mirtillo*, shown in Example 8.4, with Pallavicino's last "Cruda Amarilli" cadence in mm. 8–9 (Example 8.1) and two statements of "morire" in mm. 74 and 82 (both of which conceal consecutive P5s between the outer voices, as shown in Example 8.2).

This daring display of text-driven offenses raises the question of how Pallavicino averted Artusi's ire (at least publicly) and even earned his praise, while also being neglected by the Monteverdi brothers as a proponent of the *seconda pratica*.[18] Denis Arnold speculates that Pallavicino was "almost certainly excluded by Monteverdi for personal reasons"—the foremost of these presumably being his promotion to *maestro della musica* over Monteverdi following Wert's death in 1596.[19] As for Artusi, however, the critic's utterly divergent responses to the two Mantuans' nearly contemporaneous transgressions reinforces the possibility raised in Chapter 6 that additional, external factors—such as the composers' stature or the performance setting in which Artusi heard Monteverdi's madrigals—played a significant role in his attack.[20] As Denis Arnold concludes provocatively in his study on the *seconda pratica*: if Artusi "had attacked Wert or Pallavicino, should we ever have heard of him [Artusi]?"[21] Given Pallavicino's progressive methods in his *Cruda Amarilli*, we might ask conversely: If Artusi had, in fact, attacked Pallavicino along with Monteverdi, would we hear more of Pallavicino (and his music)?

Although more extreme, *Cruda Amarilli* is not unique in Pallavicino's Sixth Book in its daring dissonances and conspicuous parallels to works by Wert, Marenzio, and Monteverdi.[22] The opening of *A poco a poco io sento*—a setting of an anonymous lover's lament rich with references to suffering and death—for instance, contains many unorthodox dissonances and begins with a suspension-filled point of imitation that bears a striking resemblance to the opening of Monteverdi's *Ah, dolente partita*. Both works are set in forms of A-dorian—Pallavicino's in the plagal, Monteverdi's in the authentic—and begin with two voices on a unison *e″* that diverge to precipitate a series of dissonant suspensions, while the entrances of other voices add to the rendering of death-like agony. Likewise, both settings rely heavily on imitative texture to superimpose rhyming verses in *contrapposto* while varying the cadential centricity on the principal degrees (A, C, and E) with medial cadences to D and G. Pallavicino, however, goes further than Monteverdi in destabilizing the underlying mode, with more cadences *fuori del tuono*, a reframing of the A final in a phrygian context (at "angosce," anguishes), and widespread contrapuntal violations, including abandoned dissonances (e.g., leaps away from minor sevenths at "longo errore"), rearticulated suspensions, and consecutive large leaps.

The connections with another composer's work run even deeper with Pallavicino's *Deh, dolce anima mia*, the text of which is a variant reading of Amarilli's "Partiti, e ti consola" from act 3, scene 3 that appears in only one other known source: Marenzio's Seventh Book, in a setting by Florentine composer Antonio Bicci. The text (as compared to the play) reads:

Bicci (in Marenzio's Seventh Book)	Guarini, Il pastor fido
	...troppo lungamente
1 Deh, dolce anima mia,	Hai dimorato ancora.
Non pianger più se m'ami, e ti consola	Partiti; e ti consola,
Ch'infinita è la schiera	Ch'infinita è la schiera
De gl'infelici amanti.	Degli infelici amanti.
5 Vive ben altri in pianti	Vive ben altri in pianti
Sì come tu, mio core.	Sì come tu, Mirtillo. Ogni ferita
Ogni ferita ha seco il suo dolore,	Ha seco il suo dolore,
Nè se' tu solo a lagrimar d'amore.[23]	Nè se' tu solo a lagrimar d'amore.
	(Act 3, scene 3)

The madrigal text, thus, changes the passage from a nymph's rebuff of her suitor, Mirtillo (in the manner of "You've already lingered too long. Leave, and it will console you..."), to an anonymous speaker's consolation of an admirer or lover upon their separation. The only hint that the poetic voice is female comes at "tu solo" in the last verse, indicating a male addressee (unless "solo" is taken as an adverb, which further obscures the issue). Moreover, whether the separation is mutual or one-sided is not specified, but the speaker's seemingly exaggerated or even sarcastic tone—with the terms of endearment "dolce anima mia" and "mio core" giving the sense of "Oh, sweetheart, stop crying; there are plenty of others like you, dear heart"—contrasts with Amarilli's callous call for Mirtillo to stop lingering and leave. The madrigal text also replaces Mirtillo's name with the metonymic "mio core" in verse 6, and modifies the versification of lines 6–7 to create three successive lines with rhymed *-ore* endings. This particular reading proves unique to the two madrigals, yet Roman composer Antonio Cifra set a notably similar variant of the passage twice: first as a five-voice madrigal in his Second Book *a 5* (Venice: Vincenti, 1608), then as a solo aria in his *Diversi scherzi...libro secondo* (Rome: Robletti, 1613).[24]

The correlations between Bicci's and Pallavicino's pieces, however, extend beyond the text to the music as well. As Example 8.5 shows, both madrigals, for example, present the opening line in nearly identical rhythms, with an initial m6 leap downward in the Canto (although sounding a P4 in Pallavicino's work owing to the overlapping upper voices) and motion by fifths between sonorities. Both, then, venture into the extreme *durus* realm of a B-major sonority with offset homophony in verse 2. Locally, Bicci's motion to B proves more destabilizing, for the continuation of the verse leads to a cadence on B♭, the reciting pitch of the madrigal's G-hypodorian mode. Yet, Pallavicino's treatment of verses 1–2 stirs such remarkable modal ambiguity on a broader scale that it would sit comfortably on Artusi's list of modally offensive works alongside Monteverdi's *O Mirtillo* (a setting of another Amarilli speech), whose opening descending leap and overlapping voices it also resembles. Yet, whereas Monteverdi's work begins with a modally sound $\hat{3}$–$\hat{5}$ ascent in the upper voice (see Example 7.7), Pallavicino opens his G-mixolydian setting irregularly with the sonorities A–E–A⁶ before cadencing on the G final. After leading through E and B sonorities to a cadence on C (a customary cadence for the mode) in verse 2, the next verse-pair yields another shift to A, ending with a vivid allusion to the opening gesture with the same sounding upper-voice motion, *e″–b′* (mm. 8–9).

a) Pallavicino (1600)

b) Bicci (1595)

Example 8.5 Openings of Pallavicino's and Bicci's *Deh, dolce anima mia*

To this point, it remains unknown whether this assertive A cadence confirms that pitch as modal final (as suggested also by the opening sonority) or represents a *clausula peregrina* in a G-final piece with an aberrant opening. The middleground $e''-b'-e''$ upper-voice motion of mm. 1–6 supports the former reading, while the G and C cadences of verses 1 and 2 support the latter. At the same time, the disorienting A opening in a G-centered piece setting Amarilli's (modified) words recalls Pallavicino's strategies in *Cruda Amarilli*, where A functions as both a local and large-scale dissonance tied to Amarilli's bitterness in a G-dorian framework. The use of a similar pitch conflict (A vs. G) in *Deh, dolce anima mia*, where Amarilli addresses Mirtillo directly in the play, however, serves not merely as a straightforward display of Amarilli's cruelness, but also as an integrative intimation of her concealment of truth (her love, like the fundamental mode) beneath a bitter, yet superficial front (her coldness to Mirtillo, like the obfuscating effects of A). The setting, therefore, supports a reading of the text from Amarilli's perspective in the play, even while its altered text obscures this connection.

The parallels between Bicci's and Pallavicino's works continue past their openings to their settings of the remaining verses in nearly identical rhythms and often similar textures. This conspicuous kinship, in turn, strengthens the broader ties between Pallavicino's Sixth Book and Marenzio's Sixth and Seventh Books that prove especially apparent in the *Pastor fido* settings. Marenzio's *Ah, dolente partita* (1594); *Deh, Tirsi, Tirsi, anima mia* (1594); *O dolcezze amarissime d'amore* (1595); and *Ami, Tirsi, e me'l nieghi* (1594, setting a Tasso text), for example, all begin, like Pallavicino's madrigal, with prolonged exclamations with $e''-b'$ leaps in the upper voice—Pallavicino divides the leap between the Canto and Quinto to avert parallel P5s with the Basso—followed by more rapid declamation that leads from A (or in one case C) to increasingly *durus* sonorities. Marenzio's madrigals, however, are all A- and C-final works, which underscores the idiosyncrasy of Pallavicino's a–E opening for a G-mixolydian piece.

In terms of their broader effects, the similar beginnings of Marenzio's works add to both the unity of his Sixth and Seventh Books as a whole—a unity that also envelops the setting by Bicci—and their connections to Pallavicino's Sixth Book. Also adding to these kinships is the distinctive, incidental "augmented" sonority that both composers deploy for pre-cadential expressions of agony. Pallavicino had used it at "morire" in *Cruda Amarilli*, and invokes it again in *Deh, dolce anima mia* specifically at "dolore" (suffering) in verse 7, first in three parts (mm. 18–19), then with intensified dissonance in four parts (mm. 28–29).

Whereas the texts of Pallavicino's *Deh, dolce anima mia* and *Cruda Amarilli* have concordances with Marenzio's Seventh Book, *Vivrò io mai per altro amor contenta* seems to belong to a wholly separate lineage of variant *Pastor fido* texts. In the first six of its nine verses, the text departs considerably from the play but corresponds precisely with the independent reading published in Varoli's 1590 anthology, *Della nova scelta di rime*.[25] The same general version had also appeared three years earlier in Ventura's *Rime di diversi celebri poeti* (1587), but lacking verses 5 and 6.[26] These same verses (5–6) in Varoli and the madrigal, meanwhile, seem to represent an intermediate reading between the 1580s drafts and the first edition of Guarini's tragicomedy. The four printed sources read:

Ventura (1587)	*Varoli (1590) and Pallavicino (1600)*	*Il pastor fido (1589)*
Vivrò io mai per altro amor contenta,	Vivro io mai per altro Amor contenta,	Viver io fortunato
Che per quel Sol, cui lo cor mio donai,	Che per quel sol, cui lo mio cor donai?	Per altra donna mai, per altro amore?
Nè potendo il vorrei,	Ne potendo il vorrei,	Nè volendo il potrei,
Nè volendo il potrei:	Ne volendo il potrei,	Nè potendo il vorrei.
	E se pur esser de' che questo mai,	E s'esser può ch'in alcun tempo mai
	O voglia il mio volere,	
O possa il mio potere.	O possa il mio potere.	Ciò voglia il mio volere,
Prego il Ciel, & Amor che tolto pria,	Prego il Cielo, & Amor, che tolto pria	O possa il mio potere,
Ogni voler, ogni poter mi sia.	Ogni voler, ogni poter mi sia.	Prego il cielo, ed amor, che tolto pria
		Ogni voler, ogni poter mi sia.
		(Act 3, scene 6)

In the play, the passage follows *Udite, lagrimosi* in act 3, scene 6 and shows Mirtillo defending his love for Amarilli when tempted by Corisca with the prospect of another, willing lover (namely, herself). With its feminine adjective ("contenta") in verse 1 ("I will never live contentedly with another love") in place of the play's masculine "fortunato" (referring to Mirtillo), the Varoli reading distinguishes the speaker as a woman rather than a shepherd and reinforces this identification with the caption: "Piuttosto desidera una Donna innamorata, che gli sia tolto il volere, e il potere, che odiar colui ch'ama" (A woman in love wishes that her desire and power be taken away from her, rather than hate the one she loves). Whether Guarini refashioned an earlier poem for Mirtillo's speech in the play, or Mirtillo's speech took on a new, independent guise (and speaking persona) outside the play that made its way into Ventura's, Varoli's, and Pallavicino's volumes is impossible to determine from the extant sources.

In all, the alternative textual concordances of Pallavicino's three *Pastor fido* settings make it plausible that none of the texts came directly from the play itself, but from other sources—namely, Marenzio's Seventh Book and Varoli's *Della nova scelta di rime*. The versatility (and variability) of the play's texts and their placement alongside Guarini's independent poems in madrigal books of Marenzio, Pallavicino, and others further highlight the fluidity with which the texts shifted between various contexts and uses. For readers acquainted with Guarini's tragicomedy—as contemporary Mantuan courtly circles surely were—the altered scenarios and intricate intertextual allusions that these works presented might have proven an important part of their intellectual appeal.

While numerous factors seem to align Pallavicino's madrigals most closely with his Roman contemporary, the musical planning of his Sixth Book follows a marked Mantuan trend: a narrowing range of modal finals to only two or three pitches. The collection includes a variety of modes, but only two finals: G and A. In fact, all of the composer's late madrigal books show a strong preference for G and A as finals, with some D-final pieces, but very few settings with F, C, or E finals. This restriction means that there are only a handful of pieces in the lydian (or ionian) and phrygian modal pairs. Overall, Books 5–8 contain only three F-final pieces (two in Book 5 and one in Book 8) and no C- or E-final works. This selectiveness mirrors Monteverdi's focus on only two finals, G and D, in his Fifth and Sixth Books. As preserved in print, Pallavicino's madrigals soundly uphold the tradition of polyphonic madrigals for courtly chambers and intimate reading, as do the settings of Wert, Marenzio, and Monteverdi. The settings of two other Mantuan colleagues, Gastoldi and Rossi, however, introduce very different performance options to the *Pastor fido* madrigal that seem to reach beyond the conventional domains of private and polyphonic vocal performance.

Beyond Balli: Concision, Contrast, and Characterization in Gastoldi's *Pastor fido* Settings

Gastoldi produced one of the most enduring and widely printed volumes of secular music of the sixteenth century: not a collection of madrigals, but his *Balletti a cinque voci* (Venice: Amadino, 1591)—light, strophic dance pieces, most with internal repeats and "fa la la" refrains. The volume appeared in some thirty printings and three languages in Italy and north of the Alps through the mid-seventeenth century.[27] It seems logical, then, that despite Gastoldi's official role as music director of the ducal chapel of Santa Barbara—a position concerned primarily with sacred music—he was entrusted with the task of providing music for the troublesome choreographed *Gioco della cieca* for the November 1598 staging of *Il pastor fido*. The setting makes him one of three Mantuan composers known to have supplied music for stagings of the play, given Wert and Rovigo's purported yet lost music for the failed 1591–92 production. As seen in Chapter 2, evidence of the theatrical function of Gastoldi's music comes directly from the partbooks of his Fourth Book of madrigals (1602), where the piece bears the heading "Il Gioco de la cieca rapresentato alla Regina di Spagna nel Pastor fido."[28]

Raised in the territory of Bergamo, Gastoldi entered Gonzaga service by 1572 as sub-deacon of Santa Barbara and held the post of *maestro di cappella* there from 1588 until his death in 1609, while Wert (1565–96), then Pallavicino (1596–1601), and Monteverdi (1601–12) oversaw music at the court. Gastoldi, therefore, had the great fortune of serving at one of the foremost musical centers in Europe during its cultural zenith under Guglielmo and Vincenzo Gonzaga. Yet, like Pallavicino, he has also had the historical misfortune of remaining in the shadows of his influential colleagues, Wert and Monteverdi. The scant literature on Gastoldi's secular music typically only goes so far as to cite his four madrigal books and *Concenti musicali* while offering generalizing remarks on his dance music that include the mildly pejorative labels of "simplicity" and "lightness."[29] Partly to blame for the dearth of analysis, recordings, and performances of Gastoldi's madrigals is likely also the glaring lack of scholarly editions of his music. Yet, as this study of his *Pastor fido* madrigals will show, the works warrant closer consideration by scholars and performers, and rival the settings of Gastoldi's more prominent contemporaries for their original, expressive, and interpretatively rich readings of Guarini's verse.

As seen in Chapter 2, Gastoldi's fifteen *Pastor fido* settings appeared in three separate books: three in his Third Book (1598), eleven in the Fourth Book (1602), and one in the *Concenti musicali* (1604; see Table 8.1). All three volumes were dedicated to members of the Gonzaga family, either from cadet branches—Francesco, "Cavaliero di S. Iago" (Third Book) and Camillo, Count of Novellara (Fourth Book)—or in the case of the *Concenti musicali*, the heir to the Mantuan throne (Francesco). The madrigal texts, like those of Wert's settings, generally agree with the published play, in contrast to the frequent variants found in the works of Marenzio, Pallavicino, Rossi, and (in his earlier settings) Monteverdi. The only notable discrepancies are small but potentially consequential and occur in two works: *Dimmi, misero amante*—which substitutes "misero" for "povero" in the opening line—and *Tanto è possente amore*, which omits the words "caro Mirtillo" from verse 3. Several of the texts refer explicitly to the play's characters by name—four of them in the opening line (to four separate characters)—but most speak broadly enough about the nature of love and the sufferings of lovers to function equally well as independent lyrics.

Many of Gastoldi's madrigal texts stand at the fringes of the prevailing trends in the early *Pastor fido* madrigal in terms of their intrinsic qualities, role in the play, and musical fortune. While his *Gioco della cieca*, for instance, represents the first extant setting with ties to a staged performance of the play, his three treatments from the act-two chorus made him only the second composer to publish settings of the end-of-act choruses behind Rinaldo del Mel (c.1554–98)—an itinerant northern composer active in the environs of Rome in the 1580s–90s, whose *Oh bella età de l'oro* from the chorus of act 4 appeared in his Third Book *a 6* (Venice: Angelo Gardano, 1595). Gastoldi's works also draw from the speeches of a variety of characters— Mirtillo, Dorinda, Corisca, and (unusually) Amarilli's father, Titiro, along with two separate choruses—but with the notable exception of Amarilli. This omission may be explained in part by his overwhelming focus on choruses (four settings) and on Mirtillo's dialogue with Corisca in act 3, scene 6 (six settings). This latter scene would generate more madrigals than any other scene in the play over the course of the tradition, and five of its passages appeared for the first time in musical setting in Gastoldi's works.

In all, two-thirds (ten) of Gastoldi's *Pastor fido* madrigals represent the first-known settings of their texts. His works generally skirt the most fashionable passages—such as *Cruda Amarilli*; *O Mirtillo*; *Ah, dolente partita*; and *Udite, lagrimosi*—yet his 1602 treatment of Dorinda's *O misera Dorinda* from act 2, scene 2 is the second of some eighteen total settings beginning with Brescian composer Ottavio Bargagni's multi-*parte* rendering in his First Book *a5* (Venice: Gardano, 1601). At the same time, several texts that appeared first in Gastoldi's madrigal books went on to attract modest interest from later composers, including *Com'è soave cosa* (six later settings) and *M'è più dolce il penar per Amarilli* (seven).

Gastoldi's readings (like Wert's) rely heavily on homophonic declamation, often with quick rhythms and syncopation to match the accents of the text and with intermittent episodes of imitation. Improper dissonances and extreme chromaticism are rare, and notably, even textual repetition is infrequent. In place of the conventional drive to the final cadence with repeated, contrapuntal statements of the final verse or couplet, Gastoldi sometimes restates the antepenultimate and penultimate verses before ending with a single delivery of the closing line—for example, in *Dimmi, misero amante* and *Arda pur sempre o mora*. Many of his settings are, therefore, distinctively concise, lasting on average about thirty measures (breves) per piece or *parte*. Already, these approaches in text-setting distinguish Gastoldi's madrigals from the *balletti*, with their routine musical, textual, and formal repetition and more pervasive homophony, while the kinship between both genres shows in their rhythmic character and avoidance of extreme dissonance.

In his large-scale planning, Gastoldi generally avoids cadences on the modal final through the opening of a madrigal and sometimes until the terminal cadence, yet even in such cases, the modal grounding is usually conveyed through other features, such as ambitus, melodic behavior, cadential and non-cadential arrivals on other principal pitches, and prominent sonorities. This reliable preservation of the basic mode also reflects Gastoldi's restricted use of *commixtio tonorum*, and his preference for static structures in the manner of Wert that extend the opening background state until the final moments of the piece. As a composer hired under Duke Vincenzo's devout and culturally conservative father, Guglielmo Gonzaga, Gastoldi seems to apply the Counter-Reformation regard for textual clarity and the *prima pratica* approach to dissonance and mode of his sacred music to his *Pastor fido* madrigals as well. In place of the striking contrasts of texture and sonority and the vivid (sometimes transgressive) responses to impassioned moments in the text seen in the *Pastor fido* settings of Marenzio, Pallavicino, and Monteverdi, Gastoldi's settings seem to focus most on textual delivery (*pronuntiatio*)—or specifically, on the rhythmic delivery of the verse. Thus, expressions in the text that routinely inspire bold reactions in the readings of other composers—such as dissonances at allusions to pain and cruelty, or modal and cadential diversions to depict frustration or deceit—often pass with little distinction in Gastoldi's madrigals. He does, however, seem to relish opportunities for word-painting, particularly when it involves manipulations in rhythm.

The opening of *O misera Dorinda* (1602)—Dorinda's complaint about her seemingly hopeless affection for hard-hearted Silvio—illustrates many of these general features (Example 8.6).[30] The passage shows Guarini's model of pure and simple love (Dorinda) lamenting, first to herself as second person ("O misera Dorinda!"), then to her beloved Silvio ("Amoroso fanciullo"), after trying to bargain for the latter's affection by hiding his lost dog. This clarity of voice and addressee in the contexts of the play, however, becomes obfuscated in the extracted text. Hence, the revelation partway through the speech of who is speaking and the consequent reinterpretation of what had come before represent key aspects of the madrigal's interpretative play. The full passage reads:

1	O misera Dorinda! Ov'hai tu poste	O miserable Dorinda! Where have you put
	Le tue speranze? Onde soccorso attendi?	your hopes? From what do you expect help?
	In beltà che non sente ancor favilla	In beauty that feels no spark
	Di quel foco d'amor, ch'arde ogn'amante.	from that flame of love that burns every lover.
5	Amoroso fanciullo,	Amorous boy,
	Tu se' pur a me foco, e tu non ardi;	You are a flame to me, yet you do not burn;
	E tu, che spiri amore, amor non senti.	and you who inspires love, feels no love.
	Te, sotto umana forma	You, in human form,
	Di bellissima madre,	were born of the most beautiful mother,
10	Partori l'alma Dea che Cipro onora;	the divine goddess whom Cypress honors;
	Tu hai gli strali e 'l foco:	you have the arrows and the flame,
	Ben sallo il petto mio ferito e arso.	my wounded, burnt heart knows well.
	Giugni agli òmeri l'ali:	Bind wings to your shoulders:
	Sarai novo Cupido,	you would be a new Cupid,
15	Se non ch'hai ghiaccio il core,	except that you have ice for a heart,
	Né ti manca d'Amore altro che amore.	and lack nothing of Love other than love.
	(Act 2, scene 2)	

Dorinda's lament is general enough that it functions perfectly well outside its scenario in the play. Yet, the ambiguity of voice when taken outside the play stems from the absence of the first person (*io*) until verse 6 ("a me"), after the change of second-person addressee (*tu*) in verse 5. Thus, in verses 1–4, the speaker—or, indeed, the madrigal–narrator itself—calls Dorinda by name and questions her as "tu," as though this is pure second-person address from an unnamed speaker (or narrator) to Dorinda. The focus then shifts from Dorinda to the "amoroso fanciullo" in verse 5.[31] The appearance of the first person as indirect object of the "amoroso fanciullo" in verse 6—"You are a flame *to me*" ("Tu se' pur *a me* foco")—thus, recasts the scenario (particularly for those unfamiliar with the contexts here in the play) in two potential ways. Either the perspective shifts from the speaker/madrigal addressing *misera* Dorinda in vv. 1–4 to Dorinda's address to the *amoroso fanciullo* in vv. 5–16, or the madrigal, in fact, speaks not *to* (or about) Dorinda and the "amorous boy" at all, but *for* Dorinda throughout, by imparting the words she had spoken to herself and to the "novo Cupido" who wounded her heart ("il petto *mio* ferito"). The experience of hearing the madrigal, then, potentially involves not only two textual personas—Dorinda (*io/tu*) and her beloved *fanciullo* (*tu*)—but also a third one: a temporary, implicit (narrative) *io* that merges with Dorinda herself at the inward deictic, "a me," in verse 6.

As Examples 8.6 and 8.7 show, Gastoldi delineates the principal pivot in the text from Dorinda to the *fanciullo* as second person (*tu*) structurally and stylistically with a middleground 5̂–1̂ descent and a florid three-voice delivery of

Example 8.6 Gastoldi, *O misera Dorinda*, mm. 1–13

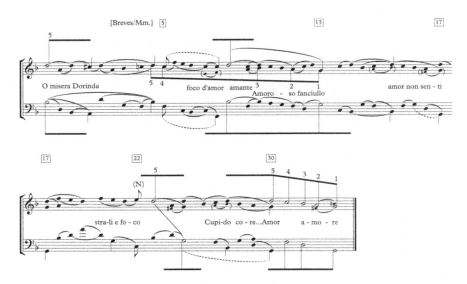

Example 8.7 Gastoldi, *O misera Dorinda*, Structural Analysis

"Amoroso fanciullo" that together end in the first, long-awaited (yet thwarted) cadence on the G-hypodorian final at the close of verse 5 (m. 13). Then, following this confirmation of the mode and shift of focus away from Dorinda, the true identity of the speaking voice comes immediately to light ("a me," mm. 13–14). Gastoldi animates the initial lines directed (as it turns out) inwardly, toward Dorinda herself, by parsing them into discrete textural and semantic units. The initial vocative, "O misera Dorinda" (mm. 1–2), leads immediately adrift in long notes and demanding leaps to A-*mi*. The following questions—marked at first by a reduction of forces from five voices to four—and response in vv. 1–4 drive in homorhythmic declamation toward the remote center of F ($\hat{7}$) at "foco d'amor" (flame of love). After this first mention of love, the texture frays into four-part imitative descents that highlight the charged words "arde" (burns) and "amante" (lover) for the remainder of verse 4 (that burns every lover). The melismatic frenzy intensifies in verse 5, drawing out the forlorn call, "Amoroso fanciullo" (amorous boy), before arriving at the delayed and frustrated cadence on the final (mm. 10–13). Finally, the speaker's declaration of the beloved's immunity to love, with the inward deictic "a me" that confirms Dorinda as first person in lines 6–7, brings the piece into modal–cadential alignment with more assertive approaches to B♭ and G thereafter.

Altogether, this first half of the piece (vv. 1–7) accomplishes several important structural and interpretive functions. First, the unusual trajectory of the initial phrase, "O misera Dorinda," from B♭ to an A-*mi* cadence in a G-hypodorian context foreshadows the tension between mode and cadence scheme to come. For the madrigal evades the G final as a cadence goal through nearly half of its length and centers instead on A-*mi* (m. 2), B♭ (m. 4), F (mm. 5 [non-cadential] and 7), and B♭ again (m. 9), before the *cadenza fuggita* on G in m. 13 and finally a stronger G cadence in m. 17. Nevertheless, the piece expresses the underlying mode through this opening by other means, including by delineating its principal intervallic species— the D-octave with its division at G (and A), and the G–D *diapente* divided at B♭—and by accentuating these key boundary pitches in the opening sonorities, B♭–D–g^6. Through its balance of modal compliance and roving cadences, the madrigal portrays a character committed in her innate love yet confounded by where it has led her in the present moment of the speech.

Second, amid this suppression of G cadences and the first-person *io* through its opening, the madrigal shows particular attention to the upper voices, both in the exclusion of the Basso from two of the first five verses, and in the creation of a "composite" upper voice in the Canto and Quinto, shown by arrows in Example 8.6. The first instances of these upper-voice exchanges are accentuated, moreover, by the Canto's striking leaps at "O misera" (m6, m. 1) and "ogni amante" (P8, m. 8). Across the piece as a whole, in fact, all of the major episodes of reduced texture involve the silencing of the Basso except one: the trio of Canto, Alto, and Basso that invokes the "amoroso fanciullo" (mm. 10–13), thus perhaps reflecting the new focus on a male addressee. The prioritizing of the upper register of the madrigal's "voice" overall intimates the underlying female perspective before and after it is made explicit by the text, and thus subtly seems to favor a reading that conforms to the play, with Dorinda as speaker throughout.

Alongside its straying cadences and steadfast mode, the first half of the madrigal conveys two essential aspects of Dorinda's character through two concurrent yet contrasting structural processes (Example 8.7). First, the static modal framework, with its firm grasp on the background *d″* (5̂) until the final verse of text, mirrors Dorinda's example of unwavering love. This persistent *d″* likewise maintains an important role on the musical surface as the upper boundary of both the Canto's and Quinto's ranges. Second, bridging the speaker's self-reference ("O misera Dorinda") in verse 1 with her address to the "amoroso fanciullo" (Silvio) in verse 6 (mm. 4–13) is a subsidiary stepwise descent through the complete G-hypodorian *diapente*, *d″–g′*, which is supported by cadences to B♭ (*d″*), F (*c″*), B♭ (*b♭′*), and finally D–G (*a′–g′*). At the foreground level, the weak consummation of this descent in an evaded G cadence at "fanciullo" (boy) seems an apt response to Dorinda's vain desire for a hopeless lover. But as a whole, the descent also seems to hint at the couple's more promising end in the play by joining the background *d″* articulated at "O misera Dorinda"—and reemphasized at "le tue speranze" (your hopes)—with *g′* and the first G cadence at "fanciullo" through a clear projection of the most assured emblem of modal identity: the *diapente* species. Hence, beneath the speaker's despair and the unsettled foreground of the music, this structural union of "misera Dorinda," "speranze," and "amoroso fanciullo" foreshadows the lovers' fortunate fate, the course to which takes root in this early turbulent encounter and comes to fruition in the scene of Monteverdi's *Ecco, Silvio* (act 4), where Silvio is transformed after seeing Dorinda wounded. From a purely analytical standpoint, this direct $\hat{5}$–$\hat{1}$ motion also illustrates how a seemingly erratic foreground and cadential plan can serve a decidedly coherent function at a deeper level: in this case, strictly supporting the degrees of the d''–g' descent.

O misera Dorinda offers but one example of common characteristics of Gastoldi's *Pastor fido* settings, including predominantly homorhythmic texture, modal clarity, deferral of cadences on the final, a suspended background, and subdued instances of dissonance and chromaticism. It also abstains completely from textual repetition and relies chiefly on stepwise voice leading. Yet this portrait is, of course, a generalization: for Gastoldi's works display such an array of exceptions that diversity must be included among their principal features. *O sfortunato e misero Mirtillo* (1602)—one of his most concise settings at only twenty breves—and *Arda pur sempre o mora* (1602), for example, are both highly imitative, while *Tu se' pur aspro a chi t'adora* (1602) combines a dynamic D-dorian structure with severe dissonances (e.g., "aspro" and "crudo") and repetitions of the final couplet that occupy one-fifth of the piece. Likewise, *O misera Dorinda*, as we have seen, has a more customary suspended background but still conveys a superficial effect of structural motion in the middleground descent of verses 1–6.

In most cases, these exceptional approaches grow out of specific affective and rhetorical demands of the verse and merely steer the conventional five-voice madrigal toward different stylistic poles. Two settings, however, stand out as belonging to different madrigal types altogether. *Baci pur bocca curiosa*—the only setting from the play in the *Concenti musicali* (1604)—has an introductory instrumental *sinfonia* and scoring for eight voices, in keeping with the rest of the collection. The *Gioco della cieca*, by contrast, is a choral dance for the stage that treats four passages for nymphs' chorus detailing the craftiness of "cieco Amor" (blind Love), while omitting the intervening dialogue of Amarilli, Mirtillo, and Corisca that occurs in the play.

Although decidedly a madrigal, Gastoldi's *Gioco* fittingly shows the more dance- and *balletto*-like side of the genre's stylistic and formal spectrum. The *prima parte* begins as though it is a strophic setting before veering off into through-composition, with the form AA'BC across its four quatrains; the *seconda* and *terza parti* begin similarly in triple meter (C3) and end with a musical–textual refrain; and stock *quinari* and *settenari* rhythmic patterns reappear throughout the piece. All of these aspects evoke the formal and phrase-level repetition expected of *balletti*, *villanelle*, *canzonette*, and other dance-like and recreational genres.[32] The setting is almost entirely homorhythmic (including at most cadences) across its four *parti*, and seldom does it stray from the modal–cadential alignment of its G-dorian grounding—a foreground feature that likewise stems from its static prolongation of the background $\hat{5}$, d''. Other features contribute to the work's "lightness" of character befitting of a pastoral game, such as nearly invariable syllabic declamation; stepwise motion in the upper voices; syncopated and dotted rhythms; few dissonances; and brief, clearly defined phrases with almost no textual repetition.

At the phrase level, Gastoldi also makes frequent use of harmonic–melodic patterns that resemble the *romanesca* and *passamezzo antico*—aria formulas rooted in traditions of dance music and improvised song—with alternations of descending P4–rising M2 (or the inverse) and bouncing P4s. The technique further aligns the piece with light, informal styles of music-making associated with dance. The opening of the piece (Example 8.8) illustrates many of these characteristics. The setting of verses 1–2 (mm. 1–5) consists entirely of *romanesca*- or *passamezzo*-like motion between the sonorities G, F, B♭, and D, with the two upper voices proceeding in stepwise motion in parallel thirds. The texture is strictly homophonic (aside from the displaced Quinto for its entrance in m. 9), with unadorned arrivals at D (non-cadentially), B♭, G, and D for the four verse-endings.

While it is relatively certain that Gastoldi's music played a role in the November 1598 staging for the Queen of Spain, precisely how it was performed—whether sung onstage by the chorus of nymphs (either dancing or not) or offstage by separate musicians (as was done, according to Guarini, for the 1584–85 Ferrarese preparations)—is open to question.[33] The scoring for two tenors, rather than two sopranos or altos, might seem incongruous in

* Begins erroneously with a semiminim rest.

Example 8.8 Gastoldi, *Cieco, Amor, non ti cred'io*, mm. 1–10

terms of verisimilitude, given that nymphs would presumably sing at higher registers. But the high tessitura of these tenors—both spanning *f–a'*—puts them approximately in an alto range in terms of written pitch. Likewise, the work's "lightness" of style, as seen in its texture, rhythmic character, and formal patterns, also pertains to its general accessibility for performance: the *Gioco* does not demand an ensemble of virtuosi or professionals, such as the duke's *concerto delle donne* or the musicians at Santa Barbara who were ordered for the performance, and thus could have been sung by the actor-dancer nymphs (depending, of course, on the physical demands of the movement). Beyond the music and texts, however, the surviving accounts of the event tell us little about how Gastoldi's work was actually performed onstage.

The *Gioco della cieca* is followed in Gastoldi's Fourth Book by two conventional madrigals that in many respects form a contrasting yet interconnected pair, despite their different contexts and speakers in the play. In this way, the works are notable for potentially demonstrating Gastoldi's attention to the relationships between madrigals in the book, as well as the coherence of the book as a whole. As we shall see, this grouping of works might also encompass a third piece situated elsewhere in the book.

Dimmi, misero amante (No. 6) comes between *Arda pur sempre o mora* and *M'è più dolce e penar per Amarilli* (both also set by Gastoldi) in Corisca's interrogation of Mirtillo in act 3, scene 6; while *O sfortunato e misero Mirtillo* (No. 7)—Mirtillo's reflective lament upon learning of Diana's curse and Amarilli's betrothal—marks the end of Mirtillo and Ergasto's dialogue in act 1, scene 2 that begins with *Cruda Amarilli*. Both of these scenes generated widespread musical interest, but Gastoldi was the first to set these specific passages to music, and they received few musical treatments thereafter. *Dimmi, misero amante* appeared in only two other settings—by Orazio Brognonico (1612) and Francesco Antonio Costa (1626)—and the six-line *O sfortunato e misero Mirtillo* in one, by Giovanni Boschetti (1613).[34]

Despite their distinct circumstances in the play, their placement on facing pages in Gastoldi's book throws the two texts, with their music, into stark relief and invites a multitude of interpretative possibilities by accentuating both their differences in the play and their similarities outside of it. The passages read:

[Corisca to Mirtillo]

1	Dimmi, misero amante,	Tell me, miserable lover,
	Con cotesta tua folle	with this your foolish
	Virtù della costanza,	virtue of constancy,
	Che cosa ami in colei che ti disprezza?	what do you love in her who despises you?
5	Ami tu la bellezza	Do you love the beauty
	Che non è tua? La gioia che non hai?	that is not yours? The joy that you do not have?
	La pietà che sospiri?	The pity for which you sigh?
	La mercé che non speri?	The mercy for which you have no hope?
	Altro non ami al fin, se dritto miri,	If you see it plainly, you love nothing other
10	Che'l tuo mal, che'l tuo duol,	than your pain, your sadness,
	che la tua morte.	your death.
	E se' sì forsennato,	And are you so fraught
	Ch'amar vuoi sempre e non esser amato?	that you want always to love and not be loved?

(Act 3, scene 6)

[Mirtillo to himself, with Ergasto]

1 O sfortunato e misero Mirtillo,	O unfortunate and miserable Mirtillo,
Tanti fieri nemici,	so many fierce enemies,
Tant'armi e tanta guerra	so many arms and so much war
Contra un cor moribondo?	against a dying heart?
5 Non bastava Amor solo,	Was Love alone not enough,
Se non s'armava a le mie pene il Fato?	so Fate, too, armed himself against
(Act 1, scene 2)	my pains?

Both texts pose a series of questions from utterly contrasting characters about the same basic matter: cruel and hopeless love. Only *O sfortunato e misero Mirtillo* identifies the suffering lover by name (Mirtillo), but both texts refer to the addressee as "misero" in their opening lines. The reading of Gastoldi's *Dimmi, misero amante* creates this connection uniquely by replacing "povero" from the play with "misero," thus also relating both texts to *O misera Dorinda* earlier in the collection. Also like Dorinda's apostrophe is the apparent concealment of the first-person *io* in both passages. In fact, apart from the initial "Dimmi" (tell me), the first person is otherwise absent from *Dimmi, misero amante*, making it nearly full second-person address, while *O sfortunato e misero Mirtillo* resembles *O misera Dorinda* in beginning as if a second-person address, only to reveal, with the meager "mio" in the last verse, that the speaker (*io*) and second person (*tu*) are one and the same—in this case, *misero* Mirtillo. Taken together, then, the two madrigals transition from an interrogation of a general *misero amante*, to identifying the lover as *misero* Mirtillo at the start of the second text, and finally to a disclosure ("mie pene") at the very end that forces a reinterpretation of the previous madrigal(s) as Mirtillo questioning his own "foolish constancy."

The pairing of the pieces in Gastoldi's Fourth Book, therefore, opens up a plurality of potential readings that play with the ambiguities of the texts: independently of one another or together as paired passages; as having the same speaker ("Mirtillo") or separate ones; as reflective speech or (with *Dimmi, misero amante*) addressing a second person; and within their own scenarios of the play (in Corisca's and Mirtillo's voices) or detached from it, as universal expressions.[35] The fact that the passages differ in how they address the *misero* lover—as *tu* in *Dimmi, misero amante*, and as *tu*-turned-*io* in *O sfortunato e misero Mirtillo*—is relatively immaterial, given that lyric poems and the play's characters use both forms of self-reference, sometimes even within a single poem or speech—as seen in *O misera Dorinda* (No. 2), where Dorinda addresses herself as *tu* in verses 1–4, then Silvio as *tu* in verses 5–16.

Gastoldi's treatment of the texts facilitates all of these potential readings by unifying the works through their visual/physical juxtaposition in the book, "misero" references, and external parameters—A-hypodorian mode, standard cleffing, and scoring for two tenors—while also distinguishing them by structural design, cadential behavior, and texture in response to their different rhetorical (and potentially speaking) characters. The first of the pair, *Dimmi, misero amante* (spoken by Corisca in the play), has a

dynamic structure with an early and protracted abandonment of the underlying mode and primary background $\hat{5}$, *e″*. As Table 8.2 and Example 8.9
show, in place of the expected confirmation of the mode and ample expansion of the initial structural pitch, the madrigal quickly moves past its first
background degree (*e″*) after just five measures to instate and sustain the
modal $\hat{4}$, *d″*, through most of the remainder of the text (vv. 3–10). Even the
first verse, despite starting and finishing on A, begins the process of weakening the A-hypodorian foundation by recasting the A-*re* final (with B♮) from
"Dimmi" as A-*mi* (with B♭) at "amante."

With this early modal betrayal, the madrigal prefigures further instability to come, where B♭ plays a central role in establishing an opposing dorian context based on D, the most frequent cadence pitch in the piece. This

Table 8.2 Gastoldi, *Dimmi, misero amante*, Structural Outline

Structural line	*e″*	*d″*	*c″*	*b′*	*a′*
Predominant Cadences	A-*re*→A-*mi*	D, G	A	G	A
Mm.	1–5	6–21	22–24	24–28	28
Verses	1–2	3–10	10–11	11–12	12

Example 8.9 Gastoldi, *Dimmi, misero amante*, mm. 1–9

modal reorientation comes with the influence of background d'' ($\hat{4}$) and the consequent emphasis of D and G as pitch centers—both foreign cadences for an A-hypodorian piece—and of D as a sonority at verse openings and endings and as a melodic boundary. The expansive period of modal–structural dissonance under the hegemony of d'' intensifies the speaker's onslaught of questions asserting the futility of love in verses 3–8. After a brief articulation of background $\hat{3}$ (c'') at a forceful A cadence at "tua morte," the fundamental line presses onward to b' at a G cadence (m. 25)—an unusual site ($\hat{7}$) for a penultimate cadence in an A-hypodorian piece—followed by a hurried presentation of the crucial A–E species before the terminal $\hat{2}$–$\hat{1}$ (b'–a') close and final cadence.

The madrigal, all told, is beset by incongruous cadences and wayward melodic/harmonic behavior that support the less stable structural pitches d'' ($\hat{4}$) and b' ($\hat{2}$). While a straightforward rendering of incompatible natures (and, hence, ill-placed love), this basic structural plan—modally inconsistent at its core, but punctuated by moments of conformity—also realizes the true character of the text's speaker in the play: Corisca, who masks her devious intent with the guise of a trustworthy friend. In Gastoldi's music, these opposing identities emerge in the contrasts between brief glimpses of modal clarity at the beginning, middle, and end—corresponding to the domains of background e'', c'', and a'—and the longer intervening spans of subversive pressures dictated by d'' and b'.

After presenting much of the text (vv. 1–9) in common fashion—lively declamation with short phrases, repeated sonorities, and dotted and syncopated rhythms—Gastoldi breaks from his customary techniques later in the piece in two notable ways: first, by setting two lines (10 and 12) uniquely in imitative counterpoint as a way to fortify their scarce but crucial endings on the A-*re* final, and second, by repeating the antepenultimate and penultimate verses (10–11) as a way to underscore a climactic moment in the text ("che la tua morte") and build anticipation for the structural denouement. At the same time, despite the scoring for two tenors, the madrigal, like *O misera Dorinda*, prioritizes the upper voices at instances of reduced texture by excluding the Basso alone or with one of the two tenors. While certain voices are highlighted in individual ways—for example, the Canto in its sole prominence at the top of the texture, and the Quinto (mm. 6–8) and then the Tenore (mm. 10–15) through metrical displacement—the clear focus on the upper register may again allude to the female voice behind the text, thus supporting a reading tied to the play that recognizes the speech as Corisca's. Gastoldi seems to make similar insinuations of the gender/identity of the poetic voice through texture and voicing for other *Pastor fido* texts where the gender and name of the speaker are withheld: for example, by highlighting the Tenore (and sometimes Alto) most frequently, including notably for first-person verbs, in Mirtillo's *Deh, bella e cara* (No. 1); and by isolating the Basso and Tenore for Titiro's entirely third-person comparison of fresh love to a rose, *Come in vago giardin rosa gentil*, particularly in the *prima parte* (and elsewhere less consistently).

Gastoldi continues his use of less habitual techniques, like imitation and text repetition, and amplifies them to greater proportions in his compact setting of *O sfortunato e misero Mirtillo*. His reading focuses more on the text's reflective character than on its message of inward torment and struggle over ill-fated love. The piece unfolds in perpetual counterpoint that adheres tightly to A-hypodorian norms, even while only insinuating arrivals on the E-*mi* cofinal and avoiding entirely cadences on the A final until the end. Along with this restricted tonal sphere (A and E-*mi*), the Canto moves in the narrow ambitus *g♯–e"*—the modal *diapente*, A–E, plus leading tone— while all of the voices spend the majority of their time outlining the fifth and fourth species A–E and E–B and the *diapente*'s division at C. This modal consistency is a product of the work's constant support of background *e"* (5̂) in a suspended structural framework (Example 8.10). In contrast to the dynamic unfolding and widespread instability of Corisca's *Dimmi, misero amante*, the tenacity of Mirtillo's lament mirrors the speaker's weary but determined heart and his state of timeless, lyric-like introspection. This effect of structural–temporal paralysis in the music also accords with this moment in the play, as the protagonist is stunned by the weighty news of Diana's curse and Amarilli's commitment.

As questions and warlike images spiral through the speaker's head, the voices in the madrigal intertwine in imitation while skirting cadences, eliding verse-endings, and shouldering the background *e"*. At only one point does the madrigal waver in its hold of the pitch: at the words "tanta guerra" (so much war), where an expanded G–D motion begets a weak middleground digression to *d"* as lower neighbor, as though the speaker (and madrigal) drops to his knees at the memory of past struggles. The commanding *e"*, however, returns in the next verse with an affective leap, *e"–g♯*, at "cor moribondo" (dying heart), the very same interval with which the madrigal begins at "O sfortunato," thus tying this restoration of *e"* to the original statements of the pitch in the Quinto (m. 1) and Canto (m. 3; see Examples 8.10 and 8.11c and d). The madrigal remains fixed in this structural state until the arrival of "Fato" (fate), the final word, which guides the madrigal to a complete and sudden end (Example 8.10). The conclusion proves fitting, as Fate always

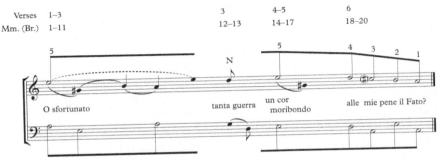

Example 8.10 Gastoldi, *O sfortunato e misero Mirtillo*, Structural Analysis

brings an end, but the decisiveness and fulfillment of this ending further seem to insinuate a promising end to the lover's war, whether that be Mirtillo's in the play or a generic "misero Mirtillo" of the lyric imagination.

While pairing *Dimmi, misero amante* and *O sfortunato e misero Mirtillo* through their mode, scoring, "misero" openings, themes of hopeless love, and placement on facing pages, Gastoldi also highlights their differing rhetorical–expressive characters with clear contrasts in textural and structural approach. Several of these features that unify the two madrigals likewise incorporate another piece, by yet another speaking character, that appears earlier in Gastoldi's Fourth Book. For the initial exclamation, "O sfortunato," in Mirtillo's lament, with its descending m6 leap, *e'–g♯* ($\hat{5}$–$\hat{\sharp 7}$), recalls the opening cry of Dorinda's *O misera Dorinda* (No. 2), where the gesture sounds a tone lower (*d''–f♯'*)—hence, in G- rather than A-hypodorian—and in homophonic declamation rather than in a point of imitation (compare

a) *O misera Dorinda* (mm. 1–2)

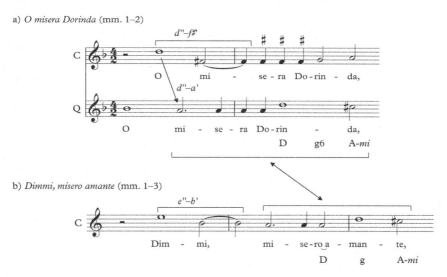

b) *Dimmi, misero amante* (mm. 1–3)

c) *O sfortunato e misero Mirtillo* (mm. 3–4)

d) *O sfortunato e misero Mirtillo* (mm. 13–14)

Example 8.11 "Misero" Leaps in Gastoldi's Fourth Book

Examples 8.11a and c). These monologues by the play's faithful but spurned lovers, Dorinda and Mirtillo, share many traits both textually and in Gastoldi's setting: not only their opening cries of "O...misero" / "O misera" and the m6 leaps that accompany them, but also steadfast structures that ultimately give way with final appeals to divine forces (*Amor* and *Fato*), widespread modal clarity despite a paucity of cadences on the final early in the piece, and an early concealment of the first-person speaker and, hence, of the fact that the speech is reflective. The kinship between the works, furthermore, dissociates them—and their loyal speakers—from Corisca's deviousness as rendered in *Dimmi, misero amante*, with its dynamic structure dominated by discord and duplicity.

From a broader perspective, the relationships between all three of these works illustrate several of the manifold forms of intertextual connections and interpretative possibility at play in Gastoldi's collection. While *Dimmi, misero amante* and *O sfortunato e misero amante* are paired on adjacent pages and with matching musical parameters, and *O misera Dorinda* and *O sfortunato* are linked through their opening exclamations and modal–structural character, all three madrigals are also bound by common "misera/o" incipits, concealments of the first-person *io*, opening leaps from the fifth degree (Example 8.11a–c), transposed versions of the same basic mode (G- and A-hypodorian), and expressions of frustrated love. Moreover, the two madrigals with the most outwardly different characters—Dorinda's *O misera Dorinda* and Corisca's *Dimmi, misero amante*—share a compelling, if discreet, association through their opening phrases, the idiosyncrasies of which may be explained as references to the other's mode. Whereas "O misera Dorinda" leads to an unusual A-*mi* cadence in a G-hypodorian context, "Dimmi, misero amante" likewise leads to A-*mi* and thereby undermines its A-*re* final. At the same time, the upper voices in both openings begin with sounding $\hat{5}$–$\hat{2}$ leaps (*d″–a′* and *e″–b′*) and end with the motion *a′–d″–c♯″* over the same sonorities, D–g–A. This gesture integrates cadential inflections to the finals of both pieces, D–g and g–A-*mi* (shown in Examples 8.11a and b). These musical cross-references become all the more pronounced given their analogous texts, "misera Dorinda" and "misero amante." The opening verses, therefore, become conflated in their melodic, harmonic, and modal/cadential behavior precisely as their texts correspond with *misera/o*.

These multi-level connections between the three *misera/o* madrigals reach across the pages of Gastoldi's book (Nos. 3, 10, and 11) and the acts of Guarini's tragicomedy (1, 2, and 3) to highlight three paradigmatic speeches from three separate facets of the play's complex plot: Dorinda's devotion to the "amoroso fanciullo" (Silvio), Mirtillo's longing for the "rigida ninfa" (Amarilli), and Corisca's devising to win over the "pastor fido" (Mirtillo). These same characters and themes appear elsewhere in the Fourth Book, including in texts drawn from two of the same scenes: Dorinda's encounter with Silvio in act 2, scene 2 (No. 10, *Tu se' pur aspro a chi t'adora*) and Mirtillo's dialogue with Corisca in act 3, scene 6 (No. 4, *Arda pur sempre o mora,* and No. 8, *Come assetato infermo*). Likewise, *Deh, bella e cara, e sì soave un tempo* (No. 1)—a two-*parte* setting from Mirtillo's humiliating confession to Amarilli in act 3, scene 3—expresses the same basic sentiments with similar imagery and language as the other Mirtillo passages in the collection.

Yet, despite these recurring themes and perspectives, the volume gives little indication of a deliberate ordering based on text, aside from the obvious focus on Guarini's play and the representation of various scenes and characters thereof. Instead, the five-voice pieces follow a general (but not entirely consistent) arrangement by certain musical parameters: system (*mollis* then *durus*), mode (dorian/hypodorian–mixolydian–lydian), and final (G, A, D, G, F), but excluding cleffing. Thus, most pieces with the same mode and final sit next to one another, with the exception of the two G-dorian works: *Deh, bella e cara* (No. 1) and the *Gioco della cieca* (No. 5). This ordering, of course, affects the *Pastor fido* settings without apparent heed to chronology, speaker, or textual theme.

At the same time, musical–textual associations, such as those between the three *miseralo* pieces, that operate internally—beneath the external parameters of system, mode, and final—seem to transcend these parameters and the physical layout of the book to join non-adjacent madrigals. Moreover, given that most of the passages in the Fourth Book were cut from the November 1598 performance in Mantua, the fact that many of them have a faint or absent first-person dimension, focusing instead on second-person address (*tu*) or third-person description, could reveal as much about what made these excerpts allegedly "superfluous" for the stage as it does about Gastoldi's (or a patron's) textual preferences. Finally, as seen in Chapter 2, Gastoldi's three settings from the chorus of act 2 also show compelling signs of unity with their common mode (G-mixolydian), matching vocal ranges, and adjacent passages, and may represent a "madrigal group" despite their appearance in separate books and the contrasting scoring *a8* for the closing "*parte*."

Altogether, Gastoldi's *Pastor fido* settings reveal a composer of much more than *balletti*, the "light," dance-style music for which he is best known: they distinguish him as a reader aware of the subtleties of the text and the makeup of its personas, with a command of the capacities of modal–structural expressivity, and with a willingness to bridge the boundaries between pieces, books, genres, and compositional approach. While the effects of cross-madrigal references and relationships are comparable to those seen in works by Marenzio, Monteverdi, and Pallavicino, they are often distinctive in their means and highlight Gastoldi's particular focus on rhythmic character and associations that embrace both text and music. The Fourth Book alone, furthermore, exhibits a range of musical, textual, and performative diversity that is exceptional for a madrigal book and unique among collections devoted largely to *Il pastor fido*. Its pages present lyric poems, excerpted monologues, and choruses with and without explicit ties to the stage; numerous voices, both male and female, discoursing on various dimensions of love (including those of young love by the elder Titiro); a spectrum of structural types and allusions within and between works; and a restrained and succinct, yet sensitive and naturalistic, treatment of the text at the surface level. His versatility in handling texts from the play, however, expands even further when considering pieces beyond the Fourth Book, including the rare example of a fully instrumental component in a *Pastor fido* setting in his 1604 *Concenti musicali*. There is, indeed, still much to be explored in Gastoldi's music.

Salamone Rossi: Marenzian Cues on a New, Mantuan Stage

Salamone Rossi (c.1570–c.1630) is not the first Jewish artist to play an important documented role in the early history of *Il pastor fido*. As seen in Chapter 2, dancer–choreographer Leone Tolosa laid the choreographic foundation of the *Gioco della cieca* for the failed Ferrarese preparations of 1584, and "Isachino hebreo"—presumably the dancer, singer, and choreographer Isacchino Massarano—was entrusted with the same task for the aborted preparations in Mantua of 1591–93. Jewish actors might also have played a larger role in these Mantuan preparations than existing records indicate, given the integral role that the Jewish theater in Mantua played in the city's cultural life at the time, including at the ducal court.[36]

Scant evidence survives of Rossi's biography—merely a handful of cursory court documents and the dedications of his music books—yet his active involvement in musical life at the Gonzaga court and his distinctive treatment by the dukes as a Jewish composer and performer attest to his stature. Following the rhetoric of his dedications (most of them to members of the Gonzaga family), Don Harràn speculates that Rossi strove in his work to secure "employment, support, recognition," and "to improve his standing in Mantuan society," all of which proved particularly challenging for a Jew in a non-Jewish environment.[37] Setting texts by Guarini, including passages from *Il pastor fido*, must also have been a key part of this strategy, given the contents of Rossi's early music books. The First Book *a5* (Venice: Amadino, 1600) is dominated by Guarini settings—thirteen out of nineteen pieces (including two from *Il pastor fido*)—along with treatments of three poems by Cesare Rinaldi, a sonnet by Angelo Grillo (Livio Celiano), and two anonymous poetic madrigals (Table 8.3). The First Book *a4* (Venice: Amadino)—published in 1614, but likely also composed around 1600—adds another seven Guarini settings (four from *Il pastor fido*) alongside nine anonymous texts, and one each by Tasso and Tommaso Stigliani (see Table 8.1). All six of his settings from the play, therefore, potentially derive from the period surrounding the 1598 productions, alongside the works of Gastoldi, Pallavicino, and Monteverdi. This early focus on Guarini distinguishes Rossi as one of the first composers to show an avid interest in the play at the beginning of his published career, as compared to his seasoned Mantuan colleagues, Wert, Pallavicino, Gastoldi, and Monteverdi; Marenzio in Rome; Monte in Prague; and others.[38]

Table 8.3 Contents of Rossi's First Book of Madrigals for Five Voices (1600)

	Piece	Textual Source	Final	System	Clef	Mode
1	*Pur venisti, cor mio*	Guarini, *Rime*	A	*durus*	G2	A-dorian
2	*Felice chi vi mira*	Guarini, *Rime*	C	*durus*	G2	C-hypolydian
3	*S'io miro in te, m'uccidi*	Rinaldi	G	*durus*	C1	G-hypomixolydian
4	*Che non fai, che non pensi*	Rinaldi	G	*durus*	C1	G-hypomixolydian
5	*Deh, com'in van chiedete*	Guarini, *Rime*	G	*mollis*	C1	G-hypodorian
6	*O com'è gran martire*	Guarini, *Rime*	G	*mollis*	C1	G-hypodorian
7	*Arsi un tempo ed amai*	Guarini, *Rime*	G	*mollis*	G2	G-dorian
8	*O donna troppo cruda*	Guarini, *Rime*	F	*mollis*	G2	F-lydian
9	*Rimanti in pace alla dolente*	Celiano	E	*durus*	C1	E-phrygian
10	*Dirmi che più non ardo?*	Rinaldi	F	*mollis*	C1	F-hypolydian
11	*Silvia, s'al suon de tuoi soavi accenti*	Anon.	F	*mollis*	C1	F-hypolydian

Per il chitarrone

12	*Ohimè, se tanto amate*	Guarini, *Rime*	G	*mollis*	G2	G-dorian
13	*Cor mio, deh non languire*	Guarini, *Rime*	G	*mollis*	G2	G-dorian
14	*Anima del cor mio*	Anon.	G	*mollis*	C1	G-hypodorian
15	*Udite, lagrimosi*	Guarini, *PF*	G	*mollis*	C1	G-hypodorian
16	*Tirsi mio, caro Tirsi*	Guarini, *PF*	G	*durus*	C1	G-hypomixolydian
17	*Parlo, misero, o taccio?*	Guarini, *Rime*	G	*durus*	C1	G-hypomixolydian

A sei voci

18	*O dolce anima mia*	Guarini, *Rime*	G	*mollis*	C1	G-hypodorian
19	*Al partir del mio sole*	Guarini, *Rime*	F	*mollis*	G2	F-lydian

Mantuan court documents contain only four payment records for Rossi between 1587 and 1622 and another entry—for provisions of wheat and wine—of 1607, with a small number of intermittent references to Rossi's involvement in musical activities during these years, including as a violist and as a contributor—alongside Gastoldi, Monteverdi, Giulio Cesare Monteverdi, and Florentine Marco da Gagliano—to five *intermedi* for the 1608 staging of Guarini's comedy *L'idropica*. Based on the irregularity of these

records and the inclusion of his payments among those for "musici straor-
dinarii"—that is, "outside" musicians that were available as needed—Rossi
seems to have served the court on an *ad hoc* basis, as his identity as a Jew
likely excluded him from any formal position. His marginalization from the
official musicians of the Gonzaga court and chapel has persisted in large
part to this day in the madrigal literature, as most studies of Mantuan music
and the early *Pastor fido* madrigal tend to neglect his work. Instead, scholars
generally acknowledge his pioneering ventures in the *madrigale concertato*,
instrumental music (as a progenitor of the trio sonata), and polyphonic music for the synagogue, while forgoing close study of the music and its distinctive treatment of the poetic texts.

Yet, the publication history of Rossi's First Book *a5* suggests that his
early madrigals found both enduring and widespread appeal among contemporary readers, for it was reprinted twice in Venice (Amadino), in
1603 and 1607, and once north of the Alps (Antwerp: Phalèse), in 1618.
This market viability perhaps stemmed not only from the book's compelling treatments of fashionable Guarini texts—the trajectory of the
Guarini vogue indeed correlates closely with the timings of the book's
printings—but also from its forward-looking versatility by endorsing the
performance of several works with either five-voice ensemble or solo soprano with instrumental accompaniment. The first edition of 1600 ad-
vertises this feature on its title page with the subtitle "con alcuni di detti
Madrigali per cantar nel Chittarrone" (with some of the aforesaid madrigals to sing with the chitarrone). The tablature "per il chittarrone" for
six of the pieces (Nos. 12–17) appears in the Canto partbook, on facing
pages with the corresponding vocal part, thus implicitly facilitating realizations with various permutations of voices and instrument: ensemble or
solo, with or without chitarrone, or some mixture thereof. These pieces
with soloistic option include the book's two *Pastor fido* settings: *Udite,
lagrimosi* and *Tirsi mio, caro Tirsi* (Table 8.3). This book represents the
earliest known *concertato* madrigals to appear in print, predating Caccini's *Nuove Musiche* (1601) and Luzzaschi's *Madrigali...per cantare et
sonare* (1601).

Rossi's First Book *a4* (1614) makes no mention of soloistic or instrumental means, which in itself might suggest an earlier conception, given
the increasing development of the continuo part across his books for five
voices. Don Harràn, likewise, cites three other factors in support of dating the four-voice works to the late 1590s or early 1600s: the omission of
"novamente composti" from the title page of the collection, formal and
textural resemblances to earlier works, and the textual focus on Guarini
with a complete absence of Marini. This latter feature runs counter to the
growing proportion of Marini settings across the composer's four previous
books of five-voice madrigals of 1600–10.[39] The Fifth Book, published in
1622, contains exclusively Marini settings.

There are three additional considerations that lend further backing to this revised dating of Rossi's *a4* collection. First is the affinity between Rossi's First Books *a5* and *a4* in having numerous textual concordances with other Mantuan books of the 1590s and 1600s, including three with Wert's Eleventh Book (1595), six with Pallavicino's Books 5–7 (1593–1604), and seven with Monteverdi's Books 2–4 (1590–1603). But these numbers are dwarfed by the eleven concordances that the two books share with Marenzio's works, all but three of which come from the latter's Books 6–8 (1594–98). Of these total tallies, nine of the concordances involve Rossi's First Book *a4*, with four tied to Pallavicino and Monteverdi, and five to Marenzio. Hence, half of the contents of the four-part volume share texts with related settings of the 1590s and early 1600s. In this respect, the *a4* works also resemble the *a5* madrigals of 1600.

In these (presumably) early Guarini-dominated books, Rossi likewise contributes to the emerging trend of setting texts from both the poet's *Rime* and *Il pastor fido*, and to the budding prominence of certain texts within this corpus. His *Rime* settings, for example, include five poems that were to become some of the foremost Guarini texts in the repertory: *Cor mio, deh non languire* (33 total known settings); *Parlo, misero, o taccio?* (32); *Felice chi vi mira* (31); *O com'è gran martire* (25), and *Deh, come in van chiedete* (19). His *Pastor fido* settings, likewise, include three passages that would become mainstays of the genre: *Ah, dolente partita* (37); *O Mirtillo* (24); and *Udite, lagrimosi* (21). Rossi was the first to set two of these fashionable texts: *Parlo, misero, o taccio?* and *Deh, come in van chiedete*, both from the *Rime*.

The second detail supporting an earlier dating of the First Book *a4* is its provenance in Mantua while including four settings from Guarini's play. As we have seen, while some thirty-two *Pastor fido* settings issued from Mantua in the years surrounding the 1598 performances, only three settings appeared after 1605. This trend alone reinforces the possibility that the four-voice madrigals, with their *Pastor fido* settings, likewise originated around 1600, alongside Rossi's settings for five voices.

The third additional factor involves the specific readings of Rossi's *Pastor fido* texts. His six settings include:

First Book *a5* (1600)
    III, 6: *Udite, lagrimosi* (Mirtillo)
    IV, 5: *Tirsi mio, caro Tirsi* (Filli/Amarilli)
First Book *a4* (1614)
    III, 1: *O dolcezze amarissime d'amore* (Mirtillo)
    III, 3: *Ah, dolente partita* (Mirtillo)
    III, 4: *O Mirtillo, Mirtillo anima mia* (Amarilli)
    III, 6: *Com'è dolce il gioire, o caro Tirsi* (Corisca)

A conspicuous trait of these madrigals is that all of their texts had appeared in Marenzio's Sixth and Seventh Books of 1594–95—not merely the same passages from the play, but also the same (or very similar) variant texts. As seen in Chapter 4, these deviations range from minor details affecting individual words or verses to more extensive and consequential reworkings.[40] Both Marenzio's and Rossi's treatments of *O Mirtillo*, for example, read "O anime in *amar* troppo infelici" in verse 7, as compared to "O anime in *amor*" in editions of the play, where "amar" could be a simple error that Rossi picked up from Marenzio's work. Rossi's setting of Mirtillo's *O dolcezze amarissime d'amore* also overlaps precisely with the text of Marenzio's work, including in its omission of six interior lines. Likewise, both composers' settings of Corisca's *Com'è dolce il gioire* append "o...Tirsi" to the opening line, but with different intermediate adjectives: "vago" in Marenzio's treatment, "caro" in Rossi's. These two madrigals, moreover, are the only known settings of this precise excerpt from the play.

Other correlations between the two composers' works surface not only in other madrigal texts—six of the texts in Rossi's First Book *a5*, for instance, had appeared in earlier settings by Marenzio[41]—but also in their musical treatment. The opening subject of Rossi's four-voice rendering of *O Mirtillo*, for example, bears a conspicuous likeness to the upper voice of Marenzio's setting of the monologue (Example 8.12). While the Canto parts of both works follow the same general contour and succession of long and short rhythms, Rossi's Tenore exhibits even closer parallels to Marenzio's Canto: both begin on the fifth degree of their respective modes, descend in similar rhythms toward the final with "O Mirtillo, Mirtillo," and complete the verse ("anima mia") in nearly matching rhythms with a stepwise rise to the cadential goal. Both settings also break the synalepha at "Mirtillo anima" that disrupts the meter of the opening *endecasillabo*. At the same time, however, the relationship of these initial cadences to the fundamental modes illustrates more broadly the contrasting degrees to which the two composers were willing to subvert modal order so early in a piece: whereas Rossi leads directly to a cadence on the A-hypodorian final, Marenzio obscures the intervallic makeup of the fundamental C *diapente*—and, by extension, the identity of the mode itself—through the early appearance of E♭ in the one-flat system before cadencing on an irregular degree, D ($\hat{2}$).[42] Such ties between the two *O Mirtillo* settings strengthen the case for their closer chronological conception. This, in turn, would further position Rossi's setting alongside Monteverdi's in the late 1590s as two of the earliest renderings of the often-set speech to follow Marenzio's inceptive treatment of 1595.[43]

The most striking correlations with the texts of Marenzio's pieces, however, appear in Rossi's five-voice treatment of Amarilli's plea to the priest Nicandro from act 4, scene 5 ("Padre mio, caro padre").[44] Like Marenzio's work, Rossi's changes the padre/figlia (father/daughter) relationship of the play to Tirsi/Filli, accordingly omits verse 3, and ends with three lines foreign to the tragicomedy:

Rossi, *Primo libro a 5 (1600)*	Guarini, *Il pastor fido*
1 **Tirsi** mio, caro **Tirsi**	Padre mio, caro padre,
E tu ancor m'abbandoni?	E tu ancor m'abbandoni?
	Padre d'unica figlia,
Cosi morir mi lasci, e non m'aiti?	Cosi morir mi lasci e non m'aiti?
Almen non mi negar gl'ultimi baci.	Almen non mi negar gl'ultimi baci:
5 Ferrirà pur duo petti un ferro solo;	Ferirà pur duo petti un ferro solo.
Verserà pur la piaga	Verserà pur la piaga
Di tua **Filli** il tuo sangue.	Di tua figlia il tuo sangue.
Tirsi, un tempo sì dolce e caro nome	Padre, un tempo sì dolce, e caro nome;
Ch'invocar non soleva indarno mai,	Ch'invocar non soleva indarno mai,
10 Soccorri a me, tua Filli;	Cosi le nozze fai
Che come vedi da spietata sorte,	De la tua cara figlia?
Condotta son a cruda et empia morte.[45]	Sposa il mattino, e vittima la sera?

a) Rossi, *O Mirtillo* (1600), mm. 1–6: Canto and Tenore.

b) Marenzio, *O Mirtillo* (1595), mm. 1–8: Canto

Example 8.12 Openings of Rossi's and Marenzio's Settings of *O Mirtillo*

Aside from a few minor orthographical disparities (abbandoni/abandoni, ferrirà/ferirà, condotta/condutta), the readings of Rossi's and Marenzio's madrigals are effectively matching variants. All of these textual parallels point strongly to the prospect that Rossi's texts came from Marenzio's madrigal books rather than the play itself. The fact that this connection to Marenzio's works encompasses Rossi's settings from both the 1600 and 1614 publications adds considerable weight to the prospect that both sets of pieces originated around the same time—namely, c.1600, as Harràn proposed.

Traces of the Roman composer's influence prove equally compelling in the musical treatments of the text. Unlike many of Gastoldi's texts that conceal the first-person *io*, here the speech establishes a strong outward presence of the speaker (*io*/Filli) as victim of the second-person addressee (*tu*/Tirsi) through verb conjugations, pronouns, and names from the outset: "*Tirsi mio ... E tu m'abbandoni? ... mi lasci? ... e non m'aiti?*" This first-person emphasis becomes a crucial aspect of Marenzio's setting through its simultaneous projection of two separate interpretive frames: one that reports the speaker's words collectively through the combined voices of the ensemble as narrator/reader, and another that centers on one voice—the Canto—for a realization of the first person's abandonment expressed in the text.[46] Throughout Marenzio's work, the Canto shifts between these roles—ensemble versus isolation—by drifting into and out of temporal and registral alignment with the other voices. This distinction of the voice reaches its climax in the speaker's ultimate plea for mercy in a verse packed with first- and second-person signifiers—"Soccori a me, tua Filli" (help me, your Filli)—where the Canto departs from a unison *d'* with the Alto and climbs alone, to the top of its modal octave, to accentuate the deictic "a me, a me," before yielding with a downward leap to join the lower voices at the non-cadential sigh, "tua Filli" (Example 8.13).

Rossi's five-voice, G-hypomixolydian reading shows marked parallels to Marenzio's work not only in its general strategy of differentiating the upper voice for the illusion of abandonment, but also in its specific treatment of individual passages. The two openings betray this kinship both textually—in

Example.8.13 Marenzio, *Tirsi mio, caro Tirsi*, mm. 42–51

a) Marenzio (1595)

b) Rossi (1600)

Example 8.14 Marenzio's and Rossi's Settings of *Tirsi mio, caro Tirsi* (vv. 1–3)

their startling transformation of Amarilli's existential plea into the abandoned Filli's lament—and musically through their similar rhythms, upper voices, and bass motion from "caro Tirsi" through verse 2; isolation of the Canto at "Così morir"; and beginnings of verse 4 ("Almen non mi negar") with matching rhythms and P4 leaps in the Canto (Example 8.14). Yet, in place of Marenzio's approximated solo Canto opening (minimally supported by the Alto) and rhythmic/registral separation of the voice at "Così," Rossi sets the Canto apart from the united lower voices metrically, with delayed and anticipated entries for verses 1, 3, and 4. Other pronounced parallels surface later in the pieces: perhaps most notably at verse 8, where both settings begin with similar D–G motions and a d''–g' leap in an offset Canto (Example 8.15), then repeat Tirsi's name and continue in like rhythms toward arrivals on their respective finals, D and G, at "nome." Indeed, with these features, Rossi seems to position his madrigal as a direct response to the late Roman composer's work.

Despite the foreground resemblances of the two works, however, Rossi sets his treatment apart in other respects. Both pieces, for instance, establish their separate modes convincingly at the outset. But in contrast to his more restrained methods in *O Mirtillo*, here Rossi introduces much more instability than Marenzio in the early lines (Example 8.14). In place of the Roman

Example 8.15 Marenzio's and Rossi's Settings of *Tirsi mio, caro Tirsi* (v. 8)

composer's cycling around sonorities on the D final for verse 1, Rossi veers sharply away from the G final to a major sonority on E, thus transforming the final to G♯ and repeating the invasive E-major sonority six times while proclaiming the central, bitter theme of the lament: "*Tirsi, e tu ancor m'ab*ban-doni?" The question leads back to G (without a true cadence), but the jarring changes across verses 1–2, G…E…G, introduce considerable instability none-theless, and reflect in modal terms the dichotomy between loyalty and aban-donment in the friction between G in its natural and altered (sharp) forms.

In terms of structural tactics, Rossi likewise diverges from Marenzio's approach of a dynamic D-dorian framework and renders the speaker's ap-peal in a static structural state on the G-hypomixolydian fifth degree, *d″*.[47] He untethers the shackled background descent only at the speaker's allu-sion to being led to a cruel death in the final verse ("Condotta son a cruda et empia morte")—a variant line that befits the situations of both the play's Amarilli and the madrigal's Filli. In keeping with the impassioned turbu-lence of the speech, this constant background proves far from serene on the musical surface, where it is unsettled first by an interrupted middleground descent, $\hat{5}$–$\hat{2}$ (*d″–a′*), in mm. 8–24 that divides the piece into two sections beginning with cries of "Tirsi," and second, with several displacements of the suspended *d″* by an upper-neighbor *e″* tied to the foreign pitch-center C (Example 8.16). From a text-expressive standpoint, the *d″–a′* interrupted descent performs a vivid enactment of abandonment in structural terms by forsaking a complete *diapente* descent (*d″–g′*) that reaches from the literal statement "m'abbandoni" at *d″* to the speaker's self-reference, "tua Filli."

Along with their superficial parallels and differing structures, Marenzio's and Rossi's settings also respond to many details of Guarini's text in con-spicuously similar ways. A prominent example comes in their matching of the poignant repetitions of the inward deictic "a me" with similar ascents to

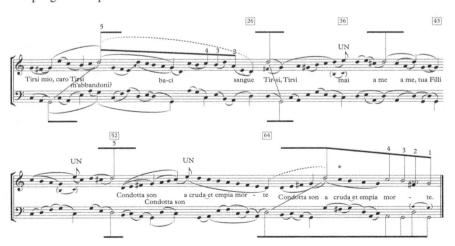

Example 8.16 Rossi, *Tirsi mio, caro Tirsi* (1600), Structural Analysis

d"—the upper modal boundary in both pieces—followed by downward leaps to close on the final for the joining of second person and self at "tua Filli." More fundamentally, both settings also, as we have seen, convey notions of abandonment by distinguishing the Canto in the polyphonic setting. Rossi, however, goes a significant step further than Marenzio in this depiction by allowing the upper voice to be truly alone—in a solo setting with instrumental accompaniment—thus forsaking entirely the communal dimension of the ensemble with which the Canto interacts in a five-voice context. The intensification of one effect (isolation), however, comes with the compromise of another: the greater interpretative potential of the multi-voice madrigal, including its casting of the Canto as "other" against the rest of the ensemble.

The strong connections between Rossi's and Marenzio's *Tirsi mio, caro Tirsi* settings add to the many ties between Marenzio's works and the broader surge of Mantuan *Pastor fido* madrigals of 1595–1600. Not only do Wert, Pallavicino, Monteverdi, and Rossi set many of the same speeches as Marenzio (sometimes with different starting or ending points) and seem to integrate aspects of Marenzio's readings into their works, but Pallavicino and Rossi also seem to have drawn their variant texts directly from Marenzio's books. In these respects, Gastoldi's settings stand out from this relatively cohesive group of first-wave composers with his more individualistic texts and less discernible references to others' works.

The traces of Marenzio's madrigals that emerge in these Mantuan settings seem to demonstrate that the Roman composer's books functioned not just as musical sources, but also as sources of text that substituted at times for the play itself. This practice further suggests that certain madrigal books—like poetic anthologies such as Varoli and Ventura—served not merely as proxies for Guarini's tragicomedy, but as sources in their own right that introduced foreign names and variant verses that became integral to the play's musical dimension, despite their inconsistencies with the dramatic work itself. Although some readers surely viewed these variants as stand-alone poems, the existence of explicit references to the tragicomedy in the book titles, dedications, captions, and written accounts (such as *L'Artusi*) of many of these madrigals, as well as implicit references to the play and its personas in the music itself, suggests that they also remained bound to the play and, thus, primarily *Pastor fido* madrigals.

In his four-voice setting of *Com'è dolce il gioire*—Corisca's seventeen-line speech from act 3, scene 6 enticing Mirtillo to take other, willing lovers (and the dialogue that generated six of Gastoldi's settings)—published in his First Book *a4*, Rossi again takes a different formal approach to a text set by Marenzio. Rossi's text reads:

1 Com'è dolce il gioire, o caro Tirsi,	How sweet it is, o dear Tirsi, to enjoy
Per gratissima donna, che t'adori	a most grateful lady who adores you
Quanto fai tu la tua	as much as you do your
Crudele ed amarissima Amarilli;	cruel and most bitter Amarilli.
5 Com'è soave cosa	What a sweet thing it is
Tanto goder quanto ami,	to enjoy what you love,
Tanto haver quanto brami;	to have what you desire,
Sentir che la tua donna	to hear that your lady
A i tuoi caldi sospiri	at your warm sighs
10 Caldamente sospiri,	warmly sighs,
E dica poi: "Ben mio,	and then says, "My love,
Quanto son, quanto miri,	all that I am, all that you look upon,
Tutto è tuo. S'io son bella,	all is yours. If I am beautiful,
A te solo son bella; a te s'adorna	to you alone am I beautiful; for you is
15 Questo viso, quest'oro e questo seno;	adorned
In questo petto mio	this face, this hair, and this bosom;
Alberghi tu, caro mio cor, non io."[48]	in this my breast
	you reside, my dear heart, not I."

On its own, the speech (introduced briefly in Chapter 4) reads as well-meaning advice gently nudging the second person to move past the cruel Amarilli and find a more compassionate, gratifying lover—an ideal *gratissima donna*. The speaker then assumes the voice of this imagined *donna* to imitate what she might say. In the play, however, this passage and its device of hypothetical speech come from the cunning Corisca and, thus, include an added layer of complexity and duplicitous intent.

With its multiple perspectives, scheming subtext (in the context of the play), and subjunctive verb tenses, the passage makes for a particularly challenging madrigal text. This might explain why the only other composer to set it to music—Scipione Cerreto, in his *L'Amarillide a tre voci* (Naples: Castantino Vitale, 1621)—placed it within a cycle-like series of five separate madrigals that treat contiguous portions of the Corisca–Mirtillo dialogue, wherein this passage is divided between the fourth (vv. 1–2) and fifth (vv. 3–17) pieces. Cerreto's setting, therefore, includes Corisca's lines leading up to the texts set by Marenzio and Rossi, wherein she attempts to lure Mirtillo into loving others (namely, her) while shifting from the past (*provasti*) and imperfect subjunctive (*provassi*), through the imperative (*provalo*), and ultimately to the future (*vedrai*), before the passage of *Com'è dolce il gioire* theorizes in the present subjective (*t'adori, ami, brami, sospiri, dica*). These earlier lines read:

Dunque, per quel ch'i' veggia,	So, from what I see,
Non *provasti* tu mai	you have never tried
Se non crudele Amor, se non sdegnoso.	love if it was not cruel and scornful.
Deh, s'una volta sola	Oh, if once only
Il *provassi* soave	you tried it sweet
E cortese e gentile!	and courteous and kind!
Provalo un poco, *provalo*; e *vedrai*	Try it a little, try it; and you will see
Com'è dolce il gioire...	how sweet it is to enjoy...

Marenzio and Rossi, then, have to convey this speculative, subjunctive, and, indeed, seductive mood from the outset of their madrigals, which begin literally mid-speech. On top of these problems of mood and verb tenses comes the challenge of Guarini's manipulations of poetic voices, perspectives, personas, and motivations. In the madrigal, what begins as a straightforward second-person address by an unnamed (and ungendered) speaker addressing Tirsi (*tu*) while contrasting the imagined *gratissima donna* with *amarissima Amarilli* ends by addressing Tirsi (*tu*) with the hypothetical (reported) voice of this ideal lady (*io*). As readers of the play would know, this ideal *donna* is, in fact, truly the speaker (Corisca) herself. Thus, the two voices—real (speaker/Corisca) and imagined (*gratissima donna*)—are, in the speaker's mind, the same. The passage as a whole, then, involves four personas—the unnamed speaker (Corisca), Tirsi/Mirtillo (*tu*), Amarilli (*lei*), and the *gratissima donna* (*lei*, then *io*)—two speaking voices (one direct, one reported), and beneath it all, the hidden prospect that the speaker is not merely imagining and impersonating this ideal *donna*, but scheming *to become* her. Rather than speaking for/as a hypothetical *donna*, the speaker is therefore secretly speaking for herself, and the two speaking "voices" of the text merge into one identity. The scenario is a tall undertaking to convey in a madrigal, but Marenzio and Rossi offer compelling solutions.

As compared to Marenzio's single-*parte* G-hypodorian setting, Rossi renders the speech in two *parti* in F-hypolydian. The texts of both settings are unique, but differ from one another only by one word in the inserted phrases of their opening lines: whereas Marenzio's setting adds "o *vago* Tirsi" to the verse in the play, Rossi's has "o *caro* Tirsi." There may be reasons for Rossi's divergence here, even if the text derived from Marenzio's work: for the phrase "o *caro* Tirsi" relates to "*caro* mio cor" in the last verse of this madrigal, as well as to the opening line of *Tirsi mio, caro Tirsi*—another madrigal that inserts "caro Tirsi" into a *Pastor fido* text. This link between the "caro Tirsi" madrigals further adds to the broader ties between Rossi's First Books *a4* and *a5*. While complicating their relationship with Guarini's tragicomedy, the insertion of "Tirsi" into both works bolsters their association with Marenzio's madrigals and any potential Amarilli–Tirsi narrative one might find therein. Moreover, the affectionate "caro" in Rossi's work makes it clearer that the speaking voice is indeed the *gratissima donna* who loves "Tirsi," and therefore may signify a textual device to overcome the complexities of the text. In Marenzio's work, "o vago Tirsi" leaves the identity of the speaker more open, including for readings associated with the composer's listeners in the Pastori della Valle Tiberina, whereby the speaker (and madrigal) playfully teases "Tirsi"—that is, potentially, Marenzio's young, music-loving patron, Virginio Orsini.

While *Tirsi mio, caro Tirsi* showed Rossi's use of a Wertian-style static structure with close adherence to the mode, his madrigals more often take after Marenzio's strategies in their dynamic dispersal of the background descent through a network of modal contexts, as seen in the latter's *O dolcezze amarissime d'amore*. In *Com'è dolce il gioire*, this modal mixture mirrors the speaker's rhetorical maneuver to steer Tirsi/Mirtillo away from "crudel ed amarissima Amarilli" and toward the idealized lover—namely (in the play), the speaker, Corisca. Duplicity, therefore, lies at the heart of Rossi's piece and offers a potential means to an end: structural fulfillment for the madrigal and love's gratification for both Tirsi (Mirtillo) and implicitly the speaker (Corisca). With its sophisticated working out of the multiple layers and readings of *Com'è dolce il gioire*, Rossi's setting is no "light" pastoral madrigal expected of the four-voice strain.

The passage displays Guarini's penchant for devices such as anaphora and parallelism with its recurrences of "Com'è," "Tanto...quanto," "caldi/caldamente sospiri," "questo," and "a te," as well as his interweaving of multiple characters and voices, including the apparent change of perspective at verse 11. Both Rossi and Marenzio similarly mark the shift in speaker with a full-voice close at "E dica poi," followed by antiphonal duo/trio statements of the imagined lover's first words: "Ben mio." The remaining verses (vv. 11–17), all in the imagined voice of the *donna*, bring contrasts in both works between high/low subgroups and the full ensemble in homophonic declamation (with offset voices in Rossi's setting) leading to polyphonic drives to the final cadence. While both renderings of the reported speech show subtle resemblances in rhythmic treatment and melodic shape at corresponding points in the text, Rossi's imitative delivery of the final verse by itself lacks the technical virtuosity and rhetorical force of Marenzio's setting of the closing couplet together, which upholds the enjambment while combining the pronominal deictics ("mio...mio...io") vertically and linearly in *contrapposto*.

Marenzio likewise seems to designate the female perspective(s) of the speech at the outset by assigning verses 1–4 to a trio of upper voices (Example 8.17a). Rossi makes no such distinction of gender, but presents the text in nearly identical rhythms to Marenzio's work, only in stricter homophony and devoid of pictorial melismas at "gioire" (Example 8.17b). Instead, Rossi focuses his opening more on a deeper-level portrayal of the speaker's true, concealed character. As Examples 8.17b and 8.18 show, his reading establishes its F-hypolydian identity forthrightly in the initial phrase, "Com'è dolce il gioire" (mm. 1–3), with an overarching motion F–C and an emphasis on F, C, and A as melodic boundaries. The completion of the verse ("o caro Tirsi"), however, brings an unsettling change with the pitch alterations F♯ and E♭ and a phrygian close on D-*mi*. Verse 2 (mm. 6–8) returns to F-hypolydian parameters for a subsidiary ("vii^{o6}–I"-type) cadence on the C cofinal, yet this marks the last clear sign of the fundamental mode until ten verses later, in the middle of the *seconda parte* (m. 55), where the madrigal cadences at last on the F final. What comes between these points (mm. 9–51) proves a remarkably distinct and protracted shift of modal parameters from the C-octave and F-hypolydian mode to the D-octave of G-hypodorian. As the examples illustrate, this G-hypodorian occupation follows immediately on the arrival of background $\hat{5}$ at the apex of a prefatory *f'–c''* ascent (vv. 1–2), and instates the potent upper-neighbor *d''* that lays the contextual groundwork for background $\hat{4}$, *b♭*, in the *seconda parte*.

Example 8.17 Marenzio's and Rossi's Settings of *Com'è dolce il gioire*, vv. 1–4

a) Detailed Reduction.

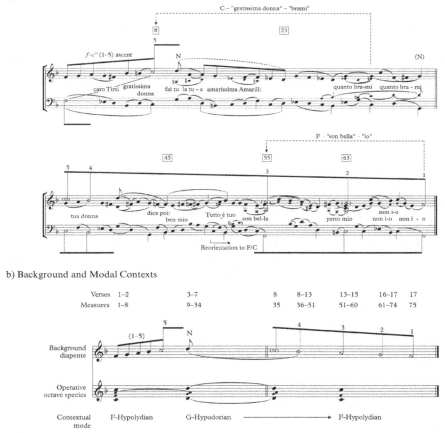

Example 8.18 Rossi, *Com'è dolce il gioire*, Structural Analysis

Rossi ties this D-octave shift precisely to the moment in the text when the speaker turns her attention from the *gratissima donna* in vv. 1–2, to her rival, Amarilli, in vv. 3–4, thus associating the interference of *d″* and the G-hypodorian mode with Amarilli's role in obstructing love's fulfillment and the speaker's will. Rossi cements this analogy between rival mode and antagonistic persona (Amarilli) through musical–textual deixis in the semantically loaded fragment "Quanto fai *tu* la *tua* [Amarilli]" (As *you* do *your* [Amarilli]), where a leap to *d″* at the pronoun "tu" (Tirsi/Mirtillo) leads directly to a foreign D cadence at the awkward line-ending "tua" (your), referring to Amarilli (Example 8.17b). The concise but assertive gesture conveys at once the second person's captivation by bitter Amarilli and her frustrating effects for both the speaker and modal order.

The Basso reinforces the new pitch center, D—and smooths over the ungainly line break—by maintaining the pitch for four uninterrupted semibreves (mm. 11–14), while the upper voices (and later the Basso) present "Crudel et amarissima Amarilli" in dissonance-filled imitation (mm. 12–19). This intense introduction of Amarilli's name ends in paired semibreves with an F sonority that reproduces the voicing of the madrigal's opening. Though prominent, the non-cadential nature of this arrival ($B\flat^6$–F) and its position between strong D cadences (mm. 11 and 23) only emphasize the diminished status of the F final in this D-octave context. For in this instance, F functions merely as an intermediate step in an expanded, intrusive *a'–d' diapente* descent through *e♭* that, in turn, transfers the upper-neighbor *d"* to the octave below (mm. 9–24; see Example 8.18a).

The change of character at "crudel ed amarissima" in terms of mode, texture, rhythm, and dissonance frames Amarilli as cruel other: the adversary of love's fulfillment and an obstacle to the speaker's aims. Rossi's reading, however, goes beyond straightforward depiction to reinforce the monologue's dual intentions in the play. For the F-hypolydian integrity that promises order and gratification, and that is frustrated by Amarilli's D modal octave, is tied not merely to the idea of requited love (the *gratissima donna*), but also to the underlying voice of the speech as a whole—namely, that of the unnamed narrator, or Corisca in the play—the implications of which play out in the *seconda parte*.

Despite the prominence of D in lines 3–5 as a sonority (sounding through over half of mm. 11–24) and as cadential goal (as both *re* and *mi*), its broader role is not as controlling modal final, but to prepare—along with two *cadenze fuggite* to B♭ (mm. 28–29)—for the idiosyncratic close of the *prima parte* on G. Rossi's ending with the *ami–brami* couplet of verses 6–7 proves conventional in formal–textual terms. Yet its termination on G proves doubly anomalous for cadencing on the modal $\hat{2}$ instead of the expected cofinal (C), and for being preceded by this very cadence on C—a fourth above the closing pitch (G)—rather than on the customary fifth above, D. This penultimate C cadence, moreover, proves inconsistent with the local G-hypodorian context, but accords instead with the fundamental (but displaced) F-hypolydian framework. The ending, therefore, represents a multi-layered confusion of modal expectations, with the normative C cadence framed as an out-of-place penultimate arrival for an atypical (but locally consistent) close on G, the second degree. This apparently ill-timed C cadence, however, proves a fitting complement to its position in the text. For, with its attachment to "brami" (Tirsi/Mirtillo's "desire"), the cadence arouses the notion of longing not only structurally—as an allusion to the past stability of the F-hypolydian mode—but also referentially, by pointing literally to the ideal beloved ("gratissima donna") in verse 2, where the one earlier C cadence brought forth the background *c"* (see Example 8.18a).

Rossi's division of the text between verses 7 and 8 is also surprising in its grammatical awkwardness, for verse 8 ("Sentir che la tua donna") contains the last of three verbs ("Sentir," to hear) dependent on the clause ("Com'è soave cosa" (v. 5). As a result, the *seconda parte* begins peculiarly in mid-thought ("To hear that your lady..."). Rossi appears to have been cognizant of this breach—thus, showing a concern for rhyme (*ami/brami*) over sense in his division of the text—for he reflects the continuing syntactical unit from the previous *parte* in the modal–structural disposition of the new opening: after a brief but futile nod to the basic mode with the sonorities C–F, the *seconda parte* resumes the G-hypodorian context from the *prima parte* while introducing the background $\hat{4}$, $b\flat$. Again, Rossi ties the structural articulation to a reference to the ideal lover, "la tua *donna*," but unlike the immediate displacement of background c'' by d'' in the *prima parte*, the madrigal maintains $b\flat$ through vv. 8–13 with consistent G-hypodorian parameters, including cadences to B♭, D-*mi*, and G (see Example 8.18). The return of the F-hypolydian mode after ten verses (over forty semibreves) of intrusion comes not with the start of the *gratissima donna*'s speech in verse 11 (despite another misleading F–C gesture there), but with her deictic and alliterative proclamation, "Tutto è tuo" (all is yours), where the gesture C–F counters a rushed f♯^{o6}–G cadence (shown in Example 8.18a). While the phrase ends with a modest B♭ cadence and final iteration of background $\hat{4}$ ("tuo"), the parallel "son bella" (I am beautiful) clauses that follow make the modal restoration complete with a simple cadence to C ("If I am beautiful"), then a forceful one to F ("to you alone I am beautiful")—the first of only two cadences on the final in the entire piece. This F arrival establishes the background $\hat{3}$, A, for now an octave below its formal register.

This decisive moment in Rossi's reading has implications beyond modal integrity. By reconciling the foreground features (F centricity) with the essential mode of the speech as a whole (F-hypolydian) precisely at the words "[io] son bella" (I am beautiful), the madrigal intimates the irony that readers of the play would recognize: that the voice of the *gratissima donna*—the *io* of "son bella"—and that of the speaker (Corisca) are one and the same. Corisca, in other words, is the ideal lover who could supplant the "crudel et amarissima Amarilli" and satisfy Tirsi/Mirtillo's desires, just as the F-hypolydian mode, with its assertive "son bella" F cadence, frees the madrigal from the G-hypodorian grip.

From this point forward (mm. 55–75), the madrigal buttresses the lady's speech with cadences that reflect the newly instated stability and that provide firm support to the remaining background steps: F, D (*a'*); C, C (*g'*); and F (*f'*). The articulations of these degrees continue the pattern of anchoring the large-scale framework with literal references to the ideal lover—"gratissima donna che t'a*dori*" (*c''*), "*donna*" (*b♭'*), "son bel*la*" (*a'*), "pet*to mio*" (*g'*), "non *io*" (*f'*)—thus integrating the notion of the *gratissima donna* with the speaker's (reported) F-hypolydian voice at the most fundamental level (see Example 8.18a). The final cadence at "io" further conveys this merging of identities—Corisca and the idealized beloved—within the F-final mode by alluding to the only other F cadence from "son bella" (m. 55) with identical voicing and a similar pre-cadential elaboration. The cadential pairing bridges the first-person references, "son bella" and "io," and their F cadential gestures to convey both the fulfillment that could come from a compassionate lover, and that this *donna* can be found in the (F-hypolydian-voiced) speaker herself.

Rossi's reading of the text is remarkable in its eloquent interweaving of identities, mode, perspectives, and foreground details in both music and text for the subtle insinuation of an antagonistic other (Amarilli) vanquished by a sympathetic beloved, and the association of this beloved with the underlying Self—the speaking *io*, or specifically Corisca, for readers who recognize her speech. The irony of this association, in turn, hinges on the text's role in the play not as friendly advice, as it reads up front, but part of Corisca's machinations to depose Amarilli (even if by death) and win Mirtillo for herself. While foregoing the motivic references, idiosyncratic cadences, and avant-garde dissonances found in many *Pastor fido* settings of Marenzio, Pallavicino, and Monteverdi, Rossi looks instead to the referential and semantic potentials of pitch-center, mode, and voicing, and to musical–textual deixis to illuminate the intricate alignments of love, rejection, rivalry, and four personas. The peculiar division of the piece in two *parti*, moreover, intensifies the modal conflict and its evocation of Amarilli's bitterness by stretching the invasive mode unconventionally across separate *parti*, hence, in turn, making the final resolution with the imagined lover's speech all the more gratifying.

A challenge of a different sort posed itself to Rossi in confronting *Ah, dolente partita*—Mirtillo's anguished farewell to Amarilli from act 3, scene 3—his setting of which also appeared in the First Book *a4*. The work shows a somewhat bolder side of the composer known for his conservativism,[49] while still relying on characteristic strategies of his other *Pastor fido* madrigals. The exceptional measures in the work may be motivated by the text, with its emotional intensity in a compact form of only eight verses, but they might also reflect Rossi's consciousness of the imposing legacy of earlier treatments of the text: some thirteen works by 1600—including by notable figures such as Marenzio, Wert, and Monteverdi—and thirty-seven by 1643.

Rossi's choice of the doleful and anomalous E-phrygian mode for the lament is unique among contemporary settings, but he treats the mode structurally in the conventionally idiosyncratic way: with a fundamental descent through the modal *diatessaron*, $\hat{8}$–$\hat{5}$ (E–B), rather than the *diapente*, beginning with a prolonged expansion of the final (e′) and finishing with a phrygian quasi-cadence (a–E) for the terminal step, $\hat{6}$–$\hat{5}$ (C–B), as shown in Example 8.19.[50] Rossi tailors this framework into a multi-dimensional portrayal of the central themes of pain (*dolente*) and parting (*partire*) that appear together in the opening cry, "Ah, dolente partita." In contrast to others' openings—Wert in five-part *contrapposto*, Marenzio with homophony and occasional offset voices, and Monteverdi with a high-voice duet leading to *contrapposto* for verses 1–3—Rossi begins with a unified E-minor

declamation of "Ah" that frays into a "parting" of the voices for a slow contrapuntal delivery of lines 1–2 (Example 8.20). The first verse leads from a
mode-affirming context of sustained E-minor and C sonorities, with a stepwise *b'–e'* descent in the Canto and continued support of background *e'*, to
an evasive g–D ending that undermines the E-phrygian character with ♭$\hat{5}$
(B♭) and ♯$\hat{2}$ (F♯). This sudden corruption of the modal *diapente* comes specifically at the contrapuntal alignment of "dolente" and "partita" (mm. 8–9)—
truly a "painful parting" in modal terms. The next verse, "Ah, fin de la mia
vita" (Ah, end of my life), quickly restores the phrygian identity, including
an ending with a phrygian quasi-cadence (a–E) to complement the notion of
death ("fin de la mia vita"). Together, these two verses (mm. 1–15) carry out
a general motion out of and back to an E-phrygian sphere, which, in turn,
creates a structural/pictorial enactment of *partire* through lower-neighbor
motion around the final, E–D–E, at the middleground level (Example 8.19).
Rossi deploys this structural *partire* gesture three times in verses 1–5—one
for each appearance of *partire* in the text ("partita," "parto," and "partire")—thus inscribing the notion of "parting" motivically in the madrigal's
opening expansion of *e'* (mm. 1–24).

   Adding to the emphasis of these "parting" figures is the constraint of the
Canto from its upper octave boundary (*e''*)—a restriction that continues
until the end of the madrigal—while instead asserting *d''* at the peak of its
ambitus. The subsidiary D "departures," therefore, eclipse the more fundamental final (*e'*) in terms of registral salience and remain the climaxes of the
piece until the final couplet. This overshadowing can be seen, for example,
in mm. 8–9, where the Alto's *d'* lower neighbor at "do-*lente*" is transferred to
the upper octave in the Canto with a m6 leap, *f♯'–d''*, at the second cry, "Ah"

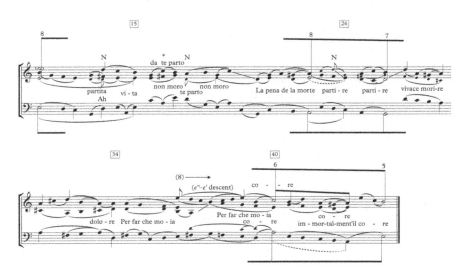

Example 8.19 Rossi, *Ah, dolente partita*, Structural Analysis

Example 8.20 Rossi, *Ah, dolente partita*, mm. 1–18

(Example 8.20). This destabilizing *d″* becomes even more pronounced when the Alto and Basso shift to E underneath it (m. 10), turning this structural neighbor tone into a pointed surface dissonance and forcing it downward through *c″* to *b′*. At the last occurrence of "partire" in verse 5, the Canto reaches *d″* again, now in a cadential motion to C. Rather than resolving the pitch upward, *d″–e″*, to fulfill its E-octave and highlight the background pitch, *e″*, the Canto instead leaps away, *d″–g′*, leaving the pre-cadential pitch hanging as a frustrated structural dissonance (see Example 8.19). The imbalance at the foreground level between structural pitch (E) and its more salient diversion (D) reflects the severity of *partire* in the text, particularly in the contexts of the play, where Mirtillo faces Amarilli's departure after having just suffered her scolding and rejection. But the temporary and ancillary nature of this dissonant "parting" pitch at the deeper level perhaps insinuates that this *partire*, too, will pass—as indeed it does for the lovers in the play.

It is the complementary notion of pain rather than parting, however, that prompts Rossi's unusual boldness. For precisely at "dolente"—with sustained E (m. 2) and C (m. 6) sonorities—the Tenore leaps a P4 to form a seventh against the Canto, whose own "resolution" down a step yields another dissonance (P4) with the Basso (Example 8.20). Soon after, at the question "Da te parto e non moro?" in verse 3 (mm. 16–17), another P4 leap—this time in the Canto, $g'-c''$—stresses the outward gesture to the second person, "Da *te*"—the source of the speaker's suffering—as an unprepared dissonance against the Alto's $f\sharp'$ (d5) and Tenore's $b-a$ (m9–m10), marked by asterisks in Examples 8.19 and 8.20. The phrase is rich in deixis and import with its merging of second-person reference ("te"), first-person verbs ("parto" and "moro"), and the notions of parting and death. The resulting discord and resolution, thus, combine these key words, "te parto" (Canto) and "e non moro" (Tenore and Alto), in the motion $f\sharp^{o6}$–e—that is, an altered phrygian quasi-cadence, the very same formation with which Marenzio renders Mirtillo's expression of death-like pain at the end of *Cruda Amarilli*. Rossi's gesture is fleeting, yet—like the incidental clashes in Monteverdi's brisk yet scandalous setting of "E più fugace" in *Cruda Amarilli*—it is offensive none-theless by contrapuntal standards. Altogether, with their basis in the text, these dissonant transgressions in verses 1–3 offer a rare glimpse of Rossi as *seconda pratica* adherent not only in his commitment to the primacy of the text, as seen in all three of these *Pastor fido* madrigals, but also in his will-ingness to breach theoretical doctrine for affective ends in a manner similar to Monteverdi's offensive means.

The initial prolongation of e' extends to verse 5, "E sento nel partire" (And I feel in parting), where juxtaposed statements of the line show the seventh degree, d', change in status from middleground diversion (mm. 25–26)—a motivic enactment of *partire, e'–d'–e'*—to a true "partire" at the background level as e' ($\hat{8}$) gives way to d' ($\hat{7}$; mm. 27–28). The new structural pitch effects a strong cadential shift toward G and D, with the latter being the only ca-dence with 5–1 bass in the entire piece.[51] Rossi then devotes the final verse to the expansion of modal $\hat{6}$, C, where the appearance of e'' as a cover tone, as expected in the phrygian framework, leads to the long-awaited fruition of the Canto's full E-octave range. The terminal $\hat{2}-\hat{1}$ ($c''-b'$) corresponds, as anticipated, with a forceful phrygian quasi-cadence, which simulates the only other cadence on the final in the piece: the fleeting phrygian quasi-ca-dence from the end of verse 2 (mm. 14–15; compare Examples 8.20 and 8.21). This last-minute allusion recalls the notion of death from "fin de la mia vita" at the closing image of an endlessly dying heart ("moia immortalmente il core") to unify the work through distant yet parallel "endings" on the E final.

Although drawing on isolated tactics of Marenzio's *Cruda Amarilli*, Rossi's madrigal may not seem to share many similarities with the Roman composer's setting of *Ah, dolente partita*—save for their identical rhyth-mic treatments of "E sento nel partire," which also pertains to Wert's and Monteverdi's settings and likely reflects the rhythms of the text more than compositional influence. Marenzio's piece, after all, uses a different mode (A-hypodorian), the antiquated *misura di breve* (cut-C), and no outlandish dissonances. But the two works do share an E modal octave and intrinsic similarities in large-scale design, including cadence plan, formal layout, and an affective use of modal structure. Because the E-phrygian background

Example 8.21 Rossi, *Ah, dolente partita*, mm. 42–46

(E–B) overlaps with the first four steps ($\hat{5}$–$\hat{2}$) of the A-hypodorian (or hy-poaeolian) framework, the two modes, as we have seen, tend to show prom-inent and misleading similarities in foreground and cadential behavior, particularly through the beginning portions of works. Marenzio's *Ah, do-lente partita*, for instance, begins—like Rossi's work—with an alternation between background *e″* ($\hat{5}$) and lower-neighbor *d″* as a structural rendering of "partita" in verses 1–2. Following similar twofold statements of verse 5, both composers likewise heed the rhetorical continuity of verses 6–7 by marking the end of verse 6 with a weak 2–1 cadence to the modal $\hat{4}$, and the end of verse 7 with a forceful 5–1 close on the modal $\hat{7}$. The inconclusiveness of these arrivals with respect to the underlying mode, in turn, compels both madrigals forward to the final verse, where E, A, and D sonorities figure prominently before the terminal close. Whether or not they are indications of direct influence, these examples elucidate the two composers' similar ap-proaches to evoking *partire* in structural terms, and to paving the way for the conclusion of the text cadentially and rhetorically, despite the basic dif-ferences in the pieces.

Other striking resemblances arise in comparing Rossi's madrigal with Monteverdi's *Ah, dolente partita* from his Fourth Book (1603)—a work that, like Marenzio's setting, makes prominent and affective use of the E modal octave in an A-hypodorian setting (see Chapter 6). These parallels are particularly evident in the madrigals' openings, where both composers depict the pain of parting ("dolente partita") with upper voices that diverge from one another while creating dissonances against the pitch E (see Ex-amples 6.1 and 8.20). In Rossi's setting, however, the sustained E sounds in both the Alto and Basso in a four-voice opening, as opposed to the poign-ant upper-voice duet and unison *e″* that begins Monteverdi's work. In fact, the nearly parallel descents E–C in the Alto and Basso through verse 1 of

Rossi's work correspond closely to the rhythmic and melodic character of Monteverdi's Quinto in mm. 1–5, only there the motion descends *toward* the A final, $\hat{5}$–$\hat{4}$–$\hat{3}$, and in Rossi's E-phrygian setting, it leads away, $\hat{8}$–$\hat{7}$–$\hat{6}$, while the Canto itself unfolds a full descending line through the modal *diapente* from $\hat{5}$ (*b′*) to $\hat{1}$ (*e′*) across the opening verse.

As a whole, Rossi's *Pastor fido* settings represent probing studies of Guarini's texts in which aspects of the verse ranging from localized import and personal deictics to overarching themes and characters' natures come to light at all levels of the musical fabric. The works are also notable for the multiple dimensions in which they operate intertextually, not only through their (often obscured) ties to the play and referential use of motives, cadences, and voicing, but also through their connections to Marenzio's (and in some cases, Monteverdi's) settings both textually and musically. This combination of external referentiality, internal self-sufficiency, and the sheer originality of Rossi's readings despite their Marenzian allusions allows for a vast range of interpretative possibilities that is further enhanced by the altered texts and character names, which loosen the direct associations with the play. The fact that Rossi achieves such far-reaching expressive ends while remaining much more guarded in his techniques than Marenzio and his Mantuan colleagues, Monteverdi and Pallavicino, attests to his skill and resourcefulness as a composer and reader.

The settings also reveal a notable technical feature of Rossi's madrigals at large, beyond their integrative and expressive use of mode and modal mixture, that has largely eluded scholars: their contrapuntal conception. This fundamentally polyphonic approach is especially apparent in the predominance of cadences with 2–1 bass motion ("vii^{o6}–I" in tonal terms) and in the distribution of the structural upper voice between various parts, similar to Monteverdi's tactic in his *Anima mia, perdona* (Chapter 6). This linearity pertains more to Rossi's madrigals for four voices than to those for five, which is perhaps not surprising, given the more limited voice leading options in a four-part context. The five-voice *Pastor fido* settings, however, also allow for optional solo performance with chittarone accompaniment, with the latter notated in tablature, which might further account for their somewhat greater vertical orientation. Indeed, with the Canto's textual and structural integrity and its more frequent diminutions and rhythmic displacement as compared to the lower voices, the five-voice settings—though still contrapuntal in nature—give indications of having been devised expressly for use in both polyphonic and monodic settings. This quality distinguishes all six works with soloistic versions—all but one of them settings of Guarini's *Pastor fido* and *Rime*—from the exclusively five-voice pieces in Rossi's First Book *a5*, which have migrating structural upper voices, incomplete texts in the Canto, and overlapping and equal upper parts.

At the same time, however, whereas Einstein stresses how well these variable solo/*a5* pieces capture "the style of the genuine monody," these monodies, though effective on contrapuntal and structural grounds, lack much of the stylistic and rhythmic distinction between the voice and instrumental part that characterizes solo madrigals of the following years, including those of Luzzaschi (1601), Caccini (1601), and others, particularly as regards vocal diminutions, where Rossi's can only be seen as allowing "room" for improvised embellishments.[52] Moreover, the solo versions of Rossi's five-voice *Pastor fido* settings also come with an interpretative sacrifice. For a key aspect of the affective force and intellectual impetus of his *Tirsi mio, caro Tirsi*, we have seen, lies in the alienation of the Canto from the rest of the ensemble—an effect that relies on an understanding that the madrigalian voice parts are inherently unified, a single "voice," whereby the Canto's separation (combined with verbal expressions of abandonment) proves a departure from the norm, highlighting that voice as an anomaly and an outcast. Although the solo version takes a step forward in terms of realism—a single singer conveys Filli/Amarilli's words and emotions—it loses the discursive interplay between the voices and the interpretative possibilities thereof.

The endorsement in Rossi's 1600 volume of a soloistic realization of multi-voice madrigals might also shed light on an implicit and even routine facet of madrigal performance in Mantua (and perhaps elsewhere) at the time. If this were the case, Rossi's methods would not have been experimental at all in terms of local practice, although putting them in print was indeed a novel step. Additionally, with its focus on Guarini texts and grouping of the optional solo/*concertato* pieces together after the strictly *a5* works, Rossi's First Book *a5* prefigures two important features of another pioneering forthcoming volume from Mantua: Monteverdi's Fifth Book of 1605, where Guarini settings predominate and the contents are divided between those with optional accompaniment and those that require it. Unlike Rossi's solo/*a5* madrigals that accommodate one medium or the other, the *a5* works with requisite accompaniment in Monteverdi's Fifth Book combine the versatility of soloistic option with the broader interpretative scope of the multi-voice madrigal.

Don Harràn has speculated that, "given the Mantuan venue of at least one of the performances [of *Il pastor fido*]...there is a reasonable possibility that one or more of Rossi's settings were written for it."[53] He then cites the madrigals of Marenzio, Giovanelli, and Gastoldi as evidence that other composers published music intended for stagings of the play in conventional madrigal books. We know well by now, however, that Gastoldi's *Gioco della cieca*—potentially along with his settings of the act-two chorus—is the only published work from this period with attested and, indeed, probable ties to the stage. Despite being impassioned settings of dramatic speeches that endorse performance soloistically, Rossi's *Pastor fido* settings give no indication of having played any theatrical or explicitly dramatic role. As we have seen, Harràn's presumption fits into a broader pattern of typecasting *Pastor fido* madrigals—particularly from this first phase of the tradition—as "dramatic" music (in the literal, mimetic sense) or more broadly theatrical (i.e., having some ties to the stage) based on factors such as text, texture, and the distinction of individual voices. As this study has shown, while the Italian madrigal took *Il pastor fido* out of the theater, the play rarely seems to have pulled the madrigal onstage. Works such as Gastoldi's *Gioco della cieca*, in other words, are isolated exceptions, while Gabriele Fattorini's twelve-*parte* rendering of the same scene in *La cieca* (1598)—with five voices reporting the speech of four characters in the manner of a collective (polyphonic) narration—proves the norm.

The Expectations of a "Pastor fido" Madrigal Reading and the Example of Artusi's Failure

We have seen how this first significant wave of Mantuan *Pastor fido* settings was split into two stages, the first distinguished by the frustrated preparations of the play of 1591–93 and Wert's madrigals of 1595, and the second, by the sumptuous productions of 1598 and 1600 and the madrigals of Gastoldi, Pallavicino, Rossi, and Monteverdi of the late 1590s and early 1600s. Despite the simultaneous interests at the Gonzaga court in both the theatrical and musical sides of the play, however, there is no documented evidence, including indications in the music itself, that any but one of these works had ties to the stage. As we saw in Chapter 2, for example, sources such as Grillo's *Breve trattato* and Gastoldi's Fourth Book tell us that the November 1598 performance for Queen Margherita of Spain involved onstage music for three specifically choral parts of the play: the *intermedi*, the *Gioco della cieca*, and (almost certainly) the end-of-act choruses. *Pastor fido* madrigals, on the other hand, seem to have occupied an entirely separate sphere in terms of performance, poetic genre, and interpretative reading, even if the readership itself overlapped to a certain extent between theatrical and madrigalian contexts.

One of the rare accounts of an off-stage madrigalian reading to survive— Artusi's discourse of 1600—reveals, as we have seen, that Monteverdi's madrigals were performed and repeated at a household gathering of musical connoisseurs in Ferrara. The event was separate from other events related to the play and to the Queen's nuptials, but took place only days before the Queen and her entourage witnessed the *Pastor fido* production in Mantua on 28 November 1598. Artusi notes specifically that these madrigals were new ("certi Madrigali nuovi") and identifies one of them not only by its text (*O Mirtillo*), but also exceptionally by its author (though misspelled) and source: "del Guerino [*sic*] tolte nel *Pastor fido*."

Artusi's treatise is, of course, tinged by its agenda of disparaging modern music for its alluring "novità."[54] Yet the scene that it sets in late 1598 Ferrara gives telling insight into the practice of performing *Pastor fido* madrigals at the time that has not been fully recognized in the madrigal literature. The audience, to begin, was aristocratic, musically knowledgeable, and evidently—based on Artusi's citation of *O Mirtillo*—aware of the origins of the texts as well as the music. This latter scenario already differs from that of *Pastor fido* madrigals conveyed in print, where textual source and authorship are seldom identified, and where the associations with Guarini's play are sometimes additionally obscured by variant texts. Second, the fact that all of the madrigals at the Ferrarese performance were uniformly re-peated seems to have stemmed not from listeners' enthusiasm, but from an expectation of close listening—from an interest in appreciating the pieces more fully through additional hearings. Finally, Artusi's account makes no reference to acting or theatrical elements, or to soloistic performance, but only to evocative movements and facial expressions by the singers ("cantanti").

The scene as a whole gives the impression of a musically enhanced poetic reading—an intimate sharing of new work that afforded equal attention to text and music, as well as time through repeated hearings for careful study and private reflection. Such expectations for considering the pieces "prop-erly"—that is, thoroughly—in fact, lie at the heart of the Monteverdi–Artusi debate: whereas Artusi's remarks show rigorous scrutiny of the music on theoretical terms, his neglect of the text leads, in Monteverdi's view, to a fun-damental misunderstanding of the works as a whole. Artusi, in other words, fails in his obligation as listener/reader—an obligation that the performance format facilitated, and that the composer (via his brother) mandates in his assertion that a full understanding of the music requires consideration "not merely of the portions or passages of the composition [i.e., devoid of text], but of its whole" ("cioè intorno non alle particelle o passaggi della cantilena solamente ma allo suo tutto").[55] As the controversy reveals, the *Pastor fido* madrigal was a musical–textual experience driven primarily by the delivery of the characters' words (*oratione*). In the specific contexts of late 1598 Fer-rara, meanwhile, the performance of these emotionally charged speeches might have served not merely as a stimulating musical–literary diversion, but also as a pastoral escape from the official matters of the Queen's visit and the concurrent devolution of the Este duchy.

As the analyses have shown, with their thorough integration of text and music in complex and subtle, immediate and far-reaching ways, the *Pastor fido* settings of Pallavicino, Gastoldi, and Rossi, too, demand the repeated hearings and close consideration of the "whole" composition that the Monteverdis expected and the Ferrarese performance allowed. As musically inscribed studies of Guarini's verse, the works are illuminating from histor-ical and analytical standpoints today, and they likely played a similar role in their own time by providing perceptive, individual, through-provoking, and sometimes playful poetic readings for performance, contemplation, and dis-cussion for all varieties of readerships, from Goretti's gathering in Ferrara and Vincenzo Gonzaga's court in Mantua to recreational musicians and solitary readers.

The major developments to the madrigal witnessed in this first wave of Mantuan *Pastor fido* settings continue through the end of Vincenzo

Gonzaga's reign in 1612, but with a shift of focus after 1605 toward Guarini's lyric verse, along with the poetry of Marini, Rinuccini, Chiabrera, Tasso, and others. For, indeed, the thrust of the *Pastor fido* madrigal as a whole turns in the early 1600s from the rapid localized expansion in Mantua and Rome to an array of smaller, often fleeting, outcroppings throughout Italy and north of the Alps in the decades that followed. These later settings incorporate many of the forward-looking tactics deployed in the early settings by Mantuan composers, such as naturalistic declamation to sustained sonorities, illicit text-driven dissonances, *concertato* medium, solo song, extreme contrasts in mode for structural–expressive ends, large-scale coherence and referentiality, and distinctions of poetic voice and perspective, not to mention the practice introduced by Marenzio and Wert of grouping numerous *Pastor fido* settings together in a single volume and connecting them with each other and to other composers' settings through textual and musical allusions. All of these techniques that flourished within the early *Pastor fido* madrigal, in fact, became integral features of the settings from the play that proliferated in the decades that followed, and, in turn, informed the conceptual and compositional frameworks of new, emerging genres and traditions of the seventeenth century.

Notes

1 See Chapter 2, note 177.
2 See the letter of Alessandro Guarini to Vincenzo Gonzaga in the Archivio di Stato (Archivio Gonzaga), busta 2677, c.349 (11 June 1599) and the letters cited in Susan Parisi, *Ducal Patronage*, 205, note 141.
3 This tally includes the 1597 *Fiori del giardino* Kaufmann collection in which Monteverdi's *Ah, dolente partita* first appeared. Not included, however, are two early settings of divergent texts associated with the play: Monteverdi's 1592 setting of a variant reading of *O primavera* (discussed in Chapter 6) and the 1588 setting of *Non sospirar, cor mio, non sospirare* by Annibale Coma, who served as organist at the Mantua Cathedral from 1570 until at least 1580, but remained active in some capacity at the Gonzaga court through 1588. Coma's setting appeared in his Second Book for four voices (Venice: Vincenti, 1588). Lucrezio Ruffolo, a composer for the Guastalla branch of the Gonzaga family, also produced five *Pastor fido* settings in his First and Third Books of five-voice madrigals (1598 and 1612), dedicated respectively to the Count (later Duke) of Guastalla, Ferrante Gonzaga, and his son, Cesare II Gonzaga.
4 Yet, see Chapter 4 on the possibility that Marenzio's settings date from as early as the late 1580s based on their textual variants.
5 Pallavicino's Sixth Book appeared in two reprints after the 1600 princeps—by Gardano (Venice) in 1606, and by Phalèse (Antwerp) in 1612. For a modern edition, see Benedetto Pallavicino, *Opera omnia*, ed. Peter Flanders, 7 vols. (Münster: American Institute of Musicology, 1983), III.
6 For the madrigal text and translation, see Chapter 5, p. 223 above
7 On Artusi's rebuttal against the mixing of distinct genera, and specifically against Vicentino's teachings and the "modern" uses thereof, see *L'Artusi*, esp. fols. 17r–21r and 37r–38v.
8 Tomlinson, *Monteverdi and the End of the Renaissance*, 97.

9 For a more complete discussion of the piece and the role of this passage therein, see Seth Coluzzi, "Speaking In (and Out of) Mode: Structure and Rhetoric in Marenzio's *O Mirtillo, Mirtillo anima mia* (1595)," *Music Theory Spectrum* 37 (2015): 253–74, esp. 265–66 and Chapter 7 above.

10 Einstein, *The Italian Madrigal*, 851–52 and James Chater, "'Cruda Amarilli': A Cross-Section," 231–34.

11 Tomlinson, *Monteverdi and the End of the Renaissance*, 117.

12 See the original Italian edition of Fabbri, *Monteverdi* (Turin: EDT/Musica, 1985), 86.

13 Massimo Ossi concludes: "For although Monteverdi clearly looks to Marenzio, and therefore to a 'non-Mantuan' model, from its opening measures Pallavicino's madrigal solidly proclaims his succession to Wert" ("Monteverdi, Marenzio, and Battista Guarini's 'Cruda Amarilli'," 321). Denis Arnold explores the prominence of Wert's declamative techniques in the music of Pallavicino, Monteverdi, and others in "'Seconda Pratica': A Background to Monteverdi's Madrigals," *Music and Letters* 38 (1957): 341–52, while Fenlon summarizes that "it is generally accepted that they [Pallavicino's last three madrigal books] were heavily influenced by Wert's late madrigals, and that they in turn played a (perhaps crucial) role in impressing Wert's later style upon the early works of Monteverdi" (*Music and Patronage*, 143).

14 Arnold, "Seconda Pratica," 350–51.

15 Artusi, *L'Artusi*, fol. 3r; G.C. Monteverdi, *Dichiaratione*.

16 "Vogliono confondere tutte le cose, che perche sono per regolarle con regole, che siano fondate sopra il vero" (*L'Artusi*, fols. 41r–v). See also Palisca's discussion of this infraction in "The Artusi–Monteverdi Controversy," 72–73.

17 For Zarlino's discussion of consecutive imperfect consonances of the same type, see *Istitutioni harmoniche*, Book 3, Chapter 29; on false relations, see Book 3, Chapter 30. False relations, of course, also fall under Artusi's prohibition of the juxtaposition of distinct *genera*.

18 In his *Conclusioni nel suono dell'organo* (Bologna: Rossi, 1609), however, Adriano Banchieri lists Pallavicino alongside Gesualdo, Fontanelli, Cavalieri, and "altri moderni" as a forebear of Monteverdi in the imitation of the text and "moderno componere" (60).

19 Arnold, "Seconda Pratica," 344.

20 Artusi allegedly knew Pallavicino's music, given his reference to it elsewhere. Even if the Sixth Book appeared too late for Artusi to evaluate in his treatise of 1600—Pallavicino's dedication is dated March of that year, eight months before that of *L'Artusi*—the theorist could have cited it in later writings of the debate. On the theorist's implicit condoning of Marenzio's more extensive modal mixture and ambiguity in his setting of *O Mirtillo* as compared to Monteverdi's setting of the same text, and its potential implications in Artusi's targeting of Monteverdi, see Chapter 6 and my "'Se vedesti qui dentro': Monteverdi's *O Mirtillo*."

21 Arnold, "Seconda Pratica," 352.

22 Kathryn Bosi Monteath traces many of the dissonances from Pallavicino's Sixth Book to his Fourth Book of 1588, where they are used more locally and sparingly, and relates them to Monteverdi's offences in "The Five-Part Madrigals of Benedetto Pallavicino," Ph.D. diss., University of Otago (1981), 174–211.

23   Oh, my sweet love,
      weep no more if you love me, and it will console you
      that endless is the number
      of unhappy lovers.
      Others live in sorrow

like you, my heart.
Each wound brings with it its suffering,
nor are you alone weeping for love.

By contrast, the passage in the play begins: "Too long / you've lingered already. / Leave, and it will console you / that endless is the number of unhappy lovers…" For a detailed comparison of the readings from Marenzio's Seventh Book with the manuscripts and early editions of the play, see Appendix A.

24 The reading in Cifra's settings begins "Deh, dolce anima mia, / Partiti e ti consola," thus diverging from that of Bicci's and Pallavicino's settings in line 2, but it also replaces Mirtillo's name with "mio core" in verse 6. Another setting of the passage by one Giuseppino—identified by John Walter Hill as Giuseppino Cenci—follows the variant of Cifra's madrigal in the opening lines but retains "Mirtillo" in verse 6, thereby strengthening the text's connection to Guarini's play. Hill mentions that the inclusion of Mirtillo's name in Cenci's monodic setting "may constitute evidence in favour of the hypothesis that it could have been used in the projected performance [by Cardinal Montalto and Michele Peretti] of 1596, and indeed may have been composed expressly for it (Hill, *Roman Monody*, I, 243–44).

25 Benedetto Varoli, *Della nova scelta di rime*, 103.

26 Licino, ed. *Rime di diversi celebri poeti* ["Ventura"], 193. Chater identifies these variants in "Un pasticcio di madrigaletti," 149. Elio Durante and Anna Martellotti discuss the Guarini texts in Pallavicino's Sixth Book and their various sources in "Il Cavalier Guarini e il Concerto delle Dame," 121–24, while noting the correspondence of *Vivrò io mai* with the Varoli edition at p. 123, note 86.

27 Megan Kaes Long provides a thorough and revealing analysis of the history, influence, and textural and tonal features of Gastoldi's 1591 and 1593 volumes of *balletti* in *Hearing Homophony: Tonal Expectation at the Turn of the Seventeenth Century* (New York: Oxford University Press, 2020), especially Chapter 2, "*La questione della lingua*: Transmission and Translation of Musical Style" (24–56).

28 Gastoldi's reputation as a composer of dance and lighter-style music grew not only from his five-voice *Balletti*, but also from the two volumes of three-part *Canzonette* and a book of three-voice *Balletti* that followed them in 1592–95. His *Canzonette a3* of 1592 also includes a final *balletto* for eight voices that bears the caption "Intermedio de Pescatori," and hence likely served as an *intermedio* for a stage work. Gastoldi, in other words, seems to have had considerable experience with music for both dance and the theatre prior to his 1598 *Gioco della cieca*. Denis Arnold ("Monteverdi: Some Colleagues and Pupils," in *The Monteverdi Companion*, ed. D. Arnold and N. Fortune [New York: Norton, 1972], 110–30, at 115) hypothesizes that the proliferation of light music by Mantuan composers (including Wert, Gastoldi, and Rossi) in the late-1580s and 1590s could stem from the influences of Agnese Argotta, Vincenzo Gonzaga's mistress beginning around 1587.

29 Arnold, for example, describes the widely disseminated *Balletti a 5* of 1591 as "so artless and naïve that they can hardly stand as 'pure' music" before acknowledging that "for dancing his pieces are perfect" ("Monteverdi: Some Colleagues and Pupils," 116).

30 Scores of the three Gastoldi madrigals analyzed here—*Dimmi, misero amante*; *O misera Dorinda*; and *O sfortunato e misero Mirtillo*—are provided in the online Support Material for this book. See the Editorial Principles (p. ix) above.

31 The use of specific names is reversed in Dorinda's speech that comes later in Gastoldi's book (but earlier in this same scene): *Tu se' pur aspro a chi t'adora, Silvio* (No. 10). Here, the passage identifies Silvio in its opening exclamation, but refers to the speaker (Dorinda) only metaphorically as a "loving and gentle

doe" ("amorosa e mansueta damma"), while bemoaning Silvio's coldness and infatuation with the hunt.

32 As Ruth DeFord notes, in "lighter" strophic genres such as the *villanella* and *canzonetta*, "the rhythm, like the formal structure, tended to be schematic, following the meter of the text, rather than the details of declamation" ("Musical Relationships between the Italian Madrigal and Light Genres in the Sixteenth Century," *Musica Disciplina* 39 [1985]: 107–68, at 112). See also Long's overview of such schemata in the works of Gastoldi, Vecchi, Morley, and others in *Hearing Homophony*, 58–85.

33 Although no performance instructions appear in the play, Guarini points out in the *Annotazioni* (53–54) that, following the example of the ancients (citing Luciano), the onstage nymphs danced but did not sing, as doing both would prove too difficult. Instead, a separate group of singers and instrumentalists provided the music from behind the scenes.

34 Giovanni Boschetto Boschetti, *Il primo libro de madrigali a cinque voci* (Rome: Robletti, 1613). Boschetti's book draws heavily from the pastoral plays of both Tasso and Guarini, with three settings from *Aminta* and four from *Il pastor fido*, and shares two *Pastor fido* texts with Gastoldi's Fourth Book and one—with the same variant opening line ("Deh, Tirsi mio gentil" in place of "Deh, Satiro gentil")—with Marenzio's Eighth Book.

35 The associations of the pieces could be expanded to the next page of the Fourth Book to include No. 8, *Come assetato infermo*, which sets a single thirteen-line statement from act 3, scene 6 in which Mirtillo compares himself and his painful desire to a thirsting sick man driven to drink a fatal poison. The text contains no character names and complements the subject of hopeless and cruel love not only of Corisca's *Dimmi, misero amante* (No. 6) from later in the same scene, but also of the preceding madrigal, *O sfortunato e misero Mirtillo* (No. 7). The connection with *Come assetato infermo* is weaker on musical grounds than that of Nos. 6 and 7, given its contrasting high cleffing and authentic A-dorian mode. However, the matching scoring (for two tenors), final (A), and modal family (dorian/aeolian)—along with the opening downward leap from 5, $e''-b'$ (discussed below)—of *Come assetato infermo* counterbalance these inconsistencies.

36 See Shlomo Simonsohn, *History of Jews in the Duchy of Mantua* (Jerusalem: Kiryath Sepher, 1977), 656–69. For an overview of court documents relating to Jewish theatrical activities in Mantua, see D'Ancona, *Origini del teatro italiano*, II, Chapter 5, "Gli Ebrei di Mantova e il teatro," 398–429. Harràn notes that the Jewish theater "became one of the major sources of theatrical entertainment for the court" in the late-sixteenth and early-seventeenth centuries, whose performances "included new and old comedies by Italian authors (e.g., Ariosto, Tasso, Muzio Manfredi) and by members of the Jewish troupe, among them Leone Summo" ("Salomone Rossi as a Composer of Theater Music," *Studi musicali* 16 [1987]: 95–131, at 109).

37 Don Harràn, "Salomone Rossi, Jewish Musician in Renaissance Italy," *Acta Musicologica* 59 (1987): 46–64, at 50.

38 Rossi's only known earlier publication is the *Canzonette a tre voci* (Venice: Amadino, 1589). Two other composers included multiple *Pastor fido* settings in their earliest publications around this same time: Ottavio Bargnani of Brescia published a total of eight passages in his *Canzonette, arie et madrigali a3–4* (Venice: Amadino, 1599) and First Book for five voices (Venice: Gardano, 1601), and Giovanni Apolloni of Arezzo included four settings in his First Book *a4* (Venice: Amadino, 1600).

39 Harràn, Introduction to Salamone Rossi, *Complete Works*, ed. Harràn, in series Corpus Mensurabilis Musicae 100, 13 vols., n.p. (Stuttgart: American Institute of Musicology: Hänssler-Verlag, 1995–2003), VII (four-voice madrigals), vii–viii.

40 See also Table 4.4 for a summary of variant texts from Marenzio's *Pastor fido* settings that reappear in later madrigals by other composers.

41 In addition to the two *Pastor fido* texts, Rossi's First Book *a5* contains settings of four other poems found in Marenzio's madrigal books, including three Guarini texts—*Ohimè, se tanto amate* (Third Book, 1582), *O dolce anima mia* (Third Book, 1582), and *Pur venisti cor mio* (Eighth Book, 1598)—and Celiano's *Rimanti in pace* (Sixth Book, 1594).

42 For a close study of Marenzio's madrigal, including its use of modal ambiguity and structural disruptions to render Amarilli's predicament, see my "Speaking In (and Out of) Mode."

43 The first settings published after Marenzio's Seventh Book appeared in 1600, in Giovanni Appolloni's First Book *a4* (1600)—the dedication of which is signed November 1599—and Philippe de Monte's *Musica sopra il pastor fido* (1600). The *terminus ante quem* for both Appolloni's and Monte's pieces, therefore, is later that of Monteverdi's work (November 1598) and roughly coincides with the proposed dating of Rossi's four-voice madrigals to c. 1600.

44 Scores of the three Rossi madrigals discussed here—*Ah, dolente partita*; *Com'è dolce il gioire, o caro Tirsi*; and *Tirsi mio, caro Tirsi*—are provided in the Support Material for this book. See the Editorial Principles (p. ix) above.

45 1 My Tirsi, dear Tirsi,   Tirsi, once so sweet and dear a name
and you, too, abandon me?   that was never invoked in vain,
So to die you leave me and do not help me?   10 help me, your Filli,
At least do not deny me the final kisses.   for, as you see, by merciless fate
5 A single blade indeed will wound two breasts;   I am led to a cruel and pitiless death.
the wound of your Filli, indeed,
will pour your blood.

46 For a more detailed study of Marenzio's madrigal, including a complete score and analytical sketch, see Seth Coluzzi, "*Tirsi mio, caro Tirsi: Il pastor fido* and the Roman Madrigal," 51–73.

47 For an analytical reduction of Marenzio's work, see Coluzzi, "*Tirsi mio, caro Tirsi*," 65 (Example 2).

48 There are several errors in the reproduction and translation of this text in John Steele's edition of the Seventh Book (Marenzio, *Il settimo libro dei madrigali a cinque voci*, ed. John Steele, vol. 3 (New York: Editions renaissantes, 1975), 82). Likewise, Chater's "*Il pastor fido* and Music: A Bibliography" notes incorrectly that Marenzio's setting omits verse 6 (175).

49 As Iain Fenlon writes, for example:

> The overwhelming conservativism of the music in all five books also characterizes the four-part volume, the very appearance of which as late as 1614 must be regarded as archaic: only a handful of books of four-part pieces were published after 1600.
>
> ("Rossi, Salamone," *Grove Music Online*, Oxford University Press.)

50 Harràn erroneously ascribes the piece to the aeolian mode in his edition of the First Book *a4* (Introduction, xvii).

51 The G and D cadences are bridged by a three-voice cadence on A in mm. 30–31 that might seem to undermine the structural authority of d' here and instead continue the support of e'. The madrigal curbs this interpretation, however, by omitting E altogether from this A cadence, thereby clarifying the gesture's role in the broader expansion of D through the outlining of the $d''-a'$ diatessaron in the upper voice and the progression toward D as cadence center in mm. 29–35 (see Example 8.19). The placement of an A cadence here also upholds the association of that pitch with literal

references to *morire* in the text, as seen at "moro" (non-cadential, m. 20), "morte" (cadence, m. 24), "morire" (cadence, m. 31), and "moia" (evaded cadence, m. 43).

52 In assessing the solo versions of Rossi's five-voice madrigals of 1600, Einstein notes the soprano's unchallenged prominence at the top of the texture, above the chittarone part and the four lower voices, and its distinctive embellishments and expressiveness before declaring Rossi "one of the first and earliest monodists, and he is much more determined and progressive than, for instance, Luzzasco Luzzaschi in his solos published in 1602 which are nothing but arrangements of *a cappella* madrigals" ("Salamone Rossi as Composer of Madrigals," *Hebrew Union College Annual* 23 [1950–51]: 383–96, at 393–94). Einstein is not entirely accurate about the discreteness of the Canto's range, as the Alto occasionally overlaps it.

53 Harràn, "Salomone Rossi as a Composer of Theater Music," 115. In his edition of the four-voice madrigals, Harràn similarly states without explanation that the *Pastor fido* settings "raise the question of possible theatrical usage for the music" (viii).

54 On Artusi's rhetoric, see Carter, "Monteverdi Responds to Artusi?"; Coluzzi, "'Se vedesti qui dentro': Monteverdi's *O Mirtillo*"; Cusick, "Gendering Modern Music"; and Ossi, *Divining the Oracle*, Chapter 1 ("The Public Debate 1").

55 G.C. Monteverdi, *Dichiaratione*, in Monteverdi's *Scherzi musicali*. Earlier Giulio Cesare takes issue specifically with Artusi's omission of the texts as part of the "whole": "in questo l'Artusi, da bon maestro piglia certe particelle, o passaggi (come lui dice) del Madregale Cruda Amarilli di mio fratello, nulla curandosi dell'oratione, tralasciandola in maniera tale, come se nulla havesse che fare con la musica."

References

Appolloni, Giovanni. *Il primo libro de madrigali a quattro voci*. Venice: Amadino, 1600.

Arnold, Denis. "Monteverdi: Some Colleagues and Pupils." In *The Monteverdi Companion*, eds. D. Arnold and N. Fortune, 110–30. New York: Norton, 1972.

———. "'Seconda Pratica': A Background to Monteverdi's Madrigals." *Music and Letters* 38 (1957): 341–52.

Artusi, Giovanni Maria. *L'Artusi, overo Delle imperfettioni della moderna musica ragionamenti dui*. Venice: Vincenti, 1600. Trans. by Oliver Strunk in *Source Readings in Music History*. New York: Norton, 1998.

Banchieri, Adriano. *Conclusioni nel suono dell'organo*. Bologna: Rossi, 1609.

Bargnani, Ottavio. *Il primo libro de madrigali a cinque voci*. Venice: Gardano, 1601.

———. *Canzonette, arie et madrigali a3–4*. Venice: Amadino, 1599.

Boschetti, Giovanni Boschetto. *Il primo libro de madrigali a cinque voci*. Rome: Robletti, 1613.

Bosi [Monteath], Kathryn. "The Five-Part Madrigals of Benedetto Pallavicino." Ph.D. diss., University of Otago, 1981.

Carter, Tim. "'E in rileggendo poi le proprie note': Monteverdi Responds to Artusi?" *Renaissance Studies* 26 (2012): 138–55.

Chater, James. "*Il pastor fido* and Music: A Bibliography." In *Guarini: la musica, i musicisti*, ed. A. Pompilio, 157–83. Lucca: Libreria Musicale Italiana Editrice, 1997.

———. "'Cruda Amarilli': A Cross-Section of the Italian Madrigal." *Musical Times* 116 (1975): 231–34.

Coluzzi, Seth. "Speaking In (and Out of) Mode: Structure and Rhetoric in Marenzio's *O Mirtillo, Mirtillo anima mia* (1595)." *Music Theory Spectrum* 37 (2015): 253–74.

———. *"Tirsi mio, caro Tirsi: Il pastor fido* and the Roman Madrigal." In *Perspectives on Luca Marenzio's Secular Music*, ed. Mauro Calcagno, 51–73. In series *Epitome musical*. Turnhout: Brepols, 2014.

———. "'Se vedesti qui dentro': Monteverdi's *O Mirtillo, Mirtillo anima mia* and Artusi's Offence." *Music and Letters* 94 (2013): 1–37.

Coma, Annibale. *Il secondo libro de madrigali a quatto voci*. Venice: Vincenti, 1588.

Cusick, Susanne. "Gendering Modern Music: Thoughts on the Monteverdi–Artusi Controversy." *Journal of the American Musicological Society* 46 (1993): 1–25.

D'Ancona, Alessandro. *Origini del teatro italiano*. 2nd ed. 3 vols. Turin: Loescher, 1891.

DeFord, Ruth. "Musical Relationships between the Italian Madrigal and Light Genres in the Sixteenth Century." *Musica Disciplina* 39 (1985): 107–68.

Durante, Elio and Anna Martellotti. "Il Cavalier Guarini e il concerto delle dame." In *Guarini: la musica, i musicisti*, ed. A. Pompilio, 91–127. Lucca: Libreria Musicale Italiana Editrice, 1997.

Einstein, Alfred. "Salamone Rossi as Composer of Madrigals." *Hebrew Union College Annual* 23 (1950–51): 383–96.

———. *The Italian Madrigal*. Trans. by A.H. Krappe, R.H. Sessions, and O. Strunk. 3 vols. Princeton, NJ: Princeton University Press, 1949.

Fabbri, Paolo. *Monteverdi*. Turin: EDT/Musica, 1985.

Fenlon, Iain. *Music and Patronage in Sixteenth-Century Mantua*. 2 vols. Oxford: Oxford University Press, 1980.

Gastoldi, Giovanni Giacomo. *Concenti musicali con le sue sinfonia a otto voci*. Venice: Amadino, 1604.

———. *Il quarto libro de madrigali a cinque voci*. Venice: Amadino, 1602.

———. *Il terzo libro de madrigali a cinque voci*. Venice: Amadino, 1598.

———. *Balletti a cinque voci*. Venice: Amadino, 1591.

Ghizzolo, Giovanni. *Madrigali et arie per sonare et cantare...libro primo*. Venice: Raverii, 1609.

Guarini, Battista. *Annotazioni sopra "Il pastor fido"*. Verona: Giovanni Tumermani, 1737. Facsimile in *La questione del 'Pastor fido.'* In series La scena e l'ombra: collana di testi e studi teatrali. Rome: Vecchiarelli, 1997.

———. *Il pastor fido, tragicommedia pastorale del molto Illustre Cavaliere Battista Guarini, ora in questa XX impressione di curiose e dotte Annotationi arrichito*. Venice: Ciotti, 1602.

Hanning, Barbara. *Of Poetry and Music's Power: Humanism and the Creation of Opera*. In series Studies in Musicology. Ann Arbor, MI: UMI Research Press, 1980.

Harràn, Don. "Salomone Rossi as a Composer of Theater Music." *Studi musicali* 16 (1987): 95–131.

———. "Salomone Rossi, Jewish Musician in Renaissance Italy." *Acta Musicologica* 59 (1987): 46–64.

Hill, John Walter. *Roman Monody, Cantata, and Opera from the Circles around Cardinal Montalto*. 2 vols. Oxford: Clarendon Press, 1997.

Kaufmann, Paul, ed. *Fiori del giardino di diversi eccellentissimi autori*. Nuremburg: Kaufmann, 1597.

Licino, Giovanni Battista, ed. *Rime di diversi celebri poeti dell'età nostra nuovamente e poste in luca*. Bergamo: Comino Ventura e compagni, 1587.

Long, Megan Kaes. *Hearing Homophony: Tonal Expectation at the Turn of the Seventeenth Century.* New York: Oxford University Press, 2020.

Marenzio, Luca. *Il settimo libro de' madrigali a cinque voci.* Venice: Gardano, 1595. Ed. by Patricia Myers in *Marenzio, the Secular Works* 14. New York: Broude Brothers, 1980.

———. *Il settimo libro dei madrigali a cinque voci* [1595]. Ed. John Steele. New York: Editions renaissantes, 1975.

Monte, Philippe de. *Musica sopra il pastor fido...libro secondo a sette voci.* Venice: Gardano, 1600.

Monteverdi, Claudio. *Scherzi musicali a tre voci.* Venice: Amadino, 1607.

Ossi, Massimo. "Monteverdi, Marenzio, and Battista Guarini's 'Cruda Amarilli'." *Music and Letters* (2008): 311–36.

———. *Divining the Oracle: Monteverdi's 'Seconda prattica.'* Chicago, IL: University of Chicago Press, 2003.

Palisca, Claude. "The Artusi–Monteverdi Controversy." In *The New Monteverdi Companion*, eds. D. Arnold and N. Fortune, 127–58. London: Faber, 1985.

Pallavicino, Benedetto. *Opera omnia.* Ed. Peter Flanders, 7 vols. Münster: American Institute of Musicology, 1983.

———. *Il sesto libro de madrigali a cinque voci.* Venice: Gardano, 1601.

Parisi, Susan. "Ducal Patronage of Music in Mantua, 1587–1627: An Archival Study." Ph.D. diss., University of Illinois at Urbana–Champaign, 1989.

Rossi, Salamone. *Complete Works.* Ed. Don Harràn. In series Corpus mensurabilis musicae 100. 13 vols. Stuttgart: American Institute of Musicology: Hänssler-Verlag, 1995–2003.

———. *Il primo libro de madrigali a quattro voci.* Venice: Amadino, 1614.

———. *Il primo libro de madrigali a cinque voci.* Venice: Amadino, 1600.

———. *Canzonette a tre voci.* Venice: Amadino, 1589.

Ruffolo, Lucrezio. *Il terzo libro de' madrigali a cinque voci con un dialogo a sette.* Venice: Vincenti, 1612.

———. *Il primo libro de madrigali a cinque voci.* Venice: Vincenti, 1598.

Simonsohn, Shlomo. *History of Jews in the Duchy of Mantua.* Jerusalem: Kiryath Sepher, 1977.

Tomlinson, Gary. *Monteverdi and the End of the Renaissance.* Oxford: Clarendon, 1987.

Varoli, Benedetto, ed. *Della nova scelta di rime di diversi eccellenti scrittori de l'età nostra parte prima.* Casalmaggiore: Antonio Guerino e compagno, 1590.

Zarlino, Gioseffo. *The Art of Counterpoint. Part three of Le istitutioni harmoniche [Venice, 1558].* Trans. by G. Marco and C. Palisca. New Haven, CT: Yale University Press, 1968.

Index